The army that carved out Japan's land empire is examined in depth in two volumes. Drawn from WW 2 period and modern Japanese and American sources the Imperial Army's corps are arranged as they were deployed in the field, each with its history and order of battle. Divisions and brigades follow in detail. In addition an index of individual units, arranged by code number, is provided to make searching easy. Over 6.000 units are identified and are represented in the two books.

Today the Japanese Army remains mysterious, in part because it was secretive by nature. These books are wide ranging and informative, but of special interest is their ability to draw back the curtain on one of the Imperial Japanese Army's most coveted secrets, the intelligence camouflage it called Tsushogo.

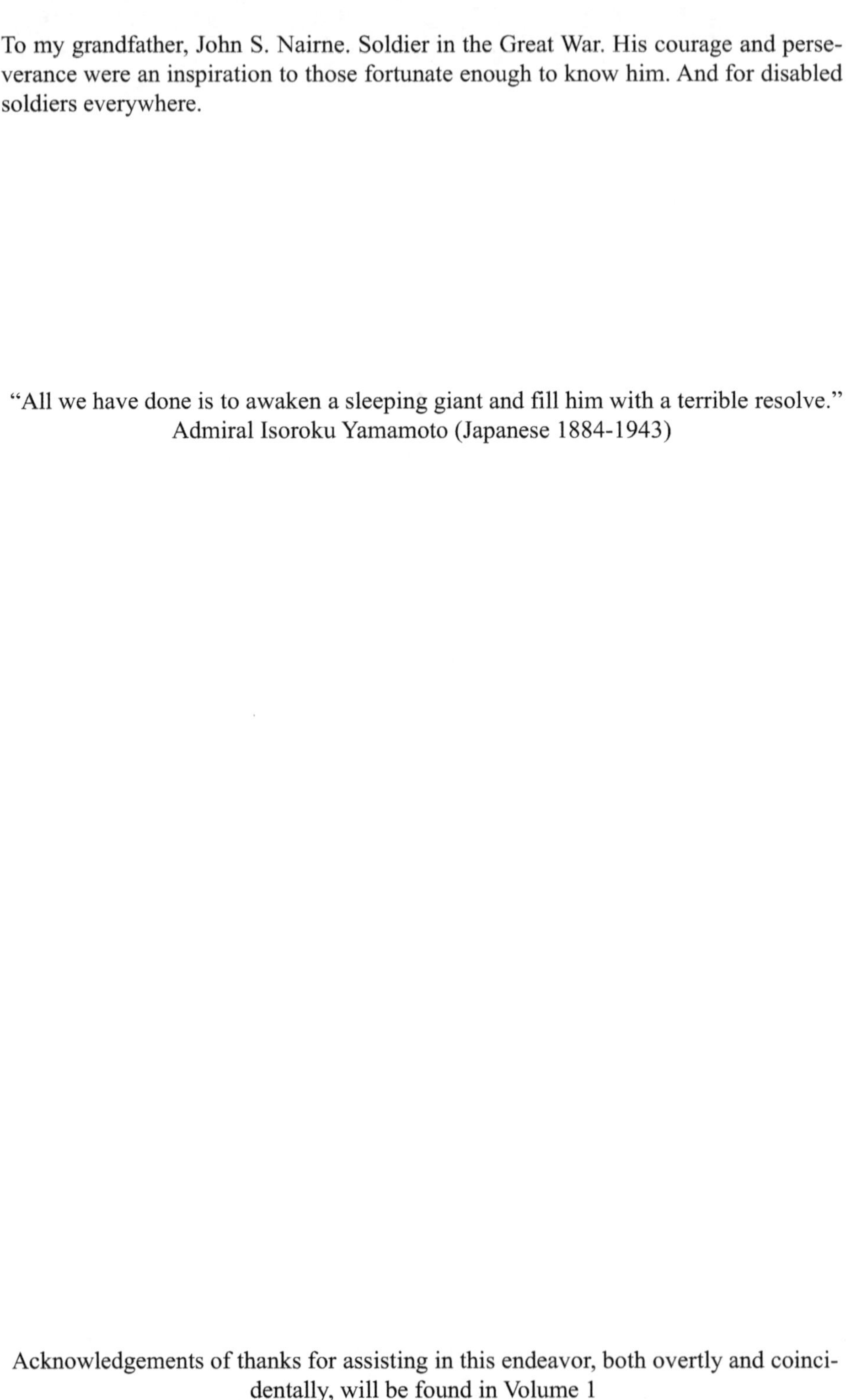

To my grandfather, John S. Nairne. Soldier in the Great War. His courage and perseverance were an inspiration to those fortunate enough to know him. And for disabled soldiers everywhere.

"All we have done is to awaken a sleeping giant and fill him with a terrible resolve."
Admiral Isoroku Yamamoto (Japanese 1884-1943)

Acknowledgements of thanks for assisting in this endeavor, both overtly and coincidentally, will be found in Volume 1

The Imperial Japanese Army
Volume 2
Conquest and Occupation 1941 to 1945

Roderick S. Grigor

This publication's sole aim is to inform for historical purposes. It has been produced without any intention of glorifying, excusing or ignoring the many horrific war crimes and atrocities the Imperial Japanese Army committed throughout the war.

Excerpts from *With the Old Breed* by Eugene B. Sledge, published by Presidio Press, an imprint of Penguin Random House, appear under fair use doctrine with the author's gratitude.

Period artifacts are from the author's collection, except where indicated.
The black and white artwork was created using war time photographs, some of which originate with Japanese print media in the 1930s and 40s but most are from soldiers' personal photo albums. In the present day the reference photographs used are in the author's possession.

December 2020

Copy editor: Elizabeth Rooney

Print ISBN: 978-1-7772728-1-4
eBook ISBN: 978-1-7772728-3-8

Address: P.O. Box 98064
970 Queen St. East
Toronto, Ontario
Canada
M4M9L9
Email: paperblossombooks@gmail.com

The typeface throughout is 10 point, Times New Roman PS MT, except photos are in 8 pt and Japanese Kanji which are 12 and 10 point MS PMincho.

Imperial Japanese Army

Conquest and Occupation 1941 to 1945

Contents: Page

Contents: Page

Contents: Page

Introduction

The Imperial Japanese Army, Volume 2: Conquest and Occupation 1941 to 1945 covers all areas of the fighting in Asia and the Pacific except Okinawa and Manchuria (Okinawa was the only major land battle fought on Japanese soil in WW2). The Imperial Japanese Navy's island garrisons and battles are also missing because the work is limited to Imperial Japanese Army units and organizations.

When I first discovered the existence of an army code name and numbering system, *Tsushogo*, it was exciting to find history that had been almost universally forgotten. Initially, as a collector of WW2 Japanese military artifacts it provided me with inside information by way of uncovering the history of items of interest. But the same information can also dispute fanciful stories, uncover hidden value and promote a better understanding of the past and the people who lived it.

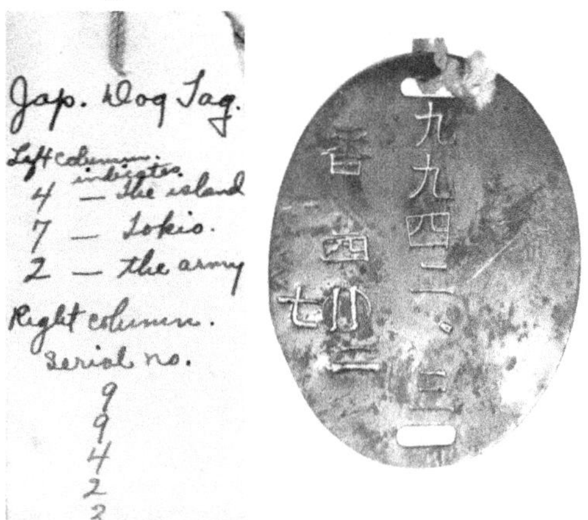

6th Air Signal Regiment tag with an invented interpretation of its code number 9942, company number 3 and soldier's personal number 472.

Collectors and dealers often cross paths with coded Japanese army items but have no idea of their meaning with good reason. They are confronting a smoke screen designed to hide unit names and strengths from a long ago enemy. Today the system continues to do the job it was designed for over 75 years ago because, as the saying goes, you can't tell the players without a program.

An easy-to-search reference book:

In chapter two orders of battle and army dispositions are arranged geographically beginning with Guadalcanal and New Guinea. Using a last-known-address protocol, Imperial Army units generally appear in the locations where history best remembers them. Within the text the juxtaposition of area armies provides a narrative that walks the reader through the Pacific and Asia towards Japan. All front line and garrison armies and much of their background and details are included

All armies directly follow their parent organization and are usually in numerical order when they share a superior. They all have activation dates, home stations, postings and commanders names. Service History sections are a year by year, date-oriented series

Fig. 1 is an excerpt from a signal soldier's service record booklet. He enlisted in 1941 and re-enlisted in 1945 as a sergeant in *Tohoku* 21401 Butai in Morioka. This was the code name for the 38th Signal Regiment, 11th Area Army. It can be found as 21401 東北 in the index of Vol. 1. Note the circle punctuation (It's in red ink in the original booklets).

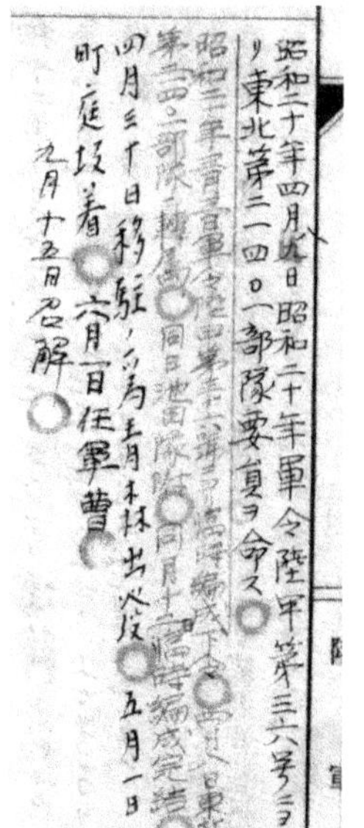

fig. 1 Service Record Booklet entries

of diary style entries covering that area's events. Punctuation between events is a circle ○ mimicking the chop marks in enlisted men's Service Record Booklets (see fig 1).

Paying the price:

As any comprehensive overview of the Asia-Pacific land war demonstrates the fighting took place almost entirely on foreign soil, protectorates notwithstanding. Until November 1944 Japan's home front population counted its casualties in dead and wounded soldiers and expended resources but otherwise remained relatively unscathed.

Volume 2:

Delineating between at home and abroad very roughly splits the army in half. As Volume 2 is about those sent outside Japan and the territories it includes all who either fought toe-to-toe with the enemy or were stranded abroad as the war moved past them, sometimes both. Volume 1 covers relatively little of the fighting but has everything concerning the organization of the army itself.

Unraveling a secret:

The two volumes contain over 6,000 individual unit entries. A Japanese-to-English numbers conversion chart makes it easy to translate code numbers on the spot.

Distributed Numbers, identified as **DN •**, were blocks of numbers assigned to army unit activating agents. They in turn assigned one number to each new unit activation. These entries can often provide a unit's origin.

During the 1940s the Imperial Army grew exponentially. Even then it only took about two months for US military intelligence to learn the identity behind a new unit code number. A system like Tsushogo could only be kept current by adding new layers and complexities. Its history is in Volume 1.

Every effort has been made to ensure the accuracy of this work. There is no doubt it contains errors and omissions, for which the author unreservedly apologizes.

Toronto
October 2020

A troop convoy en route to the invasion of the Philippines (author)

Chapter 1

Echoes of War

Impossible to prevent and almost a cliché to say, American servicemen return from war with kit bags full of souvenirs. In the Pacific hunting souvenirs was reluctantly allowed as it improved morale at the front, the US War Department mainly cautioned against the danger of booby traps and destruction of intelligence.

Circulars were distributed outlining strict regulations on collecting battlefield booty. Articles 3 and 6 of the Geneva Convention protect wounded and surrendering enemy soldiers from robbery and ill treatment and safeguard identification papers.

Soldiers were permitted to pick up small objects on the battlefield or purchase from a POW those things it was unlawful to pick up. Returning personnel were allowed to claim captured enemy equipment as personal property and transport it as luggage or send it by mail, if less than 25 lbs. That is how the history of World War 2 found its way into the attics and basements of America.

The literature reminds us of the carnage and violence soldiers endured before gaining control over a field of battle, at which point the victors often flouted regulations, especially those advocating respectful treatment of wounded and dead enemy troops. E. B. Sledge, said it in his book, *With the Old Breed,* (page 129) "*During this lull men stripped the packs and pockets of the enemy dead for souvenirs.*" "*Helmet headbands were checked for flags, packs and pockets were emptied and gold teeth were extracted. Sabers, pistols and hari-kari knives were highly prized...*" All bets were off.

Souvenir hunting and intelligence collection are two sides of the same coin. On June 29, 1942 an Australian raid on Salamaua marked the beginning of physical intelligence collection in the Pacific. For Americans it was at Guadalcanal sometime after Aug 7, 1942. Little could have been acquired prior to those dates.

Peleliu battlefield pick-up. 2nd Inf. Regt. Artillery Unit papers for a 75mm Type 95 Field Gun (author)

ATIS is created to fill a void

In October 1942 the 17th Army reached the end of its rope on the Kokoda Trail and began to retreat. Following in its wake the Allies captured 268 documents by November. As the momentum shifted sides 1,349 documents were taken from Buna in January 1943 and 1,562 from Lae the following September.

Until September 1942 the Allies suffered from a shortage of linguists fluent in Japanese. This was problematic because the timely translation of captured intelligence was a potential life saver for Australian and American soldiers.

To rectify the situation Allied Translator and Interpreter Section, SWPA., ATIS for short, was created in Melbourne on Sept 19 with Col Sidney F Mashbir commanding. The unit primarily filled its ranks with second generation (Nisei) bilingual Americans of Japanese descent, who served their country with great distinction.

In October the unit was relocated to Brisbane to be closer to General Headquarters SWPA. The new base had a document translation building, interrogation center and three cellblocks for 15 Japanese POW. Cells were omitted from the site plans and the presence of POW kept secret from the public.

Japanese military documents were often found burnt, shredded and/or rain soaked and muddy due to jungle conditions. ATIS developed techniques to lift information from material so damaged even souvenir hunters might not have bothered with it.

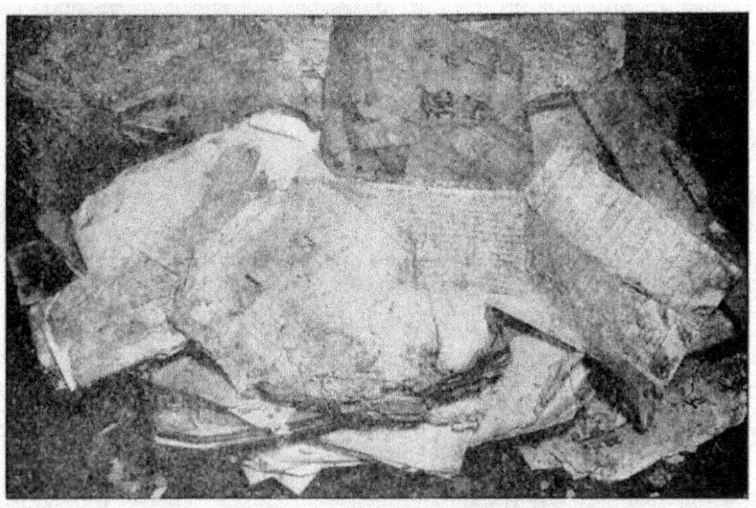

Figure 2. Captured Documents as received.

Documents found in the field. Photograph from ATIS publication, *Restoration of Captured Documents*, Publication No. 10, June 28, 1945. (ATIS)

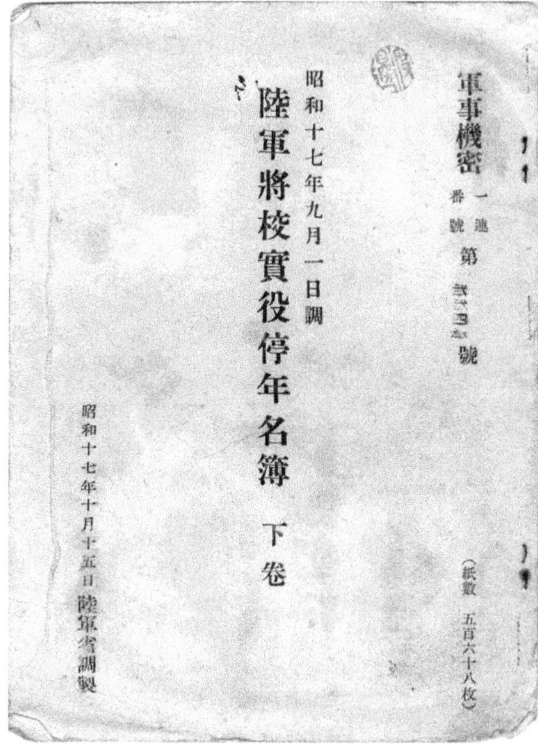

Above: Cover of the Japanese *Register of Army Officers on Active Service* a 568 page volume (image courtesy of NARA)

Battle of the Bismarck Sea legacy

On Mar 3, 1943, a convoy carrying the Japanese 51st Division was all but destroyed off New Britain's coast.

After the one-sided disaster a windfall set of documents fell into Allied hands. On Goodenough Island eight *Teiyo Maru* survivors died protecting some sealed tins that contained the *Japanese Army List*, *Register of Officers* and *Register of Reserve Officers on the Active List*, 2,700 pages in 3 vols, which were published by Japan's War Department just before November 1942. Included were a Japanese order of battle and the names and postings for every officer in the army. ATIS translated and published it as *Alphabetical List of Japanese Army Officers* ATIS Translator Section, Southwest Pacific Area, ATIS Publication No. 2, May 1943 (683 pages).

Japanese army documents

Documents relating to the army: Unit Field Files, the Miscellaneous Files, intelligence reports, service record booklets, military postal savings sheets, maps and charts, pay books, field diaries, orders, medical records, regulations, manuals, reconnaissance reports, letters, postcards, address books, photographs, magazines and newspapers. Japanese Army publications often seem undersized by Western standards.

Unit Field Files; Daily diaries were kept by all units company size or larger. Included in them were day-to-day reports of personnel and their duties, unit orders and tables of organization. At the end of the month these were bound into a single separate volume and filed with the earlier *Unit Field Files.*

Miscellaneous Files: Units bound large numbers of unrelated documents of at least some military value together and labeled them the *Miscellaneous Files.*

Service record booklets: (photo shows 14 ex.) A Company Internal Affairs Section consisted of a sergeant major, sergeant and 3 men who could write legibly. It was they who kept and updated soldier's service records in duplicate booklets at company HQ.

Pay books: (lower photos) These contained a soldier's salary deposit and withdrawal information. Used examples are less common than service record booklets.

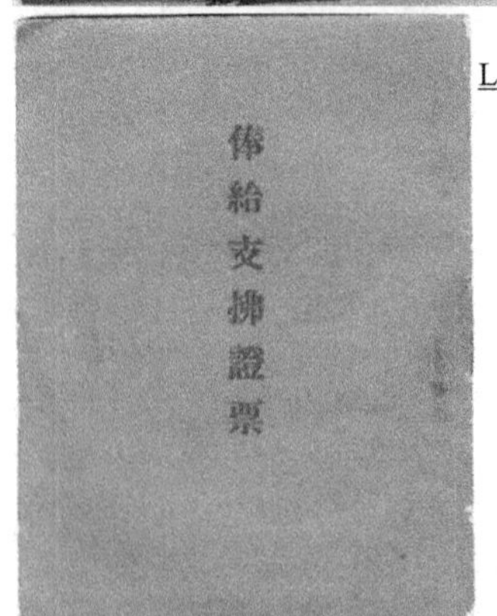

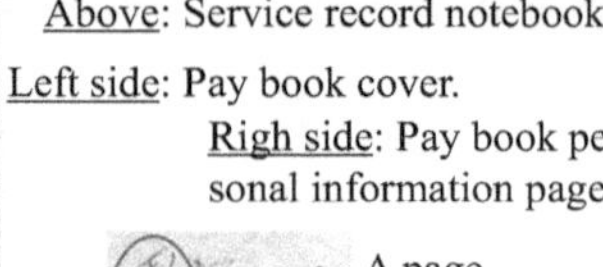

Above: Service record notebooks

Left side: Pay book cover.

Righ side: Pay book personal information page.

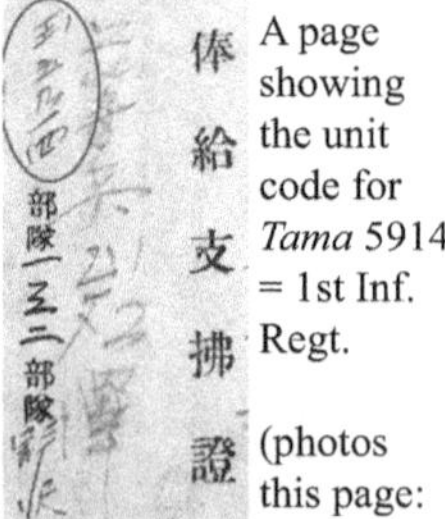

A page showing the unit code for *Tama* 5914 = 1st Inf. Regt.

(photos this page: author)

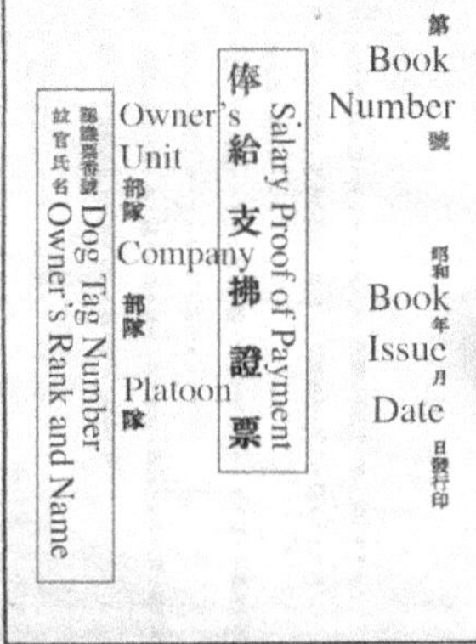

Japanese military mail

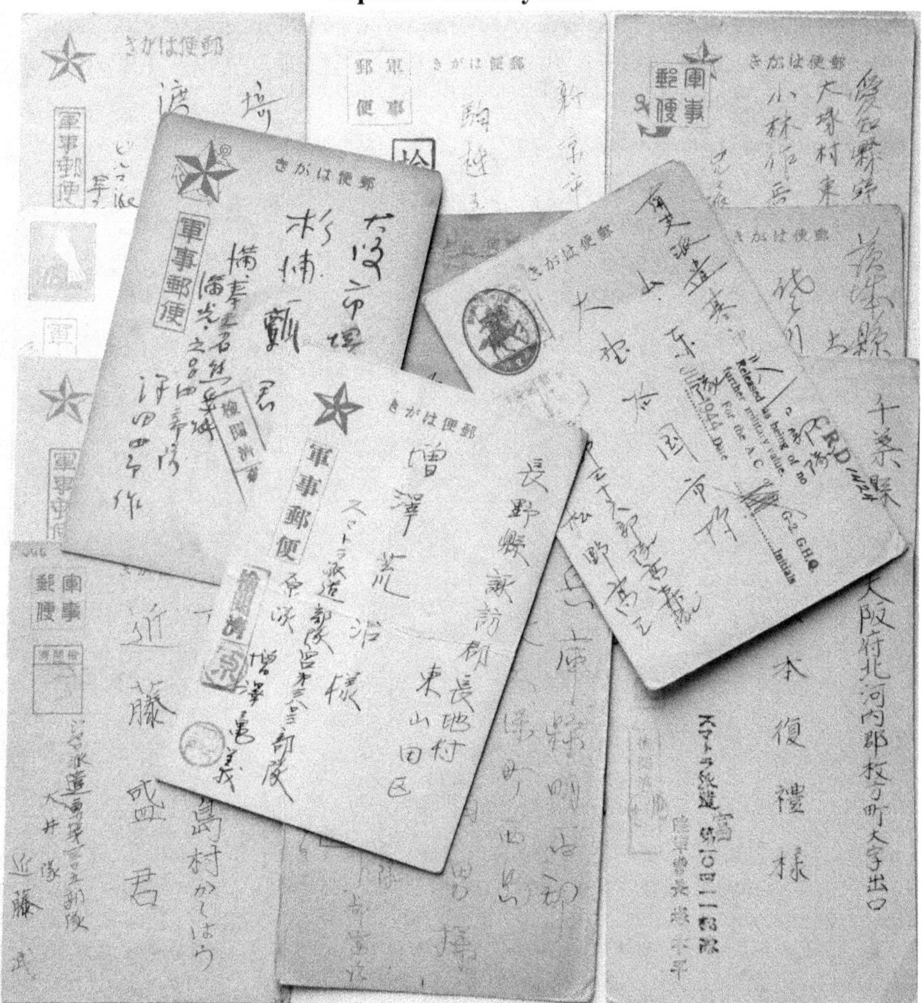

A small collection of postcards sent by Japanese soldiers from all over the Empire (author)

Japanese military mail began in September 1879 and was delivered free of charge between 1894 and 1946. In 1937, as the war escalated, it became necessary to create the Field Postal Service Section at Imperial Headquarters. Its job was to activate and manage Army Field Postal Units and their branch offices. It was also responsible for army mail delivery in cooperation with the Navy and Japan's domestic mail services. Army Field Post Office Units were responsible for keeping a record of where each army unit was located within its area of responsibility. Postcards were often made in the field using rubber-stamps on card stock instead of with printing presses.

<u>Collecting mailing addresses and dates</u>

A postcard or letter's sent/received location and date usually have everything to do with its historic value and determine how much you'd consider buying or selling one for. Pre-1945 addresses are generally read from top to bottom, right to left. The card's destination begins top right side and the return address left side. Most military mail found today was sent to Japan from overseas. After 1940 the return address is a unit's code name and number (部隊, Butai = Unit), followed by company commander's name (隊, Tai = Unit), usually in the two or three columns on the card's left side. Mail was infrequent, especially later in the war. Censorship was strict with messages limited to personal greetings, encouragement and mundane chatter.

Postcard #1: Java to Japan, arrived 8/30 1942, Date District, Fukushima Prefecture.
From 勇**1303** = 29th Inf. Regt., Yoshii Butai (3rd Battalion), Makita Tai (9th Company).
(photos on this and the facing page: author)

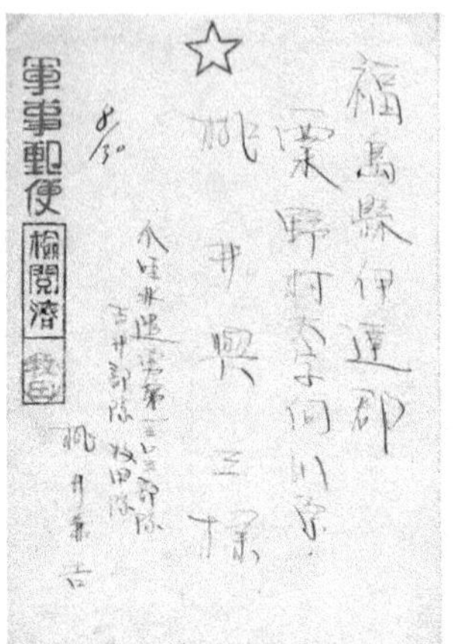

Postcard #2: (rare incoming) To the 51st Division in South China from Japan, postmarked Sept. 9, 1942.

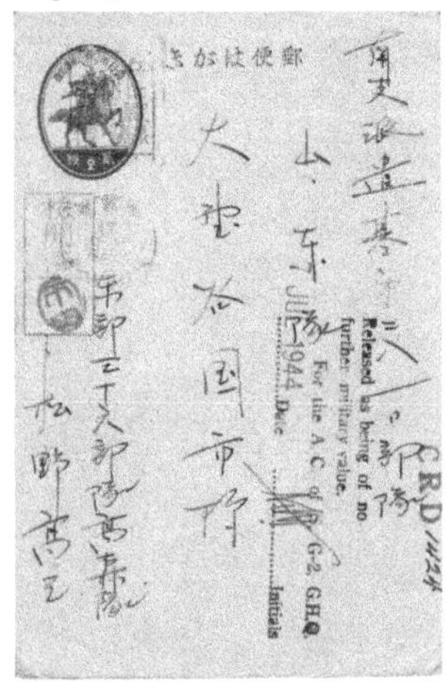

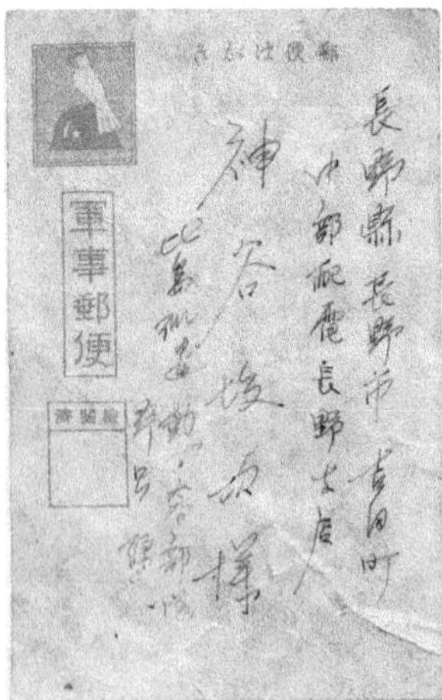

Postcard #3: (outgoing mail)
From: 105th Div. Headquarters in the Philippines.
To: Nagano Pref., Nagano City. Yoshida Machi (town)
From: 比島 Hitou (Philippines),

Postcard #1: 勇**1303** = 29th Infantry Regiment, Yoshii Butai (3rd Battalion), Makita Tai (9th Company). On Oct. 24 1942 at 0115 hours Marine Sergeant John Basilone destroyed this same infantry company during the 2nd Division's attack on Henderson Field. The story of the 9th Company's demise is touched on briefly on page 355 of Richard B. Frank's book *Guadacanal*.

Postcard #2: (rare incoming) 基**2810** = the 51st Transport Regiment., 51st Division was with the 23rd Army in South China from Sept 18, 1941 until Oct. 20 1942, when it was sent south to the 18th Army in New Guinea. In Oct 1943 this Regt. became the Lorengau Defense Unit on Manus Is. the Admiralties. US troops landed there on March 15th. Postcard captured and stamped *no further military value* by G-2 on Jul 7, 1944. The 51st Division suffered disastrously when their convoy was attacked by Allied airpower in what became known as the Battle of the Bismarck Sea.

Postcard #3: 勤**10660** = 105th Division Headquarters_ No censor mark, possibly never sent. The 105th Division was activated on Luzon, the Philippines on June 15, 1944, and attached to the Shimbu Army Group in the Manila area. In January the 82nd Infantry Brigade (also called the *Kawashima Butai*) was detached and sent to Lamon Bay/ Lucerna area while the rest of the division deployed north under the 14th Area Army's control. The US invasion of Luzon began January 9, 1945.

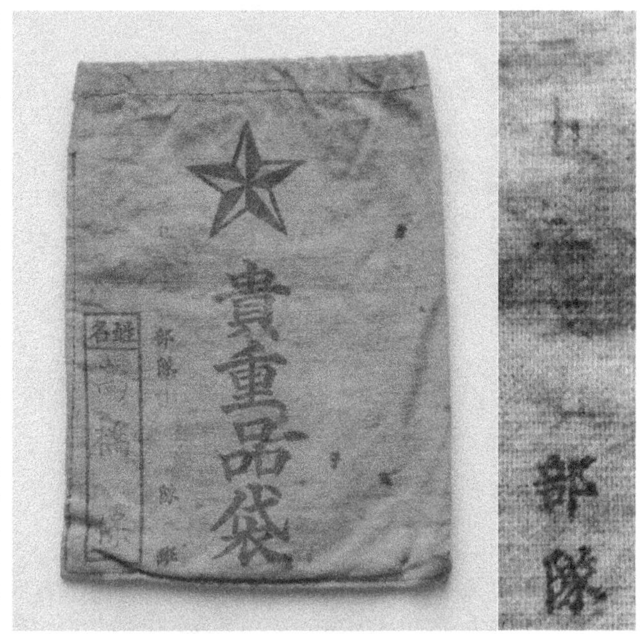

Kihochinbukuro: A valuables bag. Code number inscribed to 15375, the 48th Airfield Company served on Bacolod, Negros in the Philippines.

48th Airfield Coy, 15375; 209 men activated in Yokkaichi, Japan. Set sail from Osaka on February. 29, 1944, landed in Manila on May 11th, landed in Bacolod on the 27th.

After army aircraft ceased flying from the Bacolod area and the Americans landed, air units like this one became ad hoc infantry, machine cannon operators and transport troops until the surrender.

Army diaries

Theirs was an army of diarists who spent free time preserving the things that touched their lives. In the photo illustration, top row: The diaries illustrate common PX store examples, small pencils were housed in the spines. Soldiers serving in China and Manchuria were the original owners of these examples.

Bottom row: The two outside diaries are interesting. On the left *Memorandum* was carried by a 2nd Machine Gun Company, 36th Inf. Regt. soldier in October 1937 who tells of battles on the road to Nanking. Right side: *Notes Book* landed in the Philippines in 1941 with the 16th Division's 9th Infantry Regt. Often rifle and bayonet serial numbers, unit and dog tag info, etc., are recorded in these.

Mail call in North China, ca. 1937 (author)

Chapter 2

Conquest and Occupation

Japan's declaration of war against the United States, Britain and the Netherlands in December 1941 came a decade after the war in China began. In the intervening years the Imperial Japanese Army had become battle hardened and innovative beyond expectation. During the first six months of the Pacific War Japan shocked the world by defeating Britain and America and at the same time gaining possession of a vast area. This chapter is an overview of the war machine that briefly rivaled those of the world's great military powers.

The overseas forces of the Japanese Army are arranged according to geography. This volume begins at the outermost reaches of Empire in 1942 and travels back towards the homelands in 1945. More or less taking into account all the units and places outside Japanese waters that are part of this story in one way or another.

The chart on the next page *Army Organization for China and the Southern Area* provides headquarters locations for the army groups in this book. It can act as a visual guide for locating an army in theater, except for air armies, rail and shipping, which are out of order within the chart.

Where an army or major unit was deactivated and dispersed (usually to adjacent units) before the war ended a footprint remained but certain details were omitted from the records, e.g., units lacking authorized troop strengths, etc. (see the 19th Army, p. 70).

The Imperial Japanese Army and Navy had a long-standing rivalry that was potentially detrimental to their own side. To adjudicate Army-Navy relations Imperial General Headquarters maintained control over the islands in the Pacific. A joint cooperation agreement was made for every Army-Navy operation.

Map showing the area of responsibility assigned to each General Army

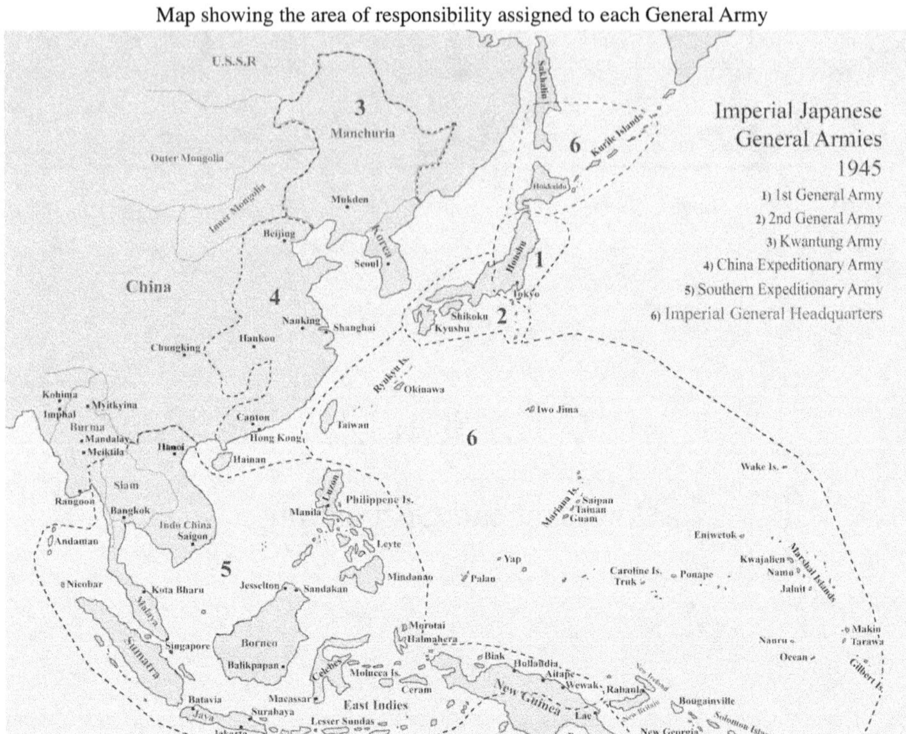

Army Organization for China and the Southern Area

1. **Imperial General Headquarters**: Tokyo; commanded the entire Japanese Army
a. under direct control: 31st Army: Truck Island, responsible Central Pacific islands
b. 8th Area Army - Rabaul, South East Pacific
b. 17th Army - Buin, Bougainville Island (formerly Guadalcanal)

2. **Southern Expeditionary Army**: - Saigon; South Asia and southwest Pacific
a. under direct control: 18th Army - Madang, New Guinea
b. 38th Army - Saigon, Vietnam
c. Burma Area Army - Moulmein, Burma
c. 28th Army - Paung, Burma; 33rd Army - Bilin, Burma
d. 7th Area Army - Singapore
d. 16th Army - Batavia, Java; 25th Army - Fort De Kock, Sumatra; 29th Army - Taiping, Malaya, 37th Army - Sangpong. Borneo
e. 14th Area Army - Manila, Philippines
e. 35th Army - Cebu Island; 41st Army - South of Manila, Philippines
f. 2nd Area Army - Manado, Celebes - (was 19th Army) deactivated June 13, 1945
f. 2nd Army -Macassar Island
g. 18th Area Army - Bangkok, Thailand
g. 15th Army - Lampang, Thailand
h. 3rd Air Army - Singapore
i. 4th Air Army - New Guinea and the Philippines (Ineffective by Apr.'44)

3. <u>China Expeditionary Army</u>: - Nanking; all of China
a. <u>under direct control</u>: 6th Army - Nanking, China
b. 13th Army - Shanghai, China
c. 23rd Army - Canton, China
d. <u>North China Area Army</u> - Beijing, China
d. 1st Army - Shanshi; 12th Army - Honan; 43rd Army - Shangtung; Mongolia Garrison Army - Kalgan, Mongolia
e. <u>6th Area Army</u> - Hankou, China
e. 11th Army - Hankou; 20th Army - Hankow, China
(Note: In central and south China air cover was supplied by the 13th Air Division, in Nanking, part of the 5th Air Army who's HQ were in Seoul, Korea.

Type 90 Field Gun deploying, limber alongside (author)

<u>Notes on army units lists</u>
Column 1 heading: Name of the army, Column 2 heading: Code name
Column 1 below: Unit names   Column 2 below: Code numbers
Parethesis (123) is the number of men authorized to serve in the unit. Please note occasionally the **actual** number of men present at the time the record was created is shown instead of the authorized number, depending on the available source.
Column 2 heading and body combine to form the unit's code name and number (called its *Tsushogo* in Japanese).
<u>Example</u>: 10th Area Army Air Intelligence Unit is *Wan* 湾4570 (2,037) with a compliment of 2,037 men.

Armies under Imperial General Headquarters' direct control

Central and Southeast Pacific Regions

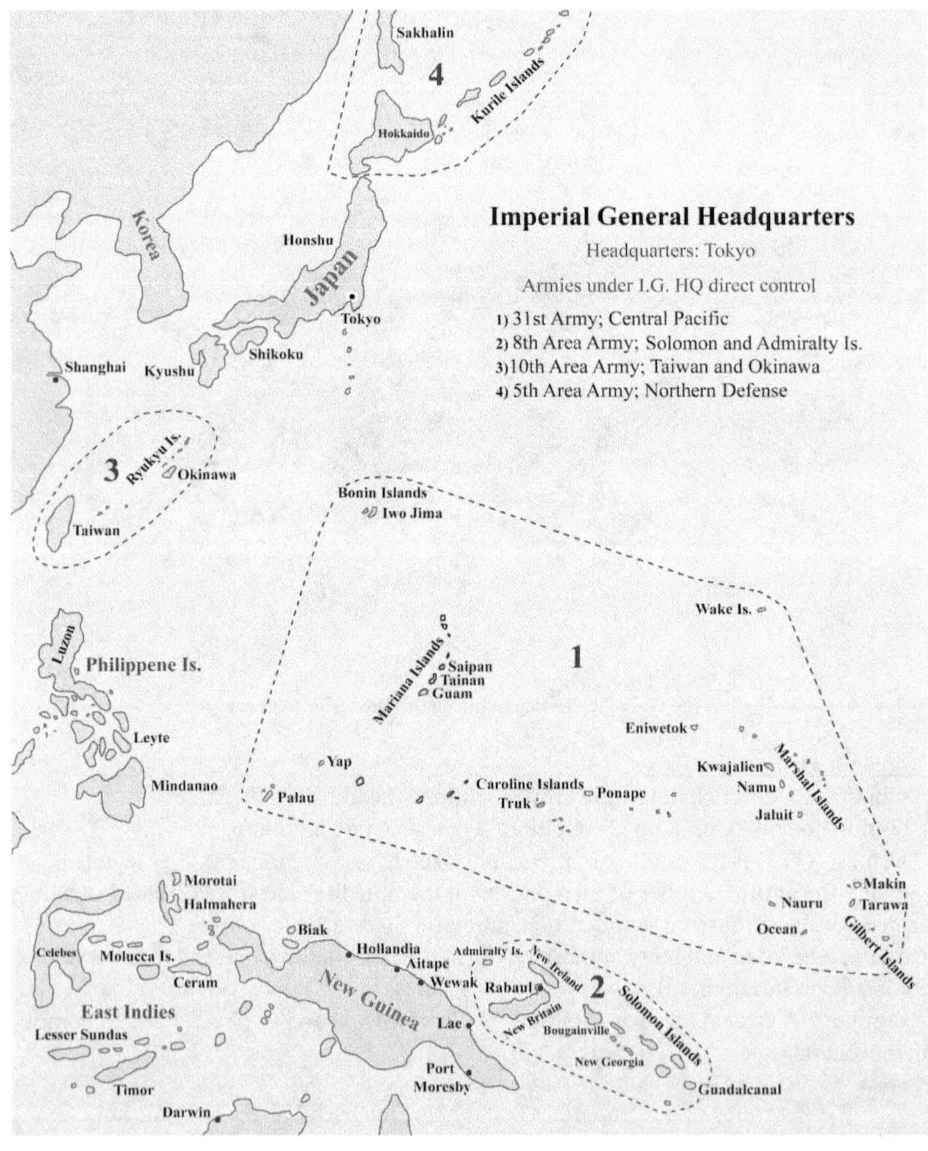

8th Area Army 剛 *Go*

The 8th Area Army headquarters was activated in Tokyo on November 16, 1942 and began operations in Rabaul on Nov. 22nd. Under I.G.HQ control it's mission was to provide a unified command for New Guinea, New Britain, New Ireland and Bougainville. Order of battle included the 17th Army, 18th Army, 6th Division, 21st I.M.B. and 12th Air Brigade. The 17th Army controlled operations in the Solomons and the 18th Army had New Guinea.

The primary supply base for the 8th Area Army was in Rabaul and the Palaus Islands acted as an intermediate base. Important front line bases included in Wewak, Hansa, Madang, Lae, Tuluvu, Garove Is. and Ervente Islands. Lt Gen Hitoshi Imamura was its commander from Nov 16th until deactivation on Sept 7, 1945.

Subordinate armies / duty dates:

17th Army from Nov 16, 1942 until Aug 15, 1945

18th Army from Nov 16, 1942 until Mar 14, 1944

Service History:

1942: Nov 6th, the 8th Area Army HQ was activated in Tokyo ○ Nov 16th to Dec 28th, Buna Detachment destroyed on New Guinea ○ Nov 22nd Lt Gen Hitoshi Imamura arrived in Rabaul by plane from Japan ○

1943: On Jan 4th the 8th Area Army rec'd orders to withdraw the 17th Army from Guadalcanal on Feb 1st and establish advantageous positions on New Guinea ○ Jan 7th the border between the 8th Area Army and the Southern Army became longitude 140 degrees ○ On Jan 13th the 18th Army withdrew from Buna to Salamaua ○ Jan 29th, Battle of Wau, New Guinea ○ Mar 1st to 3rd, half the 51st Division destroyed in the battle of the Bismarck Sea ○ June 30th US troops occupy Nassau Bay ○ Jul 28th the 4th Air Army was organized and placed under the 8th Area Army ○ Between late Aug. and mid Nov the 8th Area Army lost Buna, Munda and Guadalcanal. It became impossible to supply the front lines with the only means available, small landing craft and overland transport. Rabaul, the largest and most important base in the area, was becoming isolated. ○ At the end of Aug a plan for stockpiling supplies began and was largely completed by mid-Nov ○ Oct 1st the U.S. landed troops on Torokina Point, Bougainville. The 8th Area Army went on the defensive and 4th Air Army moved to bases between Hollandia and Madang, New Guinea ○ In Oct the 17th Division sailed from China to Rabaul ○ Dec 15th, the battle of Arawe. US troops land on Cape Merkus ○ On Dec 21st 100 fighters and bombers participate in the last of Japan's large South Pacific air raids, control over air and sea is lost, except over Rabaul and Wewak ○

1944: By January 80,000 Japanese troops are isolated on Bougainville, in Sio and on western New Britain ○ Jan 21st, the 17th Army is again ordered to destroy the enemy in Torokina ○ Early in the year food stops arriving, the army is self-sufficient ○ Feb 15th, air raids on New Ireland and Bougainville intensify after Green Is. is lost ○ Feb 29th US invades the Admiralty Is. and captured Hein Airfield ○ On Mar 6th the 2nd Battle of Torokina began. The 17th Army ordered to withdraw on Mar 25th ○ Mar 25th the 18th Army and 4th Air Army are transferred to 2nd Area Army control. The 8th Area Army warns the 17th Army supplies will stop being sent ○ By Apr 18th 5,000 refugee soldiers arrive in Rabaul and 7,500 more by May ○ In June US planes and ships in the South Pacific seem to decrease ○ In mid-July preparations for the defense of Rabaul are completed ○ In Sept air attacks on Bougainville begin to drop off. 8th Area Army

personnel are generally healthy except on Bougainville ○ In Oct air army personnel in Rabaul repair two Type 100 headquarters recon planes ○ Dec 8th regardless of branch of service all 8th Area Army units became combat units for operation *Go* ○
<u>1945</u>: By January the 8th Area Army is isolated and sits out the rest of the war. About 70% of Rabaul's defenses are comprised of 330 km of caves ○
<u>Major Units</u>: See division / brigade page for order of battle

17th Division Himeji 1907 月 *Tsuki* – Rabaul	172
38th Division Nagoya 1939 沼 *Numa* – Rabaul	182
39th Independent Mixed Brigade 1944 隆 *Chuu* – Rabaul	222-3
40th Independent Mixed Brigade 1944 隆 *Ryuu* – New Ireland	223
65th Brigade 1941 磯夏 *Natsu* – Rabaul	235

6th Air Division 洋 *Yō* – Rabaul (later attached to the 18th Army on New Guinea)

<u>Units under 8th Area Army control</u>: Rabaul	剛 *Go*	
8th Area Army Headquarters	7960 (1,387)	Rabaul
8th Area Army Intelligence Section	7960 (53)	
8th Area Army Fortification Department	11210	
8th Area Army Special Intelligence Department	11220	
8th Area Army Independent Air Unit	11254	
8th Area Army Signal Unit Headquarters	11211 (296)	
16th Signal Regiment	7591 (1,211)	
47th Signal Regiment	11216 (977)	
8th Fixed Signal Unit	11212 (150)	
9th Fixed Signal Unit	11213 (133)	
15th Fixed Signal Unit	11235	
91st Independent Wire Company	5202 (310)	
1st Independent Wireless Radio Platoon	11214 (32) was South Sea Det	
61st Independent Radio Platoon	8086 (53)	
62nd Independent Radio Platoon	8087 (53)	
9th Artillery Headquarters	11225	
7th Field Medium Artillery Regiment	1213 (1,252)	
3rd Independent Heavy Artillery Battalion	1024 (622)	
1st Independent Trench Mortar Regiment	3666 (1,054)	
1st Independent Mortar Battalion	11226 (648?)	
8th Tank Regiment	170 (1,071)	
8th Independent Rapid Firing Gun Company	unknown w/Ichiki Det (8TAS)	
19th Field Anti-Aircraft Artillery Command	9290 (53)	
39th Field Anti-Aircraft Battalion	3778	
47th Field Anti-Aircraft Battalion	8551 (667) was South Sea Det	
48th Field Anti-Aircraft Battalion	2001 (667)	
50th Field Anti-Aircraft Battalion, less the 1st Coy	3616 (667)	
36th Independent Field Anti-Aircraft Company	8031 (162)	
37th Independent Field Anti-Aircraft Company	7461 (162)	
15th Field Machine Cannon Company	1995 (99)	
14th Independent Mixed Regiment	11222 (2,080)	
36th Independent Engineer Regiment	9423 (894)	Takeshi Unit
26th Field Ordinance Depot	10347 (1,363)	

26th Field Motor Vehicle Depot	10348 (1,252)
26th Field Freight Depot	10349 (1,180)
6th Field Military Police Unit	1922 (287)
38th Independent Motor Transport Battalion	2854 (808)
Imperial Guard Division 7th Land Transport Unit	5583 (246)
31st Field Road Construction Unit	4836 (304)
86th Land Duty Company	5733 (511)
2nd Specially Established Land Duty Company	10372 (61)
3rd Specially Established Land Duty Company	10373 (61)
4th Specially Established Land Duty Company	10374 (61)
5th Specially Established Land Duty Company	10375 (61)
6th Specially Established Land Duty Company	10376 (61)
27th Specially Est Construction Duty Company	10384 (61)
6th Raiding Unit	11252 (410)
7th Raiding Unit	11253 (410)
14th Line of Communications Medical HQ	3015 (120)
67th Line of Communications Hospital	7866 (420)
103rd Line of Communications Hospital	7129 (420)
10th Casualty Clearing Unit Headquarters	4821 (117)
63rd Casualty Clearing Platoon	6408 (54)
76th Casualty Clearing Platoon	6076 / 6036 (54)
24th Field Disease Prevention / Water Supply Unit	2627 (329)
16th Line of Communications Veterinary Depot	2298 (538)
(The) Independent Sea Duty Battalion	11223
4th Shipping Transport Headquarters	6188
12th Shipping Engineer Regiment	2958 (1,099)
8th Shipping Engineer Regiment	2503
1st Independent Sea Transport Battalion	16223
14th Field Post Office Unit	3035 (251)
8th Field Horse Remount Depot	36709 (609)

17th Army 沖 *Oki*

The 17th Army began to organize May 18, 1942, its headquarters became active in Fukuoka on May 20th. Home station: Ujina. Under Southern Expeditionary Army control, its order of battle included picked formations the South Seas Detachment, Kawaguchi Detach, Aoba Detach and 41st Inf Regt (later attached to 21st I.M.B). It's mission was to occupy Port Moresby, Samoa, Fiji and New Caledonia then intercept and disrupt American-Australian lines of communications.

Imperial General Headquarters took command of the 17th Army HQ on Aug 16th and sent it to Buin. On November 15th it reorganized and was placed under 8th Area Army control Nov 16th. Lt Gen Haruyoshi Hyakutake was appointed 17th Army commander from May 18, 1942 until Apr 1, 1945, he took ill and Lt Gen Masatane Kanda succeeded him for the duration of the war.

Service History:

1942: June 8th invasion of Samoa (41st Inf Regt), New Caledonia (So Seas Det), Fiji (17th Army) and Port Moresby are put are hold (cancelled July 11th) ○ On July 21st the invasion of New Guinea begins with the Yokoyama Advanced Unit landing in Gona ○ Sept 17th, the 38th Division is transferred to the 17th Army ○ Nov 16th, 8th Area Army and 18th Army are activated ○ Nov 22nd, the 8th Area Army HQ arrived in Rabaul ○

New Guinea Campaign:

South Seas Detachment starts Kokoda Trail campaign ○ Aug. 7th *Battle of Isurava*, won by Aug 31st ○ Sept 6th to 8th *Battle of Mission Hill* ○ Sept 13th to 16th *Battle of Ioribaiwa* ○ Aug 28th the 2nd Division is attached to the 17th Army for the attack on Port Moresby ○ Sept 12th to 16th the South Seas Detachment attacks Refunto ○ Sept 23rd, South Seas Detachment withdraws to Isurava and Kokoda ○ Sept 26th Japanese advance to within sight of Port Moresby then withdraws due to supply shortages ○ Nov 15th the South Seas Detachment retreats from Oivi and Giruwa ○ On Nov 25th responsibility for Eastern New Guinea passes from the 17th Army to the 18th Army ○ See the 18th Army for New Guinea Campaign after November 25, 1942 ○

Guadalcanal Campaign:

Aug. 7th US troops land on Guadalcanal ○ Aug 20th and 21st *Battle of Tenaru River* (or *Alligator Creek*). Ichiki Detachment virtually annihilated ○ On Aug 29th the Kawaguchi Detachment landed near Taivu Point, Guadalcanal ○ On Aug 31st transports land the first wave of the Aoba Detachment ○ Sept 11th the main body of the Aoba Detachment arrives in Kamimbo Bay ○ Sept 12th to 14th Kawaguchi Detachment's attack on Henderson Field fails, *Battle of Edson's Ridge* ○ On Oct 4th 2nd Division headquarters lands on Guadalcanal and deploys to Tassafaronga ○ Oct 7th to 9th *Battle of the Matanikau River*, 2nd Division defeated by a US offensive ○ Oct 10th 17th Army headquarters lands on Guadalcanal, deploys 3 km west of Kokumbona ○ Oct 24th to 26th Battle for Henderson Field ends in failure for the 2nd Division ○ Nov 10th the 38th Division headquarters lands on Guadalcanal ○ Nov 14th, the 38th Division convoy disaster, only 4 of 11 ships reach Guadalcanal ○ On Dec 25th the 17th Army's rations are cut by 25%, the 38th Division has only 2,500 men fit for combat

1943: Jan 10th to 23rd, the battles of Mt. Austin, Galloping Horse and Sea Horse Hills, US troops take the hills near Matanikau River ○ On Jan 15th I.G.HQ orders the 17th Army to withdraw from Guadalcanal ○ Feb 1st the 38th Division left Cape Esperance and arrived at Erventa, Bougainville on Feb 2nd ○ Feb 4th the 2nd Division left Guadalcanal and landed on Erventa Feb 5th ○ Feb 7th the Matsuda Rear Guard Unit left and arrived on Erventa Feb 8th. About 33,600 men landed on Guadalcanal between Aug 1942 and Feb 1943 and by Feb 8th about 12,000 had been evacuated to Erventa ○

End of Guadalcanal ○ In February the 2nd Division was sent to the Philippines, 38th Division to Rabaul and 35th Inf Bgde to Burma ○ May 26th the Southeast Detachment was organized on Bougainville to defend New Georgia ○ June 30th US troops land on Rendova Island and wipe out the garrison ○ July 9th to Aug 4th *Battle of Munda Point*, Southeast Detachment defeated ○ Aug. 5th Munda Point evacuated ○ July 5th to 11th, battle of Enogai Inlet, US troops land to block Munda/Bairoko trail ○ July 20th *Battle of Bairoko*, US withdraws, a modest win for Japan ○ Aug 12th US attempts a small landing on Baanga Island and takes 50% casualties ○ Aug 15th (for most part a naval battle) US troops land on Vella Lavella, Americans replaced by New Zealanders in mid-Sept, fighting continued until Oct 7th when the Japanese withdrew from the island ○ Aug 20th, Baanga Is. evacuated, the garrison boating to Arundel Island ○ Aug 27th, US lands troops on Arundel Island and Japanese garrison (13th Inf Regt) evacuated by Sept 21st ○ Between Sept 22nd and Oct 2nd Southeast Detachment evacuated from Kolombangara to Choiseul in barges ○ Oct 5th, Southeast Detachment HQ is deactivated in Buin, 38th Div units sent to Rabaul ○ From Nov 1st to 3rd US troops land on Torokina Point, Bougainville. The 23rd Inf Regt, 6th Div counterattacked but the Americans held tight ○ Dec 12th the rest of the Southeast Detachment is deactivated in Rabaul ○ Dec 15th *Battle of Arawe*, the Americans land troops on Merkus Point, mainly fought a battle of attrition with the Japanese outside the wire ○ Dec 26th the 65th Brigade fought the Battle of Cape Gloucester, New Britain ○

1944: Jan 21st, the 8th Area Army ordered the 17th Army to attack Torokina (2nd battle) ○ Feb 24th the Japanese withdrew from Merkus Point ○ In late February, with less than 10 landing craft remaining, a planned counter landing in the Torokina area was abandoned ○ Mar 6th to 26th, *2nd Battle of Torokina*, the US beat off repeated attacks, Japanese finally withdraw on the 26th ○ Early to late April, the 17th Army redeployed on Bougainville, completing it with difficulty by the end of May. The plan was to cover a wide area to ensure sustainable food production ○ On June 1st the 17th Army reorganized ○ On June 24th the 38th Independent Mixed Brigade was organized from the 17th Inf Group on Bougainville ○ In early Oct Australian Troops arrive in Torokina ○ In Nov the 6th Div on western Bougainville and the 38th I.M.B. in the Torokina area report they are facing Australians ○ Nov 25th the 6th Division's West Area Defense Unit forced from the Jaba River area ○ Dec 18th *Battle of Artillery Hill*, Australian troops take it ○ Dec 30th and 31st *Battle of Pearl Ridge*, 38th I.M.B. defending ○

1945: On Jan. 1st the 38th I.M.B. retreated from Pearl Ridge after dark ○ Jan 17th the 38th I.M.B. is forced to retreat following the *Battle of Tsimba Ridge* ○ Feb 18th the 6th Div.'s West Area Defense Unit moved to Meiba and on the 20th to the Moketa area ○ Amounts of food varied from area to area, some units started conserving food in Oct and some in Jan or Feb. Those conserving rations lived on sweet potatoes and rice ○ Feb 22nd enemy planes attack Moketa from 3 sides. The West Area Defense Unit couldn't prevent enemy troops from pushing deep into rear positions ○ Feb 25th the Defense Unit is forced across the river ○ Mar 18th to Apr 5th Buliaka River operation, the 6th Div lost about 1000 men ○ Mar 28th to Apr. 6th *Battle of Slater's Knoll* is an Australian victory. From this point on the 17th Army is reduced to fighting guerilla actions ○ From Apr to Aug the 38th I.M.B. defended the Numa Numa trail in East-Central Bougainville ○ From June to Aug a special attack unit from the 13th Inf Regt is sent to disrupt and harass soft targets behind enemy lines in the Mivo River area on SW Bougainville ○

Major Units: See division / brigade page for order of battle

2nd Division* see 38th Army for last deployment 164
38th Division* see 8th Area Army for last deployment 182
(the above divisions were central in the battle for Guadalcanal)
6th Division Kumamoto 1888 明 *Akira* – Bougainville 167
38th Independent Mixed Brigade 力 *Chikara* – Bougainville 222
4th South Seas Garrison Unit (Brigade) 沖 *Oki* 6904 – Bougainville 248

Units under 17th Army control: Buin	沖 *Oki*	
17th Army Headquarters	9811 (441)	
12th Tank Regiment	1408	
3rd Trench Mortar Battalion	5533 (550)	
15th Field Air Defense Headquarters	1026	on Munda
41st Field Anti-Aircraft Battalion	6251 (528)	
59th Field Anti-Aircraft Battalion	7466 (544)	
31st Independent Field Anti-Aircraft Company	3785 (162)	
22nd Field Machine Cannon Company	3627 (105)	
23rd Field Machine Cannon Company	3617 (105)	
27th Field Machine Cannon Company	5069 (105)	
31st Field Machine Cannon Company	7465 (105)	
17th Army Signal Unit Headquarters	unknown (62)	
32nd Signal Regiment	11311	
88th Independent Wire Company	5142 (410)	
6th Independent Wireless Radio Platoon	11302 (53)	
60th Independent Wireless Radio Platoon	8085 (53)	
69th Independent Wireless Radio Platoon	11303 (53)	
70th Independent Wireless Radio Platoon	11304 (53)	
6th Independent Searchlight Company	7462	
19th Independent Engineer Regiment	8126 (421)	
39th Field Road Construction Unit	8232	
51st Construction Duty Company	8234 (511)	
55th Construction Duty Company, one section	6915	
120th Land Duty Company	7290 (511)	
96th Land Duty Company, one section	6918	
2nd Shipping Engineer Regiment	6171 (1,099)	
2nd Shipping Debarkation Unit	2947	
212th Independent Motor Transport Company	5876 (183)	
76th Line of Communications Hospital	4810 (420)	
94th Line of Communications Hospital	8201 (420)	
53rd Casualty Clearing Platoon	6012 (54)	
54th Casualty Clearing Platoon	6013 (54)	
17th Army Disease Prevention / Water Supply Unit	8607 (225)	
26th Field Ordnance Depot, one section	10347	
26th Field Motor Transport Depot, one section	10348	
26th Field Freight Depot, one section	10349	

Eastern New Guinea

South Sea Detachment:	楯 *So*
55th Infantry Group Headquarters	8414 (176)
144th Infantry Regiment	8417 (2,932)
55th Cavalry Regiment, 3rd Company	8418 (120)
55th Mountain Artillery Regiment, 1st Battalion	8420 (765)
55th Engineer Regt, 1st Company, Materials Platoon	8421 (216)

55th Division Signal Unit, an element	8422 (40)	
55th Transport Regiment, 2nd Company	8423 (615)	
55th Division Medical Unit – third of	8425 (199)	
55th Division 1st Field Hospital	8426 (182)	
55th Division Veterinary Unit, an element	8430 (30)	
55th Div. Disease Prev./Water Supply Unit	8428 (42)	one section
47th Field Anti-Aircraft Battalion, minus one coy	8551 (265)	
1st Independent Radio Platoon	11301 (32)	
1st Fixed Radio Unit	unknown (150)	
120th Land Duty Company, one platoon	7290	

South Seas Detachment total officers and men – 5,549
(Nankai Shitai) Already in Rabaul when it joined the 17th Army May 20, 1942. Under Major General Tomitaro Horii. All units from the 55th Division. Disbanded June 17, 1943, 55th Div units were shipped to the 38th Army in Burma.

Guadalcanal: (detachments in order of landing)	沖 *Oki* (33,600)	
4th Field Medium Artillery Regiment	1502 (1,477)	
10th Independent Mountain Artillery Regiment	8119	
20th Independent Mountain Artillery Battalion	No # (442)	
38th Field Anti-Aircraft Battalion	3777 (522)	
45th Field Anti-Aircraft Battalion	7016	
47th Field Anti-Aircraft Battalion, one company	8551	
76th Line of Communications Hospital, 1 section	4810	
Ichiki Detachment: (from 7th Division)	熊 *Kuma*	
28th Infantry Regiment	9208 (3,102)	
7th Engineer Regiment, 1st Company	9218	
8th Ind. Rapid Firing Gun Company (8TAS)	unknown	
Kawaguchi Detachment: (from 18th Division)	菊 *Kiku*	
35th Infantry Brigade Headquarters	8901 / 10714	
124th Infantry Regiment (reinforced)	8906	later to 31st Div.
Aoba Detachment: (from 2nd Division)	勇 *Isamu*	
2nd Infantry Group Headquarters	1330 (113)	
4th Infantry Regiment	1301 (2,719)	
2nd Reconnaissance Regiment, 4th Company	1305	
2nd Field Artillery Regt., 1st Motorized Battalion	1307	
2nd Engineer Regiment, 1st Company	1308	
2nd Division Signal Unit, 1 section	1309	
2nd Transport Regiment, 3rd Company	1310	
2nd Division Medical Unit – third of	1312 (163)	
2nd Division 2nd Field Hospital	1314 (242)	
2nd Division D. P. and Water Supply Unit – half of	1317 (98)	

Admiralties - Manus and Los Negros Islands: (2,615 + 600 navy men)
Lorengau Defense Unit:

Lorengau Defense Unit continued	基 *Moto*	
51st Transport Regiment	2810 (850)	
229th Infantry Regiment, 1st Battalion	8925 (343)	
1st Independent Mixed Regiment, 2nd Battalion	unknown (800)	
31st Sea Duty Company	3300 (289)	
63rd Independent Wireless Platoon	5203 (70)	
25th Airfield Company	11615 (37)	Los Negros Is.

Bougainville: Southeast Detachment

Southeast Detachment Headquarters	unknown	
13th Infantry Regiment	9018 明	from 6th Div
229th Infantry Regiment	8925 沼	from 38th Div
10th Ind. Mountain Artillery Regiment, 2nd Battalion	8119	
2nd Independent Rapid Firing Gun Battalion	unknown	anti tank

Central Pacific Region

31st Army 備 *Sonae*

The 31st Army's Headquarters was sent to Saipan on February 18, 1944, more administrative than a combat headquarters it was created to oversee island garrisons scattered throughout the Central Pacific Defense Zone. From Feb 25th the 31st Army reported to I.G.HQ, while the Navy's Combined Fleet provided tactical direction. Its headquarters on Saipan, Lt Gen Hideyoshi Obata was appointed commander on Feb 25th. The HQ moved to Guam on June 15th to avoid the invasion of Saipan while Obata was inspecting garrisons in the Paulus . He committed suicide Aug 11th and was replaced by Maj Gen Yoshitomo Tamura. On Aug 22nd Lt Gen Shunsaburō Mugikura became 31st Army commander and remained so until the war ended.

The Five Central Pacific Army Groups under 31st Army control

Bonin District Group: Active from Feb 25, 1944. Iwo Jima, Chichi Jima, Haha Jima and Ani Jima

Palau District Group: Active from Feb 25, 1944. Babelthuap, Peleliu, Anguar and Sonsorol Islands

Truk District Group: Active from Feb 25, 1944. Truk, Yap, Meyeron, Mortlock, Endersby, Kusaie and Ponape Islands

Northern Marianas District Group: Active from May 22, 1944. Saipan, Tinian, Pagan and Rota Islands

Southern Marianas District Group: Active from May 22, 1944. Guam

After the failure of Midway in June 1942 the Army accepted it may be fighting a battle of attrition. On Sept 30, 1943 I.G.HQ ordered operational bases in the Solomon, Caroline and Mariana Islands to become fortified positions, able to coordinate all arms counterattacks from the land, sea and air by spring 1944. The Gilbert and Marshall Is. had fallen by the time the 31st Army became active on February 25th.

Service History:
1941: The South Seas Detachment occupied Guam on Dec 10th and Wake Island on the 23rd. Japan renamed Guam "Omiya Jima" for the balance of the war ○
1942: June 5th the battle and attempted invasion of Midway ended Japan's string of military successes marking a turning point in the war ○
1943: Sept 30th emphasizing island fortifications, I.G.HQ issued operational guidance for the Pacific that conceded the turning point ○ In late Oct the 52nd Division transferred from Japan to Truk ○ On Nov 16th the 1st Amphibious Brigade, 1st, 2nd, 3rd, 4th, 5th South Pacific Detachments under Navy control and the 6th South Pacific Detachment under the 8th Area Army deployed to islands in the Central Pacific ○
1944: In early Feb the 29th Division transferred from Manchuria to Saipan ○ Feb 17th to 23rd *Battle of Eniwetok* ○ Feb 18th the 31st Army headquarters became active and shipped to Saipan ○ Feb 25th, the Bonin, Truk and Palau District Army Groups become active, while the Gilbert and Marshall Is. are already lost ○ Mar 25th, the Army and Navy reached an agreement dividing operational and administrative responsibility in the Central Pacific ○ May 22nd the Northern and Southern Mariana Army Groups become active ○ June 15th to July 7th *Battle of Saipan* ○ June 19th and 20th *A-go* operation which Americans called *The Great Marianas Turkey Shoot*. Japan lost 335 carrier planes and 3 aircraft carriers, also called *Battle of the Philippines Sea* ○ July 21st to Aug 10th *Battle of Guam* ○ July 24th to Aug 1st *Battle of Tinian* ○ Sept. 15th to Nov. 27th *Battle of Peleliu* ○ Sept. 17th to Oct. 22nd *Battle of Anguar* ○
1945: Feb. 19th to Mar. 17th Battle of Iwo Jima ○
Major Units: See division / brigade page for order of battle

14th Division Utsunomiya 1905 照 *Teru* – Babelthuap, Peleliu, Anguar	169-70
29th Division Nagoya 1941 雷 *Rai* – Guam, and Tinian Island	177
43rd Division Nagoya 1943 誉 *Homare* – Saipan Island	183-4
52nd Division Kanezawa 1940 柏 *Kashiwa* – Truk Island	187
109th Division Kofu 1937 胆 *Tan* – Iwo Jima, Chichi Jima	198-9
10th Independent Mixed Brigade 1940 備 *Sonae* – Rota Island	212
47th Independent Mixed Brigade 1944 備 *Sonae* – Saipan Island	223
48th Independent Mixed Brigade 1944 備 *Sonae* – Guam Island,	223
49th Independent Mixed Brigade 1944 備 *Sonae* – Yap Island	224
50th Independent Mixed Brigade 1944 胆 *Tan* – Meyeron Atoll	224
51st Independent Mixed Brigade 1944 備 *Sonae* – Truk Island	225
52nd Independent Mixed Brigade 1944 備 *Sonae* – Ponape Island	225
53rd Independent Mixed Brigade 1944 備 *Sonae*– Peleliu Island	225
1st Amphibious Brigade 1943 駆 *Kakeru* – Enewetok Atoll	241

Units under 31st Army control:	備 *Sonae*	
31st Army Headquarters	7920 (1,620)	
31st Army Headquarters Intelligence Section	7920 (50)	
31st Army Signal Unit	17500 (387)	
1st South Seas Detachment	11221 (1,254)	Mili Atoll
2nd South Seas Detachment	4372 (1,903)	Kusaie Is.
3rd South Seas Detachment	Reorg. into 52 I.M.B. Ponape	
4th South Seas Detachment	12501 (625)	Mortlock Is.
5th South Seas Detachment	12502	

9th Independent Engineer Regiment 4812 (894)
31st Specially Established Machine Cannon Unit 14681 (85)
32nd Specially Established Machine Cannon Unit 14682 (85)
34th Specially Established Machine Cannon Unit 14684 (85)
4th Independent Mountain Artillery Regiment 満 369 (2,677)
1st Observation Unit 12417
2nd Observation Unit 12418
1st Mobile Ordinance Repair Unit 12364 (237)
1st Sea Duty Group Headquarters unknown (120)

Truk District Group 備 *Sonae*

Truk Island: 31st Army HQ. Bypassed, Operation Hailstone Feb 17, 18, 1944

52nd Division 柏 4651 (15,422)
51st Independent Mixed Brigade 備 17564-74 (5,389)
9th Independent Engineer Regiment 4812 (894)

Yap Island: Bypassed

49th Independent Mixed Brigade 備 17542-54 (5,591)

Meyeron Atoll: Arrived April 12, 1944. Bypassed

50th Independent Mixed Brigade 胆 17554-63 (3,944)
7th Expeditionary U. reorg. as 50th I.M.B. 44/04/12

Mortlock Island: Arrived May 19, 1944. Bypassed

4th South-Seas Detachment 備 12501 (625)
Element from 51st Independent Mixed Brigade 備 17564 (132)

Endersby Island: Bypassed

11th Independent Mixed Regiment 備 17585 (2,688)

Kusaie Island: Bypassed

2nd South Seas Detachment 備 4372 (1,903)

Ponape Island: Bypassed

52nd Independent Mixed Brigade 備 17575-82 (3,194)

Eniwetok Island: Battle Feb. 17th to 23rd 1944

1st Amphibious Brigade 駆 3130-8 (5,366)

Bonin District Group: 備 *Sonae*

Iwo Jima: Battle Feb. 19th to Mar. 17th 1945

109th Division 膽 *Tan* 17501
109th Division Headquarters 17502/18301 (1,488)
109th Division Signal Unit 18305 (177)
109th Division Observation Unit 17525 (110)
109th Division Field Hospital 17526
2nd Mixed Brigade Headquarters 17512/18315 (135)

• 309th Independent Infantry Battalion	17513/18316 (579)
• 310th Independent Infantry Battalion	17514/18317 (579)
• 311th Independent Infantry Battalion	17515/18318 (579)
• 312th Independent Infantry Battalion	17516/18319 (579)
• 313th Independent Infantry Battalion	17517/18320 (579)
• 314th Independent Infantry Battalion	17518/18321 (579)
• 2nd Mixed Brigade Artillery Unit	17519/18322 (415)
• 2nd Mixed Brigade Engineer Unit	17520/18323 (221)
• 2nd Mixed Brigade Field Hospital	17521/18324 (61)
• 1st Mixed Regiment	1752218325 (1,467)
• 9th Heavy Artillery Regiment	17523/18326 (298)
• 109th Division Anti Aircraft Unit	17524/18327 (1,072) 5/22/44
• 9th Field Medium Artillery Regt., one battalion	7837 called 1st Ind. Arty Btn
• 2nd Independent Artillery Battalion	7838
Attached	膽 *Tan*
145th Infantry Regiment	11963 (3,165) from 46th Div
2nd Medium Mortar Battalion	9704 (592)
20th Independent Mortar Battalion	12710 (648)
1st Rocket Gun Company, B type	18330 (121*)
20th Specially Est. Machine Cannon Unit	18331 (85)
21st Specially Est. Machine Cannon Unit	18332 (85)
43rd Specially Est, Machine Cannon Unit	2185 (85)
44th Specially Est, Machine Cannon Unit	2186 (85)
1st Independent Machine Gun Battalion	7837 (334)
2nd Independent Machine Gun Battalion	7838 (334)
8th Independent Rapid Firing Gun Battalion	3855 (403) anti-tank
9th Independent Rapid Firing Gun Battalion	3856 (403)
10th Independent Rapid Firing Gun Battalion	6025 (403)
11th Independent Rapid Firing Gun Battalion	7179 (403)
12th Independent Rapid Firing Gun Battalion	7180 (403)
3rd Infantry Battalion, 17th Ind. Mixed Regt.	7157 (650*)
26th Tank Regiment	12076 (336*)
2nd Field Well Drilling Company	unknown (119)
5th Fortification Construction Company	2773
Iwo Jima Temporary Ordinance Depot	unknown
Iwo Jima Temporary Freight Depot	unknown
Iwo Jima Special Navigation Unit	18302
Iwo Jima Water Supply/ Purification Department	unknown

109th Division: Provided headquarters staff for the Bonin District Army Group.
Iwo Jima: Feb 19, 1945, after 3 days of bombing, the US invaded Iwo Jima. 23,000 Japanese troops defended the island. In spite of desperate efforts Mt. Suribachi fell Feb. 23rd. but the fighting continuing until the night of Mar.17th, when the commander and his remaining officers died making a suicide attack.
(000*) asterix indicates a number taken from G-2 Task Force 56 Iwo Jima Report

Chichi Jima Bypassed 備 *Sonae*

Chichi Jima continued

109th Division	膽 *Tan* 17501
109th Division Headquarters Group	17502
109th Division Signal Unit	18305
Chichi Army Hospital	17521 (129) deactiv. 5/5/44
1st Mixed Brigade Headquarters	17503/18314 (93)
• 304th Independent Infantry Battalion	17505/18307 (579) Haha J.
• 306th Independent Infantry Battalion	17507/18309 (579) Haha J.
• 307th Independent Infantry Battalion	17508/18310 (579)
• 308th Independent Infantry Battalion	17509/18311 (579)
• 1st Mixed Brigade Artillery Unit	17510/18312 (129)
• 1st Mixed Brigade Engineer Unit	17511/18313 (321)
Attached	
9th Field Medium Artillery Regiment, detachment	8737
45th Specially Established Machine Cannon Unit	2187 (85)
46th Specially Established Machine Cannon Unit	2188 (85)
17th Shipping Engineer Regiment Detachment	16701 123
2nd Independent Sea Transport Company	unknown (84)
Special Field Ordnance Depot	unknown
Special Field Munitions Dump	unknown
59th Anchorage HQ Chichi Jima Detachment	16722
Haha Jima: Bypassed	備 *Sonae*
109th Div. 1st Mixed Infantry Brigade Detachment	胆 *Tan*
• 303rd Independent Infantry Battalion	17504/18306 (579)
• 305th Independent Infantry Battalion	17506/18308 (579)
• 274th Independent Infantry Battalion	14213
• 276th Independent Infantry Battalion	14171
1st Mixed Regiment	17522 (1,467)
Ani Jima: bypassed by the U.S.	備 *Sonae*
275th Independent Infantry Battalion	unknown
Marcus Island: bypassed by the U.S.	備 *Sonae*
12th Independent Mixed Regiment	17586 (2,716)

Northern Marianas District Group 備 *Sonae*

Saipan Island: Battle June 15th to July 7th 1944

31st Army Headquarters (Administrative Personnel)	7920 (1,100)
43rd Division Nagoya 1943	誉 *Homare* (19,133)
47th Independent Mixed Brigade	備 *Sonae* (3,103)

Attached:

Northern Marianas District Group continued

18th Infantry Regiment, 1st Battalion	3219 (600)	29th Div
89th Infantry Regiment, 3rd Battalion	3476	24th Div
44th Field Machine Cannon Company	2100 (105)	
3rd Independent Mountain Artillery Regiment	5511 (845)	minus 2nd Btn
25th Anti-Aircraft Regiment	2686 (1,636)	
52nd Field Antiaircraft Artillery Battalion	4461 (667)	
43rd Independent Anti-Aircraft Company	7425 (528)	
7th Independent Engineer Regiment	7017 (894)	2nd Coy on Guam
264th Independent Motor Transport Company	6268 (183)	
265th Independent Motor Transport Company	6269 (183)	
278th Independent Motor Transport Company	7105 (183)	
9th Tank Regiment, 1st and 2nd Coys on Guam	12089 (1,071)	
60th Anchorage Headquarters	16723 (81)	
15th Infantry Regiment, one section	7757	14th Div
50th Infantry Regiment Replacement Unit	3215	29th Div
3rd Independent Tank Company	12097**	
4th Independent Tank Company	5308**	
14th Independent Trench Mortar Battalion	12586 (648)	
17th Independent Trench Mortar Battalion	12587 (648)	
29th Division Sea Transport Unit, one section	6151	29 Div
23rd Field Airfield Construction Unit	2404 (700)	
14th Field Air Repair Depot, 9th Ind. Maint. Unit	9304 (113)	
16th Shipping Engineer Regiment	16700 (1,099)	

Saipan: June 15, 1944, Saipan's unfinished defenses were stronger than any elsewhere in the Pacific so it was thought the island could delay the enemy for a considerable time. American forces pulverized the island from sea and air before landing troops on June 5th, by the 28th Japan knew it was lost. On July 6th both Vice Admiral Nagumo and Lt Gen Saito committed suicide. The last organized Japanese attack occurred early on July 7th. The loss of Saipan was thought so serious Japan's government kept it out of the news until July 18th.

Note: US forces captured the almost complete records of the 31st Army on Saipan.

Note: Saipan had straggler units formed from shipwreck survivors who fought as infantrymen.

** The 3rd and 4th Ind Tank Companies were assigned to the Palau District Group but lost heavily in a submarine attack near Saipan en route. The 118 survivors were called the 'Saipan Tank Unit'.

Tinian Island: Battle July 24th to Aug, 1st 1944	備 *Sonae*	
50th Infantry Regiment	3215 (3,162)	from 29th Div
29th Division Field Hospital	3205 (592)	
135th Infantry Regiment, 1st Battalion	11934 (1,000)	from 43rd Div

Pagan Island: Bypassed — 備 *Sonae*

Pagan Island continued	備 *Sonae*
9th Independent Mixed Regiment (Was 5th Exp Unit, reorganized on Pagan 44/05/22)	17583 (2,688)

Rota Island: Bypassed

10th Independent Mixed Brigade (final iteration)	備 *Sonae* (947)

Southern Marianas District Group	備 *Sonae*
Guam Island: Battle began July 24, 1944	
29th Division	雷 *Rai* (13,825)
48th Independent Mixed Brigade	備 *Sonae* (3,102)
Attached	
10th Independent Mixed Regiment	17584 (2,688)
25th Field Anti-Aircraft Battalion	4481 (667)
1st and 2nd Company, 9th Tank Regiment	12089
7th Independent Engineer Regiment, 2nd Company	7017
16th Shipping Engineer Regiment, 2nd Company	16700
13th Division Headquarters Detachment	6801鏡 (200)

Palau District Group:	備 *Sonae*
Babelthuap Island: Bypassed	
14th Division (split into three battle groups)	照 *Teru* (11,909)
53rd Independent Mixed Brigade	備 *Sonae* (4,263)
Attached:	
10th Independent Mixed Regiment, an element	17584
57th Line of Communications Sector Command	3965 (203)
57th Line of Communications Duty Company	3967 (511)
7th Specially Established Land Duty Company	10377 (61)
42nd Independent Motor Transport Battalion	1038
123rd Line of Communications Hospital	5223 (441)
23rd Field Airfield Construction Unit	2404 (702)
2nd South Sea Guard Unit	unknown
3rd South Sea Guard Unit	1938
23rd Field Disease Prevention / Water Supply Unit	2626 (329)
18th Army Headquarters Detached Personnel	7910
42nd Independent Anti Aircraft Company	7424
3rd Signal Regiment Replacement Unit	1244
31st Specially Established Machine Cannon Unit	14681 照 (85)
32nd Specially Established Machine Cannon Unit	14682 照 (85)
33rd Specially Established Machine Cannon Unit	14683 照 (85)
34th Specially Established Machine Cannon Unit	14684 照 (85)
35th Specially Established Machine Cannon Unit	14685 照 (85)

36th Specially Established Machine Cannon Unit	14686 尚武 (85)
37th Specially Established Machine Cannon Unit	14687 尚武 (85)
38th Specially Established Machine Cannon Unit	14688 尚武 (85)
39th Specially Established Machine Cannon Unit	14689 尚武 (85)
40th Specially Established Machine Cannon Unit	14690 尚武 (85)
30th Independent Transport Regiment	unknown
40th Sea Duty Company	5726 (511)

Peleliu Island: Battle began Sept. 15, 1944	備 *Sonae* (10,500)	
14th Division Battle Group	照 *Teru* (5,388)	
14th Division Signal Unit, one radio squad	7714 (10)	
14th Division Intendance Duty Unit	7736 (30)	
14th Division Field Hospital, one company	7770 (250)	
2nd Infantry Regiment	7746 (3,166)	
2nd Infantry Regiment Artillery Unit	7793 was 1st Bn 20th F A Regt	
15th Infantry Regiment, 3rd Battalion	7757 (1,130)	
14th Division Tank Unit (12 tanks)	4363 (130)	
14th Engineer Regiment, one company	unknown	
Attached		
346th Independent Infantry Battalion, 53rd I.M.B.	14656 (579)	
23rd Field Disease Prevention/Water Supply Unit	2626	see Babelthuap
3rd Shipping Transport Headquarters, Palau Branch	2944	

Anguar Island: Battle began Sept. 17, 1944		
59th Infantry Regiment, 1st Battalion (reinforced)	7758 照 *Teru* (about 1,500)	

Sonsorol Island: Bypassed by the U.S.		
219th Infantry Regiment, 1st Battalion	2929 東	from 35th Div

Wake Island	備 *Sonae*
65th Guard Unit (an Imperial Japanese Navy unit)	(2,000)
13th Independent Mixed Regiment	17587 (1,627)

Wake Island fell to the Imperial Navy's 2nd Maizuru NLF on Dec 23, 1941. Initial army landing was the 3rd South Seas Garrison Unit (1st Inf Btn, 1st Arty Company) on July 10, 1943 followed by the 1st Btn, 5th Ind Mixed Regiment (備5125) and 2nd Company, 16th Tank Regiment (備7591) on Jan 1, 1944. 2000 men reorganized into the 13th Ind Mixed Regt on May 22nd. Wake surrendered to the US on Sept 7, 1945.

South Asia, Pacific and Indian Ocean Regions

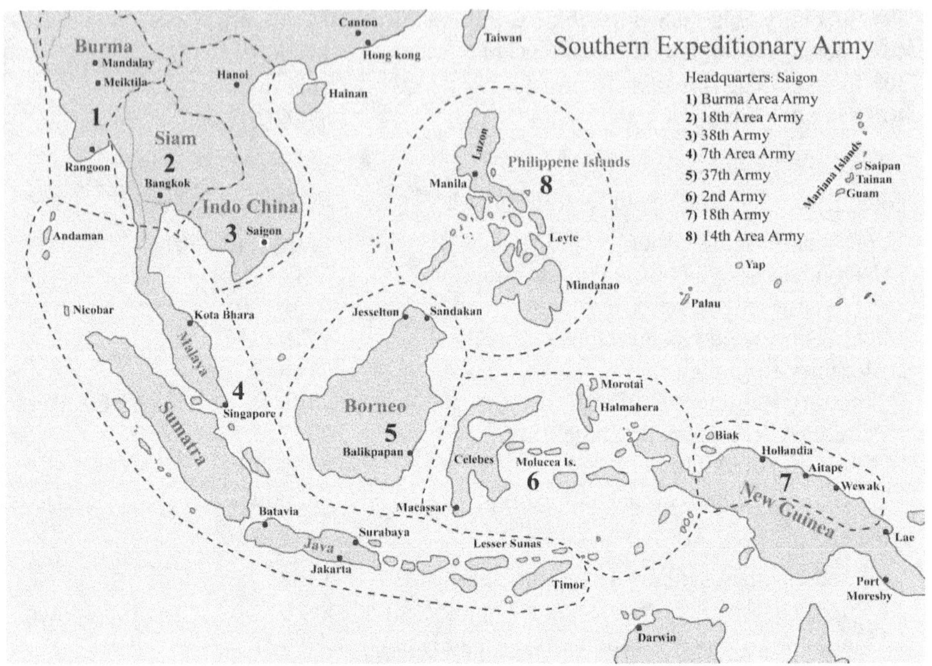

<u>**Southern Expeditionary Army**</u> 威 *i*

The Southern Expeditionary Army's order of battle had been assembled by Nov 5, 1941. Under Imperial Headquarters direction from Nov 6th, it became operational in Saigon on the 20th, moved to Singapore in March 1943, Manila on June 15, 1944 and back to Saigon on Nov 17th. The Southern Army's main supply base was in southern Indochina, Formosa served as an intermediate base and Canton China as an auxiliary base. Reserve fighting units were mainly drawn from China while service units came from Manchuria. The Southern Army Headquarters provide direction for all army operations in South Asia, the Pacific and Indian Ocean areas. Its commander was General Hisaichi Terauchi from Nov 6th until it surrendered on September 12, 1945.

Subordinate area armies / duty dates:

Burma Area Army from Mar 27, 1943 to Aug 15, 1945	Moulmein, Burma
7th Area Army from Mar 27, 1944 until deactivated Nov 15, 1945	Singapore
2nd Area Army from Apr 15, 1944 until deactivated June 13, 1945	North Sulawesi
14th Area Army from Aug 4, 1944 until deactivated Sept 2, 1945	Manila, P.I.
18th Area Army from July 15, 1945 to Aug 15, 1945	Bangkok, Thailand
Palau Area Group from Aug 21, 1944 to Aug 15, 1945	Babelthuap Is.

Subordinate armies / duty dates:

14th Army from Nov 6, 1941 to June 27, 1942	Manila. P.I.
15th Army from Nov 6, 1941 to March 27, 1943	Rangoon, Burma
16th Army from Nov 6, 1941to March 27, 1944	Batavia, Java
25th Army from Nov 6, 1941 to March 27, 1944	Fort de Kock, Sumatra

Borneo Defense Army from Apr 20, 1942 to Mar 27, 1944 Kuching, Borneo
17th Army from May 18, 1942 to Aug 16, 1942 Rabaul, New Britain
19th Army from Jan 7, 1943 to Oct 30, 1943 Ambon, to 2AA then deactivated
Thailand Garrison Army from Jan 7, 1943 to Dec 20, 1944 became 39th Army
Indochina Garrison Army from Nov 16, 1943 to Dec 20, 1944 became 38th Army
29th Army from Jan 15, 1944 to Mar 27, 1944 Taiping, Malaysia
14th Army from Mar 27, 1944 to Aug 4, 1944, Manila, became 14th Area Army
Borneo Defense Army from Sept 4, 1944 to Sept 22, 1944 became 37th Army
37th Army from Sept 22, 1944 to Sept 15, 1945 Kuching, British Borneo
38th Army from Dec 20, 1944 to Aug 15, 1945 Saigon/Hanoi, Indochina
39th Army from Dec 20, 1944 to July 14, 1945 Bangkok, became 18th Area Army
2nd Army from June 13, 1945 to Aug 15, 1945 Macassar Island
18th Army from June 17, 1945 to Sept 25, 1945 Rabaul, New Britain/Wewak, N.G.

Service History:

1941: July 22nd Japan and Indochina sign a joint defense agreement ○ On Nov 20th the Southern Expeditionary Army became operational in Saigon with General Count Terauchi commanding ○ Nov 25th Terauchi left Tokyo and arrived in Saigon Dec 5th ○ Dec 7th Pearl Harbor attacked ○ Dec 8th was X-Day, date the Japanese chose for the start of the Pacific war. Units of the Imperial Guard Division land near Bangkok, Thailand unannounced. In Malaya the 25th Army's 5th Division and elements from the 18th Division made surprise attacks on Singora, Patani and Thepha. ○ On Dec 10th the Navy sank the British battleship HMS Prince of Wales and cruiser HMS Repulse. The same day the invasion of the Philippines began with air attacks on northern Luzon airfields ○ On Dec 15th the invasion of the Dutch East Indies began. The Army's initial objectives included Borneo, Amboina, the Celebes, Timor and Sumatra ○ On Dec 16th the Kawaguchi Detachment lands in British Borneo and occupies the oilfields at Seria and Miri and Miri airfield ○ On Dec 21st Japan and Thailand sign the *Japan–Thailand Military Alliance Agreement* marking the friendly occupation of Thailand ○

1942: On Jan 11th the 16th Army captured Tarakan, Borneo ○ On Jan 12th Ambon operations began ○ Jan. 28th, the Eastern Detachment landed and Ambon fell on the 31st ○ Jan 30th the 15th Army (55th Div) crossed the Thai border into Burma, occupied Moulmein ○ Mar 9th Dutch Army surrendered to the 16th Army. Its main objective was the oil rich East Indies, secondly a speedy conquest to free up troops ○ By the end of March Southern Army control extended from south Burma to Andaman, Nicobar, Malaya and Netherlands East Indies ○ Apr 3rd, the Army relinquished control of Andaman Is. to the Navy ○ May 5th, Borneo Garrison Army headquarters became active ○ On May 18th Burma capitulates. The 15th Army is ordered to entrench itself and maintain peace ○ May 19th the Southern Fuel Depot is established in Singapore ○ June was spent mopping up, regrouping and rebuilding battle worn units ○ On June 10th confident in its gains I.G.HQ began withdrawing units from the southern area. The 10th Air Group and other air units were sent to Manchuria. ○ On June 22nd the India Independence League formed with Japanese Government support ○ On June 29th, to facilitate the introduction of military administration in the Philippines the 14th Army was transferred from Southern Army to I.G.HQ control ○ On July 9th the 3rd Air Army's headquarters became active in Singapore. ○ In July air routes were established between Hong Kong, Formosa, Philippines, Borneo, Java, Singapore, Indochina, Malaya, Sumatra, Thailand and Burma ○ July 31st the 3rd Field Railroad

Headquarters was established to oversee all Southern rail activity ○ Aug 6th, the loss of ships began to affect Southern Army operations. The 5th Division was to return to Japan but became stranded in Singapore ○ On Nov 9th the Indochina Garrison Army headquarters mobilized in Saigon ○ In November, as travel by sea continued to become ever more dangerous, construction on the Thai-Burma Railway began ○
1943: On Jan 4th Thailand Garrison Army headquarters began operations in Bangkok to manage the movement of men and supplies through Thailand ○ On Jan 15th the 19th Army became active in Batavia, Java ○ Jan 19th, Southern Army Ordinance, Motor Transport and Freight depots established ○ Feb 24th, Southern Railway Unit established to speed construction of railway lines ○ On Mar 25th Palembang Air Defense Unit was activated ○ In March the 25th Army downgraded from a field army to a garrison army in Sumatra. The Southern Army took direct control of Malaya ○ On Mar 18th the Burma Area Army became active and on the 27th attached to the Southern Army ○ In April, due to intense enemy submarine and aircraft activity, shipping to the southeast Pacific began to break down ○ On Apr 12th the 3rd Military Police Unit, Southern Army Survey Unit and Southern Army Fortifications Dept. are activated ○ Attempts to move reinforcements overland into Burma provide inadequite results ○ In early July the Southern Army requested I.G.HQ approval for an offensive in Burma, in mid-July permission was granted ○ On Oct 18th Thailand annexed Malaya's four northern provinces ○ On Oct 21st the Provisional Government for Free India was created in Burma under Chandra Bose. ○ On Nov 23rd the 2nd Area Army's headquarters arrived in Davao, Philippines ○
1944: *U-go* was seen as a proactive way to defend Burma, three divisions from the 15th Army would attack east and south of the Imphal Basin ○ On Feb 15th shipping bases in the southwest Pacific were placed under the Southern Army's direct control ○ On Apr 15th, 2nd Area Army headquarters was transferred from I.G.HQ to Southern Army control ○ On Apr 22nd the Americans made a surprise attack on the 18th Army's base in Hollandia, New Guinea ○ On Apr 29th the 33rd Army headquarters completed organizing in Rangoon ○ On May 2nd Japanese troops were forced from Eastern New Guinea ○ On May 5th the Southern Army held a meeting in Singapore to discuss the inevitable battle for the Philippines ○ On May 17th American forces began the month long *Battle of Sarmi-Wakde* ○ May 27th, the US invade Biak Island, fighting lasts until Aug 17th. ○ In May the Southern Expeditionary Army headquarters redeployed to the Philippines becoming active on June 15th ○ On June 20th the 18th Army, isolated in eastern New Guinea, was placed under Southern Army control ○ Army General Staff order an end to *U-go* on July 4th ○ On July 8th the Burma Area Army ends the *Battle of Imphal* ○ On Aug 4th the 14th Army deactivated then reactivated as the 14th Area Army. Subordinate, the 35th Army activates at the same time to operate in the central and southern Philippines ○ In early Aug the Southern Army headquarters asked I.G.HQ to move it from the Philippines to Singapore or Saigon ○ On Sept 16th protected shipping lanes are established in cooperation with the Navy to slow the loss of ships to Allied submarines and aircraft ○ On Sept 22nd the Borneo Garrison Army reorganizes into the 37th Army on Borneo and is transferred from 7th Area Army to Southern Expeditionary Army control, the General Staff felt this was a good compromise to avoid a large-scale change at a critical time ○ Between Oct 17th and 19th the Americans landed on Leyte beginning the battle for the Philippines ○ Oct 27th, the 35th Army received the 1st and 26th Divisions and the 68th Brigade ○ On November 17th permission finally arrived

for the Southern Army headquarters to move to Saigon, Indochina ○ On Dec 20th the Indochina Garrison Army headquarters becomes the 38th Army headquarters ○ 1945: Jan 1st, the 4th Air Army in the Philippines became subordinate to the 14th Area Army. Imperial General Headquarters ordered the Southern Army to hold important areas in Indochina, Thailand, Malaya and Sumatra ○ In mid-Jan the Southern Army diverted the 2nd Division from Burma and 4th Division from Sumatra to Thailand. The 2nd Division was then sent to Indochina and the 46th Division in the Flores Is. went to Singapore ○ On Jan 20th the Southern Army received orders to ship strategic materials from the Philippines to Japan ○ On Feb 5th the Southern Army was given control of the 10th Area Fleet and 4th Task Force ○ On Feb 28th with French Indochina turning hostile the Southern Army was told to use military force to control the country ○ On Apr 6th the Southern Army created the Southern Army Transportation Unit to bring all rail and shipping assets under one unified command ○ On May 8th Germany surrendered to the Allies ○ On June 5th Southern Expeditionary Army headquarters moved to Dalot, Indochina ○ On June 10th the Australians capture Labuan Island and Brunei ○ On July 1st the Australians invade Balikpapan ○ On Aug 10th the Southern Army began receiving reports that the war would soon end ○ On Aug 15th Japan's surrender was announced by the Emperor ○ On Sept 12, 1945, the Southern Army signed a surrender agreement in Singapore ○

Major Units:

No divisions or brigades under the Southern Army's direct control

Units under Southern Army HQ control:	威 *i*
Southern Army Headquarters	1160 (4,045)
Southern Army Headquarters Signal Section	1160 (33)
Southern Army L.o.C. Supervision Department	unknown
Southern Army Headquarters Staff	1601
Southern Army Fortifications Department	10413 (92)
Southern Army Special Intelligence Department	10483 (765)
Southern Army Survey Unit	15884 (30)
1st Southern Army Survey Unit	10414 (39)
2nd Southern Army Survey Unit	15885 (39)
Southern Army Signal Unit Headquarters	10316 (399)
1st Signal Unit Headquarters	2171
Southern Army Signal Unit Materials Depot	unknown (68)
1st Southern Army Signal Unit	15917 (680)
2nd Southern Army Signal Unit	15918 (847)
3rd Southern Army Signal Unit	15919 (950)
4th Southern Army Signal Unit	15920 (919)
Southern Signal Training Unit	16009 (87)
Southern Army Military Police Training Unit	10308 (263)
Southern Army Construction Training Department	10317
Southern Army Temporary Facility	15804
Southern Army Meteorological Department	18917
South. Army Disease Prev./Water Supply Dept.	9420 (295)
North Borneo District	15912
Indochina District	15913

Southern Exp. Army continued	威 *i*
North of Australia District	15914
Singapore District	15915
Southern Army Air Traffic Control Department	15910
2nd Field Replacement Unit Headquarters	4633 (102)
7th Field Replacement Unit Headquarters	10154
11th Southern Army Hospital	10312
Southern Army Fuel Depot	9800 (1,538)
Southern Army Fuel Depot Electric Company	9800 (306)
Southern Army Fuel Depot Well Drilling Company	9800 (854)
Southern Army Fuel Depot Duty Company	9800 (195)
Southern Army Air Transport Department	9326
Southern Army Aviation Department	9312 (34)
1st Air Transport Squadron	4333 (71)
2nd Air Transport Squadron	4334 (68)
Southern Army Meteorological Department	18917 (266)
Thailand POW Camp	No #
Malaysia POW Camp	No #
Saigon POW Camp	No #
Borneo POW Camp	No #
Java POW Camp	No #

French Indochina

38th Army 信 *Sin*

The 38th Army was activated in Saigon, Indochina on Dec. 20, 1944, its headquarters in Saigon until Mar 15, 1945, then Hanoi until late Sept. 1945. It served under Southern Army control from Dec 26th until it was deactivated in late Sept. 1945. Commanded by Lt Gen Yūitsu Tsuchihashi from Dec 20, 1944 until deactivation.

Service History:

1942: On Nov. 9th the Indochina Garrison Army became active in Saigon. Lacking in staff and a communications section its job was to negotiate diplomatic consessions ○
1943: On Dec. 10th the Indochina Garrison Army was placed under the Southern Expeditionary Army's control ○
1944: In March Japan's declining military fortunes brought about the decision to subjugate Indochina if the French colony began shifting allegiance. The operation would be called *Ma-go* ○ Operation *Ichi-go*, a rail corridor from Indochina to Manchuria was complete on Nov 28th. The Indochina Garrison Army sent the Ichinomiya Detachment (83rd Inf Regt, 21st Div) to meet 22nd Division troops in Suilu on the China border ○ Dec 4th the 38th Army commander Lt Gen Tsuchhashi Yuitsu landed in Indochina to replace Garrison Army commander Lt Gen Hachijiro ○ Dec 19th, with just 30,000

soldiers in Indochina Imperial HQ sent the 37th and 22nd Divisions from China. Both divisions were at half-strength from prolonged combat ○ The 38th Army was activated in Saigon on Dec 20th ○

<u>1945</u>: In January the 2nd Division was attached to the 38th Army, only the 29th Inf Regt arrived as most of the division was in central Burma. The 38th Army was placed in command of all naval land forces in Indochina. The 11th Special Naval Base Force in charge of defending Saigon-St. Jacques reported directly to the 38th Army ○ On Jan 12th a US carrier task force entered South China Sea and raided Saigon with planes leaving heavily damaged airfields and harbor facilities ○ Until Feb 28th the 38th Army maintained Indochina fairly independently but as Indochina was becoming hostile and the US threatened to land, the Southern Army was ordered to take control ○ On Mar 9th Japan demanded Indochina contribute to war funds and turn over its Army, police, rail, sea and communications. The demands arrived with a two-hour ultimatum ○ On Mar 10th Indochina refused and at 2217 the 38th Army ordered armed suppression of the French colony When resistance ended the French and Annanese were allowed to go about their business ○ A group of Indochinese fighters escaped into the mountains where small bands ambushed traffic on the Thakhek-Kratie Road ○ On March 30th the 22nd Division arrived in the Langson area but left for Thailand in mid-May ○ In April the 37th Division transferred to Thailand and the 70th I.M.B. was sent to Malaya ○ In April the 38th Army began construction on the Samnoua-Pakasno road ○ In early May the 38th Army began moving its headquarters to Hanoi (which was complete end of July) ○ By May 15th hostile forces had been eliminated from Indochina and the 38th Army began to plan defensive measures ○ In June plans were made to move 38th Army headquarters to Thakhek but the war ended before it was completed ○ The 55th Div was placed under the 38th Army's command in May but it was so battle worn and exhausted by the trip from Burma it could not be brought back to strength before September ○ In July depleted Southern Army air units were reassigned, 10,000 of the 20,000 went to the 55th Div ○ In July the 2nd Division, greatly reduced after *Ma-go*, returned from Burma. The Army made it a priority to return the Division to strength so 6,000 air force men were reassigned to it ○ On Aug 15th it was learned Japan had surrendered and cease-fighting orders arrived from Southern Army on the 17th ○ Aug 21st, 38th Army issued orders warning the troops against acts of retribution ○ The Chinese 62nd Army (Kinanghsi) and the 59th and 60th Armies (Yunnan) arrived in Indo-China on Sept 3rd and in Hanoi and Haiphong on Sept 10th ○ Japanese troops were concentrated in three areas; Mongay, Nandinh and Tourans. 38th Army HQ withdrew to 50 km south east of Hanoi and prepared to disarm. The Japanese in northern Indochina were conscripted to do service and labor jobs ○ In late Sept the British arrived in southern Indochina and proceeded to disarm Japanese troops stationed there. ○ After hostilities ended the Ntsumei Army began to fight for independence, the British enlisted former Japanese soldiers to defeat them. Former Southern Army Assistant Chief of Staff, Lt Gen Yutaka established a headquarters and recruited former 2nd and 55th Division and 5th Air Division personnel ○

<u>1946</u>: On April 3rd the first ship left Haiphong for Japan and by May repatriation from French Indochina had been completed.

<u>Major Units</u>: See division / brigade page for order of battle

2nd Division Sendai 1888 勇 *Isamu* – Saigon 164

21st Division Kanazawa 1938 討 *Tou* – Hanoi 174

37th Division Kurume 1939 冬 *Fuyu* – near Hanoi	181
55th Division Zentsuji 1940 楯 *Tate* – Phnom Penh	189
34th Independent Mixed Brigade 1943 育 *Iku* – Tourane	220-1

Note: The 55th Division's headquarters remained in Burma until the war ended.

Units under 38th Army control: Hanoi	信 *Sin*
38th Army Headquarters	7950 (540)
67th Independent Field Anti Aircraft Company	17011 (179)
34th Independent Motor Transport Company	10478 (215)
36th Specially Est. Motor Transport Company	15805 (69)
39th Specially Est. Motor Transport Company	15808 (69)
40th Independent Motor Transport Company	15809 (69)
186th Independent Motor Transport Company	10480 (194)
2nd Southern Army Hospital	6092 (163)
4th Southern Army Hospital	10307 (91)
149th Line of Communications Hospital	unknown (315) U.S. estimate
96th Casualty Clearing Platoon	unknown
38th Army Field Ordinance Depot	17012 (923)
38th Army Field Motor Transport Depot	17013 (1,269)
38th Army Field Freight Depot	17014 (756)
38th Area Army L.o.C. Veterinary Hospital	17015 (272)
38th Army Veterinary Quarantine Hospital	17016 (137)
33rd Disease Prevention and Water Supply Unit	17022
5th Southern Army Signal Unit	15922 (388)
Southern Army 1st Military Police Detachment	No # (748)

North East New Guinea

18th Army 猛 *Mo*

The 18th Army was activated in Tokyo on November 16, 1942, the same day its superior, the 8th Area Army, was activated. 18th Army headquarters were in Rabaul, New Britain from Nov 22nd until Mar. 14, 1944 and Wewak, New Guinea, with the mission of taking responsibility for Eastern New Guinea from the 17th Army. The 18th Army served under the 8th Area Army's command from Nov. 16th until Mar. 14, 1944, 2nd Area Army until June 17th and Southern Army until it was deactivated. Its initial order of battle included the South Seas Detachment, 51st Div and the 41st Inf Regt. Its commander was Lt Gen Hatazō Adachi from Nov 9, 1942 until the 18th Army was deactivated in New Guinea on September 25, 1945.

Service History:

1942: On Nov 16th the South Seas Detachment in Buna, New Guinea was placed under the 18th Army's command ○ Nov 16th to Dec 28th, Buna Detachment destroyed ○ Nov 19th, first contact with US troops ○ Nov 20th, the 65th Brigade transferred to the 18th Army from the Philippines ○ On Nov 22nd Basabua was chosen as the main supply base. Lt Gen Adachi, 18th Army commander, left Yokosuka by plane and arrived in

Rabaul on the 25th ○ On Nov 26th the 18th Army took control of eastern New Guinea from the 17th Army and ordered to secure Buna ○ Dec 6th, all army units (8,200 men) in Eastern New Guinea were placed under the 21st I.M.B. commander's control and became the Buna Detachment ○ On Dec 12th the 18th Army's commander decided to remain in Rabaul and instead send staff officers to direct operations involving the capture of Wewak, Madang and Tuluvu ○ Dec 16th, selected battle-hardened 5th Division troops sail from Rabaul to Wewak (3rd Btn, 11th I.R.) Madang (2nd Btn, 42nd I.R.) and Lae-Salamaua (3rd Btn, 21st I.R, 100 men) ○ On Dec 23rd the 51st Division was attached to the 18th Army ○ On Dec. 28th Buna Detachment evacuated Buna as the battle had become unwinnable ○

1943: On Jan 2nd Buna was lost ○ On Jan 7th the Okabe Detachment (51st Inf. Grp. HQ and 102nd I.R.) landed in Lae and began to advance on Wau village and airfield ○ On Jan 19th the 20th Division joined the 18th Army. Fighting over Buna ended in the Sananandа area ○ On Jan 28th the Okabe Detachment offensive on Wau begins with some success ○ Feb 4th Okabe withdraws when Australian reinforcements arrive ○ On Feb 11th the Buna Detachment's remnants withdraw to Lae-Salamaua ○ Feb 20th the 41st Division began landing in Wewak and Wau ○ On the 24th landing suspended with the loss of 800 men ○ *Bismarck Sea*: Feb 28th the 51st Div sailed from Rabaul in 6 large, 2 small transport ships ○ Mar 2nd the *Kyokusei Maru* was sunk. Destroyer escorts rescued about half the 1600 aboard and continued to Lae ○ On Mar 3rd bombers sank 4 of 8 destroyers and all transports, inadvertently ending the second attack on Wau ○ 18th Army HQ was sunk aboard DD *Tokitsukaze*, Lt Gen Hatazō Adachi was rescued but rescuer refused to continue to New Guinea ○ In early March the 51st Division set up a command post for survivors in Lae and began to reorganize units in the Salamaua-Lae area. Okabe rejoined the 51st Division and the 2nd echelon arrived. Buna Detachment deactivated ○ In March the 8th Shipping Engineer Regt recruited 800 men from the 170th Inf Regt ○ April and May are New Guinea's rainy season ○ On April 22nd in Lae-Salamaua the *Battles for Mubo* and *Bobdubi* began ○ On June 12th the 21st I.M.B. was deactivated ○ June 17th, South Seas Detachment is deactivated, later its units return to the 55th Div in Burma ○ June 20th the 51st Div attack on Mubo stalls, it withdraws to Mt. Tambu July 11th ○ June 28th the U.S. overruns Komiatum and Australian troops crack Bobdubi lines. ○ On Aug 2nd the 18th Army command post moves to Salamaua ○ Aug 6th, Gen Adachi leaves for Madang ○ On Aug 23rd Bobdubi is lost ○ Late-Aug, the 51st Div takes control in Lae-Salamaua and orders a general withdrawal to Madang ○ On Sept 3rd the 41st Inf Regt (21st I.M.B.) in Rabaul was removed from the 18th Army and returned to Korea ○ On Sept 5th US troops land east of Lae ○ On Sept 8th the 51st Div received orders to withdraw to Lae and construct defenses ○ On Sept 14th Salamaua is evacuated ○ Sept. 22nd, 5 to 6,000 US troops land in the Finschhafen area ○ Sept 26th, before completing deployment the 20th Div in Sio attacks Point Arndt in support of the 1st Shipping Group attack ○ Sept. 29th, the 1st Shipping Group's attack continues under 20th Division direction ○ The 18th Army commander Gen Adachi visited Nakai Detachment on Kanka Mtn. ○ 51st Div controlled the area from Sio to Gali ○ Oct 15th, the 18th Army commander boarded a ship in Madang for the Sattelberg Mtns. ○ Oct 19th arrives in Kiari, meets the 51st Div commander ○ On the 24th he sailed from Dampier to Kanomi, traveled on foot to 20th Div HQ on Sattelberg Mtn and left for Madang Nov 3rd arriving on the 13th ○ Nov 16th the Australian 9th Div began an attack on Sattelberg Mtn. ○ In mid-

Nov monsoons swell rivers, wash out bridges and disrupt communications, wet and rusting equipment and unhealthy conditions add to the misery ○ By Nov 26th the 20th Division could not muster enough strength to continue its offensive. ○ On Nov 30th the Australians began a general advance ○ On Dec 9th many battles took place but the most intense were on the coast road ○ Dec 17th enemy crossed the Lakona River so the 18th Army abandoned Finschhafen and dug in between Lakona and the north side of Sio ○ Dec 27th, the army commander left Madang for Sio and arrived at 51st Div HQ in Kiari on Dec 30th. Gen Adachi left for Sio on foot Jan 2nd ○
1944: Jan 2nd, the US lands land on Cape Gumbi and the 18th Army is relieved of Sio ○ On Jan 3rd Gen Adachi arrives in Sio, updates orders ○ Jan 6th, the 20th and 51st Divisions become the Nakano Army Group under Lt Gen Hidemitsu Nakano, 51st Div commander, with orders to withdraw to Madang ○ On Jan 7th Gen. Adachi boarded a sub and arrives safely in Madang on the 9th ○ By Jan 22nd close to 13,000 troops had arrived in Gali, the 20th Division was on the west side and the 51st Div its east, provisions were sent by sub ○ On Feb 8th Nakano Group HQ arrived in Atzer, Nakai Detachment's base of operations ○ Feb 20th the 20th Div reported to 18th Army HQ in Amron. Rested and reorganized the division left Mugil in four echelons ○ Mar 12th, weak with losses the Nakai Detachment returned to the 20th Div ○ Mar 14th, I.G.HQ placed the 18th Army under 2nd Area Army control ○ On Mar 17th Gen Adachi took an inspection tour of Alexis, Rempi and Mugil, boarded ship in Mugil and arrived in Hansa where he established a new command post on Mar 21st. The 18th Army HQ moved to Boikin ○ On Mar 24th the Nakai Detachment reached Bogia. The 41st Div in Madang split into 3 echelons, the Madang Detachment (239th I.R.) remained behind to destroy HQ installations and munitions ○ On Mar 25th the 18th Army and 4th Air Army are placed under 2nd Area Army control. 4th Air Army headquarters relocated to Hollandia ○ On Mar 30th the 4th Air Army lost 100 planes on a bomb run to Hollandia ○ On Apr 9th Gen Adachi left Hansa by sea for his Boikin HQ, arrived Apr. 11th ○ On Apr 10th Maj Gen Kitazona of the 3rd Field Transport HQ assumed command in Hollandia ○ Apr 12th, the 2nd Area Army's orders arrive, the 18th Army is to return to Hollandia-Wewak ○ By Apr 20th the 6th South Seas Detachment in Hollandia had redeployed and the Madang Detachment had withdrawn ○ On Apr 22nd the US attacked Aitape and Hollandia ○ On Apr 24th the fighting over Hollandia and Aitape ends ○ On Apr 24th Australia lands troops in Ort, 6.5 km from Madang. The army began to withdrawing from Hollandia ○ On Apr 25th the 20th Div commander left Hansa for Wewak by boat ○ Apr 26th, 18th Army HQ held a planning meeting ○ Apr 28th, 20th Div commander and his staff die in a torpedo boat attack ○ Apr. 29th the Madang Detachment arrive in Uligan and is sent to rejoin the 41st Div. ○ At the end of April the Hansa command post is shut down, HQ Liaison Section departs Hansa on May 1st ○ On May 2nd the 18th Army rec'd orders to redeploy to western New Guinea ○ On May 13th the 41st Div left Hansa for Wewak in 12 echelons ○ On May 18th Maj Gen Miyake, who was stranded with the 20th Div, became its new commander ○ On May 23rd the 41st Div's commander arrived at 18th Army HQ in Boikin ○ May 27th, submarine *RO-115* delivered supplies to the 18th Army. US troops land on Biak ○ In June soldiers from Hollandia began arriving in Sarmi, a 400 km journey with a 93% casualty rate ○ Early in June the 44th L.o.C. Guard Unit withdrew from Hansa to Wewak ○ June 17th, after being cut off from the 2nd Area Army and blocked from retreating I.G.HQ placed the 18th Army under the Southern Army's command ○ On June 25th a rear area 18th Army

command post was setup in Salup to bolster supply lines ○ On June 28th the *Battle of Driniumor River* begins east of Aitape ○ On July 5th Lt. Gen. Adachi addressed the men of the 20th and 41st Divisions. *Mo-go*, the *Battle of Aitape* began ○ On July 10th the 20th and 41st Divisions, about 10,000 men, cross the Driniumor River ○ On July 23rd the 18th Army command post began to move to Salup ○ July 25th, the 18th Army commander arrived at 41st Division HQ to direct the attack ○ July 22nd US troops land and capture Aitape ○ July 30th the 18th Army's command post moves to the village of Kiura ○ On July 31st the Americans begin a major attack ○ On Aug 1st the 41st Div assault on Sagi is successful but artillery causes heavy casualties. To direct the battle the 18th Army command post set up with 20th Div HQ 1½ km west of Atua ○ Aug 3rd, the 18th Army ended *Mo-go* ○ On Aug 4th the 20th Div. suspended combat and organized the withdrawal ○ On Aug 5th the 41st Division withdrew ○ On Aug 17th the 18th Army command post in Telau left for Mokinzan ○ On Aug 19th the 6th Air Division was deactivated but the ground units remained at their posts ○ On Aug 25th the *Battle of Aitape* ends in defeat ○ Sept 16th, the 18th Army Chief of Staff held a planning meeting on Mt. Mokin, the army intended to fight in But, East Malgip, and Wewak areas ○ Sept 17th enemy probe Smain but are repulsed by the 239th Inf. Regt ○ On Sept 20th enemy probe Malgip and near Cape Djueran but are repulsed ○ Lt Gen Adachi inspects the Kairiru and Mushu Island bases, the only shipping bases that remain near Wewak. On Sept 25th he returns to the mainland ○ Sept 29th Lt Gen Adachi inspected the Boikin Garrison Unit ○ Oct. 7th, the 18th Army orders the conservation of sea-going boats and fuel ○ On Nov 26th the Otaka Reconnaissance Unit returned after 6 months behind enemy lines ○ Dec 28th, the battle of Mt Hatayama in the Cape Djeuran highlands south of Salup in West Sepik Province began ○ A location was sought near the town of But for the 18th Army Command Post's '*Mo* But' Intelligence Center ○ 1945: From Dec 1944 to February the 18th Army promoted self-reliance through improvised farms and factories split between the 20th, 41st and 51st Divisions. By January 1945 the war was essentially over for the 18th Army ○

Major Units: See division / brigade page for order of battle

20th Division Keijo 1915 朝 *Asa* – New Guinea	173-4
41st Division Utsonomiya 1939 河 *Kawa* – New Guinea	182
51st Division Utsunomiya 1940 基 *Moto* – New Guinea	187
21st Independent Mixed Brigade 1941 西 *Nishi* deact. in Rabaul 6/12/43	215-6

Units under 18th Army control: Rabaul	猛 *Mo*	
18th Army Headquarters	7910 (458)	Rabaul
12th Field Anti Aircraft Headquarters Unit	5061 (78)	Wewak
52nd Field Anti Aircraft Battalion	7427	
56th Field Anti Aircraft Battalion	4330 (277)	
61st Field Anti Aircraft Battalion	1929 (543)	
62nd Field Anti Aircraft Battalion	1930 (543)	
63rd Field Anti Aircraft Battalion	1931 (543)	
64th Field Anti Aircraft Battalion	8050 (467)	
65th Field Anti Aircraft Battalion	6099 (549)	
50th Field Anti Aircraft Battalion, 1st Company	3616	
58th Field Anti Aircraft Battalion, 1st Company	7460 (179)	Madang
38th Independent Field Anti Aircraft Company	7467 (134)	

18th Army continued	猛 *Mo*	
41st Independent Field Anti Aircraft Company	1752 (134)	
39th Independent Anti Aircraft Company	8073 (134)	
1st Independent Field Searchlight Company	6081 (185)	
2nd Independent Field Searchlight Company	1996 (185)	
4th Independent Field Searchlight Company	1753 (185)	
7th Independent Field Searchlight Company	1932 (186)	
8th Independent Field Searchlight Company	1933 (186)	
4th Field Searchlight Battalion, 2nd Company	5066 (182)	
5th Independent Field Medium Artillery Battalion	9823 (426)	was 21st I.M.B.
15th Field Machine Cannon Company	1995 (99)	
19th Field Machine Cannon Company	7463 / 8553 (157)	
20th Field Machine Cannon Company	7464 (157)	
24th Field Machine Cannon Company	5067 (157)	
25th Field Machine Cannon Company	1225 (121)	
29th Field Machine Cannon Company	4332 (157)	
32nd Field Machine Cannon Company	1943 (106)	
33rd Field Machine Cannon Company	1944 (106)	
34th Field Machine Cannon Company	1945 (106)	
35th Field Machine Cannon Company	6078 (106)	
36th Field Machine Cannon Company	6079 (106)	
37th Field Machine Cannon Company	6080 (106)	
8th Independent Engineer Regiment	5548 (1,055)	
30th Independent Engineer Regiment	6017 (894)	
33rd Independent Engineer Regiment	3795 (894)	
36th Independent Engineer Regiment	1133 (894)	
37th Independent Engineer Regiment	1892 (894)	
3rd Signal Regiment, minus 1st Co	11400 (1,781)	Rabaul
7th Independent Wireless Radio Platoon	11401 (53)	Buna
8th Independent Wireless Radio Platoon	11402 (53)	Buna
74th Independent Wireless Radio Platoon	8054 (53)	
76th Independent Wireless Radio Platoon	8056 (53)	
46th Fixed Radio Unit	5121 (26)	
44th Line of Communications Sector Command	4817 (203)	Col. Ujihara
44th Line of Communication Guard Unit	4817 (1,035)	
44th Line of Communications Duty Company	4817 (511)	
57th Line of Communications Guard Unit	3966 (1,035)	
4th Field Transport Headquarters	6050 (37)	
39th Independent Motor Transport Battalion	4630 (808)	
225th Independent Motor Transport Company	2862 (183)	
8th Division, 9th Transport Unit	9358 (321)	
35th Field Road Construction Unit	4646 (304)	
37th Field Road Construction Unit	4020 (304)	
38th Field Road Construction Unit	8231 (304)	
40th Field Road Construction Unit	10157 (304)	
44th Field Road Construction Unit	5244 (304)	

48th Field Road Construction Unit	3605 (304)
73rd Land Duty Company, minus 1 squad	4833 (511)
76th Land Duty Company	4642 (511)
81st Land Duty Company	3031 (511)
49th Construction Duty Company	4051 (511)
90th Line of Communications Hospital	6009 (420)
112th Line of Communications Hospital	6412 (441)
117th Line of Communications Hospital	6769 (441)
46th Casualty Clearing Platoon	1006 (54)
48th Casualty Clearing Platoon	3756 (54)
73rd Casualty Clearing Platoon	6033 (54)
74th Casualty Clearing Platoon	6034 (54)
75th Casualty Clearing Platoon	6035 (54)
63rd Casualty Clearing Platoon, 1 section	6408
23rd Field D. Prev./ Water Supply Dept, one section	2626
25th Field Disease Prev/Water Supply Dept	2628 one section (see below)
27th Field Ordinance Depot	2688 (1,746)
27th Field Motor Transport Depot	2690 (1,780)
27th Field Freight Depot	2689 (1,332)

Hollandia, New Guinea (base Est. Oct. 1943)	猛 *Mo*
18th Army Headquarters (detached section)	7910
3rd Field Transport Headquarters	5702 (37) from Hansa Bay
6th South Seas Detachment	12503 (1,254)
54th Line of Communications Sector Command	6030 (203)
54th Line of Communication Guard Unit	6030 (1,034)
54th Line of Communication Transport Unit	6030
54th Line of Communications Duty Company	6030 (511)
21st Trench Mortar Battalion	8123 (963)
60th Field Anti Aircraft Battalion	8030
66th Field Anti Aircraft Battalion	6039 (545)
39th Independent Field Anti Aircraft Company	8033
40th Independent Field Anti Aircraft Company	1751 (134)
42nd Independent Field Anti Aircraft Company	9824 (150) was 21st I.M.B.
38th Field Machine Cannon Company	8052 (106)
39th Field Machine Cannon Company	8053 (106)
3rd Independent Field Searchlight Company	8032 (185)
3rd Signal Regiment, 1st Company	11400
36th Field Road Construction Unit	5734 / 5735 (304)
42nd Independent Motor Transport Battalion	1038 (808)
One section 27th Field Ordinance Depot	2688
One section 27th Field Motor Transport Depot	2690
One section 27th Field Freight Depot	2689
49th Construction Duty Company (an element?)	4051
26th Specially Est. Construction Duty Company	10383 (61)
79th Line of Communications Hospital	4614 (420)

18th Army: **Hollandia, New Guinea** continued	猛 *Mo*
113th Line of Communications Hospital	6413 (420)
23rd Disease Prevention and Water Supply Unit	2626
25th Disease Prevention and Water Supply Unit	2628 (329)
49th Anchorage Headquarters	9738
37th Sea Duty Company	3026 (511)
4th Sea Transport Battalion	6191 (536)
1st Debarkation (Landing) Unit	2946
3rd Debarkation (Landing) Unit	2948

Attached to the 18th Army:

6th Air Division: 洋 *Yō*

6th Air Division:	洋 *Yō* 9300
6th Air Division Headquarters	9301 (288)
12th Air Sector Headquarters	8340 (67)
30th Air Sector Command	8376 (25)
14th Air Brigade Headquarters	9315 (94)
• 68th Air Regiment (fighter)	9151 (322)
• 78th Air Regiment (fighter)	9152 (322)
• 208th Air Regiment (light bombers)	8328
• 63rd Air Regiment, one section	15378
20th Airfield Battalion	9606 (372)
21st Airfield Battalion	8321 (372)
25th Airfield Battalion	9615 (372)
41st Airfield Battalion	9866 (372)
47th Airfield Battalion	9607 (372)
48th Airfield Battalion	9644 (372)
51st Airfield Battalion	9608 (372)
22nd Airfield Company	15383 (208)
23rd Airfield Company	15384 (208)
24th Airfield Company	9184 (208)
26th Airfield Company	2398 (208)
33rd Airfield Company	9939 (300)
86th Airfield Company	9875 (207)
4th Field Airfield Construction Unit	9951 (79)
10th Field Airfield Construction Unit	9957 (99)
11th Field Airfield Construction Unit	9303 (490)
6th Air Navigation Unit	11701 (393)
12th Field Meteorological Unit	11702 (486)
1st Air Route Department	9315 (1,989)
14th Field Air Repair Depot	9304 (1,770)
14th Field Air Freight Depot	9305 (100)
1st Mobile Air Repair Section	9322
2nd Mobile Air Repair Section	9327
3rd Mobile Air Repair Section	9328

6th Air Division continued

4th Mobile Air Repair Section	9329	
5th Mobile Air Repair Section	9330	
7th Mobile Air Repair Section	7598	
8th Mobile Air Repair Section	7599	
73rd Land Duty Company, one squad	4833	see 18A
31st Construction Duty Company	7850 (511)	

6th Air Division: Activated in Rabaul, New Britain on Nov 24, 1942, it was assigned to the 8th Area Army from Nov 27th until July 28, 1943 and 4th Air Army until Jul 25, 1944. Its headquarters were in Rabaul until Apr 15, 1943, Wewak New Guinea until Oct 15th, Ambon until Mar 26, 1944 and Hollandia until May 31st, by then effectively destroyed as a combat unit. Deactivated July 25, 1944.

3rd Air Army 司 *Tsukasa*

The 3rd Air Army was activated on June 27, 1942 and attached to the Southern Expeditionary Army on July 10th. Its headquarters were in Singapore from July 9th under Lt Gen Michio Sugawara until May 1, 1943, Lt Gen Hideyoshi Obata until Dec. 7th and Lt Gen Hayashi Kinoshita until the war ended

Service History:

1942: On Jan 18th the 5th Air Division used air bases in northern Thailand to support Japanese forces operating against Kunming in Yunan, China ○ In March the 5th Air Division arrived in Burma with the 15th Army to support the invasion of Malaya ○ On Mar 10th the Burma Air Sector Command was activated ○ In May the 9th, 12th and 15th Field Air Depots were created under the 16th and 19th Field Air Depots to provide air repair facilities. The 16th Field Air Depot was in Indochina, Thailand and Burma. Factories were built to produce replacement parts ○ On July 9th the 3rd Air Army was activated with the 5th Air Division as a nucleus, all air units under the Southern Expeditionary Army were included in its order of battle. ○ On July 10th the 3rd Air Division was transferred to the China Expeditionary Army ○ In July a lull in operations provided time for Army General Staff to mandate that airbases in strategic areas become Air Army repair and supply bases. Air routes were established: 1) Formosa – P.I. – East Borneo – Java. 2) Formosa – P.I. – West Borneo - Singapore. 3) Hong Kong – South Indochina – East Malaya – Sumatra – Java. 4) Hong Kong – North Indochina – Thailand – West Malaya – Sumatra. 5) P.I. – South Indochina – Thailand – Burma ○ July and August, a number of Southern Army air units were transferred back to China, an event that would soon become a rarity ○ In August two radar sets arrived to partially compensate for a lack of patrol planes ○ On Aug 29th the 9th Air Brigade joined the 3rd Air Army ○ Sept 10th, an Army-Navy agreement to combine air operations in the southeast Pacific proved temporary, training and equipment differences kept the two from fully coordinating together ○ In Dec 1942 Palembang Air Defense Headquarters and the 9th Air Division were organized under the 3rd Air Army to create a unified defense. The 25th Army in Sumatra wanted both units but the Southern Army decided to attach them to the 3rd Air Army to coordinate with other air units for operational, training and replacement purposes ○

1943: On Jan 30th the 8th Air Brigade and 7th Air Division were activated ○ The 7th Air

Division was organized in Java from former 3rd Air Brigade troops and attached to the 3rd Air Army, it was responsible for Banda Sea air operations ○ In April 3rd Air Army units were assigned to intercept Allied supplies moving from India into west China ○ In April the army successfully bombed Kunming from Indochina ○ In June the 8th Air Brigade was temporarily transferred to the China Expeditionary Army. American airpower dominated south Asia and the southeast Pacific. Moving troops by land and sea became more difficult as air units were no longer able to provide direct support for ground forces ○ The 3rd Air Brigade built air bases on east Timor to extend fighter flying time, which amounted to less than 1,000 km into the southeast Pacific. The first attacks in this sector flew from these bases ○ The 7th Air Division from Java was placed under the 8th Area Army for New Guinea operations ○ On July 28th the 4th Air Army was activated in Rabaul under 8th Area Army control. Its order of battle included the 6th and 7th Air Divisions to cover operations in the Solomon Is. and New Guinea ○ In Sept the 8th Air Brigade returned from China ○ In October replacements for the 1st Air Raiding Group, 77th and 204th Air Regiments brought them up to operational strength ○ In October, the 3rd Air Army bombed Myitkyina Airfield and flew missions on Imphal for the 15th Army ○ In early December, 3rd Air Army aircraft and Navy bombers attacked Calcutta in a joint operation ○

1944: In March the 106th Air Training Brigade became active ○ In April the Southern Army took control of all army air and ground air units in south Asia that were not already under 2nd Area Army or Southern Army control ○ In May the 2nd Air Div was transferred to the Southern Army and 4th Air Division attached to the 4th Air Army. The 108th and 109th Air Training Units were sent to the Philippines ○ In May I.G.HQ issued orders that if the Philippines were attacked 3rd Air Army planes and personnel would transfer to the 4th Air Army to attack enemy transport ships. In that event the 3rd Air Army would go on the defensive ○ In June a number of air units were sent back to Japan and the 8th Air Brigade's headquarters were sent to China ○ The army planned to place a significant air presence in Halmahera to counter enemy in the New Guinea area. Attacks were limited to targeting transport ships. This was a change as I.G.HQ had previously focused on destroying enemy air power ○ In July I.G.HQ ordered most Southern Army air units to join the 4th Air Army. The entire area was in jeopardy if the Philippines were lost ○ In August the 6th Air Div HQ, 30th Air Bgde HQ, 14th Air Group and 63rd and 248th Air Units were ordered to return to Japan ○ In November combat damaged air units were sent to Japan to recover. These included the 12th and 16th Air Brigade HQ and the following Air Regts; 3rd, 14th, 19th, 26th, 30th, 62nd, 65th, 66th, 75th and 204th, many of these ended in the 6th Air Army for the final battle ○ Late 1944, the 5th Air Division shifted bases from Burma to French Indochina, its HQ arrived in Phnom Penh in March 1945, the 25th Ind. Air Brigade arrived in Saigon in Dec. its HQ following in January ○

1945: In January the 3rd Air Bgde HQ was sent to China, the 9th Air Bgde HQ to Formosa and the 7th Air Bgde HQ to Japan ○ Also in January the 21st Air Bgde, 18th, 54th, 55th, and 106th air regts were returned to their original bases in Japan ○ In February the 30th Fighter Group HQ, 6th Air Brigade HQ, 2nd, 27th, 200th and 208th Air Regts were sent to Japan, the 22nd Air Unit to Formosa and the 75th Air Unit to China ○ End of June the 35th Air Brigade HQ, 204th Air Regt (fighter), 12th Air Regt (light bomber) were sent to Formosa. After these transfers the Southern Army lacked air support for subsequent operations. Transfers continued from the 5th Air Division: 50th Air Regt (fighter) and

6th Air Regt (light bomber). 7th Air Division (HQ Java): 13th Air Regt (fighter), 61st Air Regt (heavy bomber). 9th Air Division (HQ Palembang): 21st Air Regt (fighter), 24th Air Regt (fighter), 26th Air Regt (fighter), 58th Air Regt (heavy bomber), 71st Air Squadron (fighter) ○ By now the Southern Expeditionary Army permanently lacked air support ○ On Aug 15th Japan announces its surrender and suspended hostilities ○
Ground Elements: See brigade page for order of battle
Palembang Guards Unit 1944 翔 *Sho* – Palembang, Sumatra 250
Bhutan Guards Unit 1944 盤 *Ban* – Pangkalpinang, Bangka Is. 249
Both Palembang and Bhutan Guards are affiliated with the 25th Army but under the 3rd Air Army control.

Units under 3rd Air Army control: Singapore	司 *Tsukasa*	
3rd Air Army Headquarters	9813 (348)	Singapore
3rd Air Army HQ Signal Section	9813 (95)	
1st Field Replacement Flying Unit	9915 (709)	
1st Field Replacement Flying Unit Headquarters	9915 (84)	
1st Field Replacement Flying Unit Recon. Unit	9915 (146)	
1st Field Replacement Flying Unit Fighter Unit	9915 (142)	
83rd Independent Air Command	9172	
15th Air Sector Command	高 9861 (43)	
23rd Air Sector Command	11065 (22)	
24th Air Sector Command	11078 (42)	
25th Air Sector Command	11079 (42)	
29th Air Sector Command	16637 (42)	
59th Air Sector Command	11100 (44)	
24th Airfield Battalion	9922 (372)	
27th Airfield Battalion	9923 (372)	
84th Airfield Battalion	9183 (337)	
101st Airfield Battalion	15362 (458)	N. Borneo
109th Airfield Battalion	15365 (458)	
113th Airfield Battalion	11803 (372)	
115th Airfield Battalion	16646 (372)	
117th Airfield Battalion	18438 (372)	
118th Airfield Battalion	18439 (372)	
119th Airfield Battalion	18440 (372)	
120th Airfield Battalion	18441 (372)	
121st Airfield Battalion	18442 (372)	
122nd Airfield Battalion	18443 (372)	
131st Airfield Battalion	18450 (372)	
133rd Airfield Battalion	18452 (372)	
179th Airfield Battalion	16648 (372)	
180th Airfield Battalion	16649 (372)	
5th Airfield Company	9931 (300)	
16th Airfield Company	9335 (205)	
28th Airfield Company	11059 (208)	
3rd Air Signal Headquarters	11055 (97)	
1st Air Signal Regiment	8361 (1,492)	

3rd Air Army: continued	司 *Tsukasa*	
3rd Air Signal Regiment	9616 (1,322) 2nd Co.in Burma	
3rd Air Special Signal Unit	12903 (259)	
11th Air Signal Regiment	15336 (1,322)	
3rd Fixed Signal Unit	11001	Singapore
31st Wireless Radio Unit	11084 (196)	
32nd Wireless Radio Unit	11085 (196)	
33rd Wireless Radio Unit	11086 (196)	
34th Wireless Radio Unit	11087 (196)	
35th Wireless Radio Unit	11088 (196)	
36th Wireless Radio Unit	11089 (196)	
41st Wireless Radio Unit	unknown (196)	
42nd Wireless Radio Unit	unknown (196)	
43rd Wireless Radio Unit	unknown (196)	
45th Wireless Radio Unit	11808 (196)	
46th Wireless Radio Unit	11809 (196)	
4th Air Navigational Aid Unit	11052 (192)	
2nd Air Route Unit	11058 (767)	
3rd Meteorological Regiment	11053 (1,472)	
14th Field Meteorological Unit	11090 (1,213)	
1st Field Airfield Construction Headquarters	15317 (102)	
48th Construction Duty Company	4014 (511)	
105th Field Airfield Construction Unit	15330 (149)	
110th Field Airfield Construction Unit	15335 (149)	
111th Field Airfield Construction Unit	12203 (76)	
112th Field Airfield Construction Unit	12204 (76)	
113th Field Airfield Construction Unit	12205 (76)	
115th Field Airfield Construction Unit	10805 (76)	
121st Field Airfield Construction Unit	10925 (76)	
122nd Field Airfield Construction Unit	10926 (76)	
143rd Field Airfield Construction Unit	18407 (175)	
144th Field Airfield Construction Unit	18408 (175)	
16th Field Air Repair Depot	9323 (1,991)	Borneo
19th Field Air Repair Depot	9324 (1,440)	
20th Field Air Repair Depot	11063 (1,062)	
22nd Field Air Repair Depot	11073 (1,405)	
25th Field Air Repair Depot	11074 (683)	
13th Field Air Freight Depot	11075 (1,475)	
20th Field Air Freight Depot	9320 (2,245)	
318th Independent Motor Transport Company	17622 (134)	
160th Line of Comm. Motor Transport Comp.	7338 (170)	
184th Line of Comm. Motor Transport Comp	10479 (194)	

Attached to the 3rd Air Army:

55th Air Division Singapore 1944	昭 *Akira*
55th Air Division Headquarters	19050 (196)
106th Ind. Flight Training Brigade Headquarters	11076 (36)
Southern Army 1st Air Training Unit	11056
16th Secondary Flight Training Unit	11066 (393)
17th Secondary Flight Training Unit	11067 (395)
34th Secondary Flight Training Unit	11068 (395)
37th Secondary Flight Training Unit	15358 (395)
9th Advanced Flight Training Unit	unknown (449)
18th Advanced Flight Training Unit	11094 (449)
1st Primary Flight Training Unit	18995 (1,321)
36th Secondary Flight Training Unit	15357 (431)
107th Ind. Flight Training Brigade Headquarters	15313 (39)
2nd Secondary Flight Training Unit	15314 (412)
3rd Secondary Flight Training Unit	15315 (400)
12th Secondary Flight Training Unit	15316 (395)
8th Advanced Flight Training Unit	18433 (449)
27th Advanced Flight Training Unit	11098 (502)
28th Advanced Flight Training Unit	11099 (518)
3rd Primary Flight Training Unit	18997 (1,039)
109th Ind. Flight Training Brigade Headquarters	11077 (36)
44th Secondary Flight Training Unit	11081 (395)
45th Secondary Flight Training Unit	11082 (360)
7th Advanced Flight Training Unit	18432 (449)
15th Advanced Flight Training Unit	unknown (436)
2nd Primary Flight Training Unit	18996 (1,033)
35th Secondary Flight Training Unit	11069 (395)
17th Advanced Flight Training Unit	11093 (449)
81st Airfield Battalion	9646 (372)
85th Airfield Battalion	9647 (372)
90th Airfield Battalion	9648 (372)
9th Secondary Flight Training Unit	11080
26th Advanced Flight Training Unit	11097
• 45th Ind. Air Squadron (light bomber)	18971
• 71st Independent Air Squadron	9180
18th Air Sector Command	11613
22nd Airfield Battalion	8322 (372)
104th Field Airfield Construction Unit	15329 (149)
106th Field Airfield Construction Unit	15331 (149)
109th Field Airfield Construction Unit	15334 (149)
114th Field Airfield Construction Unit	10804 (175)
120th Field Airfield Construction Unit	10924 (175)

55th Air Division: Activated on July 25, 1944, and attached to the 3rd Air Army on Dec 9th. It's headquarters were in Singapore from Dec 11th until the war ended.

<u>9th Air Division</u> Palembang, Sumatra 1943	翔 *Kakeru*	
9th Air Division Headquarters	15350 (281)	
9th Air Division Headquarters Signal Squad	15350 (79)	
8th Air Sector Command	9146 (67)	
22nd Air Sector Command	11064 (22)	
46th Airfield Battalion	9148 (372)	
76th Airfield Battalion	9624 (372)	
87th Airfield Battalion	16501 (372)	
89th Airfield Battalion	16502 (372)	
14th Airfield Company	9333 (207)	
30th Airfield Company	11060 (208)	
35th Airfield Company	15342 (208)	
37th Airfield Company	15344 (208)	
66th Airfield Company	18475 (226)	
68th Airfield Company	18476 (226)	
88th Airfield Company	9369 (207)	
7th Air Intelligence Regiment	18484 (1,164)	
14th Air Intelligence Regiment	16503 (1,689)	
18th Air Intelligence Unit	18958 (805)	
160th Line of Comm. Motor Transport Unit	7338 (194)	
• 74th Independent Air Squadron	9643 (121)	
• 87th Air Regiment (fighter)	8387 (139)	

<u>9th Air Division</u>: Activated on Dec 10, 1943 to defend the oil fields in Sumatra with headquarters in Palembang. Attached to the 3rd Air Army from Dec 28th until the war ended. The Palembang Air Defence Unit reorganized into Palembang Guards Brigade on June 1, 1944 and newly activated Pangkalanbrandan Defense Unit. In January 1945 ships could no longer sail to Japan to deliver oil so the Southern Army released the 9th Air Division from defending the Palembang and Pangkalabrandan oil fields. Both the Bhutan Guards Unit and Palembang Guards Brigade were under the 9th Air Division's command.

<u>5th Air Division</u> Phnom Penh 1942	高 *Taka*	
5th Air Division Headquarters	9638 (193)	
5th Air Division Signal Unit	9896	
4th Air Brigade Headquarters	9902 (65)	
• 64th Air Regiment	9124 (195)	Thailand
• 81st Air Regiment	2380 (247)	Indochina
1st Air Sector Command	9903 (111)	
7th Air Sector Command	9126 (67)	
15th Airfield Battalion	9921 (372)	
17th Airfield Battalion	9127 (372)	
19th Airfield Battalion	9613 (372)	
23rd Airfield Battalion	9128 (372)	
34th Airfield Battalion	9194 (372)	

5th Air Division continued

52nd Airfield Battalion	9614 (372)
82nd Airfield Battalion	9868 (372)
92nd Airfield Battalion	9870 (372)
Later 90th/92nd Joint Airfield Battalion	9648 / 9870
94th Airfield Battalion	9130 (587)
9th Airfield Company	9934 (304)
12th Airfield Company	9935 (300)
17th Airfield Company	9336 (205)
18th Airfield Company	9337 (205)
38th Airfield Company	15345 (208)
85th Airfield Company	9368 (207)
2nd Air Intelligence Regiment	9617 (1,102)
17th Air Navigation Aid Unit	9879 (235)
7th Field Airfield Construction Unit	9954 (79)
8th Field Airfield Construction Unit	9955 (79)
20th Anti-Aircraft Regiment	3505 (570)
36th Field Anti-Aircraft Battalion	4811 (522)
35th Independent Motor Transport Battalion	1388 (808)
275th Independent Motor Transport Company	3987 (183)
280th Independent Motor Transport Company	7107 (183)
281st Independent Motor Transport Company	7108 (183)
86th Line of Communication Motor Transport Unit	9893 (170)
67th Land Duty Company	3305 (511)
68th Land Duty Company	3306 (511)
80th Land Duty Company	3030 (511)
62nd Construction Duty Company	6439 (511)
75th Airfield Battalion	9645 (406)
78th Airfield Battalion	11072 (406

5th Air Division: Activated in Burma on April 14, 1942, attached to the Southern Army from Apr 14th until July 10th and 3rd Air Army until the war ended. It was based in Rangoon, Burma until Apr 15, 1945 when it was sent to Phnom Penh, Indochina for the remainder of the war.

7th Air Division Java 1943 — 襲 *Kasane*

7th Air Division Headquarters	9311
• 73rd Ind. Air Squadron (heavy bomber)	9181 (63)
• 70th Independent Air Squadron (fighter)	9641 (61)
4th Air Sector Command	9905 (113)
9th Air Sector Command	9605 / 304 (69)
32nd Air Sector Command	18486 (44)
5th Airfield Battalion	11802 (372)
28th Airfield Battalion	9924 (372)
35th Airfield Battalion	9865 (372)
68th Airfield Battalion	11804 (372)

7th Air Division continued	襲 *Kasane*
70th Airfield Battalion	11805 (372)
72nd Airfield Battalion	11806 (372)
113th Airfield Battalion	11803 (372)
7th Airfield Company	9933 (304)
15th Airfield Company	9334 (205)
27th Airfield Company	11800 (208)
29th Airfield Company	9937 (308)
31st Airfield Company	15340 (208)
34th Airfield Company	15341 (208)
39th Airfield Company	15346 (208)
40th Airfield Company	15347 (208)
41st Airfield Company	15368 (226)
43rd Airfield Company	15370 (226)
44th Airfield Company	15371 (226)
45th Airfield Company	15372 (226)
9th Field Airfield Construction Unit	9956 (79)
9th Air Signals Regiment	11057 (1,311)
8th Air Intelligence Unit	15338 (913)
298th Independent Motor Transport Company	8859 (183)
69th Land Duty Company	3307 (511)
123rd Land Duty Company	1747 (511)
43rd Construction Duty Company	3029 (511)
21st Field Aircraft Repair Depot	15348 (1,070)
21st Field Air Freight Depot	15349 (954)

7th Air Division: HQ activated in Japan on Jan 28, 1943, and shipped to Singapore on the 29th. The 7th Air Division was based in Java with the 3rd Air Army from Jan 30th until Jul 28th, the 4th Air Army until Feb 17, 1945 and 3rd Air Army until it was deactivated on July 10th.

10th Independent Air Brigade Borneo 1944

Unit	Number
10th Independent Air Brigade Headquarters	9622 / 満州715 (116)
37th Air Sector Command	司 9909 (44)
100th Airfield Battalion	15361 (458)
110th Airfield Battalion	15366 (458)
111th Airfield Battalion	15367 (458)
130th Airfield Battalion	18449 (372)
103rd Field Airfield Construction Unit	15328 (76)
145th Field Airfield Construction Unit	18409 (175)

10th Independent Air Brigade: Organized in Borneo on Oct 19, 1944 from former 10th Air Brigade personnel. It was attached to the 4th Air Army from Oct 19th until Feb 17, 1945 and 3rd Air Army until the war ended.

Southern Expeditionary Army Shipping Units 暁 *Akatsuki*

The 3rd Shipping Headquarters, under Shipping Transport Command in Japan, controlled all sea transport in the southwest. After January 1945 units in Java, Sumatra, Andaman and Nicobar Is. were placed under the 7th Area Army's control.

Southern Army Shipping Units	暁 "*Akatsuki*"	
3rd Shipping Headquarters	2944 (957)	
Shipping Signal Regiment	2955 (1,448)	
4th Shipping Engineer Regiment	6172 (1,099)	
7th Shipping Engineer Regiment	10651 (1,099)	
10th Shipping Engineer Regiment	9422 (1,099)	Andaman I.
11th Shipping Engineer Regiment	1750 (1,099)	
13th Shipping Engineer Regiment	6161 (1,099)	
14th Shipping Engineer Regiment	6162 (1,099)	
15th Shipping Engineer Regiment	6176 (1,099)	
18th Shipping Engineer Regiment	16702 (1,099)	
20th Shipping Engineer Regiment	16716 (1,099)	
7th Shipping Debarkation Unit	6187	
8th Shipping Debarkation Unit	6143	
10th Shipping Debarkation Unit	6150 (894)	
12th Shipping Debarkation Unit	6159 (894)	Burma
13th Shipping Debarkation Unit	6166 (894)	
3rd Shipping Transport Headquarters	2944	
1st Shipping Transport Battalion	6157 (557)	
2nd Shipping Transport Battalion	6189	
3rd Shipping Transport Battalion	6190 (548)	Burma
7th Shipping Transport Battalion	6158 (548)	
38th Anchorage Headquarters	6910 (151)	Burma
46th Anchorage Headquarters	6434	
47th Anchorage Headquarters	9736	
48th Anchorage Headquarters	9737 (151)	
56th Anchorage Headquarters	1741	
62nd Anchorage Headquarters	16725 / 16745 (81)	
66th Anchorage Headquarters	19778 (81)	
70th Anchorage Headquarters	15926 (209)	
11th Shipping Transport Headquarters	2952	
16th Hospital Shipping Medical Section	7142 (104)	
54th Hospital Shipping Medical Section	6776 (83)	
56th Hospital Shipping Medical Section	6779 (61)	
57th Hospital Shipping Medical Section	6780 (50)	
2nd Field Shipping Depot	2949 (1,954)	

Southern Expeditionary Army Railway Units 路 *Michi*

Early in the occupation, with the Southern Army in overall control, existing railways were taken over and managed by local army commanders. Because of numerous national borders and diverse geography, and because railways were of great importance they were all soon combined into one command and operated as a 'through service'. When Japan gained control of the Malay Peninsula, rail was the only transportation that ran its length. Although Singapore surrendered on Feb 15th it was not until March 21st that the trains in Malaya returned to service.

Service History:

1942: The 3rd Railway Transport Command was in charge of rail operations in Indochina and Thailand early in the Japanese occupation ○ The rail system outgrew the 3rd Railway Transport Command when Malaya, Burma and Sumatra joined, so 3rd Field Railway Headquarters was activated with the Command acting as its nucleus. The 3rd Field Railway Headquarters located in Kuala Lampur w/branch offices in Palembang, Hanoi, Medan, Bangkok and Padang ○ In May the 4th Railway Transport Command was activated in Java and the 6th in the Philippines to manage the railway in their areas ○ In June I.G.HQ decided to build the Thai-Burma railway based on a Thai-British study/plan ○ In Nov bomb damage to Burma's pre-war railways is repaired ○ After studying difficulties and obtaining Thailand's consent the first phase of Thai-Burma Railway construction began in early Nov. with the 2nd Railway Inspectorate in charge. First phase of construction ran from Nov until early Feb 1943 ○ In Dec railways were the target of more than half of all air attacks, 5% of the army's 200 locomotives were lost every month ○ The approx 3000 km of Burma's railways were run by the 5th Specially Established Railway Headquarters through local officials ○

1943: Late Jan, the officer overseeing railway construction died in a plane crash ○ In early Feb a plan to reduce construction time was accepted, the completion deadline was for late-Aug 1943 ○ Mid-Feb until mid-July, 2nd phase of Thai-Burma railway construction ○ Early 1943, the only supply route into Burma was from Singapore by sea, in addition to the ship shortage enemy subs and aircraft placed increased pressure on the route ○ In spring the 5th Specially Established Railway Headquarters had been exhausted by constant repairs to Burma's railways, which were down to a third of their Nov 1942 load capacity ○ Late Mar, necessary measures taken and a parallel road completed, construction continued at a rapid pace ○ In early Apr 200 motor vehicles arrived for moving supplies ○ Monsoon season, which usually begins in May came to Burma in mid Apr and Thailand in late Apr. It rained every day causing construction delays ○ In June the bridges over Mezale and Winyaw Rivers were swept away. The movement of supplies became hampered. In some places rations were cut in half or more. Cholera, malaria and other diseases became rampant within the labor force of soldiers, conscripted natives and POW ○ In June an inspection of the railway led planners to concede completion would be impossible by the end of Aug, a 2-month extension was granted ○ By the end of July a 270 km waterway had been established between Rangoon and Nike with 700 tow-boats hauling materials and supplies ○ On Aug 16th monsoon season had ended and a new railway construction commander arrived, Maj. Gen Ishida preferred to direct operations on the spot ○ On Oct 17th eastern and western sections of the tracks joined at Konkoita ○ On Aug 25th a ceremony was held to celebrate the Thai-Burma RR opening just 10 months

after the work began. It extended 415 km, had over 14 km of bridges and was built through inhospitable terrain* ○ After completion of the railway the Southern Army Railway Unit was deactivated and 2nd Railway Inspectorate, 5th Railway Regt and 1st Railway Stores Depot were sent to Burma. Maintaining the Burma-Thai Railway fell to the 4th Specially Established Railway Unit and 9th Railway Regt. There were many construction defects so every part of it needed fixing or replacing during the year that followed, enemy air attacks compounded the trouble. In the end Thai-Burma Railway barely met the needs it had been constructed to fill ○
1944: In February the Southern Army Field Railway Headquarters reorganized ○ On April 18th the 7th Area Army and 29th Army handed over control of the Malay Railway to the Southern Army Field Railway Headquarters, effective midnight on Apr 25th ○ On Sept 29th the Sumatra and Java railways were reorganized ○ At midnight on Oct 20th railway units under the Southern Army Field Railway Unit were placed under 7th Area Army control. To facilitate troop movement by rail the administration and operation passed to the 25th Army and 16th Army ○ In August the 8th Railway Regt was scheduled to upgrade the Philippine railway. While awaiting passage in Singapore elements were diverted to Sumatra and Saigon so that only the Regiment's Headquarters and half a battalion arrived in Manila Harbor on Nov 5th, too late to effect change ○
*The Japanese Army boasted the Thai-Burma Railway was its greatest achievement, at the same it attempted to hide the criminal abuses committed using forced labor on the railway's construction.

Southern Army railway units:	路 *Michi*	
Southern Army Field Railway Headquarters	義 15801 (337)	
Southern Army Field Railway Depot	15802 (525)	Naunpladuk, Th.
2nd Railway Inspectorate	5801 (69)	Kanchanaburi, Th.
5th Railway Regiment	5804 (1,784)	Thabyuzayat, B
7th Railway Regiment	2143 (1,301)	Wangyai, Thai.
9th Railway Regiment	5805 (2,543)	
10th Railway Regiment	2145 (2,560)	
11th Railway Regiment	2146 (2,560)	
1st Railway Materials Depot	5806 (158)	Nomburadokku
4th Specially Established Railway Headquarters	5838 (36)	
4th Specially Established Railway Unit	5826 (37)	
4th Specially Established Railway Engineer Unit	5828 (30)	
8th Specially Established Railway Engineer Unit	5827 (37)	Burma Area Army
5th Specially Established Railway Headquarters	5894 (36)	Burma Area Army
5th Sp. Est. Railway Bridge Construction Unit	5823 (37)	
10th Specially Established Railway Transport Unit	5821 (35)	
7th Specially Est. Railway Construction Unit	5825 (37)	Kanchanaburi, Th.
11th Specially Established Railway Transport Unit	5822 (35)	Rangoon, Burma
102nd Railway Station Command	1393 (17)	
120th Railway Station Command	4001 (17)	
121st Railway Station Command	4002 (17)	
143rd Railway Station Command	7117 (17)	
148th Railway Station Command	7034 (17)	
152nd Railway Station Command	6427 (17)	

Southern Army railway units: continued	路 *Michi*
161st Railway Station Command	9735 (17)

Western (Dutch) New Guinea

2nd Area Army 輝 *Kagayaku*

The 2nd Area Army was activated on June 27, 1942 and completed organizing on Jul 29th in Qiqihar, Manchuria. It was placed under the Kwantung Army's control July 4th as a reserve and garrison army, its headquarters in Tsitsihar. On Oct 26, 1943 the 2nd Area Army headquarters began reorganizing for the south Pacific, completed Nov 3rd. On the 3rd it left Qiqihar for Davao, Mindanao arriving Nov. 23rd. On Dec 1, 1943 the 2nd Area Army Headquarters relocated from Davao to Manado, North Sulawesi, the Celebes and became responsible for occupying strategic areas in West New Guinea, Aroe, Tanimbar, Timor and the Lesser Sunda Is. Its main supply base in Japan was Hiroshima with the advanced supply base in Manila. Depots were located in Halmahera, Ambon and Manokwari and branch depots in Solong and Makassar. The 2nd Area Army was placed under Southern Expeditionary Army control on Mar 27, 1944. Lt Gen Korechika Anami its commander from Jul 4, 1942 until Dec 26, 1944 and Lt.Gen Jō Īmura until May 29, 1945. It was deactivated June 13, 1945, at the same moment as its units and responsibilities were transferred to the 2nd Army.

Subordinate armies / duty dates:

4th Army from July 4, 1942, until Oct 30, 1943	Manchuria
6th Army from July 4, 1942, until Oct 30, 1943	Manchuria
2nd Army from Oct 30, 1943 until June 13, 1945	Manokwari, New Guinea
19th Army from Oct 30, 1943, until Feb 28, 1945	Batavia, Java
18th Army from Mar 14, 1944, until June 13, 1945	Madang, New Guinea

Service History:

1943: On Oct 26th 2nd Area Army HQ reorganized for service in the South Pacific ○ On Nov 3rd left Qiqihar, landed in Davao Nov 23rd and established a command post ○ On Dec 1st the 2nd Area Army Command Post became active ○ On Dec 25th most of the 36th Div landed in Sarmi and a detached element sent to Biak Island ○ On Dec 29th Imperial Headquarters sent the 2nd Area Army an outline of its operational boundaries and key areas ○

1944: In January disruptions to shipping began. With the situation in Burma worsening the Southern Army suspended sea transport to the 2nd Area Army for Feb to resume in Mar ○ On Jan 14th the rest of the 36th Div arrived in Sarmi ○ On Feb 1st the 33rd, 60th and 70th Air Regts from the 8th Air Div were placed under 2nd Area Army control ○ In late Feb 8th Air Div air regiments arrived in Madang and Bunda ○ On Mar 10th the 2nd

Area Army held a planning meeting in Davao, staff from 2nd Army, 19th Army and 7th Air Div attended ○ On Mar 25th the 18th Army and 4th Air Army were placed under 2nd Area Army command ○ On Apr 15th the 2nd Area Army was placed under Southern Expeditionary Army control ○ Apr 19th, I.G.HQ announced plans to construct large fortresses in western New Guinea, Palau, Mindanao and Halmahera ○ On Apr 22nd the enemy attacked rear area supply bases in Hollandia and Aitape ○ Apr 25th the 2nd Area Army's headquarters relocated from Davao to Menado, the Celebes ○ On Apr 30th, the plan (of Apr 24th) to transport the 36th Division to Hollandia was canceled ○ On May 4th the Matsuyama Detachment, 224th Inf Regt, 36th Division began to advance on Hollandia ○ On May 6th a US sub sank 3 ships carrying the 32nd and 35th Divisions in the waters off Luzon. Sailing from central China to Halmahera the convoy docked in Warmire May 9th ○ On May 10th the 15th Div was sent to Manokwari and the 32nd Div to Halmahera ○ The 2nd Area Army set its forward line between Sorong and Halmahera ○ On May 14th the 2nd Area Army commander visited 2nd Army HQ in Manokwari ○ On May 16th the Southern Army relieved the 18th Army of responsibility for recapturing Hollandia ○ May 18th, US troops landed near Tomu, opposite Wakde ○ On May 19th the Wakde garrison, one inf. company strong, was annihilated ○ May 23rd the 35th Div left Halmahera for Sorong ○ On May 27th US troops landed near Bonner Airfield on Biak Is. ○ On May 30th the 2nd Amphibious Brigade was earmarked for Biak ○ June 1st the Brigade boarded cruisers Aoba and Kinu in Davao for *Kon-go* ○ Evening of June 2nd the *Kon* convoy left Davao expecting to reach Biak on the 4th but was discovered by a B-24 on June 3rd, Combined Fleet recalled the cruisers ○ On June 4th about 40 American transports were discovered near Hollandia ○ On June 5th the Emperor commends the bravery of the Biak and Tomu Garrisons ○ On June 8th operation *Kon-go* resumed but enemy aircraft sank the destroyer carrying the 2nd Amphibious Brigade commander. The convoy arrived in Biak at 2200 ○ On June 10th the 1st Battleship Squadron, Yamato and Musashi, were assigned to *Kon-go* ○ On June 11th 300 reinforcements from Manokwari landed on Biak. Ever greater shipping losses made reinforcing Biak difficult ○ On June 15th the 2nd Amphibious Brigade was re-routed to Sorong and the 35th Div went to Biak instead ○ On June 16th Biak's Garrison abandoned the Hodalean position ○ On June 19th, with travel by ship impossible the 18th Army's headquarters received orders to stay in Aitape ○ By June 27th the Biak Detachment's complete collapse had become inevitable. The 2nd Army commander commended the 36th Div on Biak for bravery ○ On June 20th the 18th Army became isolated and was placed under Southern Expeditionary Army command ○ June 30th, US troops land in Maru on the Vogelkop Peninsula ○ On July 2nd the US invaded Noemfor Island ○ On July 16th the 36th Div HQ evacuated Manokwari and advanced on Sorong along the coast of the Vogelkop Peninsula ○ On Aug 27th the 13th Air Group, 50 planes in the 30th & 31st Air Squadrons, joined the 7th Air Div ○ Aug 30th, the Chihaya plan for Halmahera's defense was submitted to the Southern Army for approval ○ Sept 22nd, the Borneo Garrison Army became the 37th Army ○ On Sept 24th the 2nd Area Army's HQ deployed in Pinrang, South Sulawesi ○ On Oct 8th the 32nd Div received replacement troops ○ On Oct 20th US forces landed on Leyte ○ US and Australian forces on New Guinea temporarily halt attacks but continue to fight on Biak, Numpol, Sansapol, Morotai and Peleliu ○ Late Oct, the 2nd Area Army was ordered to take control of the Navy's land units in its area ○ On Oct 27th the 2nd Area Army's HQ relocates to southern Halmahera ○ Dec 26th Lt. Gen Anami is transferred

to the Air Inspectorate and replaced by Lt Gen Iimura, formerly with the 2nd Area Army General Staff ○
1945: On Feb 28th the 19th Army was deactivated and the 2nd Area Army absorbed its units ○ On Mar 26th the 46th Div was sent to join the 7th Area Army in Malaya ○ On June 13th the 2nd Area Army was deactivated and its units assigned to the 2nd Army ○
Major Units: See division / brigade page for order of battle

32nd Division Tokyo 1939 楓 *Kaede* (to the 2nd Army June 13 1945)	179
36th Division Kumamoto 1939 雪 *Yuki* (to the 2nd Army June 13 1945)	181
48th Division Taiwan 1940 海 *Umi* (to the 2nd Army June 13, 1945)	185
57th Ind. Mixed Brigade 1944 桂 *Katsura* (to the 2nd Army June 13 1945)	227
128th Ind.Mixed Brigade 1945 快捷 *Kaishou* (to 2nd Army June 13 1945)	235
2nd Amphibious Brigade 1943 巡 *Jun* (to the 2nd Army June 13 1945)	242
10th Expeditionary Unit 1944 輝 *Kagayaku* (to the 2nd Army June 13 1945)	254

Attached to the 32nd Division:

69th Field Anti-Aircraft Battalion	1999 楓 *Kaede*

Units under 2nd Area Army control: Manado 輝 *Kagayaku*

2nd Area Army Headquarters	16300	Manado
72nd Field Anti-Aircraft Battalion	12601	
73rd Field Anti-Aircraft Battalion	16305	
74th Field Anti-Aircraft Battalion, 2nd Company	7831	
20th Field Anti-Aircraft Defense Unit HQ	5757	
46th Independent Field Anti-Aircraft Company	2134	
47th Independent Field Anti-Aircraft Company	2135	
11th Independent Field Searchlight Company	2137	
45th Field Machine Cannon Company	16306	
47th Field Machine Cannon Company	1469	
1st Field Base Unit Headquarters	2130	
56th Line of Communications Sector Command	10226 (203)	
56th Line of Communications Guard Unit	10226 (1,035)	
56th Line of Communications Duty Company	10226 (511)	
30th Specially Est. Motor Transport Company	10462	
1st Specially Established Land Duty Company	10371	
36th Construction Duty Company	4828 (812)	
13th Field Meteorology Unit	15339 (972)	
123rd Field Airfield Construction Unit	15387	
124th Field Airfield Construction Unit	15388	
40th Casualty Clearing Platoon	4303	
57th Casualty Clearing Platoon	10162	
66th Casualty Clearing Platoon	6758	
2nd Area Army Field Ordinance Depot	10627 (680)	
2nd Area Army Field Motor Vehicle Depot	10628 (1,337)	
2nd Area Army Field Freight Depot	10629 (803)	
11th Debarkation Unit	6154	

Morotai, Halmahera and Western New Guinea

2nd Army 勢 *Ikioi*

The 2nd Army became active in Hanchuang, North China Aug 26 1937 and placed under North China Area Army control from Aug 31st until Apr 30, 1938, headquarters in Tungshan. On July 4th it was placed under Central China Expeditionary Army control and deactivated Dec 9th. The 2nd Army commander was Lt Gen Jūzō Nishio from Aug 26th until Apr 30, 1938 and Lt Gen Prince Naruhiko Higashikuni until Dec 9th.

Reactivation:

The 2nd Army was reactivated in Manchuria on Apr 16, 1942 and attached to the 1st Area Army from Jul 4th until Oct 30, 1943. It was placed under 2nd Area Army control for service in New Guinea and landed in Manokwari, western New Guinea between Dec 4th and 8th. On June 13, 1945 the 2nd Army was placed under Southern Army control, its headquarters deployed to Macassar in the Celebes and made responsible for Morotai, Halmahera and western New Guinea. Lt Gen Yoshio Kōzuki commanded the 2nd Army from Jul 1, 1942 until May 28, 1943, Lt Gen Ichirō Shichida until Oct. 29th and Lt Gen Fusatarō Teshima until the war ended.

On June 13, 1945, the 2nd Area Army was deactivated and its remnants placed under the 2nd Army's control, which now answered directly to the Southern Army.

Service History:

1942: On Jul 4th the 2nd Army was reactivated in Manchuria and placed under the 1st Area Army ○

1943: On Oct 30th the 2nd Army was placed under 2nd Area Army control ○ Nov 9th HQ sailed from Pusan, Korea ○ On Nov 29th the 2nd Area Army gave responsibility for Sarmi, New Guinea, the coast west of Sarmi and the Suneau Mountain Range to the 2nd Army ○ Between Dec 4th and 8th its HQ arrived in Manokwari ○ On Dec 25th, the 36th Div joined the 2nd Army and was split between Biak Is. and Sarmi where it constructed airfields and attempted farming to grow enough food to be self-sufficient ○

1944: Feb 10th, while awaiting transport from Manchuria the 14th Div was placed under 2nd Army control. While sailing south the 14th Div was redirected to the Palau Is. to join the 31st Army ○ May 17th, the US invaded Sarmi near Arare. Landed on the left bank at the mouth of the Tor River, which was undefended. The Matsuyama Detachment (224th Inf Regt, 36th Div) on its way to Hollandia turned back to confront the invasion. ○ On May 17th the US invaded Wakde Island for its airfield, which fell by May 20th ○ On May 19th the 2nd Army ordered the 36th Div including Matsuyama Detachment to destroy enemy in the Toem area ○ On May 26th, the US concentrated forces near the Sawar (Sarmi) airfield with artillery and spotter planes, the fighting was brutal ○ On May 27th the *Battle of Biak Is* began ○ On May 28th HQ and two battalions from the 219th Inf Regt landed on Noemfor Is to reinforce the single company from the 222nd I R ○ On May 30th Yoshino Unit launched a surprise attack on Arare and Toem, the fighting continued for several days ○ By June 25th the *Battle of Lone Tree Hil*l and Sarmi had been decided. Between June 27th and 30th remnants of the Japanese units were cleared ○ On May 27th the *Battle of Biak* began. Lt Gen Numata, 2nd Area Army Chief of Staff, who had been inspecting the island when the US invasion started, took command of the garrison ○ Resistance began when American troops moved inland to capture Mokmer airfield and continued until June

7th ○ On June 20th Lt Gen Numata left Biak by floatplane ○ June 22nd Col. Kuzume, 222nd I.R. commander burned the Regt's colors and committed suicide ○ Aug 17th, the fighting on Biak ended ○ July 2nd, US troops landed on Noemfor Island near Kamiri Airfield. Kamiri immediately lost ○ On Jul 4th the Americans captured Yebrurro Airstrip and the 2nd Army's HQ moved from Manokwari to Uinteshi and Idere where bago and coconuts were abundant ○ On Jul 5th Namber Airfield attacked and on the 6th it fell ○ On Jul 30th enemy landed in an unguarded place on Sansapor Point near Mar on Vogelkop Peninsula ○ There was an infantry platoon in Sansapor and invalids from the 35th Div in the Sorong area ○ Aug 16th, 400 men attempted an offensive but all were dead by the 31st ○ Control of Vogelkop Peninsula gave the Allies control of the Dampier Straits, which opened the way to the Philippines and isolated the Japanese left on New Guinea ○ In mid-Aug the 32nd Div deployed along the coast of Washire Bay on Halmahera, to defend the airfields and munitions dumps. The 2nd Area Army no longer had access to supplies or reinforcements ○ The 32nd Div plan was called *Chihaya*, the battle for Halmahera. Preparations would be complete by the end of Aug. Stranded air ground units joined front line troops when the fighting began ○ On Sept 15th the US landed troops on Gila Peninsula, Morotai. That night 7th Air Div units from Ceram and elsewhere bombed and strafed their landing site. Outnumbered by 100 to 1, weakened by hunger and disease, the army had already withdrawn ○ On Sept 24th a fortified position near Wajaboeta was overrun ○ On Sept 27th the 1st Raiding Unit arrived in Mira 5 km north of Sangowo ○ On Oct 4th the US declared Morotai secure ○ Oct 19th, the 2nd Army still had 1,100 troops on Morotai. The 2nd Raiding Company commander took control of 1st and 3rd Raiding Companies, then continued with operations throughout October but with negligible results ○ Nov 16th the Morita Detachment, 1,900 men from the 211th Inf Regt, landed in 7 large barges, 2 small barges and 4 escorts (most destroyed on the return trip) ○ On Nov 26th the remaining 2 large and 3 small barges in Galela, Halmahera ferried the Kande Group, 200 soldiers with medical equipment and food, to Morotai ○ The 2nd Army guessed at results using aerial photos and reports. They estimated about 3,000 Americans casualties by December ○ From November 21st to December 15th the Morita Unit claimed to have caused 1,200 casualties, including 160 air force personnel, fighting behind US lines ○ On December 1st the Morotai Detachment received a Unit Citation for its service in the 2nd Army ○ The US launched an offensive against the remnants of the 211th Infantry Regiment in December ○

1945: In January the Morita Unit commander was killed, Colonel Oboki replaced him ○ On Jan 14th the US claimed Morotai was clear of Japanese resistance but fighting continued until the end of the war ○ On Jan 3rd US troops attacked the 211th Inf. Regt's position ○ On Jan 5th the 211th Inf. Regt. collapsed ○ On Jan 14th US troops ended pursuit claiming 870 killed and 10 prisoners for a loss of 46 killed and 127 wounded ○ On June 13th the 2nd Area Army was deactivated. Most of its units were placed under the 2nd Army's control ○ Aug 6th, the 211th Infantry Regiment's commander was captured ○ On August 15th Japan surrendered ○ August 26th, the war on Morotai and Halmahera ended with the remnants of the 32nd Division surrendering to the US 93rd Infantry Division ○

Major Units: See division / brigade page for order of battle

5th Division Hiroshima 1888 鯉 *Koi* – Ceram Island 166

32nd Division Tokyo 1939 楓 *Kaede* – Halmahera from 2nd Area Army 179

35th Division Tokyo 1939 東 *Higashi* – New Guinea	180
36th Division Kumamoto 1939 雪 *Yuki* – Sarmi, New Guinea (from 2AA)	181
48th Division Taiwan 1940 海 *Umi* – Timor (from the 2AA)	185
57th Ind. Mixed Brigade 1944 桂 *Katsura* – Celebese Is. (from 2AA)	227
128th Ind. Mixed Brigade 1945 快捷 *Kaishou* – Halmahera (from 2AA)	235
2nd Amphibious Brigade 1943 巡 *Jun* – West New Guinea (from 2AA)	242
10th Expeditionary Unit 1944 輝 *Kagayaku* – Celebese Is. (from 2AA)	254

<u>Attached to the 35th Division</u>:	東 *Higashi*	
36th Independent Engineer Regiment	9423 (894)	Takeshi Unit
4th Independent Mountain Artillery Regiment	4734	

<u>Attached to the 36th Division</u>:	雪 *Yuki* 3521
18th Air Sector Command	11613 (26)
38th/70th Joint Airfield Battalion	8308 / 11805 (599)
5th Air Signal Regiment	9941 (1,320)
14th Field Air Freight Depot	9305 (100)
14th Field Air Repair Depot	9304 (526)
4th Air Intelligence Regiment	9302 (1,441)
13th Field Airfield Construction Unit, minus 2 Coys	15307 (275)

<u>Attached to the 48th Division</u>:	海 *Umi* 8940	
1st Specially Established Sea Transport Unit	10436 (189)	Sumbawa Is.
72nd Field Anti-Aircraft Regiment	16601	
109th Line of Communications Hospital	7015 (380)	

<u>Units under 2nd Army control</u>: Macassar	勢 *Ikioi*	
2nd Army Headquarters	16400 (601)	Macassar
2nd Army Headquarters Intelligence Section	16400 (50)	
24th Signal Regiment	10318 (1,245)	
26th Signal Regiment	16312 (1,465)	
2nd Field Signal Company	5552 (378)	
9th Independent Field Signal Company	16307 (186)	
98th Independent Wire Company	16313 (235)	
99th Independent Wire Company	16314 (310)	
100th Independent Wire Company	3170 (277)	
86th Independent Radio Platoon	12651 (57)	
87th Independent Radio Platoon	12652 (57)	
92nd Independent Radio Platoon	2542 (57)	
1st Raiding Column Headquarters	2141 (90)	
1st Raiding Company	1781 (192)	
2nd Raiding Company	1782 (192)	
3rd Raiding Company	16308 (192)	
4th Raiding Company	16309 (192)	
5th Raiding Company	16310 (192)	
6th Raiding Company	16311 (192)	
7th Raiding Company	2142 (192)	
8th Raiding Company	5762 (193)	

2nd Army continued	勢 *Ikioi*	
9th Raiding Company	5763 (192)	
10th Raiding Company	12509 (192)	
4th Tank Regiment	5058 (457)	
5th Trench Mortar Battalion	3503 (740)	
2nd Field Base Headquarters	9466	
20th Field Anti Aircraft Artillery Headquarters	5157 (53)	
32nd Field Anti Aircraft Battalion	3882 (401)	
44th Field Anti Aircraft Battalion	3959 (522)	
49th Field Anti Aircraft Battalion	1223 (667)	
53rd Field Anti Aircraft Battalion	5063 (667)	
54th Field Anti Aircraft Battalion	5065 (667)	
57th Field Anti Aircraft Battalion	4358 (667)	
68th Field Anti Aircraft Battalion	1998 (528)	
72nd Field Anti Aircraft Battalion	12601 (528)	
73rd Field Anti Aircraft Battalion	16305 (528)	
74th Field Anti Aircraft Battalion, 2nd Company	7831 (142)	
43rd Independent Field Anti Aircraft Company	2131 (162)	
44th Independent Field Anti Aircraft Company	2132 (162)	
45th Independent Field Anti Aircraft Company	2133 (162)	
48th Independent Field Anti Aircraft Company	5758 (162)	
49th Independent Field Anti Aircraft Company	5759 (162)	
50th Independent Field Anti-Aircraft Company	12506 (162)	
51st Independent Field Anti-Aircraft Company	7468 (162)	
26th Field Machine Cannon Company	4463 (136)	
41st Field Machine Cannon Company	10595 (104)	
42nd Field Machine Cannon Company	8058 (104)	
46th Field Machine Cannon Company	5760 (105)	
47th Field Machine Cannon Company	7469 (105)	
1st Specially Est. Machine Cannon Unit	16319 (85)	
2nd Specially Est. Machine Cannon Unit	16320 (85)	
3rd Specially Est. Machine Cannon Unit	16321 (85)	
4th Specially Est. Machine Cannon Unit	16322 (86)	
5th Specially Est. Machine Cannon Unit	16323 (86)	
6th Specially Est. Machine Cannon Unit	16324 (87)	
4th Field Searchlight Battalion, minus the 2nd Co.	5066 (271)	
9th Independent Field Searchlight Company	16307 (186)	
10th Independent Field Searchlight Company	2136 (186)	
12th Independent Field Searchlight Company	12602 (186)	
4th Engineer Group Headquarters	1272 (32)	
3rd Independent Engineer Regiment	5543 (1,095)	
15th Independent Engineer Regiment	8125 (937)	was in Malaya
55th Line of Communications Sector Command	10225 (203)	
55th Line of Communications Guard Unit	10225 (1,035)	
55th Line of Communications Duty Company	10225 (511)	
57th Line of Communications Sector Command	3965 (203)	

57th Line of Communications Guard Unit	3966 (1,035)	
57th Line of Communications Duty Company	3967 (511)	
51st Field Road Construction Unit	5597 (495)	
52nd Field Road Construction Unit	5599 (495)	
227th Independent Motor Transport Company	2864 (183)	
228th Independent Motor Transport Company	2865 (183)	
229th Independent Motor Transport Company	2866 (183)	
248th Independent Motor Transport Company	5708 (183)	
263rd Independent Motor Transport Company	10216 (183)	
290th Independent Motor Transport Company	9719 (182)	
13th Specially Est. Motor Transport Company	10427 (69)	
26th Specially Est. Motor Transport Company	10458 (69)	
27th Specially Est. Motor Transport Company	10459 (69)	
28th Specially Est. Motor Transport Company	10460 (69)	
33rd Specially Est. Motor Transport Company	11513 (69)	
34th Specially Est. Motor Transport Company	11514 (69)	
35th Specially Est. Motor Transport Company	11515 (69)	
1st Line of Comm. Motor Transport Company	9890 (170)	
1st Specially Established Land Duty Company	10371 (61)	
11th Specially Established Land Duty Company	10388 (61)	
35th Specially Established Land Duty Company	10443 (61)	
42nd Specially Established Land Duty Company	10469 (61)	
54th Construction Duty Company	6914 (582)	
61st Construction Duty Company	6438 (511)	
69th Construction Duty Company	15559 (511)	
70th Construction Duty Company	15560 (511)	
72nd Construction Duty Company	5889 (511)	
73rd Construction Duty Company	5871 (511)	
29th Specially Est. Construction Duty Company	10399 (61)*	
48th Specially Est. Construction Duty Company	10446 (61)	
50th Specially Est. Construction Duty Company	10448 (61)	
104th Specially Est. Construction Duty Company	1775 (61)	
13th Field Survey Unit	1373 (178)	
2nd Specially Established Sea Transport Unit	10437 (189)	
5th Field Well-Drilling Company	unknown (100)	Biak Is.
13th Field Post Office Unit	6602 (251)	
19th Field Post Office Unit	9751 (251)	
15th Southern Army Hospital	6085 (994)	
125th Line of Communications Hospital	3885 (359)	
126th Line of Communications Hospital	3886 (420)	
150th Line of Communications Hospital	16325 (172)	
18th Casualty Clearing Unit Headquarters	5280 (117)	
39th Casualty Clearing Platoon	4802 (54)	
65th Casualty Clearing Platoon	6757 (54)	
85th Casualty Clearing Platoon	7198 (54)	
87th Casualty Clearing Platoon	9771 (57)	

2nd Army continued	勢 *Ikioi*	
88th Casualty Clearing Platoon	9772 (54)	
5th Debarkation Unit	6185 (1,014)	
2nd Army Field Ordinance Depot	16401 (939)	
2nd Army Field Motor Vehicle Depot	16402 (2,132)	
2nd Army Field Freight Depot	16403 (1,303)	
2nd Disease Prevention / Water Supply Department	3170 (225)	
8th Disease Prevention / Water Supply Department	8605 (225)	
5th Field Military Police Unit	1921 (712)	
8th Field Military Police Unit	7592 (395)	
10th Field Military Police Unit	2310 (395)	
2nd Army Related Air Units (6,168)		
107th Airfield Battalion	15363 (372)	Biak Is.
108th Airfield Battalion	15364 (458)	
209th Airfield Battalion	8329 (372)	
22nd Airfield Battalion	8322 (372)	
36th Airfield Company	15343 (208)	
42nd Airfield Company	15369 (226)	
46th Airfield Company	15375 (226)	
4th Field Airfield Construction Headquarters	2400 (28)	
5th Field Airfield Construction Unit	9952 (79)	
6th Field Airfield Construction Unit	9953 (79)	
16th Field Airfield Construction Unit	15320 (648)	
17th Field Airfield Construction Unit	15321 (648)	Biak Is.
18th Field Airfield Construction Unit	15322 (648)	
19th Field Airfield Construction Unit	15323 (648)	

*Specially Established Construction Duty Companies hire an additional 675 locals

Dutch East Indies between Timor and British New Guinea

19th Army 堅 *Ken*

The 19th Army's headquarters was organized on Dec 19, 1942 and Lt Gen Nobumasa Tominaga appointed its commander on the 22nd. The headquarters became active in Batavia, Java on Jan 15, 1943, and deployed to Ambon Island Feb 20th. The 19th Army served under the Southern Expeditionary Army from Jan 7th until Oct 30th and the 2nd Area Army until it was deactivated on Feb 28, 1945 effective March 1st.

Service History:

1943: On Jan 15th the 19th Army became active in Batavia, Java. Its mission was to defend the Banda Sea area and garrison the Dutch East Indies between Timor Is. and

British New Guinea. The army was created around the 48th Div in Timor and 5th Div which was en route to the Banda Sea ○ 19th Army and 8th Area Army were separated by the line at 141 degrees latitude, which was also the boundary between Dutch and British New Guinea ○ In March the 19th Army HQ suffered difficulties transporting its subordinate units due to Allied air and sea attacks and a lack of shipping capacity ○ During May the 19th Army attempted to mobilize using small boats but made little progress ○ Oct 15th, Lt Gen Tominaga became ill and resigned and Lt Gen Kenzō Kitano became the 19th Army's commander ○
1944: On Oct 27th the 19th Army was made a subordinate to the 2nd Area Army ○
1945: Mar 1st, the 19th Army was deactivated and absorbed by the 2nd Area Army ○
Major Units: See division / brigade page for order of battle

5th Division Hiroshima 1888 鯉 *Koi* – Sunda Is. (to 2nd Army)	166
46th Division Kumamoto 1943 静 *Sei* – Lesser Sunda Is. (to 2nd Area Army)	184
48th Division Taiwan 1940 海 *Umi* – (to 2nd Area Army)	185

Units under 19th Army control: Ambon	堅 *Ken*	
19th Army Headquarters	9450	
4th Tank Regiment	5058 / 658 (457)	to 2A
3rd Field Heavy Artillery Regiment, 2nd Battalion	3766	
15th Independent Engineer Regiment	8125 (937)	to 2A
117th Field Airfield Construction Unit	11508	
118th Field Airfield Construction Unit	11509	
119th Field Airfield Construction Unit	11510	
19th Army Veterinary Hospital	5219	
19th Army Intelligence Section	11504	
39th Casualty Clearing Platoon	4802 (54)	to 2A
40th Casualty Clearing Platoon	4830 (54)	to 2A
14th Field Duty Unit Headquarters	6440	
24th Specially Established Sea Duty Company	10396	
19th Army Field Ordinance Depot	11505	
19th Army Field Motor Vehicle Depot	11506	
19th Army Field Freight Depot	11507	

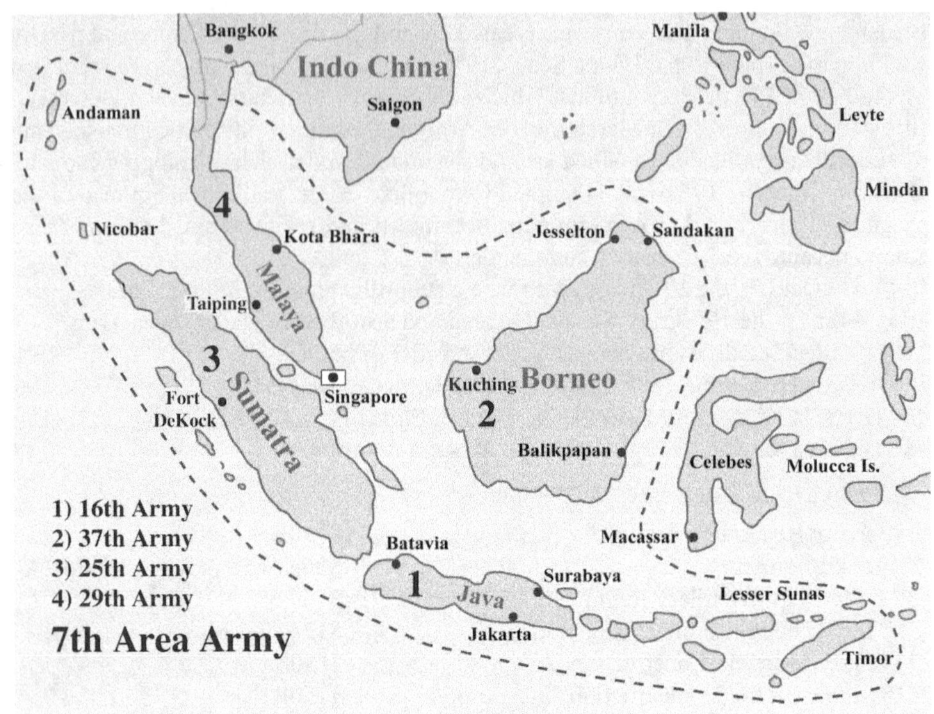

7th Area Army 岡 *Oka*

The 7th Area Army was organized on March 17, 1944, and attached to the Southern Army on Mar 27th. Its headquarters became active at midnight on April 15th in Singapore where they remained for the rest of the war. 7th Area Army's mandate was to unify Malaya, Sumatra, Java, Borneo and the Andoman and Nicobar Is. into one command. General Kenji Doihara was appointed its commander from March 22nd until April 7, 1945 and General Seishirō Itagaki until it was deactivated on Feb 22, 1946.

Subordinate armies / duty dates:

16th Army (Java) from Mar 27, 1944 until the war ended	Batavia
25th Army (Sumatra) from Mar 27, 1944 until the war ended	Fort de Kock
29th Army (Malaya) from Mar 27, 1944 until Sept 13, 1945	Taiping
Borneo Defense Army from Mar 27, 1944 until Sept 4, 1944	Kuching

(Borneo Def. became 37th Army under the Southern Army between 9/22/44 to 5/45)
37th Army (Borneo) from May 20, 1945 until Sept 15, 1945

Service History:

1944: Communications and travel throughout Japan's Empire were becoming more difficult. On Apr 15th the 7th Area Army became active in Singapore to unify command over the western Pacific area. Operations in rear areas, it was responsible for ports, shipping, rail, oil and other resources in Singapore, Malaya, Borneo, Sumatra and Java ○ In Apr there were still about 200,000 tons of shipping under the 3rd Shipping Headquarters ○ On Apr 18th the 7th Area Army and 29th Army were informed control of the Malay Railway would fall to newly activated Southern Army Field Railway Headquarters on Apr 25th ○ In May the Southern Expeditionary Army HQ moved to Manila from Singapore to supervise the defense of the Philippines ○ On May 15th

responsibility for Singapore's defense passed to the new Singapore Defense Command under the 7th Area Army's direct control ○ Late-May, the 10th Shipping Engineer Regt was sent to Andoman Is. from Sumatra to assist with sea transport ○ In July and Aug enemy planes bombed Palembang, northern Sumatra, Andaman and Nicobar Islands ○ Aug 20th the operational boundary between the 7th Area Army and 14th Area Army moved making the 7th Area Army responsible for Tawitawi Is. ○ Between July and Sept the 7th Area Army began *Sei*, the stockpiling of 1½ years supplies on isolated islands, ultimately saving their garrisons from starvation ○ On Sept 4th the Borneo Defense Army was transferred to the Southern Army's control but the 7th Area Army continued to supply it with provisions ○ Sept 16th the 7th Area Army, 3rd Shipping Transport Unit, 3rd Air Army and Navy established protected sea lanes to slow the loss of ships. The agreement was called the *Protected Sea Lanes Establishment Outline* ○ On Oct 14th the 94th Div was activated in Malaya and attached to the 29th Army ○ On Oct 20th U.S. troops invade Leyte Is., the Philippines ○ Early in Nov, as anticipated, B-29's bombed Singapore harbor destroying much infrastructure. Vital supplies and materials had already been relocated from dockside to safer locations ○ On Nov 10th at 0000 hours, the 29th Army assumed control of the Andoman and Nicobar Is. ○ On Nov 17th the Southern Army HQs moved from Manila to Saigon. Its plan was to slow the Allied advance east and fight a final battle in Thailand or Indochina ○ The 7th Area Army was given orders to transfer motor vehicles and repair facilities from Singapore and Java to Thailand and Indochina. The 7th Area Army argued that Singapore as a deep water port, transport and production hub would be a better choice for the final battle. After considering the 7th Area Army's views the Southern Army later relented ○
1945: By Jan shipping men and materials to and from Japan had become impossible ○ Protected Sea Lanes proved a failure, shipping units under the 3rd Shipping Transport Unit's control in Java, Sumatra, Andaman and Nicobar Island were instead placed under the 7th Area Army's control ○ In January the 7th Area Army planned the defense of Singapore and the strategy it would use in battle for the Malay Peninsula. The 29th Army was its buffer for Singapore and would defend transportation hubs and other strategic points ○ In mid February the Southern Army held a conference in Saigon to update strategic plans for the defense of the western Pacific area ○ On Mar 26th the 46th Div was transferred from the 2nd Area Army to the 7th Area Army for deployment in Johor. Operation *Ju-go* was a ruse designed to make it seem as though two divisions were sent from Japan, instead of redeploying one already in theater ○ On Mar 28th shipping units under 7th Area Army control were transferred to the 16th, 25th and 29th Armies. The 7th Area Army began an emergency small boat shipbuilding program for landing barges with set targets for Sept 1945 ○ In February defending Singapore passed from the 7th Area Army to the 29th Army ○ On Apr 14th the Singapore Defense Unit was activated using former Singapore Defense Command personnel ○ On Apr 16th the 46th Div was again transferred to the 39th Army in Thailand to quell civil unrest. On Apr 19th the order was cancelled over concern for Singapore ○ On May 20th the 37th Army was placed under 7th Area Army control with the understanding Borneo was to be gradually abandoned ○ By June sea transport in the southwest Pacific had shrunk to 40,000 tons of every sized vessel ○ In July Allied subs began interrupting sea traffic between Sumatra and Malaya ○ On Aug 7th the 7th Area Army transferred the 31st Div to the 29th Army ○ On Aug 15th Japan surrendered ○ Aug 25th, the Southern Army's order; all military activity must cease, came into effect ○ On Sept.12th the surrender of

the 7th Area Army was signed ○

Major Units: See division / brigade page for order of battle

46th Division Kumamoto 1943 静 *Sei* – Johor, Malaya	184
26th Independent Mixed Brigade 1943 嶽 *Gaku* – Singapore	218
Singapore Defense Unit 1944 岡 *Oka* – Singapore	250-1

Units under 7th Area Army control: Singapore	岡 *Oka*	
7th Area Army Headquarters	1615 (1,853)	
7th Area Army HQ Signal Section	1615 (33)	
13th Independent Heavy Artillery Regiment	18535	
43rd Independent Engineer Regiment	18531	
74th Land Duty Company	4834 (511)	Kuala Lampur
85th Land Duty Company	5732 (511)	
15th Specially Established Land Duty Company	10392 (61)	
Southern Army Training Unit	10482	
Singapore Military Police Unit	10308 (369)	
Southern Army Accounting Training Department	10345 (43)	Singapore
Southern Army Medical Training Department	10346 (33)	
Southern Army Reserve Officer Candidate Unit	10343	
Southern Army NCO Officer Candidate Unit	10344 (277)	
Southern Army Ordnance Manufacturing Depot	15813	
7th Area Army Ordinance Manufacturing Depot	10497 (279)	
Southern Army Fuel Depot Headquarters	unknown (720)	Singapore
Southern Army Institute of Fuel Technology	15849	Bandung Java
Java Fuel Depot	15854	Surabaya
South Sumatra Fuel Depot	15850	Palembang
Central Sumatra Fuel Depot	15851	Pekanbaru
North Sumatra Fuel Depot	15852	Pangkalanbrandan
Borneo Fuel Depot	15853	Miri
Brunei Fuel Depot	15856	Brunei
Shonan (Singapore) Oil Storage Facility	15848	Singapore
34th Field Transport Headquarters	18533	
16th Specially Est. Motor Transport Battalion	18519 (418)	
17th Specially Est. Motor Transport Battalion	18534	
17th Specially Est. Motor Transport Company	10431 (69)	
1st Specially Established Sea Transport Company	18520 (45)	
2nd Specially Established Sea Transport Company	18521 (45)	
3rd Specially Established Sea Transport Company	18522 (45)	
5th Specially Established Railway Engineer Unit	5824	
15th Specially Established Land Duty Company	10392 (61)	
47th Construction Duty Company	4013 (511)	
11th Field Post Office Unit	7853 (251)	
7th Area Army Field Ordinance Depot	10354 (943)	Singapore
7th Area Army Motor Transport Depot	10355 (1,803)	Singapore
7th Area Army Field Freight Depot	10356 (754)	Singapore
12th Line of Communications Veterinary Depot	4822 (538)	
18th Veterinary Hospital Depot	9285 (137)	

1st Southern Army Hospital	6091 (555)	Singapore
3rd Southern Army Hospital	10306 (295)	Singapore
16th Field Railway Command	18524	Singapore

Java

16th Army 治 *Osamu*

The 16th Army was activated November 5, 1941. Under Southern Expeditionary Army control from on Nov 6th it was sent to Takao, Formosa to prepare for the subjugation of the Dutch East Indies including Borneo, the Celebes, Amboina, Timor and Sumatra. The 16th Army was composed of picked units from the Kwantung Army, which included the Kawaguchi, Sakaguchi and Ito Detachments and the 2nd and 48th Divisions. On Mar 27, 1944 it was placed under 7th Area Army control and became the garrison for Java. Its headquarters were in Takao, Formosa from Nov 5th until Mar 5, 1942 and Batavia, Java until the war ended. The 16th Army was commanded by Lt Gen Hitoshi Imamura from Nov 6th until Nov 9, 1942, Lt Gen Kumakichi Harada until Apr 7, 1945 and Lt Gen Yuichirō Nagano until it was demobilized.

Service History:

1941: On Dec 16th the Kawaguchi Detachment from the 18th Div landed in Miri, Borneo, seized Miri and Seria oilfields and Miri Airfield ○ On Dec 26th the Matsumoto Detachment (3rd Btn, 146th I.R., 56th Div) organized in Davao from the Sakaguchi Detachment subjugated Jolo Is. with the loss of just two men ○

1942: On Jan 3rd the Kawaguchi Detach captured Jesselton (now Kota Kinabalu), Borneo and on the 21st the airfield near Benkayan ○ On Jan 4th the 38th Div was placed under 16th Army control for the invasion of Sumatra, the Eastern (Ito) Detach organized from the 16th Div to invade Ambon ○ On Jan 10th the Sakaguchi Detach landed on Tarakan to take its oil fields, refineries and airfield. The oil fields and other installations were already on fire ○ Jan 11th, approaching Tarakan's oilfields from the north Sakaguchi met stiff resistance. That night he captured the barracks in two attacks, the enemy surrendered at dawn. After securing the island the Navy took control and the Detachment prepared for the Balikpapan invasion ○ On Jan 24th after dark the Sakaguchi Detach landed in east Borneo near Balikpapan, by dawn the airfield had been taken without resistance ○ On the 25th bridges along the coastal road to Balikpapan City had been destroyed but the occupation continued peacefully anyway ○ On the 26th with the mopping up completed the Detachment helped to repair the airfield ○ By Jan 31st Borneo was under Japanese control ○ On Jan 28th the Ito Detach landed on Ambon and by Feb 3rd organized resistance had ended. In March the 24th Special Naval Base Force took control ○ The invasions of Bandjermasin and Java proceeded after Balikpapan. Sakaguchi split his forces in two for Bandjermasin. On Jan 30th the Overland Unit began a 100 km trek through dense mosquito infested jungle and steep terrain, 80% of his men caught malaria. Jan 27th the Sea-going Unit left Balikpapan. Feb 10th Martapoera Airfield was taken and by evening Bandjermasin collapsed without a fight ○ On Feb 15th the 38th Division invaded Sumatra occupying Palembang and Banga Is. ○ On Feb 20th the Ito Detach landed on Timor in Dili and Koepang; by 1300 hours Dili had been taken. 308 navy paratroopers airdropped near Desaoe Airfield. On Feb 21st Koepang was occupied. In southwest Timor organized resistance ended on Feb 22nd but mopping up continued until mid-Apr ○ On Mar 1st the newly mobilized 45th Div was placed under 16th Army command. Japan's objective was to capture intact the oil fields in the Dutch East Indies and quickly, to free up troops ○ On Mar 1st the 16th Army landed in eastern and western Java ○ ○ On Mar 5th the 2nd Div took Batavia and the 16th Army Headquarters made Batavia (Jakarta) home ○ Mar 7th the 48th Div took Soerabaja ○ On Mar 9th the Dutch Army surrendered ○ After subjugating Java, the 16th Army was to coast watch and assist Naval and air force units to destroy enemy at sea and prevent them entering the Java Sea ○ The 16th Army's main defenses were in eastern Java with strong points on the south coast and mobile units in Surabaya, Malang, Bandung and Batavia ○ By Mar 28th Sumatra had capitulated and its occupation was transferred from the 16th Army to the 25th Army. From Mar 1942 until the end of 1944 Java functioned as a rear area, line of communications base ○ On Apr 10th the Kawaguchi Detach transferred to the 14th Army in the Philippines to subdue the Visaya Islands ○ On Aug 28th the 2nd Div was transferred to the 17th Army and sent to Guadalcanal ○

1943: Feb 20th, responsibility for Ambon passed from the 16th Army to the 19th Army ○ On Oct 3rd Peta, the Indonesian volunteer defense army, was mobilized in Java ○

1944: On Mar 27th the 16th Army was placed in the order of battle of the new 7th Area Army. The 16th Army informed the 2nd Army it intended to mobilize as a field army if Morotai was lost ○ On Oct 20th the *Battle for Leyte Is.* began ○ By Nov 14th Leyte was lost. After that the Pacific Ocean became increasingly dangerous for Japan's ships ○

1945: On Mar 9th the 16th Army received orders to become self-reliant, if invaded to fight defensively ○ On Mar 26th the 46th Div in the Lesser Sunda Is. was placed under 7th Area Army control and sent to Malaya ○ The 16th Army provided the 46th Div with local shipping links, clothing, provisions and fuel were placed at fixed points to facilitate its movement. The seriously ill in need of medical attention were left in Java ○ The 16th Army had 10,000 combat troops and an additional 10,000 with the 48th Div. All personnel, including the Lesser Sunda island garrison, air army, civilian employees, and navy might total about 75,000. Had the Allies landed western Java would have been the main area of defense ○ On August 15th Japan surrendered ○

Major Units: See division / brigade page for order of battle

27th Independent Mixed Brigade 1943 雄 *Yu* – Bandung 218
28th Independent Mixed Brigade 1943 敬 *Kei* – Surabaya 218

Units under 16th Army control: Batavia	治 *Osamu*
16th Army Headquarters	1602 (467)
12th Field Medium Artillery Battalion	11516 (1,773)
15th Signal Regiment	1896 (934)
28th Motor Transport Regiment	1624 (764)
307th Independent Motor Transport Company	1745 (183)
5th Southern Army Hospital	10801 (308)
6th Southern Army Hospital	10802 (89)

7th Southern Army Hospital	10803 (292)
4th Railway Transport Headquarters	10314 (55)
6th Temporary Post Office Unit (replace 18th F.P.O.)	No #
16th Army Field Ordinance Depot	10360 (484)
16th Army Motor Vehicle Depot	10361 (563)
16th Army Freight Depot	10362 (406)
16th Army Military Police Unit	No # (732)

Borneo

37th Army 灘 *Nada*

The 37th Army became active in Jesselton, Borneo on Sept 22, 1944, from former Borneo Defense Army HQ personnel which had been attached to the 7th Area Army. Subordinate to the Southern Army from Sept 22nd the 37th Army was placed under 7th Area Army on May 20, 1945, with the understanding Borneo would gradually be abandoned. Lt Gen Masataka Yamawaki was commander from Sept 22nd until Dec 26th and Lt Gen Masao Baba until it was deactivated on September 15, 1945.

Service History:

1941: On Dec 16th the Kawaguchi Detachment from the 16th Army landed in Miri, Borneo and captured the Miri and Seria oilfields and Miri Airfield ○

1942: By Jan 31st the invasion of British Borneo was complete, the invasion force losing 50 killed and wounded ○ On Feb 10th the Southern Army ordered the Kawaguchi Detach to establish a military government and maintain the peace ○ On Mar 23rd the 4th Ind Mixed Regt was handed responsibility for Borneo. The Kawaguchi Detach sailed for the Philippines ○ On Apr 13th the Borneo Garrison Army HQ was organized in Tokyo ○ On May 5th Borneo Garrison Army HQ arrived in Miri and established itself in Kuching with subordinate, the 4th Ind. Mixed Regt. ○ In July the 4th Ind. Mixed Regt was reorganized into the 40th and 41st Ind. Garrison Battalions ○ In Dec the 41st Ind. Garrison Battalion was sent to Thailand (returned at the end of 1943) ○ In spite of its small size the Borneo Garrison Army kept Borneo secure ○ From Dec 1943 onward it repeatedly requested reinforcements to transition itself into a field army ○

1944: On Mar 27th the Borneo Garrison Army was attached to the new 7th Area Army ○ In April the Borneo Army headquarters were moved to Jesselton ○ On June 15th the 56th Ind. Mixed Brigade mobilized in north Borneo, the last of its 8,000 men arriving from Japan in Nov ○ By August the Borneo Army's combat strength was one mixed brigade and two independent garrison battalions ○ On Sept 4th the Borneo Garrison Army was placed under Southern Expeditionary Army control ○ On Sept 22nd the Army was deactivated and reactivated as the 37th Army ○ On Sept 27th the 25th Ind Mixed Regt was assigned to the 37th Army, it arrived in Borneo aboard battleships Fuso and Yamashiro ○ In late-Sept Borneo became the 37th Air Sector. Airbases were to be constructed in Sandakan and Jesselton for use in the Philippines campaign ○

In late-Oct the 37th Army received orders to absorb all Naval land units in Borneo ○ Reinforcements arrived late in the year, the 71st I.M.B., 20th and 22nd Ind Machinegun Btns, 103rd Field Road Construction Unit, and 147th L. of C. Hospital. While enroute to Borneo, the 26th Ind Mixed Regt was diverted to the Philippines. One company from the 18th Field Anti Aircraft Battalion made land and became stranded in Manila. Only one radio platoon and one wire company from the 4th Signal Unit landed in Borneo intact ○ At the end of Dec the two battalion garrison on Jolo Island joined the 37th Army and were shipped to Tarakan ○ In early Dec the 37th Army was given control over southern Borneo and the 22nd Special Naval Base Force in Balikpapan ○ Dec 20th all 37th Army unit commanders met in Jesselton to assign reinforcements to their various posts and promote cohesion while integrating into a fighting force ○
1945: By January only 1½ Btns of the 71st I.M.B. had arrived in Kuching ○ In March air raids on Borneo had grown so intense communications ceased between sectors and with the outside ○ Apr 2nd the U.S. Army landed the 163rd RCT on Tawi-Tawi Is. ○ In mid April the Labuan Is. and Brunei garrisons received permission to withdraw but escape by sea had become impossible, even at night. Those on Labuan were trapped. Facing destruction in Brunei the 56th I.M.B. commander led his men and resident Japanese women and children on a 40-day walk across trackless mountain terrain to the 37th Army HQ in North Borneo ○ On Apr 30th Australian troops invaded Tarakan, communications with the garrison had ended by mid May ○ On May 20th the Southern Army placed the 37th Army under 7th Area Army control with the understanding Borneo would be gradually abandoned ○ On June 10th Australian troops invaded Brunei and Labuan Island. The 500 Japanese troops on Labuan fought to the death ○ By June 22nd organized resistance had ended on Tarakan ○ On July 1st the Australian 7th Division landed in Balikpapan ○ On July 3rd the 454th Independent Infantry Battalion and 22nd Special Naval Base Force withdrew to an area north of Balikpapan. The two sides continued fighting until the war ended Aug 15th ○
Major Units: See division / brigade page for order of battle

56th Independent Mixed Brigade 1944 貫 *Kan* – north Borneo 226
71st Independent Mixed Brigade 1944 敢闘 *Kantō* – Kuching, Borneo 229

Units under 37th Army control: Sangpong	灘 *Nada*	
37th Army Headquarters	9801 (400)	Jesselton
432nd Independent Infantry Battalion	10322 (997)	Kudat
454th Independent Infantry Battalion	11012/23011 (997)	Balikpapa
455th Independent Infantry Battalion	11013/23012 (997)	Tarakan
553rd Independent Infantry Battalion	11015	
554th Independent Infantry Battalion	11016	Sandakan
774th Independent Infantry Battalion	11017	
25th Independent Mixed Regiment	12935 (2,230)	Tawitawi
20th Independent Machine Gun Battalion	3324 (334)	Sandakan
22nd Independent Machine Gun Battalion	14200 (334)	Labuan
64th Independent Field Anti-Aircraft Company	11014	
332nd Independent Motor Transport Company	11008 (183)	
103rd Field Road Construction Unit	11031 (304)	
75th Construction Duty Unit	11010 (511)	
147th Line of Communications Hospital	11011 (359)	Jesselton

11th Southern Army Hospital	10312 (89)	Jesselton
37th Army Military Police Detachment	No #	
4th Signal Unit Headquarters	12949 (62)	Jesselton
124th Independent Wire Company	12971 (310)	
125th Independent Wire Company	12972 (310)	
119th Independent Radio Company	12980 (57)	
120th Independent Radio Platoon	12981 (57)	
121st Independent Radio Platoon	12982 (57)	
1st Independent Shipping Engineer Company	16713 (333)	

Sumatra

25th Army 富 *Tomi*

The 25th Army headquarters activated in Saigon, French Indochina on June 26, 1941, from former Indochina Garrison Army headquarters personnel (split between 25th and 15th Army HQs). Placed under Imperial Headquarters control from July 5th until Nov 15th, Southern Expeditionary Army until Mar 27, 1944 and 7th Area Army until the war ended. Based in Indochina from June 26th until Dec 4th, Singora, Thailand and Kuala Lumpur, Malaysia until Feb 15, 1942, Singapore until Apr 15, 1943 and Fort de Kock, Sumatra until the war ended. Lt Gen Shōjirō Ida was 25th Army commander from June 28th until Nov. 6th, Lt Gen Tomoyuki Yamashita until July 1, 1942, Lt Gen Yaheita Saitō until Apr 8, 1943 and Lt Gen Moritake Tanabe until the war ended.

Service History:

1941: June 26th, the 25th Army HQ was organized in Indochina to invade Malaya. The Indochina Garrison Army HQ was deactivated and divided between 25th and 15th Armies HQs. Subordinates included; Imp. Guard Div, 5th, 18th and 56th Div ○ On July 5th the Imperial Guard Division arrived in Indochina ○ Nov 6th, the 25th Army joined the Southern Army's order of battle, same day as Lt. Gen. Tomoyuki Yamashita was appointed 25th Army commander ○ On Dec 8th the 25th Army began the invasion with the 18th Div landing at Kota Bharu ○ Other battles: Jitra on Dec 11th, Kampar Dec 30th to Jan 2, 1942, Slim River on Jan 6th, Gemas on Jan 14th and Maur Jan 14th. The Malaya campaign lasted until Jan 31, 1942 when the British withdrew into Singapore ○

1942: On Feb 15th Singapore surrendered to the 25th Army ○ On Mar 4th the 18th Div was transferred to the 15th Army in Burma ○ Mar 8th the Imp. Guard Div left Singapore for north and central Sumatra ○ On Mar 9th control of Sumatra passed from the 16th Army to the 25th Army, the 38th Div in Palembang and on Bangka Is. came with the territory ○ On Mar 23rd a battalion from the 18th Div and the 12th Special Naval Base Force occupied Andaman Is. ○ On Aug 6th the 5th Div in Singapore, scheduled to return to Japan, became stranded due to a lack of shipping ○ On Sept 17th the 38th Div left Sumatra to join the 17th Army in Rabaul. The 15th and 16th Ind Garrison Units, formed from replacement troops sent from Japan, replaced it. The 12th Indian Garrison Unit was reassigned to Malaya ○ On Nov 18th the stranded 5th Div sent the 5th Engineer Regiment. and two infantry battalions to Rabaul ○

1943: Jan 11th, the rest of the 5th Div was earmarked to join the 19th Army in the Tanimbar Islands ○ In March Southern Army HQ relocated to Singapore from Saigon and took operational responsibility for Malaya and the Andaman Islands ○ In March the 25th Army was downgraded from field to garrison army for Sumatra ○ On Mar 25th the Palembang Air Defence Unit was established ○ Apr 15th, the 25th Army's HQ relocated to Fort de Kock from Singapore ○ June 15th, newly activated, the 2nd Imperial Guard Div arrived in Sumatra from Thailand ○ On Sept 22nd the 4th Div joined the 25th Army's order of battle. Arrived in December ○ Nov 16th, the 15th and 16th Independent Garrison Units were reactivated as the 25th and 26th I.M.B. ○

1944: On Jan 6th the 29th Army became active in Malaya ○ In March thirty companies of the *Sumatra Volunteer Army* completed basic training and were assigned to Japanese divisions and brigades as service troops ○ On Mar 27th the 25th Army joined the 7th Area Army's order of battle ○ In May the 25th Army sent the 61st Infantry Regiment, detached from the 4th Division, to Burma for the battle of Imphal ○ On June 1st the Palembang Guards Brigade was formed from former Palembang Air Defense Unit Personnel ○

1945: On Jan 14th the 4th Div was transferred to the 39th Army in Bangkok where the 61st Infantry Regiment waited to reunite with it ○ In January the Southern Army released the 9th Air Division from defending the Palembang and Pangkalabrandan oil fields, in part because oil tankers could no longer reach Japan from Sumatra ○ May 26th, the 25th Army received orders to send a brigade to Singapore, so the 26th I.M.B. went ○ On July 23rd the Pangkalabrandan Defense Unit was ordered to relocate to Singapore ○ The reduced 25th Army planned its final battle for the Fort de Kock area. Service units and native volunteers were given the task of constructing the new defenses ○

Major Units: See division / brigade page for order of battle

2nd Imperial Guard Division Tokyo 1891 宫 *Miya* – Medan, Sumatra	164
25th Independent Mixed Brigade 1943 盤 *Ban* – Padang, Sumatra	217
Palembang Guards Brigade 1943 翔 *Sho* – Palembang (under 3rd Air Army)	250

Units under 25th Army control: Fort De Kock	富 *Tomi* 8990	
25th Army Headquarters	8991 (356)	Fort De Kock
2nd Independent Heavy Artillery Battalion	3980 (622)	Medan
1st Signal Regiment	5840 (1,523)	Fort De Kock
47th Line of Communications Guard Unit	4623 (1,036)	
94th Line of Communications Guard Unit	10936 (1,035)	
15th Field Transport Headquarters	18523 (37)	
57th Independent Motor Transport Battalion	9717 (808)	
209th Independent Motor Transport Company	5873 (183)	
235th Independent Motor Transport Company	3004 (183)	
303rd Independent Motor Transport Company	8864 (183)	Medan
15th Specially Est. Motor Transport Battalion	18518 (418)	
11th Specially Est. Motor Transport Company	10425 (69)	
16th Specially Est. Motor Transport Company	10430 (69)	Medan
18th Specially Est. Motor Transport Company	10432 (69)	

12th Disease Prevention / Water Supply Department	9362 (287)	
24th Field D. P. and Water Supply Dept., 1 Squad	2627	
13th Specially Established Land Duty Company	10390 (61)	
14th Specially Established Land Duty Company	10391 (61)	
30th Specially Est. Construction Duty Company	10411	
25th Specially Established Sea Duty Company	10397 (25)	Fort De Kock
2nd Specially Established Sea Transport Company	unknown	
9th Southern Army Hospital	10310 (289)	
10th Southern Army Hospital	10311 (161)	Medan
17th Southern Army Hospital	10499 (85)	
14th Field Meteorological Unit	11090 (1,228)	
25th Army Field Ordinance Depot	10363 (354)	
25th Army Field Motor Transport Depot	10364 (505)	
25th Army Field Freight Depot	10365 (333)	
17th Field Post Office Unit	5136 (251)	
25th Army Military Police Detachment	No # (511)	
Sumatra Volunteer Army	30 irregular companies	

Malaya

29th Army 定 *Tei*

The 29th Army was activated January 6, 1944, to garrison and administrate Malaya. Under the Southern Expeditionary Army's control from Jan 15th until Mar 27th and 7th Area Army until the war ended. The 29th Army was based in Taiping, Malaya under Lt Gen Teizō Ishiguro from Jan 7th until it was deactivated on Sept 13, 1945.

Service History:

1944: On Jan 6th the 29th Army was activated in Taiping, Malaya. The 29th Army was created to manage Southern Army administrative and guard units that were confusing the command structure in Malaya. Only the 29th Army Chief of Staff came from the Southern Army for his initial role as Malaya's Inspector of Military Administration, to smooth the transition. All other positions were filled from outside. The Military Inspectorate's duties included overseeing railways, communications, the post office in Kuala Lampur and Supreme Court, broadcasting and maritime issues in Singapore. Malay produced rubber, bauxite, iron, rice, tin and rare metals ○ On Jan 31st the 29th Army HQ moved to Taiping from Singapore ○ In February its units were deployed around Malaya. The 29th Army was joined by the 2,000 men Malayan Volunteer Army (Giyûgun) based in Johore Bahru, the 29th Army Field Freight Depot supplied them with uniforms and British rifles and machineguns. As well, 5,000 young men trained by Japanese officers and armed with hunting guns served in volunteer units in every city and town. The 29th Army wished to remain on good terms with local Chinese merchants and respected their ability to make a living, but others in the military confiscated assets hurting relations and the economy. 800,000 Chinese Malayans lived in Singapore, most were merchants suffering from the disruptions of war. To assist this population the 29th Army set aside land in Endau, Johor to distribute freely for the creation of a farming settlement ○ On Mar 27th the 29th Army was placed into the 7th Area Army's order of battle ○ On May 15th the 29th Army ceded the defense of Singapore to the new Singapore Defense Command ○ In May the 29th Army conducted war games that took into account the Burma Army's recent reversal at Imphal ○ In June the 12th Ind. Garrison Unit began work on defensive positions east and west of Gurun in Kedah, dispersing and concealing the army's ammunition and weapons ○ The 29th Army didn't have the strength to win the battle of Malaya but could effectively stall the enemy for some time ○ On Oct 14th the 94th Division was activated in Kuala Lampur from the 12th and 18th Ind Garrison Units and attached to the 29th Army ○ Nov 9th at 2400 hours, the 29th Army took command of all troops in the Andoman and Nicobar Is., including the 12th Special Naval Base Force ○

1945: In late January the 29th Army was instructed to find an assignment for the 46th Div, which it decided was to fortify the Johore Bharu area ○ In Feb the 29th Army handed over responsibility for the defense of Singapore to the 7th Area Army ○ In Mar and Apr the 29th Army built a supply base on the upper reaches of the Perak River. It planned a holding action in the Kuriku area or an attack from behind if the enemy came ashore close to Singapore ○ On Mar. 9th the 7th Area Army sent orders to the 29th Army to secure land routes into Singapore and strategic positions on the Malay Peninsula and in the Andaman and Nicobar Is. The Andaman and Nicobar garrisons had orders to hold at all costs. The 94th Div stationed on the Isthmus of Kra, fortified the defenses of Victoria Point and Phuket. Its orders were to establish relations and fight side by side with the Thai Army ○ In March the construction of fortifications in the Gunrun area fell behind schedule, so troops were brought in from Trang. The 94th Infantry Group HQ and three inf. battalions were stationed in Kuala Lampur to guard against amphibious landings ○ Also in March the 29th Army revised operational plans for the Gerik area, determining the need for a line of communications base positioned to secure the railway lines for as long as possible ○ On Mar 9th the 7th Area Army gave orders to the 29th Army to cooperate with the Singapore Defense Unit in the Johore Bharu area ○ On Mar 26th the 46th Div arrived in Singapore where the 7th Area Army deployed it to Johor to build defenses as suggested by the 29th Army in late Jan ○ On Apr 1st the U.S. invaded Okinawa ○ In April civil authorities in Malaya began an operation to suppress communism, which lasted until July ○ Apr 28th, the 70th I.M.B. joined the 29th Army, arriving in Malaya on May 23rd ○ On May 3rd Rangoon fell to British-Indian forces ○ By June the war in Burma was lost, spies arrived in Kedah to stir up trouble ○ On Jul 27th the 29th Army was notified the 37th Div would join it in Taiping, Penang, expected in Aug ○ On Aug 7th the Southern Army ordered the 31st Div in Burma to central Malaya to join the 29th Army. The 7th Area Army wished to deploy it in Singapore where it felt British Indian troops would land. In July it was assigned it to the 29th Army in Gurun, Taiping and Penang. ○ On Aug 15th Japan surrendered ○ Sept 5th, British troops landed in Singapore without opposition ○ On Sept 13th Lt Gen Ishiguro signed the surrender of the 29th Army in Kuala Lumpur ○

Major Units: See division / brigade page for order of battle

37th Independent Mixed Brigade 1944 鍛 *Tan* – Nicobar Island		222
70th Independent Mixed Brigade 1944 果敢 *Kakan* – Kuala Kangsar		229

Units under 29th Army control: Taiping 定 *Tei*

Unit	Number	Location
29th Army Headquarters	9411 (415)	Taiping
29th Army Headquarters Signal Section	9411 (18)	
1st Southwest Guard Unit	10484 (1,966)	
2nd Southwest Guard Unit	10485 (934)	
65th Independent Infantry Defense Battalion	6067 (737)	
66th Independent Infantry Defense Battalion	6068 (737)	
67th Independent Infantry Defense Battalion	6069 (737)	
210th Infantry Regiment, 3rd Battalion	4254 (1,025)	from 32nd Div
211th Infantry Regiment, 3rd Battalion	4255 (1,025)	from 32nd Div
212th Infantry Regiment, 2nd Battalion	4256 (1,025)	from 32nd Div
15th Tank Regiment	5932 (341)	
49th Independent Tank Battalion	16900	
1st Independent Field Artillery Battalion	2680 (528)	
21st Independent Field Anti-Aircraft Company	3896 (179)	
3rd Southern Army Signal Unit	15921 (62)	Singapore
97th Independent Wire Company	15800 (310)	
129th Independent Wire Company	12976 (310)	
16th Field Transport Command	2869 (37)	
224th Independent Motor Transport Company	2861 (183)	Rempang Island
4th Independent Radio Company	16901	
81st Independent Transport Company	16902	
82nd Independent Transport Company	16903	
83rd Independent Transport Company	16904	
17th Specially Est. Motor Transport Company	10431 (69)	
107th Land Duty Company	6441 (511)	
8th Southern Army Hospital	10309 (300)	Kuala Lampur
130th Line of Communications Hospital	4026 (420)	
131st Line of Communications Hospital	4027 (420)	
135th Line of Communications Hospital	7194 (420)	Kuala Lampur
61st Casualty Clearing Platoon	7007 (54)	
98th Casualty Clearing Platoon	18530 (54)	Rempang Island
29th Army Field Ordinance Depot	18527	
29th Army Field Motor Transport Depot	18528	
29th Army Field Freight Depot	18529	
29th Army Military Police Detachment	No # (615)	
2nd Independent Shipping Engineer Company	16714 (333)	Taiping
3rd Independent Shipping Engineer Company	16715 (333)	
3rd Specially Established Sea Transport Company	unknown (45)	

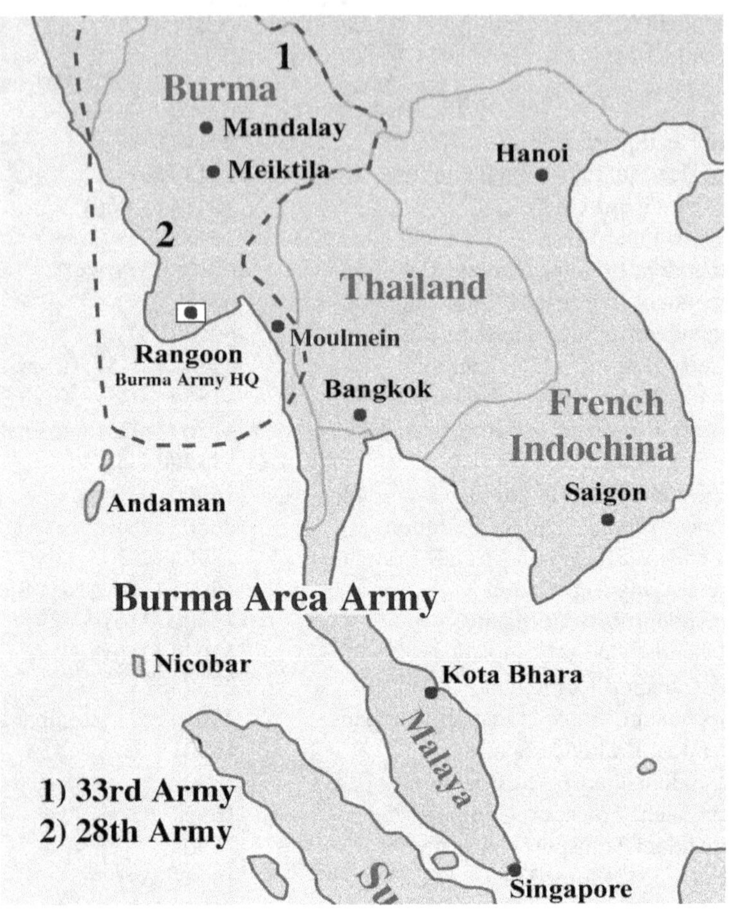

Burma

Burma Area Army 森 *Mori*

The Burma Area Army was activated in Rangoon, Burma on March 18, 1943, and placed under Southern Expeditionary Army control on March 27th. It was based in Rangoon from Mar 18th until Apr 23, 1945 and Moulmein until the war ended. Its commander was Lt Gen Masamitsu Kawabe from Mar 18th until Aug 30, 1944 and Lt Gen Heitarō Kimura until August 15, 1945.

Subordinate armies / duty dates:

15th Army from Mar 27, 1943 to July 15, 1945

28th Army from Jan 15, 1944 until the war ended

33rd Army from Apr 11, 1944 until the war ended

Service History:

1943: On Mar 18th the Burma Area Army was activated to oversee the war in Burma, its subordinate, the 15th Army reorganized and the 55th Div was detached and placed under

Burma Area Army control ○ On June 24th map maneuvers were held. It was decided the best defense would be to attack in the Imphal Plain, and afterwards establish a line of defense in the mountains to the west. It was to be an attempt to defend Burma with a display of strength ○ In July permission to go on the offensive came ○ On Aug 7th the Southern Army ordered that preparations proceed. *U-go* would begin in early 1944 ○ In August British-Indian forces deployed in depth around Akyab, showing signs of going on the offensive ○ In late August the 54th Div redeployed from Java to Burma for *U-go* ○

1944: On Jan 6th the 28th Army was activated in Rangoon ○ On the 15th it was attached to the Burma Area Army ○ *Ha-go*, *Battle of the Admin Box*, was to be a diversion for *U-go*. Begun on Feb 3rd and ending Feb 24th it was Japan's first major set back in Burma ○ In early Feb the Chinese Nationalist 1st Army marched from Assam to Hukawng Valley where it made contact with the 15th Army's 18th Div ○ On Apr 29th the 33rd Army was activated in Rangoon ○ On July 3rd the 15th and 33rd Divisions retreat ending Imphal ○ July 4th the Southern Army ended *U-go* when it became clear Imphal was a failure ○ Burma Area Army made 3 operational plans for Burma: 1) *Ban*; 15th Army counter offensive against an Allied attack in central Burma. 2) *Kan*; 28th Army defense of the Burmese west coast. 3) *Dan*; 33rd Army operations along the Tien-Mein Road ○ From Sept the Japanese army in Burma fought on the defensive ○ The Burma Area Army received orders to defend the line south of' Lashio-Mandalay and east of Irrawaddy. The 15th Army would take part in late Jan 1945 and the 28th and 33rd Armies support it where possible ○ In Nov the 49th and 53rd Divisions joined the Burma Area Army ○ In December the Burma Army completed its reorganization but enemy strength and a lack of supplies ensured plan 1, operation Ban-go would be an inevitable failure ○

1945: On Feb 4th the battle for Pokoku and Irrawaddy began ○ By mid February the enemy had massively reinforced Myitson, North Burma leaving the 33rd Army no option but to withdraw. Around the same time enemy tanks crossed the Irrawaddy River and advanced on Meiktila ○ In late Feb the 33rd Army withdrew, abandoning the Burma Road ○ On Mar 1st the Allies captured Meiktila ○ On Mar 14th 8,000 Burmese National Defense Army troops revolted against Japan ○ On March 27th the Burma Area Army put down the uprisings ○ Mar 21st, central Burma was lost when the 15th Army was forced out of Mandalay ○ On Apr 7th the Burma Area Army received orders to secure Rangoon, Toungoo and Loikaw ○ Apr 23rd, the Burma Area Army HQ left Rangoon for Moulmein ○ On May 2nd Rangoon fell to a surprise British-Indian amphibious assault the Japanese were unable to stop ○ On July 3rd the *Battle of Sittang* began. The 28th Army became trapped in western Burma, a breakout was planned for July 15th with help from the 33rd Army. Due to a communications failure the 28th Army set July 20th as the date ○ In July Burma was reorganized, most of the Burma Area Army staff officers were transferred, effectively dissolving the Burma Area Army HQ ○ On July 14th the 39th Army became the 18th Area Army in Bangkok and the battered 15th Army was placed under its command ○

Major Units: See division / brigade page for order of battle

49th Division Keijo 1943 狼 *Roo* – Thaton	186
24th Independent Mixed Brigade 1943 巌 *Gen* – Thanbyuzayat	217
72nd Independent Mixed Brigade 1944 貫徹 *Kantetu* – Hnipadaw	229
105th Independent Mixed Brigade 1945 敢威 *Kani* – Thaton	234

Units under Burma Area Army control: Moulmein	森 *Mori*	
Burma Area Army Headquarters	7900 (840)	
14th Tank Regiment	8993 (503)	
1st Independent Machinegun Company	12208 (227)	
2nd Independent Machinegun Company	12209 (227)	
3rd Independent Machinegun Company	12210 (227)	
38th Independent Rapid Firing Gun Company	12219 (145)	anti-tank guns
39th Independent Rapid Firing Gun Company	12220 (145)	
40th Independent Rapid Firing Gun Company	12221 (145)	
80th Field Machine Cannon Company	12227 (105)	
5th Field Medium Artillery Regiment	6771 (2,286)	
9th Field Medium Artillery Battalion	12222 (483)	
Southern Army Raiding Unit Headquarters	unknown	
5th Raiding Command	12218 (90)	
15th Raiding Company	12241 (192)	
16th Raiding Company	12242 (192)	
17th Raiding Company	12243 (192)	
Burma Area Army Signal Unit Headquarters	12202 (154)	
92nd Independent Wire Company	1934 (269)	
93rd Independent Wire Company	8034 (269)	
94th Independent Wire Company	10487 (269)	
71st Independent Radio Platoon	1946 (53)	
72nd Independent Radio Platoon	1947 (53)	
73rd Independent Radio Platoon	1948 (53)	
83rd Independent Radio Platoon	3178 (53)	
84th Independent Radio Platoon	3199 (53)	
85th Independent Radio Platoon	12650 (53)	
Burma Area Army L.o.C. Inspectorate General	15883 (456)	
42nd Line of Communications Sector Command	1380 (203)	
42nd Line of Communications Guard Unit	1381 (1,035)	
42nd Line of Communications Duty Company	1382 (511)	
53rd Line of Communications Sector Command	6020 (203)	
Burma Area Army Motor Transport Unit	9356 (219)	
4th Independent Engineer Regiment	3786 (617)	
20th Independent Engineer Regiment	8127 (664)	
21st Independent Engineer Regiment	27614 (862)	barracks 東部15
67th Independent Engineer Battalion	12252 (304)	
6th Independent Engineer Company	12228 (249)	
7th Independent Engineer Company	12229 (249)	
8th Independent Engineer Company	12230 (249)	
9th Independent Engineer Company	12231 (249)	
10th Independent Engineer Company	12232 (249)	
21st Bridging Materials Company	5885 (410)	
14th River Crossing Materials Company	6263 (230)	
15th River Crossing Materials Company	3964 (230)	
Southern Army Fortif. Constr. Dept., Burma Detail	10413	

33rd Field Road Construction Unit	4839 (304)	
19th Signal Regiment	10700 (2,209)	
Southern Army Special Affairs Squad	10483	
S. A Signal Unit Burma Special Investigations U.	10316	
2nd Field Transport Headquarters	1035 (37)	
5th Field Transport Headquarters	7024 (37)	
3rd Independent Transport Regiment	8613 (1,745)	
101st Independent Motor Transport Battalion	5865 (808)	
261st Independent Motor Transport Company	6060 (183)	
274th Independent Motor Transport Company	3986 (183)	
23rd Line of Comm. Motor Vehicle Command	9536	
45th Independent Motor Transport Battalion	5705 (459)	
60th Independent Motor Transport Battalion	8554 (808)	Morimoto Unit
211th Independent Motor Transport Company	5875 (183)	
226th Independent Motor Transport Company	2863 (183)	
233rd Independent Motor Transport Company	unknown (183)	
257th Independent Motor Transport Company	6056 (183)	
333rd Independent Motor Transport Company	12236 (183)	
335th Independent Motor Transport Company	12238 (183)	
1st Specially Est. Motor Transport Company	10415 (69)	
2nd Specially Est. Motor Transport Company	10416 (69)	
3rd Specially Est. Motor Transport Company	10417 (69)	
4th Specially Est. Motor Transport Company	10418 (69)	
5th Specially Est. Motor Transport Company	10419 (69)	
6th Specially Est. Motor Transport Company	10420 (69)	
7th Specially Est. Motor Transport Company	10421 (69)	
8th Specially Est. Motor Transport Company	10422 (69)	
12th Specially Est. Motor Transport Company	10426 (69)	
19th Specially Est. Motor Transport Company	10433 (69)	
20th Specially Est. Motor Transport Company	10434 (69)	
15th Field Duty Unit Headquarters	9746 (17)	
30th Field Duty Unit Headquarters	10281 (17)	
79th Land Duty Company	4645 (511)	
93rd Land Duty Company	8223 (511)	
94th Land Duty Company	8224 (511)	Fujino Unit
100th Land Duty Company	5133 (511)	
102nd Land Duty Company	5135 (511)	
131st Land Duty Company	12253 (511)	
132nd Land Duty Company	12254 (511)	
133rd Land Duty Company	12255 (511)	
134th Land Duty Company	12256 (511)	
135th Land Duty Company	12257 (511)	
136th Land Duty Company	12258 (511)	
8th Specially Established Land Duty Company	10385 (61)	
9th Specially Established Land Duty Company	10386 (61)	
10th Specially Established Land Duty Company	10387 (61)	
31st Specially Established Land Duty Company	10439 (61)	

Burma Area Army: continued	森 *Mori*	
32nd Specially Established Land Duty Company	10440 (61)	
33rd Sea Duty Company	4827 (511)	
38th Sea Duty Company	5724 (511)	
21st Specially Established Sea Duty Company	10393 (61)	
22nd Specially Established Sea Duty Company	10394 (61)	
3rd Specially Established Sea Transport Unit	10438 (189)	
53rd Construction Duty Company	6913 (511)	
60th Construction Duty Company	7044 (511)	
101st Construction Duty Company	7854 (511)	
28th Specially Est. Construction Duty Company	10398 (61)	
106th Line of Communications Hospital	7005 (362)	
107th Line of Communications Hospital	7006 (368)	Rangoon
62nd Casualty Clearing Platoon	7008 (54)	
68th Casualty Clearing Platoon	2209 (54)	
72nd Casualty Clearing Platoon	6032 (54)	
133rd Line of Communications Hospital	4046	
69th Casualty Clearing Platoon	5269 (54)	
84th Casualty Clearing Platoon	4049	
91st Casualty Clearing Platoon	6086 (54)	
94th Casualty Clearing Platoon	12239	
95th Casualty Clearing Platoon	12240 (54)	
22nd Field Disease Prevention / Water Supply Unit	2625 (329)	
26th Field Disease Prevention / Water Supply Unit	10282 (329)	
29th Field Disease Prevention / Water Supply Unit	12367 (329)	
13th Line of Communications Veterinary Hospital	4632 (538)	
21st Line of Communications Veterinary Hospital	12206 (538)	
17th Veterinary Quarantine Hospital	7055 (137)	
21st Field Motor Transport Depot	9364	
Southern Army Fuel Depot's Burma Work Depot	15855	
15th Post Office Unit	5736 (251)	
18th Post Office Unit	7054 (251)	was 16th Army
2nd Field Well Drilling Company	7841	
Burma Area Army Field Ordinance Depot	10357 (2,198)	
Burma Army Field Motor Vehicle Repair Depot	10358 (3,080)	
Burma Area Army Field Freight Depot	10359 (1,914)	
Burma Area Army Military Police Unit	No # (1,470)	

Burma Area Army Reinforcement Unit: (reserve units)

Unit	Code	Parent
61st Infantry Regiment	淀 4074 (2,181)	4th Div.
4th Field Artillery Regiment	淀 4077 (1,486)	4th Div.
157th Independent Infantry Battalion	敬 10824 (931)	28th I.M.B.
257th Infantry Regiment, 1st Section	威烈 18503	94th Div.
258th Infantry Regiment, 3rd Battalion	威烈 18504 (900)	94th Div.
94th Field Artillery Regiment, 1st Section	威烈 18505	94th Div.
158th Independent Infantry Battalion	体 15823 (931)	29th I.M.B.
159th Independent Infantry Battalion	体 15824 (931)	29th I.M.B

Burma Area Army Reinforcement Unit: continued

29th Mixed Brigade Artillery Unit, 1st Section	体 15828	29th I.M.B.
29th Mixed Brigade Signal Unit, 1st Section	体 15830	29th I.M.B

Burma Railway Units are in the Southern Army Railway Units section

Western Burma

28th Army 策 *Saku*

The 28th Army was activated in Rangoon, Burma Jan 6, 1944. Attached to the Burma Area Army on the 15th. Its headquarters was in Rangoon from Jan 18th until Feb 15th, Maudaing until May 15th, Paungde until (date unknown), Taikky until Mar 14, 1945, Allanmyo until Apr 12th, Taikky until Apr 26th, Tanbington until May 12th, Pinmezali until June 19th, Kyiyo until July 28th and Paungde until the war ended. Its commander was Lt Gen Shōzō Sakurai, (former 33rd Div Cmdr in Burma 1942), appointed on Jan 7, 1944 and arrived at headquarters on the 21st; he remained at his post until the 28th Army was deactivated in south central Burma on September 24, 1945.

Service History:

1944: British intelligence thought *Saku Shidan* was a mixed brigade from Malaya. On Jan 6th the 28th Army HQ became active in Rangoon and was responsible for the coast of Burma from Rangoon to Akayab, north along the Pegu Mountain Range to Mt Popa ○ On Jan 30th the 28th Army began operating in Maudaing ○ On Feb 15th 28th Army HQ arrived in Maudaing ○ Jan 24th the British 81st Div overran the 55th Recon Regt. in Kaladan Valley ○ *Ha-go* began on Feb 3rd with the 55th Div attacking Arakan. The Sakurai Detachment infiltrated the 7th Indian Div front lines while Kubo Btn crossed the Mayu Mtns and from Feb 6th set ambushes and raided supply lines ○ The British 15th Corps was isolated in the Box but Allied tanks countered every attempt at overrunning it ○ By Feb 22nd the Allies had received reinforcements while the Japanese had nothing but casualties, hunger and exhaustion ○ On Feb 24th the 112th Inf Regt with just 400 men left pulled back ○ On Feb 26th the Sakurai Group ceased fighting and the army withdrew to the Buthidaung-Maungdaw Road. Kubo Btn suffered greatly while extricating itself. This was Japan's first major set back in Burma ○ On Mar 1st in Kaladan Valley the 55th Reconnaissance Regt and Honjo Unit (administrative troops) counterattacked the enemy as Koba Unit flanked them west of the mountains north of Teinnyo ○ On Mar 6th *Ha-go* Phase 2 began as a defensive action ○ Mid-March the Allies forced the 55th Division to abandon north of the Buthidaung-Maungdaw Road ○ By mid-April the Koba Detach captured Sabaseik, Kaladan, Paletwa and on May 2nd Daletme ○ Apr 24th the 28th Army regrouped ○ The Brit./Indian 25th Div replaced the tank unit easing pressure on the 55th Div ○ On May 5th five infantry battalions with artillery got bogged down attacking the British near Akayab in the Mayu Mtns ○ May 15th the 28th Army HQ relocated to Paungde ○ Monsoon season began at the end of May. Kaladan was recaptured and Akayab secured until Jan 1945 ○ On July

12th the 2nd Division and most 28th Army transport units were sent to join the 33rd Army. The 28th Army received orders to defend what it occupied ○ In July the 55th Div relocated to the south coast of Burma leaving the Sakurai Group the only unit adjacent enemy lines ○ *Kan* operational plans were updated, Rangoon and Minbu with the Rangoon Defense Unit and Katsu Detach were transferred from the 15th Army to the 28th Army. Updated *Kan #1* Irrawaddy Delta area: a delaying action. *Kan #2* Yenangyaung oil fields: counterattack. *Kan #3* Rangoon area: decisive battle ○ Sept 11th Sakurai launched a surprise attack on the British and on Oct 6th attacked the Goppe Bazaar further delaying a planned Allied offensive ○ In late October the Burma Army held a conference in Rangoon and activated the 72nd I.M.B., which was added to the 28th Army and deployed to Yenangyaung ○ In December monsoon season ended. The British immediately launched an offensive along the Bay of Bengal coast ○ On Dec 26th the Sakurai Detachment, down to just 1,500 men, retreated from the Sinobin-Alethangyaw line in the Buthidaung area ○

1945: On Jan 3rd three days after the Sakurai rear guard withdrew British troops landed in Akyab. The 54th Div alone occupied Burma's west coast ○ On Jan 12th the British 25th Div landed on the Myebon Peninsula. The Myebon Unit withdrew to north of Myebon and held Hill 831 for 10 days before crossing Min River to Kani. In late January the unit covered Matsu Detachment's withdrawal. The 2nd Btn, 121st Inf R. on Ramree Island occupied prepared positions south of Yanbauk River ○ Jan 21st near Ramree Town Navy guns covered the 26th Indian Division's landing near Kyaukpyu ○ On Jan 22nd additional Allied troops landed 2 mi. south of Kangaw, the *Battle for Hill 170* began. An attack by 1st and 2nd Btns, 154th Inf R. failed and Hill 170 fell. The 54th Division ordered the Myebon Unit and Matsu Detachment to Kangaw and evacuated Ramree on Feb 9th ○ On Feb 10th the 154th I.R. 2nd and 3rd Btn briefly retook Hill 170. The Indian 81st Division attacked Kangaw from the north surrounding the Kangaw Unit's flank and rear but the 1st Recon Company rushed in and held the gap open for them as they withdrew to Tamandu ○ On Feb 16th the Indian 25th Division landed near Dokekan, the 81st and 82nd Div attacked south from Kangaw as the 25th Div attacked Tamandu from the south ○ On Feb 26th the Matsu Detach left Kolan, captured Dalet Mar 3rd ○ On Mar 9th Maj. Gen. Yamamoto of the 72nd I.M.B was assigned to Army General Staff ○ On Mar 12th the Indian 25th Div left Ramree Is. and landed in Mae where it contacted the Yamane Mixed Company, which had helped the Ramree garrison withdraw ○ By Mar 17th the Indian 25th Div was on the defensive ○ On Mar 14th 28th Army HQ redeployed to Allanmyo, reinforcements were sent from Hill 534 ○ On Mar 15th the Burma National Army left Rangoon to assist the 28th Army in Prome. Mar 27th the BNA mutinied, which the Shin-i and Shimbu Units suppressed. In rear areas morale was negatively affected and operations impacted ○ On Mar 10th the 72nd I.M.B. began an offensive in central Burma. By Mar 17th it had failed and was suspended on the 21st. The 72nd I.M.B. was directed towards Mt. Popa, its 542nd Ind Inf Btn down to just 10 men ○ Mar 27th the 3rd Btn, 121st Inf R withdrew to north of Taungup River where they stalled the enemy but lost Hill 815 to tanks and artillery on the 29th ○ End of March, *Kan #2* in the Yenangyaung oil fields began. The 54th Div split into two columns just east of Tamandu in Ann Township ○ On Apr 4th Hill 370 fell to enemy infantry with artillery, tanks and aircraft support ○ The 1st Btn, 154th IR in Legyi was surrounded after an Indian National Army battalion surrendered ○ Apr 7th the 54th Div went on the offensive. Next to Hill 990 the 3rd Btn 111th IR was nearing collapse. The right side column of the 54th Div attacked between Letmauk and Hill 990 to the south of Hill 990. ○ On Apr 8th the 2nd Btn, 111th IR occupied Shaukchon cutting off the enemy retreat to Tamandu, but without more men the area couldn't be held and so they withdrew Apr 15th ○ On Apr 9th Colonel Ohara took command of the 72nd I.M.B. East of the Arakan Mountains the situation became critical ○ The 28th Army directed the 54th Division to regroup east of Ann for future Irrawaddy operations ○ On Apr 12th the 54th Division took responsibility in the area between Salin and Sidoktaya ○ On Apr 12th the 28th Army's headquarters moved to Taikky to maintain contact with the Burma Area Army ○ On April 21st the 28th Army took command of the 2nd Btn, 121st IR ○ On Apr 25th the Yamane Composite Company lost Kagosaka Pass but took it back in repeated night attacks ○ Apr 26th the 28th Army headquarters moved from Taikky to Tanbington ○ Apr 29th the 28th Army headquarters took command of the rest of the 121st Inf Regt and withdrew it to Okpo ○ The Burma Army lost ground to the enemy causing the 28th Army to become encircled ○ On May 12th the 28th Army's headquarters arrive in Pinmezali ○ In early June the Burma Army ordered the 28th Army to break out and move to the Tenasserim area. Stage 1, withdraw to the Pegu Mtns ○ On July 20th Stage 2 was to break through on the Mandalay Road and arrive in the Sittang Plains quickly as possible ○ June 19th, the 28th Army HQ arrived in Kyiyo, reorganized by the end of June and remained until July 28th when it left for Paungde ○ The war was over by the end of the stage 3 but stage 4 would have been further movement toward south Tenasserim.

Major Units: See division / brigade page for order of battle

55th Division Zentsuji 1940 楯 *Tate* HQ only, see 38th Army (Phnom Penh) 189

Note: 壮 8416, the 143rd Infantry Regiment was detached for rest of the war

54th Division Himeji 1940 兵 *Hei* – South Burma 188

Rangoon Defense Unit 1944 森 *Mori* – Rangoon 250

Attached to the 54th Division

14th Independent Rapid firing Gun Battalion	10718 (536) anti-tank
71st Field Anti-Aircraft Battalion	8057

Units Under Control of 28th Army: Paung	策 *Saku*
28th Army Headquarters	9410 (423) Mawlamyine City
28th Army HQ Signal Section	9410 (18)
14th Ind. Rapid Firing Gun Battalion (anti tank)	10718 (536)
20th Field Road Construction Unit	9357 (120)
26th Bridging Materials Company	3790 (410)
10th River Crossing Materials Company	8627 (531)
14th Field Transport Headquarters	12235 (37)
55th Independent Motor Transport Battalion	7026 (808)
236th Independent Motor Transport Company	3005 (183)
10th Specially Est. Motor Transport Company	10424 (69)
51st Independent Transport Battalion	3751 (1,630)
9th Division 1st River Crossing Company	8132 (615)
118th Line of Communications Hospital	6770 (380)
70th Casualty Clearing Platoon	5270 (54)
71st Casualty Clearing Platoon	6031 (54)

Note: The 28th Army lacked its own signal units and relied almost entirely on existing telephone lines for wire communications. Some wireless radio units were also attached. The ad hoc Saku Group was formed to replace transport units sent to the 33rd Army.

Saku Transport Group 1944	策 *Saku*	
14th Field Transport Headquarters	森 12235 (37)	
51st Independent Transport Battalion	3751 (1,630)	
55th Independent Motor Transport Battalion	7026 (808)	
54th Transport Regiment, 3rd Company	兵 10120	
55th Transport Regiment, 3rd Company	楯 8423	
55th Division Composite Motor Transp. Company	楯 unknown	
236th Independent Motor Transport Company	3005 (183)	
101st Field Road Construction Unit	6041 (312)	Arakan
93rd Land Duty Company, 1 platoon	森 8223	

Northern and Eastern Burma

33rd Army 昆 *Kon*

The 33rd Army was actvated in Rangoon on April 8, 1944, to occupy northern and eastern Burma and prevent overland contact between India and China. It was placed under Burma Area Army control. The 33rd Army's headquarters completed organizing in Rangoon on Apr 29th. Remained in Rangoon from Apr 8th until the 30th, Mangshih until Aug 30th, Maymyo until Sept 8th, from Mongyu until late Nov, Lashio until Feb 11, 1945, Hsipaw until Mar 18th, Hsingdet until the 25th, Thazi until the 30th, Nyaungyan until Apr 3rd, an unnamed village 3 mi south of Pyawbwe until Apr 17th, Pyinmana until Apr 19th, Bilin in late May and Thaton until the war ended. Lt Gen Seizai Honda commanded the 33rd Army from Apr 8, 1944 until it was deactivated.

Service History:

1944: On Apr 8th when the 33rd Army was activated it had the 18th Div in Hukawng Valley, elite but under strength, 56th Div between China and Burma, also excellent but under strength, 24th I.M.B. near Myitkyina originally 4,500 older soldiers now 1,900. The only fresh troops were the 53rd Div, parts of which were sent elsewhere soon as they set foot in Burma. The Army's main mission was to prevent the Allies from opening an overland supply route from India into China. Myitkyina had to be defended to allow the 18th Div to withdraw from Hukawng ○ On May 8th the 53rd Div and 24th IMB advanced from Indaw. The 128th Inf. Regt advanced guard found enemy 4 mi east of Mawlu ○ On May 17th the airfield west of Myitkyina was unexpectedly lost ○ The 3rd Btn, 114th I.R., 18th Div in Namkwin, 1st Btn, 148th Inf R, 56th Div in Kamaing rushed to the city followed by the 53rd Div ○ On May 17th news Imphal had stalled and Myitkyina airfield was lost reached the 18th Div ○ Rainy season began ○ On May 19th the 56th Div arrived in Mangshih, 8 days earlier Chinese armies in Yunnan began their anticipated offensive. The 2nd Division wouldn't arrive until July ○ After the Chinese 20th Army crossed the Nu Chang River the under strength 56th Div decided to begin a mopping up action, one enemy division at a time ○ On May 28th Chinese troops set up a roadblock at Seton on the Mogaung-Kamaing Road ○ After reinforcements arrived on May 30th and June 4th the Myitkyina garrison numbered around 3,000 men ○ June 27th ○ On July 7th the 18th Div retreated from Kamaing. When it was south of Taungni it marked the end of Hukawng Valley operations ○ On its way to Myitkyina the 53rd Div passed Mogaung which was attacked soon after, making the 18th Div vulnerable to encirclement. Myitkyina was abandoned ○ In China near the Burma border the 56th Div fortified towns along the Nu Chiang River from Hpimaw in the north to Wanting in the south. Tengchung, Lameng and Lungling were central strong points ○ In May Lameng, defended by 1,260 men, had sent its ammunition to Myitkyina ○ On June 2nd Lameng was attacked. Six airdrops provided some relief ○ On June 25th Tengchung with 2,025 men came under attack ○ Mogaung was slowly being wrestled from the 53rd Div ○ On July 4th the 33rd Army received orders to drive the Chinese back across Nu Chiang River. ○ On July 5th the 53rd Div received orders to move to between Pahok and Nawnghin on the Sahmaw River to cover the 18th Div withdrawal ○ On July 8th the Burma Area Army ended the Battle of Imphal and told the 15th Army to withdraw ○ Jul 12th, the Burma Army attached the 2nd Div and 28th Army transport units to the 33rd Army ○ On Jul 13th Lungling with 2,500 defenders was smashed to bits using shells and bombs ○ Jul 23rd, the Chinese 20th Army began a new offensive ○ On Jul 25th the 33rd Army moved HQ from Maymyo to Hsenwi to get closer to Yunnan ○ On the 27th Tengchung's defenders were attacked and had to abandon the outer defenses ○ On Aug 3rd Myitkyina was abandoned. 800 survivors met a mile to the east on Aug 9th, split into three groups and walked to Mt Mara where they joined the 18th Div ○ The 18th Div marched from Taungni to Indaw to rest until mid-Aug when orders sent it to Namhkan to replace the 2nd Div ○ Aug 14th Lungling, in the Nu Chiang River area, was attacked on all sides. It seemed lost until on Aug 23rd reinforcements arrived to save the town. Control of Lungling was critical to *Dan-go* ○ Lameng, attacked by four Chinese divisions held until Sept 5th when Maj. Kanemitsu was killed and the 113th Inf. Regt's colors were burnt. In Aug the 49th Div was assigned to the 33rd Army ○ On Aug 26th three inf. btns and an artillery element from the 2nd Div left Namhkan for Mangshih ○ On Aug 2nd two Chinese divisions attacked Tengchung Castle, unable to breach the walls they dug tunnels under them to plant explosives. Aug 13th Tengchung's command post was wiped out leaving a Capt Ohta in charge ○ On Aug 14th a third Chinese division joined the attack but they still made no headway ○ Aug 19th, after an air and artillery barrage a third attack breached the south wall in seven places, the garrison now down to 640 men in the castle's southeast corner ○ Aug 22nd, a fourth attack began and on the 24th the west gate was lost. Medical supplies and munitions were air dropped on the 25th ○ Sept 1st, the southeast corner was overrun ○ Sept 11th Capt Ohta burnt the 148th Inf Regt's flag ○ On Sept 14th a 70-man banzai charge ended resistance in Tengchung. The garrison of 2,025 men held 50,000 in check for 80 days. The 33rd Army had 15,000 available troops while the Chinese 20th, 11th and 33rd Armies had 135,000 men ○ Aug 25th the 56th Div began *Dan-go* phase 1 ○ Aug 26th, the initial attack on Komatsu Hill, 3 mi south of Lungling, failed ○ On Aug 30th the 33rd Army's HQ moved to Mangshih ○ The 18th Div was slow to get to Namhkan. By the end of Aug it was 7,000 strong ○ On Sept. 7th Lameng ended with a banzai charge. That 1,260 men had held 42,000 in check for four months was inspirational to the entire army ○ By Sept 13th Lungling was clear of enemy ○ On Sept 12th the 3rd Btn, 29th Inf.

Regt had captured Hill 4 but was finished, fighting was characterized by a lack of regard for life on both sides ○ Sept 13th, it had cost 4,300 Japanese lives to pin 63,000 Chinese. By detaining three Armies in Yunnan the 11th Army was able to capture Guilin-Luichow ○ Sept 14th, after Lungling and Tengchung four Chinese divisions were freed up for elsewhere. *Dan-go* phase 1 ended ○ In early Aug the 33rd Army lost Myitkyina. Afterwards it became quiet allowing the 33rd Army to rescue the Pingka garrison and regroup ○ *Dan-Go* phase 2, in late Sept the 56th Div. formed 5 units: Lungling, Eastern, Western Northern, and Southern, relieved the 2nd Div. in Lungling and moved units from Namhkam to Wanting on the Shweli River ○ Early-Oct when it arrived in Namhkam the 18th Div was still weak from Hukwang Valley, a month later, with 3,000 replacement troops from Japan it was 9,000 strong. The 2nd Div deployed near Muse in the Shweli River Valley ○ On Oct 5th the 53rd Div withdrew to Pinwe and was transferred to the 15th Army. Lt. Gen. Honda told the Burma Area Army he could succeed without the 2nd Div and Yoshida Unit (168th Inf R). He requested they be used to provide flexibility for the overall defense of Burma ○ On Oct 28th the 2nd Div minus the Bhamo Garrison joined the Burma Area Army ○ On Oct 29th the Chinese launched a Lungling-Mangshih offensive ○ Nov 3rd, the Lungling Defense Unit withdrew to Mangshih and Yoshida Unit in Wanting and was told to watch the 56th Div rear, they were to fight flexible holding actions instead of an entrenched defense at all costs ○ On Nov 19th the 56th Div fought tenaciously from dawn until midnight when new orders arrived. Front line units were to withdraw to Chefang Pass positions ○ In early Nov the Chinese New 1st Corps advanced to Bhamo while others threatened Mandalay, they seemed to be planning to divide the 15th and 33rd Armies by cutting the rail line at Mongmit ○ In mid Nov the Yoshida Force came in contact with enemy who were attempting to outflank the 56th Div south of Shiachai ○ On Nov 30th the 56th Div regrouped and withdrew to Wanting ○ In late Aug the Bhamo Garrison was attached to the 18th Div after the 2nd Div left ○ When the 18th Div arrived in Mongmit in mid Nov Bhamo became the 33rd Army's responsibility. The garrison under Colonel Kozo Hara had 6 months food and ammunition but the defenses hadn't been completed ○ On Nov 14th Chinese troops cut communications, made probing attacks and destroyed the southern outposts ○ From mid Nov to early Dec air strikes destroyed much of their food ○ On Dec 8th the main Bhamo defenses collapsed ○ By Dec 10th the HQ was reduced to 3 officers and 5 men. A last stand was being prepared when the 18th Div and Yamazaki Unit arrived ○ In late Nov Army HQ withdrew to Lashio to direct fighting in the Mongmit and Wanting areas ○ At dawn on Dec 9th Yamazaki began the rescue of the Bhamo Garrison overrunning a number of enemy artillery positions by evening ○ On Dec 14th the Bhamo garrison escape began at 0400, in all it cost 30 men lost. Disbanded in Lashio on Dec 31st. The garrison had begun with 1,180 men but lost 580 in the siege. Yamazaki Unit lost 150 killed and 300 wounded during the rescue ○ In late Dec the 33rd Army received orders to retain the 4th Inf. Regt, 2nd Div and 168th Inf. Regt, 49th Div when the 2nd Div was transferred. Becoming a 2nd line reserve these troops were temporary and unexpected ○

1945: On Jan 8th U.S. and Chinese units went on the offensive ○ Jan 10th the 33rd Army gave the 56th Div control of Yamazaki and Ichikari Regts to unify command over the 19,800 men who faced 290,000 enemy in 20-divisions threatening the Burma Road ○ On Jan 10th the Chinese 30th and 38th Div attacked the Yamazaki Unit in Namhkan ○ On Jan 18th at night the Yamazaki Unit escaped into a gap in the Japanese lines. The

56th Div controlled 30-miles of the Burma Road between Wanting and Namhpakka but had no transports so Terada Battalion, two motor transport companies totaling 40 vehicles was sent ○ On Jan 24th Terada found the Ichikari Regt in Namhpakka surrounded and the Burma Road occupied. The convoy broke through to 56th Div HQ in Mongyu delivered gasoline, removed 1,000 casualties and several tons of ammunition. Between Jan 31st and Feb 4th the 56th Div withdrew to 8 miles south of Namhpakka ○ *Dan-Go* phase 2 ended as Chinese forces confronting the 18th Div left for central China ○ On Feb 8th the Indian 36th Division crossed the Shweli River and attacked Myitson, they were pushed back across on the 12th but their bridgehead remained intact ○ On Feb 19th the 18th Div left Mongmit for Mandalay to join *Ban-go*. Ohtsuka Butai, the 114th Inf Regt, one arty battery and one engineer coy, were left to garrison Mongmit ○ In late Feb the 18th Div left for Mandalay and the 56th Div for Hsenwi ending operation *Dan-go*. Outnumbered 15 to 1 the 33rd Army no longer had a duty to blockade the Lido Road between China and India ○ On Feb 4th the battle of Irrawaddy and Pokoku began ○ On Feb 11th the 33rd Army moved HQ to Hsipaw and reduced the front lines to Lashio, Bawdwin and Mongmit. The 15th Army, exposed and weak, needed reinforcements ○ On Feb 25th the 18th Div left Mongmit and assembled in Hsumhsai arriving in Mandalay on the 28th ○ Mar 10th the 56th Inf Regt began the attack on Meiktila ○ On Mar 14th without warning the Burma Army transferred control of Meiktila from the 15th Army to 33rd Army. 33rd Army HQ was told to direct the battle from a suburb of Kalaw, start time: 0001 hours on Mar 18th ○ The 33rd Army HQ deployed in Hsingdet with the 18th Div, 49th Div and 53rd Div under its control. Between air attacks and disrupted communications the village became untenable. On Mar 25th the HQ moved to Thazi ○ By end of March the 15th Army had been defeated and 33rd Army left exposed It was given orders to stay long enough to cover the 15th Army's retreat ○ Mar 30th the 33rd Army HQ withdrew to Nyaungyan ○ Apr 3rd to an unnamed village 3 miles south of Pyawbwe, marking the end of Meiktila. 33rd Army HQ resented the Burma Area Army's interference from 250 mi in the rear. Believing it void of the facts, it was issuing impossible directives. After *Ban-go* just ten mountain guns and six 105mm howitzers remained of 120 artillery pieces ○ On Apr 5th the 49th Div was surrounded. Breaking free the next night it left the 33rd Army HQ encircled by a pincer attack. Staff took refuge in a ravine until the enemy went north to attack the 18th Div HQ, unaware they had just flattened the 33rd Army HQ ○ On Apr 7th HQ slipped through enemy lines to join the 18th Div east of Yamethin ○ On Apr 19th the 33rd Army HQ was overrun again during the British offensive on Pyinmana. Shelling continued until dark. Afterwards approx 250 staff and wounded slipped through enemy lines and regrouped 6 miles south ○ On Apr 22nd Toungoo fell ○ On Apr 23rd the 33rd Army HQ located the 18th Div and reconnected with the 49th Div, 53rd Div and 55th Div on the 24th ○ On Apr 26th the 33rd Army HQ re-established control. After Toungoo collapsed Rangoon was next in line ○ On Apr 27th the 33rd Army was sent to the mouth of the Sittang River, the 15th Army to Moulmein and the 55th Div was placed under 15th Army command. Following Pyinmana only the Rangoon Defense Force stood between the British and Rangoon ○ On May 2nd Rangoon fell isolating the 28th Army ○ In late May the 33rd Army HQ left for Bilin ○ July 3rd, the battle of Sittang began when the 18th Div attacked Nyaungkash ○ On July 9th the British withdrew leaving the 18th Div in control of Nyaungkash and Laya ○ On July 3rd the 53rd Div crossed the Sittang River and attacked Myitkyo. By July 30th Myitkyo and Okpo had fallen and most of Abaya was burnt ○ On July 11th the 56th Div was attached to the 15th Army ○ On Aug 15th the war ended ○

Major Units: See division / brigade page for order of battle

18th Division Kurume 1907 菊 *Kiku* – Kyaikto 172

18th Division attached unit		
21st Field Medium Artillery Battalion	8121 (1,024)	
Units under control of the 33rd Army	昆 *Kon*	
33rd Army Headquarters	7901 (483)	
33rd Army HQ Signal Section	7901 (18)	
21st Independent Mixed Regiment	7136 (2,236)	
13th Independent Rapid Firing Gun Battalion	10717 (536)	anti tank unit
8th Independent Field Artillery Battalion	3148	
27th Independent Anti Aircraft Battalion	12517 (522)	
43rd Field Machine Cannon Company	8059 (105)	Rangoon Defense
102nd Field Road Construction Unit	6613 (312)	
2nd Signals Unit Headquarters	12915 (62)	
108th Independent Wire Signals Company	12911 (310)	
109th Independent Wire Signals Company	12912 (310)	
110th Independent Wire Signals Company	12913 (310)	
102nd Independent Radio Platoon	12920 (57)	
103rd Independent Radio Platoon	12921 (57)	
104th Independent Radio Platoon	12922 (57)	
22nd Bridging Materials Company	1374 (410)	
13th River Crossing Materials Company	4816 (230)	
9th Division, 1st Bridging Materials Company	8131 (564)	
2nd Independent Transport Regiment	5372 (1,706)	
61st Field Motor Transport Battalion	8856 (808)	
237th Independent Motor Transport Company	3006 (183)	
9th Specially Est. Motor Transport Company	10423 (69)	
21st Specially Est. Motor Transport Company	10435 (69)	
121st Line of Communications Hospital	2265 (362)	
60th Casualty Clearing Platoon	7134 (54)	

Thailand

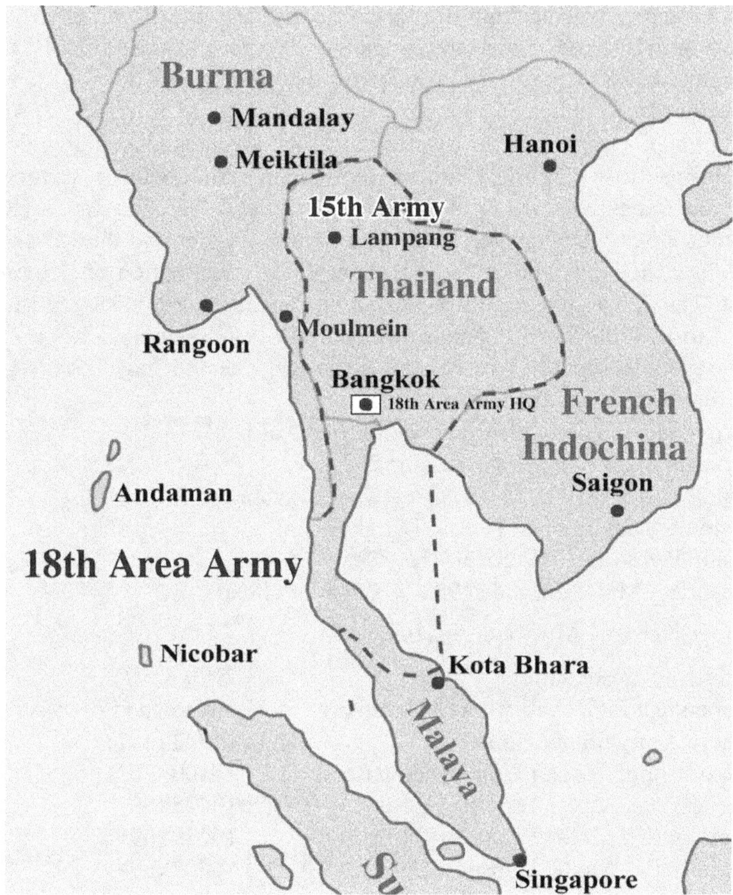

<u>18th Area Army</u> 義 *Gi*

The 18th Area Army became active in Bangkok, Thailand on July 14, 1945, from former 39th Army personnel. Created in response to Japanese forces being pushed out of Burma its purpose was to provide retreating divisions and brigades with an intact command structure for the last stand in south Asia. Its commander was Lt Gen Akito Nakamura, former 39th Army commander. The 18th Area Army answered directly to Southern Expeditionary Army HQ in Indochina.

Subordinate army / duty dates:

15th Army from July 15, 1945, until the war ended

<u>Service History</u>:

<u>1945</u>: On Mar 1st after the loss of Meiktila the war in Burma becomes un-winnable ○ On Mar 14th the Burmese National Defense Army declared war on its ally Japan ○ On Mar 21st Mandalay fell ○ On May 1st Rangoon fell. The 39th Army in Thailand was in a position to absorb displaced Burma Area Army units. The 15th Army received orders to

deploy to northern Thailand from Burma ○ In early July the 15th Army's HQ traveled from Toungoo to Bangkok and on to Lampang in northern Thailand ○ Jul 14th, the 39th Army became the 18th Area Army in Bangkok. The 15th Army HQ, 15th, 22nd, 53rd and 56th Div were placed under its command immediately ○ In July the 18th Area Army published operational plans: Priority areas included airfields in and around Bangkok, the Thai-Burma Railway, north Thailand, Tenasserim in the southeast sector, northeast Thailand and Bangkok ○ As the war was about to end the 15th Army's HQ arrived in Lampang, the 56th Div arrived at the Thai-Burma border and the 15th Div arrived in Ban Pong, Thailand. The 29th I.M.B. completed construction of defenses in the southwest. The 53rd Div was still in Burma but unable to establish contact with the 18th Area Army ○ On Aug 15th Japan surrendered ○ On September 12th in Singapore the Southern Expeditionary Army's representative, General Itagaki, surrendered all Japanese forces in the southern area ○

<u>Major Units</u>: See division / brigade page for order of battle

4th Division Osaka 1888 淀 *Yodo* – Lampang	165
15th Division Tsurugu 1905 祭 *Matsuri* – Kanchanaburi	170
22nd Division Sendai 1938 原 *Hara* – Bangkok	175
53rd Division Kyoto 1941 安 *Yasui* – Kaywe	187-8
29th Independent Mixed Brigade 1943 体 *Tai* – Prachuap	177

<u>Units under 18th Area Army control</u>: Bangkok	義 *Gi*
18th Area Army Headquarters	7970
63rd Independent Field Anti Aircraft Company	unknown (179)
6th Southern Army Signal Unit	15923 (307)
89th Line of Comm. Sector Unit Headquarters	17100 (203)
14th Specially Est. Motor Transport Company	10428 (69)
15th Specially Est. Motor Transport Company	10429 (69)
38th Specially Est. Motor Transport Company	15807 (69)
129th Land Duty Company	unknown (511)
130th Land Duty Company	unknown (511)
5th Engineer Unit Headquarters	12201 (32)
94th Casualty Clearing Platoon	unknown (54)
97th Casualty Clearing Platoon	unknown (54)
34th Field Disease Prevention / Water Supply Unit	17113
148th Line of Communications Hospital	17104 (359)
16th Southern Army Hospital	10498 (151)
18th Area Army Field Ordinance	17106 (500)
18th Area Army Field Motor Vehicle Depot	17107
18th Area Army Field Freight Depot	17108
18th Area Army L. o. C. Veterinary Depot	17110
18th Area Army Veterinary Quarantine Hospital	17109
2nd Southern Army Military Police Detachment	No # (279)

Northern Thailand

15th Army 林 *Hayashi*

The 15th Army was activated in Saigon, Indochina on Nov 5, 1941, from former Indochina Garrison Army headquarters personnel (who were split between the 15th and 25th Army HQs). Its mission was to defend north and west Burma along the border with China and India. On Nov 6th the 15th Army was placed under Southern Army control. Its 18th, 33rd, 55th and 56th Divisions arrived from Manchuria. 15th Army headquarters remained in Indochina from Nov 6th until Dec 15, 1942, Rangoon Burma until Mar 27, 1943 (when it joined the Burma Area Army), Maimyo, Burma from Apr 15th until Oct 14th, Lashio, Burma (where it was attached to the 18th Area Army) until Jul 15, 1945 and Lampang, Thailand until the war ended. The 15th Army was commanded by Lt Gen Shōjirō Īda from Nov 6th until Mar 18, 1943, Lt Gen Renya Mutaguchi until Aug 30, 1944 and Lt Gen Shihachi Katamura until it was deactivated.

Service History:

1941: On Nov 5th the 15th Army headquarters was activated in Saigon Indochina ○

1942: In early January the 15th Army began concentrating forces on Thai soil ○ Jan 20th the 55th Div crossed the Thai border into Burma ○ Jan 30th the 55th Div. occupied Moulmein ○ On Feb 14th the 55th Div won the battle of Bilin River ○ Feb 19th the 33rd Div won the battle of Sittang Bridge ○ On Mar 3rd the 33rd Div won the battle of Pegu ○ On Mar 7th the 33rd Div cleared the Taukkyan roadblock ○ On Mar 8th the 33rd and 55th Div occupied Rangoon without a fight ○ On Mar 24th the battle of Toungoo began. The 55th Div supported by the 18th Div and newly arrived 56th Div were victorious on the 30th after a hard fight ○ On Apr 1st the 15th Army went north from Tongoo and Promu ○ Apr 29th, Lashio was taken ○ On May 1st Mandalay was taken ○ May 18th, the 15th Army received orders to secure northern Burma ○ In Sept the 15th Army received orders to plan the occupation of the Assam area in India. The 18th Div commander, Lt Gen Mutaguchi, felt a lack of adequate supply and network of useable roads made the operation un-winnable ○ On Dec 17th the British Indian 14th Div began to advance from Cox's Bazaar towards Arakan ○ On Dec 23rd doubtful of the results, IGHQ suspended the Assam plan ○

1943: On Jan 7th the battle of Arakan began. British Indian troops attacked a company from the 213th Inf R, 33rd Div a mile north of Donbaik, which developed into a stalemate ○ In Feb, the 56th Div fought a Chinese division in the Salween River area, northeast Burma and the 55th Div resumed the offensive against British troops in the battle of Akyab ○ In mid Feb Ord Wingate's Chindit Brigade advanced into northern Burma ○ Mar 22nd, the 31st Div was organized in Bangkok from the 58th and 138th Inf. Regts from Malaya and 124th Inf Regt from Guadalcanal, the service units came from central and north China ○ On Mar 27th after losing the 55th Div the 15th Army joined the Burma Area Army and reorganized. It now had the 18th, 33rd, 56th and new 31st Div ○ On Apr 15th, with reorganization completed, the 15th Army HQ relocated to Maimyo ○ On May 5th the 15th Army issued a report suggesting an offensive to secure northern Burma ○ On June 17th the 15th Div was transferred from China to the 15th Army but didn't arrive in Burma until mid Jan 1944 ○ On June 24th the Burma Area Army held map maneuvers to rehearse the offensive ○ On Aug 12th orders for *U-Go*, the *Battle of Imphal* were distributed ○ Aug 25th, the 15th Army suggested destroying Chinese Army bases along the Salween River prior to the start of *U-go*. Lt Gen Mutaguchi had already drawn attention to the biggest problem facing the 15th Army; the absence of useable roads in northern Burma ○ In Sept the construction of a road crossing the Zibyu Mountain Range began as a prelude to *U-go* ○ By Oct 14th the 56th Div and part of the 18th Div had completed their Salween River objectives ○ In late Oct the Chinese 38th Div crossed into Hukawng Burma and attacked the 56th Inf Regt, 18th Div, the only Japanese unit north of Kamaing close enough for it to engage ○ On Nov 8th the 33rd Div advanced to Haka, Kalemyo and Yazagyo ○ On Dec 22nd the 15th Army presented its final plan for Imphal, suggesting that defending the line from Kohima to the high ground west of Imphal was essential for securing Burma ○

1944: On Jan 7th three divisions from the 15th Army were sent to attack from the east and south of the Imphal Basin ○ On Jan 9th the British Indian 5th and 7th Div attacked the 55th Div through railway tunnels on Burma's southwest coast by way of Maungdaw and Buthidaung ○ In early Feb the Kuomintang 1st Army marched from Assam to Hukawng and made contact with the 18th Div ○ Feb 20th the battle of Maingkwan began with US and Chinese forces surrounding the 18th Div ○ On March 2nd the 18th Div pinned the Chinese and attacked US troops ○ Mar 7th the 18th Div was forced to retreat with heavy losses ○ Mar 8th the 33rd Div crossed into Manipur State, India to begin *U-go* while the 15th Div. attacked Imphal. As fighting began the 15th Div overran Imphal ○ On Mar 15th the 15th Army crossed the Chindwin River ○ Mar 20th, after the 18th Div retreated through the Jambu Hkintang Mtns it took up positions north of the junction of several rivers around Shuduzup but fighting began before its defenses were completed ○ On Apr 3rd the 33rd Div attacked Kohima Ridge ○ On Apr 6th the 31st Div began the siege of Kohima ○ Apr 15th the 15th Army crossed the Chindwin River. The 18th Div withdrew from Tingring. It was shunted to the Malakawng Wala area and placed under 33rd Army control ○ In May Burma's rainy season prevented supplies from reaching the 15th Army ○ On June 22nd the Kohima Imphal Road was opened marking an end to the battle of Imphal ○ On July 4th the Southern Army suspended *U-go*. The Burma Army announced plans for subordinate armies to engage in coordinated but separate operations: The 15th Army: *Ban*, 28th Army: *Kan* and the 33rd Army: *Dan* ○ In mid July the 15th Army withdrew from east of Imphal to the Chindwin River to regroup ○

1945: On Jan 27th the bulk of the 2nd Div was detached from the 15th Army and sent to Indochina, its 16th Inf Regt and 2 artillery battalions remained ○ On Mar 1st Meiktila fell ○ On Mar 14th the Burmese National Defense Army declared war on its Japanese allies ○ On Mar 21st Mandalay was lost ○ May 2nd, Rangoon was captured by British Indian forces. The Burma Area Army HQ retreated from Rangoon to Moulmein where its staff were reassigned, for practical purposes it had been demobilized. The 39th Army HQ became 18th Area Army HQ and absorbed former Burma Army units including the 15th Army ○ In early July the 15th Army HQ was sent to Lampang via Bangkok to defend northern Thailand. It arrived in Lampang just prior to the end of hostilities ○

Major Units: See division / brigade page for order of battle

31st Division Bangkok 1943 烈 *Retsu* – Thaton	178
33rd Division Utsunomiya 1943 弓 *Yumi* – Nakon Patthom	179
56th Division Kureme 1940 龍 *Tatu* – South Burma	189-90

Units under the 15th Army: Lampang, Thailand	林 *Hayashi*
15th Army Headquarters	1611 (433)
1st Independent Rapid Firing Gun Battalion	3850

3rd Field Medium Artillery Regiment	3766	
18th Field Medium Artillery Regiment	1016	
59th Independent Motor Transport Battalion	5259	
102nd Independent Motor Transport Battalion	3007	
256th Independent Motor Transport Company	6055 (183)	
334th Independent Motor Transport Company	12237 (183)	Bangkok
52nd Independent Transport Company	1352	
53rd Independent Transport Company	1353	Meiktila
54th Independent Transport Company	1362	
55th Independent Transport Company	1363	
126th Land Duty Company	unknown (511)	
105th Line of Communications Hospital	7131 (362)	
124th Line of Communications Hospital	5224 (380)	
15th Casualty Clearing Unit Headquarters	7132	
38th Casualty Clearing Platoon	1357 (54)	
58th Casualty Clearing Platoon	6948 (54)	Chiang Mai
15th Army Field Ordinance Depot	10590	
15th Army Field Motor Vehicle Depot	10591	
15th Army Field Freight Depot	10592	

Bangkok, Thailand

39th Army 義 *Gi*

(became the 18th Area Army)

The former Thailand Garrison Army it became the 39th Army in Bangkok on Dec 10, 1944, and was placed under Southern Expeditionary Army control on Dec 20th. Its headquarters remained in Bangkok under Lt Gen Akito Nakamura. It was made responsible for operations extending to about 15 miles south of Ye (which is 30 miles south of Moulmein, Burma) and across the southern tip of Sullivan Island. Charged with providing security for Thailand and supply routes into Burma and Malaya. On July 14, 1945 the 39th Army became the 18th Area Army.

Service History:

1942: On Dec 21st the Japan Thailand Military Alliance was signed. The same day the Imperial Guard Division entered Thailand uninvited to invade Malaya ○ In Nov IGHQ ordered the Southern Army to build the Thailand Burma Railway ○

1943: On Jan 4th the Thai Garrison Army headquarters was established in Bangkok under Lt Gen Akito Nakamura, the former 2nd Btn, 82nd Inf Regt, 21st Div commander ○ From Feb 15th the army air force and line of communications units were posted near Bangkok ○ On Nov 16th the 29th I.M.B. began activating in Bangkok ○

1944: Jan 1st, the 29th I.M.B. completed activation ○ On Dec 8th IGHQ ordered the Southern Army to reorganize the Thailand Garrison Army into the 39th Army so it

could function as a Line of Communications base for Burma and Malaya ○
1945: On Jan 14th the 4th Div was withdrawn from Sumatra and sent to Thailand and two infantry battalions from the 24th I.M.B. in Mergui and Tavoy, Burma were placed under the 39th Army's control ○ In Feb the 39th Army took command of the 7th Field Replacement Unit and some line of communications units. The Navy ceded control over the 17th Naval Garrison Unit in Mergui to the 39th Army ○ On June 10th defensive preparations deterred rebellious Thai army and police units from open revolt ○ On July 14th the 39th Army became the 18th Area Army and the 7th Field Replacement Unit became the Bangkok Defense Unit (See 18th Area Army) ○
Major Units: See division / brigade page for order of battle

4th Division Osaka 1888 淀 *Yodo* – to 18th Area Army	165
29th Independent Mixed Brigade 体 *Karada* – to 18th Area Army	219

Units under 39th Army control: Bangkok	義 *Gi*	
39th Army Headquarters	7970	
14th Specially Est. Motor Transport Company	10428	
15th Specially Est. Motor Transport Company	10429	
7th Field Replacement Unit (Feb 1944 to July 1945)	10154	(Bangkok Def. Unit)
16th Southern Army Hospital	unknown	
2nd Southern Army Military Police Detachment	No #	

Downtown occupied Manila, the Philippines (anonymous photo)

Philippine Islands

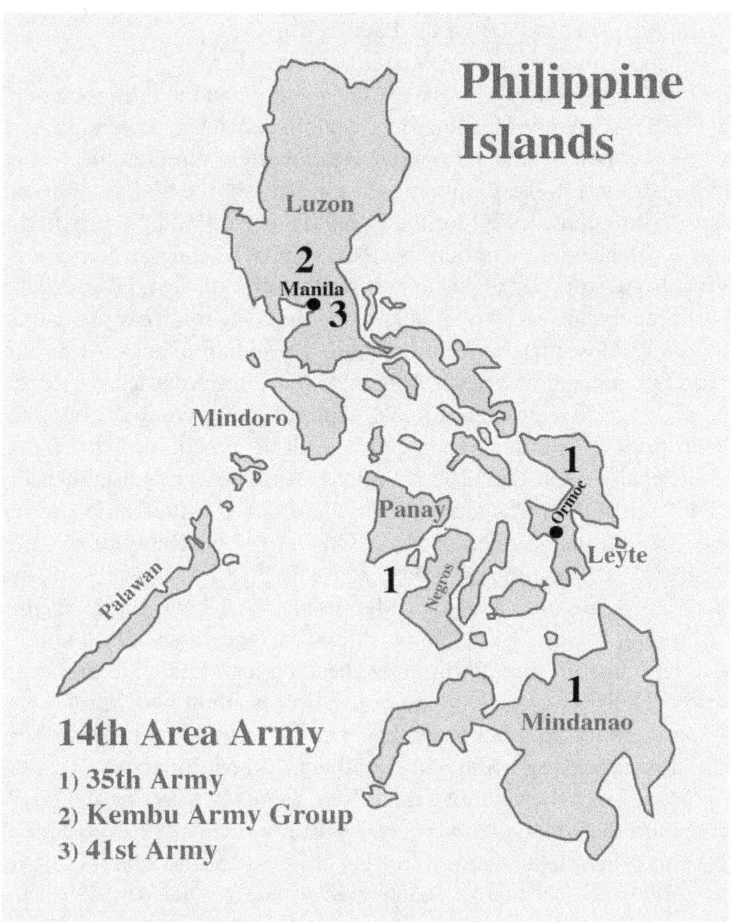

14th Area Army 尚武 *Shobu*

The 14th Area Army was activated in Manila, the Philippines on Aug 4, 1944, from former 14th Army HQ personnel and placed under Southern Expeditionary Army control the same day. The 14th Area Army HQ remained in Manila until Mar 3, 1945 and northern Luzon until the surrender. Unusually for an area army, the 14th Area Army excersised direct control over combat troops in the field through the 14th Area Army Headquarters Detached Section, which directed combat troops in the battle for Luzon. The area army also directed two independent battle groups on Luzon. The 14th Area Army's commander was Lt Gen Shigenori Kuroda from July 28th until Sept 26th and General Tomoyuki Yamashita (Tiger of Malaya) until deactivation on Sept 2, 1945.

Subordinate armies / duty dates:

35th Army from Aug 4, 1944, until Sept 2, 1945

Kembu Army Group from Oct 1944, until Sept 2, 1945

41st Army from Apr 20, 1945, until Sept 2. 1945

Service History:

1941: Nov 6th, the 14th Army headquarters became active in Taihoku, Formosa to lead the invasion and occupation of the Philippines ○ Dec 8th, X-Day, earmarked by the Japanese military as the first day of the Pacific War ○

1942: Apr 10th the Kawaguchi Detachment transferred from the 16th Army to the 14th Army to subdue the Visayas ○ On May 7th Corregidor and the Philippines surrendered ○ On May 20th, 14th Army Headquarters established itself in Manila ○ June 29th, the 14th Army was placed under Imperial Headquarters direct control to establish a military administration in the Philippines ○ On Sept 4th the 4th Div returned to Japan from Bataan. A draft constitution for the Republic of the Philippines is first read ○

1943: Under military administration in 1943 Manila became an important rear area base, transit hub and stopover for sea routes south and southeast. From 3,000 to 10,000 men were estimated to be on layover at any one time. By mid year many units passing through Manila had lost men and equipment to sea and air attacks. Arms and supplies were replaced but demand was never fully met. When the Americans landed on Luzon the chronic shortage of entrenching tools exposed many combat troops to needless danger ○ On Sept 4th another reading of the draft constitution for the Philippine Republic took place ○ On Sept 20th a National Assembly was established and three days later the Constitution was ratified ○ In Oct I.G.HQ issued orders to turn the P.I. into a supply base for the Southern Army ○ On Oct 14th the Republic of the Philippine was established ○ In Nov the 30th, 31st, 32nd and 33rd I.M.B. were organized from Ind. Garrison Units, all were active by Mar 1944 ○ After the Dampier Straits fell in December shipping became vulnerable to Allied surface vessel attacks ○

1944: Garrison units in the Philippines became careless and preoccupied with administration. Their organization, equipment and training was inferior to front line troops making them unsuitable for combat. The 14th Army had only the 16th Division available at this time ○ In May the Southern Expeditionary Army headquarters relocated to Manila, it became active there June 15th ○ In May the 30th Div left Korea for Mindanao and the Manila Anti Aircraft Unit became active ○ In June the 4th Air Army's HQ and principle air units were sent from Rabaul to Manila ○ On June 15th the 30th, 31st, 32nd and 33rd I.M.B. deactivated to become the 100th, 102nd, 103rd and 105th Divisions ○ By July casualties from New Guinea and Singapore had crowded into Manila. 10,000 stranded replacement troops from Japan were also present ○ The 1st Field Replacement Headquarters was established to organize temporary housing, supply, education and relocation for those stranded and marginally disabled ○ On July 15th the 58th I.M.B. arrived in Manila from Japan ○ July 26th, the 35th Army HQ became active on Mindanao ○ On Aug 4th the 14th Army became the 14th Area Army and the 35th Army HQ were deployed to Cebu Island ○ General Tomoyuki Yamashita was appointed overall commander in the Philippines and the 14th Area Army reorganized itself into an army for combat ○ In early Aug the Southern Army headquarters requested IGHQ allow it to move from Manila to Singapore or Saigon ○ In early Sept the 8th Div and 2nd Armored Div, which suffered losses on the voyage, began arriving ○ On Sept 22nd the 1st Div, 30th Air Group (bomber) and others were transferred to the 14th Area Army for *Sho-go* ○ On Oct 6th General Yamashita arrived in the Philippines, exchanged old HQ staff for new and increased its numbers, which raised morale throughout the army ○ In Oct the 14th Area Army created Kembu Army Group on Clark Field. It was led by the 1st Air Raiding Group commander ○ In mid

Oct a typhoon hit the Philippines ○ On Oct 18th IGHQ ordered *Sho-go*, the defense of the Philippines, to begin immediately ○ On Oct 20th the battle for Leyte began ○ In November Army General Staff transferred the 10th and 23rd Div from the 10th Area Army in Taiwan and the 19th Division in Korea to the 14th Area Army ○ By Nov 14th the battle for Leyte was lost. Under operation *Chi-go* the 35th Army extracted viable units to use elsewhere ○ On Nov 28th the 1st Air Raiding Group was placed under 4th Air Army control ○

1945: The 14th Area Army planned to defend Luzon from prepared mountain positions to the north and east of Manila ○ Jan 1st remaining 4th Air Army personnel were placed under 14th Area Army control ○ On Jan 9th the U.S. began landing troops in the Lingayan Gulf area on Luzon. Defending against three US divisions, the 23rd Div and 58th I.M.B. bore the brunt of the attack ○ On Jan 25th the assault on Clark Field and the Kembu Group began ○ By Jan 30th Clark Field was lost ○ By the end of Jan the 14th Area Army had sustained at least 6,500 casualties ○ Feb 13th, the 4th Air Army was deactivated. The 2nd and 7th Air Div and other air units were placed under 3rd Air Army control while the 4th Air Div, 1st Air Raiding Group and service units stayed on Luzon under the 14th Area Army's control ○ Feb 21st, US troops attacked the 23rd Div and 58th I.M.B. near Camp 1 in Baguio. Fighting lasted until the 23rd Div abandoned the city on Apr 26th ○ On Feb 21st the 10th Div took up positions in the Balete/Dalton Pass area and east, west and north of Puncan, building defenses and carrying out raids on San Nicolas, San Jose and Rizal ○ In late Feb communications between the 14th Area Army's northern base, Kembu Group and Shimbu Group were cut. From then on contact was sporadic by wireless radio or plane ○ On Mar 6th Shimbu Group reorganized into the 41st Army in the mountains east of Manila ○ The 2nd Tank Div, fighting on foot, and the 10th Recon Regt dug in at both Salacsac Passes ○ On Apr 1st the battle for Pass No 2 began with 150 men counterattacking Hill 504 ○ By Apr 4th 1000 men had died ○ By Apr 18th Pass No 2 was mostly in US hands ○ On Apr 20th the 41st Army (Shimbu Group) became active east of Manila ○ By Apr 24th the US had captured Hill 515 on the north side of Salacsac Pass No. 1 and on the 27th took the crest of Hill 525 ○ On Apr 28th Villa Verde Trail was blocked south of Hill 516 cutting supply lines to Pass No 1 and leaving just one route that ran through jungle south of the trail and to the east of Hill 508 ○ On Apr 26th Baguio fell ○ On May 13th the battle of Balete/Dalton Pass in the Cagayan Valley was lost ○ On May 24th Salacsac Pass No 1 fell ○ On May 5th fighting on the Villa Verde Trail began. It ended May 31st ○ May 17th Ipo Dam fell ○ On May 28th Imugan and Ariato were lost ○ By the end of May 5,750 of 8,750 men on Villa Verde trail had become casualties. By now the 2nd Tank Div had 2,300 KIA ○ Between May 28th and June 2nd the Anti Tank Unit (Army Training Unit; reserve officer candidate trainees) in the Yangiran area south of Aritao was overrun. Armed with mines the trainees used suicide tactics to destroyed 2 to 4 tanks ○ On June 1st in Ilocos Sur the 73rd and 76th Inf Regts, 19th Div began the battle of Bessang Pass ○ By June 15th the battle of Bessang Pass had been lost ○ June 3rd the Americans attacked Aritao in the Cagayan Valley, which fell on June 4th ○ The line of communications unit in Aritao withdrew to Oilan Pass and joined the 2nd Tank Div ○ The 103rd Div and 105th Div concentrated forces in the Bayombong and Bagbag Plains ○ June 5th, the south side of Bambang Hill was heavily shelled so 14th Area Army HQ Detached Section in Bambang left for Latorre that night ○ On June 6th at dawn US troops attacked Bambang ○ On June 6th, with enemy closing in and communications failing, 14th Area Army HQ Detached Section left for Wakal, northeast of Latorre ○ On June 7th US troops crossed the Magat River near Bato Bridge ○ June 8th in the evening, after failing to contact the 2nd Tank Div or 10th Div the 14th Area Army HQ Detached Section left Wakal for Kiangan. Communications with the 103rd Div had been severed ○ In mid June an attempt was made to reconnect to the 2nd Tank Div, 10th and 103rd Div, 4th Air Div ground crews and Shimbu Group, all of whom had lost communications with the 14th Area Army Headquarters ○ On June 13th American forces captured Bagbag and Echague ○ On June 21st Appari fell ○ On June 24th the Americans broke through the Payambugan Farm School area and drove west ○ At the end of June the 14th Area Army HQ Detached Section set up in Pakdan along side the line of communications headquarters unit ○ In July, 14th Area Army Headquarters Detached Section, 19th, 105th, 23rd Div, 58th I.M.B., 2nd Tank Div, Araki Detach (79th Inf Bgde, 103rd Div) retired to their last line of defense in the northern Luzon mountain wilderness. The 14th Area Army managed to regain control over the afore mentioned units, although divisions lacked equipment, artillery and munitions. They were all around a regiment more or less in strength ○ On July 4th the US declared the campaign on Luzon officially over ○ By late-July starvation and illness had killed many and afflicted all. Even under these dire conditions the 14th Area Army maintained cohesion ○ On Aug 15th Japan surrendered ○ Aug 17th the Philippine Republic was dissolved ○ On Sept 2nd the 14th Area Army was deactivated ○

<u>Major Units</u>: See division / brigade page for order of battle

Unit	Page
1st Division Tokyo 1888 玉 *Tama* – Cebu (fought on Leyte)	163-4
10th Division Himeiji 1898 鉄 *Tetsu* – San Jose sector, Luzon	168
19th Division Korea 1915 虎 *Tora* – San Fernando sector	171
23rd Division Kumamoto 1938 旭 *Asahi* – Binday area, Lingayen	175-6
26th Division Manchuria 1937 泉 *Izumi* – Leyte Island	176
103rd Division Kumamoto 1944 駿 *Shun* – Aparri sector	197
105th Division Hiroshima 1944 勤 *Kin* – Legaspi, Lamon Bay (½ w/41st A.)	198
2nd Armored Division Manchuria 1942 撃 *Geki* – San Jose, Luzon	206
58th Independent Mixed Brigade 1944 盟 *Mei* – Damortis, Lingayan	227
61st Independent Mixed Brigade 1944 鎧 *Yoroi* – Babuyan Islands	228

<u>Attached to the 10th Division</u>:

Unit	Number	Note
11th Independent Infantry Regiment	5314 (3,547)	from 26th Div.
26th Ind. Rapid Firing Gun Battalion	14203 (403)	
21st Ind. Rapid Firing Gun Company	13221	
5th Medium Trench Mortar Battalion	18808 (550)	

<u>Attached to the 23rd Division</u>

Unit	Number
51st Specially Established Machine Cannon Unit	12448 (85)
52nd Specially Established Machine Cannon Unit	12450 (85)
53rd Specially Established Machine Cannon Unit	12451 (85)
12th Field Medium Artillery Regiment	3770 (2,286)
89th Field Anti-Aircraft Regiment	2190

<u>Attached to the 103rd Division</u>

Unit	Number	Note
18th Independent Rapid Firing Gun Battalion	17653 (403)	anti-tank unit
9th Independent Tank Company	17660 (116)	

103rd Division continued

54th Specially Est. Machine Cannon Unit	12542 (85)
26th Independent Machinegun Battalion	10171 (334)
53rd Field Machine Cannon Company	2178 (105)
54th Field Machine Cannon Company	2179 (105)

Attached to the 105th Division

8th Independent Tank Company	17659 (116)
77th Field Anti Aircraft Battalion	12415 (528)
2nd Field Searchlight Battalion	3637 (271)
13th Specially Established Machine Cannon Unit	15406 (85)
14th Specially Established Machine Cannon Unit	15407 (85)
15th Specially Established Machine Cannon Unit	15408 (85)
57th Field Road Construction Unit	17635 (298)

Attached to the 2nd Armored Division

11th Specially Established Machine Cannon Unit	15404 (85)
49th Field Road Construction Unit	10059 (301)
62nd Independent Motor Transport Battalion	8857 (808)

Attached to the 58th I.M.B

16th Reconnaissance Regiment	6557 (439) from 6th Div
4th Independent Heavy Artillery Battalion (– 1 Co.)	1218

Units under 14th Area Army control: Manila	尚武 *Shobu*
14th Area Army Headquarters	1600 (1,474 total)
14th Area Army General Staff Department	1600-1
14th Area Army Adjutant Department	1600-2
14th Area Army Ordinance Department	1600-3
14th Area Army Intendance Department	1600-4
14th Area Army Physician Department	1600-5
14th Area Army Veterinary Department	1600-6
14th Area Army Legal Department	1600-7
14th Area Army Intelligence Department	1600-8
14th Area Army Records Office	1600-9
14th Area Army Telegraph Office	1600-10
14th Area Army Special Intelligence Department	1600-12
14th Area Army Medical Department	1600-13
14th Area Army Music Department	1600-15
14th Area Army Government Affairs Department	1600-18
14th Area Army Management Department	1600-19
14th Area Army Press Department	1600-20
14th Area Army Electrical Department	1600-22
14th Area Army General Administration Dept.	1600-23
14th Area Army Broadcasting Admin. Bureau	1600-24
	威 "i"

<u>14th Area Army</u> coninued	威 *i*	
4th Independent Tank Company	5308 (116)	
19th Independent Rapid Firing Gun Battalion	17654 (403)	
6th Medium Trench Mortar Battalion	12433 (550)	from 32A
7th Medium Trench Mortar Battalion	12434 (592)	
12th Field Medium Artillery Regiment	3770 (2,286)	
11th Independent Machinegun Battalion	17650 (334)	
12th Independent Machinegun Battalion	17651 (334)	
55th Field Machine Cannon Company	2180 (105)	
7th Specially Established Machine Cannon Unit	15400 (85)	
8th Specially Established Machine Cannon Unit	15401 (85)	
9th Specially Established Machine Cannon Unit	15402 (85)	
12th Specially Established Machine Cannon Unit	15405 (85)	
16th Specially Established Machine Cannon Unit	17637 (85)	
17th Specially Established Machine Cannon Unit	17638 (85)	
18th Specially Established Machine Cannon Unit	17639 (85)	
19th Specially Established Machine Cannon Unit	17640 (85)	
22nd Specially Established Machine Cannon Unit	17641 (85)	
23rd Specially Established Machine Cannon Unit	17642 (85)	
24th Specially Established Machine Cannon Unit	17643 (85)	
25th Specially Established Machine Cannon Unit	17644 (85)	
26th Specially Established Machine Cannon Unit	17645 (85)	
27th Specially Established Machine Cannon Unit	17646 (85)	
28th Specially Established Machine Cannon Unit	17647 (85)	
29th Specially Established Machine Cannon Unit	17648 (85)	
30th Specially Established Machine Cannon Unit	17649 (85)	
54th Specially Established Machine Cannon Unit	12542 (85)	
64th Specially Established Machine Cannon Unit	2194 (85)	
68th Specially Established Machine Cannon Unit	12458 (85)	
69th Specially Established Machine Cannon Unit	12459 (85)	
72nd Specially Established Machine Cannon Unit	12462 (85)	
65th Independent Engineer Battalion	6089 (790)	half to Comotes
2nd Signal Regiment	5103 (1,301)	5th Co. Okinawa
27th Signal Regiment	2527 (1,900)	
30th Signal Regiment	12616 (763)	
117th Independent Radio Platoon	12978 (57)	
118th Independent Radio Platoon	12979 (57)	
119th Independent Wire Company	12534 (310)	
120th Independent Wire Company	12535 (310)	
123rd Independent Wire Company	12970 (310)	
Army Training Unit (officer candidate trainees)	17669 (183)	anti-tank unit
14th Area Army L.o.C. Inspectorate General	15882 (533)	
85th Line of Communications Sector Command	9789 (203)	
85th Line of Communications Sector Transport Unit	9759	
88th Line of Communications Sector Command	17667 (203)	
88th Line of Communications Guard Unit	unknown (1,035)	

88th Line of Communications Duty Company	unknown (511)	
6th Field Transport Command	3626 (37)	
63rd Independent Motor Transport Battalion	1742 (808)	
210th Independent Motor Transport Company	5874 (183)	
260th Independent Motor Transport Company	6059 (183)	
319th Independent Motor Transport Company	17623 (134)	
320th Independent Motor Transport Company	17624 (134)	
321st Independent Motor Transport Company	17625 (134)	
325th Independent Motor Transport Company	17629 (134)	
327th Independent Motor Transport Company	17631 (132)	
330th Independent Motor Transport Company	17634 (134)	
6th Railway Transport Command	10315 (36)	
8th Railway Regiment	2144 (1,255)	
14th Area Army Military Police Unit	No # (2,560)	
12th Field Duty Unit Headquarters	10234 (17)	
124th Land Duty Company	1748 (511)	
37th Construction Duty Company	4829 (511)	
56th Construction Duty Company	5129 (511)	
58th Construction Duty Company	5131 (511)	
58th Field Road Construction Unit	17636 (298)	
30th Disease Prevention and Water Supply Unit	12368 (329)	
46th Specially Est. Construction Duty Company	10444 (61)	
16th Field Post Office Unit	4021 (251)	
12th Southern Army Hospital	10612 (1,099)	Manila
74th Line of Communications Hospital	4801 (380)	
129th Line of Communications Hospital	3889 (359)	
134th Line of Communications Hospital	4047 (359)	Bayombong
139th Line of Communications Hospital	9767 (421)	
16th Casualty Clearing Unit Headquarters	9723 (117)	
92nd Casualty Clearing Platoon	6087 (54)	
93rd Casualty Clearing Platoon	6088 (54)	
Southern Army Water Supply Dept. Manila Branch	9420 (295)	
14th Area Army Field Ordinance Depot	10680 / 1897 (680)	
Southern Army Manila Ordinance Repair Depot	10497	Manila
3rd Mobile Ordinance Repair Section	12366 (237)	
14th Area Army Motor Transport Depot	10681 / 1898 (1,372)	
14th Area Army Field Freight Depot	10682 / 1899 (1,686)	
2nd (Food) Cultivation Duty Unit	10682	

Kamotesu Detachment: (Camotes Islands)	威 *i*	
7th Independent Tank Company	17658 (116)	
21st Independent Trench Mortar Battalion	17656	1st & 2nd Coys
20th Independent Rapid Firing Gun Battalion	17655 (403)	
25th Independent Rapid Firing Gun Battalion	3327 (403)	
76th Field Anti-Aircraft Battalion	1970	1st & 2nd Coys
63rd Specially Established Machine Cannon Unit	2193 (85)	

14th Area Army, Kamotesu Detachment: continued	威 *i*	
65th Specially Established Machine Cannon Unit	2195 (85)	
66th Specially Established Machine Cannon Unit	2196 (85)	
67th Specially Established Machine Cannon Unit	2197 (85)	
70th Specially Established Machine Cannon Unit	12460 (85)	
71st Specially Established Machine Cannon Unit	12461 (85)	
65th Independent Engineer Battalion	6089 (894)	1/2 on Luzon
316th Independent Motor Transport Company	17620 (134)	
317th Independent Motor Transport Company	17621 (134)	
27th Signal Regiment, 1 section	2527	
138th Line of Communications Hospital	9766 (200*)	
21st Shipping Engineer Regiment	16717 (1,099)	
15th Debarkation Unit	16705	
98th Airfield Battalion	16698 (395)	
114th Airfield Battalion	16645 (395)	
32nd Airfield Company	9938 (300)	
54th Airfield Company	16654 (209)	

The Comotes Detachment (58th Independent Infantry Battalion minus 2 companies, 1 artillery company and 1 engineer platoon) was formed in Manila to suppress guerillas activities in the Comotes Islands. At night on Dec 11, 1944 both the Takahashi and Comotes Detachments arrived in Palompon. On the 18th the Comotes Detachment set sail to Comotes Island. *Taken from 'U.S. Intelligence Activities in the P.I.'

Manila Defense Force: See divisions and brigades p. 249

Southern Philippine Islands

35th Army 尚 *Shou*

35th Army Headquarters was activated on July 28, 1944, and shipped to Mindanao, the Philippines. It was placed under 14th Area Army control on Aug 4th and made responsible for the security of Leyte Island, the Visayas and Mindanao in the central and southern Philippines. Lt Gen Sosaku Suzuki was 35th Army commander from July 28, 1944 until Apr 19, 1945 and Lt Gen Gyōsaku Morozumi until deactivation. Its headquarters were on Cebu Is. from July 26th until Nov 2, 1944, Ormoc, Leyte until Dec 31, 1944 and Mindanao until it was deactivated on Sept 2, 1945.

Service History:

1944: On Aug 11th the 35th Army became operational under 14th Area Army control ○ Aug 12th Navy lookouts falsely reported U.S. troops on Samal Is. ○ On Aug 17th a planning conference was held on Cebu ○ Sept 10th, enroute to Surigao, Mindanao the 30th Div lost 16 artillery pieces in an air attack ○ On Oct 18th a typhoon swept Leyte grounding aircraft ○ Oct 19th, the 16th Div lookouts reported 10 transports in Leyte Bay ○ On the 20th US troops land near Tacloban and between Dulag and San Jose. The 35th Army had been preparing to fight a defensive battle but IGHQ wanted a decisive victory on Leyte ○ On Oct 25th Dulag Airfield fell ○ On Oct 26th Burauen airfield was lost after the 20th Inf Regt retreated to Guinarona ○ Oct 28th, key supply base Tabontabon was overrun ○ Oct. 29th, 14th Area Army staff visited 35th Army HQ on Cebu to plan ○ Oct 30th, the 35th Army's command post set up in Ormoc ○ On Nov 2nd the 35th Army HQ arrived in Ormoc ○ Nov 4th, battle of Limon, 1st Div offensive in the Managasnas area. The 41st Inf Regt, 30th Div fought in the mountains about 1¾ mile SW of Cabongaan ○ On Negros east coast near Pica Bay natives attack the garrison ○ On Nov 7th the 57th Inf Regt, 1st Div fought a battle south of Managasnas ○ Nov 8th the 26th Div arrived in Ormoc aboard three ships. The same day a typhoon and several days of heavy rain hit Leyte ○ By Nov 9th the 35th Army's headquarters knew Leyte was lost ○ Nov 11th the 26th Div came ashore but with no landing barges its munitions and supplies were still aboard when the ships left Ormoc. The 35th Army had about 48,000 troops ○ On Nov 14th the 57th Inf Regt began an attack on Managasnas as part of the 1st Div plan ○ Nov 15th the 57th Inf. Regt used Molotov cocktails against U.S. tanks ○ Nov. 20th, the 16th Div. remained on the hill west of Dagami and the 1st Div. progressed slowly near Managasnas ○ On Nov 21st four light cruisers arrived in Ormoc with 26th Div equipment, provisions and ammunition ○ On Nov 22nd about 300 aircraft attacked Ormoc sinking the ships with their cargo ○ The fresh but under equipped 26th Div was sent to Burauen ○ On Nov 26th the 1st Coy, Kaoru Air Raiding Unit attacked Burauen and Dulag airfields ○ Nov 29th and 30th, it was thought the air raiding unit was still active in the Dulag area ○ On Dec 1st the 35th Army HQ and 14th Area Army staff visited the Luni area. The troops endured continuous fighting and a lack of food. The 1st Div lost about 1,000 dead and 2,000 wounded ○ On Dec 5th the 5th Inf Regt, 8th Div landed in Palompon and the 16th Div left Dagami to recapture northern Burauen Airfield ○ On Dec 6th the 5th Inf Regt established contact with the 3rd Air Raiding Regt but they were widely scattered with few troops. The Koizumi Coy from the 13th Ind Inf Regt, 26th Div made it to the southern Burauen Airfield. US troops counterattacked in force. The 2nd Air Raiding Group landed on both airfields but failed to contact ground infiltration units. ○ On Dec 7th without reinforcements the Burauen airfield operation ended ○ 35th Army HQ remained in Lubi west of Burauen ○ On Dec 8th the Kamijo Btn, Imahori Detachment's point unit in the Ipil sugar factory, was shelled by artillery. Suffering severe losses it withdrew to northeast of Ormoc ○ Under Imahori's command the 4th Air Raiding Regt was sent to Valencia Airfield for the battle of Ormoc ○ On Dec 9th the Imahori Detachment occupied the 35th Army's Ormoc command post ○ The 68th Brigade landed in San Isidro but lost most of its artillery in an air attack ○ Dec 10th several enemy battalions landed in Ipil to attack Ormoc ○ Dec 11th, an intense mortar barrage fell on the front lines in Ormoc. Part of Ormoc fell to the enemy. The Takahashi Detachment (5th Inf Regt, 8th Div) landed in Palompon and was sent to the Ormoc area. After Burauen the 35th Army's commander escaped over mountains and through enemy controlled areas to Ormoc. 63 paras from the 4th Air Raiding Regt landed in Valencia raising the total engaged to 449 men ○ On Dec 15th the US landed troops between San Jose and Mangarin ○ Dec 16th, an attack from west of the highway came close to the 35th Army HQ. It was plain that Leyte was lost. The 35th Army HQ was attacked in Huaton, losing 10 men during the fighting it was forced to retreat to Libungao in the Kananga area ○ On Dec 19th the withdrawal to Matag-ob halted when US troops forced the HQ guard and 4th Air Raiding Regt into an engagement ○ The Takahashi Detachment supported the evacuation by engaging enemy in the Libungao area ○ On Dec 21st the 35th Army HQ withdrew to Kompisao and ordered the 1st, 16th, 26th and 102nd Div to withdraw to west of the Pagsangahan River ○ On Dec 23rd *Chi-go* operation began, its objective was to evacuate combat units from Leyte to other areas ○ The 68th Brigade on its way to Limon was withdrawn instead ○

1945: Early January, the 102nd Div HQ departed Leyte for the Visayas and the 1st Div had sent about 800 men from Leyte to Cebu in motorized barges ○ When *Chi-go* ended the 1st Field Artillery Regt commander and 2,000 troops remained on Leyte ○ At the end of January the US attacked the Takahashi Detachment and Kaneda Unit deployed SE of Kaniki Point. The Americans fought their way between the two units to just south of the 35th Army's command post ○ On Feb 1st enemy advanced to SE of Villaba, unknowingly threatening the 35th Army HQ ○ On Mar 8th the 35th Army HQ made plans to leave for Mindanao ○ On Mar 17th two boats were taken from a disabled large landing barge ○ On Mar 23rd the 35th Army commander left for Tabogon and landed the next morning ○ Mar 25th, the 35th Army HQ officially departed Leyte. In Cebu City Army staff held a conference with the 102nd and 1st Div just as the US invasion of Cebu began ○ On Mar 29th the invasion of Negros took place near Bacolod ○ April 2nd the invasion of Panay Is. took place near San Jose ○ April 8th the invasion of Jolo Is. The 55th I.M.B. defenders were crushed ○ On Apr 10th the 35th Army HQ, fifty officers aboard five small boats, set sail from Medellin, Cebu for Mindanao ○ On Apr 16th US troops invaded Mindanao ○ On Apr 17th the 35th Army commander, Lt. Gen. Sosaku Suzuki, died in a torpedo boat attack ○ On Apr 22nd Chief of Staff, Lt. Gen. Gyōsaku Morozumi, landed in Impaluto to find himself the new 35th Army commander ○ Apr. 26th US troops invade the Dumaguete area on southern Negros ○ Apr 27th American reach Santa Cruz on Mindanao and on May 3rd US 24th Div entered Davao City ○ On July 1st the United States declared the Southern Philippine campaign officially closed ○ On Sept 2nd the 35th Army acted on orders to demobilize but the news takes time to reach its isolated units ○

Major Units: See division / brigade page for order of battle

16th Division Kyoto 1905 垣 *Kaki* – Leyte Island	171
30th Division Pyongyang 1943 豹 *Hyou* – Mindanao	177-8
100th Division Nagoya 1944 拠 *Kyo* – Mindanao	195-6
102nd Division Kumamoto 1944 抜 *Nuku* – Cebu Island	196
54th Independent Mixed Brigade 1944 萩 *Hagi* – Mindanao	226
55th Independent Mixed Brigade 1944 菅 *Sugai* – Jolo Island	226
68th Brigade 1944 星 *Hoshi* – Leyte Island	235

Units under control of the 35th Army:	尚 *Shou*	
35th Army Headquarters	18200 (353)	
76th Field Anti-Aircraft Battalion	1970 (528)	
323rd Independent Motor Transport Company	17627 (134)	
324th Independent Motor Transport Company	17628 (134)	
328th Independent Motor Transport Company	17632 (132)	
329th Independent Motor Transport Company	17633 (134)	
23rd Specially Est Motor Transport Company	10455 (69)	
24th Specially Est Motor Transport Company	10456 (69)	
25th Specially Est Motor Transport Company	10457 (69)	attached 30th Div
13th Southern Army Hospital	10613 (641)	Cebu City

35th Army continued

14th Southern Army Hospital	10614 (736)	Davao City
47th Specially Est. Construction Duty Company	10445 (61)	
49th Specially Est. Construction Duty Company	10447 (61)	
22nd Field Duty Unit Headquarters	4042 (17)	
1st Signal Unit Headquarters, detached section	2171 (62)	
104th Independent Wire Company	12907 (310)	
105th Independent Wire Company	12908 (310)	
107th Independent Wire Company	12910 (310)	
98th Independent Radio Platoon	12916 (57)	
99th Independent Radio Platoon	12917 (57)	
109th Independent Radio Platoon	12390 (57)	
111th Independent Radio Platoon	12392 (57)	
112th Independent Radio Platoon	12393 (57)	
130th Independent Radio Platoon	12991 (57)	

Mountains East of Manila, Philippines

41st Army 杉 *Sugi*

The Shimbu Army Group was renamed the 41st Army on March 6, 1945, two months after the US invasion of Leyte had begun. More or less under 14th Area Army control from April 20th it was responsible for the mountainous area east of Manila. Its commander was Lt Gen Shizuo Yokoyama from Mar 19th until the war ended.

Service History:

1944: On Dec 27th the Shimbu Army Group was organized around the 8th and 105th Div and Manila Defense Force for the defense of southern Luzon ○

1945: In Jan half the 105th Div was sent to northern Luzon. ○ On Jan 9th U.S. troops began landing on Luzon near San Fabian and Lingayan ○ Jan 31st, the battle of Batangas began SW of Manila with the Fuji Group and Nosune Detach fighting in the area. Contact was lost right after the Americans arrived ○ Feb 3rd, the Shimbu Group continued preparing until the Americans had entered Manila ○ On Feb 14th at night Shimbu Group attacked the invaders. The Manila Defense Unit (Kobayashi Group) redeployed 3 inf battalions from east of San Mateo and Malikina. The Kawashima Group (82nd Inf Bgde, 105th Div) advanced 2 infantry battalions to the Rimedoios, Novaliches area ○ The Shimbu Group fought near Angat in an attempt to block enemy from moving south while the Noguchi Brigade launched infiltration attacks from south of Malinina ○ Kobayashi attacked Queson Airfield and Kawashima assaulted Kalogan Airfield, both units returned to their lines between Feb 21st and 23rd ○ On Feb 16th the Americans invaded Corregidor, the 4,500-man garrison fought until mid-March ○ On Feb 28th, suffering 16,000 casualties the 14th Area Army lost Manila ○ In early March Noguchi, Kobayashi and Kawashima coordinated a failed counterattack. It took the rest of March to establish new front lines. Each unit had its own food and sufficient ammunition but as the left flank withdrew irreplaceable equipment became lost ○ On Apr 1st US and Filipino troops attacked the 35th Air Sector Command's fortified mountain positions on the Bicol Peninsula. Fighting continued until the war ended ○ Apr 4th, the 9th Air Intelligence Unit was attacked and overrun on the Siniloan Plains, making it hard to move reinforcements around. After that US forces in the area became less aggressive ○ On Apr 20th the reorganized Shimbu Group became the 41st Army. Centered around the 8th Div and Manila Defense Force it included the Kawashima and Kobayashi Detachments on Lake Laguna's north shore, Koto and Noguchi Detachments the east shore and Fujishige Detachment on the south shore ○ In early May a noticeable reduction in US strength on the front lines indicated the 41st Army may have been bypassed ○ On May 17th the Ipo garrison was attacked on both flanks and forced to retreat ○ On May 20th US troops attack the Noguchi and Kobayashi Detachments. Mt. Purro fell and units in the Wawa Dam area became isolated ○ On May 27th the Noguchi and Kobayashi Detachments withdrew and consolidated their front lines. In May about 70% of casualties were from illness ○

<u>Major Units</u>: See division / brigade page for order of battle

8th Division Hirosaki 1898 杉 *Sugi* – East of Manila	167-8
105th Division Hiroshima 1944 勤 *Kin* – East of Manila	198
Manila Defense Force (Kobayashi Butai) 1944 尚武 *Shobu* – Manila	249

<u>Units under 41st Army control</u>:	杉 *Sugi*	
41st Army Headquarters	4732 (252)	also 8th Div. HQ
26th Independent Mixed Regiment	12936 (2,230)	Bicol
37th Independent Rapid Firing Gun Company	17668 (145)	
21st Independent Mortar Battalion	17656 (648)	
4th Medium Trench Mortar Battalion	10050 (592)	
5th Medium Trench Mortar Battalion	18808 (550)	from 32A
Manila Anti Aircraft Artillery Headquarters	10619 / 16019 (161)	
78th Field Anti-Aircraft Battalion	12519 (528)	
51st Field Machine Cannon Company	12416 (105)	
52nd Field Machine Cannon Company	12520 (105)	
10th Specially Established Machine Cannon Unit	15403 (85)	
101st Independent Radio Platoon	12919 (57)	
110th Independent Radio Platoon	12391 (57)	
123rd Independent Radio Platoon	12984 (57)	
126th Independent Radio Platoon	12987 (57)	
22nd Specially Est. Motor Transport Company	10454 (69)	
326th Specially Est. Motor Transport Company	17630 (132)	
111th Land Duty Company	9748 (511)	
63rd Line of Communications Hospital	7862 (359)	Manila
78th Line of Communications Hospital	4607 (359)	
86th Line of Communications Hospital	3762 (359)	
1st Field Replacement Unit Headquarters	4823 (88)	Manila
12th Air Signals Regiment	11807 (226)	
4th Air Special Signal Unit	12904 (259)	
5th Air Special Signal Unit	12905 (196)	
10th Air Intelligence Regiment	18916 (2,282)	

9th Air Intelligence Unit	18485 (809)
61st Surface to Air Radio Unit	10617 (196)
35th Air Sector Command	18489 (44)
147th Airfield Battalion	18491 (406)
148th Airfield Battalion	18492 (406)
149th Airfield Battalion	18493 (406)
47th Airfield Company	15374 (226)
22nd Field Airfield Construction Unit	2403 (702)
136th Field Airfield Construction Unit	18400 (175)
137th Field Airfield Construction Unit	18401 (175)
18th Shipping Air Depot	9306 (34)
144th Specially Established Sea Duty Company	19794 (61)
145th Specially Established Sea Duty Company	19795 (61)
24th Shipping Engineer Regiment	16742 (1,099)
6th Sea Raiding Squadron	16782 (110)
7th Sea Raiding Squadron	16783 (110)
8th Sea Raiding Squadron	16784 (110)
9th Sea Raiding Squadron	16785 (110)
10th Sea Raiding Squadron	16786 (110)
11th Sea Raiding Squadron	19750 (109)
13th Sea Raiding Squadron	19752 (107)
14th Sea Raiding Squadron	19753 (107)
15th Sea Raiding Squadron	19754 (107)
16th Sea Raiding Squadron	19755 (107)
17th Sea Raiding Squadron	19756 (107)
18th Sea Raiding Squadron	19757 (107)
19th Sea Raiding Squadron	19758 (107)
1st Sea Raiding Base Unit Headquarters	16737 (42)
2nd Sea Raiding Base Unit Headquarters	19770 (42)
3rd Sea Raiding Base Unit Headquarters	19771 (42)
8th Sea Raiding Base Battalion	16795 (900)
9th Sea Raiding Base Battalion	16796 (900)
10th Sea Raiding Base Battalion	16797 (900)
13th Sea Raiding Base Battalion	14210 (900)

Clark Field, Luzon, the Philippines

Kembu Army Group 尚武 *Shobu*

In October 1944 the 14th Area Army created the Kembu Army Group around the 1st Air Raiding Group HQ, which began preparations to leave Japan on Oct 22nd. About half its strength was lost in attacks during the voyage. On Dec 27th the headquarters set sail and arrived at Clark Field on Jan 8, 1945. The Raiding Group commander, Maj Gen Rikichi Tsukada was given control of the Kembu Army Group. It was deactivated September 4, 1945.

Service History:
1944: In Oct the 14th Area Army commander decided three key areas on Luzon would be held by three independent army groups. They would each inflict as much damage as possible on the Americans. Kembu Group was responsible for Clark Field and the surrounding area. There were about 30,000 men serving in the various army and navy land, sea and air units on Clark Field ○ In Oct Maj. Gen. Yamaguchi was appointed commander of Kembu Army Group and 4th Air Army Assist Chief of Staff Tsuchio leader of the Clark Field Air Army Detached Section ○
1945: Jan 6th U.S. planes bombed Calumpit Bridge making it impossible for the 2nd Tank Div to reach its Clark Field staging area. The Tank Div commander was originally chosen to be Kembu Army Group commander but circumstances kept him with his unit ○ On Jan 6th the 1st Air Raiding Group commander Maj. Gen. Tsukada was appointed to lead Kembu Group. Elements of the air raiding group had been on Clark Field since late Dec '44 ○ On Jan 25th US units attacked a plateau near Bambang on the left wing of the Kembu Group ○ On Jan 29th the Kembu Group HQ unit was attacked. After dark it withdrew to Mt. Koshinzan ○ Jan 30th, the entire Army Group retreated to 2nd line defensive positions ○ On Feb 9th the Takaya Detachment on Matsuyama Plateau received orders to retreat ○ On Feb 10th the 15th battle sector (defensive sectors created by the Navy) was hit by an attack, which was repulsed ○ On Feb 15th Americans attacked Kembu Group's left flank in the 14th battle sector and occupied Mt. Hakozaki ○ Feb 22nd, the 13th battle sector became precarious, steps were taken to prevent collapse ○ On Mar 1st Kembu Group HQ withdrew further inland ○ When the US captured the 14th battle sector, the 13th battle sector also began to crumble so it was reinforced ○ On Mar 7th Kembu Group HQ moved to Okuyama ○ On Mar 8th US troops began an assault on Mt. Koshinzan ○ Mar 11th Kembu Group HQ moved to the Kaji Plateau. Mt. Koshinzan fell isolating Kembu Group's left wing including the Takayama Detachment ○ On Mar 15th Kembu Group HQ moved to Mt. Shinzan ○ On Mar 17th U.S. troops arrived at the mountain's base north of Mt. Shinzan ○ By Mar 21st the 13th, 14th and 15th battle sectors were lost and the Takayama Detachment destroyed. Kembu Group counterattacks kept the the enemy occupied while food, munitions and medical equipment were being moved further to the rear ○ On Mar. 27th the Hoshino Battalion, 230 men remaining, retreated from Hospital Plateau ○ Mar. 28th, Kembu Group HQ withdrew from Mt. Shinzan to the foot of Mt. Pinatubo ○ Apr 6th, the Kembu Group continued to withdraw while fighting a rear guard action in the Mt. Pinatubo area ○ On Apr 16th communications with the 14th Area Army were severed ○ Apr 18th, east of Mt. Pinatubo the 1st Air Raiding Group Signal Unit was out flanked and attacked in the rear ○ On Apr 24th the retreat of the rear guard from Miharashidai Pass ended three consecutive months of fighting over Clark Field. Kembu Group HQ escaped north to the 1600 meter plateau. Short of weapons, ammo, food and medicine Kembu divided itself into 6 groups assigned to different areas: 1) line of communications units went to the mountains west of Tarlac 2) Cho Work Unit to the west of Mt. Pinatubo 3) Eguchi Detachment to mountains south of the Bamban River and west of Polloc 4) Air Depot Yamamoto Branch southwest of Mt. Pinatubo 5) Composite Signal Unit was divided between north of Iba and the mountains west of Polloc 6) Takaya Detachment ended its rear guard action and settled in an area west of Mt. Pinatubo with the Kembu Group HQ ○ May and June, men survived on sweet potatoes, by July the crops were exhausted. During that period planes flew overhead

dropping surrender leaflets ○ On Sept 1st the Kembu Group sent a messenger to Clark Field asking that 14th Area Army HQ be contacted ○ On Sept 4th the 14th Area Army sent orders for the Kembu Army Group to disarm ○

Major Units: See division / brigade page for order of battle

1st Air Raiding Group 鸞 *Ran* – Clark Field 240-1

2nd Tank Division, Manchuria 1942 撃 "Geki", 1st Btn 2nd Mech. Inf. Regt only 206

Units under Kembu Army Group control	尚武 *Shobu*	
Kembu Army Group HQ (1st Air Raid Grp HQ)	19038 (368)	
Manila Air Depot 2nd Branch	15311	
86th Line of Communications Headquarters	unknown	
14th Area Army Ordinance Depot Branch	10680	
14th Area Army Freight Depot Branch	10682	
14th Area Army Motor Transport Depot Branch	10681	
322nd Independent Motor Transport Company	17626 (134)	
14th Army Military Police Unit; Tarlac Detachment	No #	
84th Field Anti-Aircraft Battalion	12525 (521)	
137th Line of Communications Hospital	7176 (359)	
Attached:		
4th Air Division Ground Units:	翼 *Tsubasa*	
10th Air Sector Command	11620 (26)	
31st Airfield Battalion	10656 (372)	
99th Airfield Battalion	8357 (372)	
132nd Airfield Battalion	18451 (372)	
137th Airfield Battalion	18456 (372)	Hoshino Unit
150th Airfield Battalion	18494 (372)	
151st Airfield Battalion	9925 (372)	
152nd Airfield Battalion	9926 (372)	
8th Airfield Company	10657 (207)	
52nd Airfield Company	16652 (226)	
9th Air Intelligence Regiment	18485	
9th Wireless Radio Unit	18957 (212)	
25th Wireless Radio Unit	16625 (196)	
2nd Air Navigation Regiment	16612 (595)	
24th Field Airfield Construction Unit	2405 (702)	Clark Field
138th Field Airfield Construction Unit	18402 (175)	Clark Field
17th Air Signal Unit, one detached platoon	18915	
12th Air Signal Regiment, one detached platoon	11807	
10th Air Intelligence Regiment, 4th Company	18916	
96th Independent Wire Company	3177 (310)	
2nd Air Signal Headquarters, Detached Platoon	2570	
22nd Air Signal Unit	15337 (673)	
9th Radio Unit	18957 (212)	
123rd Ind Wire Company, Detached Platoon	12970	
14th Field Air Repair Depot, 8th Ind. Maint. Unit	9304 (113)	

South Pacific Region and the Philippines

4th Air Army 真 *Shin*

The 4th Air Army was activated on July 14, 1943, and placed under 8th Area Army control in Rabaul on July 28th. Subordinates included the 6th and 7th Air Divisions supporting the Solomons and New Guinea. The 4th Air Army was placed under 2nd Area Army control on Mar 14, 1944 and its headquarters relocated from Wewak to Hollandia. On April 15th it was moved again to Manodo, the Dutch East Indies to be closer to 2nd Area Army headquarters. By May 1944 Allied air power had rendered the 4th Air Army ineffective. In June 4th Air Army HQ were placed under Southern Expeditionary Army control and shipped along with the remnants of its most valuable assets to Clark Airfield in the Philippines to rebuild. The new order of battle included the 2nd Air Division, which was mainly combat aircraft and the 4th Air Division, which provided ground crew and service personnel. On Jan 1, 1945 the 4th Air Army was placed under 14th Area Army control. Destroyed again by Allied air superiority, on Jan 15th the 4th Air Army's Headquarters was relieved of responsibility for the Philippines and evacuated to Taiwan, where it was deactivated on Feb 17th. The commander of the 4th Air Army was Lt Gen Kumaichi Teramoto from July 28, 1943 until Aug 30, 1944 and Lt Gen Kyōji Tominaga until Feb 13, 1945.

Service History:

1942: On Nov 27th the newly activated 6th Air Division was assigned to the 8th Area Army. In December 6th Air Div headquarters arrived in Rabaul from Japan ○

1943: End of May, due to losses the 6th Air Division had become unfit for anything but small surprise attacks, a lack of repair facilities and the Type 3 (Ki-61 Hein) fighter's poor performance ○ In June the 7th Air Division from the Dutch East Indies joined the 8th Area Army ○ On July 28th the 4th Air Army HQ became active in Rabaul with the 6th and 7th Air Divisions as its subordinate units ○ On Aug 16th and 17th US air raids on Wewak and But destroyed 60 to 70 planes ○ In mid-Aug *Ten-go*, the destruction of enemy airbases in the Bena Bena area, was cancelled ○ By Sept 10th the entire 4th Air Army had 97 planes left, the 6th Air Division had 63 and the 7th Air Division had 34 ○ On Sept 15th another air raid on Wewak resulted in the loss of a further 30 to 40 planes, replacing them quickly became impossible ○ In early Nov US carrier planes raided Rabaul and small groups of enemy fighters launched surprise attacks on the air bases ○ From Nov 20th to 30th the 7th Air Div patrolled the area under 2nd Area Army control north of Australia ○ On Dec 15th the U.S. invaded Cape Merkus ○ Dec 26th, U.S. troops landed on Tuluvu ○ Dec 27th, America had control over the air and sea except around Rabaul and Wewak ○

1944: In early Jan the 8th Area Army requested reinforcements for 4th Air Army. I.G.HQ responded in late Jan by attaching the 8th Air Brigade to the 2nd Area Army. It reasoned it was it was easier to supply and preserve the brigade and provide direct support from outside 8th Area Army jurisdiction as the Allies controlled the air and sea around New Guinea ○ On Feb 12th the Madang operation began in support of 18th Area Army ground units and prevention of US air and sea interference ○ On Feb 29th the US invaded the Admiralties, bad weather prevented aircraft from flying ○ In mid February Naval air units left Rabaul for Truk giving America complete air superiority. The Dampier Straits fell and 8th Area Army HQ in Rabaul lost contact with its subordinate units on New Guinea ○ On Mar 25th the 4th Air Army was placed under 2nd Area Army control and its headquarters in Wewak relocated to Hollandia ○ Until Mar 30th when it lost about 70 planes during an air raid on Hollandia the 6th Air Division was the main air unit in New Guinea ○ On Apr 11th Maj. Gen. Inada became acting commander of the 6th Air Division ○ On Apr 15th the 4th Air Army HQ redeployed to Manodo in the Celebes ○ On Apr 22nd US troops landed in Humboldt Bay ○ Apr 23rd, as Hollandia was being overrun 6th Air Div personnel assembled on the west side of Lake Sentani. Southwest of the airfield 7,220 men gathered on the Genjem Plains ○ By Apr 26th the first of eleven echelons left Genjem for Sarmi ○ Apr 30th, assembly was completed and scouts sent into the jungle. The 6th Air Div commander was determined to save his pilots and key officers ○ On May 1st other echelons began to leave ○ By May 7th Hollandia had been vacated ○ May 31st, two-thirds had arrived at Tor River east of Sarmi where the 36th Div. was deployed. The infantry and other ground troops were attached to the 36th Division. About 6oo pilots, ground crew and HQ personnel informally reorganized in Sarmi ○ On June 1st the 4th Air Army HQ was sent to the Philippines with the other key personnel. They sailed from Sarmi to Rabaul then Manila to rebuild for the anticipated invasion ○ On July 25th the 6th Air Div was deactivated. About 100 men including 10 pilots managed to get to the Philippines but the majority lacked transport ○ In July IGHQ transferred 3rd Air Army combat units to the 4th Air Army in secret, reasoning if the Philippines were lost Japan's presence in Southeast Asia was doomed ○ In Aug the 2nd and 7th Air Div were attached to the 2nd Area Army ○ Sept 12th, the 2nd Air Div HQ was ordered to Bacolod, Cebu from Menado on unfounded rumors the US had landed in Davao ○ On Sept 15th the US invaded Morotai and Peleliu ○ On Sept 17th US troops landed on Suluan Island in the Philippines ○ On Oct 18th the 4th Air Army began *Sho-go* in spite of bad weather and just 50 to 70 serviceable planes. The 2nd Air Div. HQ and the 30th Fighter Group set up in Bacolod to be within range of the U.S. fleet off Leyte ○ On Oct 23rd the 4th Air Army Command Post arrived in Bacolod ○ At the end of Oct the air war for the Philippines peaked. There were 8 air bases around Bacolod. Just 140 of 317 new Type 4 (Ki-84 Frank) fighters were serviceable ○ On Nov 7th the 4th Air Army Command Post returned to Manila ○ On Nov 8th with 4th Air Army combat strength destroyed *Sho-go* ended ○ Nov 20th, with its aircraft gone the 4th Air Army reorganized. The 30th Fighter Group HQ became redundant and was assigned new duties ○ Bad weather made it hard to attack Leyte from Bacolod but US planes frequently attacked Bacolod from Morotai ○ Nov 24th the Air Army commander arrived in Lipa with new orders and to salute the Kaoru Air Raiding Unit, which launched an attack on the Burauen and Dulag airfields on Nov 26th ○ On Dec 25th the Southern Army ordered the 4th Air Army to return air units borrowed from the 3rd Air Army ○

1945: On Jan 1st the 4th Air Army was placed under 14th Area Army control, excluding its air units outside the Philippines ○ In Jan the 4th Air Div was ordered to destroy all airbases in the Manila area and join the Shimbu Army Group when US troops were close ○ On Jan 12th the 4th Air Army attacked US ships in the Lingayan Gulf, the 30th Fighter Group's last plane was destroyed during this raid ○ The 4th Air Div still had 4 recon planes. These were all that remained ○ On Feb 4th a plan was released to send 130 HQ staff, pilots and most skilled maintenance crews from the Philippines to Formosa by air, in addition 470 more were sent by ship ○ On Feb 11th about 80 planes and 120 men arrived in Taiwan from the Philippines ○ On Feb 13th I.G.HQ was advised the 4th Air Army was so reduced it could no longer perform its duties. I.G.HQ ordered the 4th Air Army to deactivate and transfer headquarters elements to Heito, Taiwan ○ Feb 17th the 4th Air Div ground crew and service units came under 14th Area Army control and the 2nd and 7th Air Div left to join the 3rd Air Army ○

Units under 4th Air Army control: Manila	眞 *Shin*	
4th Air Army Headquarters	15300 (345)	Manila
4th Air Army Headquarters Signal Section	15300 (79)	Manila
2nd Air Division Headquarters	鷲 9109	Bacalod
4th Air Division Headquarters	翼 11601	
5th Air Brigade Headquarters	11611	
13th Air Brigade Headquarters	8303	
30th Air Brigade Headquarters	5521	
6th Air Sector Command	翼 9195 (26)	
10th Air Sector Command	11620 (26)	Clark Field
11th Air Sector Command	10653 (109)	Luzon
13th Air Sector Command	9113 (26)	
31st Air Sector Command	10616 (42)	
33rd Air Sector Command	18487 (44)	
34th Air Sector Command	18488 (44)	
36th Air Sector Command	18490 (44)	
2nd Air Signal Headquarters	2570	
• 26th Air Regiment	8399	
• 30th Air Regiment (Type 1 fighter)	9198	
• 31st Air Regiment (light bomber)	9623	
• 33rd Air Regiment (fighter)	9144	
• 34th Air Regiment	11051	
• 38th Air Regiment (recon planes)	19342	
• 63rd Air Regiment	15378	
• 75th Air Regiment (light bomber)	2379 (295)	
• 83rd Air Regiment (recon/direct support)	11070	
• 95th Air Regiment	9133	
• 20th Independent Air Squadron	15382	
• 31st Independent Air Squadron	18902	
• 52nd Independent Air Squadron	10655 (63)	
33rd Secondary Air Training Unit	15356	
43rd Secondary Air Training Unit	10618	
8th Airfield Battalion	9168 (372)	
12th Airfield Battalion	9112 (372)	
14th Airfield Battalion	9114 (372)	
26th Airfield Battalion	9106 (372)	
31st Airfield Battalion	10656 (372)	Clark Field
32nd Airfield Battalion	9134 (372)	
33rd Airfield Battalion	9139 (372)	
37th Airfield Battalion	9110 (372)	
86th Airfield Battalion	8386 (372)	
99th Airfield Battalion	8357 (372)	Clark Field

102nd Airfield Battalion	16602 (458)	
103rd Airfield Battalion	16603 (458)	
123rd Airfield Battalion	18444 (372)	
124th Airfield Battalion	18445 (372)	
125th Airfield Battalion	18446 (372)	
126th Airfield Battalion	18447 (372)	
127th Airfield Battalion	18448 (372)	
134th Airfield Battalion	18453 (372)	
135th Airfield Battalion	18454 (372)	
136th Airfield Battalion	18455 (372)	
150th Airfield Battalion	18494 (372)	Clark Field
151st Airfield Battalion	9925 (372)	Clark Field
152nd Airfield Battalion	9926 (372)	Clark Field
153rd Airfield Battalion	9927 (372)	
154th Airfield Battalion	9928 (372)	
155th Airfield Battalion	9929 (372)	
8th Airfield Company	10657 (207)	Clark Field
13th Airfield Company	10658 (300)	
48th Airfield Company	15375 (226)	Negros Is.
49th Airfield Company	15376 (226)	Negros Is.
50th Airfield Company	15380 (226)	
51st Airfield Company	16651 (226)	
52nd Airfield Company	16652 (226)	Clark Field
53rd Airfield Company	16653 (226)	
24th Field Airfield Construction Unit	2405 (702)	Clark Field
125th Field Airfield Construction Unit	15389 (175)	Cagayan de Oro
126th Field Airfield Construction Unit	15390 (175)	Mindanao
127th Field Airfield Construction Unit	15391 (175)	Davao
134th Field Airfield Construction Unit	15398 (175)	Santo Domingo
135th Field Airfield Construction Unit	15399 (175)	Echague, Luzon
139th Field Airfield Construction Unit	18403 (175)	Manila, Luzon
140th Field Airfield Construction Unit	18404 (175)	Echague, Luzon
154th Field Airfield Construction Unit	18418 (175)	
11th Air Sector Command	10653 (109)	Luzon
6th Specially Est. Field Airfield Construction Unit	1600-4 (65)	Kiangan, Luzon
7th Specially Est. Field Airfield Construction Unit	1600-4 (65)	Anayan, Luzon
11th Specially Est. Field Airfield Construction Unit	15319 (65)	Terumonte
13th Specially Est. Field Airfield Construction Unit	2401 (65)	Santo Toribio
14th Specially Est. Field Airfield Construction Unit	1600-4 (65)	Bagabag, Luzon
5th Field Airfield Construction Headquarters	2401 (28)	Bacolod, Visayas
4th Specially Est. Field Airfield Construction Unit	2401 (65)	Iloilo, Visayas
5th Specially Est. Field Airfield Construction Unit	2401 (65)	Negros, Visayas
9th Specially Est. Field Airfield Construction Unit	2401 (65)	Negros, Visayas
10th Specially Est. Field Airfield Construction Unit	2401 (65)	Negros, Visayas
12th Specially Est. Field Airfield Construction Unit	2401 (65)	San Jose, Visayas

4th Air Army continued	眞 *Shin*	
3rd Field Airfield Construction Headquarters	15319 (35)	Mindanao
1st Specially Est. Field Airfield Construction Unit	2401 (65)	Davao, Mindanao
2nd Specially Est. Field Airfield Construction Unit	15319 (65)	Tacloban City
3rd Specially Est. Field Airfield Construction Unit	15319 (65)	Cagayan de Oro
8th Specially Est. Field Airfield Construction Unit	15319 (65)	Maragusan
15th Specially Est. Field Airfield Construction Unit	1600-4 (65)	Cebu Is., Visayas
56th Construction Duty Company	5629 (511)	
2nd Air Signal Headquarters	2570 (97)	
2nd Air Navigation Unit	2572 (595)	
22nd Field Meteorological Unit	10650 (732)	
6th Air Signal Regiment	9942 (1,771)	Bacolod, Silay
12th Air Signal Regiment	11807	1 platoon Kembu
17th Air Signal Unit	18915 (499)	1 pltn Kembu
22nd Air Signal Unit	15337 (673)	Clark Field
5th Wireless Radio Unit	18953 (212)	
23rd Wireless Radio Unit	16623 (196)	
24th Wireless Radio Unit	16624 (196)	
Manila Army Air Depot	風15311 (8,689)	
7th Field Air Repair Depot, 1st Ind *Maint Unit	8316 (186)	
10th Field Air Repair Depot, 1st Ind Maint Unit	8356 (113)	
10th Field Air Repair Depot, 2nd Ind Maint Unit	8356 (113)	San Carlos
11th Field Air Repair Depot, 1st Ind Maint Unit	8367 (113)	Palawan Island
11th Field Air Repair Depot, 2nd Ind Maint Unit	8367 (113)	Bambang, Luzon
12th Field Air Repair Depot, 1st Ind Maint Unit	8372 (113)	Clark Field
12th Field Air Repair Depot, 2nd Ind Maint Unit	8372 (113)	Tuguegarao
14th Field Air Repair Depot, 8th Ind Maint Unit	9304 (113)	Clark Field
16th Field Air Repair Depot, 1st Ind Maint Unit	9323 (113)	
19th Field Air Repair Depot, 1st Ind Maint Unit	9324 (113)	Mindanao
19th Field Air Repair Depot, 2nd Ind Maint Unit	9324 (113)	S. Jose del Monte
19th Field Air Repair Depot, 3rd Ind Maint Unit	9324 (113)	Negros
297th Independent Motor Transport Company	8858 (189)	
122nd Independent Radio Platoon	12983 (57)	
124th Independent Radio Platoon	12985 (57)	
125th Independent Radio Platoon	12986 (57)	
127th Independent Radio Platoon	12988 (57)	
128th Independent Radio Platoon	12989 (57)	
129th Independent Radio Platoon	12990 (57)	

*Maint = Maintenance

14th Area Army Shipping Units: 暁 *Akatsuki*

Service History:

1945: In late June the 63rd Anchorage Headquarters, commanding units in the Batulinao area, fought an American Filipino army unit to the south of Gonzaga. Nothing further was heard from them after that became known ○

3rd Shipping Transport HQ, Manila Branch	2944	Manila
61st Anchorage Headquarters	16724 (81)	
63rd Anchorage Headquarters	16746 (81)	
2nd Shipping Artillery Regiment	2954 (8,254)	
Shipping Signal Regiment, 1 Section	2955	
5th Field Shipping Depot	19806	
19th Shipping Engineer Regiment	16703 (1,099)	
25th Shipping Engineer Regiment	16743 (1,099)	
28th Shipping Engineer Regiment, 1 Section	16757	
32nd Shipping Engineer Regiment, 1 Section	19774	
1st Field Shipping Engineer Replacement Unit	6142	
144th Specially Est. Sea Duty Company	19794 (61+)*	
145th Specially Est. Sea Duty Company	19795 (61+)	
146th Specially Est. Sea Duty Company	19796 (61+)	
147th Specially Est. Sea Duty Company	19797 (61+)	
148th Specially Est. Sea Duty Company	19798 (61+)	
149th Specially Est. Sea Duty Company	19799 (61+)	
150th Specially Est. Sea Duty Company	19800 (61+)	
151st Specially Est. Sea Duty Company	19801 (61+)	
8th Sea Transport Battalion	16747	
9th Sea Transport Battalion	16748	
10th Sea Transport Battalion	16749	
1st Mobile Transport Company	16725 (87)**	
4th Mobile Transport Company	16748 (87)	
8th Mobile Transport Company	16732 (87)	
9th Mobile Transport Company	16733 (87)	
15th Mobile Transport Company	16739 (87)	
17th Mobile Transport Company	16763 (87)	
Underwater Transport Dispatch Unit	2944	
1st High Speed Transport Battalion, 1 Section	16707	
12th Sea Raiding Squadron	19751 (110)	
1st Sea Raiding Base Unit Headquarters	16787 (42)	
5th Sea Raiding Base Battalion	16794 (900)	
2nd Sea Raiding Base Unit Headquarters	19770 (42)	41st Army
6th Sea Raiding Base Battalion	19793 (900)	
14th Sea Raiding Base Battalion	3328 (900)	
15th Sea Raiding Base Battalion	3329 (900)	
16th Sea Raiding Base Battalion	3330 (900)	
3rd Sea Raiding Base Unit Headquarters	19771 (42)	
11th Sea Raiding Base Battalion	14208 (900)	
12th Sea Raiding Base Battalion	14209 (900)	

14th Area Army Shipping Units continued	暁 *Akatsuki*
17th Sea Raiding Base Battalion	2894 (900)
18th Sea Raiding Base Battalion	6680 (900)
19th Sea Raiding Base Battalion	7259 (900)
20th Sea Raiding Base Battalion	7260 (900)

* A 'Specially Established Sea Duty Company' also had + 675 local men.

**A 'Mobile Transport Company' = crew for one SS assault landing transport ship.

Ki-49 Type 100 Heavy Bomber "Helen" ground crew doing engine check (author)

China

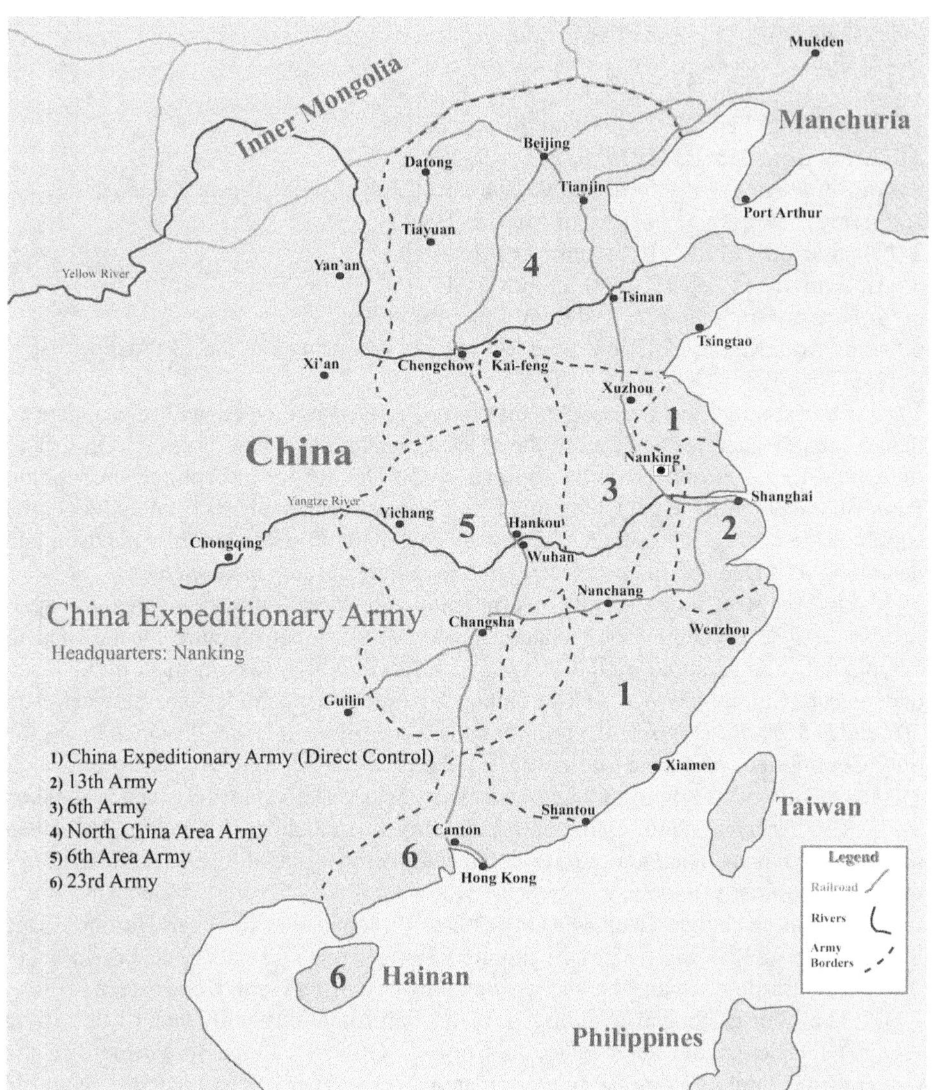

China Expeditionary Army 栄 *Sakae*

The China Expeditionary Army was activated Sept 23, 1939. Headquarters in Nanking it became operational on Oct 1st under IGHQ control. Created to unify the previously separate army commands in northern, central and south China. General Jūzō Nishio was appointed commander from Sept 22nd until Mar 1, 1941, General Shunroku Hata

until Nov 23, 1944 and General Yasuji Okamura until the China Expeditionary Army was deactivated in Hankow on September 2, 1945
Subordinate armies / duty dates:
North China Area Army from Sept 23, 1939, until the war ended
11th Army from Sept 23, 1939, until Aug 26, 1944
13th Army from Sept 23, 1939, until the war ended
21st Army from Sept 23, 1939, until Feb 9, 1940
South China Area Army from Feb 9, 1940, until July 5, 1941 (became 23rd Army)
23rd Army from July 5, 1941, until Aug 26, 1944
34th Army from July 17, 1944, until Aug 26, 1944
5th Air Army from Feb 15, 1944, until May 15, 1945
6th Area Army from Aug 26, 1944, until the war ended
6th Army from Mar 6, 1945, until the war ended (subordinate to the 13th Army)
Service History:
1939: On Sept 23rd the China Expeditionary Army was created with a mandate to defeat Japan's enemies and secure the skies, cities and occupied areas. ○ On Oct 1st the China Exp. Army became operational ○ On Dec 4th Japan captured the Kunlun Pass had the potential to cut Chunking, China's wartime capital, off from its Indochina supply route ○ Dec 18th, a large Chinese force isolated the Kunlun Pass garrison and destroyed it ○ Dec 30th, plans to retake the Kunlun Pass are abandoned ○
1940: On Mar 30th China Central Government under Wang Chingwei created by Japan in Nanching ○ On June 12th Yichang, located at a critical juncture on the road to Chongking, was captured by the 11th Army. Located at the western-most point Japan occupied in China in WW2 ○ The battle of 100 regiments took place between Aug 20th and Dec 5th. Fought over the rail lines and a coal mine in Hebei Province it was the only Communists offensive of the war ○
1941: On July 5th the South China Area Army was deactivated. Its place was taken by the 23rd Army in south China and 25th Army in Indochina ○ On July 24th Japan and Vichy France signed a mutual assistance agreement that allowed Japanese troops to occupy southern Indochina ○ Sept 17th to Oct 7th, the 1st battle of Changsha was a failed attempt to capture Changsha City ○ Dec 7th, Japan attacked Pearl Harbor ○ Dec 8th to 25th the 23rd Army's 38th Div captured Hong Kong ○ Dec 27th to Jan 15th, 11th Army's 2nd Battle of Changsha was a diversion supporting Hong Kong attack ○
1942: The Chinese began avoiding head on confrontations with Japan after Hong Kong, which created a short peace in China ○ On Jan 19th the Department of the Governor General of Hong Kong was created ○ From Apr 25th to Jul 1st the Doolittle Raid frightened Tokyo into planning the Chekiang-Kiangsi operation. IGHQ ordered the 13th Army to destroy all airbases within range of Japan ○ On July 28th IGHQ directed the China Exp. Army to leave a garrison in Chinhua to exploit the fluorite, copper and tin mined there ○ Jul 30th, repairs to the railroad had been completed ○ Aug 3rd, Chekiang/Kiangsi had been secured ○ By mid Aug the destruction of all enemy airfields in Chekiang had been completed ○ By Aug 27th the 11th Army had withdrawn to Nanchang ○ By Aug 31st the 13th Army had withdrawn to the Chinhua region marking the end of the Chekiang operation ○
1943: Feb 20th a negotiated agreement allowed the 23rd I.M.B. to pass through French leased territory on the Luichow Peninsula during a pacification operation ○ From Feb 28th veteran units continued to ship south throughout the autumn and winter of

1942. Including the 6th Div, 51st Div, 41st Div and 36th Div. In 1943 the 15th Div went to Burma and the 17th Div to Rabaul. The China Exp Army had to reorganize, four divisions were created from deactivated I.M.B.s and two I.M.B.s were activated in May. The 61st Div was sent from Japan ○ May 12th to June 3rd, the Chinese called it the Battle of West Hubei and the Japanese called it the South Yangtze River Operation. The objective was to capture 20,000 tons of shipping at Yichang and secure a passage for supplies along the Yangtze River. This was completed on May 31st and the army had withdrawn by June 6th ○
1944: Operations Apr 19th to Dec 10th. The objective of *Ichi-go* was to create a rail corridor running from north China to Indochina. Split into *Ko-go*, the northern phase along the Beijing-Wuhan railway, mainly Henan Province, and *To-go* in Hunan Province ○ By May 9th *Ko-go* had been completed ○ On May 25th *To-go* began ○ Summer 1944, the China Expeditionary Army had over a million of Japan's best trained and equipped troops but winning the war in China remained elusive. As time passed difficulties increased and the Allies delivered ever more military aid ○ In July, with the 22nd and 37th Div sent south the China Exp Army reorganized ○ On July 10th the 114th, 115th, 117th and 118th Div were created in China from deactivated brigades ○ By late July the ratio of US to Japanese aircraft was thought to be 5 to 1 ○ On Aug 22nd Army General Staff directed the China Expeditionary Army to occupy and hold certain areas along the Chekiang Coast ○ On Aug 26th the 6th Area Army was activated to unify central China. Its order of battle included the 11th, 23rd and 34th Armies ○ On Sept 27th the 20th Army's headquarters relocated to central China and was placed under 6th Area Army control. It was to garrison Hunan Province south of Ku Shui ○ From Sept 29th the battle lasted ten days before the 11th and 23rd Armies occupied Guilin and Luizhou ○ On Nov 11th the China Expeditionary Army commander visited the 6th Area Army command post in Nanyo. The commander ordered the 6th Area Army to capture Yungning (it fell on Nov 24th) and transfer two divisions from the 11th Army to Indochina ○ On Dec 10th the Ichinomiya Detachment from Indochina made contact with 22nd Division personnel from Nanning in the border town of Suilu, thus bringing operation *Ichi-go* to a successful conclusion ○
1945: On Jan 3rd the China Expeditionary Army ordered one division each from Hunan and Kwangsi into Canton to thwart Allied landings ○ In January three divisions of replacement troops were organized in Japan and sent to China. Field replacement units already in China added a further twelve mixed brigades and seven guard units ○ On Jan 22nd the China Expeditionary Army rec'd orders to prevent US planes from flying over or landing in China. It was part of a national defense zone plan with Japan at the center ○ On Jan 26th the 6th Army headquarters in Manchuria was sent to Anhui Province to direct the movement of divisions and brigades toward the central zone ○ Jan 26th the China Expeditionary Army had the entire Canton-Hankou Railway under its control ○ At the end of January Imperial Headquarters sent the 22nd and 37th Div from China to northern Indochina ○ Between Feb 1st and Apr 12th the 129th, 130th, 131st, 132nd, 133rd and 161st Div were organized from field replacement units, independent mixed and infantry brigades. The China Exp Army planned to build bases to stabilize occupied areas in north China and the lower reaches of the Yangtze River ○ In March the 43rd Army became operational in Shantung Province with the 59th Div, 5th and 9th Ind Mixed Brigades and 1st Ind Infantry Brigade ○ On Apr 3rd the 20th Army's Chihkiang operation began (ended May 9th) ○ Apr 8th marked the start of Japan's last

offensive of the war, the 20th Army's objective was to destroy US operated Chihchang Airfield ○ On May 7th Germany surrendered to the Allies ○ On May 9th the China Expeditionary Army suspend the 20th Army's Chihkiang operation ○ In May the rail corridor from Manchuria to Indochina opened by *Ichi-go* collapsed when the 23rd Army lost Nanning to a Chinese Nationalist Army ○ The 20th Army's Chihchang Airfield operation had been successful initially but by June 7th the Chinese had pushed the Japanese back to their starting point ○ On June 18th the 34th Army headquarters was sent to Manchuria ○ In June the China Expeditionary Army released its operational plans for a Soviet or American invasion, Essentially it would delay the Russians and Chinese and destroy the Americans. Plans to withdraw units in outlying areas were released on an army-by-army basis ○ On Aug 15th Japan surrendered ○ On September 2nd the China Expeditionary Army was deactivated in Hankow ○

Major Units: See division / brigade page for order of battle

Unit	Page
3rd Division Nagoya 1888 幸 *Sachi* – Wuhu	165
13th Division Sendai 1905 鏡 *Kagami* – Hsiang-Siang	169
27th Division Sakura 1938 極 *Kunyomi* – Huchow	176-7
34th Division Osaka 1939 椿 *Tsubaki* – Wuning	180
40th Division Zentsuji 1939 鯨 *Kujira* – Huchow	182
131st Division Kanazawa 1945 秋水 *Syuoui* – Yangshin, Anking	204

Under Control of the China Expeditionary Army:	栄 *Sakae*
China Expeditionary Army Headquarters	No # (2,411)
China Expeditionary Army Special Affairs Dept	9440
China Exped. Army Special Intelligence Dept.	unknown (711)
China Exped. Army Disease Prevention Dept.	unknown (389)
China Exped. Army Medical Materials Depot	unknown (1,217)
China Expeditionary Army Veterinary Department	unknown (667)
China Expeditionary Army Chemical Department	9465 (77)
China Expeditionary Army Fortification Dept	9464 (59)
China Expeditionary Army Survey Department	9463 (239)
China Expeditionary Army Field Materials Depot	9461
China Expeditionary Army Field Railway Depot	2535 (428)
China Expeditionary Army Infantry Training Unit	9436
China Expeditionary Army Artillery Training Unit	9437 (2,826)
China Expeditionary Army Engineer Training Unit	9438 (655)
Baoding Cadet Unit	1649 (779)
Central China Cadet Unit	1645 (335)
Central China NCO Quartermaster Cadet Unit	1646 (32)
Central China NCO Medic Cadet Unit	1647 (31)
Central China NCO Veterinary Cadet Unit	1648 (22)
Central China Military Police Headquarters	No # (5,602)
Central China Horse Remount Depot	1626 (435)
Central China Field Ordinance Depot	1627 (2,335)
Central China Horse Quarantine Depot	1643 (150)
Central China Disease Prev. and Water Supply Unit	1644 (1,838)
19th Field Ordinance Depot Mobile Duty Section	2636 (126)
19th Field Motor Vehicle Depot, Duty Section	2641 (196)

220th Independent Motor Transport Company	2857 (183)
282nd Independent Motor Transport Company	7028 (183)
283rd Independent Motor Transport Company	7029 (183)
292nd Independent Motor Transport Company	9721 (183)
9th Field Replacement Unit	2509
China Exp. Army 2nd Field Railway Headquarters	1430 (253)
4th Railway Department	1826 (86)
6th Railway Regiment	1435 (2,028)
13th Railway Regiment	2530 (3,362)
14th Railway Regiment	2148 (3,447)
1st Independent Railway Engineer Battalion	2151 (630)
2nd Independent Railway Engineer Battalion	2532 (630)
1st Ind. Railway Bridge Construction Battalion	2150 (575)
2nd Bridge Construction Battalion	2531
13th Independent Railway Battalion	1268 (1,034)
14th Independent Railway Battalion	1269 (1,034)
16th Independent Railway Battalion	15758 (1,034)
188th Railway Station Command	7181 (17)
189th Railway Station Command	7185 (17)
11th Armored Train Unit	1411 (1,125)
7th Independent Armored Train Company	1412

East Central China

13th Army 登 *Nobori* 7330

The 13th Army was activated September 23, 1939 in Shanghai, China from former Central China Area Army personnel. Based in Shanghai it was attached to the China Expeditionary Army on Sept 23rd. Its commander was General Jūzō Nishio from Sept 12th until Oct 26th, Lt Gen Shin'ichi Fujita until Dec 2, 1940, Lt Gen Shigeru Sawada until Oct 8, 1942, Lt Gen Sadamu Shimomura until Mar 22,1944, Lt Gen Sadashige Nagatsu until Feb 1, 1945 and Lt Gen Takurō Matsui until the 13th Army was deactivated in Hankou on Sept. 17, 1945.

Subordinate army / duty dates: (13th Army was a defacto area army May to Sept '45)
6th Army from May 28, 1945 until Sept 17, 1945

Service History:

1939: On Sept 23rd the 13th Army was activated in Shanghai China and placed under the China Exp. Army control ○ Between Dec 16th and 23rd the 13th Army's 116th Div

scored a victory at Tatungchen during the winter offensive ○
1940: On Apr 22nd the 15th and 116th Div made a pre-emptive attack on Tatungchen ○
1941: Dec 20th the 13th Army launched a diversionary attack in support of the 23rd Army's attack on Hong Kong. Enemy units around Langchi, south of Nanching and southeast of Kueichi were overrun to prevent reinforcements reaching the city ○
1942: From Apr 25th to Jul 1st the Doolittle raid on Tokyo created fears over Chekiang Province airbases within flying distance of Japan. Five divisions and two brigades from the 13th Army were sent to destroy the airfields, which were defended by 33 Chinese divisions ○ Between May 15th and 22nd the 13th Army occupied an area east of Chinhua. It destroyed the Chinese 79th Army while the others avoided risking battle. The 13th Army decided to pursue those they could to Chuhsien to force battle ○ On June 7th Chuhsien was taken. The Japanese planned to hold the Chekiang/Kiangsi railway for a month but the weather and other matters delayed departure an extra month ○ Between Jul 2nd and 20th the 13th Army captured Yungchia. A garrison remained in the Chinhua area of Chekiang Province so Japan could exploit the fluorite, copper and tin mining there ○ From July 2nd to 20th the (12th or 13th) I.M.B. hunted down British and US smuggling bases in support of the Chekiang/Kiangsi operation By July 20th Yungchia (Wenchow) had been captured and the coastline secured ○ July 28th, the (12th or 13th) I.M.B. went to Sungyang to support the Chekiang/Kiangsi and destroy enemy bases in Chekiang Province, which continued until mid August ○ By July 30th railway repairs had been completed ○ By Aug 3rd the region was secure ○ On Aug 15th in conjunction with Chekiang/Kiangsi the 13th Army entered the Chinhua region ○ On Aug 31st the 13th Army withdrew ○
1943: During spring and summer the China Expeditionary Army reorganized. The 13th Army's 15th Div was sent to the 15th Army in Burma. On May 1st the 13th Army received the 61st Div and on May 16th the 65th Div from Japan ○ From Sept 30th until Oct 10th the 13th Army marched on Kuangte to rid Anhwei Prov of guerrilla activity. Incursions into the area took place as they had back in 1937, '38 and '40. Security forces were sent to Nanling-Hsuancheng-Kuangte boundary to prevent further incidents ○
1944: From Apr 25th to May 13th the 13th Army was to draw the enemy away from the Beijing/Hankou railway for the *Ichi-go* operation ○ Apr 27th Yingshen was occupied ○ On May 8th the Luishihlipu operation was suspended ○ Between Aug 22nd and Oct 9th four battalions from the 70th Div plus five sent from Japan were to secure the Chinese coast ○ On Aug 27th the 70th Div took Lishui ○ On Sept 9th the Nashinoka Detachment captured Yungchia ○ On Sept 16th the 70th Div returned to base ○ On Sept 27th the 62nd Ind Mixed Bgde left Shanghai by boat, landed at the mouth of Lien Chang River and attacked Sungwu and Taao at daybreak ○ On Oct 2nd the 62nd I.M.B. attacked Futon, which fell on the 4th ○
1945: On May 28th the 6th Army arrived in Nanking and placed under 13th Army control. The 6th Army was to construct fortifications around Sungchiang, Chiahsing, Hangchou and Ningpo ○ On Aug 9th the 6th Army was transferred to Manchuria ○
Major Units: See division / brigade page for order of battle

60th Division Sakura 1942 矛 *Hoko* – Suchow	191
61st Division Tokyo 1943 鵄 *Tobi* – Shanghai	191-2
65th Division Nagoya 1943 専 *Sen* – Suchow	193
69th Division Hirosaki 1942 勝 *Katu* – Jiading	194
118th Division Kyoto 1944 恵 *Megumi* – Tianjin	202

161st Division Kumamoto 1945 震天 *Shinten* – Nanking 205-6
90th Independent Mixed Brigade 1945 震雷 *Shinrai* – Nanking/Yangchow 233
92nd Independent Mixed Brigade 1945 至堅 *Itaken* – Laochokao 234
6th Independent Infantry Brigade 1943 肇 *Hajime* – Anking 237
1st Independent Guard Unit 矢石 *Yaishi* – Nanking 242

Units Under Control of the 13th Army: Shanghai	登 *Nobori* 7330	
13th Army Headquarters	7331 (533)	Shanghai
10th Independent Machinegun Battalion	7358 (334)	
17th Independent Rapid Firing Gun Battalion	7359 (403)	
28th Independent Rapid Firing Gun Battalion	5767 (403)	
41st Independent Rapid Firing Gun Company	1866 (118)	
42nd Independent Rapid Firing Gun Company	1867 (118)	
2nd Independent Field Artillery Regiment	3914 (1,696)	
9th Independent Field Artillery Battalion	3149 (617)	
14th Field Medium Artillery Regiment	5520 (2,026)	
15th Ind. Field Heavy ArtilleryRegt., one battalion	5522 (1,040)	
6th Independent Heavy Artillery Battalion	1220 (626)	
21st Anti Aircraft Regiment	5302 (1,610)	
16th Trench Mortar Battalion	28247 (866)	
20th Trench Mortar Battalion	28372 (866)	
22nd Trench Mortar Battalion	28291 (866)	
2nd Independent Trench Mortar Company	12395 (326)	
65th Field Machine Cannon Company	12529 (105)	
39th Independent Engineer Regiment	4278 (591)	
60th Independent Engineer Battalion	1941 (1,684)	
10th Specially Established Engineer Company	23127 (200)	
11th Specially Established Engineer Company	23128 (200)	
12th Signal Regiment	7336 (1,330)	
35th Signal Regiment	15757 (2,238)	
121st Independent Wire Company	12536 (310)	
122nd Independent Wire Company	12537 (310)	
139th Independent Radio Platoon	23133 (57)	
140th Independent Radio Platoon	23140 (57)	
141st Independent Radio Platoon	23135 (57)	
142nd Independent Radio Platoon	23136 (57)	
56th Fixed Radio Unit	1256 (30)	
50th Line of Communications Guard Unit	1625 (1,071)	
83rd Line of Comm. Sector Unit Command	6043 (203)	
83rd Line of Communications Guard Unit	14166 (1,035)	
83rd Line of Communications Duty Company	14167 (511)	
86th Line of Communications Guard Unit	9456 (1,035)	
87th Line of Communications Guard Unit	9457 (1,035)	
29th Motor Transport Regiment	7337 (764)	
38th Motor Transport Regiment	8636 (762)	
230th Independent Motor Transport Company	5899 (183)	

13th Army: continued	登 *Nobori*
232nd Independent Motor Transport Company	7800 (183)
234th Independent Motor Transport Company	7801 (183)
258th Independent Motor Transport Company	6057 (183)
36th Sea Duty Company	3025 (511)
110th Specially Est. Construction Duty Company	14590 (61)
111th Specially Est. Construction Duty Company	14591 (61)
156th Line of Comm. (Nanking 1st) Hospital	1630 (584)
157th Line of Comm. (Shanghai 1st) Hospital	1631 (584)
170th Line of Comm. Hospital	1632 (333)
172nd Line of Comm. (Nanking 2nd) Hospital	1634 (333)
173rd Line of Communications Hospital	16150 (333)
174th Line of Communications (Xuzhou) Hospital	1651/16151 (333)
175th Line of Comm. (Shanghai 2nd) Hospital	1638 (333)
176th Line of Comm. (Zhenjiang) Hospital	1636 (333)
190th L. o. C. (Bengbu Specialty) Hospital	1637 (206)
192nd Line of Communications Hospital	9481 (206)
Shanghai POW Camp	No #
4th Field Replacement Unit	5718
11th Field Replacement Unit	11150
13th Army Veterinary Depot	7342 (297)
Central China Field Ordinance Depot	1627 (1,200)
Central China Field Motor Vehicle Depot	1628 (1,256)
Central China Field Freight Depot	1629 (931)

East Central China

6th Army 守 *Mamoyu* 6329

The 6th Army was activated in Hailar, Manchuria on August 4, 1939, to garrison the western border against Soviet incursions. Under Kwantung Army control from Aug 4th until Jul 4, 1942, 2nd Area Army until Oct 30, 1943, 3rd Area Army until Jan 25, 1945, China Expeditionary Army in Hangchow, China until May 28th and 13th Army until Aug 9th. The 6th Army's commander was Lt Gen Ryuhei Ogisu from Aug 4th until Nov 6, 1939, Lt Gen Tōji Yasui until Oct 15, 1941, Lt Gen Seiichi Kita until Mar 1, 1943, Lt Gen Teizō Ishiguro until Jan 7, 1944 and Lt Gen Jirō Sogawa until it was deactivated in Pukou, Nanjing on September 17, 1945.

Service History:
1945: Jan 25th, under China Exp Army control the 6th Army headquarters redeployed to Hangchow to reorganize replacement units. Under its watch three replacement divisions arrived from Japan, twelve mixed brigades and seven guard units were activated. After completion, the 6th Army was sent to Nanking, Anhui Province a subordinate of the 13th Army. Subsequently the 6th Army took control of the 70th and 133rd Div and 62nd, 89th and 91st I.M.B. ○ May 28th, the 6th Army arrived in Nanking where the 13th Army assigned it to constructing fortifications around Sungchiang, Chiahsing, Hangchou and Ningpo ○ On Aug 9th, the day after the Soviet declaration of war on Japan the 6th Army was transferred to Manchuria ○ The China Expeditionary Army sent 6th Army headquarters, six divisions and six independent mixed brigades north with military supplies and materials. The war ended while they were in transit.
Major Units: See division / brigade page for order of battle

70th Division Hiroshima 1942 槍 *Yari* – Fongyang	194
133rd Division Kumamoto 1945 進撃 *Shingeki* – Hangchow	205
62nd Independent Mixed Brigade 1944 操 *Misao* – Nanking Area	228
89th Independent Mixed Brigade 1945 至純 *Eijun* – Hangchow	233
91st Independent Mixed Brigade 1945 馳駆 *Chiku* – Nanking	233-4

Units Under Control of the 6th Army: Nanking	守 *Mamoyu* 6329	
6th Army Headquarters	6306 (1,732)	Nanking
29th Independent Field Artillery Battalion	1881 (617)	
255th Independent Motor Transport Company	6054 (183)	
12th Specially Established Engineer Company	23129 (200)	
171st Line of Comm. (Hangzhou) Hospital	1635 (333)	
191st Line of Communications (Jinhua) Hospital	1650 (206)	

South China

23rd Army 波 *Nami* 8110

The 23rd Army was activated July 5, 1941, from former South China Area Army personnel. Its headquarters were in Canton under Imperial HQ control from Jul 5th until Aug 12th, China Expeditionary Army until Aug 26, 1944, 6th Area Army until Mar 6, 1945, and China Exp. Army until September 17th. Its commander was Lt Gen Hitoshi Imamura from Jun 28th until Nov 6th, Lt Gen Takashi Sakai until Mar 1, 1943 and Lt Gen Hisachi Tanaka until it was deactivated in Canton on September 17, 1945.
23rd Army's predecessors: The 21st Army was activated in Moji, Japan Sept 19, 1938 and arrived in Guangzhou on Oct 11th. It was deactivated on Feb 9, 1940 and reactivated as the South China Area Army. The 22nd Army was the South China Area Army's one and only subordinate.

Service History:

1941: I.G.HQ demobilized the South China Area Army on July 5th and activated the 23rd Army in south China. The 23rd Army's initial order of battle included the 18th, 38th, 48th and 104th Div and 19th I.M.B. ○ On July 24th Japan and the Vichy France signed an agreement allowing Japanese troops into occupy southern Indochina ○ From Sept 25th until Oct 3rd the 23rd Army fought the newly formed Chinese 2nd Army to prevent the reinforcement of Changsha from Canton, this diversion provided assistance for the 11th Army in the 1st Battle for Changsha ○ In mid Nov the 1st Btn, 19th I.M.B. was assigned to garrison duty on north Hainan Island, replacing a 48th Div infantry regt ○ Dec 7th attack on Pearl Harbor ○ On Nov 6th I.G.HQ ordered the attack on Hong Kong start at the same time as the invasion of Malaya started ○ From Dec 8th to 25th the battle of Hong Kong was fought and won by the reinforced 38th Div ○ On Dec 24th the 2nd battle of Changsha began ○

1942: On Jan 19th the Department of the Governor-General of Hong Kong was created, with the China Expeditionary Army administering the colony ○ Feb 16th, the Army General Staff ordered the 23rd Army to clear Luichow Peninsula of Chinese forces (see Feb '43 for the 23rd I.M.B.) ○ By the end of April south China was peaceful. The 23rd Army received orders to march on Tsunghua and Yuantanhsu to create a diversionary attack in support of an 11th Army offensive ○

1943: In January there had been heightened Chinese activity west of Canton ○ Feb 16th to 20th three battalions from the 23rd I.M.B. captured Haikang in a surprise attack. One battalion was behind left to defend north Hainan Is. and Luichow Peninsula ○

1944: From Aug 29th until Dec 10th the 23rd Army participated in *Ichi-go*. It conducted a side operation to open a corridor along the Hsi Chiang River, creating a supply route for the 6th Area Army ○ On Sept 10th the 23rd Army begins the offensive from south China. Near Wushan the 46th and 64th Chinese Armies interfered in its advance ○ On Sept 22nd Wuchow and Tanchu were taken and the 22nd I.M.B. became responsible for rear area security ○ On Oct 24th an attack from Kueiping stalled the 23rd Army ○ On Oct 29th the 22nd Div beat and chased the enemy towards Wuhsuan and Kueihsien ○ On Nov 4th the 104th Div captured Wushan ○ Early Nov the 23rd Army sent word it was departing. Afterwards, contact with the 6th Area Army became disrupted for 10 days due to rough terrain ○ In early Nov the 11th Army found Liuchow's defenses weak ○ On Nov 9th the Luichow Airfield fell to the 104th Div (23rd Army). The same day the 11th Army and 5th Air Army attacked Guilin ○ Nov 10th Guilin Airfield was captured and the 13th Div, under 23rd Army control, entered Luichow. The two armies finally made contact ○ On Nov 11th the China Exp Army's commander visited the 6th Area Army Command Post in Nanyo with orders to capture Yungning and transfer two 11th Army divisions to Indochina ○ On Nov 24th Yungning fell without resistance ○ Nov 24th, with 22nd Div support the 23rd I.M.B. took Nanning ○ On Nov 28th the 23rd Army sent a unit from the 22nd Div in Nanning to contact the Ichinomiya Detachment from Indochina ○ Dec 10th the two met in the border town of Suilu marking the opening of the *Ichi-go* railway corridor that ran from Indochina to Manchuria. At the same time preparations were started for the anticipated Allied invasion of China ○

1945: Jan 3rd to Feb. 8th, the 23rd Army secured bridges and tunnels in the mountains between Canton and Hankou ○ From Jan 19th until 22nd four 40th Div raiding parties guarded bridges and tunnels from Lokchong to Chenhsien to prevent sabotage ○ From Jan 26th until May the Canton-Hankou Railway remained in Japanese hands ○ In May the rail corridor was closed with the loss of Nanning to a Nationalist Chinese Army ○ From June until Aug the 27th and 40th Div were temporarily attached to the 20th Army and sent to Nanchang skirmishing as they marched. The 131st Div went to Wuchang-Hankou on foot along the Canton-Hankou railway tracks. An element from the 23rd I.M.B. remained on the Luichow Peninsula while the main body went to Canton. The Swatow Detachment remained in place ○ On Aug 15th Japan surrendered ○ On Sept 17th the 23rd Army was deactivated ○

Major Units: See division / brigade page for order of battle

104th Division Nagoya 1938 鳳 *Ootori* – Suchow	197-8
129th Division Nagano 1945 英邁 *Shinki* – Tunguan	202-3
130th Division Kyoto 1945 鍾馗 *Shoki* – Chiangmiu	203
23rd Independent Mixed Brigade 1943 純 *Jun* – Swatow / Hainan Island	216-7
8th Independent Infantry Brigade 1943 肝 *Kimo* – Canton	238
13th Independent Infantry Brigade 1944 直 *Choku* – Canton	239
Hong Kong Garrison 1942 香港 – Hong Kong	249

Units under 23rd Army control: Canton	波 *Nami* 8110	
23rd Army Headquarters	8111 (788)	Canton
14th Signals Regiment	8128 (2,070)	
96th Independent Radio Platoon	2546 (59)	
61st Fixed Radio Unit	12516 (30)	
62nd Fixed Radio Unit	12653 (30)	
3rd Field Signal Company	5553 (378)	
31st Independent Mixed Regiment	23124 (2,262)	
7th Independent Field Artillery Battalion	3147	
55th Field Anti-Aircraft Battalion	3621 (667)	
99th Field Anti Aircraft Artillery Battalion	8146 (521)	
49th Field Machine Cannon Company	6093 (105)	
3rd Tank Division, Air Defense Unit 1st and 3rd Coys	3502 (294)	
59th Independent Engineer Battalion	1940 (1,684)	
8th Specially Established Engineer Company	11758 (200)	
9th Specially Established Engineer Company	11759 (200)	
102nd Specially Established Construction Duty Co.	8891 (61)	
9th Division 2nd Bridging Materials Company	8133 (564)	
6th Division 6th Land Transport Unit	8628 (261)	
8th Division 8th Land Transport Unit	8629 (321)	
12th Division 1st Land Transport Unit	8632 (261)	
14th Division 1st Land Transport Unit	8633 (261)	
15th Railway Regiment, 1st Battalion	2149 (1,100)	
13th Field Transport Command	7563 (40)	
39th Motor Transport Regiment	8637 (762)	
85th Independent Motor Transport Battalion	8147 (808)	
311th Independent Motor Transport Company	12412 (132)	
312th Independent Motor Transport Company	12413 (132)	
313th Independent Motor Transport Company	12414 (132)	
19th Independent Transport Company	8614 (397)	
20th Independent Transport Company	8615 (397)	

23rd Army: continued	波 *Nami*
21st Independent Transport Company	8616 (397)
2nd Inland Waterway Transport Unit	8638 (654)
82nd Land Duty Company	3032 (511)
56th Field Road Construction Unit	12514 (303)
66th Line of Communications Sector Command	9714 (203)
66th Sector Transport Unit	9714
66th Line of Communications Duty Company	9714 (511)
66th Line of Communications Guard Unit	9715 (1,035)
136th Line of Comm. (Guangdong) Hospital	7195 (359)
160th L. o. C. (Guangdong 1st Army) Hospital	8600 (584)
180th L.o.C. (Guangdong 2nd Army) Hospital	8601 (333)
200th L. o. C. (Hong Kong Army) Hospital	8135 (566)
7th Casualty Clearing Headquarters	8620 (33)
7th Patient Transport Headquarters	8602 (15)
4th Casualty Clearing Platoon	8603 (51)
79th Casualty Clearing Platoon	12515 (54)
23rd Army Field Ordinance Depot	17774 (937)
23rd Army Field Motor Vehicle Depot	17775 (1,015)
23rd Army Field Freight Depot	17776 (1,200)
19th Field Motor Vehicle Depot 1st Repair Squad	2641 (196)
23rd Army Veterinary Depot	8608 (194)
South China Veterinary Quarantine Depot	8609 (28)
South China Disease Prev. and Water Supply Unit	8604 (634)

Air Support: China 1945

13th Air Division: Nanking 1945	隼魁 *Hayabusa Sakigake*	
13th Air Division Headquarters	22101 (351)	
13th Air Division Headquarters Signal Squad	22101 (106)	
1st Air Brigade Headquarters	2373 (94)	
• 25th Air Regiment	2387 (275)	
• 48th Air Regiment (fighters)	16618 (284)	Liching
• 85th Air Regiment	満198 (137)	
2nd Air Brigade Headquarters	9101 (49)	
• 9th Air Regiment (fighters)	9103 (195)	Nanking
• 6th Air Regiment (light bomber)	9102 (235)	
8th Air Brigade		
• 16th Air Regiment (light bomber)	9142 (470)	
• 90th Air Regiment (light bombers)	2381 (362)	Taihsien
• 82nd Air Regiment	2383 (249)	
• 44th Air Regiment, 1 squadron (recon)	2376 (240)	Wuchin
• 54th Ind. Air Squadron (close support)	8354 (121)	Hangchou
5th Air Sector Command	9864 (56)	

13th Air Division: continued

16th Air Sector Command	9862 (45)	
26th Air Sector Command	17312 (44)	
50th Air Sector Command	16665 (44)	
56th Air Sector Command	17331 (44)	
57th Airfield Battalion	9867 (372)	
58th Airfield Battalion	17305 (372)	
59th Airfield Battalion	17306 (372)	
60th Airfield Battalion	17307 (372)	
91st Airfield Battalion	9869 (372)	
96th Airfield Battalion	8997 (372)	
104th Airfield Battalion	16604 (372)	
105th Airfield Battalion	16605 (372)	
106th Airfield Battalion	16606 (372)	
129th Airfield Battalion	17315 (372)	
168th Airfield Battalion	17323 (372)	attach 27th Div.
184th Airfield Battalion	17324 (372)	
185th Airfield Battalion	17325 (372)	
186th Airfield Battalion	17326 (372)	
217th Airfield Battalion	16697 (372)	
218th Airfield Battalion	16688 (372)	
219th Airfield Battalion	16689 (372)	
220th Airfield Battalion	16692 (372)	
1st Airfield Company	9871 (207)	
2nd Airfield Company	9872 (207)	
6th Airfield Company	9932 (300)	
19th Airfield Company	9339 (416)	
20th Airfield Company	9308 (205)	
21st Airfield Company	9309 (205)	
67th Airfield Company	9873 (207)	
69th Airfield Company	9874 (207)	
13th Line of Comm. Motor Transport Co.	9891 (170)	
64th L.o.C. Motor Transport Company	9892 (170)	
92nd L.o.C. Motor Transport Company	9894 (170)	

13th Air Division: The 13th Air Division was activated in Nanking, China on Feb 26, 1945. It joined the 5th Air Army on Mar 6th. Headquarters in Hankou, Lt Gen Kihachirō Yoshida was its commander from Mar. 7th until the war ended. Subordinate to the 5th Air Army its mission was to defend against US air attacks from the east and south sea areas as well as support ground force operations in the Chinese interior.

Service History:

1945: On May 15th the 13th Air Div moved headquarters to Nanching, all air units below the Lunghai Railway became subordinate to it, in addition to about 200 special attack (kamikaze) planes from Manchuria and Korea. All the division's pilots began combat training over the ocean to prepare for special attack missions ○ On Aug 8th the Soviets invade Manchuria. The China Exp Army ordered the 13th Air Div to move into north China. The 90th Air Regt, 54th Ind Air Squadron and 81st Air Regt

13th Air Division continued
were first to be sent ○ On Aug 14th as they deployed to airbases around Beijing reconnaissance reported a Soviet mechanized force north of Changpei ○ On Aug. 15th 20 of the 90th Air Regt's bombers attacked near Changpei as the war ended. All further action was called off whilw most of the 13th Air Division still in transit to north

Shipping Units attached to Armies in China:

2nd Shipping Transport; South China Branch	暁 *Akatsuki*	
China Expeditionary Army Sea Headquarters	unknown (172)	
65th Anchorage Headquarters	16756 (81)	China Ex. Army
67th Anchorage Headquarters	19779 (81)	China Ex. Army
101st Sea Duty Unit	2957 (603)	China Ex. Army
12th Sea Transport Battalion	19814 (548)	China Ex. Army
4th Shipping Signal Battalion	19780 (514)	
2nd Shipping Transport Headquarters	2941 (134)	
12th Shipping Group Headquarters	2945 (81)	
4th Shipping Signal Battalion, 2nd Company	19780 (232)	
29th Shipping Engineer Regiment	16758 (1,099)	
33rd Shipping Engineer Regiment	19810 (1,099)	
34th Shipping Engineer Regiment	19811 (1,099)	
64th Anchorage Headquarters	16755 (81)	23rd Army
60th Sea Duty Company, 23rd Army	1749 (511)	
111th Specially Established Sea Duty Company	1768 (61)	23rd Army
142nd Specially Established Sea Duty Company	19792 (61)	
6th Field Shipping Depot	19807 (1,224)	
8th Field Shipping Depot	19821 (649)	

Infantry regiment's color party halted on a road in China, civilians on left (author)

Central China

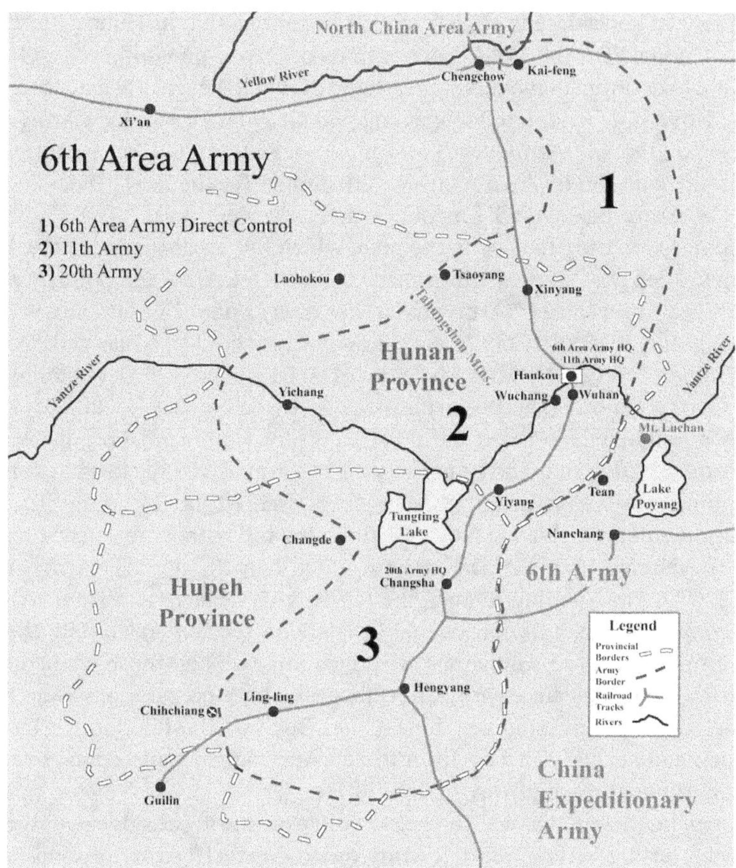

6th Area Army 統 *Tou* 17000

The 6th Area Army began organizing on Aug 26, 1944, its headquarters completed on Sept 10th. Based in the Hankou/Wuhan area it was created to fill a void in the chain of command and oversee operations in central China under the China Expeditionary Army's control. It was responsible for western occupied China from Hengyang in the south to Chengchow/Kai-feng in the north. The 6th Area Army's commander was General Yasuji Okamura from Aug 26th until Nov 22nd and General Naosaburō Okabe until it was deactivated in Hankou on Sept 17, 1945.

Subordinate armies / duty dates:

11th Army from Aug 26, 1944 until the war ended

23rd Army from Aug 26, 1944 until Mar 6, 1945

34th Army from Aug 26, 1944 until June 18, 1945

20th Army from Oct 18, 1944 until the war ended

Service History:

1944: On Aug 10th the China Expeditionary Army withdrew its command post from Hankou in anticipation of the 6th Area Army's activation ○ On Aug 29th the 11th Army began the Hunan-Kwangsi railway offensive ○ On Sept 10th the 6th Area Army became active ○ On Sept 27th the 20th Army HQ in Manchuria was placed under 6th Area Army control ○ Oct 10th, the 6th Area Army command post moves to Nanyo ○ On Oct 18th the 20th Army (a garrison and reserve army) became active in Hunan Prov, south of Ku Shui ○ On Oct 28th, the 11th Army began its offensive on Guilin. The 11th and 23rd Armies were to coordinate movements to avoid giving the enemy a chance to escape ○ In Nov the Governor General of Hong Kong was placed under 6th Area Army oversight ○ In early Nov the 23rd Army sent word it had begun moving but because of rough terrain contact with the 6th Area Army was disrupted for the next 10 days ○ In early Nov the 11th Army discovered Liuchow's defenses were weak. The 6th Area Army repeated to the 11th Army to stick to the plan, which fell on deaf ears, at the same time attempting to keep the 23rd Army informed. The 6th Area Army temporarily placed the 3rd and 13th Div from the 11th Army under 23rd Army control ○ On Nov 9th Luichow airfield fell to the 104th Div (23rd Army), the same day the 11th Army and 5th Air Army attacked Guilin ○ Nov 10th Guilin Airfield was taken and the 13th Div entered Luichow under 23rd Army control. The two armies finally made contact ○ On Nov 11th China Exp Army's commander visited the 6th Area Army Command Post in Nanyo with orders to capture Yungning and transfer two 11th Army divisions to Indochina ○ Nov 15th, Yungning was weak so the 6th Area Army ordered the 23rd Army to capture it before reinforcements arrived ○ Nov 24th Yungning fell without resistance and the 23rd I.M.B. took Nanning with 22nd Div support ○ On Nov 28th the 23rd Army sent a unit from the 22nd Div in Nanning to meet the Ichinomiya Detachment from Indochina to open the continent wide rail corridor. ○ In late Nov *Ichi-go* ended with the Chinese Kwangsi armies scattered, Hunan and Kwangsi airbases and those elements of Tang En-po's army near Tuhshan destroyed. At the same time preparations were begun for an anticipated Allied invasion of China ○ On Dec 10th the Ichinomiya Detachment from Indochina and the 22nd Div from the 6th Area Army made contact in Suilu on the Yungning/Indochina highway ○ In mid Dec the Changsha-Yoyang railway was declared open but a train that was too heavy collapsed the new bridge over the Liuyang River, during testing ○ The 6th Area Army ordered the 11th Army to send its 37th (on Dec 20th) and 22nd Div (on Jan 13th) to Indochina ○

1945: In January the 6th Area Army planned a surprise attack on the Canton-Hankou railway ○ The 20th and 23rd Armies went to secure the railway, occupy facilities along the rail line and destroy US airbases in Suichuan and Kanhsien ○ On Jan 20th the 37th Div joined the Indochina Garrison Army ○ By Jan 26th Canton-Hankou rail line has been captured and by Feb 8th the airfields also ○ On Feb 1st the 83rd, 84th and 85th I.M.B. were activated ○ In Feb, although Beijing/Hankou trains were running in Jan only 12,000 of a planned 45,000 tons of freight had made it to Wuhan. US planes bombed trains and bridges causing delays and a shortage of rolling stock. In the event of an invasion it would take days to get troops from the interior to the coast. Kwangsi Province with its tons of captured munitions would have to be abandoned ○ In Feb and Mar the 116th and 47th Div (20th Army) and three additional inf btns with 5th Air Army support were sent to destroy the Chihkiang airbase then withdraw ○ In Mar 10,000 tons of supplies arrived in Hankou but there was still a backlog of 100,000 tons (400,000 had been planned) ○ On Apr 8th the 20th Army made a costly attack on Chihkiang ○ On Apr 15th the Chihkiang operation began. The 20th Army faced 27 Chinese divisions, on top of that every 4 days a division was flown into Chihkiang from Kunming. Losses mounted and the offensive bogged down, besides that the importance of Chihkiang diminished as the war progressed. The 20th Army was to await a relief force and the 34th Army was to pull back to Yuankiang ○ In late Apr the

11th and 20th Armies began to withdraw from Kwangsi and Hunan, to be completed by the end of Aug. The 11th Army would end in Wuhan and the 20th Army north of Yoyang in the Wuhan area ○ On May 9th the China Expeditionary Army suspended its costly Chihkiang operation and ordered all units to return to their starting positions ○ In early May the tank brigade and heavy artillery went north by rail and on foot ○ In mid June the 27th and 40th Div left Canton for Kanhsien. 3,000 air ground crew, and sick and wounded from the two divisions were spread along the rail line to Wuhan ○ The 3rd Div left Chuanhsien for Changsha and was placed under 20th Army control at the border ○ The 13th Div withdrew from Ishan to Luichow and joined the 11th Army, which left for Kweilin at the end of June ○ On June 18th the 34th Army headquarters was placed under Kwantung Army control in Korea and sent to guard the border. Subordinate units remained in the Wuchang-Hankou area under 6th Area Army control. ○ Late June, the 47th Div in Siangtan-Changsha was sent north ○ End of June, the 34th Div (20th Army) withdrew through Shaoyang to Changsha. The 11th Army withdrew from Liuchow to Kweilin. Between the tank brigade, heavy artillery and 47th Div roads north became congested. The 6th Area Army distributed gasoline reserves to assist transport units. Under the Area Army's direction movement elsewhere went well ○ On July 15th the 27th, 40th and 131st Div in Kanhsien began moving northwest ○ July 20th, the 3rd and 34th Div left the Changsha-Chuchow area ○ In July the 20th Army and 23rd Army garrison troops withdrew from the Kwangtung/Hunan border making the railway vulnerable to disruptions ○ In late-July the 11th Army left Kweilin. To expedite the withdrawal it attacked Chuanhsien ○ The Japanese in China would soon become isolated so the 6th Area Army scouted out a strong defensive position ○ Roads north of Hengyang became congested and US air attacks made things worse ○ The 11th Army helped the 20th Army fortify the Shaoyang-Lingling line ○ In mid Aug 50,000 men remained in the Wuhan fortified zone after the casualties, armor, transport and divisions had left. Rumors of total surrender began in Shanghai ○ On Aug 15th Japan surrendered, by this time the 6th Area Army had been active for less than a year ○

Major Units: See division / brigade page for order of battle

132nd Division Osaka 1945 振起 *Shinki* – Yichang	204
17th Independent Mixed Brigade 1939 峰 *Mine* – Weichang	214
83rd Independent Mixed Brigade 1945 至猛 *Shimo* – Hankao	230-1
84th Independent Mixed Brigade 1945 至勇 *Shiyu* – Jiujiang	231
85th Independent Mixed Brigade 1945 至潔 *Shitatu* – Hubei	231
5th Independent Infantry Brigade 1943 悟 *Satoshi* – Jingzhao	237
7th Independent Infantry Brigade 1943 征 *Sei* – Hankou	237
11th Independent Infantry Brigade 1944 福 *Fuku* – Yingcheng	239
12th Independent Infantry Brigade 1944 善 *Zen* – Xianning	239

Units under control of the 6th Area Army: Hankow 統 *Tou* 17000

6th Area Army Headquarters	17700 (1,365)	Hankow
28th Signal Regiment	2154 (2,129)	
57th Fixed Radio Unit	1257 (30)	
58th Fixed Radio Unit	1258 (30)	
59th Fixed Wireless Radio Unit	2155 (30)	
60th Fixed Wireless Radio Unit	12511 (30)	
95th Independent Wire Company	9451 (310)	

6th Area Army: continued	統 *Tou*
131st Independent Wire Company	17793 (310)
75th Field Anti Aircraft Battalion	7832 (527)
22nd Motor Transport Regiment	1876 (760)
24th Motor Transport Regiment	3507 (760)
31st Motor Transport Regiment	5391 (764)
37th Motor Transport Regiment	3509 (764)
69th Independent Motor Transport Regiment	5073 (808)
266th Independent Motor Transport Company	6270 (183)
279th Independent Motor Transport Company	7106 (183)
310th Independent Motor Transport Company	2157 (132)
314th Independent Motor Transport Company	12512 (132)
315th Independent Motor Transport Company	12513 (132)
Imperial Guard Division 10th Land Transport Unit	5584 (246)
53rd Field Road Construction Unit	2158 (303)
11th Field Service Unit Headquarters	5582 (11)
63rd Land Duty Company	7847 (511)
46th Specially Established Land Duty Company	17746 (61)
47th Specially Established Land Duty Company	17747 (61)
48th Specially Established Land Duty Company	17748 (61)
49th Specially Established Land Duty Company	17749 (61)
50th Specially Established Land Duty Company	17750 (61)
51st Specially Established Land Duty Company	17751 (61)
52nd Specially Established Land Duty Company	17752 (61)
53rd Specially Established Land Duty Company	17753 (61)
54th Specially Established Land Duty Company	17754 (61)
55th Specially Established Land Duty Company	17755 (61)
1st Division 1st Line of Comm.Headquarters	5361 (98)
4th Division 1st Line of Comm. Headquarters	5364 (98)
7th Division 5th Land Transport Unit	5573 (246)
5th Specially Established Engineer Company	17745 (200)
6th Specially Established Engineer Company	17736 (200)
7th Specially Established Engineer Company	17757 (200)
82nd Line of Comm. Sector Unit Command	6042 (203)
51st Line of Communications Guard Unit	6107 (921)
52nd Line of Communications Guard Unit	6109 (921)
82nd Sector Transport Unit	6040
84th Line of Comm. Sector Unit Command	6044 (203)
84th Line of Communications Guard Unit	14168 (1,035)
84th Line of Communications Duty Company	14169 (511)
43rd Sea Duty Company	10230 (511)
45th Sea Duty Company	10512 (511)
54th Sea Duty Company	9742 (511)
9th Division 2nd Sea Transport Unit	5587 (246)
3rd Division 2nd Construction Unit	5588 (246)
7th Division 2nd Construction Unit	7340 (321)

108th Specially Est. Construction Duty Company	3658 (61)
9th Casualty Clearing Unit	6136 (53)
59th Casualty Clearing Platoon	7133 (54)
82nd Casualty Clearing Platoon	5820 (54)
83rd Casualty Clearing Platoon	4048 (54)
86th Casualty Clearing Platoon	7199 (54)
72nd (Baoji) Line of Communications Hospital	1366 (359)
127th Line of Communications Hospital	3887 (359)
128th Line of Communications Hospital	3888 (359)
132nd Line of Communications Hospital	4028 (359)
158th L. o. C. (Hankou 1st Army) Hospital	1639 (584)
159th Line of Comm. (Wuhan Army) Hospital	1641 (584)
177th Line of Comm. (Jiujiang Army) Hospital	1642 (333)
178th L. o. C. (Hankou 2nd Army) Hospital	1640 (333)
19th Line of Communications Veterinary Depot	9450 (538)
32nd Field Disease Prevention / Water Supply Unit	12467 (220)
34th Field Ordinance Depot	17777 (1,227)
34th Field Ordinance Depot Duty Company	17777 (450)
34th Field Motor Vehicle Depot	17778 (1,253)
34th Field Motor Vehicle Depot Duty Company	17778 (450)
34th Field Freight Depot	17779 (1,300)
34th Field Freight Depot Duty Company	17779 (670)
6th Area Army Horse Quarantine Depot	unknown (165)
6th Area Army Field Horse Remount Depot	9479 (627)
6th Area Army Military Police Unit	No # (1,440)
6th Area Army Education Unit	unknown (2,836)

Central China Railway

6th Area Army railway units	路 *Michi*
4th Field Railway Command	9449 (334)
1st Railway Regiment	栄 5571 (2,354)
3rd Railway Regiment	34101 / 1231 (1,989)
12th Railway Regiment	統 2147 (3,362)
15th Railway Regiment, minus 1st Battalion	2149 (2,262) less 1st Btn
2nd Independent Railway Engineer Labor Unit	2153 (419)
3rd Independent Railway Engineer Labor Unit	2533 (419)
4th Railway Materials Depot	2534 (158)
1st Independent Railway Engineer Battalion	2151 (419)
2nd Independent Railway Engineer Battalion	2152 (419)
187th Railway Station Command	7184 (106)
192nd Railway Station Command	7756 (106)
201st Railway Station Command	7812 (17)
202nd Railway Station Command	7813 (17)
203rd Railway Station Command	7814 (17)
204th Railway Station Command	7815 (17)
205th Railway Station Command	7816 (17)

Hunan Province / Central China

11th Army 呂 *Ro* 5501

The 11th Army began organizing on July 4, 1938, and became active in Nanking on July 15th. It served under Central China Exp Army control from July 4th until Sept 23, 1939, China Expeditionary Army until Aug 26, 1944, and 6th Area Army until it was deactivated. Its headquarters relocated from Nanking to Hankou on Dec 15, 1938. The 11th Army served under Lt Gen Yasuji Okamura from June 23rd until Mar 9, 1940, Lt Gen Waichirō Sonobe until Apr 10, 1941, Lt Gen Korechika Anami until July 1, 1942, Lt Gen Osamu Tsukada until Dec 18th, Lt Gen Isamu Yokoyama until Nov 22, 1944, Lt Gen Yoshio Kōzuki until Apr 7, 1945 and Lt Gen Yukio Kasahara until the 11th Army was deactivated in Jiujiang on Sept 17, 1945.

Service History:

1938: On Jul 15th the 11th Army became active in Nanking, China ○ On Oct 4th a coordinated pincer movement was made by the 11th Army attacking Wuhan from the east and 2nd Army attacking from the north ○ By Oct 17th the 2nd Army had taken Xinyang and the Beijing–Hankou Railway ○ On Oct 28th the 11th Army captured Wuhan ○ From Oct 26th to Nov 11th the Central China Expeditionary Army chased defeated Chinese forces ○ On Dec 15th the 11th Army received word it was to be permanently stationed in the Wuhan-Hankow area ○

1939: Mar 15th scheduled reorganization, time expired 9th and 16th Div replaced by the 33rd and 34th Div ○ On Mar 20th the 11th Army attacked Nanchang. By late Mar the 9th War Sector Army was defeated and the city taken ○ Mar 22nd, the 11th Army sent the 3rd and 16th Div and 4th Cav Brigade to defeat the Chinese 31st Army Group near Tsaoyang ○ May 1st, the April Offensive began with the 11th Army severing both wings of the Chinese Army Group by May 10th and isolating it in the mountains near Tanghsienchen. The battle was won by May 12th ○ Sept 14th to Oct 11th, the 11th Army fought *1st Battle of Changsha* against the Chinese 9th War Sector Army, inflicting losses on ten of its thirty divisions ○ On Oct 2nd the 39th and 40th Div were added and early Nov the 101st and 106th Div temporarily removed and sent to the 13th Army ○

1940: From Dec 12th until Jan 23rd a Nationalist Chinese winter offensive took place along the 11th Army's entire western front and against the 13th Army south of Hankou, by Jan 20th the attack had been beaten off but both sides suffered losses ○ On May 1st the Yichang offensive began. In Hupeh and Hunan the 11th Army was spread thin and looking for a strategic stronghold before the July rainy season began ○ June 1st, the 3rd and 39th Div crossed Han Chiang River ○ On June 12th the battle of Yichang began ○ On June 18th Yichang was captured. The 11th Army had about 10,500 casualties and the Chinese lost 60,000 ○

1941: On Mar 15th the 11th Army ordered the 33rd Div to strike southwest of Fenghsin in the Nanchang area ○ Mar 20th, the 34th Div, trapped by Chinese troops and nearly routed, was rescued by the 33rd Div and 3rd Air Bgde. All units returned to their starting positions by April 2nd ○ On May 5th the Chungyuan Plains Diversion began in support of the China Expeditionary Army north of the Yangtze but it achieve little ○ Sept 17th the *1st Changsha Operation* or *2nd Battle of Changsha* to the Chinese, the intent was to damage the 9th War Sector Army in the Changsha area. The Chinese had 30 well-equipped divisions but no air intelligence so the 11th Army had the edge. Armor and

artillery couldn't participate due to recent heavy rains. Animals couldn't carry enough supplies but discarded Chinese food and ammunition made up the shortfall ○ On Sept 28th the 4th Div and Hayabuchi Detach captured Changsha ○ Oct 1st, the 11th Army began to pull back ○ On Oct 7th the Army arrived north of the Hsinchiang River ○ Dec 7th, the attack on Pearl Harbor took place ○ From Dec 24th to Jan 6th, the *2nd Changsha Operation* or *3rd Battle of Changsha* to the Chinese, was designed to eliminate guerilla activity and support the 38th Div invasion of Hong Kong. The Chinese 20th and 99th Armies were initially routed but later rallied ○
1942: On Jan 1st the 3rd Div attacked Changsha Castle ○ On Jan 4th Changsha City was captured ○ Jan 6th, the 11th Army completed its mission and began to withdraw. The Chinese 20th, 26th, 58th, 73rd, 78th and 99th Armies harassed the Japanese turning it into a retreat ○ On Jan 13th the 11th Army crossed the Kushui River ending the action ○ Apr 25th to Jul 1st the 11th Army supported the 13th Army's Chekiang Province operation to destroy airfields within striking distance of Japan ○ Aug 27th, under orders, on Aug 15th the 11th Army concentrated on Nanchang without meeting resistance. Following Chekiang-Kiangsi the 11th Army captured Nanchang ○ From mid Dec until Jan '43 the 11th Army conducted mopped up operations in the Mt. Tapishshan area ○
1943: From Feb 15th until late-March the Chinese held a triangle north of Lake Dongting and the Yangtze, which threatened Japanese control in the area. The 11th Army was sent to destroy them and seize the triangle. A surprise attack drove the Chinese from fortified positions to Meinyang. On Feb 21st the 13th, 40th, and 58th Div destroyed the positions ○ May 5th until May 29th, the 11th Army raided south of the Yangtze River seizing 20,000 tons of small boats at Ichang and freeing up navigation on the river. The Chinese call it the *Battle of West Hubei* ○ On May 11th part 1 ended with the Chinese south of Anshang scattered ○ May 18th, part 2 ended with three Chinese divisions in the Nuanshuichieh area destroyed. In part 3 the still disorganized Chinese 87th Army was hit again ○ On May 27th the mission was completed when the vessels captured in Ichang arrived in Shahshi. On June 6th the 11th Army withdrew ○ Nov 2nd to Dec 4th the 11th Army received reinforcements for an attack north of Changde ○ On Nov 5th the 68th and 116th Div put the Chinese 44th Army to flight near Anshang ○ Nov 16th the 3rd Div and Sasaki Detach attacked and routed the Chinese 73rd Army and on Nov 21st routed the 74th Army ○ Nov 23rd, attack on Changde City ○ Dec 4th, Changde captured ○ By Dec 24th the 3rd Div and Sasaki Detach were back in their starting positions ○
1944: On Apr 19th *Ichi-go* began. The plan was to open a rail corridor from Manchuria to Indochina. The 11th Army was to capture Hengyang and open the Hengyang–Changsha–Hankou rail corridor ○ From June 3rd until mid June rain made movement difficult ○ June 18th Changsha fell to the 11th Army ○ On June 28th the siege of Hengyang began but stalled when the 68th Div commander was wounded ○ On Jul 2nd the siege was suspended due to a shortage of artillery and ammunitions, which had become mired down on muddy roads ○ From Jul 11th to 15th progress stalled ○ July 30th, the 11th Army moved headquarters to Hengyang ○ On Aug 8th Hengyang, a vital railway feeder line junction was taken after 47 days, the Chinese 10th Corps lost 15,000 of the 16,275 defenders ○ Sept 1st, Chinese 26th and 37th Armies retreated southwest while the 74th and 100th Armies went to Shaoyang. The 11th Army chased the 46th, 62nd and 79th Armies to Kiyang ○ Sept 7th the 11th Army arrived in Lingling ○ Nov 9th, Luichowhsien airfield fell ○ Nov 10th the 13th Div captured the city ○ Nov 24th, *Ichi-go* Guilin-Luichow operation began. In early Nov the 11th Army had completed

preparations, Luichow defenses were found to be weak. At the last moment, the 11th Army commander decided to attack Guilin and Liuchow at the same time. The 6th Area Army stressed maintaining coordination with the 23rd Army, so as not to give the enemy a chance of escaping. The 3rd and 13th Div were sent to attack Luichow anyway. The 11th Army was ordered to attack Ishan and its 3rd and 13th Div were temporarily placed under the 23rd Army for the attack on Luichow ○ On Nov 9th Luichow airfield fell. On the same day the 11th Army and 5th Air Army attacked Guilin ○ Nov 10th, Guilin Airfield fell and the 13th Div entered Luichow attached to the 23rd Army. The two armies made contact for the first time during the operation. The 11th Army sent the 3rd and 13th Div toward Tushan in pursuit of the Chinese ○
1945: The 11th Army withdrew from Liuchow to Kweilin ○ Apr 17th to May 3rd, the 11th Army's 3rd, 13th and 34th Div were temporarily placed under 20th Army control for withdrawal to Wuhan-Hankou ○ The 3rd and 13th Div fought the Chinese 46th Army and the 34th Div fought an enemy near Chihkiang ○ On Aug 10th the 11th Army fought the Chinese 20th and 26th Armies southwest of Chuanhsien. After Chuanhsien there was little resistance ○ On Aug 13th the 11th Army withdrew to Hunan. When it arrived in Huangpo north of Hankow it began constructing a fortified last-stand position ○
Major Units: See division / brigade page for order of battle

58th Division Kumamoto 1942 広 *Hirosi* – Hupei	190-1
22nd Independent Mixed Brigade 1942 節 *Setu* – Hengchow	216
88th Independent Mixed Brigade 1945 沖天 *Chuten* – Hupeh	232

Units under 11th Army control: Hupeh	呂 *Ro* 5501
11th Army Headquarters	5500 (574)
11th Army Signal Unit	5550
11th Army Physician Department	5501
11th Army Veterinary Depot	6118 (297)
11th Army Field Ordinance Depot	6112 (937)
17th Field Ord. Depot, 1st Mobile Repair Section	2634 (126)
16th Field Ord. Depot, 2nd Mobile Repair Section	2633 (126)
11th Army Field Motor Vehicle Repair Depot	6114 (1,023)
17th Fld Motor Vehicle Depot, 1st Mob. Repair Sect.	2639 (196)
16th Fld Motor Vehicle Depot, 1st Mob. Repair Sect.	2638 (196)
16th Fld Freight Depot, 2nd Cloths M. Repair Sect.	2643 (93)
11th Army Field Freight Depot	6116 (1,297)
1st Tank Division Air Defense Unit	12079 / 595 (1,014)
2nd Independent Mountain Artillery Regiment	5510 (2,531)
51st Independent Mountain Artillery Battalion	5513 (309)
52nd Independent Mountain Artillery Battalion	5515 (309)
15th Independent Field Heavy Artillery Regiment	5522 (1,182)
48th Field Machine Cannon Company	7833 (105)
1st Trench Mortar Battalion	5531 (883)
4th Trench Mortar Battalion	7333 (963)
41st Independent Engineer Regiment	5549 (1,684)
61st Independent Engineer Battalion	1942 (821)
2nd Specially Established Engineer Company	17742 (200)
3rd Specially Established Engineer Company	17743 (200)

4th Specially Established Engineer Company	17744 (200)
101st Specially Est. Construction Duty Company	8890 (61)
13th Signals Regiment	5555 (1,663)
8th Field Signal Company	5558 (323)
9th Field Signal Company	5559 (323)
93rd Independent Radio Platoon	2543 (59)
95th Independent Radio Platoon	2545 (59)
97th Independent Radio Platoon	2547 (59)
102nd Independent Wire Company	3172 (277)
97th Land Duty Company	6919 / 10155 (511)
98th Land Duty Company	6920 / 10156 (511)
7th Division; Bridging Materials Company	5562 (499)
8th Division; Bridging Materials Company	5563 (499)
12th Division; Bridging Materials Company	5564 (499)
14th Division; Bridging Materials Company	5565 (499)
Imperial Guard Division River Crossing Company	5566 (545)
1st Division River Crossing Company	5567 (545)
7th Division 7th Land Transport Unit	5585 (246)
7th Division 8th Land Transport Unit	5586 (246)
3rd Division 3rd Construction Unit	5589 (246)
71st Line of Communications Sector Command	5297 (203)
71st Line of Communications Guard Unit	5298 (1,035)
71st Line of Communications Duty Company	5299 (511)
81st Line of Communications Sector Command	3861 (203)
81st Line of Communications Duty Company	3861 (1,035)
81st Line of Communications Guard Unit	3861 (511)
82nd Line of Communications Guard Unit	6042 (1,035)
82nd Line of Communications Duty Company	6042 (511)
1st Field Transport Command	5860 (37)
101st Line of Communications Duty Company	5377 (100)
30th Motor Transport Regiment	5390 (764)
32nd Motor Transport Regiment	5392 (764)
33rd Motor Transport Regiment	5393 (764)
34th Motor Transport Regiment	5394 (764)
35th Motor Transport Regiment	5395 (764)
10th Field Transport Command	5371 (132)
3rd Division, 2nd Transport Company	5374
36th Motor Transport Regiment	1877 (764)
31st Independent Motor Transport Battalion	5861 (808)
32nd Independent Motor Transport Battalion	5862 (808)
33rd Independent Motor Transport Battalion	5863 (808)
49th Independent Motor Transport Battalion	6265 (808)
83rd Independent Motor Transport Battalion	7573 (808)
309th Independent Motor Transport Company	2156 (132)
4th Independent Transport Regiment	5378 (1,897)
54th Independent Transport Battalion	6000 (2,440)

11th Army: continued	呂 *Ro*
55th Independent Transport Battalion	6001 (1,028)
75th Independent Transport Battalion	5275 (2,655)
57th Independent Transport Company	4603 (430)
58th Independent Transport Company	4604 (430)
59th Independent Transport Company	4605 (430)
60th Independent Transport Company	4611 (430)
61st Independent Transport Company	4612 (430)
62nd Independent Transport Company	4613
54th Field Road Construction Unit	2159 (303)
87th Line of Communications Hospital	6002 (359)
140th Line of Communications Hospital	9768 (359)
181st Line of Communications Hospital	17781 (333)
182nd Line of Communications Hospital	17782 (333)
183rd Line of Communications Hospital	17783 (333)
5th Casualty Clearing Headquarters	6131 (33)
1st Casualty Clearing Squad	6132 (53)
3rd Casualty Clearing Squad	6134 (53)
22nd Casualty Clearing Squad	6138 (53)
45th Casualty Clearing Platoon	1005 (54)
77th Casualty Clearing Platoon	2170 (54)
78th Casualty Clearing Platoon	5765 (54)
81st Casualty Clearing Platoon	5819 (54)
89th Casualty Clearing Platoon	9774 (54)
21st Field Disease Prevention / Water Supply Unit	2624 (329)

Hupei Province / Central China

20th Army 桜 *Sakura* 7922

The 20th Army was activated on September 10, 1941, in Heilongjiang Manchuria as a garrison army on the northeastern border. Its headquarters in Chining the 20th Army served under Kwantung Army control from Sept 19th until July 4, 1942, 1st Area Army until Sept 27, 1944 and 6th Area Army in Hengchow, Hunan (arrived in China Oct 18, 1944) until the war ended. Its commander was Lt Gen Kameji Seki from Sept 11th until Mar 11, 1943, Lt Gen Masaki Honda until Apr 8, 1944 and Lt Gen Ichirō Sakanishi until it was deactivated in Changsha on Sept 17, 1945.

Service History:

1941: Sept 19th, the 20th Army in Heilongjiang Province was responsible for security along Manchuria's northeastern border with the U.S.S.R. ○

1944: Sept 27th, the 20th Army headquarters is placed under 6th Area Army control ○ On Oct 18th the 20th Army headquarters arrives in China ○ In mid Oct the 20th Army's order of battle for *Ichi-go* is comprised of units already in the 11th Army's rear area. These included the 27th, 64th, 68th and 116th Div. It is responsible for the area between Hengyang, Wunchang and Hankow ○

1945: On Jan 3rd the 20th Army is ordered to secure and prevent sabotage to bridges and tunnels in the mountains between Canton and Hankou. This task went to the 27th, 40th Div and 57th Inf Bgde from the 68th Div ○ On Jan 18th the 40th Div mobilized four raiding units to secure bridges and tunnels between Lokchong and Chenhsien ○ Jan 19th to 22nd, the rail line between Lokchong and Liangtien was secured and by Jan 26th the entire Canton-Hankou railway occupied ○ By Feb 8th the airfields had been subdued ○ The 20th Army sent the 68th Div to guard the railway tracks from Hengyang to the Kiangsi-Hunan border. The 27th and 40th Div were transferred to the 23rd Army to guard rail lines ○ On Apr 3rd the 20th Army launched an attack on Chihkiang ○ Apr 8th, the 20th Army began the last Japanese offensive of the war against Chihkiang in Hupeh Prov. Its plan was to destroy Chihkiang Airfield, which was occupied by the US 14th Air Force ○ On Apr 8th the 116th Div and Shigehiro Detachment (47th Div) moved against the Chinese 18th, 73rd, 74th and 100th Armies, with some early success ○ Apr 17th, the Sekine Detachment captured Hsinning, on Apr 27th Wuyang and May 4th Wuwutang but Chinese reinforcements trickled in ending the offensive ○ On May 6th the 47th Div arrived in China ○ On May 20th the 47th Div reached Mawangao where the Shigehiro Detachment rejoined it with orders to cover the 116th Div retreat ○ May 25th the 116th Div was safely back in Tantow and the 47th Div in Chukaopu. By June 10th all units had returned to their stations. At the close of the Chihkiang operation the 47th Div was to go to Liching and join the 43rd Army in northern China but ended the war at Chouchiakow. The 34th Div under China Expeditionary Army control was sent to the lower reaches of the Yangtze River but ended the war in Wuning ○ The 23rd Army's 27th and 40th Div were temporarily attached to the 20th Army and directed to Nanchang. The 131st Div was sent to Wuchang-Hankou along the Canton-Hankou railway. The 3rd, 13th and 34th Div from the 11th Army were temporarily assigned to the 20th Army but still heavily engaged in fighting ○

Major Units: See division / brigade page for order of battle

64th Division Hiroshima 1943 開 *Kai* – Changsha	192
68th Division Osaka 1942 檜 *Hinoki* – Hengchow	193
116th Division Kyoto 1938 嵐 *Arashi* – Hunan	201
81st Independent Mixed Brigade 1945 至強 *Shikyou* – Tsingkang	230
82nd Independent Mixed Brigade 1945 至烈 *Shiretsu* – Tsingkang	230
86th Independent Mixed Brigade 1945 秋霜 *Syuso* – Paoching	232
87th Independent Mixed Brigade 1945 震動 *Shindou* – Hengchow	232

Units under control of the 20th Army:	桜 *Sakura* 7922	
20th Army Headquarters	7907 (299)	Hengchow
20th Army Field Ordinance Depot	17771 (937)	
20th Army Field Motor Vehicle Depot	17772 (1,010)	
20th Army Freight Depot	17773 (1,413)	
20th Army Veterinary Depot	17791 (297)	
5th Independent Mountain Artillery Regiment	9435 (1,875)	
22nd Anti-Aircraft Regiment	5535 (525)	
5th Signal Regiment	1410 (1,674)	
2nd Tank Division Anti-Aircraft Unit	12104 (1,014)	
38th Independent Engineer Regiment	2968 (591)	
55th Field Road Construction Unit	5764 (303)	
184th Line of Communications Hospital	17784 (333)	

20th Army continued	桜 *Sakura*
185th Line of Comm. (Laiyang Army) Hospital	17785 (333)
24th Casualty Clearing Headquarters	17780 (117)
6th Division Bridging Materials Company	5561 (559)
16th Division 1st River Crossing Materials Co.	5568 (545)

Above: Cavalry Regiment bivouac during the 1937 Shanghai Incident. Regiment's flag with single color guard (author)

Below: Regiment's baggage train with troopers on hgh ground behind (author)

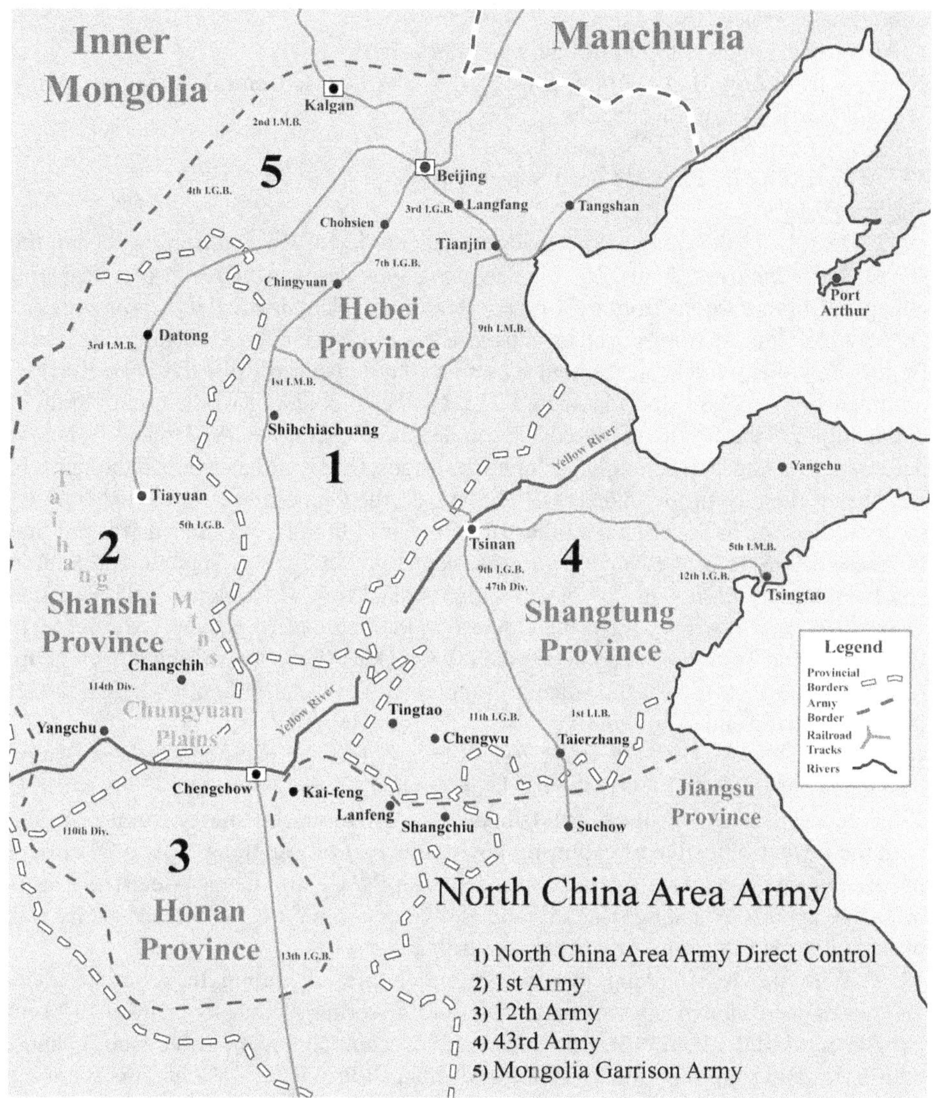

<u>North China Area Army</u> 甲 *Ko* 1400

The North China Area Army was activated on August 26, 1937, from former North China Garrison Army personnel. Headquarters in Beijing under Imperial Headquarters direction from Nov 17th until Sept 23, 1939 and China Expeditionary Army until the war ended. Its commander was General Count Hisaichi Terauchi from Aug 26th until Dec. 9, 1938, General Hajime Sugiyama until Sept 12th, General Hayao Tada until July 7, 1941, General Yasuji Okamura until Aug 25, 1944, General Naosaburō Okabe until Nov 22nd, Lt. Gen. Sadamu Shimomura until Aug 19, 1945 and Lt. Gen. Hiroshi Nemoto until the North China Area Army was deactivated in Beijing on September 17, 1945.

Subordinate armies / duty dates:
1st Army from Aug 31, 1937 until Sept 17, 1945
2nd Army from Aug 31, 1937 until July 4 1938 to Central China Exp. Army
Mongol Garrison Army from July 4, 1938 until Aug 15, 1945
12th Army from Nov 11, 1938 until Sept 17, 1945
43rd Army from Mar 22, 1943 until Sept 17, 1945

Service History:

1937: On July 7th the Marco Polo Bridge Incident (1st Inf Regt in Beijing) began the *North China Incident* ○ July 25th the *Langfang Incident* was the result of a ceasefire collapse, Chinese troops fired on a Japanese unit repairing downed telegraph wires ○ On July 26th Chinese troops fired on Japanese troops entering the Kuanganmen Gate in Beijing, in violation of an agreement. The same day Japan's ally, the East Hopei Army, mutinied in Tungchow and massacred 235 Japanese including women and children. ○ On July 29th the 5th Div captured Tianjin despite the Chinese 38th Division's heroic defense ○ On Aug 4th Beijing fell to Japanese troops, timely orders stopped the fighting and spared the city further damage ○ By Aug 8th the Chinese had evacuated Beijing, some for Paoting in South Hubei others for Chahar ○ In mid Aug Chahar was the first Japanese offensive of the *North China Incident.* By Oct Tatung, Suiyuan and Paotou had been taken ○ On Aug 26th North China Area Army headquarters was activated ○ Sept 14th, the 1st Army routed the Chinese in the battle of Chohsien ○ By Sept 24th Chingyuan and Tsanghsien had been taken ○ On Oct 14th the North China Area Army reinforced the 1st Army for the siege of Yangchu ○ On Oct 17th fighting began ○ Oct 24th the 1st Army ended pursuit ○ On Nov 16th Yangchu fell ○

1938: Feb 11th to Mar 8th, the 109th, 20th, 108th and 14th Div pacified southern Shanxi Province ○ Mar 24th to May 1st the battle of Xuzhou ○ Mar 24th to Apr 7th the battle of Taierzhuang ○ May 17th, the North China Area Army pursued enemy from Tangshan with the further objective of capturing key points east of Langfeng ○ Aug 9th to Sept 25th the North China Area Army cooperated with the Central China Area Army in its offensive against Wuchang, Hankou and Hanyang ○ On Nov 11th the 12th Army was placed under North China Area Army control ○

1939: With the Kuomintang in disarray and hopes of ending the conflict gone, guidelines were drawn up for conquering and governing Chinese territory ○ From Feb 24th until Mar 13th the 12th Army engaged in a campaign to eradicate bandit bands, their bases and supply networks in northern Jiangsu Province. Detachments spent the next few years mopping-up and fighting in small battles against guerillas, bandits and border incursions in Jiangsu ○

1940: Aug 20th to Dec 5th the North China Area Army vs. Communist 8th Route Army *Battle of 100 Regiments*. Communists managed to close the Jingxing coalmine for six months and destroy infrastructure without taking control of land, Communist victory.

1941: Dec 3rd, General Okamura introduced the *Three Alls* to pacify China's northern provinces. *Kill all, Burn all, Take all* was scorched earth retaliation for the *Battle of 100 Regiments*. This criminal policy caused as many as 2.7 million Chinese deaths from starvation and forced labor, mostly in Shandong and Hebei provinces.

1944: From Apr 19th until December the North China Area Army was involved in *Ichi-go* operations ○ In July reinforcements arrived to replace veteran divisions that had been sent elsewhere, including four new divisions for the 1st Army, 12th Army and Mongolia Garrison Army. The North China Area Army was responsible for operation

Ko-go (part of *Ichi-go)*, which ran between Beijing and Wuhan although the fighting mainly took place in Henan Prov ○ By May 9th the railway had been secured ○
1945: The North China Area Army spent the rest of the war providing security and logistical support in China ○
Major Units: See division / brigade page for order of battle

1st Independent Mixed Brigade 1939 島 *Shima* – Kwangping	209
8th Independent Mixed Brigade 1939 春 *Haru* – Shunyi	211
2nd Independent Infantry Brigade 1943 曙 *Akebono* – Shimen	236
3rd Independent Guard Unit 1945 伸張 *Shinchou* – Beijing	243
7th Independent Guard Unit 1945 至武 *Itaru Takeshi* – Baoding	244
North China Special Guard 1943 甲 *Ko* – Beijing	246

Units under the North China Area Army: Beijing	甲 *Ko* 1400	
North China Area Army Headquarters	1800 (981)	Beijing
North China Signal Training Unit	1869 (403)	
North China NCO Officer Candidate Department	1870 (227)	
NC NCO Officer Candidate Intendance Training D	1871 (29)	
NC NCO Officer Candidate Medical Training Dept	1872 (26)	
NC NCO Officer Candidate Vet, Training Dept	1873 (18)	
15th Anti-Aircraft Regiment	1409 (1,610)	
74th Field Anti-Aircraft Battalion	7831 (385)	
86th Field Anti-Aircraft Battalion	2189 (521)	
44th Independent Rapid Firing Gun Company	1874 (118)	
40th Independent Engineer Regiment	1486 (821)	
1st Specially Established Engineer Company	1487 (200)	
29th Signal Regiment	12510 (2,029)	
Independent Light Armored Car Unit	15656	
55th Fixed Radio Unit	1255 (30)	
103rd Independent Wire Company	3173 (277)	
4th Independent Engineer Company	4022 (165)	
North China Field Well Drilling Unit	1878 (183)	
6th Well Drilling Grp. (part of N.C. Well Drill Unit)	1878	
21st Motor Transport Regiment	1875 (760)	
242nd Motor Transport Company	7802 (183)	
243rd Motor Transport Company	7803 (183)	
244th Motor Transport Company	7804 (183)	
245th Motor Transport Company	7805 (183)	
5th Division 4th Land Transport Unit	1879 (321)	
1st (Inland) Water Transport Unit	1849 (872)	
23rd Field Duty Unit Headquarters	4023 (17)	
124th Specially Established Land Duty Company	5048 (61)	
125th Specially Established Land Duty Company	14955 (61)	
126th Specially Established Land Duty Company	14756 (61)	
26th Field Duty Headquarters	7189 (17)	
126th Specially Established Sea Duty Company	11174 (61)	
North China Military Police Unit	No # (2,029)	
151st L.o.C. (Beijing 1st Army) Hospital	1827 (584)	

North China Area Army continued	甲 *Ko*
152nd L.o.C. (Beijing 2nd Army) Hospital	1828 (584)
153rd Line of Comm. (Tianjin Army) Hospital	1829 (584)
154th L.o.C. (Beidaihe Army) Hospital	1830 (584)
187th Line of Comm. (Baoding Army) Hospital	1831 (206)
161st Line of Communications (Shimen) Hospital	1832 (333)
188th Line of Communications Hospital	1403 (206)
North China Field Horse Remount Depot	1801 (652)
N. China Disease Prevention / Water Supply Unit	1855 (783)
North China Decontamination Department	1887 (41)
North China Veterinary Quarantine Depot	1861 (38)
North China Field Ordinance Depot	1809 (2,325)
North China Field Motor Vehicle Depot	1813 (2,095)
• 1st North China Field Motor Vehicle Repair Unit	1813
• 3rd North China Field Motor Vehicle Repair Unit	1815
North China Field Freight Depot	1819 (3,721)
20th Line of Communications Veterinary Depot	9455 (538)
18th Railway Regiment	2152 (3,447)
115th Railway Station Command	5720 (17)
126th Railway Station Command	10054 / 8213 (17)
145th Railway Station Command	7037 (106)
151st Railway Station Command	6431 (106)
182nd Railway Station Command	6028 (17)
183rd Railway Station Command	6037 (17)
184th Railway Station Command	6038 (17)
190th Railway Station Command	17186 (17)
193rd Railway Station Command	9757 (17)
206th Railway Station Command	7817 (17)
124th Specially Established Sea Duty Company	11172 (61)
125th Specially Established Sea Duty Company	11173 (61)
126th Specially Established Sea Duty Company	11174 (61)

Shanxi Province / North West China

1st Army 乙 *Otsu* 3501

The 1st Army (its last iteration*) was activated on August 26, 1937, in Tienching, China from former China Garrison Army personnel. Its headquarters were in Tiayuan, Shanxi Prov under North China Area Army control from Aug 31st until Sept 17, 1945. Commanded by Lt Gen Kiyoshi Katsuki from Aug 26th until May 30, 1938, Lt Gen Yoshirō Umezu until Sept 7, 1939, Lt Gen Yoshio Shinozuka until June 20, 1941,

Lt Gen Yoshio Iwamatsu until Aug 1, 1942, Lt Gen Teiichi Yoshimoto until Nov 22, 1944, and Lt Gen Raishirō Sumida until it was deactivated in Taiyuan on September 17, 1945.
Note*: First mobilized for the 1st Sino-Japanese War 1894-5, deactivated. Reactivated for the Russo-Japanese War in 1904-5 then deactivated again.
Service History:
1937: Mid Aug to mid Oct participated in the Chahar operation, the first Japanese offensive of the war in China ○ Sept 14th to 24th, Battle of Taiyuan, also called Battle of Chohsien-Chingyuan. Captured Chingyuan, fighting ended when the Chinese were routed ○ Oct 12th to Nov 8th, the 20th and 109th Div occupied the Shihchiachuang-Yangchu rail line and Yangchu Plain ○ Nov. 8th, Yangchu City fell to the 5th Div, which had been temporarily attached to the 1st Army ○
1938: Feb 11th to Mar 8th, the 1st Army pursued Chinese troops to the Shanxi plains with plans to encircle and destroy them. Most escaped to south of the Yellow River, while some went to join the Communists in the mountains of Shanxi ○ Mar 8th to Apr 26th, in spite of their heavy losses Chinese resistance increased. The 1st Army withdrew to prepare for Tungshan ○ May 12th to 24th, the 1st Army assisted the 2nd Army by lending troops and support for the capture of Tungshan ○ In May the campaign in south Shanxi Province ended and the North China Area Army began mopping up hostile remnants. The 1st Army became the garrison in Shanxi Prov. with its headquarters in Taiyuan ○ The 2nd Army continued to face serious resistance from Chinese regulars and Communist guerrillas so the 1st Army lent it the 16th and 114th Div ○ In late Sept, the North China Area Army, Mongolia Army and Air Unit (activated in early Aug, deactivated on Nov 17th) contributed to the mopping up effort in north Shanxi ○
1939: Jul 3rd to Aug 21st the Chinese had 80,000 Nationalist and 20,000 Communist fighters in east Shanxi ○ On July 13th the 1st Army captured Changchih ○ By July 21st six Chinese div were still active in the area ○ Sept 9th, the mopping up continues ○
1940: Apr 17th to early May the 1st Army planned to destroy Kuomintang south of Changchih but another enemy force appeared near Hsiangning. Both withdrew before they could be engaged. Mopping up operations temporarily drove the enemy forces from south Shanxi ○ Aug 20th, the battle of 100 regiments. The Communist 18th Army Group attacked Shichiachuang-Yangchu railway lines and industrial buildings. The Jingxing coal mine was destroyed and Japanese garrisons in the area suffered heavy losses ○ Aug 30th to Dec 3rd, the destruction caused by the Communists was temporary. The 1st Army chased them back to their bases in the mountains and destroyed some of the bases. After that the Communists offered little organized resistance ○
1941: On May 7th the 1st Army attacked the Chinese 15th, 27th (Kuomintang) and 93rd (Communist) Armies in west Shanxi. A dust storm hid Japanese movements surprising the Chinese 15th Army, which was defeated. The 27th and 93rd Armies withdrew ○
1944: On July 10th the 114th Div was re-activated and placed under 1st Army control ○ Apr 18th to Dec 10th, *Ichi-go* was the 1st Army's last major action of the war. It's mission was to open and secure railway lines between Beijing and Hankou ○
1945: The 1st Army spent the remainder of the war as the garrison in Shanxi where it was deactivated on September 17, 1945 ○
Major Units: See division / brigade page for order of battle
114th Division Mizonokuchi 1937 将 *Sye* – Taiyuan 200
3rd Independent Mixed Brigade 1938 造 *Tukuru* – Hsingsiang 209

10th Independent Infantry Brigade 1943 固 *Ko* – Taiyuan	238
14th Independent Infantry Brigade 1944 塁 *Rui* – Tuanfu	239-40
5th Independent Guard Unit 1945 至隆 *Yoshitaka* – Yuncheng	243

Units under 1st Army control: Taiyuan	乙 *Otsu* 3501	
1st Army Headquarters	3500 (262)	Taiyuan
9th Signal Regiment	3506 (1,605)	
24th Independent Mountain Artillery Battalion	1890 (991)	
81st Field Machine Cannon Company	15651 (105)	
1st Independent Transport Regiment	3510 (1,745)	
27th Motor Transport Regiment	3508 (760)	
162nd L. o. C. (Taiyuan Army) Hospital	1835 (333)	
163rd Line of Comm. (Linfen Army) Hospital	1838 (333)	
164th L. o. C. (Liancheng Army) Hospital	1839 (333)	
194th L. o. C. (Changzhi Army) Hospital	1837 (206)	
195th L. o. C. (Yangquan Army) Hospital	1833 (206)	
196th Line of Communications Hospital	1836 (206)	
North China Field Freight Depot, Teigen Branch	1824	

North Cental China

12th Army 仁 *Hito* 4220

The 12th Army was activated in north China November 9, 1938, and placed under North China Area Army control on Nov 11th, headquarters in Chenghsien, Henan Prov. After the Wuhan-Hankou operation (May 30th to Oct. 28, 1938) the newly occupied areas in Henan Province and Licheng area became the 12th Army's responsibility* until Sept 1, 1944 when Licheng and its Japanese garrison were placed under North China Area Army control. Its commander was Lt Gen Kamezō Suetaka from Nov 9th until Sept 12, 1939, Lt Gen Sadakata Īda until Mar 1, 1941, Lt Gen Kazutsugu Tsuchihashi until Mar 1, 1943, Lt Gen Seiichi Kita until Feb 7, 1944, Lt Gen Eitarō Uchiyama until Apr 7, 1945 and Lt Gen Takashi Takamori until it was deactivated in Chengchow on Sept 17, 1945.

Note: *But also active in Shandong and Jiangsu Provinces.

Service History:

1938: Nov 11th, 12th Army was placed under North China Area Army control ○

1939: On Feb 24th the 12th Army was sent to Kiangsu Province to attack the Chinese 57th and 89th Armies and subdue Tunghai and the Huaiyin supply base ○ On Mar 2nd Huaiyin captured ○ On Mar 4th Tunghai was captured ○ On Mar 13th Tunghai/Huaiyin ended with the Chinese retreating and the 12th Army mopping up ○ June 29th, the 12th Army left Shangchiu and Lanfeng, drove the enemy from Chengwu and Tingtao and cleared western Shandong Province of hostile forces ○

1940 to 1943: The 12th Army's headquarters were in Chenghsien. During this time it served as a garrison for pacified areas of Honan and Lichen ○

1944: On July 17th newly mobilized, the 115th and 117th Div were placed under 12th Army control ○ Apr 19th, the 12th Army was assigned to secure the rail lines from Beijing to Hankou for operation *Ichi-go* ○ On Apr 19th the 37th Div (1st Army) took Chenghsien supported by the 7th I.M.B. (12th Army) ○ May 19th the 12th Army received orders to take Loyang ○ On May 25th Loyang fell to the 12th Army ○ Mar 27th the 4th Cav Brigade took Laohokao airfield but failed to capture the city ○

1945: On Mar 22nd the 12th Army began its offensive on Laohokou but as the 110th and 115th Div approached Nanyang the attack was halted. The 115th and 3rd Armored Div occupied the Likuanchiao-Laohokou line instead, the 110th Div took Hsihsiakou ○ Mar 27th, Laohokou airfield was recaptured ○ On Mar 31st the Yoshitake Detachment and a medium artillery regiment took Nanyang. Bad roads and rain prevented some units from reaching their starting positions before April 2nd ○ On Apr 8th the 115th Div captured Laohokao with artillery support. The 34th Army blocked reinforcements from arriving in Laohokao from the south. Following the operation the 12th Army returned to performing garrison duties ○ May 30th, the 117th Div was sent to Taonan, Manchuria to serve in the new 44th Army ○ Deactivated in Chengchow on Sept 17th ○

Major Units: See division / brigade page for order of battle

110th Division Himeji 1938 鷺 *Sagi* – Loyang	199-200
115th Division Asahikawa 1944 北 *Kita* – Laohokow	201
3rd Armored Division Tsudanuma 1942 滝 *Taki* – Chenghsien	206-7
4th Cavalry Brigade 1909 成 *Sei* – Honan Province	240
6th Independent Guard Unit 1945 至毅 *Itaru Takeshi* – Baoding	243-4
10th Independent Guard Unit 1945 至敏 *Itaru Toshi* – Chengchow	244-5
13th Independent Guard Unit 1945 疾風 *Hayate* –Suiping	245-6
14th Independent Guard Unit 1945 紫電 *Shiden* – Yanchang / Xianyang	246

Units under 12th Army control: Chengchow	仁 *Hito* 4220	
12th Army Headquarters	4221 (267)	Chengchow
10th Signal Regiment	4222 (1,605)	
25th Motor Transport Regiment	4223 (1,092)	deact 7/10/45
26th Motor Transport Regiment	4224 (1,092)	deact 7/10/45
7th Division 4th Land Transport Unit	4225 (321)	
6th Field Medium Artillery Regiment	3504 (1,696)	
1st Independent Mountain Artillery Battalion	1485 (991)	
43rd Independent Rapid Firing Gun Company	1868 (118)	
82nd Field Machine Cannon Company	15652 (105)	
83rd Field Machine Cannon Company	15653 (105)	
84th Field Machine Cannon Company	15654 (105)	
87th Land Duty Company	4016 (511)	
24th Bridging Materials Company	4618 (680)	
25th Bridging Materials Company	4619 (410)	
31st Bridging Materials Company	6415 (410)	
168th L. o. C. (Xinxiang Army) Hospital	1834 (333)	
169th Line of Communications Hospital	1402 (333)	
186th Line of Communications (Kaifeng) Hospital	1845 (206)	
189th Line of Communications Hospital	1413 (206)	
North China Field Freight Depot, Sairen Branch	1825	

North East China

43rd Army 秀嶺 *Shurei* 17201

The 43rd Army became operational March 10, 1945, and placed under North China Area Army control on Mar 22nd. Its headquarters were in Tsinan, Shantung where it as a garrison army. Its initial order of battle included the 59th Div, 5th and 9th I.M.B. and 1st Ind Inf Bgde. The 43rd Army commander was Lt Gen Tadayasu Hosokawa from Mar 31, 1945 until it was deactivated in Tsinan on September 17, 1945.

Service History:

1945: From Mar to Aug the 43rd Army worked to fortify Shantung's coastline as a potential invasion target ○ By Aug 15th half the planned fortifications on the coast and a third of those around Changtien had been completed. In the event of an American invasion the 43rd Army planned a campaign of harassment using guerrilla tactics against enemy attempts to establish air and naval bases. The objective being to inflict as many casualties as possible ○

Major Units: See division / brigade page for order of battle

Unit	Page
47th Division Hirosaki 1943 弾 *Dan* – Yenching	184-5
5th Independent Mixed Brigade 1938 桐 *Kiri* – Tsingtao	210
9th Independent Mixed Brigade 1939 谷 *Tani* – Tientsin	211-2
1st Independent Infantry Brigade 1943 幹 *Kan* – Chucheng	236
9th Independent Guard Unit 1945 至剛 *Itaru Tsuyoshi* – Shantung	244
11th Independent Guard Unit 1945 至鋭 *Surudoi* – Shantung	245
12th Independent Garrison Unit 1945 至厳 *Itaru Gen* – Tsingtao	245

Units under control of the 43rd Army: Tsinan	秀嶺 *Shurei* 17201	
43rd Army Headquarters	17200 (270)	Tsinan
18th Trench Mortar Battalion	28371 (866)	
19th Trench Mortar Battalion	28248 (866)	
45th Independent Rapid Firing Gun Company	1888 (118)	
21st Motor Transport Regiment	1895 (760)	
63rd Fixed Radio Unit	12470 (26)	
64th Fixed Radio Unit	12471 (26)	
155th Line of Comm. (Jinan Army) Hospital	1841 (584)	
165th L. o. C. (Qingdao Army) Hospital	1840 (333)	
197th L. o. C. (Yanzhou Army) Hospital	1842 (206)	

Zhangjiakou Evacuation Unit: Hebei (Mongolia)	戍 *Inu*
Evacuation Unit Headquarters	5301 (196)
23rd Motor Transport Regiment	1304 / 5304 (760)
166th Line of Communications Hospital	1846 (333)
167th Line of Communications Hospital	1847 (333)
198th Line of Communications Hospital	1848 (206)
199th Line of Communications Hospital	1844 (206)

Mongolia

Mongolia Garrison Army 戊 *Bo* 5300

The Mongolia Garrison Army was activated in Kalgan, Inner Mongolia on July 4, 1938, from former Mongolia Garrison Group personnel. It was created to secure Inner Mongolia and Chahar Province along the China-Mongolia border. With headquarters in Kalgan it served under the North China Area Army from July 7th until the war ended. Its commander was Lt Gen Shigeru Hasunama from July 4th until Aug 31, 1939, General Hajime Sugiyama until Sept 12th, Lt Gen Naosaburō Okabe until Sept 29, 1940, Lt Gen Masataka Yamawaki until Jan 20, 1941, Lt Gen Shigetarō Amakasu until Mar 2, 1942, Lt Gen Ichirō Shichida until May 28, 1943, Lt Gen Yoshio Kōzuki Nov 22, 1944 and Lt Gen Nemoto Hiroshi until at least August 26, 1945. The Mongolia Garrison Army was deactivated in Tulung.

Service History:

1940: On Jan 28th the Mongolia Garrison Army began the first Houtao offensive to destroy active enemy units and guerillas ○ By Mar 1st resistance had been crushed and the army returned to base ○ On Mar 21st the second battle of Houtao began. The Chinese 35th Army attacked Wuyuian in retaliation for the first Houtao offensive ○ On Mar 22nd a Japanese relief column crossed the Wuchia River but the Chinese army broke dykes, caused flooding and forced an end to the pursuit ○ By Mar 29th all Mongolia Garrison Army units had returned to their starting positions ○

1944: On July 17th the newly activated 118th Div was placed under Mongolia Garrison Army control ○

1945: May 28th, the 118th Div was transferred to the 13th Army in Hebei. IGHQ issued orders to defend south of the Abagapeitzufu and Pailingmiao line. By now the best units in the Mongolia Garrison Army had been transferred to the Southern Expeditionary Army, 12th and 13th Armies, leaving only the 2nd I.M.B. and 4th Ind Guard Brigade. IGHQ planned to have two divisions join the Mongolia Army. ○ With the Soviets threatening to invade, the China Expeditionary Army ordered the 118th Div, attached to the 13th Army, to rejoin the Mongolia Garrison Army but the war ended before it arrived ○ By Aug 15th part of the division was just south of Wanchuan ○ On Aug 9th the Soviets invaded Inner Mongolia. Fortifications had been completed in the areas close to Wanchuan, Tatung and Fengchen ○ On Aug 14th an element from the 4th Ind Guard Unit skirmished with a Soviet mechanized unit and returned to base ○ On Aug 18th the Russians attacked the fortified positions near Wanchuan. Civilian evacuees were protected by the 2nd I.M.B. ○ On Aug 20th the Russians rejected 5 offers of truce and continued to attack the lines but were repulsed ○ By Aug 21st all the civilians had been evacuated and the brigade left for Nankou ○ On Aug 26th the 2nd Independent Mixed Brigade arrived in Nankou ○

Major Units: See division / brigade page for order of battle

2nd Independent Mixed Brigade 1938 響 *Hibiki* – Beijing	209
4th Independent Guard Unit 1945 至誠 *Sisei* – Fengchen	243

Units under the Mongolia Garrison Army: Kalgan 戊 *Bo* 5300

Mongolia Garrison Army Headquarters	5301 (196)	Kalgan
23rd Motor Transport Regiment	1304 / 5304 (760)	
Mongolia Garrison Army Intelligence Department	5309 (66)	
130th Independent Wire Company	12977 (310)	
131st Independent Wire Company	unknown (310)	

<u>Mongolia Garrison Army</u>: continued	戍 *Bo*
166th L. o. C. (Zhangjiakou Army) Hospital	1846 (333)
167th Line of Communications (Datong) Hospital	1847
198th Line of Communications (Baotou) Hospital	1848
199th L. o. C. (Pingdiquanzhen) Hospital	1844

Type 97 'Chi-ha' medium tanks, the backbone of Japan's armored forces (author)

End of Overseas Armies

Chapter 3

Overseas Divisions and Brigades

Over time the Army activated 168 infantry divisions, in addition there were 3 Imperial guard, 4 armored and 4 anti-aircraft divisions. The first twenty mobilized between 1888 and 1915 and were Permanent Divisions, except for the 13th, 15th, 17th and 18th that were temporary activations for wartime. Between 1868 and 1938 the Army never had more than twenty divisions in total. Jumping ahead, one hundred and fifty-four divisions had been in service by the time Japan surrendered in August 1945.

Infantry divisions were comprised of a group of 3 to 4 infantry regiments supported by permanent reconnaissance, engineer and artillery units. Transport, signal, ordinance, medical, veterinary and other service units kept the division self-sufficient as a small town when it was in the field. Some divisions were formed around independent infantry battalions instead of regiments, this kind retained the two-infantry brigade structure.

Divisions were classified in three different ways, *A* type: strengthened, added firepower and/or personnel: *B* type: standard and *C* type: light, equipped for garrison duty and security work.

Divisions and Brigades Activated in Occupied and Contested Areas:

Conscription normally filled the ranks when it came to troop replacement and unit activation in Japan, Korea and Taiwan, with its large Japanese civil population Manchuria was another area the army drew on later. As the war progressed and evolving circumstances necessitated change new divisions and brigades began to activate in occupied areas. The manpower for these came from replacement units, surplus replacement personnel and service units, stranded remnants of relocated divisions and brigades and recovered hospital patients. They were standard 丙 C type divisions except the 48th Division and 2nd Guard Division, which were created as

strengthened 甲 A types.
Activations abroad began on Feb 10, 1938 with the 2nd, 3rd and 6th Independent Mixed Brigades in North China and continued throughout the country for the rest of the war. As the army was xenophobic by nature native populations in occupied countries were normally excluded from joining, the exception being entry into manual labor units.
The first activation outside China was the 21st Independent Mixed Brigade in Hanoi, French Indochina on June 26, 1941 and the first division was the 31st Division in Bangkok on Mar 22, 1943. Field activations would sometimes occur if hostilities were anticipated and the local garrison units were ill-equipped to deal with it.

Divisions and brigades:
Left side column: Formal unit name.
Right side column: Code name and number (parentheses; personnel strength)
Service History: with a date shows battle participation.
Classifying Japanese Army Divisions:
甲 *A*: Shown as (A type) Strengthened; augmented firepower and/or personnel.
乙 *B*: Shown as (B type) Standard.
丙 *C*: Shown as (C type) Security, lighter in composition.
Mojifu (Code name): shown at top of unit code number list. These are an organization's kanji code name and are shown with their Romaji pronunciation.
Manchu: 満州, used by units whose code numbers originate in the Kwantung Army.
Note: Disease Prevention and Water Supply Units = D. P. & Water Supply Unit

Imperial Guard Division

Imperial Guard Division Tokyo 1891		
2nd Imperial Guard Division 1943	宮 *Miya* 3814 (14,843)	
Konoe 2nd Division Headquarters	3800 (298)	
Konoe 2nd Division Signal Unit	3810 (187)	
Konoe 2nd Division Ordinance Duty Unit	3812 (131)	
Konoe 2nd Division Medical Unit	3813 (533)	
Konoe 2nd Division 1st Field Hospital	3814 (228)	
Konoe 2nd Division 2nd Field Hospital	3817 (235)	
Konoe 2nd Infantry Group Headquarters	3801 (87)	
• Konoe 3rd Infantry Regiment (Kōhu)	3802 (2,580)	
• Konoe 4th Infantry Regiment (Sakura)	3803 (2,580)	
• Konoe 5th Infantry Regiment (Tokyo)	3804 (3,964)	
• Konoe 2nd Cavalry Regiment	3806 (418)	
• Konoe 2nd Field Artillery Regiment	3808 (1,024)	
• Konoe 2nd Engineer Regiment	3809 (544)	Thai-Burma RR
• Konoe 2nd Transport Regiment	3811 (494)	
• Konoe 2nd Sea Transport Unit	6146 (1,542)	

Imperial Guard Division: (A type) Activated Tokyo Dec 14, 1891. Home station: Tokyo. Became triangular Nov 30, 1940. With Eastern District Army from July 7, 1937 until June 26, 1940, 22nd Army until Nov 19th, South China Area Army until July 5, 1941, 25th Army in Saigon for the invasion of Malaya on Nov 8, 1941. During the invasion the Div. lost favor with Gen. Yamashita for insubordination, later sidelined to Sumatra.

Service History: China, Indochina, Malaya, Sumatra

Infantry Divisions

1st Division Tokyo 1888	玉 *Tama* 5911 (12,000)
1st Division Headquarters	5912 (252)
1st Division Signal Unit	5922 (240)
1st Division Ordinance Duty Unit	5924 (40)
1st Division Medical Unit	5925 (491)
1st Division 1st Field Hospital	5926 (287)
1st Division 4th Field Hospital	5929 (284)
1st Division D. P. & Water Supply Unit	1201 (100)
1st Division Anti-Gas Unit	5917
1st Division Infantry Group	
• 1st Infantry Regiment (Azabu)	5914 (2,200)
• 49th Infantry Regiment (Kofu)	5915 (2,200)
• 57th Infantry Regiment (Sakura)	5916 (2,200)
• 1st Cavalry Regiment	5918 (200)
• 1st Field Artillery Regiment	5920 (1,700)

1st Division continued

• 1st Engineer Regiment	5521 (600)
• 1st Transport Regiment	5923 (1,200)

1st Division: (A type) Activated Tokyo May 14, 1888. Home station: Tokyo. Lost the 3rd Inf Regt becoming triangular Jul. 16, 1940. With the Kwantung Army from July 7, 1937 until July 15,1938, 4th Army until July 24, 1944, Imperial HQ until Sept. 22nd, 14th Area Army until Oct 27th and 35th Army landed on Leyte Oct 30th, destroyed by Jan 1, 1945.
4th Expeditionary Unit (Yap Is): Detached from the 1st and 12th Div Feb 21, 1944.
6th Expeditionary Unit (Guam): Detached from the 11th, 12th and 1st Div Feb 21, 1944.
Service History: Manchuria: Kanchazu Is Incident June 29 1937 China: Marco Polo Bridge Incident July 7 1937. Philippines: Leyte Oct 20 1944, Bohol Island 4/11/45.

2nd Division Sendai 1888	勇 *Isamu* 1320 (13,755)
2nd Division Headquarters	1339 (305)
2nd Division Signal Unit	1309 (182)
2nd Division Ordinance Duty Unit	1311 (123)
2nd Division Medical Unit	1312 (491)
2nd Division 1st Field Hospital	1313 (242)
2nd Division 2nd Field Hospital	1314 (242)
2nd Division 4th Field Hospital	1315 (247)
2nd Division D. P. & Water Supply Unit	1317 (196)
2nd Division Veterinary Unit	1316 (47)
2nd Infantry Group Headquarters	1330 (93) detach. Jan 30, 1942
• 4th Infantry Regiment (Sendai)	1301 (2,719)
• 16th Infantry Regiment (Shibata)	1302 (2,719)
• 29th Infantry Regiment (Wakamatsu)	1303 (2,719)
• 2nd Recon (Cavalry) Regiment	1305 (439)
• 2nd Field Artillery Regiment	1307 (1,738)
• 2nd Engineer Regiment	1308 (827)
• 2nd Transport Regiment	1310 (381)

2nd Division: (A type) Activated Sendai May 14, 1888. Home station: Sendai. Lost the 30th Inf Regt, becoming triangular Jul. 16, 1940. With the Kwantung Army from July 7, 1937 until July 21, 1938, 3rd Army until Nov 6, 1941, 16th Army until Aug 28, 1942, 17th Army until Mar 16, 1943, 14th Army (never sent to the Philippines) until Sept 13th, Southern Expeditionary Army until Jan 15, 1944, 28th Army until July 12th, 33rd Army until Oct 28th, Burma Area Army until Jan 27, 1945, 28th Army until May 23rd and 38th Army in Saigon until the war ended. The 29th I.R. burnt its flag on Henderson Field, Guadalcanal.
Note: Katayama Detachment: Manchuria: Akiyama Heights Sept 6 1939.
Aoba Detachment: 2nd Inf Group HQ and 4th Inf Regt Java Mar 1 1942, Guadalcanal.
Service History: Manchuria: Harbin Jan 25 1932. Mongolia: Chahar Aug 8 1937. Java: Invasion Mar 1 1942. Sumatra: Invasion Feb 14 1942. Guadalcanal: Matanikau River October 7 1942, Henderson Field October 24 1942. Burma: Bhamo November 8 1944.

3rd Division Nagoya 1888	幸 *Sachi* 3741 (18,882)
3rd Division Headquarters	3700 (362)
3rd Division Signal Unit	3710 (233)
3rd Division Ordinance Duty Unit	3712 (95)
3rd Division Medical Unit	3713 (400)
3rd Division 1st Field Hospital	3714 (301)
3rd Division 2nd Field Hospital	3715 (301)
3rd Division 4th Field Hospital	3717 (309)
3rd Division Veterinary Unit	3720 (119)
3rd Infantry Group Headquarters	3701
• 6th Infantry Regiment (Nagoya)	3702 (4,098)
• 34th Infantry Regiment (Shizuoka)	3703 (4,102)
• 68th Infantry Regiment (Gifu)	3704 (4,098)
• 3rd Cavalry Regiment	3706 (452)
• 3rd Field Artillery Regiment	3708 (1,959)
• 3rd Engineer Regiment	3709 (901)
• 3rd Transport Regiment	3711 (1,170)

3rd Division: (A type) Activated Nagoya May 14, 1888. Home station: Nagoya. Lost the 18th Inf Regt becoming triangular Jul 31, 1941. With the Eastern District Army from July 7, 1937 until Aug 15th, Shanghai Expeditionary Force until Feb 14, 1938, Central China Expeditionary Army until Aug 22nd, 2nd Army until Dec 9th, 11th Army until Apr 18, 1945 and China Expeditionary Army in Wuhu until it was deactivated in Pukou.
Service History: China: 2nd Shanghai Aug 23 1937, Suixian May 3 1938, Beijing-Hankou Railway Oct 4 1938, Hisiangtung May 1 1939, 1st Changsha Sept 14 1939, Yichang May 31 1940, South Henan Jan 30 1941, Chungyuan May 5 1941, 2nd Changsha Dec 24 1941, 3rd Changsha Jan 1 1942, Mt. Tapishshan Dec/Jan 1943, Changde Nov 16 1943, Luichow Nov 9 1944.

4th Division Osaka 1888	淀 *Yodo* 4066 (11,068)
4th Division Headquarters	4050 (295)
4th Division Signal Unit	4080 (210)
4th Division Ordinance Duty Unit	4083 (131)
4th Division Medical Unit	4084 (533)
4th Division 1st Field Hospital	4091 (228)
4th Division 4th Field Hospital	4094 (232)
4th Division D. P. & Water Supply Unit	4096 (239)
4th Infantry Group Headquarters	4071
• 8th Infantry Regiment (Osaka)	4072 (2,181)
• 37th Infantry Regiment (Sakai)	4073 (2,181)
• 61st Infantry Regiment (Wakayama)	4074 (2,181)
• 4th Cavalry Regiment	4075 (418)
• 4th Field Artillery Regiment	4077 (1,486)
• 4th Engineer Regiment	4079 (259)
• 4th Transport Regiment	4081 (494)

4th Division: (A type) Activated in Osaka May 14, 1888. Home station: Osaka. Lost the 70th Inf Regt, becoming triangular Mar. 9, 1940. With the Kwantung Army from Jul 7, 1937 until Jul 1, 1940, 11th Army until Nov 8, 1941, Imperial HQ until Feb 10, 1942, 14th Army until June 12th, Central District Army in Japan (reorganized) Sept 22, 1943, 25th Army in Sumatra until Jan 14, 1945, 39th Army until July 15th and 18th Area Army in Lampang, Thailand until the war ended. Led by Lt. Gen. Tomoyuki Yamashita 9/23/39 to 7/22/40.
Service History: China: Yichang May 31 1940, South Henan Jan 30 1941, Chungyuan May 5 1941, 2nd Changsha Sept 17 1941. Philippines: Bataan Apr 3 1942, Corregidor May 5 1942.

5th Division Hiroshima 1888	鯉 *Koi* 5191 (15,242)
5th Division Headquarters	5171 (360)
5th Division Signal Unit	5181 (235)
5th Division Ordinance Duty Unit	5183 (107)
5th Division Medical Unit	5184 (533)
5th Division 2nd Field Hospital	5186 (228)
55h Division 4th Field Hospital	5188 (233)
5th Infantry Group Headquarters	5172 (87)
• 11th Infantry Regiment (Hiroshima)	5173 (3,165)
• 21st Infantry Regiment (Hamada)	5174 (3,972)
• 42nd Infantry Regiment (Yamaguchi)	5175 (3,165)
• 5th Cavalry Regiment	5177 (418)
• 5th Field Artillery Regiment	5179 (1,486)
• 5th Engineer Regiment	5180 (759)
• 5th Transport Regiment	5182 (494)

5th Division: (A type) Activated in Hiroshima May 14, 1888, Home station: Hiroshima. Became motorized July 7, 1937. Lost the 41st Inf Regt becoming triangular in June 1941. With Army General Staff from July 7, 1937 until the 27th, China Garrison Army until Aug 31st, North China Area Army until Mar 30, 1938, 2nd Army until July 4th, North China Area Army until Sept 19th, 21st Army until Nov 29th, 12th Army until Sept 5, 1939, Kwantung Army until Sept 29th, Imperial HQ until Oct 16th, 21st Army, which became the 22nd Army on Feb 9, 1940, until Oct 12, 1940, Imperial HQ until Nov 6, 1941, 25th Army until Aug 6, 1942 (stranded in Singapore), 19th Army from Jan 11th until Feb 28, 1945, and 2nd Army. Sunda Is. garrison on Ceram Island until the war ended.
Note: Kawamura Detachment (41st Inf Regt) Philippines: Lingayan Apr 5, 1942, Panay Apr 16 1942, Mindanao Apr 22, 1942 (41st I.R. joined 21st I.M.B. in New Guinea on Apr 1, 1943).
Service History: China: Tianjin, Jul 29 1937, Taiyuan Sept 14 1937, Pingxingguan Sept 25 1937, Yangchu Nov 8 1937, Taierzhuang Mar 24 1938, Xuzhou May 10 1938, Canton Oct 12 1938, Kunlun Pass Dec 18 1939, Kohoku Feb 24 1940, Ssulo Mar 31 1940. Indochina: Lang Son Sept 22 1940. Malaya: Invasion Dec 8, 1941, Jitra Dec 11 1941, Gurun Dec 14 1941, Slim River Jan 6 1942, Muar Jan 14 1942, Singapore Feb 8 1942 (Div rec'd a citation for heroism). Indonesia: Ceram Is. garrison

6th Division Kumamoto 1888	明 *Akira* 9016 (20,909)	
6th Division Headquarters	9015 (448)	
6th Division Signal Unit	9026 (239)	
6th Division Ordinance Duty Unit	9028 (121)	
6th Division Medical Unit	9029 (913)	
6th Division 1st Field Hospital	9030 (236)	
6th Division 2nd Field Hospital	9031 (236)	
6th Division 4th Field Hospital	9033 (243)	
6th Division Veterinary Unit	9034 (119)	
6th Infantry Group Headquarters	9017 (92)	Iwasa Unit
• 13th Infantry Regiment (Kumamoto)	9018 (3,843)	
• 23rd Infantry Regiment (Miyakonojo)	9019 (3,843)	
• 45th Infantry Regiment (Kagoshima)	9020 (3,843)	
• 6th Cavalry Regiment	9022 (452)	
• 6th Field Artillery Regiment	9024 (3,186)	
• 6th Engineer Regiment	9025 (898)	
• 6th Transport Regiment	9027 (2,289)	

6th Division: (A type) Activated Kumamoto May 14, 1888. Home station: Kumamoto. Lost the 47th Inf Regt becoming triangular Nov 30, 1940. With the China Garrison Army from July 27, 1937 until Aug 31, 1937, 1st Army until Oct 20th, 10th Army until Feb 14, 1938, Central China Expeditionary Army until July 4th, 11th Army until Nov 16, 1942, 8th Area Army until Nov 20th and 17th Army on Bougainville until the war ended.
Note: Southeast Detachment: 13th Inf. Regt. w/artillery, created May 26, 1943. Operated independently but served under the 6th Div on Bougainville from mid-1944 on.
Service History: Manchuria: Rehe Feb 21 1933. China: 2nd Shanghai Nov 5 1937, Nanking Dec 9 1937, Beijing-Hankou Railway Oct 4 1938, 1st Changsha Sept 14 1939, Yichang May 1 1940, 2nd Changsha Dec 27 1941. Bougainville: 1st Torokina Nov 1 1943, 2nd Torokina Mar 6 1944, Buliaka River Mar 18 1945, Mivo River June 1945.

8th Division Hirosaki 1898	杉 *Sugi* 4732 (12,740)	
8th Division Headquarters	4700 (252)	
8th Division Signal Unit	4755 (240)	
8th Division Ordinance Duty Unit	4767 (41	as of Jul 1940)
8th Division 2nd Field Hospital	4792 (278)	
8th Division 4th Field Hospital	4794 (284)	
8th Division Anti-Gas Unit	4770 (10)	
8th Division D. P. & Water Supply Unit	1202 (250)	
8th Division Veterinary Unit	4780 / 満648 (71)	
8th Infantry Group Headquarters	unknown (6)	Fujishige Detach.
• 5th Infantry Regiment (Aomori)	4715 (2,500)	Takahashi Detach.
• 17th Infantry Regiment (Akita)	4717 (2,500)	
• 31st Infantry Regiment (Hirosaki)	4711 (2,500)	
• 8th (Recon) Cavalry Regiment	4728 (320)	
• 8th Field Artillery Regiment	4738 (2,200)	

8th Division continued	
• 8th Engineer Regiment	4748 (900)
• 8th Transport Battalion	4768 (1,200)

8th Division: (A type) Activated in Hirosaki Oct 1, 1898. Home station: Hirosaki. Lost the 32nd Inf Regt becoming triangular Oct 1, 1939. With the Eastern District Army from July 7, 1937 until Oct 1st, Kwantung Army until Jan 13, 1938, 3rd Army until Sept 19, 1941, 20th Army until July 18, 1944, Imperial HQ until Aug 4th, and 14th Area Army until Apr 20, 1945 and 41st Army on Luzon, destroyed by June 1945. 41st Army (Shimbu Army Group) used the 8th Division's code name "Sugi".
3rd Expeditionary Unit: Enderby Is., detached from the 8th Div on Feb 21, 1944.
Takahashi Detachment: 5th Inf Regt on Leyte Is., Ormoc/Libungao Dec 19 1944.
Fujishige Detachment: 8th Div. Inf. Group HQ in Batangas SW of Manila Jan 31 1945.
Service History: Manchuria: Rehe Feb 21 1933. China: 2nd Shanghai Aug 13 1937. Philippines: south Luzon Feb 3 1945.

10th Division Himeji 1898	鉄 *Tetsu* 5425 (12,000)	
10th Division Headquarters	5410 (250)	
10th Division Signal Unit	5453 (240)	
10th Division Ordinance Duty Unit	4883 (93)	
10th Division 1st Field Hospital	5457 (242)	
10th Division 2nd Field Hospital	5458 (278)	
10th Division 3rd Field Hospital	5459 (242)	
10th Division 4th Field Hospital	5460 (284)	
10th Division D. P. & Water Supply Unit	5462 (100)	
10th Division Anti-Gas Unit	5455 (10)	as of Jul 6 1940
10th Division Veterinary Unit	5461 (52)	
10th Infantry Group Headquarters	5445 (93)	
• 10th Infantry Regiment (Okayama)	5448 (2,200)	
• 39th Infantry Regiment (Himeji)	5446 (2,200)	
• 63rd Infantry Regiment (Matsue)	5447 (2,200)	
• 10th Cavalry Regiment	5450 (200)	
• 10th Field Artillery Regiment	5451 (1,700)	
• 10th Engineer Regiment	5452 (600)	
• 10th Transport Regiment	5454 (1,200)	

10th Division: (A type) Activated in Himeji October 1, 1898. Home station: Himeji. Lost the 40th Inf Regt and became triangular July 30, 1940. With the China Garrison Army from July 27, 1937 until Aug 31st, 2nd Army until Nov 29, 1938, North China Area Army until Aug 11, 1939, Imperial HQ until Aug 1, 1940, Kwantung Army until July 4, 1944, Imperial HQ until Aug 4th, 10th Area Army until Nov 20th and 14th Area Army in Cagayan Valley, Luzon. Of the 10th Div's 17,000 men about 2,000 survived the war. In Feb 1945 the Oyabu Butai (359th Ind Inf Btn, 105th Div) is attached.
1st Expeditionary Unit (Saipan): Detached from 25th, 24th and 10th Div Feb 21, 1944.
10th Expeditionary Unit (Halmahera): 10th Inf Grp HQ detach from Div Apr 4 1944.

Service History: China: Taierzhuang Mar 24 1938, Xuzhou May 10 1938, Wuhan late Aug 1938, Beijing-Hankou Railway Oct 4 1938. Luzon Philippines: Zig Zag Pass Jan 31 1945, Balete Pass Feb 21 1945, Salacsac Pass Apr 24 1945.

13th Division Sendai 1905	鏡 *Kagami* 6800 (19,087)	
13th Division Headquarters	6801 (362)	
13th Division Signal Unit	6813 (233)	
13th Division Ordinance Duty Unit	6818 (95)	
13th Division Medical Unit	6814 (400)	
13th Division 1st Field Hospital	6815 (301)	
13th Division 2nd Field Hospital	6816 (301)	
13th Division 4th Field Hospital	6817 (309)	
13th Division Veterinary Unit	6819 (119)	
13th Infantry Group Headquarters	6802 (79)	deactivated 5/1/43
• 65th Infantry Regiment (Wakamatsu)	6805 (4,098)	
• 104th Infantry Regiment (Sendai)	6804 (4,098)	
• 116th Infantry Regiment (Sakata)	6806 (4,098)	
• 17th Cavalry Regiment		deactivated in 1937
• 13th Division Cavalry Unit	6808	
• 19th Mountain Artillery Regiment	6809 (2,620)	
• 13th Engineer Regiment	6811 (901)	
• 13th Transport Regiment	6812 (1,170)	

13th Division: (C type) Activated in Jōetsu, Niigata on April 1, 1905, and deactivated due to cost cutting May 1, 1925. Reactivated in Sendai Sept 9, 1937. Home station: Sendai. Lost the 58th Inf Regt becoming triangular Mar 22, 1943. Shanghai Expeditionary Army from Sept 11th until Feb 14, 1938, Central China Expeditionary Army until July 4th, 2nd Army until Dec 9th, 11th Army until April 18, 1945 and China Expeditionary Army Hsiang-Siang, Luizhou until the war ended. Deactivated in Jiujiang on September 17, 1945.

Service History: China: 2nd Shanghai Oct 1 1937, Nanking Dec 9 1937, Suixian May 3 1938, Wuhan Aug 1938, Beijing-Hankou Railway Oct 4 1938, 1st Changsha Sept 14 1939, Yichang May 1 1940, Meinyang Feb 15 1943, Liuchow Nov 9 1944.

14th Division Utsunomiya 1905	照 *Teru* 7702 (11,909)	
14th Division Headquarters	7713 (351)	
14th Division Signal Unit	7714 (233)	
14th Division Intendance Duty Unit	7780 (133)	
14th Division Ordinance Duty Unit	7736 (107)	
14th Division 2nd Field Hospital	7782 (242)	
14th Division 3rd Field Hospital	7783 (242)	
14th Division 4th Field Hospital	7784 (247)	
14th Division D. P. & Water Supply Unit	7781 (196)	
14th Division Infantry Group Headquarters		deactivated 5/1/43
• 2nd Infantry Regiment (Mito)	7746 (3,166)	Peleliu Is.

14th Division continued	照 *Teru*	
• 15th Infantry Regiment (Takasaki)	7757 (3,964)	3rd Btn Peleliu
• 59th Infantry Regiment (Utsunomiya)	7768 (3,166)	1st Btn Anguar
• 18th Cavalry Regiment (until Sept. 1940)	満405	
• 14th Recon Regiment (from Sept. 1940)	満405 (439)	reorg 3/5/44
• 14th Division Tank Unit	4363 (130) Amano Unit, Peleliu	
• 20th Field Artillery Regiment	7793 / 満818	reorg 3/5/44
• 14th Division Machine Cannon Unit	unknown (340)	
• 14th Engineer Regiment	unknown (875)	reorg 3/5/44
• 14th Transport Regiment	7725 (1,170)	
• 14th Division Sea Transport Unit	6147 (1,542)	

14th Division: (A type) Activated Utsunomiya July 6, 1905. Home station: Utsunomiya. Lost the 50th Inf Regt and became triangular July 16, 1941. With the Eastern District Army from July 7th until Aug 31, 1937, 1st Army until Sept 19, 1939, Imperial HQ until Aug 1, 1940, Eastern District Army until Aug 23rd, 6th Army until Dec 3, 1941, Kwantung Army until July 4, 1942, 2nd Area Army until Oct 30, 1943, 3rd Area Army until Feb 10, 1944, 2nd Army until Mar 2nd, 31st Army until Aug 21, 1945 and Southern Expeditionary Army on Babethuap Is. until the war ended. By Nov 16, 1943 the 3 field hospitals had reorganized into 14th Div Field Hospital 照7770 with 530 personnel. Note: Became an Ocean Division (3 battle groups + shipping unit) on Nov 16, 1943, left Tateyama Tokyo Apr 7, 1944, and arrived in the Palaus Islands on Apr 24th.
Service History: China: 1st Shanghai Jan 28 1932. Manchuria: Rehe Feb 21 1933. China: Lanfeng May 10 1938. Palaus Islands: Peleliu Sept 15 1944, Anguar Sept 17 1944.

15th Division Tsuruga 1905	祭 *Matsuri* 7361 (13,173)	
15th Division Headquarters	7379 (657)	
15th Division Signal Unit	7363 (239)	
15th Division Ordinance Duty Unit	7364 (95)	deactivated 11/14/44
15th Division Medical Unit	7369 (257)	
15th Division 1st Field Hospital	7360 (242)	
15th Division 2nd Field Hospital	7365 (242)	
15th Division 4th Field Hospital	7374 (247)	deactivated 11/14/44
15th Division Veterinary Unit	7373 (52)	
15th Division Infantry Group Headquarters	7362 (92)	
• 51st Infantry Regiment (Kyoto)	7370 (2,790)	
• 60th Infantry Regiment (Kyoto)	7368 (2,790)	
• 67th Infantry Regiment (Tsuruga)	7371 (2,790)	
• 15th Cavalry Regiment	7376 (540)	deactivated 3/5/44
• 21st Field Artillery Regiment	7378 (1,357)	
• 15th Engineer Regiment	7367 (644)	
• 15th Transport Regiment	7372 (1,021)	

15th Division: (C type) Activated April 1, 1905, deactivated due to cost cutting May 1, 1925. Reactivated in Nagoya on Apr 4, 1938. Home station: Tsurugu. With the Central China Expeditionary Army from July 15th until Sept 23, 1939, 13th Army until Mar 15,

1943, China Expeditionary Army until June 1st, 15th Army until July 15, 1945 and 18th Area Army in Kanchanaburi, Thailand until the war ended.
Service History: China: Tatungchen Apr 22 1940, Zhejiang Jiangxi May 27 1942. Burma: Imphal Apr 3 1944, Mandalay Mar 7 1945.

16th Division Kyoto 1905	垣 *Kaki* 6550 (14,555)	
16th Division Headquarters	6551 (310)	
16th Division Signal Unit	6560 (187)	
16th Division Ordinance Duty Unit	6562 (123)	
16th Division Medical Unit	6563 (491)	
16th Division 1st Field Hospital	6564 (242)	
16th Division 2nd Field Hospital	6565 (242)	
16th Division 3rd Field Hospital	6566 (242)	
16th Division 4th Field Hospital	6567 (247)	
16th Division D. P. & Water Supply Unit	6569 (196)	
16th Division Veterinary Unit	6568 (52)	
16th Infantry Group Headquarters*	6553 (79)	deactivated 6/15/44
• 9th Infantry Regiment (Kyoto)	6554 (2,881)	
• 20th Infantry Regiment (Fukuchiyama)	6555 (2,881)	
• 33rd Infantry Regiment (Tsu)	6556 (2,881)	
• 16th Cavalry Regiment	6557 (439)	
• 22nd Field Artillery Regiment	6558 (1,766)	
• 16th Engineer Regiment	6559 (875)	
• 16th Transport Regiment	6561 (749)	

16th Division: (A type) Activated in Kyoto July 18, 1905. Home station: Kyoto. Lost the 38th Inf Regt became triangular Sept 16, 1940. With Imperial Headquarters from July 7, 1937 until Aug 31st, 2nd Army until Oct 30th, Shanghai Expeditionary Army until Jan 15, 1938, North China Area Army until July 4th, 2nd Army until Dec 9th, 11th Army until July 11, 1939, Imperial Headquarters until Aug 1, 1940, Central District Army until Nov 6, 1941, 14th Army until Aug 4, 1944 and 35th Army, destroyed on Leyte by Dec 1944.
Note: *Kimura Detachment; 20th I.R., 122nd I.R., Philippines: Legaspi Dec 12 1941
Service History: China: 2nd Shanghai Nov 12 1937, Nanking Dec 9 1937, Suixian May 3 1938, Xuzhou May 10 1938, Wuhan June 23 1938, Beijing-Hankou Railway Oct 4 1938, Hisiangtung May 1 1939. Philippines: Bicol Peninsula Dec 12 1941, Leyte Oct 17 1944.

17th Division Himeji 1907	月 *Tsuki* 7380 (17,507)
17th Division Headquarters	7381 (436)
17th Division Signal Unit	7389 (232)
17th Division Ordinance Duty Unit	7391
17th Division Medical Unit	unknown
17th Division 1st Field Hospital	7392 (276)
17th Division 2nd Field Hospital	7395 (300)

17th Division continued

17th Infantry Group Headquarters	7382 (55)	
• 53rd Infantry Regiment (Tottori)	7384 (4,089)	
• 54th Infantry Regiment (Okayama)	7385 (4,089)	
• 81st Infantry Regiment	7386 (4,098)	
• 17th Division Reconnaissance Unit	7398	
• 23rd Field Artillery Regiment	7387 (1,939)	
• 17th Engineer Regiment	7388 (899)	
• 17th Transport Regiment	7390 (1,160)	
• 2nd Mixed Regiment	7397	
• 6th Mixed Regiment	7399	
Attached		
54th Engineer Regiment	10118 (913)	from the 54th Div

17th Division: (C type) Activated November 30, 1907, deactivated due to cost cutting May 1, 1925. Reactivated in Himeji April 4, 1938. Home station: Himeji. With the Central China Expeditionary Army from July 15th until Sept 23, 1939, 13th Army until May 1, 1943, North China Area Army until Sept 15th and 8th Area Army in Rabaul New Britain until the war ended.
Note: 17th Inf Group HQ detached June 24, 1944 became the 38th Ind Mixed Brigade on Bougainville.
Service History: China: Wuhan June 23 1938, South Henan Jan 30 1941. New Guinea: New Britain: Cape Gloucester Dec 15 1943.

18th Division Kurume 1907	菊 *Kiku* 8918 (11,073)	
18th Division Headquarters	8900 (450)	
18th Division Signal Unit	8910 (239)	
18th Division Ordinance Duty Unit	8912	deact. 11/14/44
18th Division Medical Unit	8913 (600)	
18th Division 1st Field Hospital	10715 (242)	
18th Division 2nd Field Hospital	8914 (242)	deact. 11/14/44
18th Division 3rd Field Hospital	8915 (247)	
18th Division D. P. & Water Supply Unit	10716 (239)	deact. 11/14/44
18th Division Veterinary Unit	8917 (52)	
18th Infantry Group Headquarters	8901 / 10714	deact. 11/14/44
• 55th Infantry Regiment (Omura)	8902 (2,140)	
• 56th Infantry Regiment (Kurume)	8903 (2,140)	
• 114th Infantry Regiment (Fukuoka)	8905 (2,140)	
• 18th Mountain Artillery Regiment	8908 (1,575)	
• 12th Engineer Regiment	8909 (644)	
• 12th Transport Regiment	8911 (604)	
Attached		
21st Field Medium Artillery Battalion	8121 (1,024)	

18th Division: (C type) Activated Nov 13, 1907, deactivated due to cost cutting May 1, 1925. Reactivated in Kurume Sept 9, 1937. Home station: Kurume. Lost the 124th Inf

Regt becoming triangular Apr 30, 1943. With the 10th Army from Oct 10th until Feb 14, 1938, Central China Expeditionary Army until Sept 19th, 21st Army until Feb 9, 1940, South China Area Army until July 5, 1941, 23rd Army until Nov 6th, 25th Army until Mar 4, 1942, 15th Army until Apr 15, 1944, 33rd Army until Feb 28, 1945 and 15th Army until the war ended.
Note: Kawaguchi Detach., 35th Inf Bgde HQ, 124th Inf R., activated Nov 20, 1941. Borneo: Invasion Dec 16, 1941, Philippines Apr 1, 1941, Guadalcanal Aug 28, 1942.
Service History: China: 2nd Shanghai Nov 5 1937, Canton Oct 12 1938. Malaya: Invasion Dec. 8, 1941, Singapore Feb 8 1942. Burma: Toungoo Mar 24 1942, Salween River Oct 14 1943, Maingkwan Feb 20 1944, Meiktila Mar 12 1945, Sittang July 3 1945

19th Division Ranan, Korea 1915	虎 *Tora* 8530 (15,986)	
19th Division Headquarters	8500 (300)	
19th Division Signal Unit	8512 (239)	
19th Division Ordinance Duty Unit	8514	deactivated 2/17/45
19th Division Medical Unit	8515	deactivated 2/17/45
19th Division 1st Field Hospital	8518 (242)	
19th Division 2nd Field Hospital	8519 (242)	deactivated 2/17/45
19th Division 4th Field Hospital	8521 (249)	
19th Division D. P. & Water Supply Unit	8517 (196)	
19th Division Veterinary Unit	8516	
19th Division Anti-Gas Unit	8507	deactivated 2/17/45
19th Infantry Group Headquarters	8501	deactivated 11/16/44
• 73rd Infantry Regiment (Ranan)	8502 (2,917)	
• 75th Infantry Regiment (Hoeryong)	8505 (2,110)	
• 76th Infantry Regiment (Ranan)	8506 (1,303)	
• 19th Cavalry Regiment	8508 (722)	
• 25th Mountain Artillery Regiment	8510 (2,307)	
• 19th Engineer Regiment	8511 (961)	
• 19th Transport Regiment	8513 (749)	

19th Division: (A type) Activated in Ranan, Korea Dec 24, 1915. Home station: Ranan. Lost the 74th Inf Regt and became triangular Nov 1, 1942. With the Korea District Army from July 7th until Nov 20, 1944 and 14th Area Army on Luzon, destroyed by June 1945.
8th Expeditionary Unit (Truk Is.): Detached from the 19th Div. on Feb 21, 1944.
Service History: China: Changkufeng Jul 25 1938. Philippines: Baguio Feb 21 1945, Bessang Pass June 1 1945, Mankiyan/Tacbo Jul 14 1945.

20th Division Korea 1915	朝 *Asa* 2086 (18,507)
20th Division Headquarters	2099 (359)
20th Division Signal Unit	2061 (239)
20th Division Ordinance Duty Unit	2063 (112)
20th Division Medical Unit	2064 (822)

20th Division continued

20th Division 1st Field Hospital	2065 (277)
20th Division 2nd Field Hospital	6072 (277)
20th Division 3rd Field Hospital	6073
20th Division 4th Field Hospital	6074 (284)
20th Division D. P. & Water Supply Unit	2067 (239)
20th Division Anti-Gas Unit	2056
20th Division Veterinary Unit	2066 (125)
20th Infantry Group Headquarters	2051 (90)
• 78th Infantry Regiment (Yongsan)	2053 (3,843)
• 79th Infantry Regiment (Yongsan)	2054 (3,843)
• 80th Infantry Regiment (Daegu)	2055 (3,843)
• 20th Cavalry Regiment	2057
• 26th Field Artillery Regiment	2059 (3,156)
• 20th Engineer Regiment	2060 (898)
• 20th Transport Regiment	2062 (1.166)

20th Division: (A type) Activated in Yongsan, Korea December 24, 1915. Home station: Keijo. Lost the 77th Inf Regt and became triangular July 27, 1941. With the Korea District Army from July 7, 1937 until July 11th, China Garrison Army until Aug 31st, 1st Army until July 11, 1939, Korea District Army until Nov 30, 1942, 17th Army until Mar 2, 1944 and 18th Army on New Guinea until the war ended.
Service History: China: Beijing July 25 1937, Taiyuan Sept 14 1937, Yangchu Oct 12 1937, New Guinea: Salamaua Jul 2 1943, Ramu Val. Sept 19 1943, Finschhafen Sept 26 1943, Sattelberg Nov 17 1943, Driniumor July 10 1944, Aitape Wewak Sepik Nov 1944.

21st Division Kanazawa 1938	討 *Utsu* 4230 (13,864)
21st Division Headquarters	4231 (136)
21st Division Signal Unit	4239 (178)
21st Division Ordinance Duty Unit	4241 (122)
21st Division Medical Unit	4242 (376)
21st Division 1st Field Hospital	4243 (239)
21st Division 2nd Field Hospital	4244 (246)
21st Division D. P. & Water Supply Unit	4246 (196)
21st Division Veterinary Unit	4245 (48)
21st Division Infantry Group Headquarters	4233 (12)
• 62nd Infantry Regiment (Toyama)	4234 (3,190)
• 82nd Infantry Regiment (Toyama)	4235 (3,190)
• 83rd Infantry Regiment (Kanazawa)	4236 (3,190)
• 51st Mountain Artillery Regiment	4237 (1,688)
• 21st Engineer Regiment	4238 (401)
• 21st Transport Regiment	4240 (652)

21st Division: (C type) Activated in Kanazawa April 4, 1938. Home station: Kanazawa. With the North China Area Army from July 15th until Nov 11th, 12th Army until Nov.6, 1941, Southern Expeditionary Army until Dec 2, 1943, Indochina Garrison Army until

Dec 20, 1944 and 38th Army in Hanoi, Vietnam until the war ended.
Service History: China: Hundred Regiments Aug 20 1940, South Shanxi May 7 1941. Philippines: Invasion Feb 26 1942. Indochina: 2nd Indochina Mar 9 1945.

22nd Division Sendai 1938	原 *Hara* 7949 (15,183)	
22nd Division Headquarters	7930 (378)	
22nd Division Signal Unit	7937 (219)	
22nd Division Ordinance Duty Unit	7941 (95)	
22nd Division Field Hospital	7939 (998)	
22nd Division Veterinary Unit	7940 (65)	
22nd Infantry Group Headquarters	7931 (12)	deactivated 5/1/43
• 84th Infantry Regiment (Sendai)	7934 (3,667)	
• 85th Infantry Regiment (Wakamatsu)	7935 (3,667)	
• 86th Infantry Regiment (Yamagata)	7936 (3,667)	
• 52nd Mountain Artillery Regiment	6739 (1,191)	
• 22nd Engineering Regiment	7933 (424)	
• 22nd Transport Regiment	7938 (812)	

22nd Division: (C type) Activated in Utsunomiya April 4, 1938, from 14th Depot Division troops. Home station: Sendai. With the Central China Expeditionary Army from July 15th until Sept 23, 1939, 13th Army until Feb 1, 1944, 23rd Army until Jan 13, 1945, Southern Army until Mar 26th, 38th Army until July 15th and 18th Area Army in Bangkok, Thailand until the war ended. Note: Opened Ichi-go rail corridor from Manchuria by meeting the Ichinomiya Detachment in Longzhou on the Indochina border Dec 10, 1944.
Service History: China: Hsiaoshan Jan 22 1940, Zhejiang/Jiangxi May 27 1942, Yungning Nov 15 1944. Indochina: 2nd Indochina Incident Mar 9 1945.

23rd Division Kumamoto 1938	旭 *Asahi* 1168 (14,298)	
23rd Division Headquarters	1103 (250)	
23rd Division Signal Unit	1172 (239)	
23rd Division Ordinance Duty Unit	1190 (81)	
23rd Division Medical Unit	1188 (699)	
23rd Division 1st Field Hospital	1189 (242)	
23rd Division 2nd Field Hospital	9050 (242)	
23rd Division 4th Field Hospital	9052 (247)	
23rd Division D. P. & Water Supply Unit 23rd	1206 (196)	
Division Anti-Gas Unit	unknown	
23rd Division Veterinary Unit	1194 (52)	
23rd Division Infantry Group	満887 (6)	as of Jul 6 1940
• 64th Infantry Regiment (Kumamoto)	1111 (2,910)	
• 71st Infantry Regiment (Kagoshima)	1125 (2,910)	
• 72nd Infantry Regiment (Miyokonojo)	1128 (2,910)	
• 23rd Reconnaissance Regiment	1136 (439)*	
• 13th / 17th Field Artillery Regiments	1163 (1,636)	

23rd Division continued

• 23rd Engineer Regiment	1167 (898)
• 23rd Transport Regiment	1175 (749)

23rd Division: (A type) Activated in Kumamoto April 4, 1938. Home station: Kumamoto. With the Kwantung Army from Sept 11th until Aug 14, 1939 (destroyed at Nomonhan by Aug 3rd), rebuilt in northeast China, 6th Army until Sept 22, 1944, Kwantung Army until Oct 24th, 6th Army until Dec 11th and 14th Area Army, destroyed on Luzon by June 1945.
*Comprised of a cavalry troop and a tankette company.
Note: 64th Inf Regt sunk *Akitsu Maru* Nov 15, 1944
Note: 23rd Div HQ, Signal, 1st Fld Hosp., 1st Btn 71st Inf Regt, 2nd Btn 72nd Inf Regt, 1st Co. 23rd Eng Regt. sunk aboard *Mayasan Maru* on Nov 17, 1944.
Service History: Manchuria: Nomonhan May 11 1939. Philippines: Lingayan Jan 9 1945, Baguio Feb 21 1945.

26th Division Manchuria 1937	泉 *Izumi* 5310 (13,359)
26th Division Headquarters	5311 (229)
26th Division Signal Unit	5320 (219)
26th Division Ordinance Duty Unit	5322 (95)
26th Division Field Hospital	5324 (351)
26th Division Veterinary Unit	1194 (45)
26th Division Infantry Group	
• 11th Ind. Infantry Regiment (Tsu)	5314 (3,547)
• 12th Ind. Infantry Regiment (Gifu)	5315 (3,547)
• 13th Ind. Infantry Regiment (Shizuoka)	5316 (3,547)
• 26th Cavalry Regiment	5317
• 11th Independent Field Artillery Regiment	5318 (882)
• 26th Engineer Regiment	5319 (401)
• 26th Transport Regiment	5321 (502)

26th Division: (C type) Activated in Manchuria Sept 30, 1937, from former 11th I.M.B. troops. Home station: Nagoya. With the Kwantung Army until Jan 4, 1938, Mongolia Garrison Army until July 4, 1944, 14th Area Army until Oct 27th and 35th Army on Leyte (landed Nov 11th), destroyed by Dec 23, 1944.
Service History: Manchuria: Nomonhan May 11 1939. China: Wuyuan Mar 16 1940, Hundred Regiments Aug 20 1940. Philippines: Leyte Nov 9 1944.

27th Division Sakura 1938	極 *Kiwame* 2915 (19,035)
27th Division Headquarters	2900 (361)
27th Division Signal Unit	2901 (233)
27th Division Ordinance Duty Unit	2908 (95)
27th Division Medical Unit	2913 (400)
27th Division 1st Field Hospital	2912 (301)
27th Division 2nd Field Hospital	2918 (304)

27th Division continued

27th Division 4th Field Hospital	2919 (311)	
27th Division Veterinary Unit	2911 (119)	
27th Division Infantry Group		
• 1st China Garrison Inf. Regt (Beijing)	2902 (4,104)	
• 2nd China Garrison Inf. Regt (Tianjin)	2904 (4,104)	
• 3rd China Garrison Inf. Regt (Beijing)	2906 (4,104)	
• 27th Mountain Artillery Regiment	2905 (3,161)	
• 27th Engineer Regiment	2907 (901)	
• 27th Transport Regiment	2909 (1,170)	
Attached		
168th Airfield Battalion	17323 (406)	

27th Division: (C type) Activated in Beijing June 21, 1938, from former China Garrison Brigade troops. Home station: Sakura. With the 11th Army from July 4th until Nov 29th, North China Area Army until Sept 11, 1939, China Expeditionary Army until June 16, 1943, Kwantung Army until Feb 1, 1944, 6th Area Army until Jan 2, 1945, 20th Army until Mar 6th, 23rd Army until Apr 18th and China Expeditionary Army in Huchow until it was deactivated in Shanghai on September 17, 1945.
Service History: China: Wuhan June 24 1938, Hundred Regiments Aug 20 1940, Canton-Hankou Railway garrison Mar 6 1945.

29th Division Nagoya 1941	雷 *Rai* 3229 (13,825)	
29th Division Headquarters	3200 (361)	
29th Division Signal Unit	3295 (235)	
29th Division Ordinance Duty	3277 (106)	
29th Division Intendance Duty Unit	3299 (133)	
29th Division Field Hospital	3205 (592)	Tinian
29th Division Infantry Group		
• 18th Infantry Regiment (Toyohashi)	3219 (3,671)	
• 38th Infantry Regiment (Nara)	3211 (3,162)	
• 50th Infantry Regiment (Matsumoto)	3215 (3,162)	Tinian
• 29th Division Tank Unit	3264 / 4364 (130)	Guam
• 29th Transport Regiment	3203 (128)	
• 29th Division Sea Transport Unit	6151 (1,542)	

29th Division: (A type) Activated in Manchuria on July 22, 1941. Home station: Nagoya. With the Kwantung Army from Apr 1st until Feb 10, 1944, Eastern District Army until Feb 25th and 31st Army on Guam but with some units on Saipan and Tinian.
Service History: Mariana Is: Saipan June 5 1944, Guam Jul 21 1944, Tinian Jul 24 1944.

30th Division Pyongyang 1943	豹 *Hyou* 12020 (13,417)
30th Division Headquarters	2021 (301)
30th Division Signal Unit	12031 (187)

30th Division continued

30th Division Ordinance Duty Unit	12033 (79)
30th Division Medical Unit	12034 (662)
30th Division 1st Field Hospital	12035 (217)
30th Division 2nd Field Hospital	12036 (242)
30th Division 4th Field Hospital	12038 (223)
30th Division D. P. & Water Supply Unit	12040 (185)
30th Division Veterinary Unit	12039 (48)
30th Division Infantry Group	
• 41st Infantry Regiment (Fukuyama)	12023 (2,763)
• 74th Infantry Regiment (Hamhung)	12024 (2,857)
• 77th Infantry Regiment (Pyongyang)	12025 (2,857)
• 30th Cavalry Regiment	12027 (381)
• 30th Field Artillery Regiment	12029 (1,554)
• 30th Engineer Regiment	12030 (875)
• 30th Transport Regiment	12032 (726)
Attached	
25th Specially Est. Motor Transport Coy	10457 (69)

30th Division: (C type) Activated in Pyongyang, Korea May 14, 1943. Home station: Pyongyang. With the Korea District Army until Apr 1, 1944, 14th Army until Aug 4th and 35th Army on Mindanao until it was deactivated September 7, 1945.
Note: 41st Inf Regt was with the 5th Div. and then the 21st I.M.B. prior to joining.
Service History: Philippines: Leyte Oct 20 1944, Kabacan Apr 22 1945.

31st Division Bangkok 1943	烈 *Retsu* 10720 (11,073)	
31st Division Headquarters	10701 (450)	
31st Division Signal Unit	10705 (239)	
31st Division Ordinance Duty Unit	10707 (81)	
31st Division Medical Unit	10708 (600)	deact. 11/14/44
31st Division 1st Field Hospital	10709 (242)	
31st Division 2nd Field Hospital	10710 (242)	deact. 11/14/44
31st Division 3rd Field Hospital	10711 (247)	
31st Division D. P. & Water Supply Unit	10713 (196)	deact. 11/14/44
31st Division Veterinary Unit	10712 (52)	
31st Infantry Group Headquarters	10721 (92)	deact.11/14/44
• 58th Infantry Regiment (Takada)	10352 (2,140)	
• 124th Infantry Regiment (Fukuoka)	8906 (2,140)	
• 138th Infantry Regiment (Nara)	10353 (2,140)	
• 31st Mountain Artillery Regiment	10703 (1,575)	
• 31st Engineering Regiment	10704 (644)	
• 31st Transportation Regiment	10706 (604)	

31st Division: (C type) Activated Bangkok, Thailand Mar 22, 1943. Home station: Kofu. With the 15th Army from June 15th until Aug 7, 1945 (mostly destroyed at Kohima) and 29th Army until the war ended with remnants in Bangkok.

31st Division continued
Note: 58th Inf Regt came from the 12th Div and 124th Inf R. (Kawaguchi Detach. Borneo, the P.I., Guadalcanal) from the 18th Div and the 138th Inf Regt from the 116th Div.
Service History: Burma: Sangshak Mar 19 1944, Kohima Apr 4 1944.

32nd Division Tokyo 1939	楓 *Kaede* 4250 (12,659)
32nd Division Headquarters	4251 (343)
32nd Division Signal Unit	4259 (233)
32nd Division Ordinance Duty Unit	4261 (95)
32nd Division Medical Unit	4262 (367)
32nd Division 1st Field Hospital	4263 (277)
32nd Division 2nd Field Hospital	4264 (308)
32nd Division Veterinary Unit	4265 (119)
32nd Division Infantry Group	
• 210th Infantry Regiment (Kofu)	4254 (2,567)
• 211th Infantry Regiment (Tokyo)	4255 (2,567)
• 212th Infantry Regiment (Sakura)	4256 (2,567)
• 32nd Field Artillery Regiment	4257 (1,682)
• 32nd Engineer Regiment	4258 (872)
• 32nd Transport Regiment	4260 (970)

32nd Division: (C type) Activated in Tokyo Feb. 7, 1939. Home station: Tokyo. With the 12th Army until Apr 17, 1944, 14th Army until Apr 28th, 2nd Area Army until June 13, 1945 and 2nd Army on Halmahera until the war ended. Deactivated Sept 30, 1945.
Service History: China: Zhejiang Jiangxi May 27 1942. Morotai: Sept 15 1944.

33rd Division Utsunomiya 1943	弓 *Yumi* 10722 (8,327)	
33rd Division Headquarters	6820 (301)	
33rd Division Signal Unit	6827 (238)	
33rd Division Ordinance Duty Unit	6929 (113)	
33rd Division Medical Unit	6830 (257)	
33rd Division 1st Field Hospital	6831 (242)	
33rd Division 2nd Field Hospital	6832 (242)	
33rd Division Veterinary Unit	6833 (52)	
33rd Division D. P. & Water Supply Unit	6834 (198)	
33rd Infantry Group Headquarters	6821 (9)	deactivated 5/1/43
• 213th Infantry Regiment (Mito)	6822 (2,298)	
• 214th Infantry Regiment (Utsunomiya)	6823 (2,298)	"Bayakko Butai"*
• 215th Infantry Regiment (Takasaki)	6824 (2,298)	
• 33rd Mountain Artillery Regiment	6825 (1,524)	
• 33rd Engineer Regiment	6826 (338)	
• 33rd Transport Regiment	6828 (324)	

33rd Division: (C type) Activated in Sendai Feb 2, 1939. Home station: Utsunomiya. With 11th Army from Mar 15th until Nov 6, 1941 and 15th Army, arrived in Bangkok on Jan 10, 1942. The 213th Inf R. and two battalions from the 33rd Mountain Artillery

33rd Division continued
Regt arrived in late March, in Thailand with the 15th Army when the war ended.
*"White Tigers Unit" (白虎部隊)
Service History: China: 1st Changsha Sept 14 1939, Shanggao Mar 15 1941, South Shanxi May 7 1941 Burma: Rangoon Feb 8 1942, Sittang Bridge Feb 19 1942, Pegu Mar 3 1942, Taukkyan Roadblock Mar 7 1942, Shwedaung Mar 29 1942, Yenangyaung Apr 11 1942, Arakan Jan 7 1943, Chin Hills Nov 8 1943, Admin Box Feb 4 1944, Imphal Mar 8 1944, Pakkoku/Kahnla Feb 5 1945.

34th Division Osaka 1939	椿 *Tsubaki* 6855 (14,304)
34th Division Headquarters	6840 (630)
34th Division Signal Unit	6848 (287)
34th Division 1st Field Hospital	6852 (1,004)
34th Division Veterinary Unit	6854 (65)
34th Infantry Group Headquarters	6841 (?)
• 216th Infantry Regiment (Osaka)	6842 (3,787)
• 217th Infantry Regiment (Osaka)	6843 (3,787)
• 218th Infantry Regiment (Wakayama)	6844 (3,787)
• 34th Engineer Regiment	6847 (901)
• 34th Transport Regiment	6849 (812)
• 34th Division Artillery Unit	unknown (583) active 7/10/45

34th Division: (C type) Activated in Osaka Feb 7, 1939. Home station: Osaka. With the 11th Army from Mar 15th until April 18, 1945 and China Expeditionary Army in Wuning until it was deactivated in Pukou, Nanjing on September 17, 1945.
Service History: China: Shanggao Mar 15 1941, Changsha Sept 25 1941, Chihkiang Apr 17 1945

35th Division Tokyo 1939	東 *Higashi* 2935 (11,989)	
35th Division Headquarters	2937 (452)	
35th Division Signal Unit	2924 (219)	
35th Division Medical Unit	2931	
35th Division Field Hospital	2932 (357)	
35th Division Veterinary Unit	2934 (45)	deactivated 6/24/44
35th Division Infantry Group		
• 219th Infantry Regiment (Kofu)	2929 (3,427)	Noemfoor Is.
• 220th Infantry Regiment (Tokyo)	2920 (3,427)	
• 221st Infantry Regiment (Sakura)	2921 (3,427)	1,482 men on Biak
• 35th Engineer Regiment	2925 (178)	
• 35th Transport Regiment	2927 (502)	
Attached		
36th Independent Engineer Regiment	9423 剛 (894)	Takeshi Unit
4th Ind. Mountain Artillery Regiment	4734	

35th Division: (C type) Activated in Asahikawa Feb 7, 1939. Home station: Tokyo. With the North China Area Army from Apr 1st until Apr 10, 1942, 12th Army until Feb

25, 1944, 31st Army's Palau Group until Mar 15th and 2nd Army on Halmahera until it was deactivated on September 30, 1945.
Service History: China: South Shanxi May 7 1941, Taihang Mtns. Apr 27 1943. New Guinea: Noemfoor July 2 1944, Sansapor July 30 1044.

36th Division Kumamoto 1939	雪 *Yuki* 3521 (12,674)	
36th Division Headquarters	3520 (359)	226 men on Biak
36th Division Signal Unit	3528 (235)	
36th Division Ordinance Duty Unit	3530 (107)	
36th Division Intendance Unit	3531 (123)	
36th Division Field Hospital	3532 (755)	189 on Biak
36th Division Infantry Group		
• 222nd Infantry Regiment (Hirosaki)	3523 (3,964)*	2,103 on Biak
• 223rd Infantry Regiment (Akita)	3524 (3,165)	
• 224th Infantry Regiment (Akita)	3525 (3,165)	
• 36th Division Tank Company	10596 (130)	64 on Biak
• 36th Mountain Artillery Regiment	3526	one btn on Biak
• 36th Engineer Regiment	3527	240 on Biak
• 36th Division Transport Unit	3529 (131)	106 on Biak
• 36th Division Sea Transport Unit	6144 (1,542)	
Attached (see 2nd Army for the rest)		
52nd Construction Duty Company	8235 (511)	on Biak

36th Division: (C type) Activated in Hirosaki Feb 7, 1939. Home station: Hirosaki. With the 1st Army from Apr 1st until Oct 30, 1943, reorganized into an ocean division Oct 20th, 2nd Area Army until Dec 6th, 19th Army until Dec 25th and 2nd Army in Sarmi. *222nd Inf Regt on Biak, flag burnt 6/22/44. One battalion on Noemfoor Is.
Service History: China: Hundred Regiments Aug 20 1940, South Shanxi May 7 1941. New Guinea: Wakde-Sarmi May 17 1944, Biak May 27 1944, Noemfoor July 2 1944

37th Division Kurume 1939	冬 *Fuyu* 3540 (15,465)
37th Division Headquarters	3541 (239)
37th Division Signal Unit	3548 (219)
37th Division Ordinance Duty Unit	3550 (95)
37th Division 2nd Field Hospital	3552 (998)
37th Division Veterinary Unit	3554 (65)
37th Infantry Group Headquarters	3542 (26)
• 225th Infantry Regiment (Kumamoto)	3543 (3,667)
• 226th Infantry Regiment (Miyakonoji)	3544 (3,667)
• 227th Infantry Regiment (Kagoshima)	3545 (3,667)
• 37th Mountain Artillery Regiment	3546 (1,612)
• 37th Engineer Regiment	3547 (424)
• 37th Transport Regiment	3549 (812)

37th Division: (C type) Activated in Kurume Feb. 7, 1939. Home station: Kurume.

37th Division continued
With the 1st Army in Shanxi from Apr. 1st until Mar. 11, 1944, 12th Army until July 17th, 11th Army until Dec. 20th, 38th Army near Hanoi until July 27, 1945, and 29th Army in Malaya until the war ended, deactivated in Indochina on September 14, 1945.
Service History: China: South Shanxi May 7 1941, Kweilin Nov 9 1944. Indochina: 2nd Indochina Incident Mar 9 1945.

38th Division Nagoya 1939	沼 *Numa* 8920 (14,074)
38th Division Headquarters	8921 (154)
38th Division Signal Unit	8929 (201)
38th Division Ordinance Duty Unit	8931 (121)
38th Division Medical Unit	8932
38th Division 1st Field Hospital	8933 (238)
38th Division 2nd Field Hospital	8934 (245)
38th Division Veterinary Unit	8935 (49)
38th Division Infantry Group	
• 228th Infantry Regiment (Nagoya)	8924 (3,377)
• 229th Infantry Regiment (Gifu)	8925 (3,377)
• 230th Infantry Regiment (Shizuoka)	8926 (2,925)
• 38th Mountain Artillery Regiment	8927 (1,688)
• 38th Engineer Regiment	8928 (592)
• 38th Transport Regiment	8930 (657)
3rd Mixed Regiment*	8936 (2,935)

38th Division: (C type) Activated in Nagoya June 30, 1939. Home station: Nagoya. With the 21st Army from Oct 2nd until Feb 9, 1940, South China Area Army until Jul 5, 1941, 23rd Army until Jan 4, 1942, 16th Army until Mar 9th, 25th Army until Sept 17th, 17th Army until Apr 16, 1943 and 8th Area Army in Rabaul until the war ended. The Division nickname "Swampers" came from a swampy area in south China it had garrisoned.
*Shoji Detachment: 230th Inf. Regt., also called the 3rd Mixed Regt: Java Mar 1 1942, Guadalcanal Oct 14 1942, on 6/24/44 joined the 40th I.M.B. on New Ireland.
Ito/Eastern Detachment: 38th Inf. Group HQ, 228th Inf Regt: Ambon Jan 30 1942, Timor Feb 20 1943, Guadalcanal Nov 8, 1942.
229th Inf. Regt became Southeast Detachment May 26, 1943. 1st Btn on Los Negros.
Service History: China: Hong Kong Dec 8 1941, Sumatra: Palembang Feb 13 1942. Guadalcanal Nov 10 1942, Munda Point Jul 22 1943, New Britain Dec 15 1943.

40th Division Zentsuji 1939	鯨 *Kujira* 6895 (14,236)	
40th Division Headquarters	6880 (630)	
40th Division Signal Unit	6888 (219)	
40th Division Field Hospital	6892 (1,004)	
40th Division Veterinary Unit	6894 (65)	
40th Infantry Group Headquarters	6881 (79)	deactivated 5/1/43
• 234th Infantry Regiment (Marugame)	6882 (3,787)	

40th Division continued

• 235th Infantry Regiment (Tokushima)	6883 (3,787)	
• 236th Infantry Regiment (Kochi)	6884 (3,787)	
• 40th Cavalry Regiment	6885 (678)	deactivated 5/1/43
• 40th Mountain Artillery Regiment	6886 (583)	deactivated 5/1/43
• 40th Engineer Regiment	6887 (901)	
• 40th Transport Regiment	6889 (812)	
• 40th Division Artillery Unit	unknown (583)	active 710/45

<u>40th Division</u>: (C type) Activated in Zentsuji June 30, 1939. Home station: Zentsuji. With the 11th Army from Oct 2nd, until Aug 26, 1944, 6th Area Army from Oct 2nd until Mar 6, 1945, 23rd Army until June 17th and China Expeditionary Army in Huchow until it was deactivated in Pukou, Nanjing on September 17, 1945.
<u>Service History</u>: China: South Henan Jan 30 1941, 2nd Changsha Dec 27 1941, Meinyang Feb 15 1943, Guilin Nov 9 1944, Canton-Hankou Railway Jan 3 1945, Canton-Hankou Railway garrison Mar 6 1945.

41st Division Utsunomiya 1939	河 *Kawa* 3560 (18,148)	
41st Division Headquarters	3561 (450)	
41st Division Signal Unit	3570 (239)	
41st Division Ordinance Duty Unit	3571 (121)	
41st Division Medical Unit	3572 (822)	
41st Division 1st Field Hospital	3573 (238)	
41st Division 2nd Field Hospital	3574 (245)	
41st Division 3rd Field Hospital	3576 (277)	
41st Division Veterinary Unit	3575 (49)	
41st Infantry Group Headquarters	3563 (11)	deactivated 5/1/43
• 237th Infantry Regiment (Mito)	3564 (3,843)	
• 238th Infantry Regiment (Takasaki)	3565 (3,843)	
• 239th Infantry Regiment (Utsunomiya)	3566 (3,843)	
• 41st Cavalry Regiment	No # (?)	
• 41st Mountain Artillery Regiment	3567 (2,090)	
• 41st Engineer Regiment	3568 (898)	
• 41st Transport Regiment	3569 (1,166)	

<u>41st Division</u>: (C type) Activated in Utsunomiya June 30, 1939. Home station: Utsunomiya. With the 1st Army from Oct 2nd until Apr 10, 1942, North China Area Army until Nov 16th and 8th Area Army until Dec 1st and 18th Army on New Guinea until the war ended.
<u>Service History</u>: China: Hundred Regiments Aug 20 1940. South Shanxi May 7 1941. New Guinea: Driniumor July 10 1944, Aitape, Weak, Sepik Nov 1944.

43rd Division Nagoya 1943	誉 *Homare* 11930 (19,133)
43rd Division Headquarters	11931 (415)
43rd Division Signal Unit	11939 (235)

43rd Division Ordinance Duty Unit	11941 (107)	
43rd Division Intendance Service Unit	11949 (123)	
43rd Division Field Hospital	11943 (592)	
43rd Division D. P. & Water Supply Unit	11947 (109)	
43rd Infantry Group Headquarters	11932	deactivated 2/6/45
• 118th Infantry Regiment (Shizuoka)	11933 (3,156)	
• 135th Infantry Regiment (Nagoya)	11934 (3,156)	3rd Btn to Tinian
• 136th Infantry Regiment (Gifu)	11935 (3,156)	
• 43rd Recon Regiment	11936	reorganized 4/7/44
• 43rd Field Artillery Regiment	11937	reorganized 4/7/44
• 43rd Engineer Regiment	11938	reorganized 4/7/44
• 43rd Transport Regiment	11940 (131)	

43rd Division: (C type) Activated in Nagoya May 14, 1943, from former 63rd Ind. Inf. Group personnel. Home station: Nagoya. With the Central District Army from June 1st until Apr 7, 1944, re-organized into an ocean division Apr 7th, with the 31st Army, Northern Marianas Army Group on Saipan.
Service History: Mariana Islands: Saipan June 15 1944, Tinian Jul 24, 1944.

46th Division Kumamoto 1943	静 *Sei* 11960 (13,231)	
46th Division Headquarters	11961 (359)	
46th Division Signal Unit	11966 (235)	
46th Division Ordinance Duty Unit	11968 (107)	
46th Division Field Hospital	11969 (758)	
46th Division Intendance Duty Unit	11970 (2,123)	
46th Division Infantry Group		
• 123rd Infantry Regiment (Kumamoto)	11962 (3,165)	
• 145th Infantry Regiment (Ōita)	11963 (3,165)	Iwo Jima
• 147th Infantry Regiment (Miyakonojō)	11964 (3,165)	
• 46th Division Tank Unit	12500 (130)	Lesser Sundae Is.
• 46th Division Transport Unit	11967 (131)	Rempang Island

46th Division: (C type) Activated in Kumamoto May 14, 1943, from former 66th Ind Inf Group and 6th Depot Division personnel. Home station: Kumamoto. Western District Army until Oct 22nd, 19th Army Lesser Sunda Is. until Feb 28, 1945, 2nd Area Army until Mar 26th, 29th Army until June 21st and the 7th Area Army in Johor State, Malaya until the war ended. Note: 145th I.R stranded on Saipan diverted to Iwo Jima.
Service History: East Indies and Malaya: garrison. Japan: Iwo Jima Feb 19 1945.

47th Division Hirosaki 1943	弾 *Dan* 11990
47th Division Headquarters	11991 (361)
47th Division Signal Unit	12002 (239)
47th Division Ordinance Duty Unit	11995 (112)
47th Division Medical Unit	11998 (1,109)
47th Division 1st Field Hospital	12011 (301)
47th Division 2nd Field Hospital	12012 (301)

47th Division continued

47th Division 4th Field Hospital	12014 (309)
47th Division D. P. & Water Supply Unit	12009 (239)
47th Division Veterinary Unit	12008 (119)
47th Division Infantry Group	
• 91st Infantry Regiment (Akita)	12018 (3,836)
• 105th Infantry Regiment (Akita)	12017 (3,836)
• 131st Infantry Regiment (Hirosaki)	12016 (3,836)
• 47th Cavalry Regiment	12019 (832)
• 47th Mountain Artillery Regiment	12000 (3,222)
• 47th Engineer Regiment	12001 (961)
• 47th Transport Regiment	12003 (1,014)

47th Division: (C type) Activated in Hirosaki May 14, 1943, from former 67th Ind. Inf Group personnel. Home station: Hirosaki. With the Northern Army until Mar 16, 1944, 5th Area Army until July 5th, Imperial Headquarters until Nov 15th, 6th Area Army (20th Army) in China until June 17, 1945, and 43rd Army in Yenching until the war ended. Deactivated in Hankou.
12th Expedit. Unit (P.I.) spun off Jun 13, '44, 47th Div Inf. Grp, became 57th I.M.B.
Shigehiro Detachment arrived early and fought in the Chihchiang Airfield offensive.
Service History: China: Chihchiang Apr 15 1945.

48th Division Formosa 1940	海 *Umi* 8940 (12,893)	
48th Division Headquarters	8940 (300)	
48th Division Signal Unit	8948 (187)	
48th Division Ordinance Duty Unit	8950 (131)	
48th Division Medical Unit	8951 (533)	
48th Division 1st Field Hospital	8952 (228)	
48th Division 4th Field Hospital	8953 (233)	
48th Infantry Group Headquarters	8941 (87)	
• 1st Formosa Infantry Regiment (Taipei)	8942 (2,580)	
• 2nd Formosa Infantry Regiment (Tainan)	8943 (2,580)	
• 47th Infantry Regiment (Ōita)	8944 (2,580)	
• 48th Cavalry Regiment	8945 (418)	
• 48th Mountain Artillery Regiment	8946 (1,783)	
• 48th Engineer Regiment	8947 (759)	
• 48th Transport Regiment	8949 (494)	
Attached		
1st Special Sea Transport Unit	10436 勢	Sumbawa Island
4th Tank Regiment	5058 (142)	
72nd Field Anti Aircraft Regiment	16601	
109th Line of Communications Hospital	7015	

48th Division:(A type) Activated on Hainan Is. China Nov. 30, 1940, from former Formosa Mixed Brigade personnel. Home station: Formosa. Equipped with truck and bicycle units earmarked to storm Singapore after traveling the length of the Malay Peninsula. With the South China Area Army from Jan 6, 1941, until July 5th, 23rd Army

48th Division continued
until Aug. 12th, Formosa District Army until Nov 6th, 14th Army until Jan 14, 1942, 16th Army until Jan 7, 1943, 19th Army until Feb 28, 1945, 2nd Area Army until June 13th and 2nd Army on Timor until the war ended.
Service History: Philippines: Invasion Dec 12 1941, East Java: Invasion Mar 1 1942.

49th Division Seoul, Korea 1943	狼 *Rō* 18700 (15,497)
49th Division Headquarters	18701 (300)
49th Division Signal Unit	18708 (239)
49th Division Ordinance Duty Unit	18710 (81)
49th Division Medical Unit	18711 (699)
49th Division 1st Field Hospital	18712 (242)
49th Division 2nd Field Hospital	18713 (242)
49th Division 4th Field Hospital	18714 (249)
49th Division Veterinary Unit	18715 (52)
49th Division D. P. & Water Supply Unit	18716 (196)
49th Division Infantry Group	
• 106th Infantry Regiment (Seoul)	18702 (2.881)
• 153rd Infantry Regiment (Seoul)	18703 (2.881)
• 168th Infantry Regiment (Seoul)	18704 (2.881)
• 49th Cavalry Regiment	18705 (543)
• 49th Mountain Artillery Regiment	18706 (2,307)
• 49th Engineer Regiment	18707 (962)
• 49th Transport Regiment	18709 (749)

49th Division: (C type) Activated in Seoul, Korea May 27, 1944, from former 64th Ind. Inf Group personnel. Home station: Seoul. With the Korea District Army until May 31, 1944, departed Pusan June 20 1944 and landed in Singapore on July 19th, Burma Area Army until Aug, 33rd Army until (?) and Burma Area Army until the war ended.
Katsu Detachment: 153I.R., 3rd Btn 49Art Regt, with the 28th Army in western Burma
Service History: Burma: Meiktila Feb 26 1945, Sittang July 3 1945.

51st Division Utsunomiya 1940	基 *Moto* 2833 (20,497)	
51st Division Headquarters	2800 (430)	
51st Division Signal Unit	2809 (239)	
51st Division Ordinance Duty Unit	2811 (112)	
51st Division Medical Unit	2812 (1,103)	
51st Division 1st Field Hospital	2813 (277)	
51st Division 2nd Field Hospital	2814 (277)	
51st Division 3rd Field Hospital	2815 (277)	
51st Division 4th Field Hospital	2816 (284)	
51st Division Veterinary Unit	2817 (200)	
51st Infantry Group Headquarters	2801 (92)	Okabe Unit
• 66th Infantry Regiment (Utsunomiya)	2802 (3,928)	Araki Unit
• 102nd Infantry Regiment (Mito)	2803 (3,928)	
• 115th Infantry Regiment (Fukushima)	2804/4824 (3,928)	

51st Division continued

• 51st Cavalry (Recon.) Regiment	2805 (774)	Umboi Island
• 14th Field Artillery Regiment	2807 (2,135)	
• 51st Engineer Regiment	2808 (898)	
• 51st Transport Regiment	2810 (1,815)	Manus Island

51st Division: (B type) Activated in Utsunomiya between Aug 3 and 7, 1941, from 14th Depot Division personnel. Home station: Utsunomiya. With the Eastern District Army from Sept 7th until Aug 1, 1941, Kwantung Army for "Kwantung Army Special Maneuvers" until Sept 18th, 23rd Army until Oct 20 1942, 17th Army until Dec 23rd and 18th Army on New Guinea until the war ended.
Note: Over 1/3 of personnel drowned in battle of Bismarck Sea, 3/1/43 (18th Army). Okabe Detachment (51st Inf. Group HQ) Buna Jan 7 1943, Mubo Jan 12, Wau Jan 27. By Oct 1943 the 51st Transport Regt was the Lorengau Defense Unit on Manus Is.
Service History: China: Garrison. Bismarck Sea: Mar 1 1943. New Guinea: Mubo May 9 1943, Bobdubi Hill May 14 1943, Salamaua Sept 11 1943. Bougainville: Arawe (2 inf co.) Dec 15 1943. Admiralties: Los Negros Feb 29 1944, Manus Is. Mar 15 1944.

52nd Division Kanezawa 1940	柏 *Kashiwa* 4651 (15,422)	
52nd Division Headquarters	4650 (487)	
52nd Division Signal Unit	4662 (235)	
52nd Division Ordinance Duty Unit	4664 (107)	
52nd Division Intendance Service Unit	4675 (115)	
52nd Division Field Hospital	4676 (755)	
52nd Division Infantry Group	unknown	deactivated 12/4/43
• 69th Infantry Regiment (Toyama)	4654 (2,874)	
• 107th Infantry Regiment (Kanazawa)	4655 (3,643)	
• 150th Infantry Regiment (Matsumoto)	4656 (2,874)	
• 52nd Division Tank Unit	4672 / 2131 (130)	
• 52nd Division Transport Unit	4673 (131)	
• 52nd Division Sea Transport Unit	4674 / 6145 (1,542)	
• 8th Independent Artillery Regiment	unknown	

52nd Division: (C type) Activated in Kanezawa July 10, 1940, from 9th Depot Division personnel. Home station: Kanezawa. With the Eastern District Army from Oct 1st until deactivated June 27, 1942, reactivated Sept 2, 1943, reorganized into an *ocean division* Oct 20, 1943, Eastern District Army from Feb 22, 1944 until Feb 25th and 31st Army, Truk District Group until the war ended.
Service History: Truk Island: garrison.

53rd Division Kyoto 1941	安 *Yasui* 10016 (14,737)
53rd Division Headquarters	10017 (295)
53rd Division Signal Unit	10031 (239)
53rd Division Ordinance Duty Unit	10034 (81)
53rd Division Medical Unit	10035 (699)

53rd Division continued

53rd Division 1st Field Hospital	10036 (242)
53rd Division 2nd Field Hospital	10037 (242)
53rd Division 4th Field Hospital	10039 (247)
53rd Division D. P. & Water Supply Unit	10041 (196)
53rd Division Veterinary Unit	10040 (52)
53rd Infantry Group Headquarters	10019 (92) deactivated 6/15/44
• 119th Infantry Regiment (Tsuruga)	10020 (2,917)
• 128th Infantry Regiment (Kyoto)	10021 (2,917)
• 151st Infantry Regiment (Tsu)	10022 (2,917)
• 53rd Cavalry Regiment	10024 (402)
• 53rd Field Artillery Regiment	10027 (1,116)
• 53rd Engineer Regiment	10030 (906)
• 53rd Transport Regiment	10032 (749)

53rd Division: (C type) Activated in Kyoto September 16, 1941, from 16th Depot Division personnel. Home station: Kyoto. With the Central District Army (Chubu) until Nov 15, 1943, Southern Expeditionary Army until Jan 11, 1944, Burma Area Army until Apr 8th, 33rd Army until Oct 5th, 15th Army until July 14, 1945, and 18th Area Army (near the Thai-Burma border but unable to contact the 18th Area Army) until the war ended.
On Apr 24, 1944 the 151 Inf Regt was attached the 15th Army and the 3rd Btn 119th Inf Regt to the 56th Div.
Note: 8th Ind. Anti-Tank Company, formerly with the Ichiki Detachment on Guadalcanal joined the 53rd Division July 11, 1942.
Service History: Burma: Sittang Jul 3 1945.

54th Division Himeji 1940	兵 *Hei* 10109 (14,807)
54th Division Headquarters	10100 (250)
54th Division Signal Unit	10119 (239)
54th Division Ordinance Duty Unit	10121 (81)
54th Division Medical Unit	10122 (699)
54th Division 1st Field Hospital	10123 (242)
54th Division 2nd Field Hospital	10124 (242)
54th Division 4th Field Hospital	10126 (247)
54th Division D. P. & Water Supply Unit	10128 (196)
54th Division Veterinary Unit	10127 (52)
54th Infantry Group Headquarters	12207 (92)
• 111th Infantry Regiment (Himeji)	10112 (2,910)
• 121st Infantry Regiment (Tottori)	10113 (2,910)
• 154th Infantry Regiment (Okayama)	10114 (2,910)
• 54th Cavalry Regiment	10115 (439)
• 54th Field Artillery Regiment	10117 (1,636)
• 54th Engineer Regiment	10118 (913) attached to 17th Div
• 54th Transport Regiment	10120 (749)

54th Division: (B type) Activated in Himeji July 10, 1940, from 10th Depot Division personnel. Home station: Himeji. With the Central District Army in Himeji from Aug 4th until Feb 16, 1943, Imperial Headquarters until Mar 27th, Burma Area Army until Jan 15, 1944, and 28th Army in South Burma until the war ended.
Service History: Burma: Hill 170 Jan 22 1945, Sittang July 3 1945.

55th Division Zentsuji 1940	楯 *So* 8413 (15,844)
55th Division Headquarters	8400 (304)
55th Division Signal Unit	8422 (239)
55th Division Ordinance Duty Unit	8424 (81)
55th Division Medical Unit	8425 (700)
55th Division 1st Field Hospital	8426 (182)
55th Division 2nd Field Hospital	8427 (242)
55th Division 4th Field Hospital	8429 (247)
55th Division D. P. & Water Supply Unit	8428 (196)
55th Division Veterinary Unit	8430 (73)
55th Infantry Group Headquarters	8414 (131)
• 112th Infantry Regiment (Marugame)	8415 (2,933)
• 143rd Infantry Regiment (Tokushima)	8416 (2,933)
• 144th Infantry Regiment (Kōchi)	8417 (2,905)
• 55th Cavalry Regiment	8418 (667)
• 55th Mountain Artillery Regiment	8420 (2,296)
• 55th Engineer Regiment	8421 (906)
• 55th Transport Regiment	8423 (749)

55th Division: (B type) Activated in Zentsuji, Kagawa Prefecture July 10, 1940, from 11th Depot Division personnel. Home station: Zentsuji. With the Western District from Aug. 1st, Army until Nov 6, 1941, 15th Army until Mar 27, 1943, Burma Area Army until Jan 15, 1944, 28th Army until July 11, 1945 (its headquarters remained in Paung with 28th Army) and 38th Army in Phnom Penh, Vietnam until the war ended,
Note: South Seas Detachment (55th Inf Group HQ, 144th Inf Regt) activated Sept 27, 1941. New Guinea: Isurava Aug 26, 1942, Kokoda Oct 4th, Oivi Oct 29th. Deactivated and returned to the 55th Div. June 17, 1943.
Sakurai Detachment: (55th I.G. HQ, 143rd Inf Regt, I/213th Inf Regt, I,III/122nd Inf Regt) Admin Box Feb 4 1944, Goppe Bazaar Oct 6 1944, Hill 162 Dec 10 1944,
Service History: Burma: Invasion Jan 22 1942, Moulmein Jan 30 1942, Bilin River Feb 14 1942, Rangoon Mar 8 1942, Yunnan-Burma Road Campaign Mar 18 1942, Toungoo Mar 24 1942, Akyab Feb 1943, Admin Box Feb 4 1944, Sittang July 3 1945.

56th Division Kurume 1940	龍 *Tatu* 6703 (15,471)
56th Division Headquarters	6701 (304)
56th Division Signal Unit	6741 (239)
56th Division Ordinance Duty Unit	6743 (81)

56th Division continued

56th Division Headquarters	6701 (304)	
56th Division Signal Unit	6741 (239)	
56th Division Ordinance Duty Unit	6743 (81)	
56th Division Medical Unit	6744 (699)	
56th Division 1st Field Hospital	6745 (242)	
56th Division 2nd Field Hospital	6746 (242)	
56th Division 4th Field Hospital	6748 (247)	
56th Division D. P. & Water Supply Unit	6747 (196)	
56th Division Veterinary Unit	6749 (52)	
56th Infantry Group Headquarters	6733	deactivated 7/15/44
• 113th Infantry Regiment (Fukuoka)	6734 (2,881)	
• 146th Infantry Regiment (Ōmura)	6735 (2,903)	
• 148th Infantry Regiment (Kurume)	6736 (2,881)	
• 56th Reconnaissance Regiment	6737 (439)	
• 56th Field Artillery Regiment	6739 (1,636)	
• 56th Engineer Regiment	6740 (913)	
• 56th Transport Regiment	6742 (749)	

56th Division: (B type) Activated in Kurume July 10, 1940, from 12th Depot Division personnel. Home station: Kurume. With the Western District Army from Aug 1st, until Nov 27, 1941, 25th Army until Mar 4, 1942, 15th Army until Apr 7, 1944, 33rd Army until July 11, 1945 and 15th Army on the southern Thai-Burma border until the war ended.

Note: Sakaguchi Detach. (56th Inf. Group HQ, 146th Inf. Regt.) Tarakan: Jan 7 1942, Balikpapan Jan 23 1942, Java: Invasion Mar 1 1942. Returned to the 56th Div. in Apr. 1942.

Service History: Burma: Yunnan-Burma Road Campaign Mar 18 1942, Toungoo Mar 24 1942, Mawchi Apr 13 1942, Lashio Apr 29 1942, Salween River Feb 1943, Lashio Jan 1944, Myitkyina May 3 1944, Ramou/Mount Song June 4 1944, Lameng June-Sept 1944.

58th Division Kumamoto 1942	広 *Hirosi* 2304 (16,463)
58th Division Headquarters	2305 (669)
58th Division Signal Unit	7319 (413)
58th Division Field Hospital	7309 (996)
58th Division Veterinary Unit	2309 / 2039 (64)
51st Infantry Brigade	7303
51st Infantry Brigade Headquarters	2306 (135)
• 92nd Independent Infantry Battalion	7312 (1,475)
• 93rd Independent Infantry Battalion	7313 (1,475)
• 94th Independent Infantry Battalion	7314 (1,475)
• 95th Independent Infantry Battalion	7315 (1,475)
52nd Infantry Brigade	7304
52nd Infantry Brigade Headquarters	2307 (133)

58th Division continued

• 96th Independent Infantry Battalion	7316 (1,475)	
• 106th Independent Infantry Battalion	7317 (1,475)	
• 107th Independent Infantry Battalion	7310 (1,475)	
• 108th Independent Infantry Battalion	7311 (1,475)	
• 58th Engineer Regiment	7318 (901)	Suzuki Unit
• 58th Division Transport Unit	2308 (782)	
• 58th Division Artillery Unit	unknown (583)	

58th Division: (C type) Activated in North China Feb. 2, 1942, from former 18th I.M.B personnel. Home station: Kumamoto, Japan. With the 11th Army in Hangzhow from Feb 27, 1942 until it was deactivated in Kingian on September 17, 1945. Inherited the 18th I.M.B.'s code name.
Service History: China: Meinyang Feb 15 1943, Guilin Nov 9 1944.

60th Division Sakura 1942	矛 *Hoko* 7305 (13,795)
60th Division Headquarters	2315 (265)
60th Division Signal Unit	2324 (398)
60th Division Field Hospital	3854 (349)
60th Division Veterinary Unit	2326 (44)
55th Infantry Brigade Headquarters	2316 (122)
• 46th Independent Infantry Battalion	2317 (1,324)
• 47th Independent Infantry Battalion	2318 (1,324)
• 48th Independent Infantry Battalion	2319 (1,324)
• 49th Independent Infantry Battalion	2320 (1,324)
56th Infantry Brigade Headquarters	2321 (122)
• 50th Independent Infantry Battalion	2322 (1,324)
• 112th Independent Infantry Battalion	3851 (1,324)
• 113th Independent Infantry Battalion	3852 (1,324)
• 114th Independent Infantry Battalion	3853 (1,324)
• 60th Division Trench Mortar Unit	23130 (577)
• 60th Division Engineer Unit	2323 (901)
• 60th Division Transport Unit	2325 (417)

60th Division: (C type) Activated in Shanghai, China February 2, 1942, from former 11th I.M.B. personnel. Home station: Sakura. With the 13th Army in Suchow from April 10th until it was deactivated in Shanghai on September 17, 1945. Inherited the 11th I.M.B. code name.
Service History: China: Suchow.

61st Division Tokyo 1943	鵄 *Tobi* 3060 (13,412)
61st Division Headquarters	3061 (189)
61st Division Signal Unit	3066 (398)
61st Division Field Hospital	3068 (349)

61st Division continued

61st Division Veterinary Unit	3069 (44)	
61st Division Infantry Group		
• 101st Infantry Regiment (Tokyo)	3062 (3,479)	
• 149th Infantry Regiment (Kofu)	3063 (3,479)	
• 157th Infantry Regiment (Sakura)	3064 (3,479)	
• 61st Trench Mortar Unit	23131 (577)	
• 61st Engineer Regiment	3065 (901)	deactivated 2/1/45
• 61st Transport Regiment	3067 (615)	deactivated 2/1/45

61st Division: (C type) Activated in Tokyo March 13, 1943, from former 61st Ind Inf Group personnel. Home station: Tokyo. With the 13th Army in Shanghai from March 16th until it was deactivated in Shanghai on September 17, 1945.
Service History: China: garrison Nanking until Feb 1945, Shanghai.

64th Division Hiroshima 1943	開 *Kai* 7971 (12,313)
64th Division Headquarters	7980 (902)
64th Division Signal Unit	7988 (398)
64th Division Field Hospital	7989 (357)
64th Division Veterinary Unit	9428 (45)
64th Division Intendance Service Unit	7986 (502)
69th Infantry Brigade Headquarters	9426 (156)
• 51st Independent Infantry Battalion	7981 (1,283)
• 52nd Independent Infantry Battalion	7982 (1,283)
• 53rd Independent Infantry Battalion	7983 (1,283)
• 131st Independent Infantry Battalion	8011 (1,283)
70th Infantry Brigade Headquarters	9427 (156)
• 54th Independent Infantry Battalion	7984 (1,283)
• 55th Independent Infantry Battalion	7985 (1,283)
• 132nd Independent Infantry Battalion	8012 (1,283)
• 133rd Independent Infantry Battalion	8013 (1,283)
• 64th Division Engineer Unit	7987 (901)
• 64th Division Transport Unit	7986 (302)
• 64th Division Artillery Unit	unknown (583)

64th Division: (C type) Activated in Hubei, China May 1, 1943, from former 12th I.M.B. personnel. Home station: Hiroshima, Japan. With the 13th Army until Mar 15, 1944, China Expeditionary Army until Jul 17th, 11th Army until Aug 26th, 6th Area Army until Oct 19th and 20th Army in Changsha until it was deactivated in Sianyin Sept 6, 1945.
Service History: China: Jiangbei.

65th Division Nagoya 1943	専 *Sen* 7972 (13,637)
65th Division Headquarters	7990 (276)
65th Division Signal Unit	7993 (398)
65th Division Field Hospital	7999 (357)

65th Division continued

65th Division Veterinary Unit	9434 (45)
71st Infantry Brigade Headquarters	9429 (156)
• 56th Independent Infantry Battalion	7994 (1,283)
• 57th Independent Infantry Battalion	7995 (1,283)
• 58th Independent Infantry Battalion	7996 (1,283)
• 59th Independent Infantry Battalion	7997 (1,283)
72nd Infantry Brigade Headquarters	9430 (156)
• 60th Independent Infantry Battalion	7998 (1,283)
• 134th Independent Infantry Battalion	9431 (1,283)
• 135th Independent Infantry Battalion	9432 (1,283)
• 136th Independent Infantry Battalion	9433 (1,283)
• 13th Independent Artillery Battalion	9990 (583)
• 13th Independent Engineer Battalion	7992 (901)
• 65th Division Transport Unit	7991 (615)

65th Division: (C type) Activated in Anhui Prov. China May 1, 1943, from former 13th I.M.B. personnel (71st I. Bgde.). Home station: Nagoya. With the 13th Army in Suchow, China from May 1st until the war ended. Deactivated in Suchow on Sept 23, 1945.
Service History: China: Lu'an and Suchow.

68th Division Osaka 1942	檜 *Hinoki* 7320 (16,091)
68th Division Headquarters	2327 (982)
68th Division Signal Unit	2336 (413)
68th Division Field Hospital	6098 (697)
68th Division Veterinary Unit	2338 (64)
57th Infantry Brigade Headquarters	2328 (133)
• 61st Independent Infantry Battalion	2329 (1,475)
• 62nd Independent Infantry Battalion	2330 (1,475)
• 63rd Independent Infantry Battalion	2331 (1,475)
• 64th Independent Infantry Battalion	2332 (1,475)
58th Infantry Brigade Headquarters	2333 (133)
• 65th Independent Infantry Battalion	2334 (1,475)
• 115th Independent Infantry Battalion	6095 (1,475)
• 116th Independent Infantry Battalion	6096 (1,475)
• 117th Independent Infantry Battalion	6097 (1,472)
• 68th Division Engineer Unit	2335 (901)
• 68th Division Transport Unit	2337 (782)
• 68th Division Artillery Unit	unknown (583)

68th Division: (C type) Activated in Hupei, China Feb 2, 1942, from former 14th I.M.B. personnel (57th I. Bgde.). Home station: Osaka, Japan. With the 11th Army until Aug 26, 1944, 6th Area Army until Oct 19th and 20th Army in Hengchow until the war ended. Deactivated in Hengchow. Inherited the 14th I.M.B.s code name.
Service History: China: Changde/Anshang Nov 5 1943, Hengyang June 28 1944.

69th Division Hirosaki 1942	勝 *Katu* 2355 (14,024)	
69th Division Headquarters	2356 (187)	
69th Division Signal Unit	4219 (398)	
69th Division Field Hospital	5231 (349)	
69th Division Veterinary Unit	4217 (44)	
59th Infantry Brigade Headquarters	4211 (117)	
• 82nd Independent Infantry Battalion	4212 (1,324)	
• 83rd Independent Infantry Battalion	4213 (1,324)	
• 84th Independent Infantry Battalion	4214 (1,324)	
• 85th Independent Infantry Battalion	4215 (1,324)	
60th Infantry Brigade Headquarters	2358 (117)	
• 86th Independent Infantry Battalion	4216 (1,324)	
• 118th Independent Infantry Battalion	5228 (1,324)	
• 119th Independent Infantry Battalion	5229 (1,324)	
• 120th Independent Infantry Battalion	5230 (1,324)	
• 69th Division Machine Cannon Unit	1498 (577)	
• 69th Division Engineer Unit	4218 (901)	deactivated 2/1/45
• 69th Division Transport Unit	2359 (508)	

69th Division: (C type) Activated in Linfen, Shanxi Prov. China Feb 2, 1942, from former 16th I.M.B personnel (59th I. Bgde.). Home station: Hirosaki, Japan. With the 1st Army from Apr 10th until May 28, 1945 and 13th Army in Jiading until it was deactivated in Shanghai on September 17, 1945. Inherited the 16th I.M.B.s code name.
Service History: China: Shanxi, Jiading.

70th Division Hiroshima 1942	槍 *Yari* 7300 (12,449)	
70th Division Headquarters	2339 (256)	
70th Division Signal Unit	2347 (330)	
70th Division Field Hospital	7155 (349)	
70th Division Veterinary Unit	2349 (44)	
61st Infantry Brigade Headquarters	2340 (122)	
• 102nd Independent Infantry Battalion	2341 (1,274)	
• 103rd Independent Infantry Battalion	2342 (1,274)	
• 104th Independent Infantry Battalion	2343 (1,324)	
• 105th Independent Infantry Battalion	2344 (1,324)	
62nd Infantry Brigade Headquarters	2345 (122)	
• 121st Independent Infantry Battalion	7152 (1,324)	
• 122nd Independent Infantry Battalion	7153 (1,324)	
• 123rd Independent Infantry Battalion	7154 (1,324)	
• 124th Independent Infantry Battalion	6874 (1,324)	
• 70th Division Machine Cannon Unit	11154	
• 70th Division Trench Mortar Unit	23132 (577)	
• 70th Division Engineer Unit	2346 (901)	deactivated 2/1/45
• 70th Division Transport Unit	2348 (472)	
• 4th Independent Security Battalion	7172	

70th Division: (C type) Activated in Central China Feb 2, 1942, from former 20th I.M.B (61st I. Bgde.). Home station: Hiroshima, Japan. With the 13th Army from Apr 10th until July 15, 1945 and 6th Army in Jiaxing until the war ended. Deactivated in Kuchen Sept 23, 1945. One of six divisions in transit to Manchuria with 6th Army Headquarters when the war ended. Inherited the 20th I.M.B.s code name.
Service History: China: Zhejiang Jiangxi May 27 1942, Lishui Aug 27 1944.

94th Division Osaka 1944	威烈 *Iretsu* (14,225)
94th Division Headquarters	18501 (438)
94th Division Signal Unit	18507 (239)
94th Division Ordinance Duty Unit	18509 (81)
94th Division Medical Unit	18510 (699)
94th Division 1st Field Hospital	18511 (277)
94th Division 4th Field Hospital	18512 (277)
94th Division D. P. & Water Supply Unit	18513 (196)
94th Infantry Group Headquarters	18514 (92)
• 256th Infantry Regiment (Osaka)	18502 (2,881)
• 257th Infantry Regiment (Osaka)	18503 (2,881)
• 258th Infantry Regiment (Osaka)	18504 (2,881)
• 94th Field Artillery Regiment	18505 (1,636)
• 94th Engineer Regiment	18506 (898)
• 94th Transportation Regiment	18508 (749)

94th Division: (C type) Activated in Kuala Lampur, Malaysia Oct 14, 1944, from former 12th and 18th Independent Garrison Unit personnel. Home station: Osaka, Japan. With the 29th Army from Oct 14th until surrendering in Sungei Patani on Oct 8, 1945.
Service History: Malaysia: Kedah.

100th Division Nagoya 1944	拠 *Kyo* 10600 (13,304)
100th Division Headquarters	10620 (292)
100th Division Signal Unit	10626 (347)
100th Division Field Hospital	12419 (366)
100th Division D. P. & Water Supply Unit	12421 (181)
100th Division Veterinary Unit	12420 (49)
75th Infantry Brigade Headquarters	10675 (56)
75th Brigade Signal Unit	10636 (132)
75th Brigade Labor Unit	10637 (159)
• 163rd Independent Infantry Battalion	10621 (997)
• 164th Independent Infantry Battalion	10622 (997)
• 165th Independent Infantry Battalion	10623 (997)
• 166th Independent Infantry Battalion	10624 (997)
76th Infantry Brigade Headquarters	10676 (56)
76th Division Signal Unit	10647 (132)
76th Brigade Labor Unit	10648 (159)
• 167th Independent Infantry Battalion	10625 (997)

100th Division continued

• 168th Independent Infantry Battalion	10638 (997)
• 352nd Independent Infantry Battalion	10639 (997)
• 353rd Independent Infantry Battalion	10646 (997)
• 100th Division Artillery Unit	10649 (510)
• 100th Division Engineer Unit	10683 (2,022)
• 100th Division Transport Unit	10684 (867)

100th Division: (C type) Activated Mindanao, the Philippines June 15, 1944, from former 30th I.M.B. personnel. Home station: Nagoya, Japan. With the 14th Army from June 15th until Aug 4th and 35th Army on Mindanao until it was deactivated on Sept 7, 1945. Inherited the 30th I.M.B.s code name.

Service History: Philippines: Mindanao: Ising Nov 1944, Cotabato Jan 1945, Davao Apr 27 1945.

102nd Division Kumamoto 1944	抜 *Batu* 10602 (13,304)	
102nd Division Headquarters	10630 (292)	
102nd Division Signal Unit	10635 (347)	
102nd Division Field Hospital	12422 (366)	
102nd Division D. P. & Water Supply Unit	12424 (181)	
102nd Division Veterinary Unit	12423 (49)	
77th Infantry Brigade Headquarters	10677 (56)	
77th Brigade Signal Unit	10686 (132)	
77th Brigade Labor Unit	10687 (159)	Kono Unit
• 170th Independent Infantry Battalion	10632 (997)	
• 171st Independent Infantry Battalion	10633 (997)	
• 172nd Independent Infantry Battalion	10634 (997)	
• 354th Independent Infantry Battalion	10685 (997)	
78th Infantry Brigade Headquarters	10678 (56)	
78th Brigade Signal Unit	10694 (132)	
78th Brigade Labor Unit	10695 (159)	
• 169th Independent Infantry Battalion	10631 (997)	
• 173rd Independent Infantry Battalion	10688 (997)	
• 174th Independent Infantry Battalion	10689 (997)	
• 355th Independent Infantry Battalion	10693 (997)	
• 102nd Division Field Artillery Unit	10696 (510)	
• 102nd Division Engineer Unit	10697 (2,022)	
• 102nd Division Transport Unit	10698 (867)	

102nd Division: (C type) Activated in the Vizaya Islands, P.I. June 15, 1944, from former 31st I.M.B. personnel. Home station: Kumamoto, Japan. With the 14th Army until Aug 4, 1944 and 35th Army (35th Army was deactivated Apr 19, 1945) on Cebu and Negros. Inherited the 31st I.M.B. code name.

Service History: Philippines: Leyte Oct 20 1944, Bohol Island Apr 11, 1945.

103rd Division Kumamoto 1944	駿 *Shun* 10603 (13,304)	
103rd Division Headquarters	10640 (292)	
103rd Division Signal Unit	10645 (347)	
103rd Division Field Hospital	12521 (366)	
103rd Division D. P. & Water Supply Unit	12523 (181)	
103rd Division Veterinary Unit	12522 (49)	
79th Infantry Brigade Headquarters	10679 (56)	Araki Unit
79th Brigade Signal Unit	10601 (132)	
79th Brigade Labor Unit	10604 (159)	
• 175th Independent Infantry Battalion	10641 (997)	
• 176th Independent Infantry Battalion	10642 (997)	
• 178th Independent Infantry Battalion	10644 (997)	
• 356th Independent Infantry Battalion	10699 (997)	
80th Infantry Brigade Headquarters	10690 (56)	Yaguchi Unit
80th Brigade Signal Unit	17617 (132)	
80th Brigade Labor Unit	17618 (159)	
• 177th Independent Infantry Battalion	10643 (997)	
• 179th Independent Infantry Battalion	17614 (997)	
• 180th Independent Infantry Battalion	17615 (997)	
• 357th Independent Infantry Battalion	17616 (997)	
• 103rd Division Field Artillery Unit	17619 (510)	
• 103rd Division Engineer Unit	10606 (2,022)	
• 103rd Division Transport Unit	10607 (867)	

103rd Division: (C type) Activated on Luzon, the Philippines June 15, 1944, from former 32nd I.M.B personnel. Home station: Kumamoto. With the 14th Area Army (Aparri garrison) from June 15th until it surrendered on Sept 10, 1945. It was reduced to less than 200 men in the Cagayan area trying to rejoin the army in late July. Inherited the 32nd I.M.B.s code name.

Service History: Philippines: Aparri Jan 9 1945, Orioung Pass June 11 1945.

104th Division Nagoya 1938	鳳 *Ootori* 8975 (15,350)
104th Division Headquarters	8974 (396)
104th Division Signal Unit	8978 (219)
104th Division Ordinance Duty Unit	8965 (95)
104th Division Medical Unit	8973
104th Division 2nd Field Hospital	8962 (699)
104th Division Veterinary Unit	8966 (65)
104th Division Infantry Group	
• 108th Infantry Regiment (Osaka)	8964 (3,427)
• 137th Infantry Regiment (Osaka)	8972 (3,787)
• 161st Infantry Regiment (Wakayama)	8963 (3,787)
• 104th Tank Regiment	8974
• 104th Field Artillery Regiment	8961 (1,417)
• 104th Engineer Regiment	8969 (424)

104th Division continued

• 104th Transport Regiment	8976 (812)	

104th Division: (C type) Activated in Osaka June 16, 1938, from former 4th Depot Div troops. Home station: Nagoya. Lost the 170th Inf Regt becoming triangular Jan 13, 1941. With the 21st Army from Sept 19th until Feb 9, 1940, South China Area Army until July 5, 1941 and 23rd Army in Suchow. Deactivated in Canton on Sept 17, 1945. Service History: China: Canton Oct 12 1938, Wushan Nov 4 1944, Liuchow Nov 9 1944, Canton-Hankou Railway Jan 3 1945.

105th Division Hiroshima 1944	勤 *Kin* 10605 (13,304)	
105th Division Headquarters	10660 (292)	
105th Division Signal Unit	10664 (347)	
105th Division Field Hospital	12361 (366)	
105th Division D. P. & Water Supply Unit	12363 (181)	
105th Division Veterinary Unit	12362 (49)	
81st Infantry Brigade Headquarters	10691 (56)	Noguchi Unit
81st Brigade Signal Unit	10667 (132)	
81st Brigade Labor Unit	10668 (159)	
• 181st Independent Infantry Battalion	10661 (997)	
• 182nd Independent Infantry Battalion	10662 (997)	
• 183rd Independent Infantry Battalion	10665 (997)	
• 185th Independent Infantry Battalion	10666 (997)	
82nd Infantry Brigade Headquarters	10692 (56)	Kawashima Unit
82nd Brigade Signal Unit	10673 (132)	
82nd Brigade Labor Unit	10674 (159)	
• 184th Independent Infantry Battalion	10669 (997)	
• 186th Independent Infantry Battalion	10670 (997)	
• 358th Independent Infantry Battalion	10671 (997)	
• 359th Independent Infantry Battalion	10672 (997)	to 10th Div.
• 105th Division Artillery Unit	10663 (510)	
• 105th Division Engineer Unit	10608 (2,022)	
• 105th Division Transport Unit	10609 (867)	

105th Division: (C type) Activated Luzon, the Philippines June 15, 1944, from former 33rd I.M.B. personnel. Home station: Hiroshima. With the 41st Army, about half the division was later deployed to north Luzon under 14th Area Army control.

Note: Kawashima Detachment (82nd Inf. Bgde) Jan. 1945, Lamon Bay and Lucena

Service History: Philippines: Luzon Jan 9 1945.

109th Division Kofu 1944	膽 *Tan* 17501
109th Division Headquarters	17502 /18301 (1,488)
109th Division Signal Unit	18305 (177)
109th Division Observation Unit	17525 / 18328 (110)
109th Division Field Hospital	17526

109th Division continued

Chichi Jima Field Hospital	17527 (129) deactiv. 5/22/44
1st Mixed Brigade Headquarters	17503 / 18304 (93)
• 303rd Independent Infantry Battalion	17504 / 18306 (579)
• 304th Independent Infantry Battalion	17505 / 18307 (579)
• 305th Independent Infantry Battalion	17506 / 18308 (579)
• 306th Independent Infantry Battalion	17507 / 18309 (579)
• 307th Independent Infantry Battalion	17508 / 18310 (579)
• 308th Independent Infantry Battalion	17509 / 18311 (579)
• 1st Mixed Brigade Artillery Company	17510 / 18312 (129)
• 1st Mixed Brigade Engineer Company	17511 / 18313 (321)
• 2nd Mixed Brigade Headquarters	17512 / 18315 (135)
• 309th Independent Infantry Battalion	17513 / 18316 (579)
• 310th Independent Infantry Battalion	17514 / 18317 (579)
• 311th Independent Infantry Battalion	17515 / 18318 (579)
• 312th Independent Infantry Battalion	17516 / 18319 (579)
• 313th Independent Infantry Battalion	17517 / 18320 (579)
• 314th Independent Infantry Battalion	17518 / 18321 (579)
• 2nd Mixed Brigade Artillery Unit	17519 / 18322 (415)
• 2nd Mixed Brigade Engineer Unit	17520 / 18323 (221)
• 2nd Mixed Brigade Field Hospital	17521 / 18324 (61)
• 1st Mixed Regiment	17522 / 18325 (1,467)
• 109th Heavy Artillery Regiment	17523 / 18326 (534)
• 109th Division Anti-Aircraft Unit	17524/18327 (1,072) de 5/22/44
• 1st Independent Artillery Battalion	7837
• 2nd Independent Artillery Battalion	7838

109th Division: (C type) Activated in Kanazawa on August 26, 1937. Home station: Kanazawa. With the North China Area Amy from Aug 31st until Mar 30, 1938 and 1st Army until it was deactivated on December 24, 1938.
Reactivated in the Ogasawara Is. May 22, 1944. Home station: Kofu. With 31st Army until destroyed on Iwo Jima. Note: The 1944 order of battle is shown here.
Service History 1937-8: China: Yangchu Oct. 12, 1937.
Service History 1944-5: Japan: Iwo Jima: Feb 19 1945.

110th Division Himeji 1938	鷺 *Sagi* 3905 (14,362)
110th Division Headquarters	3906 (547)
110th Division Signal Unit	3916 (529)
110th Division Ordinance Duty Unit	3918 (95)
110th Division Field Hospital	3919 (1,004)
110th Division Veterinary Unit	3920 (65)
110th Division Infantry Group	
• 110th Infantry Regiment (Himeji)	3911 (3,667)
• 139th Infantry Regiment (Himeji)	3908 (3,667)
• 163rd Infantry Regiment (Matsue)	3912 (3,667)

110th Division continued

• 110th Division Cavalry Unit	3913 (460)
• 110th Division Artillery Unit	3914 (727)
• 110th Division Engineer Unit	3915 (901)
• 110th Division Transport Unit	3917 (812)

110th Division: (C type) Activated in Himeji June 16, 1938, from 10th Depot Division personnel. Home station: Himeji. Lost the 140th Inf Regt and became triangular Apr 16, 1942. With the North China Area Army from June 25th until Mar 22, 1945 and 12th Army in Loyang until it was deactivated in Chengchow.
Service History: China: Nanyang March 31 1945.

114th Division Mizonokuchi 1937	将 *Sye* 1459 (11,891)
114th Division Headquarters	1460 (175)
114th Division Signal Unit	1465 (329)
114th Division Field Hospital	15610 (352)
114th Division Veterinary Unit	15611 (45)
83rd Infantry Brigade	15600
83rd Infantry Brigade Headquarters	15601 (50)
• 199th Independent Infantry Battalion	1461 (1,233)
• 200th Independent Infantry Battalion	1462 (1,233)
• 201st Independent Infantry Battalion	1463 (1,233)
• 202nd Independent Infantry Battalion	1464 (1,233)
84th Infantry Brigade	15602
84th Infantry Brigade Headquarters	15603 (50)
• 381st Independent Infantry Battalion	15604 (1,233)
• 382nd Independent Infantry Battalion	15605 (1,233)
• 383rd Independent Infantry Battalion	15606 (1,233)
• 384th Independent Infantry Battalion	15607 (1,233)
• 114th Division Field Artillery Unit	15759 (583)
• 114th Division Engineer Unit	15608 (901)
• 114th Division Transport Unit	15609 (567)

114th Division: (C type) Activated Utsunomiya Oct 12, 1937. Home station: Utsunomiya. With the 10th Army From Oct 20th until Feb 10, 1938, North China Army until Nov 11th and 12th Army until it was deactivated August 12, 1939.
Reactivated in North China on July 10, 1944, from 14th Depot Division troops and 3rd Ind Inf Brigade troops. Home station: Mizonoguchi, Japan. With the 1st Army in Taiyuan, Shanxi Province until it was deactivated in Taiyuan on September 17, 1945.
Service History 1937-9: China: 2nd Battle Shanghai Nov 5 1937, Xuzhou May 10 1938.
Service History 1944-5: China: Shanxi garrison.

115th Division Asahikawa 1944	北 *Kita* 2970 (11,891)	
115th Division Headquarters	2971 (184)	
115th Division Signal Unit	2979 (330)	
115th Division Field Hospital	15619 (352)	
115th Division Veterinary Unit	15620 (45)	
85th Infantry Brigade	unknown	
85th Infantry Brigade Headquarters	2978 (50)	
• 26th Independent Infantry Battalion	2972 (1,233)	
• 27th Independent Infantry Battalion	2973 (1,233)	
• 28th Independent Infantry Battalion	2974 (1,233)	
• 29th Independent Infantry Battalion	2975 (1,233)	
86th Infantry Brigade	15612	
86th Infantry Brigade Headquarters	15613 (50)	
• 30th Independent Infantry Battalion	2976 (1,233)	
• 385th Independent Infantry Battalion	15614 (1,233)	
• 386th Independent Infantry Battalion	15615 (1,233)	
• 387th Independent Infantry Battalion	15616 (1,233)	
• 115th Division Artillery Unit	No # (583)	
• 115th Division Engineer Unit	15617 (901)	deactivated 7/19/45
• 115th Division Transport Unit	15618 (867)	

115th Division: (C type) Activated in North China July 10, 1944, from former 7th I.M.B. personnel (became 85th Inf. Bgde.). Home station: Asahikawa. With the 12th Army in Laohekou from July 17th until it was deactivated in Fancheng on September 17, 1945.

Service History: China: Laohekou Apr 8 1945, Henan Province garrison.

116th Division Kyoto 1938	嵐 *Arashi* 6217	
116th Division Headquarters	6200 (362)	
116th Division Signal Unit	6226 (301)	
116th Division Ordinance Duty Unit	6228 (95)	
116th Division Medical Unit	6229 (400)	
116th Division 1st Field Hospital	6230 (301)	
116th Division 2nd Field Hospital	6231 (301)	
116th Division 4th Field Hospital	6233 (309)	
116th Division Veterinary Unit	6234 (119)	activated 5/1/43
116th Division Infantry Group		
• 109th Infantry Regiment (Kyoto)	6213 (4,218)	
• 120th Infantry Regiment (see note)	6212 (4,218)	
• 133rd Infantry Regiment (Tsu)	6214 (4,218)	
• 120th Cavalry Regiment	1653	
• 122nd Field Artillery Regiment	6222 (1,959)	
• 116th Engineer Regiment	6225 (901)	
• 116th Transport Regiment	6227 (1,170)	

116th Division: (C type) Activated in Kyoto, May 15, 1938. Home station: Kyoto.

116th Division continued
Lost the 138th Inf. Regt. became triangular Dec 25, 1942. With the Central China Expeditionary Army from May 20th until Sept 23, 1939, 13th Army until Feb 1, 1944, 11th Army until Oct 19th and 20th Army in Muchang, Hunan where it was deactivated on Sept 17, 1945. Note: 120th Inf Regt's home station is in Fukuchiyama.
Service History: China: Nanking Dec 9 1937, Tatungchen Dec. 16 1939, Jiangxi May 27 1942, Anshang Nov 5 1943, Hengyang June 22 1944, Chihchiang Apr 15 1945.

118th Division Kyoto 1944	恵 *Megumi* 15633 (11,866)	
118th Division Headquarters	10284 (175)	
118th Division Signal Unit	15761 (329)	
118th Division (Mito) Field Hospital	15644 (327)	
118th Division Veterinary Unit	15645 (45)	
89th Infantry Brigade	15634	
89th Infantry Brigade Headquarters	15635 (50)	
• 223rd Independent Infantry Battalion	10285 (1,233)	
• 224th Independent Infantry Battalion	10286 (1,233)	
• 225th Independent Infantry Battalion	6046 (1,233)	
• 226th Independent Infantry Battalion	6047 (1,233)	
90th Infantry Brigade	15636	
90th Infantry Brigade Headquarters	15637 (50)	
• 392nd Independent Infantry Battalion	15638 (1,233)	
• 401st Independent Infantry Battalion	15639 (1,233)	
• 402nd Independent Infantry Battalion	15640 (1,233)	
• 403rd Independent Infantry Battalion	15641 (1,233)	
• 118th Division Trench Mortar Unit	15756 (577)	activated 2/1/45
• 118th Division Engineer Unit	15642 (901)	
• 118th Division Transport Unit	15643 (867)	

118th Division: (C type) Activated in Datong, North China July 10, 1944, from former 9th Ind Inf Bgde personnel (became Div HQ and 89th Inf Bgde). Home station: Kyoto. With the Mongolia Garrison Army from July 17th until May 28, 1945 and 13th Army in Tianjin and Zhangjiakou, Hebei until it was deactivated in Tianjin on September 22, 1945.
Inherited the 9th Independent Infantry Brigade's code name.
Service History: Mongolia: garrison. China: Shanghai garrison.

129th Division Nagano 1945	英邁 *Shimbu* 8639/8640
129th Division Headquarters	8641 (121)
129th Division Signal Unit	8654 (330)
129th Division Ordinance Duty Unit	8656 (95)
129th Division Field Hospital	8657 (487)
129th Division D. P. & Water Supply Unit	8659 (239)
129th Division Veterinary Unit	8658 (119)
91st Infantry Brigade Headquarters	8642 (153)

129th Division continued		
• 98th Independent Infantry Battalion	8643 (1,348)	
• 278th Independent Infantry Battalion	8644 (1,348)	
• 279th Independent Infantry Battalion	8983 (1,348)	
• 280th Independent Infantry Battalion	8646 (1,348)	to 5th Area Army
92nd Infantry Brigade Headquarters	8647 (153)	
• 101st Independent Infantry Battalion	8648 (1,348)	
• 588th Independent Infantry Battalion	8649 (1,348)	
• 589th Independent Infantry Battalion	8650 (1,348)	
• 590th Independent Infantry Battalion	8651 (1,348)	
• 129th Division Artillery Unit	8652 (756)	
• 129th Division Engineer Unit	8653 (401)	
• 129th Division Transport Unit	8655 (576)	

129th Division: (C type) Activated in Daya Bay, China April 12, 1945, from former 19th IMB personnel. Home station: Nagano. With the 23rd Army in Tunguan, China from Apr 20th until it was deactivated in Canton-Swatow on September 22nd.
Service History: China: Dongguan garrison.

130th Division Kyoto 1945	鍾馗 *Shoki* 8612
130th Division Headquarters	8611 (345)
130th Division Signal Unit	8987 (330)
130th Division Ordinance Duty Unit	8670 (95)
130th Division 1st Field Hospital	8671 (487)
130th Division 2nd Field Hospital	8672 (487)
130th Division D. P. & Water Supply Unit	8674 (239)
130th Division Veterinary Unit	8673 (119)
93rd Infantry Brigade Headquarters	8661 (153)
• 97th Independent Infantry Battalion	8981 (1,348)
• 99th Independent Infantry Battalion	8983 (1,348)
• 100th Independent Infantry Battalion	8934 (1,348)
• 277th Independent Infantry Battalion	8662 (1,348)
94th Infantry Brigade Headquarters	8664 (153)
• 281st Independent Infantry Battalion	8665 (1,348)
• 620th Independent Infantry Battalion	8666 (1,348)
• 621st Independent Infantry Battalion	8667 (1,348)
• 622nd Independent Infantry Battalion	8668 (1,348)
• 130th Division Artillery Unit	8985 (3,161)
• 130th Division Engineer Unit	8986 (901)
• 130th Division Transport Unit	8669 (864)

130th Division: (C type) Activated in south China April 12, 1945, from former 19th I.M.B. personnel. Home station: Kyoto. With the 23rd Army in Chiangmiu, Guangdong from April 20th until it was deactivated in Swatow on September 22nd.
Service History: China: Zhongshan, Shantou garrison.

131st Division Kanazawa 1945	秋水 *Syusui* 17800
131st Division Headquarters	17801 (950)
131st Division Signal Unit	17807 (330)
131st Division Ordinance Duty Unit	17809 (95)
131st Division Field Hospital	17890 (491)
131st Division Veterinary Unit	17899 (119)
95th Infantry Brigade Headquarters	17803 (51)
• 591st Independent Infantry Battalion	17891 (1,549)
• 592nd Independent Infantry Battalion	17892 (1,549)
• 593rd Independent Infantry Battalion	17893 (1,549)
• 594th Independent Infantry Battalion	17894 (1,549)
96th Infantry Brigade Headquarters	17805 (51)
• 595th Independent Infantry Battalion	17895 (1,549)
• 596th Independent Infantry Battalion	17896 (1,549)
• 597th Independent Infantry Battalion	17897 (1,549)
• 598th Independent Infantry Battalion	17898 (1,549)
• 131st Division Engineer Unit	17806 (901)
• 131st Division Transport Unit	17808 (1,263)
• 131st Division Artillery Unit	unknown (583) activate 7/10/45

131st Division: (C type) Activated in Wuhan, China Feb 1, 1945, from former 27th and 40th Div personnel. Home station: Kanazawa. With the 23rd Army from Mar 6th until June 17th and China Expeditionary Army in Yangshin, Anking where it was deactivated on September 17th.

Service History: China:

132nd Division Osaka 1945	振起 *Shinki* 17720
132nd Division Headquarters	17721 (950)
132nd Division Signal Unit	17727 (330)
132nd Division Ordinance Duty Unit	17737 (95)
132nd Division Field Hospital	17738 (491)
132nd Division Veterinary Unit	17739 (119)
97th Infantry Brigade Headquarters	17723 (51)
• 599th Independent Infantry Battalion	17729 (1,549)
• 600th Independent Infantry Battalion	17730 (1,549)
• 601st Independent Infantry Battalion	17731 (1,549)
• 602nd Independent Infantry Battalion	17732 (1,549)
98th Infantry Brigade Headquarters	17725 (51)
• 603rd Independent Infantry Battalion	17733 (1,549)
• 604th Independent Infantry Battalion	17734 (1,549)
• 605th Independent Infantry Battalion	17735 (1,549)
• 606th Independent Infantry Battalion	17736 (1,549)
• 132nd Division Artillery Unit	unknown (583) activated 710/45
• 132nd Division Engineer Unit	17726 (901)
• 132nd Division Transport Unit	17728 (1,263)

132nd Division: (C type) Activated in Wuhan, China Feb 1, 1945, from former 39th and 68th Depot Div personnel. Home station: Osaka. With the 34th Army from Mar 6th until June 17th and 6th Area Army in Yichang. Deactivated in Hankow on Sept 17th. Service History: China: Yichang.

133rd Division Kumamoto 1945	進撃 *Shingeki* 23051	
133rd Division Headquarters	23052 (755)	
133rd Division Signal Unit	23066 (330)	
133rd Division Ordinance Duty Unit	23068 (95)	
133rd Division Field Hospital	23069 (491)	
133rd Division Veterinary Unit	23070 and 23124 (119)	
99th Infantry Brigade	23053	
99th Infantry Brigade Headquarters	23054 (51)	
• 607th Independent Infantry Battalion	23055 (1,549)	
• 608th Independent Infantry Battalion	23056 (1,549)	
• 609th Independent Infantry Battalion	23057 (1,549)	
• 610th Independent Infantry Battalion	23058 (1,549)	
100th Infantry Brigade	23059	
100th Infantry Brigade Headquarters	23060 (51)	
• 611th Independent Infantry Battalion	23061 (1,549)	
• 612th Independent Infantry Battalion	23062 (1,549)	
• 613th Independent Infantry Battalion	23063 (1,549)	
• 614th Independent Infantry Battalion	23064 (1,549)	
• 133rd Division Artillery Unit	23971 (453)	activated 710/45
• 133rd Division Engineer Unit	23065 (901)	
• 133rd Division Transport Unit	23067 (1,263)	

133rd Division: (C type) Activated in Guilin, China Feb 1, 1945, from former 65th and 70th Div personnel. Home station: Kumamoto, Japan. With the 13th Army from Mar 6th until Jul 15th and 6th Army in Hangchow and deactivated in Wanking on Sept 17th. Service History: China: Hangchow.

161st Division Kumamoto 1945	震天 *Shinten* 23137
161st Division Headquarters	23138 (329)
161st Division Signal Unit	23152 (330)
161st Division Ordinance Duty Unit	23154 (95)
161st Division 1st Field Hospital	23155 (487)
161st Division 2nd Field Hospital	23156 (487)
161st Division D. P. & Water Supply Unit	23158 (239)
161st Division Veterinary Unit	23157 (119)
101st Infantry Brigade Headquarters	23140 (153)
• 475th Independent Infantry Battalion	23141 (1,348)
• 476th Independent Infantry Battalion	23142 (1,348)
• 477th Independent Infantry Battalion	23143 (1,348)
• 528th Independent Infantry Battalion	23086 (1,348)
102nd Infantry Brigade Headquarters	23145 (153)

161st Division continued

• 478th Independent Infantry Battalion	23146 (1,348)
• 479th Independent Infantry Battalion	23147 (1,348)
• 480th Independent Infantry Battalion	23148 (1,348)
• 481st Independent Infantry Battalion	23149 (1,348)
• 161st Division Artillery Unit	23150 (462)
• 161st Division Engineer Unit	23151 (901)
• 161st Division Transport Unit	23153 (977)

161st Division: (C type) Activated in Shanghai April 12, 1945. Home station: Kumamoto. With the 13th Army in Shanghai, China from Apr 20th, arrived in Nanking on Aug 13th while redeploying to Manchuria, it was deactivated in Nanking on September 17th.
Service History: China: Shanghai coastal defense. Manchuria: reached Nanking in transit.

Armored Divisions

2nd Armored Division Manchuria 1942	撃 *Geki* 12090 (7,200 P.I.)	
2nd Tank Division Headquarters	12091 (100)	
2nd Tank Division Signal Unit	12096 (120)	
2nd Tank Division Maintenance Unit	12106 (500)	
3rd Tank Brigade Headquarters	12093 (10)	
• 6th Tank Regiment (Osaka)	12094 (800)	
• 7th Tank Regiment (Osaka)	12095 (800)	
• 10th Tank Regiment (Osaka)	12098 (800)	
• 2nd Mechanized Infantry Regiment	12100 (1,500)	Clark Field
• 2nd Tank Division Rapid Firing Gun Unit	12103 (200)	
• 2nd Mechanized Artillery Regiment	12104 (1,200)	
• 2nd Tank Division Engineer Regiment	12105 (800)	
• 2nd Tank Division Transport Regiment	12107 (400)	
• 88th Transport Regiment	17667	

2nd Armored Division: Activated Manchuria June 24, 1942. Home station: Manchuria. With the 1st Mechanized Army from July 4th until Oct 30, 1943, 1st Area Army until July 24, 1944, Imperial General Headquarters until Aug 4th and 14th Area Army on Luzon the Philippines where it was destroyed. Authorized strength reduced from 17,781 to 7,200 for service in the Philippines. Fought as infantry from late Feb 1945.
Service History: Philippines: Luzon Jan 23 1945, Clark Field Jan 25 1945, Salacsac Pass Apr 24 1945.

3rd Armored Division Tsudanuma 1942	滝 *Taki* 5350 (12,738)	
3rd Tank Division Headquarters	5340 (158)	
3rd Tank Division Field Hospital	unknown (180)	activ. 7/10/45
3rd Tank Division D. P. & Water Supply Unit	unknown (100)	activ. 7/10/45
3rd Tank Division Maintenance Unit	5348 (878)	

3rd Armored Division continued

6th Tank Brigade Headquarters	5349 (48)
• 13th Tank Regiment (Tsudanuma)	5509 (1,291)
• 17th Tank Regiment (Tsudanuma)	1450 (1,291)
• 3rd Mechanized Infantry Regiment	5342 (3,549)
• 3rd Tank Division Rapid firing Gun Unit	5343 (506)
• 3rd Mechanized Artillery Regiment	5346 (1,666)
• 3rd Tank Reconnaissance Unit	5345 (856)
• 3rd Tank Engineer Unit	5347 (1,449)
• 3rd Tank Transport Unit	5355 (1,015)

3rd Armored Division: Activated in North China June 24, 1942, from former 1st Cavalry Brigade personnel. Home station: Tsudanoma, Japan. With the North China Area Army until December 19th, Mongolia Garrison Army until April 2, 1944, and 12th Army in Beijing until the war ended.
Service History: China: Luoyang May 13 1944.

Roadside rest in China (author)

End of Divisions

Brigades

The Imperial Japanese Army was well known for its bicycle soldiers (author)

Independent Brigades:

Independent mixed brigades (I.M.B.) were the most numerous. The infantry component was typically one or two regiments or three to six independent battalions. Operational support for them came from their own signal, artillery and engineer units.

In the army as a whole there were 116 I.M.B. in addition to 14 infantry, 9 armored, 1 airborne, 1 mobile and 4 amphibious brigades.

1st Independent Mixed Brigade 1939	島 *Shima* 2960 (4,572)	
1st Brigade Headquarters	2961 (231)	
• 72nd Independent Infantry Battalion	2962 (1,549)	
• 73rd Independent Infantry Battalion	2963 (1,549)	
• 74th Independent Infantry Battalion	2964 (1,549)	
• 75th Independent Infantry Battalion	2965 (1,549)	
• 76th Independent Infantry Battalion	2966 (1,549)	
• 1st Brigade Artillery Unit	2967 (582)	activated 2/1/45
• 1st Brigade Engineer Unit	1891 (531)	activated 2/1/45
• 1st Brigade Signal Unit	2969 (175)	

1st I.M.B.: Activated in Tokyo on March 17, 1934. With the Kwantung Army from July 7, 1937 until July 13th, China Garrison Army until Aug 16th and Kwantung Army until it was deactivated on August 12, 1938.
Reactivated in the Yellow River area on July 22, 1939, from former 109th Division personnel. Home station: Toyama. With the North China Area Army in Kwangping until it was deactivated in Shihchiachuang, China (order of battle shown is 2nd activation).
Service History: China: Taiyuan Sept 14 1937, Hundred Regiments Aug 20 1940.

2nd Independent Mixed Brigade 1938	響 *Hibiki* 5330 (4,581)	
2nd Brigade Headquarters	5331 (242)	
• 1st Independent Infantry Battalion	5332 (1,549)	
• 2nd Independent Infantry Battalion	5333 (1,549)	
• 3rd Independent Infantry Battalion	5334 (1,549)	
• 4th Independent Infantry Battalion	5335 (1,549)	
• 5th Independent Infantry Battalion	5336 (1,549)	
• 2nd Brigade Artillery Unit	5337 (582)	activated 2/1/45
• 2nd Brigade Engineer Unit	5338 (531)	activated 2/1/45
• 2nd Brigade Signal Unit	5339 (175)	

2nd I.M.B.: Activated in Beijing on Feb 10, 1938. Home station: Osaka. With the Mongolia Garrison Army from Mar 12, 1938 until it was deactivated in Beijing.
Service History: China: Baotou Dec 22 1939, Hundred Regiments Aug 20 1940, Inner Mongolia Aug 18 1945.

3rd Independent Mixed Brigade 1938	造 *Tukuru* 3580 (4,583)	
3rd Brigade Headquarters	3581 (242)	
• 6th Independent Infantry Battalion	3582 (1,549)	
• 7th Independent Infantry Battalion	3583 (1,549)	
• 8th Independent Infantry Battalion	3584 (1,549)	
• 9th Independent Infantry Battalion	3585 (1,549)	
• 10th Independent Infantry Battalion	3586 (1,549)	
• 3rd Brigade Artillery Unit	3587 (582)	activated 2/1/45
• 3rd Brigade Engineer Unit	3588 (531)	activated 2/1/45
• 3rd Brigade Signal Unit	3589 (175)	

3rd I.M.B.: Activated in Beijing on Feb 10, 1938. Home station: Sendai. With the 1st Army in Hsingsiang, China until it was deactivated in Shanxi Province on 9/17/45.
Service History: China: Hundred Regiments Aug 20 1940.

4th Independent Mixed Brigade 1938	石 *Ishi* 3590
4th Brigade Headquarters	3591 (147)
• 11th Independent Infantry Battalion	3592 (811)
• 12th Independent Infantry Battalion	3593 (811)
• 13th Independent Infantry Battalion	3594 (811)
• 14th Independent Infantry Battalion	3595 (811)
• 15th Independent Infantry Battalion	3596 (811)
• 4th Brigade Artillery Unit	3598 (581)
• 4th Brigade Engineer Unit	3599 (531)
• 4th Brigade Signal Unit	3597 (175)

4th I.M.B.: Activated in Kyoto, Japan Feb 10, 1938. Home station: Unknown. With the 1st Army in China from Feb 8th until Apr 30, 1943, deactivated May 1st to establish the 63rd Infantry Brigade, 62nd Div.
A previous 4th Mixed Brigade arrived in Manchuria on Dec. 7, 1931.
Service History: China: Hundred Regiments Aug 20 1940.

5th Independent Mixed Brigade 1938	桐 *Kiri* 4270 (4,583)
5th Brigade Headquarters	4271 (242)
• 16th Independent Infantry Battalion	4272 (1,549)
• 17th Independent Infantry Battalion	4273 (1,549)
• 18th Independent Infantry Battalion	4274 (1,549)
• 19th Independent Infantry Battalion	4275 (1,549)
• 20th Independent Infantry Battalion	4276 (1,549)
• 5th Brigade Artillery Unit	4277 (582)
• 5th Brigade Engineer Unit	4289 (531)
• 5th Brigade Signal Unit	4279 (175)

5th I.M.B.: Activated in Tianjin, China on Mar. 23, 1938. Home station: Mito. With the 2nd Army from Mar 23, 1938 until Sept.22, 1939, 12th Army until Aug 26, 1944 and 43rd Army in Tsingtao where it was deactivated when the war ended.
Service History: China: Tsingtao garrison.

6th Independent Mixed Brigade 1939	秋 *Aki* 4280
6th Brigade Headquarters	4281 (unknown)
• 21st Independent Infantry Battalion	4282
• 22nd Independent Infantry Battalion	4283
• 23rd Independent Infantry Battalion	4284
• 24th Independent Infantry Battalion	4285
• 25th Independent Infantry Battalion	4286

6th Independent Mixed Brigade continued

• 6th Brigade Artillery Unit	4287
• 6th Brigade Engineer Unit	4288
• 6th Brigade Signal Unit	4289

6th I.M.B.: Activated in Chengchow, China Feb 10, 1938. Home station: Gifu. With the 12th Army until April 30, 1943 when it was deactivated on May 1st in Beijing to establish the 64th Infantry Brigade, 62nd Division.
Service History: China: Licheng area garrison.

7th Independent Mixed Brigade 1939	北 *Kita* 2970
7th Brigade Headquarters	2971 (147)
• 26th Independent Infantry Battalion	2972 (850)
• 27th Independent Infantry Battalion	2973 (850)
• 28th Independent Infantry Battalion	2974 (850)
• 29th Independent Infantry Battalion	2975 (850)
• 30th Independent Infantry Battalion	2976 (850)
• 7th Brigade Artillery Unit	2977
• 7th Brigade Signal Unit	2979 (173)

7th I.M.B.: Activated in Tianjin, China Jan 14, 1939. Home station: Asahikawa. With the North China Area Army from Jan 14th until Apr 10, 1942 and 12th Army until Jul 9, 1944. Deactivated on July 10, 1944 to establish the 85th Infantry Brigade, 115th Div.'s headquarters and 115th Division Signal Unit.
Service History: China: Hundred Regiments Aug 20 1940.

8th Independent Mixed Brigade 1939	春 *Haru* 2980 (4,960)
8th Brigade Headquarters	2989 (446)
• 31st Independent Infantry Battalion	2981 (1,549)
• 32nd Independent Infantry Battalion	2982 (1,549)
• 33rd Independent Infantry Battalion	2983 (1,549)
• 34th Independent Infantry Battalion	2984 (1,549)
• 35th Independent Infantry Battalion	2985 (1,549)
• 8th Brigade Artillery Unit	2986 (582)
• 8th Brigade Engineer Unit	2987 (531)
• 8th Brigade Signal Unit	2988 (175)

8th I.M.B.: Activated in Yellow River, China Jan 14, 1939. Home station: Tokyo. With the North China Area Army in Shunyi until it was deactivated in Beijing Sept 17, 1945. Note: An earlier iteration of the 8th I.M.B. arrived in Manchuria Nov 11, 1931.
Service History: China: Hundred Regiments Aug 20 1940.

9th Independent Mixed Brigade 1939	谷 *Tani* 4200 (4,775)
9th Brigade Headquarters	4201 (231)
• 36th Independent Infantry Battalion	4202 (1,549)

9th Independent Mixed Brigade continued

• 37th Independent Infantry Battalion	4203 (1,549)
• 38th Independent Infantry Battalion	4204 (1,549)
• 39th Independent Infantry Battalion	4205 (1,549)
• 40th Independent Infantry Battalion	4206 (1,549)
• 9th Brigade Artillery Unit	4207 (582) activated Feb 1 1945
• 9th Brigade Engineer Unit	4208 (531) activated Feb 1 1945
• 9th Brigade Signal Unit	4209 (175)

9th I.M.B.: Activated in Taiyuan, China Jan 14, 1939. Home station: Kofu. With the 1st Army from Jan 14th until April 10, 1942, North China Area Army until March 22, 1945 and 43rd Army in Tientsin until the war ended. Deactivated in Tientsin.
Service History: Hundred Regiments Aug 20 1940, South Shanxi May 7 1941.

10th Independent Mixed Brigade 1939	衣 *Koromo* 4290
10th Brigade Headquarters	4291 (unknown)
• 41st Independent Infantry Battalion	4292
• 42nd Independent Infantry Battalion	4293
• 43rd Independent Infantry Battalion	4294
• 44th Independent Infantry Battalion	4295
• 45th Independent Infantry Battalion	4296

10th I.M.B.: Activated in Jinan, China Jan 14, 1939. Home station: Unknown. With the 12th Army in Jiangsu Province from Jan 14th until Feb 2, 1942, deactivated in Shandong to establish the 53rd Infantry Brigade, 59th Division. (An unrelated 10th I.M.B. was later activated to garrison Rota Is. in the Northern Marianas. Source: Akira Takizawa web page Japanese Garrisons on Bypassed Pacific Islands)
Service History: China: Shandong garrison.

11th Independent Mixed Brigade 1937	矛 *Hoko*
11th Brigade Headquarters	1068 (unknown)
• 46th Independent Infantry Battalion	2317
• 47th Independent Infantry Battalion	2318
• 48th Independent Infantry Battalion	2319
• 49th Independent Infantry Battalion	2320
• 50th Independent Infantry Battalion	2322

11th I.M.B.: Activated in Japan on Oct 15, 1934. Home station: Unknown. With the Kwantung Army from July 7 to 12 1937, China Garrison Army until Aug 26th and Kwantung Army until Sept 30, 1937 when the 11th I.M.B. was deactivated to form the 26th Division in Manchuria._
Reactivated in Japan on Jan 14, 1939. With the Central China Expeditionary Army from Jan 14th until Sept 23rd and 13th Army until it was deactivated in Shanghai Feb 2, 1942, to become the 55th Infantry Brigade, 60th Division.
Service History 1934-7: China: Nankou Aug 8 1937, Taiyuan Sept 14 1937.
Service History 1939-42: China:

12th Independent Mixed Brigade 1939	望 *Bou*
12th Brigade Headquarters	1074 (unknown)
• 51st Independent Infantry Battalion	1418
• 52nd Independent Infantry Battalion	1419
• 53rd Independent Infantry Battalion	1420
• 54th Independent Infantry Battalion	1423
• 55th Independent Infantry Battalion	1424

12th I.M.B.: Activated in China on Jan 14, 1939. Home station: Unknown. With the Central China Expeditionary Army from Jan 14th until Aug 31st and 13th Army until May 1, 1943 when it was deactivated in Hankou to form the 69th and 70th Infantry Brigades, 64th Division.
Service Record: China: Yenchang summer 1941, Zhejiang Jiangxi May 27 1942.

13th Independent Mixed Brigade 1939	倭 *Wa*
13th Brigade Headquarters	2267 (unknown)
• 56th Independent Infantry Battalion	2031
• 57th Independent Infantry Battalion	2032
• 58th Independent Infantry Battalion	2033
• 59th Independent Infantry Battalion	2034
• 60th Independent Infantry Battalion	2036

13th I.M.B.: Activated in China January 14, 1939. Home station: Unknown. With the Central China Expeditionary Army from Jan 14th until August 1st and 13th Army until May 1, 1943. Deactivated in Guangzhou May 1st to establish the 71st Inf. Brigade, 65th Division.
Service History: China: Zhejiang Jiangxi May 27 1942.

14th Independent Mixed Brigade 1939	檜 *Hinoki*
14th Brigade Headquarters	334 (unknown)
• 61st Independent Infantry Battalion	1435
• 62nd Independent Infantry Battalion	1436
• 63rd Independent Infantry Battalion	1437
• 64th Independent Infantry Battalion	1438
• 65th Independent Infantry Battalion	1440

14th I.M.B.: Activated in Jiangxi, China on January 14, 1939. Home station: Unknown. With the 11th Army in Hsiaochihkou, Hubei from Jan 14th until Feb 2, 1942 when it was deactivated to form the 57th Infantry Brigade, 68th Division.
Service History: China: Luchan Apr. 17, 1939, Changha Sept 25 1941.

15th Independent Mixed Brigade 1939	陣 *Jin* (冑 *Chuu*)
15th Brigade Headquarters	2991 (unknown)
• 77th Independent Infantry Battalion	2992

15th Independent Mixed Brigade continued

- 78th Independent Infantry Battalion 2993
- 79th Independent Infantry Battalion 2994
- 80th Independent Infantry Battalion 2995
- 81st Independent Infantry Battalion 2996

15th I.M.B.: Activated in north China on July 22, 1939. Home station: Unknown. With the North China Area Army from Jul 22nd until May 1, 1943 when it was deactivated in Beijing to establish the 66th and 67th Infantry Brigades, 63rd Division.
Service History: Hundred Regiments Aug 20 1940

16th Independent Mixed Brigade 1939 勝 *Katu*

16th Brigade Headquarters 2047 (unknown)
- 82nd Independent Infantry Battalion 2048
- 83rd Independent Infantry Battalion 2049
- 84th Independent Infantry Battalion 2050
- 85th Independent Infantry Battalion 2051
- 86th Independent Infantry Battalion 2053

16th I.M.B.: Activated in Shanxi Province, China Nov 7, 1939. Home station: Unknown. With the 1st Army from Nov 7th until Feb 2, 1942 when it was deactivated in Linfen, Shanxi to establish the 59th Infantry Brigade, 69th Division.
Service History: China: South Shanxi May 7 1941.

17th Independent Mixed Brigade 1939 峰 *Mine* (5,167)

17th Brigade Headquarters 8100 (205)
- 87th Independent Infantry Battalion 8101 (1,549)
- 88th Independent Infantry Battalion 8102 (1,549)
- 89th Independent Infantry Battalion 8103 (1,549)
- 90th Independent Infantry Battalion 8105 (1,549)
- 91st Independent Infantry Battalion 8106 (1,549)

- 17th Brigade Artillery Unit 8107 (421)
- 17th Brigade Engineer Unit 8108 (178)
- 17th Brigade Signal Unit 8109 (175)

17th I.M.B.: Activated in Shanghai, China Nov 7, 1939. Home station: Sakura. With the 13th Army from Nov 2nd until Oct 14, 1942, 11th Army until Apr 15, 1944, Wuhan Garrison Army until July 7th, 34th Army until June 17, 1945 and 6th Area Army in Wuchang where it was war deactivated.
Service History: China:

18th Independent Mixed Brigade 1939 広 *Kou*

18th Brigade Headquarters 1203 (unknown)
- 92nd Independent Infantry Battalion 1204

18th Independent Mixed Brigade continued

• 93rd Independent Infantry Battalion	1205
• 94th Independent Infantry Battalion	1206
• 95th Independent Infantry Battalion	1207
• 96th Independent Infantry Battalion	1209

18th I.M.B.: Activated in Jiangxi, China Nov 7, 1939, from former 136th Inf Bgde HQ, 106th Div troops. With the 11th Army Nov 7th until Feb 2, 1942 when it was deactivated to form the 51st Infantry Brigade, 58th Division. Its code numbers were reissued to the 11th, 12th, 23rd, 24th and 28th Division's Disease Prevention and Water Supply Units.
Service History: China: Yichang May 31 1940, Hupei Nov 25 1940, South Henan Jan 30 1941, Chungyuan May 5 1941.

19th Independent Mixed Brigade 1940	潮 *Shio*	
19th Brigade Headquarters	8980 (183)	
• 97th Independent Infantry Battalion	8981 (819)	
• 98th Independent Infantry Battalion	8982 (819)	
• 99th Independent Infantry Battalion	8983 (819)	
• 100th Independent Infantry Battalion	8984 (819)	
• 101st Independent Infantry Battalion	8988 (819)	activ. Feb 15 1944
• 19th Brigade Artillery Unit	8985 (577)	
• 19th Brigade Engineer Unit	8986 (288)	
• 19th Brigade Signal Unit	8987 (207)	

19th I.M.B.: Activated in Guangzhou, China on Nov 30, 1940. Home station: Kurume. With the South China Area Army from Dec 6, 1940 until July 5, 1941 and 23rd Army until April 12, 1945. Deactivated on Apr 12th and divided between the 129th and 130th Division activations.
Service History: China: Swatow garrison (Swatow, later north Hainan Island).

20th Independent Mixed Brigade 1940	槍 *Yari*
20th Brigade Headquarters	2403 (unknown)
• 102nd Independent Infantry Battalion	2404
• 103rd Independent Infantry Battalion	2405
• 104th Independent Infantry Battalion	2406
• 105th Independent Infantry Battalion	2407

20th I.M.B.: Activated in Shanghai, China on Nov 30, 1940. Home station: Unknown. With the 11th Army from Dec 6th until Oct 15, 1941 and 13th Army until. It was deactivated on Feb 2, 1942 to establish the 61st Infantry Brigade, 70th Division.
Service History: China:

21st Independent Mixed Brigade 1941	西 *Nishi*
21st Brigade Headquarters	unknown

21st Independent Mixed Brigade continued		
• 170th Infantry Regiment (Sasayama)	unknown	fr. 104th Div 1/13/41
• 41st Infantry Regiment (Hiroshima)	5176	joined 4/1/43
• 21st Brigade Tank Unit	7591	
• 21st Brigade Artillery Unit	9823	
• 21st Brigade Anti-Aircraft Unit	9824 (150) 42nd I.Fld. A.A. Co.	
• 21st Brigade Signal Unit	unknown	

21st I.M.B.: Activated in Hanoi, Indochina on June 26, 1941, from former Indochina Expeditionary Army personnel, 170th Inf Regt, and the 5th Ind Field Heavy Artillery Btn. Home station: Unknown. With the 25th Army in Indochina from July 5th until Nov 6th, Southern Exp. Army until Sept 14, 1942, Imperial Headquarters (left Saigon Oct 21st arrived Guam Nov 5th, 2nd Btn, 170th iR [Sekine Unit] detached, the rest sail to New Guinea) until Oct 28th, 17th Army until Nov 16th, 8th Area Army until Nov 26th and 18th Army (became Buna Detachment on Dec. 6, 1942) until it was deactivated on June 12, 1943.

Notes: The 170th I.R. lost its flag in a ship sinking. March 1943. 800 men from the 170th I.R. join the 8th Shipping Engineer Regt to fill a manpower shortage. The 41st Inf Regt joins the Buna Detachment on Apr 1st. On June 22nd former 21st I.M.B. troops join the 3rd South Seas Garrison Unit. In Rabaul the 41st I.R. was removed from the 18th Army on Sept 3, 1943, returned to Korea rebuilt and absorbed by the new 30th Division.

Service History: Indochina: New Guinea: Buna Nov 16 1942.

22nd Independent Mixed Brigade 1942	節 *Setu* 9444 (5,810)
22nd Brigade Headquarters	9400 (224)
• 66th Independent Infantry Battalion	9401 (1,549)
• 70th Independent Infantry Battalion	9402 (1,549)
• 71st Independent Infantry Battalion	9403 (1,549)
• 125th Independent Infantry Battalion	9404 (1,549)
• 126th Independent Infantry Battalion	9405 (1,549)
• 127th Independent Infantry Battalion	9406 (1,549)
• 22nd Brigade Artillery Unit	9407 (439)
• 22nd Brigade Engineer Unit	9408 (178)
• 22nd Brigade Signal Unit	9409 (175)

22nd I.M.B.: Activated in Guangzhou, China Nov 27, 1942, from 1st Independent Infantry Unit personnel. Home station: Sakura. With the 23rd Army from Nov 27th until May 28, 1945 and 11th Army in Hengchow until the war ended.

Service History: China: Hunan-Kwangsi Railway Aug 29 1944.

23rd Independent Mixed Brigade 1943	純 *Jun* 9445 (5,187)
23rd Brigade Headquarters	9841 (271)
• 128th Independent Infantry Battalion	9842 (1,549)
• 129th Independent Infantry Battalion	9843 (1,549)

23rd Independent Mixed Brigade continued

• 130th Independent Infantry Battalion	9844 (1,549)
• 247th Independent Infantry Battalion	9848 (1,549)
• 248th Independent Infantry Battalion	9849 (1,549)
• 23rd Brigade Artillery Unit	9845 (592)
• 23rd Brigade Engineer Unit	9846 (178)
• 23rd Brigade Signal Unit	9847 (175)
• 23rd Brigade Transport Unit	9850

23rd I.M.B.: Activated on Formosa on Jan 18, 1943. Home station: Unknown. Landed in Guangzhou Bay, China in Feb 1943. With the 23rd Army in Canton from Jan 18th until it was deactivated on September 17, 1945.
Service History: China: Luichow-Hainan Is Feb 20 1943, Nanning Nov 15 1944, Luichow garrison Nov 28 1944.

24th Independent Mixed Brigade 1943	巌 *Gen* (4,607)	
24th Brigade Headquarters	15814 (165)	
• 138th Independent Infantry Battalion	15815 (931)	
• 139th Independent Infantry Battalion	15816 (931)	
• 140th Independent Infantry Battalion	15817 (931)	deactiv. 11/14/44
• 141st Independent Infantry Battalion	15818 (931)	
• 24th Brigade Artillery Unit	15819 (360)	
• 24th Brigade Engineer Unit	15820 (180)	
• 24th Brigade Signal Unit	15821 (178)	

24th I.M.B.: Activated in Burma Nov 16, 1943, from former 54th Inf. Group HQ personnel. Home station: Yamagata. With the Burma Area Army until March 1, 1944, 15th Army until April 7th, 33rd Army until June 15th and Burma Area Army in Thanbyuzayat until the war ended.
Service History: Burma:

25th Independent Mixed Brigade 1943	盤 *Ban* (4,607)
25th Brigade Headquarters	10908 (165)
• 142nd Independent Infantry Battalion	10909 (931)
• 143rd Independent Infantry Battalion	10910 (931)
• 144th Independent Infantry Battalion	10911 (931)
• 145th Independent Infantry Battalion	10912 (931)
• 25th Brigade Artillery Unit	10913 (360)
• 25th Brigade Engineer Unit	10914 (180)
• 25th Brigade Signal Unit	10915 (178)

25th I.M.B.: Activated in Northern Sumatra Nov 16, 1943, from former 15th Ind Garrison Unit personnel. Home station: Osaka. With the 25th Army from Nov 16th until the war ended.
Service History: Sumatra:

26th Independent Mixed Brigade 1943	嶽 *Gaku* (4,607)	
26th Brigade Headquarters	10916 (165)	
• 146th Independent Infantry Battalion	10917 (931)	
• 147th Independent Infantry Battalion	10918 (931)	
• 148th Independent Infantry Battalion	10919 (931)	Palembang
• 149th Independent Infantry Battalion	10920 (931)	
• 26th Brigade Artillery Unit	10921 (360)	
• 26th Brigade Engineer Unit	10922 (180)	
• 26th Brigade Signal Unit	10923 (178)	

26th I.M.B.: Activated in South Sumatra Nov.16, 1943, from former 16th Ind Garrison Unit personnel. Home station: Hirosaki. With the 25th Army from Nov 16th until May 26, 1945 and 7th Area Army in Singapore until the war ended.
Service History: Sumatra:

27th Independent Mixed Brigade 1943	雄 *Yu* (4,607)
27th Brigade Headquarters	10810 (165)
• 150th Independent Infantry Battalion	10811 (931)
• 151st Independent Infantry Battalion	10812 (931)
• 152nd Independent Infantry Battalion	10813 (931)
• 153rd Independent Infantry Battalion	10814 (931)
• 27th Brigade Artillery Unit	10815 (360)
• 27th Brigade Engineer Unit	7178 (180)
• 27th Brigade Signal Unit	10816 (178)

27th I.M.B.: Activated in West Java Nov 16, 1943, from former 13th Ind Garrison Unit personnel. Home station: Hamada. With the 16th Army in Badung, Bali until the war ended.
Service History: Java: Bali garrison.

28th Independent Mixed Brigade 1943	敬 *Kei* (4,607)
28th Brigade Headquarters	10820 (165)
• 154th Independent Infantry Battalion	10821 (931)
• 155th Independent Infantry Battalion	10822 (931)
• 156th Independent Infantry Battalion	10823 (931)
• 157th Independent Infantry Battalion	10824 (931)
• 28th Brigade Artillery Unit	10825 (360)
• 28th Brigade Engineer Unit	5218 (180)
• 28th Brigade Signal Unit	10826 (178)

28th I.M.B.: Activated in East Java Nov 16, 1943, from former 14th Ind Garrison Unit personnel. Home station: Akita. With the 16th Army around Surabaya until the war ended.
Service History: Java: Surabaya garrison.

29th Independent Mixed Brigade 1943	体 *Tai* (5,338)	
29th Brigade Headquarters	15822 (165)	
• 158th Independent Infantry Battalion	15823 (931)	
• 159th Independent Infantry Battalion	15824 (931)	
• 160th Independent Infantry Battalion	15825 (931)	
• 161st Independent Infantry Battalion	15826 (931)	
• 162nd Independent Infantry Battalion	15827 (931)	
• 671st Independent Infantry Battalion	unknown	activated 4/14/45
• 29th Brigade Artillery Unit	15828 (556)	
• 29th Brigade Engineer Unit	15829 (898)	
• 29th Brigade Signal Unit	15830 (178)	

29th I.M.B.: Activated in Bangkok on Nov 16, 1943, from former 6th Field Replacement Unit personnel. Home station: Kyoto. With the Thai Garrison Army until Dec 20, 1944, 39th Army until July 15, 1945 and 18th Area Army in Prachuap, Thailand until the war ended. The 159th Ind Inf Btn and Engineer Unit worked on the Thai-Burma Railway. For the last month of the war the 158th and 159th Ind Inf Btns, 1st Section each the 29th Bgde Artillery Unit and Signal Unit were attached to the Burma Area Army Reinforcement Unit.
Service History: Thailand.

30th Independent Mixed Brigade 1943	拠 *Kyo*
30th Brigade Headquarters	10620 (unknown)
• 163rd Independent Infantry Battalion	10521
• 164th Independent Infantry Battalion	10622
• 165th Independent Infantry Battalion	10623
• 166th Independent Infantry Battalion	10624
• 167th Independent Infantry Battalion	10625
• 168th Independent Infantry Battalion	10638
• 30th Brigade Signal Unit	10626

30th I.M.B.: Activated in Davao, Philippines Nov 16, 1943, from former 11th Ind Garrison Unit personnel. Home station: Unknown. With the 14th Army from Nov 16th until June 15, 1944 when it was deactivated to establish the 100th Div HQ, and 75th and 76th Inf Brigades.
Service History: Philippines:

31st Independent Mixed Brigade 1943	抜 *Batu*
31st Brigade Headquarters	10630 (unknown)
• 169th Independent Infantry Battalion	10631
• 170th Independent Infantry Battalion	10632
• 171st Independent Infantry Battalion	10633
• 172nd Independent Infantry Battalion	10634
• 173rd Independent Infantry Battalion	10688
• 174th Independent Infantry Battalion	10689 3rd & 4th Coys to Palawan

• 31st Brigade Signal Unit 10635

31st I.M.B.: Activated in the Philippines on Nov 16, 1943, from 10th Ind Garrison Unit troops. Home station: Unknown. With the 14th Army from Nov 16th until June 15, 1944 when it was deactivated to establish the 102nd Div HQ, and 77th and 78th Inf Brigades.
Service History: Philippines:

32nd Independent Mixed Brigade 1943	駿 *Shun*
32nd Brigade Headquarters	10640 (unknown)
• 175th Independent Infantry Battalion	10641
• 176th Independent Infantry Battalion	10642
• 177th Independent Infantry Battalion	10643
• 178th Independent Infantry Battalion	10644
• 179th Independent Infantry Battalion	17614
• 180th Independent Infantry Battalion	17615
• 356th Independent Infantry Battalion	10699
• 357th Independent Infantry Battalion	17616
• 32nd Brigade Signal Unit	10645

32nd I.M.B.: Activated on Luzon, Philippines Nov 16, 1943, from 17th Ind Garrison Unit troops. Home station: Unknown. With the 14th Army from Nov 16th until June 15, 1944 when it was deactiv. to form the 103rd Div HQ, and 79th and 80th Inf Brigades.
Service History: Philippines:

33rd Independent Mixed Brigade 1943	育 *Iku*
33rd Brigade Headquarters	10660 (unknown)
• 181st Independent Infantry Battalion	10661
• 182nd Independent Infantry Battalion	10662
• 183rd Independent Infantry Battalion	10665
• 186th Independent Infantry Battalion	10670
• 33rd Brigade Artillery Unit	10663
• 33rd Brigade Signal Unit	10664

33rd I.M.B.: Activated south Luzon, Philippines Nov 16, 1943. Two battalions from the 142nd Inf Regiment, 65th I.M.B. were reorganized into 181st and 182nd Ind Inf Btns, who with the 183rd and 186th Ind Inf Battalions were sent from Zentsuji Japan to become the 33rd I.M.B. Home station: Unknown. With the 14th Army from Nov 16th until June 15, 1944, it was deactivated to establish the 105th Div HQ and 81st and 82nd Inf Bgds.
Service History: Philippines:

34th Independent Mixed Brigade 1944	育 *Iku* 7819 (2,745 on 1/31/45)
34th Brigade Headquarters	7820 (165)
• 187th Independent Infantry Battalion	7821 (931)
• 188th Independent Infantry Battalion	7822 (931)
• 189th Independent Infantry Battalion	7823 (931)

• 190th Independent Infantry Battalion	7824 (931)	
• 672nd Independent Infantry Battalion	17017 (931)	activated 4/14/45
• 673rd Independent Infantry Battalion	17018 (931)	activated 4/14/45
• 674th Independent Infantry Battalion	17019 (931)	activated 4/14/45
• 675th Independent Infantry Battalion	17020 (931)	activated 4/14/45
• 34th Brigade Artillery Unit	7825 (360)	
• 34th Brigade Engineer Unit	7826 (180)	
• 34th Brigade Signal Unit	7827 (178)	

34th I.M.B.: Activated in French Indochina on Nov 16, 1943, from former 3rd Field Replacement Unit personnel. Home station: Tokyo. With the Indochina Garrison Army, which became the 38th Army, on Dec. 20, 1944 in Indochina until the war ended.
Service History: Indochina: 2nd Indochina incident Mar 9 1945.

35th Independent Mixed Brigade 1944	教 *Kyou* (6,651)
35th Brigade Headquarters	15832 (185)
• 251st Independent Infantry Battalion	15833 (958)
• 252nd Independent Infantry Battalion	15834 (958)
• 253rd Independent Infantry Battalion	15835 (958)
• 254th Independent Infantry Battalion	15836 (958)
• 255th Independent Infantry Battalion	15837 (958)
• 256th Independent Infantry Battalion	15838 (958)
• 257th Independent Infantry Battalion	2558 (958)
• 35th Brigade Artillery Unit	15839 (360)
• 35th Brigade Engineer Unit	2559 (180)
• 35th Brigade Signal Unit	2560 (178)

35th I.M.B.: Activated in the Andaman Islands Feb 10, 1944, from former 1st Southwest Garrison Unit personnel (the 257th Ind Inf Btn landed in Malaya in July '44). Home station: Mizonokuchi. With the 29th Army in Port Blair until the war ended.
Service History: Andaman Islands: Andaman garrison.

36th Independent Mixed Brigade 1944	練 *Ren* (3,757)
37th Brigade Headquarters	15840 (165)
• 262nd Independent Infantry Battalion	15841 (958)
• 263rd Independent Infantry Battalion	15842 (958)
• 264th Independent Infantry Battalion	15843 (958)
• 265th Independent Infantry Battalion	2561 (958) deactivated 11/14/44
• 37th Brigade Artillery Unit	2562 (360)
• 37th Brigade Engineer Unit	2563 (180)
• 37th Brigade Signal Unit	2564 (178)

36th I.M.B.: Activated in the Nicobar Islands Feb 10, 1944, from former 2nd Inf. Group HQ and 8th Inf Regt personnel. Home station: Kashiwa. With the 29th Army on Nicobar Is. until the war ended.
Service History: Nicobar Islands: Nicobar Is. garrison.

37th Independent Mixed Brigade 1944	鍛 *Tan* (3,757)
37th Brigade Headquarters	15844 (165)
• 262nd Independent Infantry Battalion	15845 (958)
• 263rd Independent Infantry Battalion	15846 (958)
• 264th Independent Infantry Battalion	15847 (958)
• 265th Independent Infantry Battalion	2565 (958) deactivated 11/14/44
• 37th Brigade Artillery Unit	2566 (360)
• 37th Brigade Engineer Unit	2567 (180)
• 37th Brigade Signal Unit	2568 (178)

<u>37th I.M.B.</u>: Activated in the Nicobar Islands Feb 10, 1944, from former 4th and 32nd Division, 15th Inf. Group HQ and 2nd Southwest Garrison Unit personnel. Home station: Osaka. With the 29th Army on Nicobar I. until the war ended.
<u>Service History</u>: Nicobar Islands: Nicobar Is. garrison.

38th Independent Mixed Brigade 1944	力 *Chikara*
38th Brigade Headquarters	11306 (55)
• 81st Infantry Regiment	7386 (4,089)
• 53rd Infantry Regiment, 3rd Battalion	7384 (1,336)
• 54th Infantry Regiment, 2nd Battalion	7385 (1,336)
• 38th Brigade Artillery Unit	11307 (131)
• 38th Brigade Engineer Unit	11308 (180)
• 38th Brigade Signal Unit	11309 (178)
• 38th Brigade Medical Unit	11310
Attached	
17th Field Artillery Regiment, 1st Battalion	1152 旭
10th Ind. Mountain Artillery Regt, 1 section	20900 睦
17th Division Medical Unit, 1 section	unknown 月
17th Engineer Regiment, 1 section	7388 月
64th Casualty Clearing Platoon	6409 (54)
12th Shipping Engineer Company, 1 section	unknown

<u>38th I.M.B.</u>: Activated Bougainville June 24, 1944, from former 17th Inf Group HQ and 4th South Seas Garrison Unit personnel. Home station: Gifu. With 17th Army on Bougainville until the war ended.
<u>Service History</u>: Bougainville: Artillery Hill Dec 18 1944, Pearl Ridge Dec 30 1944, Tsimba Ridge Jan 17 1945, Numa Numa Trail Apr 1945.

39th Independent Mixed Brigade 1944	隆 *Chuu* 11230
39th Brigade Headquarters (Takasaki)	11231 (55)
• 4th Mixed Regiment (Takasaki)	11232 (3,377)
• 5th Mixed Regiment (Mito)	11233 (3,377)
• 39th Brigade Signal Unit (Utsunomiya)	11234 (178)
• 39th Brigade Field Hospital (Utsunomiya)	11236 (179)

<u>39th I.M.B.</u>: Activated in Rabaul, New Britain June 24, 1944. Home station: Takasaki. With the 8th Area Army on New Britain until the war ended.
Note: a former unrelated 39th Mixed Bgde was in Mukden Sept 21, 1931.
<u>Service History</u>: New Britain Dec 15 1943.

40th Independent Mixed Brigade 1944	隆 *Ryuu* 11240 (4,161)
40th Brigade Headquarters	11241 (55)
• 230th Infantry Regiment	8926 (3,377)
• 34th Independent Mixed Regiment	11250 (3,000)
• 35th Independent Mixed Regiment	11251 (1,910)
• 40th Brigade Artillery Unit	11242 (131)
• 40th Brigade Engineer Unit	11243 (180)
• 40th Brigade Signal Unit	11244 (178)
• 40th Brigade Transport Unit	11245 (350)
• 40th Brigade Field Hospital	11246 (149)

<u>40th I.M.B.</u>: Activated in Munda, New Ireland June 24, 1944, from former 38th Inf Group personnel (Shoji Detachment: Java, Guadalcanal). Home station: Nagoya. With the 8th Area Army on New Ireland until the war ended.
<u>Service History</u>: New Ireland:

47th Independent Mixed Brigade 1944	備 *Bi* (3,103)
47th Brigade Headquarters	17528 (152)
• 315th Independent Infantry Battalion	17529 (579)
• 316th Independent Infantry Battalion	17530 (579)
• 317th Independent Infantry Battalion	17531 (579)
• 318th Independent Infantry Battalion	17532 (579)
• 47th Brigade Artillery Unit	17533 (415)
• 47th Brigade Engineer Unit	17534 (221)

<u>47th I.M.B.</u>: Activated on Saipan May 22, 1944, from former 1st Expeditionary Unit (landed Apr 19th) and 15th Inf Regt personnel. Home station: Osaka. With the 31st Army's Northern Marianas District Group, destroyed on Saipan.
<u>Service History</u>: Northern Marianas: Saipan June 15 1944.

48th Independent Mixed Brigade 1944	備 *Bi* (3,102)
48th Brigade Headquarters	17535 (152)
• 319th Independent Infantry Battalion	17536 (579)
• 320th Independent Infantry Battalion	17537 (579)
• 321st Independent Infantry Battalion	17538 (579)
• 322nd Independent Infantry Battalion	17539 (579)
• 48th Brigade Artillery Unit	17540 (415)
• 48th Brigade Engineer Unit	17541 (221)

48th I.M.B.: Activated on Guam May 22, 1944, from former 6th Expeditionary Unit personnel. Home station: Marugame. With the 31st Army, Southern Marianas District Group, destroyed on Guam.
Service History: Southern Marianas: Guam: July 21 1944.

49th Independent Mixed Brigade 1944	備 *Bi* (5,591)
49th Brigade Headquarters	17542 (153)
• 323rd Independent Infantry Battalion	17543 (579)
• 324th Independent Infantry Battalion	17544 (579)
• 325th Independent Infantry Battalion	17545 (579)
• 326th Independent Infantry Battalion	17546 (579)
• 327th Independent Infantry Battalion	17547 (579)
• 328th Independent Infantry Battalion	17548 (579)
• 329th Independent Infantry Battalion	17549 (579)
• 330th Independent Infantry Battalion	17550 (579)
• 49th Brigade Artillery Unit	17551 (415)
• 49th Brigade Anti-Aircraft Unit	17552 (170)
• 49th Brigade Engineer Unit	17553 (221)

49th I.M.B.: Activated Yap Island May 22, 1944, from former 4th Expeditionary Unit personnel. Home station: Unknown. With the 31st Army, Palau Area Group on Yap Island (bypassed) until the war ended. 9th Expeditionary Unit sinking survivors joined the 327th I.I.B. and 330th Ind Infantry Btn.
Service History: Palau Islands: Yap Island garrison.

50th Independent Mixed Brigade 1944	胆 *Tan* (3,944)
50th Brigade Headquarters	17554 (153)
• 331st Independent Infantry Battalion	17555 (579)
• 332nd Independent Infantry Battalion	17556 (579)
• 333rd Independent Infantry Battalion	17557 (579)
• 334th Independent Infantry Battalion	17558 (579)
• 335th Independent Infantry Battalion	17559 (579)
• 50th Brigade Artillery Unit	17561 (415) *
• 50th Brigade Anti Aircraft Unit	17562 (170) **
• 50th Brigade Tank Unit	17560 (92)
• 50th Brigade Engineer Unit	17563 (221) ***

50th I.M.B.: Activated on Mayeron Atoll May 22, 1944, from former 5th South Seas Detachment and 7th Expeditionary Unit (landed Apr. 12th) personnel. Home station: Mizonokuchi. With the 31st Army, Truk District Group on Meyeron Island (bypassed by the U.S.).
* 17561 was the 3rd Battalion, 42nd Field Artillery Regiment
** 17562 was the 3rd Company, 52nd Anti Aircraft Battalion
*** 17563 was the 3rd Battalion. 24th Engineer Regiment
Service History: Truk District: Mayeron Island garrison.

51st Independent Mixed Brigade 1944	備 *Sonae* (5,389)	
51st Brigade Headquarters	17564 (153)	
• 336th Independent Infantry Battalion	17565 (579)	
• 337th Independent Infantry Battalion	17566 (579)	
• 338th Independent Infantry Battalion	17567 (579)	
• 339th Independent Infantry Battalion	17568 (579)	
• 340th Independent Infantry Battalion	17569 (579)	
• 341st Independent Infantry Battalion	17570 (579)	
• 51st Brigade 1st Artillery Unit	17571 (415)	
• 51st Brigade 2nd Artillery Unit	17572 (415)	
• 51st Brigade Anti-Aircraft Unit	17573 (711)	
• 51st Brigade Engineer Unit	17574 (221)	

51st I.M.B.: Activated on Mortlock Island May 22, 1944, from former 2nd Expeditionary Unit and 8th Expeditionary Unit (landed May 19th) personnel. Home station: Wakamatsu. With the 31st Army, Truk District Group on Mortlock Island, bypassed by U.S. forces.
Service History: Truk District: Mortlok Island garrison.

52nd Independent Mixed Brigade 1944	備 *Sonae* (3,194)	
52nd Brigade Headquarters	17575 (152)	
• 342nd Independent Infantry Battalion	17576 (579)	
• 343rd Independent Infantry Battalion	17577 (579)	
• 344th Independent Infantry Battalion	17578 (579)	
• 345th Independent Infantry Battalion	17579 (579)	
• 52nd Brigade Tank Unit	17580 (92)	
• 52nd Brigade Artillery Unit	17581 (415)	
• 52nd Brigade Engineer Unit	17582 (221)	

52nd I.M.B.: Activated on Ponape Island May 22, 1944, from 3rd South Seas Detachment and 2nd Battalion, 5th Ind. Mixed Regt. personnel. Home station: Sendai. With the 31st Army, Truk Area Group on Ponape Island until the war ended. Ponape bypassed by U.S. forces.
Service History: Truk Area Group: Ponape Island garrison.

53rd Independent Mixed Brigade 1944	備 *Sonae* 14650 (4,263)	
53rd Brigade Headquarters	14653 (153)	
• 346th Independent Infantry Battalion	14656 (579)	on Peleliu
• 347th Independent Infantry Battalion	14657 (579)	
• 348th Independent Infantry Battalion	14658 (579)	
• 349th Independent Infantry Battalion	14659 (579)	
• 350th Independent Infantry Battalion	14660 (579)	
• 351st Independent Infantry Battalion	14661 (579)	
• 53rd Brigade Artillery Unit	14670 (415)	
• 53rd Brigade Engineer Unit	14671 (221)	

53rd I.M.B.: Activated in the Palau Islands May 22, 1944, from former 57th Line of Communications Guard Unit personnel. Home station: Kashiwa. With the 31st Army, Palau District Group on Babelthuap Island. 346th Ind. Inf. Btn fought on Peleliu.
Service History: Palau District Group: Babelthuap garrison, Peleliu Sept 15 1944.

54th Independent Mixed Brigade 1944	萩 *Hagi* (3,877)
54th Brigade Headquarters	17600 (168)
• 360th Independent Infantry Battalion	17601 (997)
• 361st Independent Infantry Battalion	17602 (997)
• 362nd Independent Infantry Battalion	17603 (997)
• 54th Brigade Artillery Unit	17604 (360)
• 54th Brigade Engineer Unit	17605 (180)
• 54th Brigade Signal Unit	17606 (178)

54th I.M.B.: Activated in Manila, Philippines June 15, 1944, from Sendai recruits. Home station: Wakamatsu. With the 14th Army from June 15th until Aug 4th and 35th Army on Mindanao until it was deactivated on September 7, 1945.
Service History: Philippines: Leyte Oct 20 1944.

55th Independent Mixed Brigade 1944	菅 *Sugai* (3,875)	
55th Brigade Headquarters	17607 (155)	
• 363rd Independent Infantry Battalion	17608 (999)	
• 364th Independent Infantry Battalion	17609 (997)	on Leyte
• 365th Independent Infantry Battalion	17610 (997)	
• 55th Brigade Artillery Unit	17611 (361)	
• 55th Brigade Engineer Unit	17612 (182)	
• 55th Brigade Signal Unit	17613 (178)	

55th I.M.B.: Activated in Manila, Philippines on June 15, 1944, from former 6th, 61st and 119th Inf Regt Replacement personnel. Home station: Hirosaki. With the 14th Army from June 15th, until Dec 15th and 35th Army on Jolo Island. Left Manila for Cebu on Sept 4, 1944 and arrived on Jolo Island Oct 5th where it was later destroyed.
Service History: Philippines: Jolo Apr 8 1945.

56th Independent Mixed Brigade 1944	貫 *Turanaka* (6,869)
56th Brigade Headquarters	15890 (169)
• 366th Independent Infantry Battalion	15891 (997)
• 367th Independent Infantry Battalion	15892 (997)
• 368th Independent Infantry Battalion	15893 (997)
• 369th Independent Infantry Battalion	15894 (997)
• 370th Independent Infantry Battalion	15895 (997)
• 371st Independent Infantry Battalion	15896 (997)
• 56th Brigade Artillery Unit	15897 (360)
• 56th Brigade Engineer Unit	15898 (180)

56th Independent Mixed Brigade continued

• 56th Brigade Signal Unit	15899 (178)

56th I.M.B.: Activated north Borneo June 15, 1944, completed when personnel from Japan arrived in November. Home station: Unknown. With the Borneo Defense Army, which became the 37th Army on Sept 20, 1944. Ended the war in Borneo with the 37th Army.
Service History: Borneo: North Borneo June 10, 1945.

57th Independent Mixed Brigade 1944	桂 *Katsura* (6,868)	
57th Brigade Headquarters	15900 (168)	
• 372nd Independent Infantry Battalion	15901 (997)	
• 373rd Independent Infantry Battalion	15902 (997)	
• 374th Independent Infantry Battalion	15903 (997)	deactiv. Feb.'45
• 375th Independent Infantry Battalion	15904 (997)	
• 376th Independent Infantry Battalion	15905 (997)	
• 377th Independent Infantry Battalion	15906 (997)	
• 57th Brigade Artillery Unit	15907 (360)	
• 57th Brigade Engineer Unit	15908 (180)	
• 57th Brigade Signal Unit	15909 (178)	

57th I.M.B.: Activated in Kanazawa on June 15, 1944, from former 47th Infantry Group personnel. Home station: Kanazawa. With the 2nd Area Army from June 15th until June 13, 1945 and 2nd Army in the Celebes until the war ended.
Service History: Sunda Islands: Celebes garrison.

58th Independent Mixed Brigade 1944	盟 *Mei* 7201 (5,440)	
58th Brigade Headquarters	7203 (348)	
• 378th Independent Infantry Battalion	7204 (575)	[from 1,363]
• 379th Independent Infantry Battalion	7205 (575)	[from 1,363]
• 380th Independent Infantry Battalion	7206 (575)	[from 1,363]
• 544th Independent Infantry Battalion	17662 (806)	
• 545th Independent Infantry Battalion	17663 (806)	
• 546th Independent Infantry Battalion	17664 (806)	
• 58th Brigade Artillery Unit	7207 (478)	deactivated 5/20/45
• 58th Brigade Infantry Gun Unit	17665 (493)	
• 58th Brigade Rapid firing Gun Unit	unknown (145)	
• 58th Brigade Engineer Unit	7208 (161)	
• 58th Brigade Signal Unit	unknown (145)	

58th I.M.B.: Activated in Hirosaki on June 22, 1944, from former 12th Expeditionary Unit personnel. Home station: Hirosaki. With the 2nd Area Army in Hirosaki from June 22nd until July 4th and 14th Army in Manila from July 15th. Deployed to Lingayan Bay remnants deactivated on September 11, 1945.
Service History: Philippines: Lingayan Jan 6 1945, Baguio Feb 21 1945.

61st Independent Mixed Brigade 1944	鎧 *Yoroi* (3,240)	
61st Brigade Headquarters	10291 (100)	
• 302nd Independent Infantry Battalion	1790 (562)	
• 405th Independent Infantry Battalion	10292 (562)	
• 406th Independent Infantry Battalion	10293 (562)	
• 407th Independent Infantry Battalion	10294 (562)	
• 408th Independent Infantry Battalion	10295 (562)	
• 409th Independent Infantry Battalion	10296 (562)	
• 61st Brigade Artillery Unit	10297 (650)	
• 61st Brigade Engineer Unit	10298 (174)	
• 61st Brigade Signal Unit	10299 (156)	

61st I.M.B.: Activated in the Philippines on July 10, 1944. Home station: Kyoto. With the 14th Army in the Babuyan Islands (one battalion deployed to each important island) and 10th Area Army, which was given responsibility for the Babuyans in June 1945. The 61st I.M.B. surrendered in September 1945.

Service History: Philippines: Babuyan Islands garrison.

62nd Independent Mixed Brigade 1944	操 *Misao*	
62nd Brigade Headquarters	6467 (184)	
• 410th Independent Infantry Battalion	6468 (1,348)	
• 411th Independent Infantry Battalion	6469 (1,348)	
• 412th Independent Infantry Battalion	6470 (1,348)	
• 413th Independent Infantry Battalion	6471 (1,348)	
• 414th Independent Infantry Battalion	6472 (1,348)	
• 625th Independent Infantry Battalion	2487 (1,348)	activated 2/1/45
• 62nd Brigade Artillery Unit	6473 (560)	
• 62nd Brigade Engineer Unit	6474 (526)	
• 62nd Brigade Signal Unit	6475 (226)	
• 62nd Brigade Work Duty Unit	23075 (511)	activated 2/1/45
• 62nd Brigade Field Hospital	23077 (491)	activated 2/1/45
• 62nd Brigade Veterinary Unit	23078	
Attached		
10th Ind. Field Heavy Artillery Battalion	23073 (443)	
54th Ind. Field Anti Aircraft Company	unknown (161)	
64th Field Machine Cannon Company	12528 (105)	

62nd I.M.B.: Activated in Shikoku, Japan July 10, 1944. Home station: Marugame. With the 13th Army in Shanghai, China until May 15, 1945 and 6th Army in Hangchow, it was deactivated in Sunkiang.

Service History: China: Fuchou Oct 2 1944.

70th Independent Mixed Brigade 1944	果敢 *Kakan* (5,995)
70th Brigade Headquarters	17001 (165)

70th Independent Mixed Brigade continued

• 428th Independent Infantry Battalion	17002 (997)	
• 429th Independent Infantry Battalion	17003 (997)	
• 430th Independent Infantry Battalion	17004 (997)	
• 431st Independent Infantry Battalion	17005 (997)	
• 676th Independent Infantry Battalion	unknown (997)	activ. 4/14/45
• 677th Independent Infantry Battalion	unknown (997)	activ. 4/14/45
• 70th Brigade Tank Unit	17006 (125)	
• 70th Brigade Artillery Unit	17007 (360)	
• 70th Brigade Engineer Unit	17008 (180)	
• 70th Brigade Signal Unit	17009 (178)	

70th I.M.B.: Activated in Saigon Sept 18, 1944, from former Saigon Defense Unit personnel. Home station: Mizonokuchi. With the Indochina Garrison Army (becomes the 38th Army on Dec 20th) until May 23, 1945 and 29th Army Kuala Kangsar, Malaya until the war ended.
Service History: Indochina: Malaya: Taiping area defense.

71st Independent Mixed Brigade 1944	敢闘 *Kantō* (4,871)
71st Brigade Headquarters	11000 (165)
• 538th Independent Infantry Battalion	11001 (997)
• 539th Independent Infantry Battalion	11002 (997)
• 540th Independent Infantry Battalion	11003 (997)
• 541stIndependent Infantry Battalion	11004 (997)
• 71st Brigade Artillery Unit	11005 (360)
• 71st Brigade Engineer Unit	11006 (180)
• 71st Brigade Signal Unit	11007 (178)

71st I.M.B.: Activated in south Borneo Oct 14, 1944. Home station: Fukuoka. With the 37th Army in Kuching, Borneo until the war ended. By January only 1½ Btns were in service, with the bulk of the unit still shipping in from Japan.
Service History: Borneo: Kuching garrison.

72nd Independent Mixed Brigade 1944	貫徹 *Kantetsu* 12211 (4,871)
72nd Brigade Headquarters	12212 (165)
• 187th Independent Infantry Battalion	7821 (997)
• 188th Independent Infantry Battalion	7822 (997)
• 542nd Independent Infantry Battalion	12213 (997)
• 543rd Independent Infantry Battalion	12214 (997)
• 72nd Brigade Artillery Unit	12215 (360)
• 72nd Brigade Engineer Unit	12216 (180)
• 72nd Brigade Signal Unit	12217 (178)

72nd I.M.B.: Activated in Yenangyaung, Burma Nov 14, 1944, from former 61st Inf Regt and 33rd Inf Group HQ personnel, a total of 2,200 officers and men completed mobilizing in late January. Home station: Mizonokuchi. With the 28th Army in the

72nd Independent Mixed Brigade continued
Yenangyaung oil fields from Dec 17th until July 15, 1945, and Burma Area Army in Hnipadaw until the war ended.
Service History: Burma: Pokoku Jan 14 1945.

81st Independent Mixed Brigade 1945	至強 *Shikyo* 17810
81st Brigade Headquarters	17811 (352)
• 484th Independent Infantry Battalion	17812 (1,549)
• 485th Independent Infantry Battalion	17813 (1,549)
• 486th Independent Infantry Battalion	17814 (1,549)
• 487th Independent Infantry Battalion	17815 (1,549)
• 488th Independent Infantry Battalion	17816 (1,549)
• 81st Brigade Artillery Unit	17817 (612)
• 81st Brigade Engineer Unit	17818 (526)
• 81st Brigade Signal Unit	17819 (226)

81st I.M.B.: Activated in Hunan, China Mar 10, 1945, from former 1st Field Replacement Unit personnel. Home station: Utsunomiya. With the 20th Army in Tsingkang, Hunan from Mar 6th until it was deactivated in Changsha on September 17th.
Service History: China: Tsingkang garrison.

82nd Independent Mixed Brigade 1945	至烈 *Shiretsu* 17820
82nd Brigade Headquarters	17821 (352)
• 489th Independent Infantry Battalion	17822 (1,549)
• 490th Independent Infantry Battalion	17823 (1,549)
• 491st Independent Infantry Battalion	17824 (1,549)
• 492nd Independent Infantry Battalion	17825 (1,549)
• 493rd Independent Infantry Battalion	17826 (1,549)
• 82nd Brigade Artillery Unit	17827 (612)
• 82nd Brigade Engineer Unit	17828 (526)
• 82nd Brigade Signal Unit	17829 (226)

82nd I.M.B.: Activated in Hunan Feb 1, 1945, from former 2nd Field Replacement Unit personnel. Home station: Toyama. With the 20th Army in Tsingkang, Hunan from March 6th until it was deactivated in Changsha on September 17th.
Service History: China: Tsingkang garrison.

83rd Independent Mixed Brigade 1945	至猛 *Shimō1* 7830
83rd Brigade Headquarters	17831 (352)
• 494th Independent Infantry Battalion	17832 (1,549)
• 495th Independent Infantry Battalion	17833 (1,549)
• 496th Independent Infantry Battalion	17834 (1,549)
• 497th Independent Infantry Battalion	17835 (1,549)
• 498th Independent Infantry Battalion	17836 (1,549)

83rd Independent Mixed Brigade continued

• 83rd Brigade Artillery Unit	17837 (631)
• 83rd Brigade Engineer Unit	17838 (587)
• 83rd Brigade Signal Unit	17839 (226)

83rd I.M.B.: Activated in Hankou Feb 1, 1945, from former 5th Field Replacement Unit personnel. Home station: Wakayama. With the 34th Army from Mar. 6th until June 17th and 6th Area Army in Hankou where it was deactivated on September 17th.
Service History: China: Hankou garrison.

84th Independent Mixed Brigade 1945	至勇 *Shiyū* 17840
84th Brigade Headquarters	17841 (352)
• 499th Independent Infantry Battalion	17842 (1,549)
• 500th Independent Infantry Battalion	17843 (1,549)
• 501st Independent Infantry Battalion	17844 (1,549)
• 502nd Independent Infantry Battalion	17845 (1,549)
• 503rd Independent Infantry Battalion	17846 (1,549)
• 84th Brigade Artillery Unit	17847 (612)
• 84th Brigade Engineer Unit	17848 (526)
• 84th Brigade Signal Unit	17849 (226)

84th I.M.B.: Activated in Qiqihair Manchuria on Feb 1, 1945, from former 9th Field Replacement Unit personnel. Home station: Mizonokuchi. With the 6th Area Army in Huangmei China from Mar 6th until it was deactivated in Kuikiang on September 17th.
Service History: China: Huangmei garrison.

85th Independent Mixed Brigade 1945	至潔 *Shiketsu* 17850	
85th Brigade Headquarters	17851 (352)	Endo Unit
• 504th Independent Infantry Battalion	17852 (1,549)	
• 505th Independent Infantry Battalion	17853 (1,549)	
• 506th Independent Infantry Battalion	17854 (1,549)	
• 507th Independent Infantry Battalion	17855 (1,549)	
• 508th Independent Infantry Battalion	17856 (1,549)	
• 85th Brigade Artillery Unit	17857 (612)	
• 85th Brigade Engineer Unit	17858 (526)	
• 85th Brigade Signal Unit	17859 (226)	

85th I.M.B.: Activated in Kohoku Feb 1, 1945, from former 10th Field Replacement Unit personnel. Home station: Toyama. With the 34th Army from Mar 6th until June 17th and 6th Area Army in Yingching, Hubei. It was deactivated in Hankou on September 17th.
Service History: China: Yingching garrison.

86th Independent Mixed Brigade 1945	秋霜 *Shūsō* 17860
86th Brigade Headquarters	17861 (352)
• 509th Independent Infantry Battalion	17862 (1,549)
• 510th Independent Infantry Battalion	17863 (1,549)
• 511th Independent Infantry Battalion	17864 (1,549)
• 512th Independent Infantry Battalion	17865 (1,549)
• 513th Independent Infantry Battalion	17866 (1,549)
• 86th Brigade Artillery Unit	17867 (612)
• 86th Brigade Engineer Unit	17868 (526)
• 86th Brigade Signal Unit	17869 (226)

86th I.M.B.: Activated in Hunan, China on Feb 1, 1945. Home station: Sendai. With the 20th Army in Paoching from Mar 6th until it was deactivated Sept 17th in Weichang.
Service History: China: Paoching garrison.

87th Independent Mixed Brigade 1945	震動 *Shindo* 17870
87th Brigade Headquarters	17871 (352)
• 514th Independent Infantry Battalion	17872 (1,549)
• 515th Independent Infantry Battalion	17873 (1,549)
• 516th Independent Infantry Battalion	17874 (1,549)
• 517th Independent Infantry Battalion	17875 (1,549)
• 518th Independent Infantry Battalion	17876 (1,549)
• 87th Brigade Artillery Unit	17877 (612)
• 87th Brigade Engineer Unit	17878 (526)
• 87th Brigade Signal Unit	17879 (226)

87th I.M.B.: Activated in Hunan, China Feb 1, 1945. Home station: Marugame. With the 20th Army in Hengyang from Mar 6th until it was deactivated September 17th in Kuikiang.
Service History: China: Hengyang garrison.

88th Independent Mixed Brigade 1945	沖天 *Chuten* 17880
88th Brigade Headquarters	17881 (352)
• 519th Independent Infantry Battalion	17882 (1,549)
• 520th Independent Infantry Battalion	17883 (1,549)
• 521st Independent Infantry Battalion	17884 (1,549)
• 522nd Independent Infantry Battalion	17885 (1,549)
• 523rd Independent Infantry Battalion	17886 (1,549)
• 88th Brigade Artillery Unit	17887 (612)
• 88th Brigade Engineer Unit	17888 (526)
• 88th Brigade Signal Unit	17889 (226)

88th I.M.B.: Activated in Guangxi Province, China Feb 1, 1945. Home station: Omura. With the 11th Army in Hupei from Mar 6th, it was deactivated on September 17th in Weichang.
Service History: China: Hubei garrison.

89th Independent Mixed Brigade 1945	至純 *Shijun* 23080
89th Brigade Headquarters	23081 (284)
• 524th Independent Infantry Battalion	23082 (1,348)
• 525th Independent Infantry Battalion	23083 (1,348)
• 526th Independent Infantry Battalion	23084 (1,348)
• 527th Independent Infantry Battalion	23085 (1,348)
• 528th Independent Infantry Battalion	23086 (1,348)
• 89th Brigade Artillery Unit	23087 (560)
• 89th Brigade Engineer Unit	23088 (537)
• 89th Brigade Signal Unit	23089 (226)
• 89th Brigade Transport Unit	23090 (167)
• 89th Brigade Fatigue Duty Unit	23091 (511)
• 89th Brigade Field Hospital	23092 (491)
• 89th Brigade Veterinary Unit	23093 (119)
• 89th Brigade Water Purification Unit	23094 (239)
Attached	
9th Independent Machinegun Battalion	7357 (334)
63rd Field Machine Cannon Company	12527 (105)
53rd Ind. Field Anti-Aircraft Company	2174 (161)

89th I.M.B.: Activated in Wenzhou, China Feb 1, 1945. Home station: Hirosaki. With the 13th Army from Mar 6th until Apr 8th and 6th Army in Hangchow until it was deactivated on September 17th in Shanghai.
Service History: China: Hangzhou garrison.

90th Independent Mixed Brigade 1945	震雷 *Shinrai* 23095
90th Brigade Headquarters	23096 (352)
• 626th Independent Infantry Battalion	23097 (1,549)
• 627th Independent Infantry Battalion	23098 (1,549)
• 628th Independent Infantry Battalion	23099 (1,307)
• 629th Independent Infantry Battalion	23100 (1,549)
• 630th Independent Infantry Battalion	23101 (1,549)
• 90th Brigade Artillery Unit	23102 (739)
• 90th Brigade Engineer Unit	23103 (587)
• 90th Brigade Signal Unit	23104 (284)

90th I.M.B.: Activated in Jiangsu, China Feb 1, 1945, from former 4th Field Replacement Unit personnel. Organization completed about Feb 25th. Home station: Shizuoka. With the 13th Army in the Nanking/Yangchow area from Mar 6th until it was deactivated on September 17th in Shanghai.
Service History: China: Nanking garrison.

91st Independent Mixed Brigade 1945	馳駆 *Chiku* 23105
91st Brigade Headquarters	23106 (352)
• 631st Independent Infantry Battalion	23107 (1,549)

91st Independent Mixed Brigade continued

• 632nd Independent Infantry Battalion	23108 (1,549)
• 633rd Independent Infantry Battalion	23109 (1,549)
• 634th Independent Infantry Battalion	23110 (1,549)
• 635th Independent Infantry Battalion	23111 (1,549)
• 91st Brigade Artillery Unit	23112 (612)
• 91st Brigade Engineer Unit	23113 (526)
• 91st Brigade Signal Unit	23114 (226)

91st I.M.B.: Activated in Ningbo on Feb 1, 1945, from former 11th Field Replacement Unit personnel. Home station: Kurume. With the 13th Army from Mar 6th until Apr 8th and 6th Army in Ningbo where it was deactivated on September 25th.
Service History: China: Ningbo garrison.

92nd Independent Mixed Brigade 1945	至堅 *Shiken*
92nd Brigade Headquarters	11160 (352)
• 615th Independent Infantry Battalion	11161 (1,549)
• 616th Independent Infantry Battalion	11162 (1,549)
• 617th Independent Infantry Battalion	11163 (1,549)
• 618th Independent Infantry Battalion	11164 (1,549)
• 619th Independent Infantry Battalion	11165 (1,549)
• 92nd Brigade Artillery Unit	11166 (612)
• 92nd Brigade Engineer Unit	11167 (526)
• 92nd Brigade Signal Unit	11168 (226)

92nd I.M.B.: Activated in Shanxi on Feb 1, 1945, from former 12th Field Replacement Unit personnel. Home station: Kyoto. With the 13th Army in Laohokou, Hubei from Mar 6th until it was deactivated in Chengping.
Service History: China:

105th Independent Mixed Brigade 1945	敢威 *Kani* 12245
105th Brigade Headquarters	12246 (171)
• 451st Independent Infantry Battalion	12247 (997)
• 452nd Independent Infantry Battalion	12248 (997)
• 453rd Independent Infantry Battalion	12249 (997)
• 105th Brigade Artillery Unit	12250 (545)
• 105th Brigade Engineer Unit	12251
• 105th Brigade Signal Unit	12252
• 11th Field Heavy Artillery Battalion	No # (1,773)

105th I.M.B.: Activated in Rangoon, Burma on Feb 17, 1945, from former Rangoon I.M.B. personnel (3,174 Japanese-Rangoon residents). Home station: Tokyo. With the Burma Area Army from Feb 27th until May 3rd and 28th Army until the war ended. Attached to the Rangoon Defense Unit.
Service History: Burma: Pegu Apr 28 1945.

128th Independent Mixed Brigade 1945	快捷 *Kaishou*
128th Brigade Headquarters	16331 (163)
• 768th Independent Infantry Battalion	16332 (997)
• 769th Independent Infantry Battalion	16333 (997)
• 770th Independent Infantry Battalion	16334 (997)
• 771st Independent Infantry Battalion	16335 (997)
• 772nd Independent Infantry Battalion	16336 (997)
• 773rd Independent Infantry Battalion	16337 (997)
• 128th Brigade Engineer Unit	16338 (180)
• 128th Brigade Signal Unit	16339 (178)

128th I.M.B.: Activated Halmahera, the Moluccas on May 29, 1945, from former 1st Field Base Unit HQ personnel. Home station: Unknown. With the 2nd Area Army from May 29th until June 13th and 2nd Army on Halmahera Island until the war ended.
Service History: Indonesia: Halmahera Island garrison.

(Independent) Brigades

65th Brigade 1941	夏 *Natsu* (3,168)
65th Brigade Headquarters	9855 (155)
• 141st Infantry Regiment (Marugame)	9853 (2,671)
• 65th Brigade Engineer Unit	9856 (138)
• 65th Brigade Signal Unit	9857 (67)
• 65th Brigade Field Hospital	9858 (149)

65th Brigade: Activated in Hiroshima Oct 8, 1941, from former 65th Independent Infantry Group personnel. Home station: Yokosuka. With the 14th Army from Oct 8th until Nov 20 1942, 18th Army until March 14, 1944 and 8th Area Army in Rabaul until the war ended.
Service History: Philippines: Invasion Dec 12 1941. New Britain: Cape Gloucester Dec 15 1943.

68th Brigade 1944	星 *Hoshi* 10000 (5,959)
68th Brigade Headquarters	10001 (169)
• 126th Infantry Regiment (Mito)	10005 (3,654)
• 68th Brigade Artillery Unit	10006 (1,420)
• 68th Brigade Engineer Unit	10004 (282)
• 68th Brigade Signal Unit	10003 (202)
• 68th Brigade Medical Unit	10007 (245)

68th Brigade: (Not an I.M.B.) Activated in Siping, Manchuria on June 19, 1944, from former Koshurei (Gongzhuling) Army School students. Home station: Mito. The 3rd Inf Battalion was added to the 126th Inf Regt in Taiwan from 50th and 66th Div troops. With the Formosa Army (10th Area Army from Sept 22nd on) until Oct 27th and 35th Army on Leyte (landed in San Isidro Dec 9th), destroyed by July 12, 1945.
Service History: Philippines: Leyte Oct 20 1944.

Independent Infantry Brigades

1st Independent Infantry Brigade 1943	幹 *Miki* 1422 (5,987)
1st Brigade Headquarters	1423 (177)
• 191st Independent Infantry Battalion	1424 (1,427)
• 192nd Independent Infantry Battalion	1425 (1,427)
• 193rd Independent Infantry Battalion	1436 (1,427)
• 194th Independent Infantry Battalion	1437 (1,427)
•1st Brigade Signal Unit	1438 (111)

1st I.I.B.: Activated in Yanzhou, China on Dec 10, 1943. Home station: Mizonokuchi. With the 12th Army from Feb 1, 1944 until Aug 26th, North China Area Army until Mar 22, 1945 and 43rd Army in Zhucheng until it was deactivated in Qingdao.
Service History: China:

2nd Independent Infantry Brigade 1943	曙 *Akebono* 1439 (5,987)
2nd Brigade Headquarters	1453 (180)
• 195th Independent Infantry Battalion	1454 (1,427)
• 196th Independent Infantry Battalion	1455 (1,427)
• 197th Independent Infantry Battalion	1456 (1,427)
• 198th Independent Infantry Battalion	1457 (1,427)
• 2nd Brigade Signal Unit	1458 (111)

2nd I.I.B. Activated in Zhengding, China on Dec 10, 1943. Home station: Osaka. With the North China Area Army from Feb 1, 1944 until it was deactivated in Shijiazhuang Hebei (spelling also appears as Schuihchianchuang).
Service History: China:

3rd Independent Infantry Brigade 1943	将 *Sye* 1459
3rd Infantry Brigade Headquarters	1460
• 199th Independent Infantry Battalion	1461
• 200th Independent Infantry Battalion	1462
• 201st Independent Infantry Battalion	1463
• 202nd Independent Infantry Battalion	1464
3rd Brigade Signal Unit	1465

3rd I.I.B.: Activated in Fenyang, China on Dec 10, 1943. Home station: Unknown. With the 1st Army from Feb 1, 1944 until July 10th when it was deactivated to establish the 114th Division HQ, signal unit and 83rd Infantry Brigade.
Service History: China:

4th Independent Infantry Brigade 1943	弘 *Hiroshi*
4th Brigade Headquarters	1466
• 203rd Independent Infantry Battalion	1467
• 204th Independent Infantry Battalion	1468

4th Independent Infantry Brigade continued

• 205th Independent Infantry Battalion	1469
• 206th Independent Infantry Battalion	1470
4th Brigade Signal Unit	1471

4th I.I.B.: Activated in Jinan, China Dec 10, 1943. Home station: Unknown. With the 12th Army from Feb 1, 1944 until July 10th when it was deactivated to form the 117th Division's signal unit and 87th Infantry Brigade.
Service History: China:

5th Independent Infantry Brigade 1943	悟 *Satori* 6100 (5,985)
5th Brigade Headquarters	6101 (175)
• 207th Independent Infantry Battalion	6102 (1,427)
• 208th Independent Infantry Battalion	6103 (1,427)
• 209th Independent Infantry Battalion	6104 (1,427)
• 210th Independent Infantry Battalion	6105 (1,427)
• 5th Brigade Signal Unit	6106 (111)

5th I.I.B.: Activated in Jiangling, China December 10, 1943. Home station: Shizuoka. With the 11th Army from Feb 1, 1944 until April 8th, Wuhan Garrison Army until Jul 17th, 34th Army until June 17, 1945 and 6th Area Army in Zhengzhou, it was deactivated in Hankow.
Service History: China:

6th Independent Infantry Brigade 1943	肇 *Hajime* 7350 (5,985)
6th Brigade Headquarters	7351 (177)
• 211th Independent Infantry Battalion	7352 (1,427)
• 212th Independent Infantry Battalion	7353 (1,427)
• 213th Independent Infantry Battalion	7354 (1,427)
• 214th Independent Infantry Battalion	7355 (1,427)
• 6th Brigade Signal Unit	7356 (111)

6th I.I.B.: Activated in China on Dec 10, 1943, from former 22nd Infantry Group HQ personnel. Home station: Gifu. With the 13th Army in Anqing from Feb 1, 1944 until the war ended. It was deactivated in Anqing.
Service History: China:

7th Independent Infantry Brigade 1943	征 *Sei* 9447 (5,985)
7th Brigade Headquarters	9448 (175)
• 215th Independent Infantry Battalion	5592 (1,427)
• 216th Independent Infantry Battalion	5593 (1,427)
• 217th Independent Infantry Battalion	5594 (1,427)
• 218th Independent Infantry Battalion	5595 (1,427)
• 7th Brigade Signal Unit	5596 (111)

7th I.I.B.: Activated in China Dec 10, 1943, from former 116th Inf Group HQ personnel. Home station: Toyama. With the 11th Army from Feb 4, 1944 until April 15th, Wuhan Garrison Army until July 17th, 34th Army until June 17, 1945 and 6th Area Army in Nanjing where it was deactivated.
Service History: China:

8th Independent Infantry Brigade 1943	肝 *Kimo* 8137 (5,987)
8th Brigade Headquarters	8138 (177)
• 219th Independent Infantry Battalion	7828 (1,427)
• 220th Independent Infantry Battalion	7829 (1,427)
• 221st Independent Infantry Battalion	3321 (1,427)
• 222nd Independent Infantry Battalion	3322 (1,427)
• 8th Brigade Signal Unit	2875 (111)

8th I.I.B.: Activated in China on Dec 10, 1943, from former 104th Inf Group HQ personnel. Home station: Wakamatsu. With the 23rd Army in Canton until it was deactivated on September 22, 1945.
Service History: China: Canton-Hankou Railway Jan 3 1945.

9th Independent Infantry Brigade 1943	恵 *Megumu*
9th Brigade Headquarters	10284 (163)
• 223rd Independent Infantry Battalion	10285 (1,233)
• 224th Independent Infantry Battalion	10286 (1,233)
• 225th Independent Infantry Battalion	6046 (1,233)
• 226th Independent Infantry Battalion	6047 (1,233)
• 9th Brigade Signal Unit	5761 (330)

9th I.I.B.: Activated in China on Dec 10, 1943, from former 3rd Inf Group HQ personnel. Home station: Kyoto. With the 12th Army from Feb 1, 1944, until Jul 10th when it was deactivated to establish the 118th Division Headquarters and 89th Infantry Brigade.
Service History: China: Luoyang Apr 17 1944.

10th Independent Infantry Brigade 1943	固 *Katame* 1493 (5,987)
10th Brigade Headquarters	3141 (177)
• 227th Independent Infantry Battalion	6794 (1,427)
• 228th Independent Infantry Battalion	6795 (1,427)
• 229th Independent Infantry Battalion	7038 (1,427)
• 230th Independent Infantry Battalion	6459 (1,427)
• 10th Brigade Signal Unit	7160 (111)

10th I.I.B.: Activated in China on Dec 10, 1943,, from former 28th Inf Group HQ personnel. Home station: Fukuoka. With the 1st Army in Taiyuan, Shanxi from Feb. 1, 1944 until it was deactivated in Shanxi Province on September 17, 1945.
Service History: China:

11th Independent Infantry Brigade 1944	福 *Huku* (5,985)
11th Brigade Headquarters	5580 (175)
• 231st Independent Infantry Battalion	5581 (1,427)
• 232nd Independent Infantry Battalion	5582 (1,427)
• 233rd Independent Infantry Battalion	5583 (1,427)
• 234th Independent Infantry Battalion	5584 (1,427)
• 11thBrigade Signal Unit	5585 (111)

11th I.I.B.: Activated in Xinyang China on Feb 15, 1944. Home station: Osaka. With the China Expeditionary Army from Feb 15th until Apr 15th, Wuhan Garrison Army until July 17th, 34th Army until June 17, 1945 and 6th Area Army in Yingcheng Hubei. It was deactivated in Hankou on September 17th.
Service History: China:

12th Independent Infantry Brigade 1944	善 *Zen* 7343 (5,985)
12th Brigade Headquarters	7344 (177)
• 235th Independent Infantry Battalion	7345 (1,427)
• 236th Independent Infantry Battalion	7346 (1,427)
• 237th Independent Infantry Battalion	7347 (1,427)
• 238th Independent Infantry Battalion	7348 (1,427)
• 12th Brigade Signal Unit	7349 (111)

12th I.I.B.: Activated in Xianning, China on Dec 1, 1943. Home station: Yamaguchi. With the China Expeditionary Army from Feb 15, 1944 until April 15th, Wuhan Garrison Army until July 17th, 34th Army until June 17, 1945 and 6th Area Army in Xianning until the war ended.
Service History: China:

13th Independent Infantry Brigade 1944	直 *Choku* 8139 (5,987)
13th Brigade Headquarters	8140 (45)
• 239th Independent Infantry Battalion	8141 (1,427)
• 240th Independent Infantry Battalion	8142 (1,427)
• 241st Independent Infantry Battalion	8143 (1,427)
• 242nd Independent Infantry Battalion	8144 (1,427)
• 13th Brigade Signal Unit	8145 (111)

13th I.I.B.: Activated in China on Dec 10, 1943. Home station: Tokushima. With the 23rd Army in Chaoching from Feb 15, 1944 until deactivated in Canton Sept 22, 1945.
Service History: China:

14th Independent Infantry Brigade 1944	塁 *Rui* 1472 (5,987)
14th Brigade Headquarters	1473 (168)
• 243rd Independent Infantry Battalion	1474 (1,427)
• 244th Independent Infantry Battalion	1475 (1,427)

14th Independent Infantry Brigade continued	
• 245th Independent Infantry Battalion	1476 (1,427)
• 246th Independent Infantry Battalion	1477 (1,427)
• 14th Brigade Signal Unit	1478 (111)

14th I.I.B.: Activated in Luhan, China on Feb 15, 1944. Home station: Osaka. With the 1st Army in Tianfu until it was deactivated in Shanxi Province on Sept 17, 1945
Service History: China:

Cavalry Brigade

4th Cavalry Brigade 1909	成 *Nari* 5359 (3,149)
4th Cavalry Brigade Headquarters	5351 (45)
• 25th Cavalry Regiment	5352 (1,109)
• 26th Cavalry Regiment	5353 (1,109)
• 4th Cavalry Brigade 1st Tank Unit	286
• 4th Cavalry Brigade Artillery Unit	5356 (415)
• 4th Cavalry Brigade Transport Unit	5358 (490)

4th Cavalry Brigade: Activated in Nagoya April 4, 1909. Home station: Nagoya. With the Cavalry Group in Manchuria from July 7, 1937 to Dec 1, 1942, and Honan Province with 12th Army until the war ended.
Service History: Manchuria: Rehe Feb 21 1933. China: Suixian May 3 1938, South Shanxi May 7 1941, Laohokou Mar 27 1944

Air Raiding Brigade (Paratroops and Glider)

Army Regulation Kō No.93, Dec 1, 1941 created the 1st Air Raiding Brigade

1st Raiding Group 1941	鸞 *Ran* (9,835)	
1st Raiding Group Headquarters	19038 (368)	to Clark Field, P.I.
1st Air Raiding Brigade Headquarters	19150 (33)	
1st Air Raiding Brigade Signal Unit	19151 (164)	
• 1st Air Raiding Regiment	9947 (468)	
• 2nd Air Raiding Regiment	19039 (468)	Palembang 2/14/42
2nd Air Raiding Brigade Headquarters	19040 (140)	
• 3rd Air Raiding Regiment	9948 (894)	Buri P.I. 12/6/44
• 4th Air Raiding Regiment	9949 (894)	a few join Buri raid
1st Glider Infantry Transport Wing	19052 (430)	
• 1st Glider Infantry Regiment	19045 (848)	
• 2nd Glider Infantry Regiment	19046 (848)	
• 1st Raiding Machine Cannon Raiding Unit	19047 (308)	
• 1st Raiding Engineer Battalion	19048 (250)	
• 1st Raiding Signal Unit	19044	

Air Raiding Group continued

1st Raiding Brigade 1944	帥 *Sui* - attach 6th Air A. 5/2/45	
1st Raiding Brigade Headquarters	9944	2/30/41 to 8/31/45
• 1st Infantry Raiding Regiment	9945 (894)	11/30/44 to 8/26/45
• 2nd Infantry Raiding Regiment	9946 (894)	11/30/44 to 8/31/45
• 1st Raiding Tank Unit	19049 (465)	
• 1st Raiding Maintenance Unit	19051 (340)	
101st Airfield Company	19043 (174)	
102nd Airfield Company	19152 (179)	
103rd Airfield Company	19053 (179)	

1st Air Raiding Group: First activated Nittabaru Airfield, Kyushu, Dec 1, 1941, later elements on Nov 30, 1944. Home station: Takanabe. With the 1st Air Army until Oct 22, 1944, Raiding Group HQ and the Air Raiding Group joined the 4th Air Army Nov 28th in P.I., 3rd and 4th Air Raiding Regt arrived in Manila by Nov 11th for Burauen raid, Maj Gen Tsukada became commander of Kembu Army Group Jan 6, 1945. Sailed for the Philippines in early Dec, losing men to attacks on the voyage. 1st Air Raiding Group HQ left Japan Dec 27th and landed on Clark Field Jan 8, 1945. U.S. Intelligence Bulletin Apr 7, 1945 estimated each Air Raiding Regt had 35 transport planes. The 1st Inf Raiding Bgde remained in Japan. Note: Activated in 1943 the 5th Air Raiding Regt was converted to the 2nd Glider Inf Regt in Nov/Dec 1944.
Service History: Sumatra: Palembang Feb 14 1942. Philippines: Leyte: Burauen Airfields Dec 6 1944. Luzon: Clark Field Jan 25 1945. Japan: Okinawa: Yontan Field May 25 1945

Amphibious Brigades

1st Amphibious Brigade 1943	駆 *Kakeru* 3139 (5,366)	
1st Amphibious Brigade Headquarters	3130 (120)	Parry Is.
• 1st Amphibious Battalion	3131 (1,036)	2nd Co. Parry Is.
• 2nd Amphibious Battalion	3132 (1,036)	Kwajalein Is.
• 3rd Amphibious Battalion	3133 (1,036)	Engebi Is.
• 1st Amphib. Bgde Machine Cannon Unit	3134 (76)	
• 1st Amphibious Brigade Tank Unit	3135 (66)	3 tanks each Island
• 1st Amphibious Brigade Engineer Unit	3136 (243)	
• 1st Amphibious Brigade Signal Unit	3137 (139)	
• 1st Amphibious Brigade Medical Unit	3138 (190)	
• 1st Amphibious Brigade Transport Unit	6152 (1,542)	

1st Amphibious Brigade: Activated in Manchuria on Nov 16, 1943, from former 3rd Ind Garrison Unit personnel. Home station: Wakamatsu. Attached to the 4th Fleet from Nov 16th (landed on Enewetok Jan 4th) until Feb 25, 1944 and 31st Army until the war ended (some 1st Amphibious Bgde units on other islands were by-passed).
Service History: Enewetok Atoll: Feb. 17 1944 (HQ, 1st Am. Btn & Tank Unit destroyed)

2nd Amphibious Brigade 1943	巡 *Meguru* 3189 (5,486)
2nd Amphibious Brigade Headquarters	3180 (122)
• 1st Amphibious Battalion	3181 (1,036)
• 2nd Amphibious Battalion	3182 (1,036)
• 3rd Amphibious Battalion	3183 (1,036)
• 2nd Amphib. Bgde Machine Cannon Unit	3184 (76)
• 2nd Amphibious Brigade Tank Unit	3185 (66)
• 2nd Amphibious Brigade Engineer Unit	3186 (243)
• 2nd Amphibious Brigade Signal Unit	3187 (139)
• 2nd Amphibious Brigade Medical Unit	3188 (190)
• 2nd Amphibious Brigade Transport Unit	6153 (1,542) deactivated 3/4/45

2nd Amphibious Brigade: Activated in Manchuria on Nov 16, 1943, from former 29th Inf Group HQ, 70th and 150th L.o.C. Guard Unit personnel. Home station: Kurume. With the 2nd Area Army, New Guinea (departed Dalian, Manchuria on Apr 12, 1944) until Jan 4, 1945 and 2nd Army in New Guinea until the war ended.
Service History: New Guinea:

Independent Guard Units

1st Independent Guard Unit 1945	矢石 *Siseki* 23115
1st Independent Guard Unit Headquarters	23116 (341)
• 1st Independent Guard Battalion	23117 (1,385)
• 2nd Independent Guard Battalion	23118 (1,385)
• 3rd Independent Guard Battalion	23119 (1,385)
• 4th Independent Guard Battalion	23120 (1,385)
• 5th Independent Guard Battalion	23121 (1,385)
• 6th Independent Guard Battalion	23122 (1,385)
• 1st Independent Guard Pioneer Unit	23123 (231)

1st I.G.U.: Activated in China on February 1, 1945. Home station: Mizonokuchi. With the 13th Army in Nanking from March 9th until it was deactivated.

2nd Independent Guard Unit 1945	至成 *Sisei* 17760
2nd Independent Guard Unit Headquarters	17761 (341)
• 7th Independent Guard Battalion	17762 (1,385)
• 8th Independent Guard Battalion	17763 (1,385)
• 9th Independent Guard Battalion	17764 (1,385)
• 10th Independent Guard Battalion	17765 (1,385)
• 11th Independent Guard Battalion	17766 (1,385)
• 12th Independent Guard Battalion	17767 (1,385)
• 2nd Independent Guard Pioneer Unit	17768 (231)

2nd I.G.U.: Activated in China on Feb 1, 1945. Home station: Utsunomiya. With the 20th Army in Changsha from March 6th until it was deactivated.

3rd Independent Guard Unit 1945	伸張 *Sinchō* 15657
3rd Independent Guard Unit Headquarters	15658 (341)
• 13th Independent Guard Battalion	15659 (1,385)
• 14th Independent Guard Battalion	15660 (1,385)
• 15th Independent Guard Battalion	15661 (1,385)
• 16th Independent Guard Battalion	15662 (1,385)
• 17th Independent Guard Battalion	15663 (1,385)
• 18th Independent Guard Battalion	15664 (1,385)
• 3rd Independent Guard Pioneer Unit	15665 (231)

3rd I.G.U.: Activated in Beijing, China on Feb 1, 1945. Home station: Sendai. With the North China Area Army in Beijing from March 6th until it was deactivated.

4th Independent Guard Unit 1945	至誠 *Sisei* 15666
4th Independent Guards Unit Headquarters	15667 (341)
• 19th Independent Guard Battalion	15668 (1,365)
• 20th Independent Guard Battalion	15669 (1,365)
• 21st Independent Guard Battalion	15670 (1,365)
• 22nd Independent Guard Battalion	15671 (1,365)
• 23rd Independent Guard Battalion	15672 (1,365)
• 24th Independent Guard Battalion	15673 (1,365)
• 4th Independent Guards Pioneer Unit	15674 (235)

4th I.G.U.: Activated in China on Feb 1, 1945, from former 2nd I.M.B. and 118th Div. personnel. Home station: Akita. With the Mongolia Garrison Army in Zhangjiakou, Mongolia from March 6th and in Fengchen when the war ended.

5th Independent Guard Unit 1945	至隆 *Siriū* 15675
5th Independent Guard Unit Headquarters	15676 (341)
• 25th Independent Guard Battalion	15677 (1,385)
• 26th Independent Guard Battalion	15678 (1,385)
• 27th Independent Guard Battalion	15679 (1,385)
• 28th Independent Guard Battalion	15680 (1,385)
• 29th Independent Guard Battalion	15681 (1,385)
• 30th Independent Guard Battalion	15682 (1,385)
• 5th Independent Guard Pioneer Unit	15683 (231)

5th I.G.U.: Activated in China on Feb.1, 1945. Home station: Tsu. With the 1st Army in Yuncheng from April 6th until the war ended.

6th Independent Guard Unit 1945	至毅 *Siki* 15684
6th Independent Guard Unit Headquarters	15685 (341)
• 31st Independent Guard Battalion	15686 (1,385)

6th Independent Guard Unit continued

• 32nd Independent Guard Battalion	15687 (1,385)
• 33rd Independent Guard Battalion	15688 (1,385)
• 34th Independent Guard Battalion	15689 (1,385)
• 35th Independent Guard Battalion	15690 (1,385)
• 36th Independent Guard Battalion	15691 (1,385)
• 6th Independent Guard Pioneer Unit	15692 (231)

6th I.G.U.: Activated in China on Feb 1, 1945. Home station: Marugame. With the 12th Army in the Posiang area from March 6th until the war ended.

7th Independent Guard Unit 1945	至武 *Sibu* 15693
7th Independent Guard Unit Headquarters	15694 (341)
• 37th Independent Guard Battalion	15695 (1,385)
• 38th Independent Guard Battalion	15696 (1,385)
• 39th Independent Guard Battalion	15697 (1,385)
• 49th Independent Guard Battalion	15698 (1,385)
• 41st Independent Guard Battalion	15699 (1,385)
• 42nd Independent Guard Battalion	15700 (1,385)
• 7th Independent Guard Pioneer Unit	15701 (231)

7th I.G.U.: Activated in China on Feb 1, 1945. Home station: Fukuoka. With the North China Area Army in the Baoding, Hopeh area from March 6th until the war ended.

9th Independent Guard Unit 1945	至剛 *Sigō* 15702
9th Independent Guard Unit Headquarters	15703 (256)
• 43rd Independent Guard Battalion	15704 (1,385)
• 44th Independent Guard Battalion	15705 (1,385)
• 45th Independent Guard Battalion	15706 (1,385)
• 46th Independent Guard Battalion	15707 (1,385)
• 47th Independent Guard Battalion	15708 (1,385)
• 48th Independent Guard Battalion	15709 (1,385)
• 9th Independent Guard Pioneer Unit	15710 (231)

9th I.G.U.: Activated in Tsinan, China on Feb 1, 1945. Home station: Wakamatsu. With the 43rd Army in the Shantung area from April 20 until the war ended.

10th Independent Guard Unit 1945	至敏 *Sibin* 15711
10th Independent Guard Unit Headquarters	15712 (256)
• 49th Independent Guard Battalion	15713 (1,385)
• 50th Independent Guard Battalion	15714 (1,385)
• 51st Independent Guard Battalion	15715 (1,385)
• 52nd Independent Guard Battalion	15716 (1,385)

10th Independent Guard Unit continued

• 53rd Independent Guard Battalion	15717 (1,385)
• 54th Independent Guard Battalion	15718 (1,385)
• 10th Independent Guard Pioneer Unit	15719 (231)

10th I.G.U.: Activated in China on Apr 12, 1945. Home station: Yamagata. With the 43rd Army from April 20th until May 28th and 12th Army in Chengchow until the war ended.

11th Independent Guard Unit 1945	至鋭 *Siei* 15220
11th Independent Guard Unit Headquarters	15721 (256)
• 55th Independent Guard Battalion	15722 (1,385)
• 56th Independent Guard Battalion	15723 (1,385)
• 57th Independent Guard Battalion	15724 (1,385)
• 58th Independent Guard Battalion	15725 (1,385)
• 59th Independent Guard Battalion	15726 (1,385)
• 60th Independent Guard Battalion	15727 (1,385)
• 11th Independent Guard Pioneer Unit	15728 (231)

11th I.G.U.: Activated in Tsinan, China on Apr 12, 1945. Home station: Sendai. With the 43rd Army from April 20th until May 28th and 12th Army in Shantung until the war ended.

12th Independent Guard Unit 1945	至厳 *Sigen* 15729
12th Independent Guard Unit Headquarters	15730 (256)
• 61st Independent Guard Battalion	15731 (1,365)
• 62nd Independent Guard Battalion	15732 (1,365)
• 63rd Independent Guard Battalion	15733 (1,365)
• 64th Independent Guard Battalion	15734 (1,365)
• 65th Independent Guard Battalion	15735 (1,365)
• 66th Independent Guard Battalion	15736 (1,365)
• 12th Independent Guard Pioneer Unit	15737 (235)

12th I.G.U.: Activated in China on Apr 12, 1945. Home station: Tsu. With the 12th Army from April 20th until May 28th and 43rd Army in Tsingtao, Shantung until the war ended.

13th Independent Guard Unit 1945	疾風 *Situpu* 15738
13th Independent Guard Unit Headquarters	15739 (256)
• 67th Independent Guard Battalion	15740 (1,365)
• 68th Independent Guard Battalion	15741 (1,365)
• 69th Independent Guard Battalion	15742 (1,365)
• 70th Independent Guard Battalion	15743 (1,365)
• 71st Independent Guard Battalion	15744 (1,365)

13th Independent Guard Unit continued

• 72nd Independent Guard Battalion	15745 (1,365)
• 13th Independent Guard Pioneer Unit	15746 (235)

13th I.G.U.: Activated in China on Apr 12, 1945. Home station: Nagoya. With the 12th Army in the Suiping area from April 20th until the war ended.

14th Independent Guard Unit 1945	紫電 *Siden* 15747
14th Independent Guard Unit Headquarters	15748 (256)
• 73rd Independent Guard Battalion	15749 (1,365)
• 74th Independent Guard Battalion	15750 (1,365)
• 75th Independent Guard Battalion	15751 (1,365)
• 76th Independent Guard Battalion	15752 (1,365)
• 77th Independent Guard Battalion	15753 (1,365)
• 78th Independent Guard Battalion	15754 (1,365)
• 14th Independent Guard Pioneer Unit	15755 (235)

14th I.G.U.: Activated in China on Apr. 12, 1945. Home station: Kanagawa. With the 12th Army in the Yanchang-Xianyang area, Shaanxi from April 20th until the war ended.

Independent Garrison Units

North China Special Guard Unit 1943	甲 *Ko* 1419 (5,889)
North China Special Garrison Headquarters	1420
• 1st Special Garrison Battalion	1414
• 2nd Special Garrison Battalion	1415
• 3rd Special Garrison Battalion	1416
• 4th Special Garrison Battalion	1417
• 5th Special Garrison Battalion	1418
• 6th Special Garrison Battalion	1479
• 7th Special Garrison Battalion	1480
• 8th Special Garrison Battalion	1481
• 9th Special Garrison Battalion	1482
• 10th Special Garrison Battalion	1483
North China Sp. Garrison Training Unit	1419

North China Special Garrison Unit: Activated in Tianjin, China on Aug 24, 1943. With the North China Area Army from Sept 20, 1943 until the war ended.
Service History: China: Beijing garrison.

12th Independent Garrison Unit 1942	定 *Tei*
12th Ind. Garrison Unit Headquarters	10902

12th Independent Garrison Unit continued	
43rd Ind. Infantry Garrison Battalion	10903
44th Ind. Infantry Garrison Battalion	10904
45th Ind. Infantry Garrison Battalion	10905
46th Ind. Infantry Garrison Battalion	10906
47th Ind. Infantry Garrison Battalion	10907

12th Ind. Garrison Unit: Activated in Sumatra Sept 26, 1942. With the 25th Army in Singapore until Mar 30, 1943, Southern Expeditionary Army until Jan 15, 1944 and 29th Army in Kuala Lumpur, Malaysia until Oct 16, 1944, when it was deactivated to become the 94th Division.

1st South Seas Garrison Unit 1943	剛 *Go*
1st South Seas Garrison Unit 1st Company	unknown
1st South Seas Garrison Unit 2nd Company	
1st South Seas Garrison Unit 3rd Company	
1st South Seas Garrison Unit 4th Company	
1st South Seas Garrison Unit Artillery Co.	

1st South Seas Garrison Unit: Activated in Shizuoka, Japan on Apr 12, 1943. About 800 men with the 8th Area Army from Apr 12th until their transport was sunk off Jaluit Atoll May 20th. In November the survivors became part of the 1st South Seas Detachment 2nd Battalion.

1st South Seas Detachment 1943	剛 *Go*	
1st South Seas Detachment 1st Battalion	11221	
1st South Seas Detachment 2nd Battalion	4372	
1st South Seas Detachment 3rd Battalion	unknown	
1st South Seas Detachment 4th Battalion	12501 (625)	activated 2/16/43
1st South Seas Detachment 5th Battalion	12502 (625)	
1st South Seas Detachment 6th Battalion	12503 (625)	activated 2/16/43

1st South Seas Detachment: Activated on Mili Atoll, Marshall Islands on Nov 16, 1943, from former 122nd Inf. Regt and 1st So. Seas Garrison Unit personnel. Home station: Takasaki.

2nd South Seas Garrison Unit 1943	備 *Bi*
2nd Garrison Infantry Group Headquarters	4372
• 19th Independent Garrison Battalion	4372
• 20th Independent Garrison Battalion	4372
• 21st Independent Garrison Battalion	4372
• 2nd South Seas Tank Company	12501
• 2nd South Seas Artillery Company	unknown
• 2nd South Seas Mountain Artillery Co.	unknown

2nd South Seas Garrison Unit: Activated in Kagoshima April 12, 1943. With the Eastern District Army until May 19th, Combined Fleet (navy) until Feb 25, 1944 and 31st Army on Kusaie (Kosrae) Island until the war ended. By-passed by American troops.
Service History: Caroline Islands: Kusaie garrison.

3rd South Seas Garrison Unit 1943	備 *Bi*
3rd South Seas Garrison Headquarters	unknown
• 1st 3rd South Seas Garrison Battalion	
• 2nd 3rd South Seas Garrison Battalion	
• 3rd 3rd South Seas Garrison Battalion	
• 3rd South Seas Garrison Unit Tank Unit	
• 3rd South Seas Garrison Unit Signal Unit	

The 3rd South Seas Garrison Unit: Activated in Rabaul, New Britain June 12, 1943, from former 21st I.M.B. personnel. With the Imperial Navy from June 12th (arrived Wake Is on July 10th) until Feb 25, 1944, and 31st Army until becoming the 13th I.M.R. on May 22, 1944. Wake surrendered Sept 7, 1945.
Note: Wake Is. fell to the Maizuru 2nd Special Naval Landing force on Dec 23, 1941. About half the garrison was army although the navy retained control until the war ended.
Service History: Wake Atoll: Wake garrison.

4th South Seas Garrison Unit 1943	沖 *Oki*
4th South Seas Garrison Headquarters	6094 (79)
• 1st 4th South Seas Garrison Battalion	6094 (650)
• 2nd 4th South Seas Garrison Battalion	6094 (651)
• 3rd 4th South Seas Garrison Battalion	6094 (651)
• 4th South Seas Garrison 1st Artillery Co.	6094 (264)
• 4th South Seas Garrison 2nd Artillery Co.	6094 (264)
• 4th South Seas Garrison 3rd Artillery Co.	6094 (264)
• 4th South Seas Garrison Signal Unit	6094 (117)

4th South Seas Garrison Unit: Activated in Wakayama on June 12, 1943. Home station: Osaka. With Imperial Headquarters from June 26th until July 22nd, Combined Fleet (navy) on Buka Island, Bougainville until Nov 1st and 17th Army on Bougainville Island until the war ended. Matsuda Unit absorbed into the new 38th I.M.B. on June 24, 1944.
Service History: New Guinea: Buka Island garrison. Bougainville: 2nd Torokina Mar 6 1944

Locale Defense Units

Bhutan Guards Unit 1944	盤 *Ban*	
Bhutan Guards Headquarters	2138 (282)	
• 104th Anti-Aircraft Regiment	15381 (1,066)	
• 102nd Machine Cannon Battalion	2139 (458)	
Bhutan Guards Unit	2140 (167)	

Bhutan Guards Unit: Activated in Pangkalpinang, Bangka Is. on June 1, 1944, from the former Bhutan Air Defence Unit (est. Dec 10, 1943). Also called the Pangkalpinang Guards Unit, affiliated with the 25th Army but under control of the 9th Air Division, 3rd Air Army in Sumatra.

Hong Kong Garrison 1942	波 *Nami* (3,134)	
Hong Kong Guard Headquarters	8138 (80)	
• 67th Independent Infantry Battalion	8114 (809)	activated 1/25/39
• 68th Independent Infantry Battalion	8115 (809)	activated 1/25/39
• 69th Independent Infantry Battalion	8116 (809)	activated 1/25/39
• Hong Kong Guard Artillery Unit	8139 (627)	
• Hong Kong Military Hospital	No #	
Attached		
• 51st Independent Mountain Gun Battalion	5513	
• 11th Field Transport Headquarters	unknown (17)	
• 31st Independent Transport Battalion	unknown	
• 32nd Independent Transport Battalion	unknown	
• 33rd Independent Transport Battalion	unknown	

Hong Kong Defense Garrison: Activated in Hong Kong on Jan 19, 1942, from former 1st Ind. Inf. Unit personnel. Home station: Osaka. With the Governor General of Hong Kong from Jan 27th until Dec 11, 1944 and the 23rd Army until the war ended.

Manila Defense Unit (Kobayashi) 1944	尚武 *Shobu*	
Manila Defense Force Headquarters	17661 (122)	
22nd Field Medium Artillery Regiment	4328 (949)	
13th Independent Machinegun Battalion	17652 (334)	
25th Independent Machinegun Battalion	5766 (334)	
23rd Ind. Rapid Firing Gun Battalion	5243 (403)	anti tank
20th Ind. Medium Artillery Battalion	17657 (748)	
3rd Rocket Gun Battalion	12384 (845)	
4th Ind. Heavy Artillery Battalion, 1 Battery	1218	

Manila Defense Unit: Activated in Manila, the Philippines on Oct 14, 1944, 6 days before the U.S. invaded Leyte Island. With the 14th Area Army from Oct 14th until Apr 20, 1945 and 41st Army until it's destroyed on Luzon. (Also called the Kobayashi Group)

Palembang Guards Brigade 1943	翔 *Sho* 12508
Palembang Guards Brigade Headquarters	10366 (185)
• 101st Anti-Aircraft Regiment	10367 (1,218)
• 102nd Anti-Aircraft Regiment	10368 (1,066)
• 103rd Anti-Aircraft Regiment	10369 (1,066)
• 101st Machine Cannon Battalion	1949 (861)
• 101st Strategic Balloon Unit	15811 (396)
• 57th Specially Est. Machine Cannon Unit	2191 (85)
• 58th Specially Est. Machine Cannon Unit	2192 (85)
• 59th Specially Est. Machine Cannon Unit	12454 (85)
• 60th Specially Est. Machine Cannon Unit	12455 (85)
• 61st Specially Est. Machine Cannon Unit	12456 (85)
• 62nd Specially Est. Machine Cannon Unit	12457 (85)
• Palembang Guard Signal Unit	12507 (332)
• Palembang Guard Unit	12508 (504)

Palembang Guards Brigade: Activated in Palembang, Sumatra June 1, 1944, from former Palembang Air Defence Unit (est. Mar 25, 1943) personnel. Affiliated with the 25th Army but under control of the 9th Air Division in Sumatra.

Rangoon Defense Unit 1944	森 *Mori*
Rangoon Defense Unit Headquarters	12200 (258)
33rd Field Anti-Aircraft Battalion	3893 (465)
35th Field Anti-Aircraft Battalion	3895 (465)
51st Field Anti-Aircraft Battalion	3629 (681)
58th Ind. Field Anti-Aircraft Company	12223 (179)
59th Ind. Field Anti-Aircraft Company	12224 (179)
60th Ind. Field Anti-Aircraft Company	12225 (179)
61st Ind. Field Anti-Aircraft Company	12226 (179)
70th Field Anti-Aircraft Battalion	10593 (528)
71st Field Anti-Aircraft Battalion	8057 (536)
43rd Field Machine Cannon Company	8059 (105)

Rangoon Defense Unit: Activated on June 1, 1944, from the former Rangoon Air Defence Unit (est. July 26. 1943) personnel. With the Burma Area Army from June 1st until Sept 20th, 28th Army until reorganized Mar 20, 1945 as the Rangoon Anti-Aircraft Unit attached to the Rangoon Defense Unit, Burma Area Army until May 3rd, 28th Army until the war ended.

Singapore (Shonan) Defense Unit 1945	岡 *Oka*
Singapore Guards Headquarters	18500 (357)
Singapore Guards HQ Signal Section	18500 (185)
• 79th Independent Guard Battalion	18525 (1,385)
• 80th Independent Guard Battalion	18526 (1,385)
• 48th Field Anti Aircraft Battalion	2001 (280)

Singapore Defense Unit continued

• 94th Field Anti-Aircraft Battalion	1957 (521)
• 25th Independent Artillery Battalion	18515 (460)
• 78th Field Machine Cannon Company	18516 (105)
• 79th Field Machine Cannon Company	18517 (105)

In the last weeks of the war soldiers from the remnants of other units reorganized.

1st Provisional Mixed Battalion	No #
2nd Provisional Mixed Battalion	No #
3rd Provisional Mixed Battalion	No #

Singapore Defense Unit: Activated in Singapore Apr 14, 1945, from Singapore Defense Command units to defend against air raids and provide ground security. With the 7th Area Army from Apr 14th until the war ended. Singapore was called Shonan by Japan.

Expeditionary Units

1st Expeditionary Unit 1944	国 *Kuni* (5,500)
25th Infantry Group Headquarters	4702
40th Infantry Regiment, 3rd Btn.	4904
14th Infantry Regiment, 3rd Btn.	4903
25th Engineer Regiment, 3rd Company	4908
10th Infantry Regiment, 3rd Btn.	5448 鉄
10th Field Artillery Regiment, 3rd Btn.	5451 鉄
89th Infantry Regiment, 3rd Btn.	3476 山
Attached:	
3rd Independent Mountain Artillery Regiment	

1st Exp. Unit: Activated in Mudanjiang, Manchuria on Feb 21, 1944, from 25th, 24th and 10th Division personnel. With the Kwantung Army from Feb 21st until the 25th and 31st Army, landed on Saipan Mar 19th. Reorganized into the 47th I.M.B. on May 22nd.

2nd Expeditionary Unit 1944	武 *Take* (2,500) 2552
7th Infantry Regiment, 3rd Btn.	1524 (880)
19th Infantry Regiment, 3rd Btn.	1528 (880)
9th Mountain Artillery Regiment, 1st Btn.	1546 (837)
9th Engineer Regiment, 3rd Company	1559

2nd Exp. Unit: Activated in Mudanjiang, Manchuria on Feb 21, 1944, from 9th Division personnel. With the Kwantung Army from Feb 21st until the 25th and 31st Army, Truk District Group, landed on Mortlok Is. May 19th, became the 51st I.M.B May 22nd .

3rd Expeditionary Unit 1944	杉 *Sugi* (3,500) 2553
8th Infantry Group Headquarters	unknown
5th Infantry Regiment, 1st Btn.	4715
17th Infantry Regiment, 1st Btn.	4717
31st Infantry Regiment, 3rd Btn.	4711
8th Field Artillery Regiment, 3rd Btn.	4738
8th Engineer Regiment, 3rd Company	4748

3rd Exp. Unit: Activated in Suiyang, Manchuria on Feb 21, 1944, from 8th Division personnel. With the Kwantung Army from Feb 21st until the 25th and 31st Army, landed on Enderby Island on Mar 23rd. Reorganized into the 11th Ind Mixed Regt May 27th.

4th Expeditionary Unit 1944	玉 *Tama* 2554
12th Infantry Group Headquarters	unknown
1st Infantry Regiment, 2nd Btn.	5915
49th Infantry Regiment, 3rd Btn.	5916
57th Infantry Regiment, 3rd Btn.	5918
1st Field Artillery Regiment, 3rd Btn.	5920
1st Engineer Regiment, 3rd Company	5521
Joined March 4, 1944	劍 *Ken* (3,500)
24th Infantry Regiment, 3rd Btn.	8703
46th Infantry Regiment, 3rd Btn.	8705
48th Infantry Regiment, 3rd Btn.	8707
24th Field Artillery Regiment, 3rd Btn.	8722
18th Engineer Regiment, 3rd Company	8745

4th Exp. Unit: Activated in Dongning, Manchuria on Feb 21, 1944, from 1st and 12th Division personnel. With the Kwantung Army from Feb 21st until the 25th and 31st Army, Palau District Group, landed on Yap Island Apr 24th. Became the 49th I.M.B. May 22nd.

5th Expeditionary Unit 1944	命 *Mei* (3,000) 2555
71st Infantry Group Headquarters	4355
87th Infantry Regiment, 3rd Btn.	4322
88th Infantry Regiment, 3rd Btn.	4323
71st Mountain Artillery Regiment, 1st Btn.	4324
71st Engineer Regiment, 3rd Company	13273

5th Exp. Unit: Activated in Hunchun, Manchuria Feb 21, 1944, from 71st Division personnel. With the Kwantung Army from Feb 21st until the 25th and 31st Army, Northern Marianas District Group on Pagan Is. Reorganized into the 9th Ind. Mixed Regt. on May 22nd.

6th Expeditionary Unit 1944	錦 *Nishiki* (8,000) 2556
11th Infantry Group Headquarters	unknown
12th Infantry Regiment, 3rd Btn.	2425
43rd Infantry Regiment, 3rd Btn.	2435
44th Infantry Regiment, 1st Btn.	2445
11th Mountain Artillery Regiment, 3rd Btn.	2465
11th Engineer Regiment, 3rd Company	2475
<u>12th Div. Units</u>	劍 *Ken* to 4th Exp. Unit 3/4/44
24th Infantry Regiment, 3rd Btn.	8703
46th Infantry Regiment, 3rd Btn.	8705
48th Infantry Regiment, 3rd Btn.	8707
24th Field Artillery Regiment, 3rd Btn.	8722
18th Engineer Regiment, 3rd Company	8745
<u>1st Div. units joined March 4, 1944</u>	玉 *Tama*
1st Infantry Regiment, 2nd Btn.	5914
49th Infantry Regiment, 3rd Btn.	5915
57th Infantry Regiment, 3rd Btn.	5916
1st Field Artillery Regiment, 3rd Btn.	5920
1st Engineer Regiment, 3rd Company	5521

<u>6th Exp. Unit</u>: Activated in Hukin, Manchuria Feb 21, 1944, from the 11th and 12th Div, 1st Division units joined in March. With the Kwantung Army from Feb 21st until the 25th and 31st Army, Southern Marianas District Group, landed on Guam March 20th. Reorganized into the 48th I.M.B. and 10th Ind Mixed Regt on May 22nd.

7th Expeditionary Unit 1944	山 *Yama* (2,500) 2557
22nd Infantry Regiment, 1st Btn.	3474
32nd Infantry Regiment, 3rd Btn.	3475
42nd Field Artillery Regiment, 3rd Btn.	3480
24th Engineer Regiment, 3rd Company	3481

<u>7th Exp. Unit</u>: Activated in Dongan, Manchuria on Feb 21. 1944, from 24th Div units. With the Kwantung Army from Feb 21st until the 25th and 31st Army, Truk District Group, landed on Mereyon Island Apr 12th. Became the 50th I.M.B. on May 27th.

8th Expeditionary Unit 1944	Unknown (4,000)
2nd Ind. Garrison Unit Headquarters	8502 (972)
73rd Infantry Regiment, 3rd Btn.	8505 (703)
75th Infantry Regiment, 3rd Btn.	8506 (434)
76th Infantry Regiment, 3rd Btn.	8510 (769)
25th Mountain Artillery Regiment, 3rd Btn.	8510
19th Engineer Regiment, 3rd Company	8511

<u>8th Exp. Unit</u>: Activated in Changchun, Manchuria on Feb 21, 1944, from the 2nd Ind Garrison Unit HQ and 19th Division personnel. With the Korea Army from Feb 21st until the 25th and 31st Army, Truk District Group, landed on Truk Mar 25th.

8th Expeditionary Unit continued
Became the 51st I.M.B. on May 22nd.

9th Expeditionary Unit 1944	山 *Yama* (3,500)
24th Infantry Group Headquarters	
12th Independent Garrison Battalion	
14th Independent Garrison Battalion	
28th Independent Garrison Battalion	

9th Exp. Unit: Activated in Manchuria on Apr 4, 1944, from former 24th Inf Group HQ and 8th Ind Garrison Unit personnel. With the 31st Army, Northern Mariana District Group from Apr 4th, convoy sunk May 16th, landed on Saipan May 18th. Survivors joined the 49th I.M.B. on Yap; 12th I.G.B. to the 330th I.I.B. and 14th and 28th I.G.B. to the 327th I.I.B

10th Expeditionary Unit 1944	輝 *Kagayaku* 12901 (3,500)
10th Infantry Group Headquarters	5445
22nd Independent Garrison Battalion	5043
23rd Independent Garrison Battalion	5045
30th Independent Garrison Battalion	14022

10th Exp. Unit: Activated in Jiamusi, Manchuria on Apr 8, 1944, from former 10th Inf Group HQ and 5th and 6th Ind Garrison Unit personnel. Home station: Kofu. With the Kwantung Army on Halmahera Is. the Celebes by June 13th, 2nd Area Army from Aug 4th until June 13th 1945 and 2nd Army on Halmahera Is. until the war ended.

11th Expeditionary Unit 1st Kurile Islands Group 1944	北部 *Hokubu* (2,500)
1st Kurile (57th Infantry Group) Headquarters	7210 (100)
2nd Independent Garrison Battalion	14012 (800)
4th Independent Garrison Battalion	14014 (800)
29th Independent Garrison Battalion	14021 (800)

11th Expeditionary Unit / 1st Kurile Islands Group: Activated in Manchuria on Apr 8, 1944, from former 57th Inf Group HQ, 1st and 5th Ind Garrison Unit personnel. Home station: Sakura. With the 27th Army until Jan 22, 1945, and 5th Area Army until July 16th when it was deactivated in Hokkaido. The 57th I.G. HQ Unit returned to the Kuriles to form the 129th I.M.B. Originally the 11th Expeditionary Unit, the 1st Kurile Islands Group received its name after arriving in the Kuriles.

12th Expeditionary Unit 1944	Unknown
47th Infantry Group Headquarters	unknown
91st Infantry Regiment, 1st Btn.	12018
105th Infantry Regiment, 3rd Btn.	12017

12th Expeditionary Unit continued

131st Infantry Regiment, 3rd Btn.	12016
47th Mountain Artillery Regiment, 2nd Btn.	12000
47th Engineer Regiment, 2nd Company	12001
47th Division Signal Unit, an element	12002

12th Exp. Unit: Activated in Hirosaki, Japan on June 13, 1944, from 47th Division personnel. In Hirosaki with the 2nd Area Army from June 13th until 22nd when it was reorganized into the 58th I.M.B. The 58th I.M.B. was attached to the 14th Army in the P.I. July 4th.

South Seas Detachment 1941	楯 *So* (5,549)
55th Infantry Group Headquarters	8414 (176)
144th Infantry Regiment	8417 (2,932)
55th Cav. Regiment, 3rd Company, 1st Pltn	8418 (120)
55th Mountain Artillery Regt, 1st Battalion	8420 (550)
55th Engineer Regiment, 1st Company	8421 (216)
55th Division Materials Platoon, an element	8421 in the Engineer Company
55th Division Signal Unit, an element	8422 (40)
55th Transport Regiment, 2nd Company	8423 (615)
1/3 of the 55th Division Medical Unit	8425 (199)
55th Division 1st Field Hospital	8426 (182)
55th Div. Water Supply Unit, an element	8428 (42)
55th Division Veterinary Unit, an element	8430 (30)
47th Field Anti-Aircraft Battalion	8551 (265)
1st Independent Wireless Radio Platoon	11214 (32)
1st Fixed Radio Unit	unknown (150)

South Seas Detachment: (Nankai Shitai) Activated on Chichijima, Bonin Islands on Sept 27, 1941, from 55th Division personnel, mobilization was completed on Oct 4th. With Imperial Headquarters from Nov 16th until May 18, 1942, 17th Army from May 20th (to New Caledonia but invasion was cancelled) until Nov 16th and 18th Army until Apr 1, 1943, deactivated June 17, 1943 and returned to the 55th Division in Burma.
Note: Nov 23, 1942, withdrawing along the Kokoda Trail Major General Tomitaro Horii, detachment commander, drowned crossing the Kumusi River in New Guinea.
Service History: Guam: Dec 7 1941, New Guinea: Rabaul Jan 23 1942, Buna Aug 16 ’42.

End of Divisions and Brigades

Horse-drawn transport wagons crossing a pontoon bridge (author)

Japanese Army pontoon bridge straining under a truck in New Guinea (anonymous photo captured by army engineer Cpl Royer. Background information courtesy WWHAM, Alliance, Ohio)

Chapter 4

Code Numbers for Units Overseas

Code names and numbers were used to conceal unit strengths, arm of service, duty, and common names, so says Article 2 of the *Rules on the Wartime Code Names of Army Units*. Turned on its head, this eighty-year-old system reveals hierarchical unit relationships, which may otherwise have been lost. Kanji names assigned to a parent formation are, by extension, the code name for its subordinate units as well.

Code names are another feature of the Imperial Army that require close attention. Consult a dictionary and most kanji have several meanings, so it's important to know which one is correct. In JACARs archives there is an incomplete syllabary chart that provides kana sounds for code names (JACAR ref. code: C12121216500). The correct code name pronunciations appear in this book next to the armies, divisions and brigades they are associated with in romaji form (atop each formation's order of battle). Due to space restrictions it was decided to provide these instead of English translations, which for most part can be readily found by searching.

Charter documents on the rules for code-naming army units:

1 - July 10, 1940, *Detailed Rules of Army Peacetime Formation*

2 - September 10, 1940, *1941 Detailed Rules for Army Mobilization Plan*

3 - November 14, 1940, *The Rules on Code Names of Units in Manchuria*

4 - October 9, 1942, *Matters on the Code Names of Units in China*

5 - 1942, *Main Points for the Reformation of Military Preparedness*

6 - February 26, 1944, *Matters on the Code Names of Units that are Subordinate or Commanded by the Southern (Expeditionary) Army*

7 - Autumn 1944, *Detailed Rules of Delegated Martial Order in Southern Areas*

Index of Sequential Unit Code Numbers
for Units Sent Overseas

"On account of insufficient materials, completeness may not be expected."
1st Demobilization Bureau, Dec. 26, 1945

Soldiers in China crossing a bridge built by army engineers (author)

Abbreviations identifying parent unit(s):
Army (A) with a number indicates the army (2A) is the 2nd Army
Area Army (AA)
General Army (GA)
Air General Army (AGA)
Imperial General Headquarters (GHQ)
Air Army (AirA)
Air Division (AirDiv)
Burma Area Army (BAA)
China Expeditionary Army (CA)
Continental Railway (CRR)
Japan (homeland) Railway (RR)
Kembu Army Group (KeG), the Philippines
Mongolia Garrison Army (MGA)
Army Shipping Corps, Japan (ASC)
Southern Army Shipping (SoS)
Southern Army Railway (SRR)
6th Air Division, 18th Army (6AirDiv 18A)
Southern Expeditionary Army (SA)
Tokyo Bay Army (TBC)
Tokyo Defense Army (TDA)
I.M.B. = Independent Mixed Brigade
I.I.G.B. = Independent Infantry Garrison/Guard Battalion
Japan's Army Districts:
North (*Hokubu* 北部) Army District (HoB)
Northeast (*Tohoku* 東北) Army District (ToH)
East (*Tobu* 東部) Army Distinct (ToB)
East Sea (*Tokai* 東海) Army District (ToK)
Central (*Chubu* 中部) Army District (ChB)
Central Country (*Chugoku* 中国) Army District (ChG)
Shikoku (*Shikoku* 四国) Armu District (Shikoku)
West (*Seibu* 西部) Army District (SeB)
Korea (*Chosen* 朝鮮) Divisional District (KoD)
Formosa (*Wan* 湾) Army District (FoD)
Kwantung Army (満州, 満, 徳) also called the *Kantō* Army. Some units have the 2 or 3 digit code #s issued in Manchuria in addition to the standard Tsushogo code. (KA)

Code numbers:
1. DN • Distributed Numbers: An activating unit was assigned a code # from a (DN) block of #'s. **2.** Units listed twice may be detached elements, units that share the same number or a unit converted to another type or joined to another organization but retaining its original number. All **DN •** are listed in both volumes
As war progressed certain independent mixed brigades were converted to divisions. At the time, in some cases, they also received new code names and numbers while retaining their formal names; those units may also be listed twice.
DN • Apr 1945 distribution: From blocks of numbers distributed in April 1945
DN • not distributed: Does **not** mean numbers in this block were not used.

0	1	2	3	4	5	6	7	8	9	10
○	一	二	三	四	五	六	七	八	九	十

Code # - Code Kanji - Formal Unit Name - (Parental Affiliation) - Page No.

152 呂 (拓) 3rd Tank Regiment (11A) - N/A
170 剛 8th Tank Regiment (8AA) - 24
198 満州 85th Air Regiment (13AirDiv 5AirA) - 136
286 成 4th Cavalry Brigade (NCAA) - N/A
318 尚武 10th Temporary Field Duty Company (14AA) - N/A
334 檜 14th Independent Mixed Brigade Headquarters, became 68th Div (11A) - 213
369 満 4th Independent Mountain Artillery Regiment (31A) - 32
394 尚武 1st Temporary Transport Company (14AA) - N/A
405照 14th Division Reconnaissance Regiment (31A) - 170
419 尚武 Shobu Temporary Line of Comms. Veterinary Depot (14AA) - N/A
420 尚武 Shobu Temporary Army Horse Convalescence Depot (14AA) - N/A
595 / 12079 呂 1st Tank Division Anti-Aircraft Unit (11A) - 146
642 栄 2nd Sea Transport Battalion (CA) - N/A
658 / 5058 堅 4th Tank Regiment (19A) - 71
818 満州 / 7793 照 20th Field Artillery Regiment, 14th Div (31A) - 170
DN • 1000-49 Tokyo Divisional District
1005 呂 45th Casualty Clearing Platoon (11A) - 148
1006 猛 46th Casualty Clearing Platoon (18A) - 49
1016 林 18th Field Medium Artillery Regiment (15A) - 101
1024 剛 3rd Independent Heavy Artillery Battalion (8AA) - 25
1026 沖 15th Field Air Defense Headquarters (17A) - 28
1035 森 2nd Field Transport Headquarters (BAA) - 87
1038 備 42nd Independent Motor Transport Battalion, Palau Is. (31A) - 36
DN • 1050-99 東部 *Tobu* Army District
DN • 1050–99, 晴 *Hare*, 1st Anti-Aircraft Division, Apr. 1945 distribution
1068 矛 11th Independent Mixed Brigade Headquarters (13A) - 212
1074 望 12th Independent Mixed Brigade Headquarters, later 64th Div (13A) - 213
DN • 1100-49 薩 *Satsu,* Kumamoto Divisional District
1103 旭 23rd Division Headquarters (14AA) - 175
1111 旭 64th Infantry Regiment, 23rd Div (14AA) - 175
1125-8 旭 23rd Division (14AA) - 175-6
1133 猛 36th Independent Engineer Regiment (18A) - 48
1136 旭 23rd Reconnaissance Regiment, 23rd Div. (14AA) - 175
1152 旭 17th Field Artillery Regiment (23Div 14AA) - 175
1160 威 Southern Expeditionary Army Headquarters (I.G.HQ) - 41
1163-94 旭 23rd Division (14AA) - 175
1194 泉 26th Division Veterinary Unit (14AA) - 176
DN • 1200-99 徳 *Toku,* Kwantung (Kantō) Army
1201 玉 1st Division Disease Pretension and Water Supply Unit (35A) - 163
1202 杉 8th Division Disease Pretension and Water Purification Unit (41A) - 167
1203-9 広 18th Independent Mixed Brigade, became the 58th Division (11A) - 214-5
1213 剛 7th Field Medium Artillery Regiment (8AA) - 24
1218 威 58th Independent Mixed Brigade (14AA) - 227

1220 登 6th Independent Heavy Artillery Battalion (13A) - 131
1223 勢 49th Field Anti-Aircraft Battalion (2A) - 68
1225 猛 25th Field Machine Cannon Company (18A) - 48
1244 備 3rd Signal Regiment Replacement Unit, Babelthuap Is. (31A) - 36
1255 甲 55th Fixed Radio Unit (NCAA) - 153
1256 甲 56th Fixed Radio Unit (13A) - 131
1257 甲 57th Fixed Radio Unit (6AA) - 141
1258 展 58th Fixed Radio Unit (6AA) - 141
1268 栄 13th Independent Railway Battalion (CA) - 129
1269 栄 14th Independent Railway Battalion (CA) - 129
1272 猛 4th Engineer Group Headquarters (2A) - 68
1280 猛 4th Railway Engineer Unit (18A) - N/A
DN • 1300-99 仙 *Sen,* Sendai Divisional District
1301-39 勇 2nd Division (38A) - 164
1301-17 勇 Aoba Detachment, Guadalcanal (17A) - 29
1304 / 5304 戍 23rd Motor Transp. Regt, Zhangjiakou Evac Unit (MGA) - 158/159
1305 勇 2nd Reconnaissance (Cavalry) Regiment, 2nd Division (38A) - 164
1330 勇 2nd Division Infantry Group HQ, Aoba Detachment (17A, 38A) - 29, 164
1352 林 52nd Independent Transport Company (15A) - 101
1353 林 53rd Independent Transport Company (15A) - 101
1357 林 38th Casualty Clearing Platoon (15A) - 101
1362 林 54th Independent Transport Company (15A) - 101
1363 林 55th Independent Transport Company (15A) - 101
1366 栄 72nd (Baoji) Line of Communications Army Hospital (6AA) - 143
1373 勢 13th Field Survey Unit (2A) - 69
1374 昆 22nd Bridging Materials Company (33A) - 96
1380 森 42nd Line of Communications Sector Command (BAA) - 86
1381 森 42nd Line of Communications Guard Unit (BAA) - 86
1382 岡 42nd Line of Communications Duty Company (BAA) - 86
1388 高 35th Independent Motor Transport Battalion (5AirDiv 3AirA) - 57
1393 路 102nd Railway Station Command (SRR) - 61
DN • 1400-99 甲 *Ko*, North China Area Army
1400 甲 North China Area Army, as a Unit (CA) - 153
1401 甲 North China Chinese Language Education Unit (NCAA) - N/A
1402 仁 169th Line of Communications (Zhengzhou) Hospital (12A) - 157
1403 甲 188th Line of Communications Hospital (NCAA) - 154
1404 甲 North China War Dog Training Compound (NCAA) - N/A
1405 甲 North China Pigeon Training Office (NCAA) - N/A
1407 甲 North China Area Army Prison (NCAA) - N/A
1408 沖 12th Tank Regiment (17A) - 28
1409 甲 15th Anti-Aircraft Regiment (NCAA) - 153
1410 桜 5th Signal Regiment (20A) - 149
1411 栄 11th Armored Train Unit (CA) - 129
1412 栄 7th Independent Armored Train Company - 129
1413 仁 189th Line of Communications Hospital (12A) - 157
1414-20 甲 North China Special Garrison Unit (NCAA) - 246
1418-24 望 12th Independent Mixed Brigade (13A) - 213

0	1	2	3	4	5	6	7	8	9	10
〇	一	二	三	四	五	六	七	八	九	十

1422-5 幹 1st Independent Infantry Brigade (43A) - 235
1430 栄 2nd Field Railway Headquarters (CA) - 129
1435-40 檜 14th Independent Mixed Brigade, became 68th Div (20A) - 213
1435 栄 6th Railway Regiment (CA) - 129
1436-8 幹 1st Independent Infantry Brigade (43A) - 236
1439 曙 2nd Independent Infantry Brigade, brigade number, not a unit (NCAA) - 236
DN • 1440-5 甲 *Ko*, not used - North China Area Army
DN •1446 甲 *Ko*, not used - North China Area Army
1450 滝 17th Tank Regiment, 3rd Armored Div (12A) - 206
1453-8 曙 2nd Independent Infantry Brigade (NCAA) - 236
1459-65 将 114th Division (1A) - 200
1469 輝 47th Field Machine Cannon Company (2AA) - 64
1472-8 塁 14th Independent Infantry Brigade (1A) - 239-40
1480-83 甲 North China Special Garrison Unit (NCAA) - 246
1485 仁 1st Independent Mountain Artillery Battalion (12A) - 157
1486 甲 40th Independent Engineer Regiment (NCAA) - 153
1487 甲 1st Specially Established Engineer Company (NCAA) - 153
1493 固 10th Independent Infantry Brigade, bgde number not a unit (1A) - 238
1498 勝 69th Division Machine Cannon Unit (13A) - 194
DN • 1500-99 澤 *Sawa*, Kanazawa Divisional District
1502 沖 4th Field Medium Artillery Regiment, Guadalcanal (17A) - 29
DN • 1600-99 Not Distributed
1600 尚武 14th Area Army Headquarters (SA) - 107
1600-1 尚武 14th Area Army General Staff Department (14AA) - 107
1600-2 尚武 14th Area Army Adjutant Department (14AA) - 107
1600-3 尚武 14th Area Army Ordinance Department (14AA) − 107
1600-4 尚武 14th Area Army Intendance Department (14AA) - 107
1600-4 威 7th Specially Established Field Airfield Construction Unit (4AirA) - 121
1600-4 威 11th Specially Established Field Airfield Construction Unit (4AirA) - 121
1600-4 威 14th Specially Est. Field Airfield Construction Unit (4AirA) - 121
1600-4 威 15th Specially Established Field Airfield Construction Unit (4AirA) - 122
1600-5 尚武 14th Area Army Physician Department (14AA) - 107
1600-6 尚武 14th Area Army Veterinary Department (14AA) - 107
1600-7 尚武 14th Area Army Legal Department (14AA) - 107
1600-8 尚武 14th Area Army Intelligence Department (14AA) - 107
1600-9 尚武 14th Area Army Records Office (14AA) - 107
1600-10 尚武 14th Area Army Telegraph Office (14AA) - 107
1600-12 尚武 14th Area Army Special Intelligence Department (14AA) - 107
1600-13 尚武 14th Area Army Medical Department (14AA) - 107
1600-15 尚武 14th Area Army Music Department (14AA) - 107
1600-18 尚武 14th Area Army Government Affairs Department (14AA) - 107
1600-19 尚武 14th Area Army Management Department (14AA) - 107
1600-20 尚武 14th Area Army Press Department (14AA) - 107
1600-22 尚武 14th Area Army Electrical Department (14AA) - 107

1600-23 尚武 14th Area Army General Administration Department (14AA) - 107
1600-24 尚武 14th Area Army Broadcasting Administration Bureau (14AA) - 107
1601 威 Southern Army Headquarters Staff (14AA, SA) - 41
1602 治 16th Army Headquarters (7AA) - 76
1611 林 15th Army Headquarters (18AA) - 100
1615 岡 7th Area Army Headquarters (SA) - 74
1624 治 28th Motor Transport Regiment (16A) - 76
1625 登 50th Line of Communications Guard (13A) - 131
1626 栄 Central China Horse Remount Depot (CA) - 128
1627 栄 Central China Field Ordinance Depot (CA) - 128
1627 登 Central China Field Ordinance Depot (13A) - 132
1628 登 Central China Field Motor Vehicle Depot (13A) - 132
1629 登 Central China Field Freight Depot (13A) - 132
1630 登 156th Line of Communications (Nanking 1st Army) Hospital (13A) - 132
1631 登 157th Line of Communications (Shanghai 1st Army) Hospital (13A) - 132
1632 登 170th Line of Communications Hospital (13A) - 132
1634 登 172nd Line of Communications (Nanking 2nd Army) Hospital (13A) - 132
1635 栄 171st Line of Communications (Hangzhou Army) Hospital (6A) - 133
1636 登 176th Line of Communications (Zhenjiang Army) Hospital (13A) - 132
1637 専 190th Line of Comms. (Bengbu Specialty Army) Hospital (13A) - 132
1638 登 175th Line of Communications (Shanghai 2nd Army) Hospital (13A) - 132
1639 統 158th Line of Communications (Hankou 1st Army) Hospital (6AA) - 143
1640 統 178th Line of Communications (Hankou 2nd Army) Hospital (6AA) - 143
1641 栄 159th Line of Communications (Wuhan Army) Hospital (6AA) - 143
1642 統 177th Line of Communications (Jiujiang Army) Hospital (6AA) - 143
1643 栄 Central China Horse Quarantine Depot (CA) - 128
1644 栄 Central China Disease Prevention and Water Supply Unit (CA) - 128
1645 栄 Central China Cadet Unit (CA) - 128
1646 栄 Central China NCO Quartermaster Cadet Unit (CA) - 128
1647 栄 Central China NCO Medic Cadet Unit (CA) - 128
1648 栄 Central China NCO Veterinary Cadet Unit (CA) - 128
1649 栄 Baoding Cadet Unit (CA) - 128
1650 登 191st Line of Communications (Jinhua) Hospital (6A) - 133
1651/16151 登 174th Line of Communications (Xuzhou) Hospital (13A) - 132
1653 嵐 120th Cavalry Regiment, 116th Division (20A) - 201
DN • 1700-99 湾 *Wan*, Formosa (Taiwan) Army
1741 暁 56th Anchorage Headquarters (SS) - 59
1742 尚武 63rd Independent Motor Transport Battalion (14AA) - 109
1745 灘 307th Independent Motor Transport Company (16A) - 76
1747 襲 123rd Land Duty Company (7AirDiv 3AirA) - 58
1748 威 124th Land Duty Company (14AA) - 109
1749 波 60th Sea Duty Company (23A) - 138
1750 暁 11th Shipping Engineer Regiment (SS) - 59
1751 猛 40th Independent Field Anti Aircraft Company (18A) - 49
1752 猛 41st Independent Field Anti-Aircraft Company (18A) - 48
1753 猛 4th Independent Field Searchlight Company (18A) - 48
1768 波 111th Specially Established Sea Duty Company (23A) - 138

0	1	2	3	4	5	6	7	8	9	10
〇	一	二	三	四	五	六	七	八	九	十

1775 勢 104th Specially Established Construction Duty Company (2A) - 69
1781 勢 1st Raiding Company (2A) - 67
1782 勢 2nd Raiding Company (2A) - 67
1790 鎧 61st Independent Mixed Brigade (14AA) - 228
DN • 1800-99 甲 *Ko*, North China Area Army
1800 甲 North China Area Army Headquarters (NCAA) - 153
1801 甲 North China Field Horse Remount Depot (NCAA) - 154
1809 甲 North China Field Ordinance Depot (NCAA) - 154
1813 甲 North China Field Motor Vehicle Depot (NCAA) - 154
1813 甲 1st North China Field Motor Vehicle Repair Unit (NCAA) - 154
1815 甲 3rd North China Field Motor Vehicle Repair Unit (NCAA) - 154
1819 甲 North China Field Freight Depot (NCAA) - 154
1820 甲 North China Field Freight Depot Headquarters (NCAA) - N/A
1821 甲 North China Field Freight Beijing Branch Depot (NCAA) - N/A
1822 甲 North China Field Freight Shimen Branch Depot (NCAA) - N/A
1823 甲 North China Field Freight Daito Branch Depot (NCAA) - N/A
1824 乙 North China Field Freight Depot, Teigen Branch (1A) - 156
1825 仁 North China Field Freight Depot, Sairen Branch (12A) - 157
1826 栄 4th Railway Department (CA) - 129
1827 甲 151st Line of Communications (Beijing 1st) Hospital (NCAA) - 153
1828 甲 152nd Line of Communications (Beijing 2nd) Hospital (NCAA) - 154
1829 甲 153rd Line of Communications (Tianjin) Hospital (NCAA) - 154
1830 甲 154th Line of Communications (Beidaihe) Hospital (NCAA) - 154
1831 甲 187th Line of Communications (Baoding) Hospital (NCAA) - 154
1832 甲 161st Line of Communications (Shimen) Hospital (NCAA) - 154
1833 乙 195th Line of Communications (Yangquan) Hospital (1A) - 156
1834 仁 168th Line of Communications (Xinxiang) Hospital (12A) - 157
1835 乙 162nd Line of Communications (Taiyuan) Hospital (1A) - 156
1836 乙 196th Line of Communications Hospital (1A) - 156
1837 乙 194th Line of Communications (Changzhi) Hospital (1A) - 156
1838 乙 163rd Line of Communications (Linfen) Hospital (1A) - 156
1839 乙 164th Line of Communications (Liancheng) Hospital (1A) - 156
1840 秀嶺 165th Line of Communications (Qingdao) Hospital (43A) - 158
1841 秀嶺 155th Line of Communications (Jinan) Hospital (43A) - 158
1842 秀嶺 197th Line of Communications (Yanzhou) Hospital (43A) - 158
1844 戊 199th Line of Communications (Pingdiquanzhen) Hospital (MGA) - 158/160
1845 仁 186th Line of Communications (Kaifeng) Hospital (12A) - 157
1846 戊 166th Line of Communications (Zhangjiakou) Hospital (MGA) - 158/160
1847 戊 167th Line of Communications (Datong) Hospital (MGA) - 158/160
1848 戊 198th Line of Communications (Baotou) Hospital (MGA) - 158/160
1849 甲 1st (Inland) Water Transport Unit (NCAA) - 153
1855 甲 North China Disease Prevention and Water Supply Unit (NCAA) - 154
1861 甲 North China Veterinary Quarantine Depot (NCAA) - 154
1866 登 41st Independent Rapid Firing Gun Company (13A) - 131

1867 登 42nd Independent Rapid Firing Gun Company (13A) - 131
1868 仁 43rd Independent Rapid Firing Gun Company (12A) - 157
1869 甲 North China Signal Training Unit (NCAA) - 153
1870 甲 North China NCO Officer Candidate Department (NCAA) - 153
1871 甲 N. China NCO Officer Candidate Intendance Training D. (NCAA) - 153
1872 甲 N. China NCO Officer Candidate Medical Training Dept (NCAA) - 153
1873 甲 N. China NCO Officer Candidate Veterinary Training D. (NCAA) - 153
1874 甲 44th Independent Rapid Firing Gun Company (NCAA) - 153
1875 甲 21st Motor Transport Regiment (NCAA) - 153
1876 統 22nd Motor Transport Regiment (6AA) - 142
1877 呂 36th Motor Transport Regiment (11A) - 147
1878 甲 North China Well Drilling Unit (NCAA) - 153
1878 甲 6th Well Drilling Group; Sub Unit (NCAA) - 153
1879 甲 5th Division 4th Land Transport Unit (NCAA) - 153
1881 守 29th Independent Field Artillery Battalion (6A) - 133
1887 甲 North China Decontamination Department (NCAA) - 154
1888 秀嶺 45th Independent Rapid Firing Gun Company (43A) - 158
1890 乙 24th Independent Mountain Artillery Battalion (1A) - 156
1891 島 1st Independent Mixed Brigade Engineer Unit (NCAA) - 209
1892 猛 37th Independent Engineer Regiment (18A) - 48
1895 秀嶺 21st Motor Transport Regiment (43A) - 158
1896 治 15th Signal Regiment (16A) - 76
1897 尚武 22nd Field Ordinance Depot (14A) - N/A
1897 尚武 14th Area Army Field Ordinance Depot (14AA) - 109
1898 尚武 22nd Field Motor Transport Depot (14A) - N/A
1899 尚武 22nd Field Freight Depot (14A) - N/A
DN • 1900-99 東部 *Tobu* Army District
1921 勢 5th Field Military Police Unit (2A) - 70
1922 剛 6th Field Military Police Unit (8AA) - 25
1929 猛 61st Field Anti-Aircraft Battalion (18A) - 47
1930 猛 62nd Field Anti-Aircraft Battalion (18A) - 47
1931 猛 63rd Field Anti-Aircraft Battalion (18A) - 47
1932 猛 7th Independent Field Searchlight Company (18A) - 48
1933 猛 8th Independent Field Searchlight Company (18A) - 48
1934 森 92nd Independent Wire Company (BAA) - 86
1938 備 3rd South Seas Guard Unit (31A) - 36
1940 波 59th Independent Engineer Battalion (23A) - 135
1941 登 60th Independent Engineer Battalion (13A) - 131
1942 呂 61st Independent Engineer Battalion (11A) - 146
1943 猛 32nd Field Machine Cannon Company (18A) - 48
1944 猛 33rd Field Machine Cannon Company (18A) - 48
1945 猛 34th Field Machine Cannon Company (18A) - 48
1946 森 71st Independent Radio Platoon (BAA) - 86
1947 森 72nd Independent Radio Platoon (BAA) - 86
1948 森 73rd Independent Radio Platoon (BAA) - 86
1949 翔 101st Machine Cannon Btn. (Palembang Guards Brigade 3AirA) - 250
1957 岡 94th Field Anti-Aircraft Battalion, Singapore Defense Unit (7AA) - 251

0	1	2	3	4	5	6	7	8	9	10
〇	一	二	三	四	五	六	七	八	九	十

DN • 1960-69 not used *Tobu* Army District
DN • 1960 – 1969 東部 *Tobu* Army District, not distributed
1970 尚 76th Field Anti-Aircraft Battalion, minus 1st & 2nd Coy.s (35A) - 112
1970 威 76th Field Anti-Aircraft Battalion, 1st & 2nd Coy.s Camotes (14AA) - 109
DN • 1972 – 1984 東部 *Tobu* Army District, not distributed
DN • 1986 – 1989 東部 *Tobu* Army District, not distributed
1995 剛 15th Field Machine Cannon Company (8AA) - 24
1995 猛 15th Field Machine Cannon Company (18A) - 48
1996 猛 2nd Independent Field Searchlight Company (18A) - 48
1997 – 1st Anti-Aircraft Field Training Unit (Unknown) - N/A
1998 勢 68th Field Anti-Aircraft Battalion (2A) - 68
1999 輝 69th Field Anti-Aircraft Battalion, att. 32nd Div. (2AA) - 64
DN • 2000-99 Imperial Palace District
2001 剛 48th Field Anti-Aircraft Battalion (8AA) - 24
2001 岡 48th Field Anti Aircraft Battalion, Singapore Defense Unit (7AA) - 250
2002 and 7464 猛 20th Field Machine Cannon Company (18A) - 48
2031-6 倭 13th Independent Mixed Brigade (13A) - 213
2039/2309 広 58th Division Veterinary Unit, 58th Div (11A) - 190
2047-53 勝 16th Independent Mixed Brigade (1A) - 214
2051-67 朝 20th Division (18A) - 173-4
2086 朝 20th Division's number, not a unit (18A) - 173
2100 昆 44th Field Machine Cannon Company, Saipan (31A) - 35
2101 備 15th Fortress Engineer Unit, Ogasawara Group, Chichi Jima (31A) - N/A
2130 輝 1st Field Base Unit Headquarters (2AA) - 64
2131 and 4672 柏 52nd Division Tank Unit, Truk District (31A) - 187
2131 輝 43rd Independent Field Anti Aircraft Company (2A) - 68
2132 輝 44th Independent Field Anti Aircraft Company (2A) - 68
2133 輝 45th Independent Field Anti Aircraft Company (2A) - 68
2134 輝 46th Independent Field Anti Aircraft Company (2AA) - 64
2135 輝 47th Independent Field Anti Aircraft Company (2AA) - 64
2136 輝 10th Independent Field Searchlight Company (2A) - 68
2137 輝 11th Independent Field Searchlight Company (2AA) - 64
2138 盤 Bhutan Guards Headquarters, Bhutan (3AirA) - 249
2139 翔 102nd Machine Cannon Battalion, Bhutan (3AirA) - 249
2140 盤 Bhutan Guards Unit, Bhutan (3AirA) - 249
2141 勢 1st Raiding Column Headquarters (2A) - 67
2142 勢 7th Raiding Company (2A) - 67
2143 路 7th Railway Regiment (SRR) - 61
2144 尚武 8th Railway Regiment (14AA) - 109
2145 路 10th Railway Regiment (SRR) - 61
2146 路 11th Railway Regiment (SRR) - 61
2147 統 12th Railway Regiment (6AA) - 143
2148 栄 14th Railway Regiment (CA) - 129
2149 路 15th Railway Regiment, central China (CA) - 143

2149 波 15th Railway Regiment, 1st Battalion (23A) - 135
2150 栄 1st Independent Railway Bridge Construction Battalion (CA) - 129
2151 栄 1st Independent Railway Engineer Battalion (CA) - 129
2152 路 2nd Independent Railway Engineer Battalion (CA) - 143
2152 甲 18th Railway Regiment (CA) - 154
2153 統 2nd Independent Railway Engineer Labor Unit (6AA) - 143
2154 統 28th Signal Regiment (6AA) - 141
2155 統 59th Fixed Wireless Radio Unit (6AA) - 141
2156 呂 309th Independent Motor Transport Company (11A) - 147
2157 統 310th Independent Motor Transport Company (6AA) - 142
2158 統 53rd Field Road Construction Unit (6AA) - 142
2159 呂 54th Field Road Construction Unit (11A) - 148
2170 呂 77th Casualty Clearing Platoon (11A) - 148
2171 威 1st Signal Unit Headquarters (SA) - 41
2171 威 1st Signal Unit Headquarters, detached section (35A) - 113
2174 至純 89th Independent Mixed Brigade (6A) - 233
2178 駿 53rd Field Machine Cannon Company, att. 103rd Div (14AA) - 107
2179 駿 54th Field Machine Cannon Company, att. 103rd Div (14AA) - 107
2180 尚武 55th Field Machine Cannon Company (14AA) - 108
2185 備 43rd Specially Established Machine Cannon Unit, Iwo Jima (31A) - 33
2186 備 44th Specially Established Machine Cannon Unit, Iwo Jima (31A) - 33
2187 備 45th Specially Established Machine Cannon Unit (31A) - 34
2188 備 46th Specially Established Machine Cannon Unit (31A) - 34
2189 甲 86th Field Anti-Aircraft Battalion (NCAA) - 153
2190 威 89th Field Anti-Aircraft Regiment, att. 23rd Div (14AA) - 106
2191 昭 57th Specially Established Machine Cannon Unit (9AirDiv 3AirA) - 250
2192 翔 58th Specially Established Machine Cannon Unit (9AirDiv 3AirA) - 250
2193 尚武 63rd Specially Est. Machine Cannon Unit, Camotes Is. (14AA) - 110
2194 尚武 64th Specially Established Machine Cannon Unit (14AA) - 108
2195 尚武 65th Specially Est. Machine Cannon Unit, Camotes Is. (14AA) - 110
2196 尚武 66th Specially Est. Machine Cannon Unit, Camotes Is. (14AA) - 110
2197 尚武 67th Specially Est. Machine Cannon Unit, Camotes Is. (14AA) - 110
DN • 2200-99 松 *Mutu*, Asahikawa Divisional District
2209 森 68th Casualty Clearing Platoon (BAA) - 88
2265 昆 121st Line of Communications Hospital (33A) - 96
2267 倭 13th Independent Mixed Brigade Headquarters (13A) - 212
2298 剛 16th Line of Communications Veterinary Depot (8AA) - 25
DN • 2300-49 栄 *Sakae*, China Expeditionary Army
2304-09 広 58th Division (11A) - 190-1
2310 勢 10th Field Military Police Unit (2A) - 70
2317-22 矛 11th Independent Mixed Brigade, became the 60th Div (13A) - 212
2315-26 矛 60th Division (13A) - 191
2327-38 檜 68th Division (20A) - 193
2339-49 槍 70th Division (6A) - 194
DN • 2350-60 甲 *Ko*, North China Area Army
2355-9 勝 69th Division (13A) - 194
DN • 2361-99 Not Distributed

0	1	2	3	4	5	6	7	8	9	10
〇	一	二	三	四	五	六	七	八	九	十

2373 隼魁 1st Air Brigade Headquarters (13AirDiv 5AirA) - 136
2376 隼魁 44th Air Regiment, 1 squadron (13AirDiv 5AirA) - 136
2379 燕 75th Air Regiment (4AirA) - 120
2380 隼 81st Air Regiment, Indochina (5AirDiv 3AirA) - 56
2381 隼魁 90th Air Regiment (13AirDiv 5AirA) - 136
2383 隼魁 82nd Air Regiment (13AirDiv 5AirA) - 136
2387 隼魁 25th Air Regiment (13AirDiv 5AirA) - 136
2398 剛 26th Airfield Company (6AirDiv, 18A) - 50
DN • 2400-99 四國 *Shikoku* Army District
2400 勢 4th Field Airfield Construction Headquarters (2A) - 70
2401 威 3rd Field Airfield Construction Headquarters (4AirA) - 122
2401 威 5th Field Airfield Construction Headquarters (4AirA) - 121
2401 威 1st Specially Established Field Airfield Construction Unit (4AirA) - 122
2401 威 4th Specially Established Field Airfield Construction Unit (4AirA) - 121
2401 威 5th Specially Established Field Airfield Construction Unit (4AirA) - 121
2401 威 9th Specially Established Field Airfield Construction Unit (4AirA) - 121
2401 威 10th Specially Established Field Airfield Construction Unit (4AirA) - 121
2401 威 12th Specially Established Field Airfield Construction Unit (4AirA) - 121
2401 威 13th Specially Established Field Airfield Construction Unit (4AirA) - 121
2403-7 槍 20th Independent Mixed Brigade, became 70th Div (11A) - 215
2403 杉 22nd Field Airfield Construction Unit (41A) - 115
2404 備 23rd Field Airfield Construction Unit, Saipan, *evidence for both* (31A) - 35
2404 備 23rd Field Airfield Construction Unit, Babelthuap Is. (31A) - 36
2405 威 24th Field Airfield Construction Unit (KeG 14AA and 4AirA) - 117, 121
2487 操 625th Independent Infantry Battalion, 62nd I.M.B. (6A) - 228
2503 剛 8th Shipping Engineer Regiment (8AA) - 25
2509 栄 9th Field Replacement Unit (CA) - 129
2527 尚武 27th Signal Regiment (14AA) - 108
2527 威 27th Signal Regiment, 1 section, Comotes Detach. (14AA) - 110
2530 栄 13th Railway Regiment (CA) - 129
2531 栄 2nd Bridge Construction Battalion (CA) - 129
2532 栄 2nd Independent Railway Engineer Battalion (CA) - 129
2533 統 3rd Independent Railway Engineer Labor Unit (6AA) - 143
2534 路 4th Railway Materials Depot, central China (CA) - 143
2535 栄 China Expeditionary Army Field Railway Depot (CA) - 128
2542 勢 92nd Independent Radio Platoon (2A) - 67
2543 呂 93rd Independent Radio Platoon (11A) - 147
2545 呂 95th Independent Radio Platoon (11A) - 147
2546 波 96th Independent Radio Platoon (23A) - 135
2547 波 97th Independent Radio Platoon (11A) - 147
DN • 2550-99 Not Distributed
2554 備 1st Engineer Regiment 3rd Company – detached (31A) - N/A
2558-60 教 35th Independent Mixed Brigade (29A) - 221
2561-4 練 36th Independent Mixed Brigade (29A) - 221

2565-8 鍛 37th Independent Mixed Brigade (29A) - 222
2570 威 2nd Air Signal Headquarters (4AirA) - 117, 122
2572 威 2nd Air Navigation Unit (4AirA) - 122
DN • 2600-99 徳 *Toku*, Kwantung (Kantō) Army
2624 呂 21st Field Disease Prevention and Water Supply Dept. (11A) - 148
2625 森 22nd Field Disease Prevention and Water Supply Dept. (BAA) - 88
2626 備 23rd Field Disease Prevention and Water Supply Dept. Palau Is. (31A) - 36
2626 猛 23rd Field Disease Prevention and Water Supply Dept., 1 section (18A) - 50
2627 剛 24th Field Disease Prevention and Water Supply Dept. (8AA) - 25
2627 富 24th Field Disease Prev. and Water Supply Dept., 1 section (25A) - 81
2628 猛 25th Field Disease Prevention and Water Supply Dept. (18A) - 50
2633 呂 16th Field Ordnance Depot, 2nd Mobile Repair Section (11A) - 146
2633 甲 16th Army Ordinance Depot, 1st Mobile Repair Section (NCAA) - N/A
2634 呂 17th Field Ordnance Depot, 1st Mobile Repair Section (11A) - 146
2636 栄 19th Field Ordinance Depot Mobile Duty Section (CA) - 128
2638 呂 16th Field Motor Vehicle Depot, 1st Mobile Repair Section (11A) - 146
2639 呂 17th Field Motor Vehicle Depot, 1st Mobile Repair Section (11A) - 146
2641 栄 19th Field Motor Vehicle Depot, Duty Section (CA) - 129
2641 波 19th Field Motor Vehicle Depot 1st Mobile Repair Squad (23A) - 136
2643 呂 16th Field Freight Depot, 2nd Mobile Clothing Repair Section (11A) - 146
2680 定 1st Independent Field Artillery Battalion (29A) - 83
2686 備 25th Anti-Aircraft Regiment, Saipan (31A) - 35
2688 猛 27th Field Ordinance Depot (18A) - 49
2689 猛 27th Field Freight Depot (18A) - 49
2690 猛 27th Field Motor Transport Depot (18A) - 49
DN • 2700-99 西部 *Seibu* Army District
2773 備 5th Fortification Construction Duty Company, Iwo Jima (31A) - 33
DN • 2800-99 丸 *Maru*, Utsunomiya Divisional District
2800-33 基 51st Division (18A) - 186-7
2810 51st Transport Regiment, Lorengau Def. Unit, Manus Island (17A) - 30
2854 剛 38th Independent Motor Transport Battalion (8AA) - 25
2857 栄 220th Independent Motor Transport Company (CA) - 129
2861 定 224th Independent Motor Transport Company (29A) - 83
2862 猛 225th Independent Motor Transport Company (18A) - 48
2863 森 226th Independent Motor Transport Company (BAA) - 87
2864 勢 227th Independent Motor Transport Company (2A) - 69
2865 勢 228th Independent Motor Transport Company (2A) - 69
2866 勢 229th Independent Motor Transport Company (2A) - 69
2875 肝 8th Independent Infantry Brigade (23A) - 238
2894 暁 17th Sea Raiding Base Battalion (14AA) - 124
DN • 2900-99 甲 *Ko*, North China Area Army
2900-19 極 27th Division (CA) - 176-7
2920-35 東 35th Division (2A) - 180
2941 栄 2nd Shipping Transport Headquarters (CA) - 138
2944 威 3rd Shipping Transport Headquarters, Palau Branch (SoS) - 37
2944 暁 3rd Shipping Transport Headquarters, Manila Branch (14AA) - 123
2944 暁 Underwater Transport Dispatch Unit (14AA) - 123

0	1	2	3	4	5	6	7	8	9	10
○	一	二	三	四	五	六	七	八	九	十

2945 暁 12th Shipping Group Headquarters (CA) - 138
2946 猛 1st Debarkation Unit (18A) - 50
2947 沖 2nd Shipping Debarkation Unit (17A) - 28
2948 猛 3rd Debarkation Unit (18A) - 50
2949 暁 2nd Field Shipping Depot (SoS) - N/A
2954 暁 2nd Shipping Artillery Regiment (14AA) - 123
2955 暁 Shipping Signal Regiment (SoS) - 59
2955 暁 Shipping Signal Regiment, 1 Section (14AA) - 123
2957 暁 101st Sea Duty Unit (CA) - 138
2958 剛 12th Shipping Engineer Regiment (8AA) - 25
2961-69 島 1st Independent Mixed Brigade (NCAA) - 209
2968 桜 38th Independent Engineer Regiment (20A) - 149
2929 東 219th Infantry Regiment, 1st Battalion 35th Div., Sonsorol Is. (31A) - 37
2970-9 北 7th Independent Mixed Brigade, became the 115th Div (12A) - 211
2970-9 北 115th Division (12A) - 201
2980-9 春 8th Independent Mixed Brigade (NCAA) - 211
2991-6 冑 15th Independent Mixed Brigade (NCAA) - 213-4
DN • 3000-99 *Yō*, Tokyo Divisional District
3004 富 235th Independent Motor Transport Company (25A) - 80
3005 策 236th Independent Motor Transport Company, Saku Group (28A) - 91,92
3006 昆 237th Independent Motor Transport Company (33A) - 96
3007 林 102nd Independent Motor Transport Battalion (15A) - 101
3015 剛 14th Line of Communications Medical Unit Headquarters (8AA) - 25
3025 登 36th Sea Duty Company (13A) - 132
3026 猛 37th Sea Duty Company, Hollandia (18A) - 50
3029 司 43rd Construction Duty Company (7AirDiv 3AirA) - 58
3030 高 80th Land Duty Company (5AirDiv 3AirA) - 57
3031 猛 81st Land Duty Company (18A) - 49
3032 波 82nd Land Duty Company (23A) - 136
3035 剛 14th Field Post Office Unit (8AA) - 25
3060-69 鶏 61st Division (13A) - 191-2
DN • 3100-99 徳 *Toku*, Kwantung (Kantō) Army
3130-9 駆 1st Amphibious Brigade (31A) - 241
3141 固 10th Independent Infantry Brigade (1A) - 237
3147 波 7th Independent Field Artillery Battalion (23A) - 135
3148 昆 8th Independent Field Artillery Battalion (33A) - 96
3149 登 9th Independent Field Artillery Battalion (13A) - 131
3170 勢 2nd Disease Prevention and Water Supply Unit (2A) - 70
3170 輝 100th Independent Wire Company (2A) - 67 (both are unit 3170)
3172 波 102nd Independent Wire Company (11A) - 147
3173 甲 103rd Independent Wire Company (NCAA) - 153
3177 尚武 96th Independent Wire Company, (KeG) - 117
3178 森 83rd Independent Radio Platoon (BAA) - 86
3180-9 巡 2nd Amphibious Brigade (2AA) - 242

3199 森 84th Independent Radio Platoon (BAA) - 86
DN • 3200-99 張 "Hari" Nagoya Divisional District
3200-99 雷 29th Division (31A) - 177
3215 雷 50th Infantry Regiment, 29th Division, Tinian Is. (31A) - 35
3215 雷 50th Infantry Regiment Replacement Unit, 29th Div., Saipan (31A) - 35
3205 雷 29th Division Field Hospital, 29th Division, Tinian Is. (31A) - 35
3219 雷 18th Infantry Regiment, 1st Battalion, 29th Div Saipan (31A) - 35
3264 / 4364 雷 29th Division Tank Unit, 29th Div (31A) - 177
DN • 3300-99 仙 *Sen*, Sendai Divisional District
3300 剛 31st Sea Duty Company, Lorengau Manus Island (8AA) - 30
3305 高 67th Land Duty Company (5AirDiv 3AirA) - 57
3306 司 68th Land Duty Company (5AirDiv 3AirA) - 57
3307 襲 69th Land Duty Company (7AirDiv 3AirA) - 58
3321-2 肝 8th Independent Infantry Brigade (23A) - 238
3324 灘 20th Independent Machine Gun Battalion (37A) - 78
3327 威 25th Independent Rapid Firing Gun Battalion, Camotes (14AA) - 109
3328 暁 14th Sea Raiding Base Battalion (14AA) - 123
3329 暁 15th Sea Raiding Base Battalion (14AA) - 123
3330 暁 16th Sea Raiding Base Battalion (14AA) - 123
DN • 3400-99 薩 *Satsu*, Kumamoto Divisional District
3476 山 89th Infantry Regiment, 3rd Battalion, 24th Div. Saipan (31stA) - 35
DN • 3500-49 甲 "Ko" North China Area Army
3500 乙 1st Army Headquarters (NCAA) - 156
3501 乙 1st Army (NCAA) - 156
3502 滝 3rd Tank Division, Air Defense Unit 1st and 3rd Coys (23A) − 135
3503 勢 5th Trench Mortar Battalion (2A) - 68
3504 仁 6th Field Medium Artillery Regiment (12A) - 157
3505 高 20th Anti-Aircraft Regiment (5AirDiv 3AirA) - 57
3506 乙 9th Signal Regiment (1A) - 156
3507 統 24th Motor Transport Regiment (6AA) - 142
3508 乙 27th Motor Transport Regiment (1A) - 156
3509 統 37th Motor Transport Regiment (6AA) - 142
3510 乙 1st Independent Transport Regiment (1A) - 156
DN • 3511-19 乙 *Otsu*, 1st Army, not used
3520-32 雪 36th Division (2A) - 181
DN • 3536-9 雪 36th Division, not used
3540-54 冬 37th Division (38A) - 181
DN • 3550-75 丸 *Maru*, Utsunomiya Divisional District
3560-76 河 41st Division (18A) - 183
DN • 3576-99 Not Distributed
DN • 3577-79 石 62nd Division, not used
3581-9 造 3rd Independent Mixed Brigade (1A) - 209
3590-6 石 4th Independent Mixed Brigade, became the 62nd Div (1A) - 210
DN • 3600-99 徳 *Toku*, Kwantung (Kantō) Army
3605 猛 48th Field Road Construction Unit (18A) - 49
3616 剛 50th Field Anti-Aircraft Battalion, less 1st Coy (8AA) - 24
3616 猛 50th Field Anti-Aircraft Battalion, 1st Company (18A) - 47

0	1	2	3	4	5	6	7	8	9	10
〇	一	二	三	四	五	六	七	八	九	十

3617 沖 23rd Field Machine Cannon Company (17A) - 28
3621 波 55th Field Anti-Aircraft Battalion (23A) - 135
3626 威 6th Field Transport Command (14AA) - 109
3627 沖 22nd Field Machine Cannon Company (17A) - 28
3629 森 51st Field Anti-Aircraft Battalion, Rangoon Defense Unit (BAA) - 250
3637 威 2nd Field Searchlight Battalion, attached 105th Div (14AA) - 107
3658 統 108th Specially Established Construction Duty Company (6AA) - 143
3666 剛 1st Independent Trench Mortar Regiment (8AA) - 24
DN • 3700-99 張 *Hari*, Nagoya Divisional District
3701-41 幸 3rd Division (CA) - 165
3751 策 51st Independent Transport Battalion, Saku Group (28A) - 91, 92
3756 猛 48th Casualty Clearing Platoon (18A) - 49
3762 杉 86th Line of Communications Hospital (41A) - 114
3766 林 3rd Field Medium Artillery Regiment (15A) - 101
3766 堅 3rd Field Medium Artillery Regiment, 2nd Battalion (19A) - 71
3770 威 12th Field Medium Artillery Regiment, att. 23rd Div (14AA) - 108
3777 沖 38th Field Anti-Aircraft Battalion, Guadalcanal (17A) - 29
3778 剛 39th Field Anti-Aircraft Battalion (8AA) - 24
3785 沖 31st Independent Field Anti-Aircraft Company (17A) - 28
3786 林 4th Independent Engineer Regiment (BAA) - 86
3790 策 26th Bridging Materials Company (28A) - 91
3795 猛 33rd Independent Engineer Regiment (18A) - 48
3801-17 宮 2nd Guards Division (25A) - 163
3850 林 1st Independent Rapid Firing Gun Battalion (15A) - 100
3851-4 矛 60th Division (13A) - 191
3855 備 8th Independent Rapid Firing Gun Battalion, Iwo Jima (31A) - 33
3856 備 9th Independent Rapid Firing Gun Battalion, Iwo Jima (31A) - 33
3861 呂 81st Line of Communications Sector Command (11A) - 146
3861 呂 81st Line of Communications Duty Company (11A) - 146
3861 呂 81st Line of Communications Guard Unit (11A) - 146
3882 輝 32nd Field Anti-Aircraft Battalion (2A) - 68
3885 勢 125th Line of Communications Hospital (2A) - 69
3886 勢 126th Line of Communications Hospital (2A) - 69
3887 統 127th Line of Communications Hospital (6AA) - 143
3888 統 128th Line of Communications Hospital (6AA) - 143
3889 威 129th Line of Communications Hospital (14AA) - 109
3893 森 33rd Field Anti-Aircraft Battalion, Rangoon Defense Unit (BAA) - 250
3895 森 35th Field Anti-Aircraft Battalion, Rangoon Defense Unit (BAA) - 250
3896 定 21st Independent Field Anti-Aircraft Company (29A) - 83
DN • 3900-99 Nagano District
3905-20 鷲 110th Division (12A) - 199-200
3921-52 鷲 110th Division, not used
3914 登 2nd Independent Field Artillery Regiment (13A) - 131
3959 勢 44th Field Anti-Aircraft Battalion (2A) - 68

3964 森 15th River Crossing Materials Company (BAA) - 86
3965 胆 52nd Line of Communications Sector Command (31A, 2A) - 36, 69
3966 猛 57th Line of Communications Guard Unit (18A, 2A) - 48, 69
3967 胆 57th Line of Communications Duty Company (31A, 2A) - 36, 69
3980 富 2nd Independent Heavy Artillery Battalion (25A) - 80
3986 森 274th Independent Motor Transport Company (BAA) - 87
3987 高 275th Independent Motor Transport Company (5AirDiv 3AirA) - 57
DN • 4000-49 中部 *Chubu* Army District
4001 威 120th Railway Station Command (SRR) - 61
4002 威 121st Railway Station Command (SRR) - 61
4013 岡 47th Construction Duty Company (7AA) - 74
4014 司 48th Construction Duty Company (3AirA) - 54
4015 猛 49th Construction Duty Company (18A) - 49
4016 仁 87th Land Duty Company (12A) - 157
4020 猛 37th Field Road Construction Unit (18A) - 48
4021 威 16th Field Post Office Unit (14AA) - 109
4022 甲 4th Independent Engineer Company (NCAA) - 153
4023 甲 23rd Field Duty Unit Headquarters (NCAA) - 153
4026 定 130th Line of Communications Hospital (29A) - 83
4027 定 131st Line of Communications Hospital (29A) - 83
4028 統 132nd Line of Communications Hospital (6AA) - 143
4042 尚 22nd Field Duty Unit Headquarters (35A) - 113
4046 森 133rd Line of Communications Hospital (BAA) - 88
4047 威 134th Line of Communications (Bayombong) Hospital (14AA) - 109
4048 統 83rd Casualty Clearing Platoon (6AA) - 143
4049 森 84th Casualty Clearing Platoon (BAA) - 88
DN • 4050-99 攝 *Setu*, Osaka Divisional District
4050-96 淀 4th Division (18AA) - 165
4051 猛 49th Construction Duty Company (18A) - 49
4066 淀 4th Division, division #, not a unit (18AA) - 165
4074 淀 61st Infantry Regiment, 4th Division (reserve unit BAA) - 88
4077 淀 4th Field Artillery Regiment, 4th Division (reserve unit BAA) - 88
DN • 4100-55 中部 *Chubu* Army District
DN • 4156-99 Not Distributed
DN • 4200-99 甲 *Ko*, North China Area Army
4200-9 谷 9th Independent Mixed Brigade (43A) - 211-2
4211-9 勝 69th Division (13A) - 194
4215 勝 85th Independent Infantry Battalion, 69th Div (13A) - 194
4220 仁 12th Army, number for the 12th Army as a whole (NCAA) - 157
4221 仁 12th Army Headquarters (NCAA) - 157
4222 仁 10th Signal Regiment (12A) - 157
4223 仁 25th Motor Transport Regiment (12A) - 157
4224 仁 26th Motor Transport Regiment (12A) - 157
4225 仁 7th Division 4th Land Transport Unit (12A) - 157
4226-29 not used (12A)
4230-45 討 21st Division (38A) - 174
4250-65 楓 32nd Division (2AA) - 179

0	1	2	3	4	5	6	7	8	9	10
○	一	二	三	四	五	六	七	八	九	十

4254 楓 210th Infantry Regiment, 3rd Battalion, from 32nd Div (29A) - 83
4255 楓 211th Infantry Regiment, 3rd Battalion, from 32nd Div (29A) - 83
4256 楓 212th Infantry Regiment, 2nd Battalion, from 32nd Div (29A) - 83
4271-6 桐 5th Independent Mixed Brigade (43A) - 210
4278 呂 39th Independent Engineer Regiment (13A) - 131
4279 桐 5th Independent Mixed Brigade Signal Unit, 5th I.M.B. (43A) - 210
4280-9 秋 6th Independent Mixed Brigade, became the 62nd Div (32A) - 211
4289 桐 5th Independent Mixed Brigade Engineer Unit (43A) - 210
4290-6 衣 10th Independent Mixed Brigade, later 59th Div (12A) - 212
DN • 4300-4499 満州 *Manshu*, Kantō Army
4303 輝 40th Casualty Clearing Platoon (2AA) - 64
4328 尚武 22nd Field Medium Artillery Regt., Manila Defense Force (14AA) - 249
4330 猛 56th Field Anti-Aircraft Battalion (18A) - 47
4332 猛 29th Field Machine Cannon Company (18A) - 48
4333 威 1st Air Transport Squadron (SA) - 42
4334 威 2nd Air Transport Squadron (SA) - 42
4354 隼魁 54th Independent Air Squadron (13AirDiv 5AirA) - 136
4358 勢 57th Field Anti-Aircraft Battalion (2A) - 68
4363 照 14th Division Tank Unit, 14th Div. Peleliu Is. (SA) - 37, 170
4364 / 3264 雷 29th Division Tank Unit, 29th Div (31A) - 177
4372 備 2nd South Seas Detachment, Kusaie Is. (31A) - 31
4461 備 52nd Field Antiaircraft Artillery Battalion, Saipan (31A) - 35
4463 勢 26th Field Machine Cannon Company (2A) - 68
4481 備 25th Field Anti-Aircraft Battalion, Guam (31A) - 36
DN • 4500-99 湾 *Wan*, Formosa (Taiwan) Army
DN • 4600-99 澤 *Sawa*, Kanazawa Divisional District
4603 呂 57th Independent Transport Company (11A) - 148
4604 呂 58th Independent Transport Company (11A) - 148
4605 呂 59th Independent Transport Company (11A) - 148
4607 杉 78th Line of Communications Hospital (41A) - 114
4611 呂 60th Independent Transport Company (11A) - 148
4612 呂 61st Independent Transport Company (11A) - 148
4613 呂 62nd Independent Transport Company (11A) - 148
4614 猛 79th Line of Communications Hospital (18A) - 49
4618 仁 24th Bridging Materials Company (12A) - 157
4619 仁 25th Bridging Materials Company (12A) - 157
4623 富 47th Line of Communications Guard Unit (25A) - 80
4630 猛 39th Independent Motor Transport Battalion (18A) - 48
4632 森 13th Line of Communications Veterinary Hospital (BAA) - 88
4633 威 2nd Field Replacement Unit Headquarters (SA) - 42
4642 猛 76th Land Duty Company (18A) - 49
4645 森 79th Land Duty Company (BAA) - 87
4646 猛 35th Field Road Construction Unit (18A) - 48
4650-76 柏 52nd Division (31A) - 187

DN • 4700-99 陸 *Riku*, Hirosaki Divisional District
4700-94 杉 8th Division (41A) - 167-8
4732 杉 8th Division, not a unit (41A) - 167
4732 杉 41st Army Headquarters (14AA) - 114
4734 東 4th Ind. Mountain Artillery Regiment, attached 35th Div. (2A) - 180
4738 杉 8th Field Artillery Regiment, 8th Div (41A) - 167
4748 杉 8th Engineer Regiment, 8th Div (41A) - 168
4755 杉 8th Division Signal Unit, 8th Div (41A) - 167
4801威 74th Line of Communications Hospital (14AA) - 109
4802 治 39th Casualty Clearing Platoon, from 19th Army to 2nd Army (2A) - 69, 71
4810 沖 76th Line of Communications Hospital (17A) - 29
4811 高 36th Field Anti-Aircraft Battalion (5AirDiv 3AirA) - 57
4812 備 9th Independent Engineer Regiment (31A) - 32
4816 林 13th River Crossing Materials Company (33A) - 96
4817 猛 44th Line of Communications Sector Command (18A) - 48
4817 猛 44th Line of Communication Guard Unit (18A) - 48
4817 猛 44th Line of Communications Duty Company (18A) - 48
4821 剛 10th Casualty Clearing Unit Headquarters (8AA) - 25
4822 岡 12th Line of Communications Veterinary Hospital (7AA) - 74
4823 杉 1st Field Replacement Unit Headquarters (41A) - 114
4827 森 33rd Sea Duty Company (BAA) - 88
4828 輝 36th Construction Duty Company (2AA) - 64
4829 威 37th Construction Duty Company (14AA) - 109
4830 堅 40th Casualty Clearing Platoon, from 19th Army to 2nd Army (19A) - 71
4833 猛 73rd Land Duty Company, minus one squad (18A) - 48
4833 洋 73rd Land Duty Company, one squad (6AirDiv, 8AA) - 51
4834 岡 74th Land Duty Company (7AA) - 74
4836 剛 31st Field Road Construction Unit (8AA) - 25
4839 森 33rd Field Road Construction Unit (BAA) - 87
4883 鉄 10th Division Ordinance Duty Unit (14AA) - 168
DN • 4900-49 攝 *Setu*, Osaka Divisional District
DN • 4950-99 Not Distributed
DN • 5000-99 徳 *Toku*, Kwantung (Kantō) Army
5043-5 勢 10th Infantry Group (2AA) - 168
5045 勢 23rd Independent Garrison Battalion, 10th Expeditionary Unit (2A) - 254
5048 甲 124th Specially Established Land Duty Company (NCAA) - 153
5058 勢 4th Tank Regiment, from 19th Army to 2nd Army (19A) (2A) - 68, 71
5061 猛 12th Field Anti Aircraft Headquarters Unit (18A) - 47
5063 勢 53rd Field Anti Aircraft Battalion (2A) - 68
5065 勢 54th Field Anti Aircraft Battalion (2A) - 68
5066 勢 4th Field Searchlight Battalion, minus 2nd Co. (2A) - 68
5066 猛 4th Field Searchlight Battalion, 2nd Company (18A) - 48
5067 猛 24th Field Machine Cannon Company (18A) - 48
5069 沖 27th Field Machine Cannon Company (17A) - 28
5073 統 69th Independent Motor Transport Regiment (6AA) - 142
DN • 5100-99 中国 *Chugoku* Army District
5103 尚武 2nd Signal Regiment (14AA) - 108

0	1	2	3	4	5	6	7	8	9	10
〇	一	二	三	四	五	六	七	八	九	十

5121 猛 46th Fixed Radio Unit (18A) - 48
5125 備 5th Independent Mixed Regiment, Wake Is. (31A) - 37
5129 尚武 56th Construction Duty Company (14AA) - 109
5131 尚武 58th Construction Duty Company (14AA) - 109
5133 森 100th Land Duty Company (BAA) - 87
5135 森 102nd Land Duty Company (BAA) - 87
5136 富 17th Field Post Office Unit (25A) - 81
5142 沖 88th Independent Wire Company (17A) - 28
5157 勢 20th Field Anti-Aircraft Artillery Headquarters (2A) - 68
5171-91 鯉 5th Division (2A) - 166
5173 矛 11th Infantry Regiment, 5th Division (13A) - 166
5176 西41st Infantry Regiment, 21st I.M.B. (18A) - 216
DN • 5200-99 陸 *Riku*, Hirosaki Divisional District
5202 剛 91st Independent Wire Company (8AA) - 24
5203 剛 63rd Independent Radio Platoon, Lorengau, Manus Is. (17A) - 30
5218 敬 28th Independent Mixed Brigade Engineer Unit (16A) - 218
5219 堅 19th Army Veterinary Hospital (19A) - 71
5223 備 123rd Line of Communications Hospital (31A) - 36
5224 林 124th Line of Communications Hospital (15A) - 101
5228-31 勝 69th Division (13A) - 194
5259 林 59th Independent Motor Transport Battalion (15A) - 101
5243 武 23rd Ind. Rapid Firing Gun Battalion, Manila Def. Unit (14AA) - 249
5244 猛 44th Field Road Construction Unit (18A) - 48
5269 森 69th Casualty Clearing Platoon (BAA) - 88
5270 森 70th Casualty Clearing Platoon (28A) - 91
5275 呂 75th Independent Transport Battalion (11A) - 148
5280 勢 18th Casualty Clearing Unit Headquarters (2A) - 69
5297 呂 71st Line of Communications Sector Command (11A) - 147
5298 呂 71st Line of Communications Guard Unit (11A) - 147
5299 呂 71st Line of Communications Duty Company (11A) - 147
DN • 5300-49 張 "Hari" Nagoya Divisional District
5300 戍 Mongolia Garrison Army (NCAA) - 160
5301 戍 Mongolia Garrison Army/Evac Unit Headquarters (NCAA) - 158/159
5302 登 21st Anti-Aircraft Regiment (13A) - 131
DN • 5305-6 戍 not used Mongolia Garrison Army
5304 / 1304 戍 23rd Motor Transp. Regt., Zhangjiakou Evac Unit (43A) - 158/159
5308 威 4th Independent Tank Company (14AA) - 108
5308 備 4th Independent Tank Company/Saipan Tank Unit (31A) - 35
5309 戍 Mongolia Garrison Army Intelligence Department - 159
5310-24 泉 26th Division (14AA) - 176
5314 威 11th Independent Infantry Regiment, att. 10th Div (14AA) - 106, 176
5331-9 響 2nd Independent Mixed Brigade (MGA) - 209
5340-55 滝 3rd Armored Division (12A) - 206-7
DN • 5350-99 甲 *Ko*, North China Area Army

5351-8 成 4th Cavalry Brigade (NCAA) - 240
5350 滝 3rd Armored Division, not a unit (12A) - 206
5359 成 4th Cavalry Brigade, not a unit (NCAA) - 240
5361 統 1st Division 1st Line of Communications Headquarters (6AA) - 142
5364 統 4th Division 1st Line of Communications Headquarters (6AA) - 142
5371 呂 10th Field Transport Command (11A) - 147
5372 昆 2nd Independent Transport Regiment (33A) - 96
5374 呂 3rd Division, 2nd Transport Company (11A) - 147
5377 呂 101st Line of Communications Duty Company (11A) - 147
5378 呂 4th Independent Transport Regiment (11A) - 147
5390 呂 30th Motor Transport Regiment (11A) - 147
5391 統 31st Motor Transport Regiment (6AA) - 142
5392 呂 32nd Motor Transport Regiment (11A) - 147
5393 呂 33rd Motor Transport Regiment (11A) - 147
5394 呂 34th Motor Transport Regiment (11A) - 147
5395 呂 35th Motor Transport Regiment (11A) - 147
DN • 5400-49 越 *Etsu*, Nagano Divisional District
5410-62 鉄 10th Division (14AA) - 168, 10th Expeditionary Unit - 254
DN • 5450-99 Not Distributed
DN • 5500-99 栄 *Sakae,* China Expeditionary Army
5500 呂 11th Army Headquarters (6AA) - 146
5501 呂 11th Army, number for the 11th Army as a whole (6AA) - 146
5501 呂 11th Army Physician Department (11A) - 146
5509 滝 13th Tank Regiment, 3rd Armored Division (12A) - 147
5510 桜 2nd Independent Mountain Artillery Regiment (11A) - 146
5511 備 3rd Independent Mountain Artillery Regiment (31A) - 35
5513 呂 51st Independent Mountain Artillery Battalion (11A) - 146
5515 呂 52nd Independent Mountain Artillery Battalion (11A) - 146
5520 登 14th Field Medium Artillery Regiment (13A) - 131
5521 真 30th Air Brigade Headquarters (4AirA) - 120
5522 呂 15th Independent Field Heavy Artillery Regiment (11A) - 146
5522 登 15th Independent Field Heavy Artillery Regt, one battalion (13A) - 131
5531 呂 1st Trench Mortar Battalion (11A) - 146
5533 沖 3rd Trench Mortar Battalion (17A) - 28
5535 桜 22nd Anti-Aircraft Regiment (20A) - 149
5543 勢 3rd Independent Engineer Regiment (2A) - 68
5548 猛 8th Independent Engineer Regiment (18A) - 48
5549 呂 41st Independent Engineer Regiment (11A) - 146
5550 呂 11th Army Signal Unit (11A) - 146
5552 勢 2nd Field Signal Company (2A) - 67
5553 呂 3rd Field Signal Company (23A) - 135
5555 呂 13th Signals Regiment (11A) - 147
5558 呂 8th Field Signal Company (11A) - 147
5559 呂 9th Field Signal Company (11A) - 147
5561 桜 6th Division Bridging Materials Company (20A) - 150
5562 呂 7th Division; Bridging Materials Company (11A) - 147
5563 呂 8th Division; Bridging Materials Company (11A) - 147

0	1	2	3	4	5	6	7	8	9	10
〇	一	二	三	四	五	六	七	八	九	十

5564 呂 12th Division; Bridging Materials Company (11A) - 147
5565 呂 14th Division; Bridging Materials Company (11A) - 147
5566 呂 Imperial Guard Division River Crossing Company (11A) - 147
5567 呂 1st Division River Crossing Company (11A) - 147
5568 桜 16th Division 1st River Crossing Materials Company (20A) - 150
5571 **路** 1st Railway Regiment, central China (CA) - 143
5573 統 7th Division 5th Land Transport Unit (6AA) - 142
5580-5 福 11th Independent Infantry Brigade (6AA) - 239
5582 統 11th Field Service Unit Headquarters (6AA) - 142
5583 剛 Imperial Guard Division 7th Land Transport Unit (8AA) - 25
5584 統 Imperial Guard Division 10th Land Transport Unit (6AA) - 142
5585 呂 7th Division 7th Land Transport Unit (11A) - 147
5586 呂 7th Division 8th Land Transport Unit (11A) - 147
5587 統 9th Division 2nd Sea Transport Unit (6AA) - 142
5588 統 3rd Division 2nd Construction Unit (6AA) - 142
5589 呂 3rd Division 3rd Construction Unit (11A) - 147
5592-6 征 7th Independent Infantry Brigade (6AA) - 237-8
5597 勢 51st Field Road Construction Unit (2A) - 69
5599 勢 52nd Field Road Construction Unit (2A) - 69
DN • 5600-5749 蔵 *Zō*, Tokyo Divisional District
5629 尚武 56th Construction Duty Company (4AirA) - 122
5702 猛 3rd Field Transport Headquarters, Hollandia (18A) - 49
5705 森 45th Independent Motor Transport Battalion (BAA) - 87
5708 勢 248th Independent Motor Transport Company (2A) - 69
5718 登 4th Field Replacement Unit (13A) - 132
5720 甲 115th Railway Station Command (NCAA) - 154
5724 森 38th Sea Duty Company (BAA) - 88
5726 備 40th Sea Duty Company, Babelthuap, Paulus Is. (31A) - 37
5732 岡 85th Land Duty Company (7AA) - 74
5733 剛 86th Land Duty Company (8AA) - 25
5734 / 5735 猛 36th Field Road Construction Unit, Hollandia (18A) - 49
5736 森 15th Post Office Unit (BAA) - 88
DN • 5750-99 中部 *Chubu* Army District
5757 輝 20th Field Anti-Aircraft Defense Unit HQ (2AA) - 64
5758 輝 48th Independent Field Anti Aircraft Company (2A) - 68
5759 輝 49th Independent Field Anti Aircraft Company (2A) - 68
5760 輝 46th Field Machine Cannon Company (2A) - 68
5762 勢 8th Raiding Company (2A) - 67
5763 勢 9th Raiding Company (2A) - 68
5764 桜 55th Field Road Construction Unit (20A) - 149
5765 呂 78th Casualty Clearing Platoon (11A) - 148
5766 杉 25th Ind. Machinegun Battalion, Manila Def. Force (41A) - 249
5767 登 28th Independent Rapid Firing Gun Battalion (13A) - 131
5775 輝 20th Field Anti-Aircraft Defense Unit Headquarters (2AA) - N/A

5801 路 2nd Railway Inspectorate (SRR) - 61
5804 路 5th Railway Regiment (SRR) - 61
5805 路 9th Railway Regiment (SRR) - 61
5806 路 1st Railway Materials Depot (SSR) - 61
5809 / 5895 森 5th Specially Est. Railway Unit Headquarters (BAA) - 61
5819 呂 81st Casualty Clearing Platoon (11A) - 148
5820 統 82nd Casualty Clearing Platoon (6AA) - 143
5821 路 10th Specially Established Railway Transport Unit (SRR) - 61
5822 路 11th Specially Established Railway Transport Unit (SRR) - 61
5822 路 Marai 11th Specially Established Railway Materials Depot (SRR) -61
5823 路 5th Specially Established Railway Bridge Construction Unit (SRR) - 61
5824 岡 5th Specially Established Railway Engineer Unit (7AA) - 74
5825 森 7th Specially Established Railway Construction Unit (SRR) - 61
5826 路 4th Specially Established Railway Unit (SRR) - 61
5827 路 8th Specially Established Railway Engineer Unit (SRR) - 61
5828 路 4th Specially Established Railway Engineer Unit (SRR) - 61
5838 路 4th Specially Established Railway Headquarters (SRR) - 61
5840 富 1st Signal Regiment (25A) - 80
5860 呂 1st Field Transport Command (11A) - 147
5861 呂 31st Independent Motor Transport Battalion (11A) - 147
5862 呂 32nd Independent Motor Transport Battalion (11A) - 147
5865 森 101st Independent Motor Transport Battalion (BAA) - 87
5871 勢 73rd Construction Duty Company (2A) - 69
5873 富 209th Independent Motor Transport Company (25A) - 80
5874 威 210th Independent Motor Transport Company (14AA) - 109
5875 森 211th Independent Motor Transport Company (BAA) - 87
5876 沖 212th Independent Motor Transport Company (17A) - 28
5885 森 21st Bridging Materials Company (BAA) - 86
5889 勢 72nd Construction Duty Company (2A) - 69
5894 森 5th Specially Established Railway Headquarters (BAA) - 61
5895 路 / 5809 5th Specially Established Railway Unit Headquarters (SRR) - 61
5899 登 230th Independent Motor Transport Company (13A) - 131
DN • 5900-49 満州 *Manshu*, Kantō Army
5911-29 玉 1st Division (14AA) - 163-4
5932 定 15th Tank Regiment (29A) - 83
DN • 5950-99 Not Distributed
DN • 6000-49 中部 *Chubu* Army District
6000 呂 54th Independent Transport Battalion (11A) - 147
6001 波 55th Independent Transport Battalion (11A) - 148
6002 呂 87th Line of Communications Hospital (11A) - 148
6009 猛 90th Line of Communications Hospital (18A) - 49
6012 沖 53rd Casualty Clearing Platoon (17A) - 28
6013 沖 54th Casualty Clearing Platoon (17A) - 28
6017 猛 30th Independent Engineer Regiment (18A) - 48
6020 森 53rd Line of Communications Sector Command (BAA) - 86
6020 森 53rd Line of Communications Duty Unit (BAA) - N/A
6025 備 10th Independent Rapid Firing Gun Battalion, Iwo Jima (31A) - 33

0	1	2	3	4	5	6	7	8	9	10
〇	一	二	三	四	五	六	七	八	九	十

6028 甲 182nd Railway Station Command (NCAA) - 154
6030 猛 54th Line of Comm. Sector Command, Hollandia (18A) - 49
6030 猛 54th Line of Comm. Guard Unit, Hollandia (18A) - 49
6030 猛 54th Line of Comm. Transport Unit, Hollandia (18A) - 49
6030 猛 54th Line of Comm. Duty Company, Hollandia (18A) - 49
6031 策 71st Casualty Clearing Platoon (28A) - 91
6032 森 72nd Casualty Clearing Platoon (BAA) - 88
6033 猛 73rd Casualty Clearing Platoon (18A) - 49
6034 猛 74th Casualty Clearing Platoon (18A) - 49
6035 猛 75th Casualty Clearing Platoon (18A) - 49
6036 and 6076 剛 76th Casualty Clearing Platoon (8AA) - 25
6037 甲 183rd Railway Station Command (NCAA) - 154
6038 甲 184th Railway Station Command (NCAA) - 154
6039 猛 66th Field Anti-Aircraft Battalion, Hollandia (18A) - 49
6040 統 82nd Sector Transport Unit (6AA) - 142
6041 策 101st Field Road Construction Unit, Saku Group (28A) - 92
6042 統 82nd Line of Communications Sector Unit Command (6AA) - 142
6042 呂 82nd Line of Communications Guard Unit (11A) - 147
6042 呂 82nd Line of Communications Duty Company (11A) - 147
6043 登 83rd Line of Communications Sector Unit Command (13A) - 131
6044 統 84th Line of Communications Sector Unit Command (6AA) - 142
6046-7 恵 118th Division (13A) - 202
DN • 6050-99 攝 *Setu*, Osaka Divisional District
6050 猛 4th Field Transport Headquarters (18A) - 48
6054 守 255th Independent Motor Transport Company (6A) - 133
6055 林 256th Independent Motor Transport Company (15A) - 101
6056 森 257th Independent Motor Transport Company (BAA) - 87
6057 登 258th Independent Motor Transport Company (13A) - 132
6059 尚武 260th Independent Motor Transport Company (14AA) - 109
6060 森 261st Independent Motor Transport Company (BAA) − 87
6067 定 65th Independent Infantry Defense Battalion (29A) - 83
6068 定 66th Independent Infantry Defense Battalion (29A) - 83
6069 定 67th Independent Infantry Defense Battalion (29A) - 83
6072 朝 20th Division 2nd Field Hospital (18A) - 174
6073 朝 20th Division 3rd Field Hospital (18A) - 174
6074 朝 20th Division 4th Field Hospital (18A) - 174
6075 猛 75th Casualty Clearing Platoon (18A) - 49
6076 / 6036 剛 76th Casualty Clearing Platoon (8AA) - 25
6078 猛 35th Field Machine Cannon Company (18A) - 48
6079 猛 36th Field Machine Cannon Company (18A) - 48
6080 猛 37th Field Machine Cannon Company (18A) - 48
6081 猛 1st Independent Field Searchlight Company (18A) - 48
6085 勢 15th Southern Army Hospital (2A) - 69
6086 森 91st Casualty Clearing Platoon (BAA) - 88

6087 尚武 92nd Casualty Clearing Platoon (14AA) - 109
6088 尚武 93rd Casualty Clearing Platoon (14AA) - 109
6089 尚武 65th Independent Engineer Battalion, split in half (14AA) - 108
6089 威 65th Independent Engineer Battalion, half Comotes Detach. (14AA) - 108
6091 威 1st Southern Army Hospital (7AA) - 74
6092 威 2nd Southern Army Hospital (38A) - 44
6093 波 49th Field Machine Cannon Company (23A) - 135
6094 沖 4th South Seas Garrison Unit (17A) - 28
6095-8 檜 68th Division (20A) - 193
6099 猛 65th Field Anti-Aircraft Battalion (18A) - 47
DN • 6100-10 栄 *Sakae*, China Expeditionary Army
6100-6 悟 5th Independent Infantry Brigade (6AA) - 237
6107 統 51st Line of Communications Guard Unit (6AA) - 142
6109 統 52nd Line of Communications Guard Unit (6AA) - 142
DN • 6111-99 暁 *Akatsuki*, Shipping Corps Headquarters
6112 呂 11th Army Field Ordinance Depot (11A) - 146
6114 呂 11th Army Field Motor Vehicle Repair Depot (11A) - 146
6116 呂 11th Army Field Freight Depot (11A) - 146
6118 呂 11th Army Veterinary Depot (11A) - 146
6127 呂 21st Field Hospital (11A) - N/A
6131 呂 5th Casualty Clearing Headquarters (11A) - 148
6132 呂 1st Casualty Clearing Squad (11A) - 148
6134 呂 3rd Casualty Clearing Squad (11A) - 148
6136 統 9th Casualty Clearing Unit (6AA) - 143
6138 呂 22nd Casualty Clearing Squad (11A) - 148
6142 暁 1st Field Shipping Engineer Replacement Unit (14AA) - 123
6143 暁 8th Debarkation Unit (SoS) - 59
6144雪 36th Division Sea Transport Unit (2AA) - 181
6145 / 4672 柏 52nd Division Sea Transport Unit, Truk District (31A) - 187
6146 宮 Konoe 2nd Sea Transport Unit, Imperial Guard (25A) - 163
6147照 14th Division Sea Transport Unit (31A) - 170
6150 暁 10th Debarkation Unit (SoS) - 59
6151 雷 29th Division Sea Transport Unit (31A) - 35, 177
6152 駆 1st Amphibious Brigade (31A) - 241
6153 巡 2nd Amphibious Brigade (2AA) - 242
6154 暁 11th Debarkation Unit (2AA) - 64
DN • 6157-99 四國 *Shikoku* Army District
6157 暁 1st Sea Transport Battalion (SoS) - 59
6158 暁 7th Sea Transport Battalion (SoS) - 59
6159 暁 12th Shipping Debarkation Unit (SoS) - 59
6161 暁 2nd Shipping Group attached 38th IMB (17A) - 222
6161 暁 13th Shipping Engineer Regiment (SoS) - 59
6162 暁 14th Shipping Engineer Regiment (SoS) - 59
6166 暁 13th Debarkation Unit (SoS) - 59
6170 暁 1st Shipping Engineer Regiment, 1st Company (18A) - N/A
6171 暁 2nd Shipping Engineer Regiment (17A) - 28
6172 暁 4th Shipping Engineer Regiment (SoS) - 59

0	1	2	3	4	5	6	7	8	9	10
〇	一	二	三	四	五	六	七	八	九	十

6173 猛 5th Shipping Engineer Regiment (18A) - N/A
6176 暁 15th Shipping Engineer Regiment (SoS) - 59
6185 勢 5th Debarkation Unit (2A) - 70
6187 暁 7th Debarkation Unit (SoS) - 59
6188 剛 4th Shipping Transport Headquarters (8AA) - 25
6189 暁 2nd Sea Transport Battalion (SoS) - 59
6190 森 3rd Sea Transport Battalion (SoS) - 59
6191 猛 4th Sea Transport Battalion (18A) - 50
6194 暁 3rd Wake (Island Shipping) Depot - N/A
DN • 6200-99 洛 *Raku*, Kyoto Divisional District
6200-34 嵐 116th Division (20A) - 201
6251 沖 41st Field Anti-Aircraft Battalion (17A) - 28
6263 森 14th River Crossing Materials Company (BAA) - 86
6265 呂 49th Independent Motor Transport Battalion (11A) - 147
6268 備 264th Independent Motor Transport Company, Saipan (31A) - 35
6269 備 265th Independent Motor Transport Company, Saipan (31A) - 35
6270 統 266th Independent Motor Transport Company (6AA) - 142
DN • 6300-49 德 *Toku*, Kwantung (Kantō) Army
6306 守 6th Army Headquarters (13A) - 133
6329 守 6th Army (CA) - 133
DN • 6350-99 Not Distributed
6354 守 8th Border Garrison Artillery (6A) - N/A
DN • 6400-99 四國 *Shikoku* Army District
6408 剛 63rd Casualty Clearing Platoon (8AA) - 25
6408 猛 63rd Casualty Clearing Platoon, one Section (18A) - 49
6409 沖 64th Casualty Clearing Platoon; attached 38th IMB (17A) - 222
6412 猛 112th Line of Communications Hospital (18A) - 49
6413 猛 113th Line of Communications Hospital (18A) - 50
6415 仁 31st Bridging Materials Company (12A) - 157
6427 路 152nd Railway Station Command (SRR/CRR) - 61
6431 仁 151st Railway Station Command (12A) - 153
6434 暁 46th Anchorage Headquarters (SoS) - 59
6438 勢 61st Construction Duty Company (2A) - 69
6439 司 62nd Construction Duty Company (5AirDiv 3AirA) - 57
6440 堅 14th Field Duty Unit Headquarters (19A) - 71
6441 岡 107th Land Duty Company (29A) - 83
6459 固 10th Independent Infantry Brigade (1A) - 237
6467-75 操 62nd Independent Mixed Brigade (6A) - 228
DN • 6500-49 德 *Toku*, Kwantung (Kantō) Army
DN • 6550-99 洛 *Raku*, Kyoto Divisional District
6550-69 **垣** 16th Division (35A) - 171
6558 垣 22nd Field Artillery Regiment, 16th Div (35A) - 171
DN • 6600-99 澤 *Sawa*, Kanazawa Divisional District
6602 勢 13th Field Post Office Unit (2A) - 69

6613 昆 102nd Field Road Construction Unit (33A) - 96
6680 暁 18th Sea Raiding Base Battalion (14AA) - 124
DN • 6700-99 黒 *Kuro*, Kureme Divisional District
6701-49 龍 56th Division (15A) - 190
6757 勢 65th Casualty Clearing Platoon (2A) - 69
6758 輝 66th Casualty Clearing Platoon (2AA) - 64
6769 猛 117th Line of Communications Hospital (18A) - 49
6770 策 118th Line of Communications Hospital (28A) - 91
6771 森 5th Field Medium Artillery Regiment (BAA) - 86
6776 暁 54th Hospital Shipping Medical Section (SoS) - 59
6779 暁 56th Hospital Shipping Medical Section (SoS) - 59
6780 暁 57th Hospital Shipping Medical Section (SoS) - 59
6794-5 固 10th Independent Infantry Brigade (1A) - 237
DN • 6800-19 仙 *Sen*, Sendai Divisional District
6800-19 鏡 13th Division (CA) - 169
6801 鏡 13th Division Headquarters Detachment, Guam (31A) - 36
DN • 6820-39 丸 *Maru*, Utsunomiya Divisional District
6820-34 弓 33rd Division (15A) - 179
DN • 6840-55 攝 *Setu*, Osaka Divisional District
6840-55 椿 34th Division (CA) - 180
DN • 6860-79 Hiroshima Divisional District
6874 槍 124th Independent Infantry Battalion, 70th Division (6A) - 194
DN • 6880-6905 四國 *Shikoku* Divisional District
6880-94 鯨 40th Division (CA) - 182-3
DN • 6910-49 越 *Etsu*, Nagano Divisional District
6910 森 38th Anchorage Headquarters (BAA) - 59
6913 森 53rd Construction Duty Company (BAA) - 88
6914 勢 54th Construction Duty Company (2A) - 69
6915 沖 55th Construction Duty Company, one section (17A) - 28
6918 沖 96th Land Duty Company, one section (17A) - 28
6919 呂 97th Land Duty Company (11A) - 147
6920 呂 98th Land Duty Company (11A) - 147
6948 林 58th Casualty Clearing Platoon (15A) - 101
DN • 6950-99 Not Distributed
DN • 7000-99 薩 *Satsu*, Kumamoto Divisional District
7005 森 106th Line of Communications Hospital (BAA) - 88
7006 森 107th Line of Communications Hospital (BAA) - 88
7007 定 61st Casualty Clearing Platoon (29A) - 83
7008 森 62nd Casualty Clearing Platoon (BAA) - 88
7015 勢 109th Line of Communications Hospital; att. 48th Div. (2A) - 67
7016 沖 45th Field Anti Aircraft Battalion, Guadalcanal (17A) - 29
7017 備 7th Independent Engineer Regiment, minus 2nd Coy Saipan (31A) - 35
7017 備 7th Independent Engineer Regiment, 2nd Company, Guam (31A) - 36
7024 森 5th Field Transport Headquarters (BAA) - 87
7026 策 55th Independent Motor Transport Battalion, Saku Group (28A) - 91, 92
7028 栄 282nd Independent Motor Transport Company (CA) - 129
7029 栄 283rd Independent Motor Transport Company (CA) - 129

0	1	2	3	4	5	6	7	8	9	10
○	一	二	三	四	五	六	七	八	九	十

7034 路 148th Railway Station Command (SRR/CRR) - 61
7037 甲 145th Railway Station Command (NCAA) - 154
7038 固 229th Independent Infantry Battalion, 10th I.I.B. (1A) - 238
7044 森 60th Construction Duty Company (BAA) - 88
7054 森 18th Field Post Office Unit (BAA) - 88
7055 森 17th Veterinary Quarantine Hospital (BAA) - 88
DN • 7100-99 中国 *Chugoku* Army District
7105 備 278th Independent Motor Transport Company, Saipan (31A) - 35
7106 統 279th Independent Motor Transport Company (6AA) - 142
7107 高 280th Independent Motor Transport Company (5AirDiv 3AirA) - 57
7108 高 281st Independent Motor Transport Company (5AirDiv 3AirA) - 57
7117 路 143rd Railway Station Command (SRR) - 61
7129 剛 103rd Line of Communications Hospital (8AA) - 25
7131 林 105th Line of Communications Hospital (15A) - 101
7132 林 15th Casualty Clearing Unit Headquarters (15A) - 101
7133 統 59th Casualty Clearing Platoon (6AA) - 143
7134 昆 60th Casualty Clearing Platoon (33A) - 96
7136 昆 21st Independent Mixed Regiment (33A) - 96
7142 暁16th Hospital Shipping Medical Section (SoS) - 59
7152-4 槍 121st to 124th Independent Infantry Battalion, 70th Div (6A) - 194
7155 槍70th Division Field Hospital (6A) - 194
7157 備 17th Independent Mixed Regiment, 3rd Btn. Iwo Jima (31A) - 33
7160 固 10th Independent Infantry Brigade (1A) - 238
7172 槍 4th Independent Security Battalion, 70th Div (6A) - 194
7176 威 137th Line of Communications (Clark Field) Hospital (KeG) - 117
7179 備 11th Independent Rapid Firing Gun Battalion, Iwo Jima (31A) - 33
7180 備 12th Independent Rapid Firing Gun Battalion, Iwo Jima (31A) - 33
7181 栄 188th Railway Station Command (CA) - 129
7184 路 187th Railway Station Command (6AA) - 143
7185 栄 189th Railway Station Command (CA) - 129
7189 甲 26th Field Duty Headquarters (NCAA) - 153
7194 定 135th Line of Communications Hospital (29A) - 83
7195 波 136th Line of Communications (Guangdong) Hospital (23A) - 136
7198 勢 85th Casualty Clearing Platoon (2A) - 69
7199 統 86th Casualty Clearing Platoon (6AA) - 143
DN • 7200-99 陸 *Riku*, Hirosaki Divisional District
7201盟 58th Independent Mixed Brigade, not a unit (14AA) - 227
7203-8 盟 58th Independent Mixed Brigade (14AA) - 227
7259 暁 19th Sea Raiding Base Battalion (14AA) - 124
7260 暁 20th Sea Raiding Base Battalion (14AA) - 124
7290 沖 120th Land Duty Company (17A) - 29
DN • 7300-49 栄 *Sakae*, China Expeditionary Army
7300 槍 70th Division (6A) - 194
7303 広 51st Infantry Brigade, brigade code # 58th Div (11A) - 190

7304 広 52nd Infantry Brigade, brigade code # 58th Div (11A) - 190-1
7305 矛 60th Division (13A) - 191
7312-19 広 58th Division (11AA) - 190-1
7320 檜 68th Division, division #, not a unit (20A) - 193
7330 登 13th Army (CA) - 131
7331 登 13th Army Headquarters (CA) - 131
7333 呂 4th Trench Mortar Battalion (11A) - 146
7336 登 12th Signal Regiment (13A) - 131
7337 登 29th Motor Transport Regiment (13A) - 131
7338 翔 160th Line of Communications Motor Transport Unit (3AirA) - 54
7340 統 7th Division 2nd Construction Unit (6AA) - 142
7342 登 13th Army Veterinary Depot (13A) - 132
7343-9 善 12th Independent Infantry Brigade (6AA) - 239
DN • 7350-79 洛 *Raku*, Kyoto Divisional District
7350-6 肇 6th Independent Infantry Brigade (13A) - 237
7357 至純 9th Independent Machinegun Battalion, 89th I.M.B. (6A) - 233
7358 登 10th Independent Machinegun Battalion (13A) - 131
7359 登 17th Independent Rapid Firing Gun Battalion (13A) - 131
7361-79 祭 15th Division (18AA) - 170
DN • 7380-99 越 *Etsu*, Nagano Divisional District
7380-97 月 17th Division (8AA) - 171-2
7382-6 力 38th Independent Mixed Brigade (17A) - 222
DN • 7400-49 朝鮮 Korea Army
7424 備 42nd Independent Anti Aircraft Company, Babelthuap (31A) - 36
7425 備 43rd Independent Anti Aircraft Company, Saipan (31A) - 35
7427 猛 52nd Field Anti Aircraft Battalion (18A) - 47
DN • 7450-99 South Jeolla Divisional District (KoD)
7460 猛 58th Field Anti-Aircraft Battalion, 1st Company (18A) - 47
7461 剛 37th Independent Field Anti-Aircraft Company (8AA) - 24
7462 沖 6th Independent Searchlight Company (17A) - 28
7463 / 8553 猛 19th Field Machine Cannon Company (18A) - 48
7464 / 2002 猛 20th Field Machine Cannon Company (18A) - 48
7465 沖 31st Field Machine Cannon Company (17A) - 28
7466 沖 59th Field Anti Aircraft Battalion (17A) - 28
7467 猛 38th Independent Field Anti Aircraft Company (18A) - 47
7468 輝 51st Independent Field Anti Aircraft Company (2A) - 68
7469 勢 47th Field Machine Cannon Company (2A) - 68
DN • 7500-99 徳 *Toku*, Kwantung (Kantō) Army
7563 波 13th Field Transport Command (23A) - 135
7573 呂 83rd Independent Motor Transport Battalion (11A) - 147
7591 剛 16th Signal Regiment (8AA) - 24
7591 備 16th Tank Regiment, 2nd Company deact., Wake Is. (31A) - 37
7592 勢 8th Field Military Police Unit (2A) - 70
7598 洋 7th Mobile Air Repair Section (6AirDiv, 8AA) - 51
7599 洋 8th Mobile Air Repair Section (6AirDiv, 8AA) - 51
DN • 7600-99 中部 *Chubu* Army District
DN • 7700-99 丸 *Maru*, Utsunomiya Divisional District

0	1	2	3	4	5	6	7	8	9	10
〇	一	二	三	四	五	六	七	八	九	十

7702-84 照 14th Division (31A) - 169-70
7702 照 14th Division's #, not a unit (31A) - 169
7713-4 照 14th Division Units (31A) - 169
7714 照 14th Division Signal Unit, one radio squad, Peleliu (31A) - 37
7725 照 14th Transport Regiment, 14th Div. (31A) - 170
7736 照 14th Division Ordinance Duty Unit (31A) - 169
7736 照 14th Division Ordinance Duty Unit, one squad, Peleliu (31A) - 37, 169
7746 照 2nd Infantry Regiment, 14th Division (31A) - 37
7756 統 192nd Railway Station Command (6AA) - 143
7757 照 15th Infantry Regiment, 3rd Battalion, 14th Division Peleliu (31A) - 37, 170
7757 照 15th Infantry Regiment, one section 14th Div. Saipan (31A) - 35
7768 照 59th Infantry Regiment, one section 14th Div. Saipan (31A) - 37, 170
7770 照 14th Division Field Hospital, one company Peleliu (31A) - 37
7780-4 照 14th Division Units (31A) - 169-70
7793 照 20th Field Artillery Regiment, 14th Div. (31A) - 37, 170
DN • 7800-99 蔵 *Zō*, Tokyo Divisional District
7800 登 232nd Independent Motor Transport Company (13A) - 132
7801 登 234th Independent Motor Transport Company (13A) - 132
7802 甲 242nd Motor Transport Company (NCAA) - 153
7803 甲 243rd Motor Transport Company (NCAA) - 153
7804 甲 244th Motor Transport Company (NCAA) - 153
7805 甲 245th Motor Transport Company (NCAA) - 153
7812 統 201st Railway Station Command (6AA) - 143
7813 統 202nd Railway Station Command (6AA) - 143
7814 統 203rd Railway Station Command (6AA) - 143
7815 統 204th Railway Station Headquarters (6AA) - 143
7816 統 205th Railway Station Headquarters (6AA) - 143
7817 甲 206th Railway Station Headquarters (NCAA) - 154
7819-20 育 34th Independent Mixed Brigade (38A) - 220-1
7819 育 34th Independent Mixed Brigade, brigade # not a unit - 220
7820 育 34th I.M.B. Headquarters 34th I.M.B. (38A) - 220
7821 貫徹 187th Independent Infantry Battalion, 72nd IMB (BAA) - 229
7821 育 187th Independent Infantry Battalion, 34th I.M.B. (38A) - 220
7822 貫徹 188th Independent Infantry Battalion, 72nd IMB (BAA) - 229
7822 育 188th Independent Infantry Battalion, 34th I.M.B. (38A) - 220
7823育 189th Independent Infantry Battalion, 34th I.M.B. (38A) - 220
7824育 190th Independent Infantry Battalion, 34th I.M.B. (38A) - 221
7828 肝 219th Independent Infantry Battalion, 8th Ind. Inf. Bgd (23A) - 238
7829 肝 220th Independent Infantry Battalion, 8th Ind. Inf. Bgd (23A) -238
7830 富 Unknown unit # 2 Butai, Tanaka Tai, Aoshima Tai (25A) postcard
7831 甲 74th Field Anti-Aircraft Battalion, less the 2nd Company (NCAA) - 153
7831 輝 74th Field Anti-Aircraft Battalion, 2nd Company (2A) - 64
7832 統 75th Field Anti-Aircraft Battalion (6AA) - 142
7833 呂 48th Field Machine Cannon Company (11A) - 146

7837 備 1st Independent Machine Gun Battalion, Iwo Jima (31A) - 33
7838 備 2nd Independent Machine Gun Battalion, Iwo Jima (31A) - 33
7841 森 2nd Field Well Drilling Company (BAA) - 88
7847 統 63rd Land Duty Company (6AA) - 142
7850 洋 31st Construction Duty Company (6AirDiv 8AA) - 51
7853 岡 11th Field Post Office Unit (7AA) - 74
7854 森 101st Construction Duty Company (BAA) - 88
7862 杉 63rd Line of Communications Hospital (41A) - 114
7866 剛 67th Line of Communications Hospital (8AA) - 25
DN • 7900-29 Not Distributed
7900 森 Burma Area Army Headquarters (SA) - 86
7901 昆 33rd Army Headquarters (BAA) - 96
7907 桜 20th Army Headquarters (6AA) - 149
7910 猛 18th Army Headquarters (SA) - 47
7910 猛 18th Army Headquarters detached personnel, Babelthuap Is. (31A) - 36
7910 猛 18th Army Headquarters detached personnel, Hollandia (31A) - 49
7920 備 31st Army Headquarters (I.G.HQ) - 31, 34
7922 桜 20th Army (6AA) - 149
DN • 7930-49 仙 *Sen*, Sendai Divisional District
7930-49 原 22nd Division (8AA) - 175
DN • 7950-60 Not Distributed
7950 信 38th Army Headquarters (SA) - 44
7960 剛 8th Area Army Headquarters (SA) - 24
DN • 7961-99 栄 *Sakae*, China Expeditionary Army
7970 義 39th Army Headquarters, later 18th A.A. HQ (SA) - 102
7970 義18th Area Army Headquarters (SA) - 98
7971-89 開 64th Division (20A) - 192
7972-99 専 65th Division (13A) - 192-3
DN • 8000-99 西部 *Seibu* Army District
8011-3 開 64th Division (20A) - 192
8030 猛 60th Field Anti Aircraft Battalion, Hollandia (18A) - 49
8031 剛 36th Independent Field Anti-Aircraft Company (8AA) - 24
8032 猛 3rd Independent Field Searchlight Company, Hollandia (18A) - 49
8033 猛 39th Independent Field Anti Aircraft Company, Hollandia (18A) - 49
8034 森 93rd Independent Wire Company (BAA) - 86
8050 猛 64th Field Anti-Aircraft Battalion (18A) - 47
8052 猛 38th Field Machine Cannon Company (18A) - 49
8053 猛 39th Field Machine Cannon Company (18A) - 49
8054 猛 74th Independent Wireless Radio Platoon (18A) - 48
8056 猛 76th Independent Wireless Radio Platoon (18A) - 48
8057 策 71st Field Anti-Aircraft Battalion, attached to 54th Div. (28A) - 91
8058 勢 42nd Field Machine Cannon Company (2A) - 68
8059 昆 43rd Field Machine Cannon Company (33A) - 96
8073 猛 39th Independent Anti Aircraft Company (18A) - 48
8085 沖 60th Independent Wireless Radio Platoon (17A) - 28
8086 剛 61st Independent Radio Platoon (8AA) - 24
8087 剛 62nd Independent Radio Platoon (8AA) - 24

0	1	2	3	4	5	6	7	8	9	10
○	一	二	三	四	五	六	七	八	九	十

DN • 8100-20 Not Distributed
8100-9 峰 17th Independent Mixed Brigade (6AA) - 214
8110 波 23rd Army (CA) - 135
8111 波 23rd Army Headquarters (CA) - 135
8114 波 67th Independent Infantry Battalion, Hong Kong Defense Unit (23A) - 249
8115 波 68th Independent Infantry Battalion, Hong Kong Defense Unit (23A) - 249
8116 波 69th Independent Infantry Battalion, Hong Kong Defense Unit (23A) - 249
8119 沖 10th Independent Mountain Artillery Regiment, Guadalcanal (17A) - 29
8119 沖 10th Ind. Mountain Artillery Regt. 2nd Battalion, Bougainville (17A) - 29
DN • 8121-49 栄 *Sakae*, China Expeditionary Army
8121 敏 21st Field Medium Artillery Battalion, attached to the 18th Div (33A) - 96
8123 猛 21st Trench Mortar Battalion, Hollandia (18A) - 49
8125 勢 15th Independent Engineer Regiment, 19th Army to 2nd Army (2A) - 68, 71
8126 沖 19th Independent Engineer Regiment (17A) - 28
8127 森 20th Independent Engineer Regiment (BAA) - 86
8128 波 14th Signals Regiment (23A) - 135
8131 昆 9th Division, 1st Bridging Materials Company (33A) - 96
8132 策 9th Division, 1st River Crossing Company (28A) - 91
8133 波 9th Division, 2nd Bridging Materials Company (23A) - 135
8135 波 200th Line of Communications (Hong Kong Army) Hospital (23A) - 136
8137 肝 8th Independent Infantry Brigade – brigade only, not a unit (23A) - 238
8138 肝 8th Independent Infantry Brigade Headquarters (23A) - 238
8138 波 Hong Kong Defense Unit Headquarters (23A) - 249
8139 波 Hong Kong Artillery Unit (23A) - 249
8139 直 13th Independent Infantry Brigade – brigade #, not unit (23A) - 249
8140-5 直 13th Independent Infantry Brigade (23A) - 239
8146 波 99th Field Anti Aircraft Battalion (23A) - 135
8147 波 85th Independent Motor Transport Battalion (23A) - 135
DN • 8150-59 Not Distributed
DN • 8160-99 栄 *Sakae*, China Expeditionary Army
DN • 8200-99 洛 *Raku*, Kyoto Divisional District
8201 沖 94th Line of Communications Hospital (17A) - 28
8213 / 10054 甲 126th Railway Station Command (NCAA) - 154
8223 森 93rd Land Duty Company (BAA) - 87
8223 森 93rd Land Duty Company, 1 platoon, Saku Group (28A) - 92
8224 森 94th Land Duty Company (BAA) - 87
8231 猛 38th Field Road Construction Unit (18A) - 48
8232 沖 39th Field Road Construction Unit (17A) - 28
8234 沖 51st Construction Duty Company (17A) - 28
8235 勢 52nd Construction Duty Company, attached 36th Div (2A) - 181
8235 雪 36th Division (2AA) - 181
8303 威 13th Air Group Headquarters (4AirA) - 120
8308 / 11805 勢 38th/70th Joint Airfield Battalion, attached 36th Div (2A) - 67
8316 靖 7th Field Air Repair Depot 1st Ind. Maintenance Unit (4AirA) - 122

8321 洋 21st Airfield Battalion (6AirDiv, 18A) - 50
8322 勢 22nd Airfield Battalion, formerly with the 55AirDiv (2A) - 70
8321 洋 21st Airfield Battalion (6AirDiv, 8AA) - 50
8322 勢 22nd Airfield Battalion was 55AirDiv (2A) - 55, 70
8328 洋 208th Flying Regiment (6AirDiv, 8AA) - 50
8329 勢 209th Airfield Battalion (2A) - 70
8340 洋 12th Air Sector Headquarters (6AirDiv, 8AA) - 50
8354 隼魁 54th Independent Air Squadron (13AirDiv 5AirA) - 136
8356 翼 10th Field Air Repair Depot, 1st and 2nd Ind. Maint. Units (4AirA) - 122
8357 威 99th Airfield Battalion (KeG) - 117, 120
8361 司 1st Air Signals Regiment (3AirA) - 53
8367 翼 11th Field Air Repair Depot, 1st and 2nd Ind. Maint Unit (4AirA) - 122
8372 翼 12th Field Air Repair Depot, 1st and 2nd Ind. Maintenance Unit (4AirA) - 122
8376 洋 30th Air Sector Command (6AirDiv 8AA) - 50
8386 翼 86th Airfield Battalion (4AirA) - 120
8387 翔 87th Air Regiment (9AirDiv, 3AirA) - 56
8399 誠 26th Air Regiment (4AirA) - 120
DN • 8400-49 四國 *Shikoku* Divisional District
8400-30 楯 55th Division (38A, Headquarters w/28A) - 189
8414-28 楯 Nanto (South-East) Detachment later 55 Div, 38A (17A) - 28-9
8418 壮 55th Cavalry Regiment (28A) - 189
8423 策 55th Transport Regiment, 3rd Company, Saku Group (28A) - 92
DN • 8450-8549 Not Distributed
8500-30 虎 19th Division (14AA) - 173
8510-11 虎 8th Expeditionary Unit, Truk (31A) - 173
DN • 8550-99 South Jeolla Divisional District (Korea)
8551 剛 47th Field Anti-Aircraft Battalion, formerly w/South Seas Det. (8AA) - 24
8551 剛 47th Field Anti-Aircraft Battalion, one company Guadalcanal (17A) - 29
8553 and 7463 猛 19th Field Machine Cannon Company (18A) - 48
8554 森 60th Independent Motor Transport Battalion (BAA) - 87
DN • 8600-99 栄 *Sakae*, China Expeditionary Army
8600 波 160th Line of Communications (Guangdong 1st Army) Hospital (23A) - 136
8601 波 180th Line of Communications (Guangdong 2nd Army) Hospital (23A) - 136
8602 波 7th Patient Transport Headquarters (23A) - 136
8603 波 4th Casualty Clearing Unit Squad (23A) - 136
8604 波 South China Disease Prevention and Water Supply Unit (23A) - 136
8605 勢 8th Disease Prevention and Water Supply Unit (2A) - 70
8607 沖 17th Army Disease Prevention and Water Supply Unit (17A) - 28
8608 波 23rd Army Veterinary Depot (23A) - 136
8609 波 South China Veterinary Quarantine Depot (23A) - 136
8611 鍾馗 130th Division Headquarters (23A) - 203
8612 鍾馗 130th Division, division's number, not a unit (23A) - 203
8613 森 3rd Independent Transport Regiment (BAA) - 87
8614 波 19th Independent Transport Company (23A) - 135
8615 波 20th Independent Transport Company (23A) - 135
8616 波 21st Independent Transport Company (23A) - 136
8620 波 7th Casualty Clearing Unit Headquarters (23A) - 136

0	1	2	3	4	5	6	7	8	9	10
〇	一	二	三	四	五	六	七	八	九	十

8627 策 10th River Crossing Materials Company (28A) - 91
8628 波 6th Division 6th Transport Unit (23A) - 135
8629 波 8th Division 8th Transport Unit (23A) - 135
8632 波 12th Division 1st Transport Unit (23A) - 135
8633 波 14th Division 1st Transport Unit (23A) - 135
8636 登 38th Motor Transport Regiment (13A) - 131
8637 波 39th Motor Transport Regiment (23A) - 135
8638 波 2nd Inland Waterway Transport Unit (23A) - 136
8639-59 英邁 129th Division (23A) - 202-3
8661-74 鍾馗 130th Division (23A) - 203
DN • 8700-99 黒 *Kuro*, Kureme Divisional District
8737 備 9th Field Medium Artillery Regiment, detachment (31A) - 34
DN • 8800-49 Not Distributed
DN • 8850-99 漢 *Kan*, Keijo Divisional District Seoul, Korea
8852 尚武 26th Independent Motor Transport Battalion (14AA) - N/A
8853 森 73rd Line of Communications Sector Command (BAA) - N/A
8854 森 73rd Line of Communications Guard Unit (BAA) - N/A
8855 森 73rd Line of Communications Duty Company (BAA) - N/A
8856 昆 61st Field Motor Transport Battalion (33A) - 96
8857 威 62nd Ind. Motor Transport Battalion, att. 2nd Armored Div (14AA) - 107
8858 威 297th Independent Motor Transport Company (4AirA) - 122
8859 襲 298th Independent Motor Transport Company (7AirDiv 3AirA) - 58
8864 富 303rd Independent Motor Transport Company (25A) - 80
8890 策 101st Specially Established Construction Duty Company (11A) - 147
8891 波 102nd Specially Established Construction Duty Company (23A) - 135
DN • 8900-39 栄 *Sakae*, China Expeditionary Army
8900-17 菊 18th Division (33A) - 172
8906 烈 124th Infantry Regiment, 31st Division (15A) - 178
8906 菊 124th Infantry Regiment (reinforced) Kawaguchi Det. (17A) - 29
8920-36 沼 38th Division (8AA) - 182
8925 沼 229th Infantry Regiment, 1st Battalion, Lorengau Manus Is. (17A) - 30
8925 沼 229th Infantry Regiment, Southeast Detach., Bougainville (17A) - 30
8934-87 鍾馗 130th Division (23A) - 203
DN • 8940-53 湾 *Wan*, Formosa (Taiwan) Army
8940-53 海 48th Division (16A) - 185
DN • 8954-64 Not Distributed
8961-78 鳳 104th Division (23A) - 197-8
DN • 8965-99 栄 *Sakae*, China Expeditionary Army
8980-7 潮 19th Independent Mixed Brigade (23A) - 215
8983 英邁 129th Division (23A) - 202-3
8990 富 25th Army (7AA) - 80
8991 富 25th Army Headquarters (7AA) - 80
8993 森 14th Tank Regiment (BAA) - 86
8997 隼魁 96th Airfield Battalion (13AirDiv 5AirA) - 137

DN • 9000-20 薩 *Satsu* Kumamoto Divisional District
9015-34 明 6th Division (17A) - 167
9018 明 13th Infantry Regiment, Southeast Detachment, Bougainville (17A) - 30
DN • 9021-49 Gifu Air Division
DN • 9050-99 湾 "Wan" Formosa (Taiwan) Army
9050-2 旭 23rd Division (14AA) - 175-6
DN • 9100-49 薩 *Satsu*, Kumamoto Divisional District
9101 隼魁 2nd Air Brigade Headquarters (13AirDiv 5AirA) - 136
9102 隼魁 9th Air Regiment (13AirDiv 5AirA) - 136
9103 隼魁 6th Air Regiment (13AirDiv 5AirA) - 136
9106 威 26th Airfield Battalion (4AirA) - 120
9109 鷲 2nd Air Division Headquarters (4AirA) - 120
9110 威 37th Airfield Battalion (4AirA) - 120
9112 威 12th Airfield Battalion (4AirA) - 120
9113 翼 13th Air Sector Command (4AirA) - 120
9114 威 14th Airfield Battalion (4AirA) - 120
9123 威 27th Air Regiment (4AirA) - N/A
9124 高 64th Air Regiment (5AirDiv, 3AirA) - 56
9126 高 7th Air Sector Command (5AirDiv 3AirA) - 56
9127 高 17th Airfield Battalion (5AirDiv 3AirA) - 56
9128 高 23rd Airfield Battalion (5AirDiv 3AirA) - 56
9130 高 94th Airfield Battalion (5AirDiv 3AirA) - 57
9132 燕 74th Air Regiment (4AirA) - N/A
9133 燕 95th Air Regiment (4AirA) - 120
9134 威 32nd Airfield Battalion (4AirA) - 120
9135 洋 14th Air Brigade Headquarters (6AirDiv 8AA) - 50
9139 威 33rd Airfield Battalion (4AirA) - 120
9142 隼魁 16th Air Regiment (13AirDiv 5AirA) - 136
9144 富 33rd Air Regiment (4AirA) - 120
9146 翔 8th Air Sector Command (9AirDiv 3AirA) - 56
9148 翔 46th Airfield Battalion (9AirDiv 3AirA) - 56
DN • 9150-99 Gifu Air Division
9151 洋 68th Air Regiment (6AirDiv 8AA) - 50
9152 洋 78th Air Regiment (6AirDiv 8AA) -50
9168 威 8th Airfield Battalion (4AirA) - 120
9172 司 83rd Independent Air Command (3AirA) - 53
9180 昭 71st Independent Air Squadron (55AirDiv 3AirA) - 55
9181 司 73rd Independent Air Squadron (7AirDiv 3AirA) - 57
9183 司 84th Airfield Battalion (3AirA) - 53
9184 洋 24th Airfield Company (6AirDiv 18A) - 50
9194 高 34th Airfield Battalion (5AirDiv 3AirA) -56
9195 翼 6th Air Sector Command (4AirA) - 120
9198 司 30th Air Regiment (4AirA) - 120
DN • 9200-99 松 *Mutu*, Asahikawa Divisional District
9208 熊 28th Infantry Regiment, Ichiki Det. Guadalcanal (17A) - 29
9218 熊 7th Engineer Regiment, 1st Company w/Ichiki Det. Guadalcanal (17A) - 29
9285 森 18th Veterinary Hospital Depot (7AA) - 74

0	1	2	3	4	5	6	7	8	9	10
○	一	二	三	四	五	六	七	八	九	十

9290 剛 19th Field Anti Aircraft Artillery Command (8AA) - 24
DN • 9300-49 Gifu Air Division
9300 洋 6th Air Division, # not a unit (8AA) - 50
9301 洋 6th Air Division Headquarters (8AA) - 50
9302 輝 4th Air Intelligence Regiment, att. 36th Div. (2A) - 67
9303 洋 11th Field Airfield Construction Unit (6AirDiv 8AA) - 50
9304 洋 14th Field Air Repair Depot (8AirDiv 18A) - 50
9304 洋 14th Field Air Repair Depot, was 6AirDiv, attached 36th Div (2A) - 67
9304 洋 14th Field Air Repair Depot, 8th Ind. Maint. Unit, Luzon (4AirA) - 117, 122
9304 洋 14th Field Air Repair Depot, 9th Ind. Maintenance Unit, Saipan (31A) - 35
9305 輝 14th Field Air Freight Depot, attached 36th Div. (2A) - 67
9306 杉 18th Shipping Air Depot (41A) - 115
9308 隼魁 20th Airfield Company (13AirDiv 5AirA) - 137
9309 隼魁 21st Airfield Company (13AirDiv 5AirA) - 137
9311 襲 7th Air Division Headquarters (7AirDiv 3AirA) - 57
9312 威 Southern Army Aviation Department (SA) - 42
9315 洋 14th Air Brigade Headquarters (6AirDiv 8AA) - 50
9315 洋 1st Air Route Department (6AirDiv 8AA) - 50
9320 司 20th Field Air Freight Depot (3AirA) - 54
9322 洋 1st Mobile Air Repair Section (6AirDiv 8AA) - 50
9323 司 16th Field Air Repair Depot (3AirA) - 54
9324 司 19th Field Air Repair Depot (3AirA) - 54
9324 眞 19th Field Air Repair Depot, 1st to 3rd Ind. Maint. Units (14AirA) - 122
9326 威 Southern Army Air Transport Department (SA) - 42
9327 洋 2nd Mobile Air Repair Section (6AirDiv 8AA) - 50
9328 洋 3rd Mobile Air Repair Section (6AirDiv 8AA) - 50
9329 洋 4th Mobile Air Repair Section (6AirDiv 8AA) - 51
9330 洋 5th Mobile Air Repair Section (6AirDiv 8AA) - 51
9333 昭 14th Airfield Company (9AirDiv 3AirA) - 56
9334 襲 15th Airfield Company (7AirDiv 3AirA) - 58
9335 司 16th Airfield Company (3AirA) - 53
9336 高 17th Airfield Company (5AirDiv 3AirA) - 57
9337 高 18th Airfield Company (5AirDiv 3AirA) - 57
9339 隼魁 19th Airfield Company (13AirDiv 5AirA) - 137
DN • 9350-99 徳 *Toku*, Kwantung (Kantō) Army
9356 森 Burma Area Army Motor Transport Unit (BAA) - 86
9357 策 20th Field Road Construction Unit (28A) - 91
9358 猛 8th Division, 9th Transport Unit (18A) - 48
9362 富 12th Disease Prevention and Water Supply Unit (25A) - 81
9364 森 21st Field Motor Transport Depot (BAA) - 88
9368 隼魁 85th Airfield Company (5AirDiv 3AirA) - 57
9369 昭 88th Airfield Company (9AirDiv 3AirA) - 56
DN • 9400-20 Not Distributed
9400-9 節 22nd Independent Mixed Brigade (11A) - 216

9410 策 28th Army Headquarters (BAA) - 91
9411 定 29th Army Headquarters (7AA) - 83
9420 威 Southern Army Disease Prevention and Water Supply Dept. (SA) - 41
9420 尚武 Southern Army D. P., Water Supply Dept. Manila Branch (14AA) - 109
DN • 9421-99 栄 *Sakae*, China Expeditionary Army
9421 猛 9th Shipping Engineer Regiment (18A) - N/A
9422 暁 10th Shipping Engineer Regiment (SoS) - 59
9423 猛 36th Independent Engineer Regiment (8AA) - 48
9425 開 69th Infantry Brigade, brigade id # 64th Div (20A) - 192
9426-8 開 64th Division (20A) - 192
9429-34 専 65th Division (13A) - 192-3
9435 桜 5th Independent Mountain Artillery Regiment (20A) - 149
9436 栄 China Expeditionary Army Infantry Training Unit (CA) - 128
9437 栄 China Expeditionary Army Artillery Training Unit (CA) - 128
9438 栄 China Expeditionary Army Engineer Training Unit (CA) - 128
9440 栄 China Expeditionary Army Special Affairs Department (CA) - 128
9444 節 22nd Independent Mixed Brigade, not a unit (11A) - 216
9445 純 23rd Independent Mixed Brigade, not a unit (23A) - 216-7
9447 征 7th Independent Infantry Brigade, brigade code # (6AA) - 237
9448 征 7th Independent Infantry Brigade Headquarters (6AA) - 237
9449 **路** 4th Field Railway Command, central China (CA) - 143
9450 賢 19th Army Headquarters (SA) - 71 (both 9450 are correct)
9450 統 19th Line of Communications Veterinary Depot (6AA) - 143
9451 統 95th Independent Wire Company (6AA) - 141
9455 甲 20th Line of Communications Veterinary Depot (NCAA) - 154
9456 登 86th Line of Communications Guard Unit (13A) - 131
9457 登 87th Line of Communications Guard Unit (13A) - 131
9461 栄 China Expeditionary Army Field Materials Depot (CA) - 128
9463 栄 China Expeditionary Army Survey Department (CA) - 128
9464 栄 China Expeditionary Army Fortification Department (CA) - 128
9465 栄 China Expeditionary Army Chemical Department (CA) - 128
9466 勢 2nd Field Base Headquarters (2A) - 68
9479 統 6th Area Army Field Horse Remount Depot (6AA) - 143
9481 登 192nd Line of Communications Hospital (13A) - 132
DN • 9500-49 松 *Mutu*, Asahikawa Divisional District
9536 森 23rd Line of Comm. Motor Transport Command (BAA) - 87
DN • 9550-99 北部 *Hokubu* Army District
DN • 9600-99 Gifu Air Division
9605 / 304 司 9th Air Sector Command (7AirDiv 3AirA) - 57
9606 洋 20th Airfield Battalion (6AirDiv 18A) - 50
9607 洋 47th Airfield Battalion (6AirDiv 18A) - 50
9608 洋 51st Airfield Battalion (6AirDiv 18A) - 50
9612 隼魁 14th Air Signal Regiment (13AirDiv 5AirA) - N/A
9613 高 19th Airfield Battalion (5AirDiv 3AirA) - 56
9614 高 52nd Airfield Battalion (5AirDiv 3AirA) - 57
9615 洋 25th Airfield Battalion (6AirDiv 8AA) - 50
9616 司 3rd Air Signal Regiment (3AirA) - 54

0	1	2	3	4	5	6	7	8	9	10
○	一	二	三	四	五	六	七	八	九	十

9616 司 3rd Air Signal Regiment, 2nd Co. in Burma (3AirA) - N/A
9617 高 2nd Air Intelligence Regiment (5AirDiv 3AirA) - 57
9622 司 10th Independent Air Brigade Headquarters (3AirA) - 58
9623 威 31st Air Regiment (4AirA) - 120
9624 翔 76th Airfield Battalion (9AirDiv 3AirA) - 56
9638 高 5th Air Division Headquarters (5AirDiv 3AirA) - 56
9641 司 70th Independent Flying Squadron (7AirDiv 3AirA) - 57
9643 翔 74th Independent Flying Squadron (9AirDiv 3AirA) - 56
9644 洋 48th Airfield Battalion (6AirDiv, 8AA) - 50
9645 高 75th Airfield Battalion (5AirDiv 3AirA) - 57
9646 高 81st Airfield Battalion (55AirDiv 3AirA) - 55
9647 昭 85th Airfield Battalion (55AirDiv 3AirA) - 55
9648 昭 90th Airfield Battalion (55AirDiv 3AirA) - 55
9648/9870 高 Later 90th/92nd Joint Airfield Battalion (5AirDiv 3AirA) - 57
DN • 9700-49 県 *Kuro*, Kurume Divisional District
9704 備 2nd Medium Mortar Battalion, Iwo Jima (31A) - 33
9714 波 66th Line of Communications Sector Command (23A) - 136
9714 波 66th Sector Transport Unit (23A) - 136
9714 波 66th Line of Communications Duty Unit (23A) - 136
9715 波 66th Line of Communications Guard Unit (23A) - 136
9717 富 57th Independent Motor Transport Battalion (25A) - 80
9719 輝 290th Independent Motor Transport Company (2A) - 69
9721 栄 292nd Independent Motor Transport Company (CA) - 129
9723 尚武 16th Casualty Clearing Unit Headquarters (14AA) - 109
9735 路 161st Railway Station Command (SRR) - 62
9736 暁 47th Anchorage Headquarters (SoS) - 59
9737 暁 48th Anchorage Headquarters (SoS) - 59
9738 猛 49th Anchorage Headquarters (18A) - 50
9742 統 54th Sea Duty Company (6AA) - 142
9746 森 15th Field Duty Unit Headquarters (BAA) - 87
9748 杉 111th Land Duty Company (41A) - 114
DN • 9750-99 西部 *Seibu* Army District
9751 勢 19th Field Post Office Unit (2A) - 69
9757 甲 193rd Railway Station Command (NCAA) - 154
9758 路 194th Railway Station Command (CA) - N/A
9759 尚武 85th Line of Communications Sector Transport Unit (14AA) - 108
9766 威 138th Line of Communications Hospital, Comotes Detach. (14AA) - 110
9767 威 139th Line of Communications Hospital (14AA) - 109
9768 呂 140th Line of Communications Hospital (11A) - 148
9771 勢 87th Casualty Clearing Platoon (2A) - 70
9772 勢 88th Casualty Clearing Platoon (2A) - 70
9774 呂 89th Casualty Clearing Platoon (11A) - 148
9789 尚武 85th Line of Communications Sector Command (14AA) - 108
DN • 9800-49 東部 *Tobu* Army District

9800 威 Southern Army Fuel Depot (SA) - 42
9801 灘 37th Army Headquarters (7AA) - 78
9811 沖 17th Army Headquarters (8AA) - 28
9813 司 3rd Air Army Headquarters (3AirA) - 53
9815 司 1st Field Replacement Flying Unit (3AirA) - 53
9823 西 21st Ind. Mixed Bgde Artillery Unit, same as 5th Ind Hvy Art Btn (18A) - 216
9823 猛 5th Independent Field Medium Artillery Battalion (18A) - 48
9824 西 21st Ind. Mixed Brigade Anti-Aircraft Unit, same as 42nd AA Co (18A) - 216
9824 猛 42nd Independent Field Anti-Aircraft Company (18A) - 49
9841-50 純 23rd Independent Mixed Brigade (23A) - 216-7
DN • 9850-99 栄 *Sakae*, China Expeditionary Army
9851-8 夏 65th Brigade (8AA) - 235
9861 高 15th Air Sector Command (3AirA) - 53
9862 隼魁 16th Air Sector Command (13AirDiv 5AirA) - 137
9864 隼魁 5th Air Sector Command (13AirDiv 5AirA) - 136
9865 司 35th Airfield Battalion (7AirDiv 3AirA) - 57
9866 洋 41st Airfield Battalion (6AirDiv, 18A) - 50
9867 隼魁 57th Airfield Battalion (13AirDiv 5AirA) - 137
9868 高 82nd Airfield Battalion (5AirDiv 3AirA) - 57
9869 隼魁 91st Airfield Battalion (13AirDiv 5AirA) - 137
9870 昭 92nd Airfield Battalion (5AirDiv 3AirA) - 57
9870 / 9648 - 90th/92nd Joint Airfield Battalion (5AirDiv 3AirA) - 57
9871 隼魁 1st Airfield Company (13AirDiv 5AirA) - 137
9872 隼魁 2nd Airfield Company (13AirDiv 5AirA) - 137
9873 隼魁 67th Airfield Company (13AirDiv 5AirA) - 137
9874 隼魁 69th Airfield Company (13AirDiv 5AirA) - 137
9875 洋 86th Airfield Company (6AirDiv, 8AA) - 50
9879 司 17th Air Navigation Aid Unit (5AirDiv 3AirA) - 57
9890 治 1st Line of Communications Motor Transport Company (2A) - 69
9891 隼魁 13th L. of C. Motor Transport Company (13AirDiv 5AirA) - 137
9892 隼魁 64th L. of C. Motor Transport Company (13AirDiv 5AirA) - 137
9893 高 86th Line of Communication Motor Transport Unit (5AirDiv 3AirA) - 57
9894 隼 92nd L. of C. Motor Transport Company (13AirDiv 5AirA) - 137
9896 高 5th Air Division Signal Unit (5AirDiv 3AirA) - 56
DN • 9900-99 Gifu Air Division
9902 威 4th Air Brigade Headquarters (5AirDiv 3AirA) - 56
9903 高 1st Air Sector Command (5AirDiv 3AirA) - 56
9905 司 4th Air Sector Command (7AirDiv 3AirA) - 57
9909 司 37th Air Sector Command (10th Ind. Air Brigade 3AirA) - 58
9915 司 1st Field Replacement Flying Unit Headquarters (3AirA) - 53
9921 高 15th Airfield Battalion (5AirDiv 3AirA) - 56
9922 司 24th Airfield Battalion (3AirA) - 53
9923 司 27th Airfield Battalion (3AirA) - 53
9924 司 28th Airfield Battalion (7AirDiv 3AirA) - 57
9925 威 151st Airfield Battalion (KeG 14AA and 4AirA) - 117, 121
9926 威 152nd Airfield Battalion (KeG 14AA and 4AirA) - 117, 121
9927 威 153rd Airfield Battalion (4AirA) - 121

0	1	2	3	4	5	6	7	8	9	10
〇	一	二	三	四	五	六	七	八	九	十

9928 威 154th Airfield Battalion (4AirA) - 121
9929 威 155th Airfield Battalion (4AirA) - 121
9931 司 5th Airfield Company (3AirA) - 53
9932 隼魁 6th Airfield Company (13AirDiv 5AirA) - 137
9933 襲 7th Airfield Company (7AirDiv 3AirA) - 58
9934 高 9th Airfield Company (5AirDiv 3AirA) - 57
9935 昭 12th Airfield Company (5AirDiv 3AirA) - 57
9937 襲 29th Airfield Company (7AirDiv 3AirA) - 58
9938 / 15374 威 32nd Airfield Company, Comotes Detach. (14AA) - 110
9939 洋 33rd Airfield Company (6AirDiv, 8AA) - 50
9941 輝 5th Air Signal Regiment, attached 36th Div (2A) - 67
9942 威 6th Air Signal Regiment (4AirA) - 122
9947 鸞 1st Air Raiding Regiment (KeG 14AA) - 240-1
9948 鸞 3rd Air Raiding Regiment (KeG 14AA) - 240-1
9949 鸞 4th Air Raiding Regiment (KeG 14AA) - 240-1
9951 猛 4th Field Airfield Construction Unit (6AirDiv, 8AA) - 50
9952 勢 5th Field Airfield Construction Unit (2A) - 70
9953 勢 6th Field Airfield Construction Unit (2A) - 70
9954 高 7th Field Airfield Construction Unit (5AirDiv 3AirA) - 57
9955 高 8th Field Airfield Construction Unit (5AirDiv 3AirA) - 57
9956 司 9th Field Airfield Construction Unit (7AirDiv, 3AirA) - 58
9957 洋 10th Field Airfield Construction Unit (6AirDiv, 8AA) - 50
DN • 10000-15, 星 *Hoshi*, 68th Brigade
10000-7 星 68th Brigade (14AA) - 235
DN • 10016-99, 洛 *Raku*, Kyoto Divisional District
10016-41 安 53rd Division (BAA) - 187-8
10050 杉 4th Medium Trench Mortar Battalion (41A) - 114
10054 / 8213 甲 126th Railway Station Command (NCAA/CRR) - 154
10059 威 49th Field Road Construction Unit, att. 2nd Armored Div (14AA) - 107
DN • 10100-99, 兵 *Hei*, 54th Division
10100-28 兵 54th Division (28A) - 188
10118 月 54th Engineer Regiment, attached 17th Div. (8AA) - 172
10120 兵54th Transport Regiment, 3rd Company, Saku Group (28A) - 92
10154 威 7th Field Replacement Unit Headquarters (SA) - 42
10154 義 7th Field Replacement Unit, Bangkok Defense Unit (39A) - 102
10155 / 6919 策 97th Land Duty Company (11A) - 147
10156 / 6920 策 98th Land Duty Company (11A) - 147
10157 猛 40th Field Road Construction Unit (18A) - 48
10162 輝 57th Casualty Clearing Platoon (2AA) - 64
10171 駿 26th Independent Machinegun Battalion, att. 103rd Div (14AA) - 107
DN • 10200-99, 洛 *Raku*, Kyoto Divisional District
10216 輝 263rd Independent Motor Transport Company (2A) - 69
10225 勢 55th Line of Communications Sector Command (2A) - 68
10225 勢 55th Line of Communications Guard Unit (2A) - 68

10225 勢 55th Line of Communications Duty Company (2A) - 68
10226 輝 56th Line of Communications Sector Command (2AA) - 64
10226 輝 56th Line of Communications Guard Unit (2AA) - 64
10226 輝 56th Line of Communications Duty Company (2AA) - 64
10230 統 43rd Sea Duty Company (6AA) - 142
10234 尚武 12th Field Duty Unit Headquarters (14AA) - 109
10281 森 30th Field Duty Unit Headquarters (BAA) - 87
10282 森 26th Field Disease Prevention and Water Supply Unit (BAA) - 88
10284-6 恵 118th Division (13A) - 202
10291-9 鎧 61st Independent Mixed Brigade (14AA) - 228
DN • 10300-499, 威 *i*, Southern Expeditionary Army, April 1945 distribution
10306 岡 3rd Southern Army Hospital (SA) - N/A
10307 信 4th Southern Army Hospital (38A) - 44
10308 威 Southern Army Military Police Training Unit (SA) - 41
10308 岡 Singapore Military Police Unit (7AA) - 74
10309 威 8th Southern Army Hospital (29A) - 83
10310 威 9th Southern Army Hospital (25A) - 81
10311 威 10th Southern Army Hospital (25A) - 81
10312 威 11th Southern Army Hospital (37A) - 79
10314 治 4th Railway Transport Headquarters (16A) - 77
10315 尚武 6th Railway Transport Command (14AA) - 109
10316 威 Southern Army Signal Unit Headquarters (SA) - 41
10316 森 Southern Army Signal Unit Burma Special Investigation Unit (BAA) - 87
10317 威 Southern Army Construction Training Department (SA) - 41
10318 勢 24th Signal Regiment (2A) - 67
10322 灘 432nd Independent Infantry Battalion (37A) - 78
10343 岡 Southern Army Reserve Officer Candidate Unit (7AA) - 74
10344 岡 Southern Army NCO Officer Candidate Unit (7AA) - 74
10345 岡 Southern Army Accounting Training Department (7AA) - 74
10346 岡 Southern Army Medical Training Department (7AA) - 74
10347 剛 26th Field Ordinance Depot (8AA) - 24
10347 沖 26th Field Ordnance Depot, one section (17A) - 28
10348 剛 26th Field Motor Transport Depot (8AA) - 25
10348 沖 26th Field Motor Transport Depot, one section (17A) - 28
10349 剛 26th Field Freight Depot (8AA) - 25
10349 沖 26th Field Freight Depot, one section (17A) - 28
10352-3 烈 31st Division (15A) - 178
10354 岡 7th Area Army Field Ordinance Depot (7AA) - 74
10355 岡 7th Area Army Motor Vehicle Repair Depot (7AA) - 74
10356 岡 7th Area Army Field Freight Depot (7AA) - 74
10357 森 Burma Area Army Field Ordinance Depot (BAA) - 88
10358 森 Burma Area Army Field Motor Transport Depot (BAA) - 88
10359 森 Burma Area Army Field Freight Depot (BAA) - 88
10360 治 16th Army Field Ordinance Depot (16A) - 77
10361 治 16th Army Motor Vehicle Depot (16A) - 77
10362 治 16th Army Freight Depot (16A) - 77
10363 富 25th Army Field Ordinance Depot (25A) - 81

0	1	2	3	4	5	6	7	8	9	10
〇	一	二	三	四	五	六	七	八	九	十

10364 富 25th Army Field Motor Vehicle Depot (25A) - 81
10365 富 25th Army Field Freight Depot (25A) - 81
10366 翔 Palembang Guards Unit Headquarters, Palembang (3AirA) - 250
10367 翔 101st Anti-Aircraft Regiment, Palembang (3AirA) - 250
10368 翔 102nd Anti-Aircraft Regiment, Palembang (3AirA) - 250
10369 翔 103rd Anti-Aircraft Regiment, Palembang (3AirA) - 250
10371 輝 1st Specially Established Land Duty Company (2A) - 69
10372 剛 2nd Specially Established Land Duty Company (8AA) - 25
10373 剛 3rd Specially Established Land Duty Company (8AA) - 25
10374 剛 4th Specially Established Land Duty Company (8AA) - 25
10375 沖 5th Specially Established Land Duty Company (8AA) - 25
10376 剛 6th Specially Established Land Duty Company (8AA) - 25
10377 備 7th Specially Established Land Duty Company, Palau (31A) - 36
10378 猛 16th Specially Established Sea Duty Company (18A) - N/A
10379 猛 17th Specially Established Sea Duty Company (18A) - N/A
10380 猛 18th Specially Established Sea Duty Company (18A) - N/A
10381 猛 19th Specially Established Sea Duty Company (18A) - N/A
10382 猛 20th Specially Established Sea Duty Company (18A) - N/A
10383 猛 26th Specially Established Construction Duty Company (18A) - 49
10384 剛 27th Specially Established Construction Duty Company (8AA) - 25
10385 森 8th Specially Established Land Duty Company (BAA) - 87
10386 森 9th Specially Established Land Duty Company (BAA) - 87
10387 森 10th Specially Established Land Duty Company (BAA) - 87
10388 勢 11th Specially Established Land Duty Company (2A) - 69
10390 富 13th Specially Established Land Duty Company (25A) - 81
10391 富 14th Specially Established Land Duty Company (25A) - 81
10392 岡 15th Specially Established Land Duty Company (7AA) - 74
10393 森 21st Specially Established Sea Duty Company (BAA) - 88
10394 森 22nd Specially Established Sea Duty Company (BAA) - 88
10397 富 25th Specially Established Sea Duty Company (25A) - 81
10398 森 28th Specially Established Construction Duty Company (BAA) - 88
10399 勢 29th Specially Established Construction Duty Company (2A) - 69
10400 – 91st Independent Airfield Company - N/A
10411 富 30th Specially Established Construction Duty Company (25A) - 81
10413 威 Southern Army Fortification Department (SA) - 41
10413 森 Southern Army Fortification Construction Dept. Burma Detail (BAA) - 86
10414 威 Southern Army 1st Survey Unit (SA) - 41
10415 森 1st Specially Established Motor Transport Company (BAA) - 87
10416 森 2nd Specially Established Motor Transport Company (BAA) - 87
10417 森 3rd Specially Established Motor Transport Company (BAA) - 87
10418 森 4th Specially Established Motor Transport Company (BAA) - 87
10419 森 5th Specially Established Motor Transport Company (BAA) - 87
10420 森 6th Specially Established Motor Transport Company (BAA) - 87
10421 森 7th Specially Established Motor Transport Company (BAA) - 87

10422 森 8th Specially Established Motor Transport Company (BAA) - 87
10423 昆 9th Specially Established Motor Transport Company (33A) - 96
10424 策 10th Specially Established Motor Transport Company (28A) - 91
10425 富 11th Specially Established Motor Transport Company (25A) - 80
10426 森 12th Specially Established Motor Transport Company (BAA) - 87
10427 輝 13th Specially Established Motor Transport Company (2A) - 69
10428 義 14th Specially Established Motor Transport Company (18AA) - 98, 102
10429 義 15th Specially Established Motor Transport Company (18AA) - 98, 102
10430 定 16th Specially Established Motor Transport Company (25A) - 80
10431 定 17th Specially Established Motor Transport Company (29A) - 83
10432 富 18th Specially Established Motor Transport Company (25A) - 80
10433 森 19th Specially Established Motor Transport Company (BAA) - 87
10434 森 20th Specially Established Motor Transport Company (BAA) - 87
10435 昆 21st Specially Established Motor Transport Company (33A) - 96
10436 勢 1st Specially Established Sea Transport Unit, att. 48th Div (2A) - 67
10437 勢 2nd Specially Established Sea Transport Unit (2A) - 69
10438 森 3rd Specially Established Sea Transport Unit (BAA) - 88
10439 森 31st Specially Established Land Duty Company (BAA) - 87
10440 森 32nd Specially Established Land Duty Company (BAA) - 88
10443 勢 35th Specially Established Land Duty Company (2A) - 69
10444 尚武 46th Specially Established Construction Duty Company (14AA) - 109
10445 尚 47th Specially Established Construction Duty Company (35A) - 113
10446 勢 48th Specially Established Construction Duty Company (2A) - 69
10447 尚 49th Specially Established Construction Duty Company (35A) - 113
10448 勢 50th Specially Established Construction Duty Company (2A) - 69
10449 51st Specially Established Sea Duty Company - N/A
10450 勢 52nd Specially Established Sea Duty Company (2A) - N/A
10451 暁 53rd Specially Established Sea Duty Company (2A?) - N/A
10452 暁 54th Specially Established Sea Duty Company (2A?) - N/A
10453 暁 55th Specially Established Sea Duty Company (2A?) - N/A
10454 杉 22nd Specially Established Motor Transport Company (41A) - 114
10455 尚 23rd Specially Established Motor Transport Company (35A) - 112
10456 尚 24th Specially Established Motor Transport Company (35A) - 112
10457 尚 25th Specially Established Motor Transport Company (35A) - 112
10458 治 26th Specially Established Motor Transport Company (2A) - 69
10459 治 27th Specially Established Motor Transport Company (2A) - 69
10460 勢 28th Specially Established Motor Transport Company (2A) - 69
10462 輝 30th Specially Established Motor Transport Company (2AA) - 64
10469 勢 42nd Specially Established Land Duty Company (2A) - 69
10473 暁 56th Specially Established Sea Duty Company (2A?) - N/A
10474 暁 57th Specially Established Sea Duty Company (2A?) - N/A
10475 暁 58th Specially Established Sea Duty Company (2A?) - N/A
10476 暁 59th Specially Established Sea Duty Company (2A?) - N/A
10477 暁 60th Specially Established Sea Duty Company (2A?) - N/A
10478 信 34th Independent Motor Transport Company (38A) - 44
10480 信 186th Independent Motor Transport Company (38A) - 44
10482 岡 Southern Army Training Unit (7AA) - 74

0	1	2	3	4	5	6	7	8	9	10
○	一	二	三	四	五	六	七	八	九	十

10483 威 Southern Army Special Intelligence Department (SA) - 41
10483 森 Southern Army Burma Special Affairs Squad (BAA) - 87
10484 定 1st Southwest Guard Unit (29A) - 83
10485 定 2nd Southwest Guard Unit (29A) - 83
10487 森 94th Independent Wire Company (BAA) - 86
10497 岡 7th Area Army Ordinance Manufacturing Depot - 74
10497 威 Southern Army Manila Ordinance Repair Shop (SA) - 109
10498 威 16th Southern Army Hospital (18AA) - 98
10499 富 17th Southern Army Hospital (25A) - 81
DN • 10500-49, Not Distributed
10512 暁 45th Sea Duty Company (6AA) - 142
10590 林 15th Army Field Ordinance Depot (15A) - 101
10591 林 15th Army Field Motor Vehicle Depot (15A) - 101
10592 林 15th Army Field Freight Depot (15A) - 101
10593 森 70th Field Anti-Aircraft Battalion, Rangoon Defense Unit (BAA) - 250
10595 勢 41st Field Machine Cannon Company (2A) - 68
10596雪 36th Division Tank Company (2AA) - 181
DN • 10600 – 10699, 尚武 *Shobu*, 14th Area Army, Apr. 1945 distribution
10600-75 抛 100th Division (35A) - 195-6
10601 駿 79th Brigade Signal Unit, 103rd Div (14AA) - 197
10602-98 抜 102nd Division (35A) - 196
10603-79 駿 103rd Division (14AA) - 197
10604 駿 79th Brigade Labor Unit, 103rd Div (14AA) - 197
10605-92 勤 105th Division (41A) - 198
10606 駿 103rd Division Engineer Unit (14AA) - 198
10607 駿 103rd Division Transport Unit (14AA) - 198
10608 勤 105th Division Engineer Unit (14AA) - 198
10609 勤 105th Division Transport Unit (14AA) - 198
10612 尚武 12th Southern Army Hospital (14AA) - 109
10613 尚 13th Southern Army (Cebu City) Hospital (35A) - 112
10614 尚 14th Southern Army (Davao City) Hospital (35A) - 113
10616 翼 31st Air Sector Command (4AirA) - 120
10617 威 61st Surface to Air Radio Unit (41A) - 115
10618 威 43rd Secondary Air Training Unit (4AirA) - 120
10619 / 16019 杉 Manila Anti Aircraft Artillery Headquarters (41A) - 114
10620-38 抛 30th Independent Mixed Brigade; became 100th Div (14AA) - 219
10627 輝 2nd Area Army Field Ordinance Depot (2AA) - 64
10628 輝 2nd Area Army Field Motor Vehicle Depot (2AA) - 64
10629 輝 2nd Area Army Field Freight Depot (2AA) - 64
10630-5 抜 31st Independent Mixed Brigade; became 102nd Div (14AA) - 219-2
10640-99 駿 32nd Independent Mixed Brigade; became 103rd Div (14AA) - 220
10650 翼 22nd Field Meteorological Unit (4AirDiv 4AirA) - 122
10651 暁 7th Shipping Engineer Regiment (SoS) - 59
10653 翼 11th Air Sector Command Headquarters (4AirA) - 120

0	1	2	3	4	5	6	7	8	9	10
○	一	二	三	四	五	六	七	八	九	十

11012/23011 灘 454th Independent Infantry Battalion (37A) - 78
11013/23012 灘 455th Independent Infantry Battalion (37A) - 78
11014 灘 64th Independent Field Anti-Aircraft Company (37A) - 78
11015 灘 553rd Independent Infantry Battalion (37A) - 78
11016 灘 554th Independent Infantry Battalion (37A) - 78
11017 灘 774th Independent Infantry Battalion (37A) - 78
11031 灘 103rd Field Road Construction Unit (37A) - 78
DN • 11050-11149, 司 *Tsukasa*, 3rd Air Army, Apr. 1945 distribution
11051 洋 34th Air Regiment (4AirA) - 120
11052 司 4th Air Navigational Aid Unit (3AirA) - 54
11053 司 3rd Meteorological Regiment (3AirA) - 54
11055 司 3rd Air Signals Headquarters (3AirA) - 53
11056 昭 Southern Army 1st Air Training Unit (55AirDiv 3AirA) - 55
11057 司 9th Air Signals Regiment (7AirDiv 3AirA) - 58
11058 司 2nd Air Route Unit (3AirA) - 54
11059 司 28th Airfield Company (3AirA) - 53
11060 翔 30th Airfield Company (9AirDiv 3AirA) - 56
11063 司 20th Field Aircraft Repair Depot (3AirA) - 54
11064 翔 22nd Air Sector Command (9AirDiv 3AirA) - 56
11065 司 23rd Air Sector Command (3AirA) - 53
11066 昭 16th Secondary Flight Training Unit (55AirDiv 3AirA) - 55
11067 昭 17th Secondary Flight Training Unit (55AirDiv 3AirA) - 55
11068 昭 34th Secondary Flight Training Unit (55AirDiv 3AirA) - 55
11069 昭 35th Secondary Flight Training Unit (55AirDiv 3AirA) - 55
11070 司 83rd Air Regiment (4AirA) - 120
11072 高 78th Airfield Battalion (4AirA) - N/A
11073 司 22nd Field Aircraft Repair Depot (3AirA) - 54
11074 司 25th Field Aircraft Repair Depot (3AirA) - 54
11075 司 13th Field Air Freight Depot (3AirA) - 54
11076 昭 106th Independent Flight Training Brigade (55AirDiv 3AirA) - 55
11077 昭 109th Independent Flight Training Brigade (55AirDiv 3AirA) - 55
11078 司 24th Air Sector Command (3AirA) - 53
11079 司 25th Air Sector Command (3AirA) - 53
11080 昭 9th Secondary Flight Training Unit (55AirDiv 3AirA) - 55
11081 昭 44th Secondary Flight Training Unit (55AirDiv 3AirA) - 55
11082 昭 45th Secondary Flight Training Unit (55AirDiv 3AirA) - 55
11084 司 31st Wireless Radio Unit (3AirA) - 54
11085 司 32nd Wireless Radio Unit (3AirA) - 54
11086 司 33rd Wireless Radio Unit (3AirA) - 54
11087 司 34th Wireless Radio Unit (3AirA) - 54
11088 司 35th Wireless Radio Unit (3AirA) - 54
11089 司 36th Wireless Radio Unit (3AirA) - 54
11090 司 14th Field Meteorological Unit (25A) - 81
11093 昭 17th Advanced Flight Training Unit (55AirDiv 3AirA) - 55

11094 昭 18th Advanced Flight Training Unit (55AirDiv 3AirA) - 55
11097 昭 26th Advanced Flight Training Unit (55AirDiv 3AirA) - 55
11098 昭 27th Advanced Flight Training Unit (55AirDiv 3AirA) - 55
11099 昭 28th Secondary Flight Training Unit (55AirDiv 3AirA) - 55
DN • 11150-99, 遠征 *Sizume*, 44th Army, Apr. 1945 distribution
11100 司 59th Air Sector Command (3AirA) - 53
11150 登 11th Field Replacement Unit (13A) - 132
11160-8 至堅 92nd Independent Mixed Brigade (13A) - 234
11172 甲 124th Specially Established Sea Duty Company (NCAA) - 154
11173 甲 125th Specially Established Sea Duty Company (NCAA) - 154
11174 甲 126th Specially Established Sea Duty Company (NCAA) - 154
DN • 11200-99, 剛 *Go*, 8th Area Army, Apr. 1945 distribution
11210 剛 8th Area Army Fortification Department (8AA) - 24
11211 剛 8th Area Army Signal Unit Headquarters (8AA) - 24
11212 剛 8th Fixed Signal Unit (8AA) - 24
11213 猛 9th Fixed Signal Unit (8AA) - 24
11214 剛 1st Independent Wireless Radio Platoon, was So Seas Det (8AA) - 24, 29
11216 剛 47th Signal Regiment (8AA) - 24
11220 剛 8th Area Army Special Intelligence Department (8AA) - 24
11221 備 1st South Seas Detachment, activated Dec 16, 1943 (31A) - 31
11222 剛 14th Independent Mixed Regiment (8AA) - 24
11223 剛 (The) Independent Sea Duty Battalion (8AA) - 25
11225 剛 9th Artillery Headquarters (8AA) - 24
11226 剛 1st Independent Mortar Battalion (8AA) - 24
11230-6 隆 39th Independent Mixed Brigade (8AA) - 222
11235 剛 15th Fixed Signal Unit (8AA) - 24
11240-51 隆 40th Independent Mixed Brigade (8AA) - 223
11252 剛 6th Raiding Unit (8AA) - 25
11253 剛 7th Raiding Unit (8AA) - 25
11254 剛 8th Area Army Independent Air Unit (8AA) - 24
DN • 11300-99, 沖 *Oki*, 17th Army, Apr. 1945 distribution
11301 剛 1st Independent Wireless Radio Platoon (8AA) - 24
11302 猛 6th Independent Wireless Radio Platoon (17A) - 28
11303 沖 69th Independent Wireless Radio Platoon (17A) - 28
11304 沖 70th Independent Wireless Radio Platoon (17A) - 28
11306-10 力 38th Independent Mixed Brigade (17A) - 222
11311 沖 32nd Signal Regiment (17A) - 28
DN • 11400-99, 猛 *Mo*, 18th Army, Apr. 1945 distribution
11400 猛 3rd Signal Regiment, minus 1st Company (18A) - 48
11400 猛 3rd Signal Regiment, 1st Company, Hollandia (18A) - 49
11401 猛 7th Independent Wireless Radio Platoon (18A) - 48
11402 猛 8th Independent Wireless Radio Platoon (18A) - 48
DN • 11500-99, Not Distributed
11504 堅 19th Army Intelligence Section (19A) - 71
11505 堅 19th Army Field Ordinance Depot (19A) - 71
11506 堅 19th Army Field Motor Vehicle Depot (19A) - 71
11507 堅 19th Army Field Freight Depot (19A) - 71

0	1	2	3	4	5	6	7	8	9	10
○	一	二	三	四	五	六	七	八	九	十

11508 堅 117th Field Airfield Construction Unit (19A) - 71
11509 堅 118th Field Airfield Construction Unit (19A) - 71
11510 堅 119th Field Airfield Construction Unit (19A) - 71
11513 治 33rd Specially Established Motor Transport Company (2A) - 69
11514 治 34th Specially Established Motor Transport Company (2A) - 69
11515 治 35th Specially Established Motor Transport Company (2A) - 69
11516 治 12th Field Medium Artillery Battalion (16A) - 76
DN • 11600-99, 翼 *Tsubasa*, 4th Air Division
11601 翼 4th Air Division Headquarters (4AirA) - 120
11611 威 5th Air Brigade Headquarters (4AirA) - 120
11613 昭 18th Air Sector Command, 36th Div (2A) - 67
11615 剛 25th Airfield Company, Los Negros Is. (8AA) -30
11620 翼 10th Air Sector Command (KeG 14AA and 4AirA) - 117, 120
11701 洋 6th Air Navigation Unit (6AirDiv 18A) - 50
11702 洋 12th Field Meteorological Unit (6AirDiv, 18A) - 50
11758 波 8th Specially Established Engineer Company (23A) - 135
11759 波 9th Specially Established Engineer Company (23A) - 135
DN • 11800 – 11899, 襲 *Shu*, 7th Air Division
11800 司 27th Airfield Company (7AirDiv 3AirA) - 58
11802 昭 5th Airfield Battalion (55AirDiv 3AirA) - 57
11803 司 113th Airfield Battalion (7AirDiv 3AirA) - 58
11804 司 68th Airfield Battalion (7AirDiv 3AirA) - 57
11805 / 8308 司 38th/70th Joint Airfield Battalion (36th Div, 2A) - 67
11806 司 72nd Airfield Battalion (7AirDiv 3AirA) - 58
11807 杉 12th Air Signals Regiment (41A) - 114
11807 威 12th Air Signal Regiment, one platoon (KeG 14AA and 4AirA) - 117, 122
11808 司 45th Wireless Radio Unit (3AirA) - 54
11809 司 46th Wireless Radio Unit (3AirA) - 54
DN • 11900-29, 勲 *Isao*, 42nd Division
DN • 11930-49, 誉 *Homare*, 43rd Division
11930-49 誉 43rd Division (31A) - 183-4
11934 誉 135th Infantry Regt., 1st Battalion, 43rd Div on Tainan (31A) - 35
DN • 11950-59, Not Distributed
DN • 11960-89, 静 *Sei*, 46th Division
11960-70 静 46th Division (7AA) - 184
11963 静 145th Infantry Regiment, 46th Div, Iwo Jima (31A) - 33
DN • 11990-12014, 弾 *Dan*, 47th Division
11990-12019 弾 47th Division (43A) - 184-5
DN • 12015-19, Not Distributed
DN • 12020-49, 緑 *Midori*, Heijo Divisional District (Korea)
12020-40 豹 30th Division (35A) - 177-8
DN • 12050-69, 徳 *Toku*, Kwantung (Kantō) Army, Apr. 1945 distribution
DN • 12071-89, 拓 *Taku*, 1st Armored Division
12076 備 26th Tank Regiment, Iwo Jima (31A) - 33

12079 / 595 呂 1st Tank Division Air Defense Unit (11A) - 146
12089 備 9th Tank Regiment, Saipan (31A) - 35
12089 備 9th Tank Regiment, 1st and 2nd Coys on Guam (31A) - 36
DN • 12090-109, 撃 *Geki*, 2nd Armored Division
12090-8 撃 2nd Armored Division (14AA) - 206
12097 備 3rd Independent Tank Company (31A) - 35
12100-7 撃 2nd Tank Division (14AA) - 206
12104 桜 2nd Tank Division Anti-Aircraft Unit (20A) - 149
DN • 12110-99, 桜 *Sakura*, 20th Army, Apr. 1945 distribution
DN • 12200-99, 森 *Mori*, Burma Area Army, Apr. 1945 distribution
12200 森 Rangoon Anti-Aircraft Unit HQ, Rangoon Defense Unit (BAA) - 250
12201 義 5th Engineer Unit Headquarters (18AA) - 98
12202 森 Burma Area Army Signal Unit Headquarters (BAA) - 86
12203 司 111th Field Airfield Construction Unit (3AirA) - 54
12204 司 112th Field Airfield Construction Unit (3AirA) - 54
12205 司 113th Field Airfield Construction Unit (3AirA) - 54
12206 森 21st Line of Communications Veterinary Hospital (BAA) - 88
12208 森 1st Independent Machinegun Company (BAA) - 86
12209 森 2nd Independent Machinegun Company (BAA) - 86
12210 森 3rd Independent Machinegun Company (BAA) - 86
12211-7 貫徹 72nd Independent Mixed Brigade, Rangoon Defense Unit (BAA) - 250
12218 森 5th Raiding Command (BAA) - 86
12219 森 38th Independent Rapid Firing Gun Company (BAA) - 86
12220 森 39th Independent Rapid Firing Gun Company (BAA) - 86
12221 森 40th Independent Rapid Firing Gun Company (BAA) - 86
12222 森 9th Field Medium Artillery Battalion (BAA) - 86
12223 森 58th Ind. Field Anti-Aircraft Company Rangoon Defense Unit (BAA) - 250
12224 森 59th Ind. Field Anti-Aircraft Company Rangoon Def. Unit (BAA) - 250
12225 森 60th Ind. Field Anti-Aircraft Company Rangoon Def. Unit (BAA) - 250
12226 森 61st Ind. Field Anti-Aircraft Company Rangoon Def. Unit (BAA) - 250
12227 森 80th Field Machine Cannon Company (BAA) - 86
12228 森 6th Independent Engineer Company (BAA) - 86
12229 森 7th Independent Engineer Company (BAA) - 86
12230 森 8th Independent Engineer Company (BAA) - 86
12231 森 9th Independent Engineer Company (BAA) - 86
12232 森 10th Independent Engineer Company (BAA) - 86
12233 森 90th Line of Communications Sector Command (BAA) - N/A
12234 森 91st Line of Communications Sector Command (BAA) - N/A
12235 策 14th Field Transport Headquarters, Saku Group (28A) - 91, 92
12236 森 333rd Independent Motor Transport Company (BAA) - 87
12237 林 334th Independent Motor Transport Company (15A) - 101
12238 森 335th Independent Motor Transport Company (BAA) - 87
12239 森 94th Casualty Clearing Platoon (BAA) - 88
12240 森 95th Casualty Clearing Platoon (BAA) - 88
12241 森 15th Raiding Company (BAA) - 86
12242 森 16th Raiding Company (BAA) - 86
12243 森 17th Raiding Company (BAA) - 86

0	1	2	3	4	5	6	7	8	9	10
○	一	二	三	四	五	六	七	八	九	十

12245-52 敢威 105th Independent Mixed Brigade (BAA) - 234
12252 森 67th Independent Engineer Battalion (BAA) - 86
12253 森 131st Land Duty Company (BAA) - 87
12254 森 132nd Land Duty Company (BAA) - 87
12255 森 133rd Land Duty Company (BAA) - 87
12256 森 134th Land Duty Company (BAA) - 87
12257 森 135th Land Duty Company (BAA) - 87
12258 森 136th Land Duty Company (BAA) - 87
DN • 12300-99, 東部 *Tobu* Army District, Apr. 1945 distribution
12361-3 勤 105th Division (41A) - 198
12364 備 1st Mobile Ordinance Repair Unit (31A) - 32
12366 尚武 3rd Mobile Ordinance Repair Unit (14AA) - 109
12367 森 29th Field Disease Prevention and Water Supply Unit (BAA) - 88
12368 尚武 30th Disease Prevention and Water Supply Unit (14AA) - 109
12384 武 3rd Rocket Launcher Battalion, Manila Defense Force (41A) - 249
12390 尚 109th Independent Radio Platoon (35A) - 113
12391 杉 110th Independent Radio Platoon (41A) - 114
12392 尚 111th Independent Radio Platoon (35A) - 113
12393 尚 112th Independent Radio Platoon (35A) - 113
12395 登 2nd Independent Trench Mortar Company (13A) - 131
DN • 12400-99, 中部 *Chubu* Army District, Apr. 1945 distribution
12412 波 311th Independent Motor Transport Company (23A) - 135
12413 波 312th Independent Motor Transport Company (23A) - 135
12414 波 313th Independent Motor Transport Company (23A) - 135
12415 威 77th Field Anti Aircraft Battalion, attached 105th Div (14AA) - 107
12416 杉 51st Field Machine Cannon Company (41A) - 114
12417 備 1st Observation Unit (31A) - 32
12418 備 2nd Observation Unit (31A) - 32
12419-21 抛 100th Division (35A) - 195-6
12422-4 抜 102nd Division (35A) - 196
12433 球 6th Medium Trench Mortar Battalion (14AA) - 108
12434 尚武 7th Medium Trench Mortar Battalion (14AA) - 108
12448 威 51st Specially Est. Machine Cannon Unit, att. 23rd Div (14AA) - 106
12450 威 52nd Specially Est. Machine Cannon Unit, att. 23rd Div (14AA) - 106
12451 威 53rd Specially Est. Machine Cannon Unit, att. 23rd Div (14AA) - 106
12454 定 59th Specially Est. Machine Cannon Unit, Palembang (3AirA) - 250
12455 翔 60th Specially Est. Machine Cannon Unit, Palembang (3AirA) - 250
12456 翔 61st Specially Est. Machine Cannon Unit, Palembang (3AirA) - 250
12457 定 62nd Specially Est. Machine Cannon Unit, Palembang (3AirA) - 250
12458 尚武 68th Specially Established Machine Cannon Unit (14AA) - 108
12459 尚武 69th Specially Established Machine Cannon Unit (14AA) - 108
12460 尚武 70th Specially Established Machine Cannon Unit, Comotes (14AA) - 110
12461 尚武 71st Specially Established Machine Cannon Unit, Comotes (14AA) - 110
12462 尚武 72nd Specially Established Machine Cannon Unit (14AA) - 108

12467 統 32nd Field Disease Prevention and Water Supply Unit (6AA) - 143
12470 秀嶺 63rd Fixed Radio Unit (43A) - 158
12471 秀嶺 64th Fixed Radio Unit (43A) - 158
DN • 12500-99, 西部 *Seibu* Army District, Apr. 1945 distribution
12500 静 46th Division Tank Unit (7AA) - 184
12501 備 4th South Seas Detachment (31A) - 31, 32
12502 備 5th South Seas Detachment (31A) - 31
12503 猛 6th South Seas Detachment, in Hollandia (18A) - 49
12506 輝 50th Independent Field Anti-Aircraft Company (2A) - 68
12507 翔 Palembang Guard Signal Unit (9AirDiv 3AirA) - 250
12508 翔 Palembang Guards Unit (9AirDiv 3AirA) - 250
12509 勢 10th Raiding Company (2A) - 68
12510 甲 29th Signal Regiment (NCAA) - 153
12511 統 60th Fixed Wireless Radio Unit (6AA) - 141
12512 統 314th Independent Motor Transport Company (6AA) - 142
12513 統 315th Independent Motor Transport Company (6AA) - 142
12514 波 56th Field Road Construction Unit (23A) - 136
12515 波 79th Casualty Clearing Platoon (23A) - 136
12516 波 61st Fixed Radio Unit (23A) - 135
12517 昆 27th Independent Anti Aircraft Battalion (33A) - 96
12519 杉 78th Field Anti-Aircraft Battalion (41A) - 114
12520 杉 52nd Field Artillery Company (41A) - 114
12521-3 駿 103rd Division (14AA) - 197
12525 尚武 84th Field Anti Aircraft Battalion (KeG 14AA) - 117
12527 至純 63rd Field Machine Cannon Company, 89 IMB (6A) - 233
12528 操 64th Field Machine Cannon Company, 62 IMB (6A) - 228
12529 登 65th Field Machine Cannon Company (13A) - 131
12534 尚武 119th Independent Wire Company (14AA) - 108
12535 杉 120th Independent Wire Company (14AA) - 108
12536 登 121st Independent Wire Company (13A) - 131
12537 登 122nd Independent Wire Company (13A) - 131
12542 尚武 54th Specially Est. Machine Cannon Unit, 103rd Div (14AA) - 108
12586 備 14th Independent Trench Mortar Battalion, Saipan (31A) - 35
12587 備 17th Independent Trench Mortar Battalion, Saipan (31A) - 35
DN • 12600-99, 達 *Tatsu*, 5th Area Army, Apr. 1945 distribution
12601 輝 72nd Field Anti-Aircraft Battalion (2A) - 64
12602 輝 12th Independent Field Searchlight Company (2A) - 68
12616 威 30th Signal Regiment (14AA) - 108
12650 森 85th Independent Radio Platoon (BAA) - 86
12651 勢 86th Independent Radio Platoon (2A) - 67
12652 勢 87th Independent Radio Platoon (2A) - 67
12653 波 62nd Fixed Radio Unit (23A) - 135
DN •12700-99, 朝鮮 Korea Army District
12700 秀嶺 43rd Army Headquarters (NCAA) - 158
12710 備 20th Independent Mortar Battalion, Iwo Jima (31A) -33
DN • 12800-99, 湾 *Wan*, 10th Area Army, Apr. 1945 distribution (Taiwan)
DN • 12900-99, 徳 *Toku*, Kwantung (Kantō) Army, Apr. 1945 distribution

0	1	2	3	4	5	6	7	8	9	10
〇	一	二	三	四	五	六	七	八	九	十

12901 輝 10th Expeditionary Unit Headquarters (2AA) - 254
12903 司 3rd Air Special Signal Unit (3AirA) - 54
12904 杉 4th Air Special Signal Unit (41A) - 114
12905 杉 5th Air Special Signal Unit (41A) - 114
12907 威 104th Independent Wire Company (35A) - 113
12908 威 105th Independent Wire Company (35A) - 113
12910 威 107th Independent Wire Company (35A) - 113
12911 昆 108th Independent Wire Company (33A) - 96
12912 昆 109th Independent Wire Company (33A) - 96
12913 昆 110th Independent Wire Company (33A) - 96
12915 昆 2nd Signals Unit Headquarters (33A) - 96
12916 尚 98th Independent Radio Platoon (35A) - 113
12917 尚 99th Independent Radio Platoon (35A) - 113
12919 杉 101st Independent Radio Platoon (41A) - 114
12920 昆 102nd Independent Radio Platoon (33A) - 96
12921 昆 103rd Independent Radio Platoon (33A) - 96
12922 昆 104th Independent Radio Platoon (33A) - 96
12935 灘 25th Independent Mixed Regiment (37A) - 78
12936 杉 26th Independent Mixed Regiment (41A) - 114
12949 灘 4th Signal Unit Headquarters (37A) - 79
12970 振武 123rd Independent Wire Company (KeG 14AA) - 108, 117
12971 灘 124th Independent Wire Company (37A) - 79
12972 灘 125th Independent Wire Company (37A) - 79
12976 定 129th Independent Wire Company (29A) - 83
12977 戊 130th Independent Wire Company (MGA) - 159
12978 尚武 117th Independent Radio Platoon (14AA) - 108
12979 尚武 118th Independent Radio Platoon (14AA) - 108
12980 灘 119th Independent Radio Company (37A) - 79
12981 灘 120th Independent Radio Platoon (37A) - 79
12982 灘 121st Independent Radio Platoon (37A) - 79
12983 威 122nd Independent Radio Platoon (4AirA) - 122
12984 杉 123rd Independent Radio Platoon (41A) - 114
12985 威 124th Independent Radio Platoon (4AirA) - 122
12986 威 125th Independent Radio Platoon (4AirA) - 122
12987 杉 126th Independent Radio Platoon (41A) - 114
12988 威 127th Independent Radio Platoon (4AirA) - 122
12989 威 128th Independent Radio Platoon (4AirA) - 122
12990 尚武 129th Independent Radio Platoon (4AirA) - 122
12991 尚 130th Independent Radio Platoon (35A) - 113
DN • 13000-99, 鋭 *Ei*, 1st Area Army, Apr. 1945 distribution
13075-8 操 62nd Independent Mixed Brigade (6A) - 228
DN • 13100-99, 強 *Kyou*, 3rd Area Army, Apr. 1945 distribution
DN • 13200-49, 徳 *Toku*, Kwantung (Kantō) Army
13221 威 21st Independent Rapid Firing Gun Company, att. 10th Div (14AA) - 106

DN • 13250-99, Not Distributed
DN • 13300-99, 東部 *Tobu* Army District, Apr. 1945 distribution
DN • 13301-7 not used, *Tobu* Army District
DN • 13348-50 not used, *Tobu* Army District
DN • 13380-99 not used *Tobu* Army District
DN • 13400-99, 中部 *Chubu* Army District, Apr. 1945 distribution
DN • 13500-99, 西部 *Seibu* Army District, Apr. 1945 distribution
DN • 13600-99, 達 *Tatsu*, 5th Area Army, Apr. 1945 distribution
DN • 13700-99, 朝鮮 Korea (Chosen) Army
DN • 13800-99, 湾 *Wan*, 10th Area Army, Apr. 1945 distribution (Taiwan)
DN • 13900-99, 徳 *Toku*, Kwantung (Kantō) Army, Apr. 1945 distribution
DN • 14000-99, 遠征 *Sizume*, 44th Army, Apr. 1945 distribution
14022 勢 30th Ind. Garrison Battalion, 10th Expeditionary Unit (2AA) - 254
DN • 14100-49, 緑 *Midori*, Heijo Divisional District (Korea)
DN • 14150-14199 攝 *Setu*, Osaka Divisional District
14166 登 83rd Line of Communications Guard Unit (13A) - 131
14167 登 83rd Line of Communications Duty Company (13A) - 131
14168 統 84th Line of Communications Guard (6AA) - 142
14169 統 84th Line of Communications Duty Company (6AA) - 142
14171 備 274th Independent Infantry Battalion, att. 109th Div Chichi Jima (31A) -34
DN • 14200-99, 蔵 *Zō*, Tokyo Divisional District
14200 灘 22nd Independent Machine Gun Battalion (37A) - 78
14203 威 26th Independent Rapid Firing Gun Battalion, att. 10th Div (14AA) - 106
14208 暁 11th Sea Raiding Base Battalion (14AA) - 123
14209 暁 12th Sea Raiding Base Battalion (14AA) - 123
14210 暁 13th Sea Raiding Base Battalion (41A) - 115
14213 備 274th Independent Infantry Battalion, att. 109th Div Chichi Jima (31A) -34
DN • 14300-49, 張 *Hari*, Nagoya Divisional District
DN • 14350-99, 薩 *Satsu*, Kumamoto Divisional District
DN • 14400-99, 徳 *Toku*, Kwantung (Kantō) Army
DN • 14500-99, Not Distributed
14590 登 110th Specially Established Construction Duty Company (13A) - 132
14591 登 111th Specially Established Construction Duty Company (13A) - 132
DN • 14600-799, 徳 *Toku*, Kwantung (Kantō) Army
15650 備 53rd Independent Mixed Brigade, not a unit (31A) - 225
14653-71 備 53rd Independent Mixed Brigade (31A) - 225
14656 備 346th Independent Infantry Battalion, detached to Peleliu (31A) - 37
14681 備 31st Specially Established Machine Cannon Unit (31A) - 32, 36
14682 備 32nd Specially Established Machine Cannon Unit (31A) - 32, 36
14683 備 33rd Specially Established Machine Cannon Unit (31A) - 36
14684 備 34th Specially Established Machine Cannon Unit (31A) - 32, 36
14685 備 35th Specially Established Machine Cannon Unit (31A) - 36
14686 備 36th Specially Established Machine Cannon Unit (31A) - 37
14687 備 37th Specially Established Machine Cannon Unit (31A) - 37
14688 備 38th Specially Established Machine Cannon Unit (31A) - 37
14689 備 39th Specially Established Machine Cannon Unit (31A) - 37
14690 備 40th Specially Established Machine Cannon Unit (31A) - 37

0	1	2	3	4	5	6	7	8	9	10
〇	一	二	三	四	五	六	七	八	九	十

14756 甲 126th Specially Established Land Duty Company (NCAA) - 153
DN • 14800-99, Not Distributed
DN • 14900-49, Not Distributed
DN • 14950-99, 徳 *Toku*, Kwantung (Kantō) Army
14955 甲 125th Specially Established Land Duty Company (NCAA) - 153
DN • 15000-49, Not Distributed
DN • 15050-99, 中国 *Chugoku* Army District
DN • 15100-49, 黒 *Kuro*, Kureme Divisional District
DN • 15150-99, 漢 *Kan*, Keijo Divisional District (Korea)
DN • 15200-99, 徳 *Toku*, Kwantung (Kantō) Army, Apr. 1945 distribution
DN • 15300-49, Not Distributed
15300 真 4th Air Army Headquarters (14AA) - 120
15307 輝 13th Field Airfield Construction Unit, att. 36 Div less 2 coys (2A) - 67
15311 威 Manila Army Air Depot (4AirA) - 122
15311 威 Manila Air Depot, 2nd Branch (KeG) - 117
15313 昭 107th Independent Flight Training Brigade HQ (55AirDiv 3AirA) - 55
15314 昭 2nd Secondary Flight Training Unit (55AirDiv 3AirA) - 55
15315 昭 3rd Secondary Flight Training Unit (55AirDiv 3AirA) - 55
15316 昭 12th Secondary Flight Training Unit (55AirDiv 3AirA) - 55
15317 司 1st Field Airfield Construction Headquarters (3AirA) - 54
15319 威 3rd Field Airfield Construction Headquarters (4AirA) - 122
15319 威 2nd Specially Established Field Airfield Construction Unit (4AirA) - 122
15319 威 3rd Specially Established Field Airfield Construction Unit (4AirA) - 122
15319 威 8th Specially Established Field Airfield Construction Unit (4AirA) - 122
15319 威 11th Specially Established Field Airfield Construction Unit (4AirA) - 121
15320 勢 16th Field Airfield Construction Unit (2A) - 70
15321 勢 17th Field Airfield Construction Unit (2A) - 70
15322 輝 18th Field Airfield Construction Unit (2A) - 70
15323 勢 19th Field Airfield Construction Unit (2A) - 70
15328 103rd Field Airfield Construction Unit (10th Ind. Air Bgde 3AirA) - 58
15329 昭 104th Field Airfield Construction Unit (55AirDiv 3AirA) - 55
15330 司 105th Field Airfield Construction Unit (3AirA) - 54
15331 昭 106th Field Airfield Construction Unit (55AirDiv 3AirA) - 55
15334 昭 109th Field Airfield Construction Unit (55AirDiv 3AirA) - 55
15335 司 110th Field Airfield Construction Unit (3AirA) - 54
15336 司 11th Air Signal Regiment (3AirA) - 54
15337 威 22nd Air Signal Unit (KeG 14AA and 4AirA) - 117, 122
15338 司 8th Air Intelligence Unit (7AirDiv 3AirA) - 58
15339 司 13th Field Meteorological Unit (2AA) - 64
15340 司 31st Airfield Company (7AirDiv 3AirA) - 58
15341 司 34th Airfield Company (7AirDiv 3AirA) - 58
15342 翔 35th Airfield Company (9AirDiv 3AirA) - 56
15343 勢 36th Airfield Company (2A) - 70
15344 翔 37th Airfield Company (9AirDiv 3AirA) - 56

15345 高 38th Airfield Company (5AirDiv 3AirA) - 57
15346 司 39th Airfield Company (7AirDiv 3AirA) - 58
15347 司 40th Airfield Company (7AirDiv 3AirA) - 58
15348 司 21st Field Aircraft Repair Depot (7AirDiv 3AirA) - 58
15349 司 21st Field Air Freight Depot (7AirDiv 3AirA) - 58
DN • 15350, 翔 *Kakeru*, 9th Air Division Headquarters
15350 翔 9th Air Division Headquarters (9AirDiv 3AirA) - 56
DN • 15351-99, Not Distributed
15356 威 33rd Secondary Flight Training Unit (4AirA) - 120
15357 昭 36th Secondary Flight Training Unit (55AirDiv 3AirA) - 55
15358 昭 37th Secondary Flight Training Unit (55AirDiv 3AirA) - 55
15361 司 100th Airfield Battalion (10th Ind. Air Brigade 3AirA) - 58
15362 司 101st Airfield Battalion (3AirA) - 53
15363 勢 107th Airfield Battalion (2A) - 70
15364 勢 108th Airfield Battalion (2A) - 70
15365 司 109th Airfield Battalion (3AirA) - 53
15366 司 110th Airfield Battalion (10th Ind. Air Brigade 3AirA) - 58
15367 司 111th Airfield Battalion (10th Ind. Air Brigade 3AirA) - 58
15368 司 41st Airfield Company (7AirDiv 3AirA) - 58
15369 昭 42nd Airfield Company (2A) - 70
15370 司 43rd Airfield Company (7AirDiv 3AirA) - 58
15371 司 44th Airfield Company (7AirDiv 3AirA) - 58
15372 司 45th Airfield Company (7AirDiv 3AirA) - 58
15373 勢 46th Airfield Company (2A) - 70
15374 翼 47th Airfield Company (41A) - 115
15375 威 48th Airfield Company (4AirA) - 121
15376 威 49th Airfield Company (4AirA) - 121
15378 洋 63rd Flying Regiment (4AirA) - 120
15378 洋 63rd Air Regiment, one section (6AirDiv 18A) - 50
15380 威 50th Airfield Company (4AirA) - 121
15381 盤 104th Anti-Aircraft Regiment, Bhutan (3AirA) - 249
15382 威 20th Independent Air Squadron (4AirA) - 120
15383 猛 22nd Airfield Company (6AirDiv, 18A) - 50
15384 猛 23rd Airfield Company (6AirDiv, 18A) - 50
15387 輝 123rd Field Airfield Construction Unit (2AA) - 64
15388 輝 124th Field Airfield Construction Unit (2AA) - 64
15389 威 125th Field Airfield Construction Unit (4AirA) - 121
15390 威 126th Field Airfield Construction Unit (4AirA) - 121
15391 威 127th Field Airfield Construction Unit (4AirA) - 121
15398 輝 134th Field Airfield Construction Unit (4AirA) - 121
15399 威 135th Field Airfield Construction Unit (4AirA) - 121
DN • 15400-99, 眞 *Shin*, 4th Air Army
15400 尚武 7th Specially Established Machine Cannon Unit (14AA) - 108
15401 尚武 8th Specially Established Machine Cannon Unit (14AA) - 108
15402 尚武 9th Specially Established Machine Cannon Unit (14AA) - 108
15403 尚武 10th Specially Established Machine Cannon Unit - N/A
15404 威 11th Sp. Est. Machine Cannon Unit, att. 2nd Armored Div (14AA) - 107

0	1	2	3	4	5	6	7	8	9	10
〇	一	二	三	四	五	六	七	八	九	十

15405 威 12th Specially Established Machine Cannon Unit (14AA) - 108
15406 威 13th Specially Est. Machine Cannon Unit, att. 105th Div (14AA) - 107
15407 威 14th Specially Est. Machine Cannon Unit, att. 105th Div (14AA) - 107
15408 威 15th Specially Est. Machine Cannon Unit, att. 105th Div (14AA) - 107
DN • 15500, Not Distributed
DN • 15501-49, 監 Kantō Army Supply Inspectorate Department
DN • 15550-99, 松 *Mutu*, Asahikawa Divisional District
15559 勢 69th Construction Duty Company (2A) - 69
15560 勢 70th Construction Duty Company (2A) - 69
DN • 15600-799, 甲 *Ko*, North China Area Army, Apr. 1945 distribution
15600-11 将 114th Division (1A) - 200
15600 将 83rd Infantry Brigade, brigade id # 114th Div (1A) - 200
15602 将 84th Infantry Brigade, brigade id # 114th Div (1A) - 200
15612-20 北 115th Division (12A) - 201
15612 北 86th Infantry Brigade, brigade id # 115th Div (12A) - 201
15633-45 恵 118th Division (13A) - 202
15634 恵 89th Infantry Brigade, brigade id # 118th Div (13A) - 202
15636 恵 90th Infantry Brigade, brigade id # 118th Div (13A) - 202
15651 乙 81st Field Machine Cannon Company (1A) - 156
15652 仁 82nd Field Machine Cannon Company (12A) - 157
15653 仁 83rd Field Machine Cannon Company (12A) - 157
15654 仁 84th Field Machine Cannon Company (12A) - 157
15656 甲 Independent Light Armored Car Unit (NCAA) - 153
15657-65 伸張 3rd Independent Guard Unit (NCAA) - 243
15666-74 至誠 4th Independent Guards Unit (MGA) - 243
15676-83 至隆 5th Independent Guard Unit (1A) - 243
15685-92 至毅 6th Independent Guard Unit (12A) - 244
15693-701 至武 7th Independent Guard Unit (NCAA) - 244
15702-10 至剛 9th Independent Guard Unit (43A) - 244
15711-9 至敏 10th Independent Guard Unit (12A) - 244-5
15721-8 至鋭 11th Independent Guard Unit (43A) - 245
15730-7 至厳 12th Independent Guard Unit (43A) - 245
15738-46 疾風 13th Independent Guard Unit (12A) - 245-6
15747-55 紫電 14th Independent Guard Unit (12A) - 246
15757 登 35th Signal Regiment (13A) - 131
15758 栄 16th Independent Railway Battalion (CA) - 129
15759 将 114th Division Field Artillery Unit (1A) - 200
DN • 15800-6299, 威 *i*, Southern Expeditionary Army, Apr. 1945 distribution
15800 定 97th Independent Wire Company (29A) - 83
15801 義 Southern Army Field Railway Headquarters (SRR) - 61
15802 路 Southern Army Field Railway Depot (SRR) - 61
15804 威 Southern Army Temporary Facilities (SA) - 41
15805 信 36th Specially Est. Motor Transport Company (38A) - 44
15807 義 38th Specially Est. Motor Transport Company (18AA) - 98

15808 信 39th Specially Est. Motor Transport Company (38A) - 44
15809 信 40th Independent Motor Transport Company (38A) - 44
15811 翔 101st Strategic Balloon Unit, Palembang Guard Brigade (3AirA) - 250
15813 岡 Southern Army Ordnance Manufacturing Depot (7AA) - 74
15814-21 巌 24th Independent Mixed Brigade (BAA) - 217
15822-30 体 29th Ind. Mixed Brigade (18AA) - 219
15823 体 158th Ind. Infantry Battalion, 29th IMB (BAA reserve) - 88, 219
15824 体 159th Ind. Infantry Battalion, 29th IMB (BAA reserve) - 88, 219
15828 体 129th Mixed Brigade Artillery Unit, 1st Section (BAA reserve) - 89, 219
15830 体 29th Mixed Brigade Signal Unit, 1st Section (BAA reserve) - 89
15832-9 教 35th Independent Mixed Brigade (29A) - 221
15840-3 練 36th Independent Mixed Brigade (29A) - 221
15844-7 鍛 37th Independent Mixed Brigade (29A) - 222
15848 威 Singapore Oil Storage Facility (SA) - 74
15849 岡 Southern Army Institute of Fuel Technology (7AA) - 74
15850 岡 South Sumatra Fuel Depot (7AA) - 74
15851 岡 Central Sumatra Fuel Depot (7AA) - 74
15852 威 North Sumatra Fuel Depot (SA) - 74
15853 威 Borneo Fuel Depot (SA) - 74
15854 岡 Java Fuel Depot (7AA) - 74
15855 森 Southern Army Fuel Depot's Burma Work Depot (BAA) - 88
15856 威 Brunei Fuel Depot (SA) - 74
15882 尚武 14th Area Army Line of Comm. Inspectorate General (14AA) - 108
15883 森 Burma Area Army Line of Comm. Inspectorate General (BAA) - 86
15884 威 Southern Army Survey Unit (SA) - 41
15885 威 2nd Southern Army Survey Unit (SA) - 41
15890-99 貫 56th Independent Mixed Brigade (37A) - 226-7
15900-9 桂 57th Independent Mixed Brigade (2AA) - 227
15910 威 Southern Army Air Traffic Control Department (SA) - 42
15912 威 North Borneo District (SA) - 41
15913 威 Indochina District (SA) - 41
15914 威 North of Australia District (SA) - 42
15915 威 Singapore District (SA) - 42
15917 威 1st Southern Army Signal Unit (SA) - 41
15918 威 2nd Southern Army Signal Unit (SA) - 41
15919 威 3rd Southern Army Signal Unit (SA) - 41, 74
15920 威 4th Southern Army Signal Unit (SA) - 41
15921 定 3rd Southern Army Signal Unit (29A) - 83
15922 威 5th Southern Army Signal Unit (38A) - 44
15923 威 6th Southern Army Signal Unit (18AA) - 98
15926 暁 70th Anchorage Headquarters (SoS) - 59
16009 威 Southern Signal Training Unit (SA) - 41
16019 / 10619 杉 Manila Anti Aircraft Artillery Headquarters (41A) - 114
16150 登 173rd Line of Communications Hospital (13A) - 132
16151 登 174th Line of Communications (Xuzhou) Hospital (13A) - 132
16223 剛 1st Independent Sea Transport Battalion (8AA) - 25
DN • 16300-99, 輝 *Kagayaku*, 2nd Area Army, Apr. 1945 distribution

0	1	2	3	4	5	6	7	8	9	10
〇	一	二	三	四	五	六	七	八	九	十

16300 輝 2nd Area Army Headquarters (SA) - 64
16305 輝 73rd Field Anti-Aircraft Battalion (2AA) - 68
16306 輝 45th Field Machine Cannon Company (2AA) - 64
16307 輝 9th Independent Field Searchlight Company (2A) - 68
16308 勢 3rd Raiding Company (2A) - 67
16309 勢 4th Raiding Company (2A) - 67
16310 勢 5th Raiding Company (2A) - 67
16311 勢 6th Raiding Company (2A) - 67
16312 勢 26th Signal Regiment (2A) - 67
16313 輝 98th Independent Wire Company (2A) - 67
16314 輝 99th Independent Wire Company (2A) - 67
16319 輝 1st Specially Established Machine Cannon Unit (2A) - 68
16320 輝 2nd Specially Established Machine Cannon Unit (2A) - 68
16321 輝 3rd Specially Established Machine Cannon Unit (2A) - 68
16322 輝 4th Specially Established Machine Cannon Unit (2A) - 68
16323 輝 5th Specially Established Machine Cannon Unit (2A) - 68
16324 輝 6th Specially Established Machine Cannon Unit (2A) - 68
16325 勢 150th Line of Communications Hospital (2A) - 69
16331-9 快捷 128thIndependent Mixed Brigade (2A) - 235
DN • 16400-99, 勢 *Ikioi*, 2nd Army, April 1945 distribution
16400 勢 2nd Army Headquarters (SA) - 67
16401 勢 2nd Army Field Ordinance Depot (2A) - 70
16402 勢 2nd Army Field Motor Vehicle Depot (2A) - 70
16403 勢 2nd Army Field Freight Depot (2A) - 70
DN • 16500-99, 翔 *Kakeru*, 9th Air Division
16501 翔 87th Airfield Battalion (9AirDiv 3AirA) - 56
16502 翔 89th Airfield Battalion (9AirDiv 3AirA) - 56
16503 翔 14th Air Intelligence Regiment (9AirDiv 3AirA) - 56
DN • 16600-99, 羽 *Hane*, 2nd Air Army, Apr. 1945 distribution
16601勢 72nd Field Anti Aircraft Regiment, att. to 48th Div (16A) - 185
16602 威 102nd Airfield Battalion (4AirA) - 121
16603 威 103rd Airfield Battalion (4AirA) - 121
16604 隼魁 104th Airfield Battalion (13AirDiv 5AirA) - 137
16605 隼魁 105th Airfield Battalion (13AirDiv 5AirA) - 137
16606 隼魁 106th Airfield Battalion (13AirDiv 5AirA) - 137
16612 威 2nd Air Navigation Regiment (KeG 14AA) - 117
16618 隼魁 48th Air Regiment (13AirDiv 5AirA) - 136
16623 威 23rd Wireless Radio Unit (4AirA) - 122
16624 威 24th Wireless Radio Unit (4AirA) - 122
16625 威 25th Wireless Radio Unit (KeG) - 117
16637 司 29th Air Sector Command (3AirA) - 52
16645 威 114th Airfield Battalion, Comotes Detach. (14AA) - 110
16646 備 115th Airfield Battalion (3AirA) - 52
16648 司 179th Airfield Battalion (3AirA) - 52

16649 司 180th Airfield Battalion (3AirA) - 52
16651 威 51st Airfield Company (4AirA) - 121
16652 威 52nd Airfield Company (KeG 14AA and 4AirA) - 117, 121
16653 威 53rd Airfield Company (4AirA) - 121
16654 威 54th Airfield Company, Comotes Detachment (14AA) - 110
16665 隼魁 50th Air Sector Command (13AirDiv 5AirA) - 137
16688 隼魁 218th Airfield Battalion (13AirDiv 5AirA) - 137
16689 隼魁 219th Airfield Battalion (13AirDiv 5AirA) - 137
16692 隼魁 220th Airfield Battalion (13AirDiv 5AirA) - 137
16697 隼魁 217th Airfield Battalion (13AirDiv 5AirA) - 137
16698 威 98th Airfield Battalion, Comotes Detachment (14AA) - 110
DN • 16700-99, 暁 *Akatsuki*, Army Shipping Corps Headquarters
16700 備 16th Shipping Engineer Regiment, Saipan (31A) - 35
16700 備 16th Shipping Engineer Regiment, 2nd Company, Guam (31A) - 36
16701 備 17th Shipping Engineer Regiment (31A) - 34
16702 暁 18th Shipping Engineer Regiment (SoS) - 59
16703 暁 19th Shipping Engineer Regiment (14AA) - 123
16705 暁 15th Debarkation Unit, Camotes Islands (14AA) - 110
16707 暁 1st High Speed Transport Battalion, 1 Section (14AA) - 123
16713 灘 1st Independent Shipping Engineer Company (37A) - 79
16714 定 2nd Independent Shipping Engineer Company (29A) - 83
16715 定 3rd Independent Shipping Engineer Company (29A) - 83
16716 暁 20th Shipping Engineer Regiment (SoS) - 59
16717 暁 21st Shipping Engineer Regiment, Camotes Islands (14AA) - 110
16722 暁 59th Field Anchorage Headquarters, Chichi Jima Detach. (31A) - 34
16723 備 60th Anchorage Headquarters, Saipan (31A) - 35
16724 暁 61st Anchorage Headquarters (14AA) - 123
16725 / 16745 暁 62nd Anchorage Headquarters (SoS) - 59
16725 暁 1st Mobile Transport Company (14AA) - 123
16725 / 16745 暁 62nd Anchorage Headquarters (SoS) - 59
16732 暁 8th Mobile Transport Company (14AA) - 123
16733 暁 9th Mobile Transport Company (14AA) - 123
16736 暁 12th Mobile Transport Company (CA) - N/A
16737 暁 1st Sea Raiding Base Unit Headquarters (41A) - 115, 124
16737 暁 13th Mobile Transport Company - N/A
16738 暁 14th Mobile Transport Company - N/A
16739 暁 15th Mobile Transport Company (14AA) - 123
16742 暁 24th Shipping Engineer Regiment (41A) - 115
16743 暁 25th Shipping Engineer Regiment (14AA) - 123
16745 / 16725 暁 62nd Anchorage Headquarters (SoS) - 59
16746 暁 63rd Anchorage Headquarters (14AA) - 123
16747 暁 8th Sea Transport Battalion (14AA) - 123\
16748 暁 9th Sea Transport Battalion (14AA) - 123
16748 暁 4th Mobile Transport Company (14AA) - 123
16749 暁 10th Sea Transport Battalion (14AA) - 123
16755 波 64th Anchorage Headquarters (23A) - 138
16756 栄 65th Anchorage Headquarters (CA) - 138

0	1	2	3	4	5	6	7	8	9	10
〇	一	二	三	四	五	六	七	八	九	十

16757 暁 28th Shipping Engineer Regiment, 1 Section (14AA) - 123
16758 暁 29th Shipping Engineer Regiment (CA) - 138
16763 暁 17th Mobile Transport Company (14AA) - 123
16782 杉 6th Sea Raiding Squadron (41A) - 115
16783 杉 7th Sea Raiding Squadron (41A) - 115
16784 杉 8th Sea Raiding Squadron (41A) - 115
16785 杉 9th Sea Raiding Squadron (41A) - 115
16786 杉 10th Sea Raiding Squadron (41A) - 115
16787 暁 1st Sea Raiding Base Unit Headquarters (14AA) - 123
16794 暁 5th Sea Raiding Base Battalion (14AA) - 123
16795 暁 8th Sea Raiding Base Battalion (41A) - 115
16796 暁 9th Sea Raiding Base Battalion (41A) - 115
16797 暁 10th Sea Raiding Base Battalion (41A) - 115
DN • 16800-99, 策 *Saku*, 28th Army, Apr. 1945 distribution
DN • 16900-99, 定 *Tei*, 29th Army, Apr. 1945 distribution
16900 定 49th Independent Tank Battalion (29A) - 83
16901 定 4th Independent Radio Company (29A) - 83
16902 定 81st Independent Transport Company (29A) - 83
16903 定 82nd Independent Transport Company (29A) - 83
16904 定 83rd Independent Transport Company (29A) - 83
DN • 17000-99, 信 *Sin*, 38th Army, Apr. 1945 distribution
17000 統 6th Area Army (CA) - 141
17001-9 果敢 70th Independent Mixed Brigade (29A) - 229
17011 信 67th Independent Field Anti Aircraft Company (38A) - 44
17012 信 38th Army Field Ordinance Depot (38A) - 44
17013 信 38th Army Field Motor Transport Depot (38A) - 44
17014 信 38th Army Field Freight Depot (38A) - 44
17015 信 38th Area Army Line of Communications Veterinary Hospital (38A) - 44
17016 信 38th Army Veterinary Quarantine Hospital (38A) - 44
17017-20 育 34th Independent Mixed Brigade (38A) - 220-1
17022 信 33rd Disease Prevention and Water Supply Unit (38A) - 44
DN • 17100-99, 義 *Gi*, 39th Army, Apr. 1945 distribution
17100 義 89th Line of Communications Sector Unit Headquarters (18AA) - 98
17104 義 148th Line of Communications Hospital (18AA) - 98
17106 義 18th Area Army Field Ordinance (18AA) - 98
17107 義 18th Area Army Field Motor Transport Depot (18AA) - 98
17108 義 18th Area Army Field Freight Depot (18AA) - 98
17109 義 18th Area Army Veterinary Quarantine Hospital (18AA) - 98
17110 義 18th Area Army Line of Comm. Veterinary Depot (18AA) - 98
17113 義 34th Field Disease Prevention and Water Supply Unit (18AA) - 98
17186 栄 190th Railway Station Command (NCAA) - 154
DN • 17200-99, 秀嶺 *Shurei*, 43rd Army, Apr. 1945 distribution
17200 秀嶺 43rd Army Headquarters (NCAA) - 158
17201 秀嶺 43rd Army (as a whole) (NCAA) - 158

DN • 17300-99, 隼 *Hayabusa*, 5th Air Army
17305 隼魁 58th Airfield Battalion (13AirDiv 5AirA) - 137
17306 隼魁 59th Airfield Battalion (13AirDiv 5AirA) - 137
17307 隼魁 60th Airfield Battalion (13AirDiv 5AirA) - 137
17312 隼魁 26th Air Sector Command (13AirDiv 5AirA) - 137
17315 隼魁 129th Airfield Battalion (13AirDiv 5AirA) - 137
17323 隼魁 168th Airfield Battalion, att. 27th Div (CA) - 137
17324 隼魁 184th Airfield Battalion (13AirDiv 5AirA) - 137
17325 隼魁 185th Airfield Battalion (13AirDiv 5AirA) - 137
17326 隼魁 186th Airfield Battalion (13AirDiv 5AirA) - 137
17331 隼魁 56th Air Sector Command (13AirDiv 5AirA) - 137
DN • 17400-49, 北部 *Hokubu*, 27th Army
DN • 17450-99, Not Distributed
DN • 17500-99, 備 *Sonae*, 31st Army, Apr. 1945 distribution
17501-27 and 18301-28 膽 109th Division (31A) - 198-9
17502/18301 胆 109th Division Headquarters - 32
17503/18314 胆 1st Mixed Brigade Headquarters, 109th Div (31A) – 34
17504/18306 胆 303rd Independent Infantry Battalion, 109th Div (31A) - 34
17505/18307 胆 304th Independent Infantry Battalion, 109th Div (31A) – 34
17506/18308 胆 305th Independent Infantry Battalion, 109th Div (31A) - 34
17507/18309 胆 306th Independent Infantry Battalion, 109th Div (31A) - 34
17508/18310 胆 307th Independent Infantry Battalion, 109th Div (31A) - 34
17509/18311 胆 308th Independent Infantry Battalion, 109th Div (31A) - 34
17510/18312 胆 1st Mixed Brigade Artillery Unit, 109th Div (31A) - 34
17511/18313 胆 1st Mixed Brigade Engineer Unit, 109th Div (31A) - 34
17513/18316 胆 309th Independent Infantry Battalion, 109th Div (31A) - 33
17514/18317 胆 310th Independent Infantry Battalion, 109th Div (31A) - 33
17515/18318 胆 311th Independent Infantry Battalion, 109th Div (31A) - 33
17516/18319 胆 312th Independent Infantry Battalion, 109th Div (31A) - 33
17517/18320 胆 313th Independent Infantry Battalion, 109th Div (31A) - 33
17518/18321 胆 314th Independent Infantry Battalion, 109th Div (31A) - 33
17519/18322 胆 2nd Mixed Brigade Artillery Unit, 109th Div (31A) - 33
17520/18323 胆 2nd Mixed Brigade Engineer Unit, 109th Div (31A) - 33
17523 膽 *9th* Heavy Artillery Regiment, 109th Div. (31A) - 33
17528-35 備 47th Independent Mixed Brigade (31A) - 223
17535-42 備 48th Independent Mixed Brigade (31A) - 223
17542-54 備 49th Independent Mixed Brigade, Yap Is. (31A) - 32, 224
17554-63 胆 50th Independent Mixed Brigade, Meyeron Atoll (31A) - 32, 224
17564-74 備 51st Independent Mixed Brigade, Truk, Mortlock Is. (31A) - 32, 225
17575-82 備 52nd Independent Mixed Brigade, Ponape Is. (31A) - 32, 225
17583 備 9th Independent Mixed Regiment, Pagan Is. (31A) - 36
17584 備 10th Independent Mixed Regiment, Guam Is. (31A) - 36
17585 備 11th Independent Mixed Regiment, Truk Dist., Endersby Is. (31A) - 32
17586 備 12th Independent Mixed Regiment, Marcus Is. (31A) - 34
17587 備 13th Independent Mixed Regiment, Wake Is. (31A) - 37
DN • 17600-99, 尚武 *Shobu*, 14th Area Army, Apr. 1945 distribution
17600-6 萩 54th Independent Mixed Brigade (35A) - 226

0	1	2	3	4	5	6	7	8	9	10
〇	一	二	三	四	五	六	七	八	九	十

17607-13 菅 55th Independent Mixed Brigade (35A) - 226
17614-6 駿 32nd Independent Mixed Brigade, later 103rd Div (14AA) - 220
17614-9 駿 103rd Division (14AA) - 197
17620 威 316th Ind. Motor Transport Company, Camotes Is. (14AA) - 110
17621 威 317th Ind. Motor Transport Company, Camotes Is. (14AA) - 110
17622 司 318th Independent Motor Transport Company (3AirA) - 54
17623 威 319th Independent Motor Transport Company (14AA) - 109
17624 威 320th Independent Motor Transport Company (14AA) - 109
17625 威 321st Independent Motor Transport Company (14AA) - 109
17626 威 322nd Independent Motor Transport Company (KeG) - 117
17627 尚 323rd Independent Motor Transport Company (35A) - 112
17628 尚 324th Independent Motor Transport Company (35A) - 112
17629 威 325th Independent Motor Transport Company (14AA) - 109
17630 杉 326th Independent Motor Transport Company (41A) - 114
17631 威 327th Independent Motor Transport Company (14AA) - 109
17632 尚 328th Independent Motor Transport Company (35A) - 112
17633 尚 329th Independent Motor Transport Company (35A) - 112
17634 威 330th Independent Motor Transport Company (14AA) - 109
17635勤 57th Field Road Unit, attached 105th Division (14AA) - 107
17636 威 58th Field Road Construction Unit (14AA) - 109
17637 威 16th Specially Established Machine Cannon Unit (14AA) - 108
17638 威 17th Specially Established Machine Cannon Unit (14AA) - 108
17639 威 18th Specially Established Machine Cannon Unit (14AA) - 108
17640 威 19th Specially Established Machine Cannon Unit (14AA) - 108
17641 威 22nd Specially Established Machine Cannon Unit (14AA) - 108
17642 威 23rd Specially Established Machine Cannon Unit (14AA) - 108
17643 威 24th Specially Established Machine Cannon Unit (14AA) - 108
17644 威 25th Specially Established Machine Cannon Unit (14AA) - 108
17645 威 26th Specially Established Machine Cannon Unit (14AA) - 108
17646 威 27th Specially Established Machine Cannon Unit (14AA) - 108
17647 威 28th Specially Established Machine Cannon Unit (14AA) - 108
17648 威 29th Specially Established Machine Cannon Unit (14AA) - 108
17649 威 30th Specially Established Machine Cannon Unit (14AA) - 108
17650 威 11th Independent Machinegun Battalion (14AA) - 108
17651 威 12th Independent Machinegun Battalion (14AA) - 108
17652 武 13th Ind. Machinegun Battalion, Manila Def. Unit (14AA) - 249
17653 威 18th Independent Rapid Firing Gun Btn., 103rd Div (14AA) - 106
17654 威 19th Independent Rapid Firing Gun Battalion (14AA) - 108
17655 威 20th Independent Rapid Firing Gun Battalion, Comotes (14AA) - 109
17656 杉 21st Independent Mortar Battalion minus 1st & 2nd Coys (41A) - 114
17656 威 21st Ind. Mortar Battalion, 1st and 2nd Coys, Comotes (14AA) - 109
17657 杉 20th Independent Medium Artillery Btn., Manila Def. (41A) - 249
17658 威 7th Independent Tank Company, Camotes Detachment (14AA) - 109
17659 勤 8th Independent Tank Company, attached 105th Div (41A) - 107

17660 駿 9th Independent Tank Company, attached 103rd Div (14AA) - 106
17661 武 Manila Defense Force Headquarters (41A) - 249
17662-5 盟 58th Independent Mixed Brigade (14AA) - 227
17667 尚武 88th Line of Communications Sector Command (14AA) - 108
17668 杉 37th Independent Rapid Firing Gun Company (41A) - 114
17669 尚武 Army Training Unit (officer candidate trainees) (14AA) - 108
DN • 17700-899, 統 *Tou*, 6th Area Army, Apr. 1945 distribution
17700 統 6th Area Army Headquarters (6AA) - 141
17720-39 振起 132nd Division (6AA) - 205
17736 統 6th Specially Established Engineer Company (6AA) - 142
17742 呂 2nd Specially Established Engineer Company (11A) - 146
17743 呂 3rd Specially Established Engineer Company (11A) - 146
17744 呂 4th Specially Established Engineer Company (11A) - 147
17745 統 5th Specially Established Engineer Company (6AA) - 142
17746 統 46th Specially Established Land Duty Company (6AA) - 142
17747 統 47th Specially Established Land Duty Company (6AA) - 142
17748 統 48th Specially Established Land Duty Company (6AA) - 142
17749 統 49th Specially Established Land Duty Company (6AA) - 142
17750 統 50th Specially Established Land Duty Company (6AA) - 142
17751 統 51st Specially Established Land Duty Company (6AA) - 142
17752 統 52nd Specially Established Land Duty Company (6AA) - 142
17753 統 53rd Specially Established Land Duty Company (6AA) - 142
17754 統 54th Specially Established Land Duty Company (6AA) - 142
17755 統 55th Specially Established Land Duty Company (6AA) - 142
17757 統 7th Specially Established Engineer Company (6AA) - 142
17771 桜 20th Army Field Ordinance Depot (20A) - 149
17772 桜 20th Army Field Motor Vehicle Depot (20A) - 149
17773 桜 20th Army Freight Depot (20A) - 149
17774 波 23rd Army Field Ordinance Depot (23A) - 136
17775 波 23rd Army Field Motor Vehicle Depot (23A) - 136
17776 波 23rd Army Field Freight Depot (23A) - 136
17777 統 34th Field Ordinance Depot (6AA) - 143
17778 統 34th Field Motor Vehicle Depot (6AA) - 143
17779 統 34th Field Freight Depot (6AA) - 143
17780 桜 24th Casualty Clearing Department Headquarters (20A) - 150
17781 呂 181st Line of Communications Hospital (11A) - 148
17782 呂 182nd Line of Communications Hospital (11A) - 148
17783 呂 183rd Line of Communications Hospital (11A) - 148
17784 桜 184th Line of Communications Hospital (20A) - 149
17785 桜 185th Line of Communications (Laiyang Army) Hospital (20A) - 150
17791 桜 20th Army Veterinary Depot (20A) - 149
17793 統 131st Independent Wire Company (6AA) - 142
17800-99 秋水 131st Division (CA) - 203
17810-19 至強 81st Independent Mixed Brigade (20A) - 230
17820-29 至烈 82nd Independent Mixed Brigade (20A) - 230
17830-9 至猛 83rd Independent Mixed Brigade (6AA) - 230-1
17840-9 至勇 84th Independent Mixed Brigade (6AA) - 231

0	1	2	3	4	5	6	7	8	9	10
○	一	二	三	四	五	六	七	八	九	十

17850-9 至潔 85th Independent Mixed Brigade (6AA) - 231
17860-9 秋霜 86th Independent Mixed Brigade (20A) - 232
17870-9 震動 87th Independent Mixed Brigade (20A) - 232
17888-9 沖天 88th Independent Mixed Brigade (BAA) - 232
DN • 17900-99, Not Distributed
DN • 18000-99, 展 *Ten*, 34th Army, Apr. 1945 distribution
DN • 18100-99, 富士 *Fuji*, 36th Army, Apr. 1945 distribution
DN • 18200-99, 尚 *Shou*, 35th Army, Apr. 1945 distribution
18200 尚 35th Army Headquarters (14AA) - 112
DN • 18300-99, 膽 *Tan*, 109th Division
18301-28 and 17501-27 膽 109th Division (31A) - 32-3, 34, 198-9
18301/17502 胆 109th Division Headquarters - 32
18302 備 Iwo Jima Special Navigation Unit (31A) - 33
18305 膽 109th Division Signal Unit (31A) - 34, 198
18306/17504 胆 303rd Independent Infantry Battalion, 109th Div (31A) - 34
18307/17505 胆 304th Independent Infantry Battalion, 109th Div (31A) – 34
18308/17506 胆 305th Independent Infantry Battalion, 109th Div (31A) - 34
18309/17507 胆 306th Independent Infantry Battalion, 109th Div (31A) - 34
18310/17508 胆 307th Independent Infantry Battalion, 109th Div (31A) - 34
18311/17509 胆 308th Independent Infantry Battalion, 109th Div (31A) - 34
18312/17510 胆 1st Mixed Brigade Artillery Unit, 109th Div (31A) – 34
18313/17511 胆 1st Mixed Brigade Engineer Unit, 109th Div (31A) – 34
18314/17503 胆 1st Mixed Brigade Headquarters, 109th Div (31A) – 34
18316/17513 胆 309th Independent Infantry Battalion, 109th Div (31A) - 33
18317/17514 胆 310th Independent Infantry Battalion, 109th Div (31A) - 33
18318/17515 胆 311th Independent Infantry Battalion, 109th Div (31A) - 33
18319/17516 胆 312th Independent Infantry Battalion, 109th Div (31A) - 33
18320/17517 胆 313th Independent Infantry Battalion, 109th Div (31A) - 33
18321/17518 胆 314th Independent Infantry Battalion, 109th Div (31A) - 33
18322/17519 胆 2nd Mixed Brigade Artillery Unit, 109th Div (31A) - 33
18323/17520 胆 2nd Mixed Brigade Engineer Unit, 109th Div (31A) - 33
18330 備 Rocket Gun Company, B type (31A) - 33
18331 備 20th Specially Established Machine Cannon Unit, Iwo Jima (31A) - 33
18332 備 21st Specially Established Machine Cannon Unit, Iwo Jima (31A) - 33
DN • 18400-99, Not Distributed
18400 杉 136th Field Airfield Construction Unit (41A) - 115
18401 杉 137th Field Airfield Construction Unit (41A) - 115
18402 威 138th Field Airfield Construction Unit (KeG) - 117
18403 威 139th Field Airfield Construction Unit (4AirA) - 121
18404 威 140th Field Airfield Construction Unit (4AirA) - 121
18407 司 143rd Field Airfield Construction Unit (3AirA) - 54
18408 司 144th Field Airfield Construction Unit (3AirA) - 54
18409 威 145th Field Airfield Construction Unit (10th Ind Air Bgde 3AirA) - 58
18418 眞 154th Field Airfield Construction Unit (4AirA) - 121

18432 昭 7th Advanced Flight Training Unit (55AirDiv 3AirA) - 55
18433 昭 8th Advanced Flight Training Unit (55AirDiv 3AirA) - 55
18438 司 117th Airfield Battalion (3AirA) - 53
18439 司 118th Airfield Battalion (3AirA) - 53
18440 司 119th Airfield Battalion (3AirA) - 53
18441 司 120th Airfield Battalion (3AirA) - 53
18442 司 121st Airfield Battalion (3AirA) - 53
18443 司 122nd Airfield Battalion (3AirA) - 53
18444 威 123rd Airfield Battalion (4AirA) - 121
18445 威 124th Airfield Battalion (4AirA) - 121
18446 威 125th Airfield Battalion (4AirA) - 121
18447 鷲 126th Airfield Battalion (4AirA) - 121
18448 威 127th Airfield Battalion (4AirA) - 121
18449 司 130th Airfield Battalion (10th Ind. Air Brigade 3AirA) - 58
18450 威 131st Airfield Battalion (3AirA) - 53
18451 威 132nd Airfield Battalion (KeG) - 117
18452 威 133rd Airfield Battalion (3AirA) - 53
18453 威 134th Airfield Battalion (4AirA) - 121
18454 威 135th Airfield Battalion (4AirA) - 121
18455 威 136th Airfield Battalion (4AirA) - 121
18456 威 137th Airfield Battalion (KeG, 14AA) - 117
18475 翔 66th Airfield Company (9AirDiv 3AirA) - 56
18476 翔 68th Airfield Company (9AirDiv 3AirA) - 56
18484 翔 7th Air Intelligence Regiment (9AirDiv 3AirA) - 56
18485 威 9th Air Intelligence Unit (41A and KeG 14AA) - 115, 117
18486 襲 32nd Air Sector Command (7AirDiv 3AirA) - 57
18487 威 33rd Air Sector Command (4AirA) - 120
18488 威 34th Air Sector Command (4AirA) - 120
18489 杉 35th Air Sector Command (41A) - 115
18490 威 36th Air Sector Command (4AirA) - 120
18491 杉 147th Airfield Battalion (41A) - 115
18492 杉 148th Airfield Battalion (41A) - 115
18493 杉 149th Airfield Battalion (41A) - 115
18494 威 150th Airfield Battalion (KeG 14AA and 4AirA) - 117, 121
DN • 18500-99, 岡 *Oka*, 7th Area Army, Apr. 1945 distribution
18500-26 岡 Singapore Defense Unit (7AA) - 250-1
18501-14 威烈 94th Division (29A) - 195
18503 威烈 257th Infantry Regiment, 1st Section (BAA reserve) - 88
18504 威烈 258th Infantry Regiment, 3rd Battalion (BAA reserve) - 88
18505 威烈 94th Field Artillery Regiment, 1st Section (BAA reserve) - 88
18518 富 15th Specially Established Motor Transport Battalion (25A) - 80
18519 岡 16th Specially Established Motor Transport Battalion (7AA) - 74
18520 岡 1st Specially Established Sea Transport Company (7AA) - 74
18521 岡 2nd Specially Established Sea Transport Company (7AA) - 74
18522 岡 3rd Specially Established Sea Transport Company (7AA) - 74
18523 富 15th Field Transport Headquarters (25A) - 80
18524 岡 16th Field Railway Headquarters - N/A

0	1	2	3	4	5	6	7	8	9	10
○	一	二	三	四	五	六	七	八	九	十

18527 定 29th Army Field Ordinance Depot (29A) - 83
18528 定 29th Army Field Motor Transport Depot (29A) - 83
18529 定 29th Army Field Freight Depot (29A) - 83
18530 定 98th Casualty Clearing Platoon (29A) - 83
18531 岡 43rd Independent Engineer Regiment (7AA) - 74
18533 岡 34th Field Transport Headquarters (7AA) - 74
18534 岡 17th Specially Established Motor Transport Battalion (7AA) - 74
18535 岡 13th Independent Heavy Artillery Regiment (7AA) - 74
DN • 18600-99, 昆 *Kon*, 33rd Army, April 1945 distribution
DN • 18700-49, 狼 *Rō*, 49th Division
18700-16 狼 49th Division (BAA) - 186
DN • 18750-99, Not Distributed
DN • 18800-99, 球 *Kyu*, 32nd Army, April 1945 distribution
18808 尚武 5th Medium Trench Mortar Battalion, att. 10th Div (14AA) - 106
18808 杉 5th Medium Trench Mortar Battalion (41A) - 114
DN • 18900-1 誠 *Makoto*, 8th Air Division Formosa
DN • 18902-49, Not Distributed
18902 威 31st Independent Air Squadron (4AirA) - 120
18915 威 17th Air Signal Unit (4AirA) - 122
18915 威 17th Air Signal Unit, 1 platoon (KeG 14AA) - 117
18916 杉 10th Air Intelligence Regiment (41A and KeG 14AA) - 114, 117
18917 威 Southern Army Meteorological Department (SA) - 41
18953 威 5th Wireless Radio Unit (4AirA) - 122
18957 威 9th Wireless Radio Unit (KeG 14AA) - 117
18958 翔 18th Air Intelligence Unit (9AirDiv 3AirA) - 56
18971 昭 45th Independent Air Squadron (55AirDiv 3AirA) - 55
18995 昭 1st Primary Flight Training Unit (55AirDiv3AirA) - 55
18996 昭 2nd Primary Flight Training Unit (55AirDiv 3AirA) - 55
18997 昭 3rd Primary Flight Training Unit (55AirDiv 3AirA) - 55
19038 鸞 1st Air Raid Group Headquarters, later Kembu HQ (14AA) - 240
19038 鸞 Kembu Army Group Headquarters (KeG 14AA) - 117
19039 鸞 2nd Air Raiding Regiment (KeG, 14AA) - 240
19040 鸞 2nd Air Raiding Brigade Headquarters (KeG, 14AA) - 240
19043 帥 101st Airfield Company, 1st Raiding Brigade (6AirA) - 241
19044 鸞 1st Raiding Signal Unit (KeG, 14AA) - 240
19045 鸞 1st Glider Infantry Regiment (KeG, 14AA) - 240
19046 鸞 2nd Glider Infantry Regiment (KeG, 14AA) - 240
19047 鸞 1st Raiding Machine Cannon Raiding Unit (KeG, 14AA) - 240
19048 鸞 1st Raiding Engineer Battalion (KeG, 14AA) - 240
DN • 19050, 昭 *Akira*, 55th Air Division
19050 昭 55th Air Division Headquarters, air training (55AirDiv, 3AirA) - 55
DN • 19051-99, 昭 *Akira*, 55th Air Division
19052 鸞 1st Glider Infantry Transport Wing (KeG, 14AA) - 230
DN • 19100-49, 誠 *Makoto*, 8th Air Division

DN • 19150-249, 燕 *Tsubame*, 1st Air Army, Apr. 1945 distribution
19150 鸞 1st Air Raiding Brigade Headquarters (KeG, 14AA) - 240
19151 鸞 1st Air Raiding Brigade Signal Unit (KeG, 14AA) - 240
DN • 19250-349, 鏑 *Cabra*,1st Air Division
19342 眞 38th Air Regiment (4AirA) - 120
DN • 19350-449, 空 *Kyoku*, 51st Air (Training) Division
DN • 19450-99, Not Distributed
DN • 19500, 靖 *Yasu*, 6th Air Army Headquarters
DN • 19501-699, Not Distributed
DN • 19700, 蓬 *Hō*, 50th Division
DN •19701-49, 湾 *Wan*, Formosa (Taiwan) Army
DN • 19750-899, 暁 *Akatsuki*, Army Shipping Corps Headquarters
19750 杉 11th Sea Raiding Squadron (41A) - 115
19751 暁 12th Sea Raiding Squadron (14AA) - 123
19752 暁 13th Sea Raiding Squadron (41A) - 115
19753 暁 14th Sea Raiding Squadron (41A) - 115
19754 暁 15th Sea Raiding Squadron (41A) - 115
19755 暁 16th Sea Raiding Squadron (41A) - 115
19756 暁 17th Sea Raiding Squadron (41A) - 115
19757 暁 18th Sea Raiding Squadron (41A) - 115
19758 暁 19th Sea Raiding Squadron (41A) - 115
19770 暁 2nd Sea Raiding Base Unit Headquarters (41A) - 115, 123
19771 暁 3rd Sea Raiding Base Unit Headquarters (41A) - 115, 123
19774 暁 32nd Shipping Engineer Regiment (1 Section, 14AA) -123
19778 暁 66th Anchorage Headquarters (SoS) - 59
19779 栄 67th Anchorage Headquarters (CA) - 138
19780 栄 4th Shipping Signal Battalion (CA) - 138
19780 暁 4th Shipping Signal Battalion, 2nd Company (23A) - 138
19792 波 142nd Specially Established Sea Duty Company (23A) - 138
19793 暁 6th Sea Raiding Base Battalion (14AA) - 123
19794 暁 144th Specially Established Sea Duty Company (41A) - 123
19795 暁 145th Specially Established Sea Duty Company (41A) - 123
19796 暁 146th Specially Established Sea Duty Company (14AA) - 123
19797 暁 147th Specially Established Sea Duty Company (14AA) - 123
19798 暁 148th Specially Established Sea Duty Company (14AA) - 123
19799 暁 149th Specially Established Sea Duty Company (14AA) - 123
19800 暁 150th Specially Established Sea Duty Company (14AA) - 123
19801 暁 151st Specially Established Sea Duty Company (14AA) - 123
19806 暁 5th Field Shipping Depot (14AA) - 123
19807 暁 6th Field Shipping Depot (23A) - 138
19810 栄 33rd Shipping Engineer Regiment (CA) - 138
19811 暁 34th Shipping Engineer Regiment (CA) - 138
19814 暁 12th Sea Transport Battalion (CA) - 138
19821 暁 8th Field Shipping Depot (23A) - 138
DN • 19900-99, 昭 *Akira*, 55th Air (Training) Division
DN • 20100-99, 祐 *Yū*, 108th Division
DN • 20200-99, Not Distributed

0	1	2	3	4	5	6	7	8	9	10
〇	一	二	三	四	五	六	七	八	九	十

DN • 20300-99, 公 *Kimi*, 112th Division
DN • 20400-99, 宰 *Sai*, 119th Division
DN • 20500-49, 凪 *Nagi*, 107th Division
DN • 20550-9, 祐 *Yū*, 108th Division
DN • 20600-49, Not Distributed
DN • 20650-99, 公 *Kimi*, 112th Division
DN • 20700-49, 宰 *Sai*, 119th Division
DN • 20750-99, 陸 *Riku*, Hirosaki Divisional District
DN • 20750-99, 陸 *Riku*, Hirosaki Divisional District
DN • 20800-49, 張 *Hari*, Nagoya Divisional District
DN • 20850-99, 攝 *Setu*, Osaka Divisional District
DN • 20900-49, 黒 *Kuro*, Kurume Divisional District
DN • 20950-99, 松 *Mutu*, Asahikawa Divisional District
DN • 21000-49, Not Distributed
DN • 21050-99, 城 *Shiro*, 5th Army, April 1945 distribution
DN • 21100-49, Not Distributed
DN • 21150-99, 奏 *So*, 79th Division
DN • 21200-99, 靖 *Yasu*, 6th Air Army, April 1945 distribution
DN • 21300-49, 陽 *Yo*, 40th Army, April 1945 distribution
DN • 21350-400, Not Distributed
DN • 21401-600, 東北 *Tohoku* Army District
DN • 21601-800, 東海 *Tokai* Army District, Apr. 1945 distribution
DN • 21801-900, 紺 *Kon*, 52nd Air (Training) Division
DN • 21901-2000, 宙 *Chu*, 53rd Air (Training) Division
DN • 22001-50, 漢 *Kan*, Keijo Divisional District (Korea)
DN • 22051-100, 護東 *Gotō*, 140th Division, April 1945 distribution
DN • 22101-200, 隼魁 *Hayabusa Sakigake*, 13th Air Division, 5AirA
22101 隼魁 13th Air Division Headquarters (5AirA, CA) - 136
DN • 22201-50, 護仙 *Gosen*, 142nd Division
DN • 22251-300, 護古 *Goko*, 143rd Division
DN • 22301-50, 護阪 *Gohan*, 144th Division
DN • 22351-400, 護州 *Gosyu*, 145th Division
DN • 22401-50, 護南 *Gonan*, 146th Division
DN • 22451-500, 護北 *Gohoku*, 147th Division
DN • 22501-50, 護朝 *Gosen*, 150th Division
DN • 22551-600, 護宇 *Gou*, 151st Division
DN • 22601-50, 護沢 *Gotaku*, 152nd Division
DN • 22651-700, 護京 *Gokyo*, 153rd Division
DN • 22701-50, 護路 *Goro*, 154th Division
DN • 22751-800, 護土 *Godo*, 155th Division
DN • 22801-50, 護西 *Gosei*, 156th Division
DN • 22851-900, 護弘 *Goko*, 157th Division
DN • 22901-50, 護鮮 *Gosen*, 160th Division
DN • 22951-23050, 達 *Tatsu*, 5th Area Army

23011/11012 灘 454th Independent Infantry Battalion (37A) - 78
23012/11013 灘 455th Independent Infantry Battalion (37A) - 78
DN • 23051-200, 登 *Nobori*, 13th Army, April 1945 distribution
23051-71 進撃 133rd Division (6A) - 205
23073 操 10th Independent Field Heavy Artillery Battalion, 62 IMB (6A) - 228
23080-94 至純 89th Independent Mixed Brigade (6A) - 233
23086 震天 528th Independent Infantry Battalion, 161st Division (13A) - 205
23095-104 震雷 90th Independent Mixed Brigade (13A) - 233
23105-14 馳駆 91st Independent Mixed Brigade (6A) - 234
23116-23 矢石 1st Independent Guard Unit (13A) - 242
23124 波 31st Independent Mixed Regiment (23A) - 135
23124 進撃133rd Division Veterinary Unit (6A) - 205
23127 登 10th Specially Established Engineer Company (13A) - 131
23128 登 11th Specially Established Engineer Company (13A) - 131
23129 守 12th Specially Established Engineer Company (6A) - 133
23130 矛 60th Division Trench Mortar Unit (13A) - 191
23131 鵄 61st Division Trench Mortar Unit (13A) - 192
23132 槍 70th Division Trench Mortar Unit (6A) - 194
23133 登 139th Independent Radio Platoon (13A) - 131
23135 登 141st Independent Radio Platoon (13A) - 131
23136 登 142nd Independent Radio Platoon (13A) - 131, 158
23137-58 震天 161st Division (13A) - 205-6
23140 登 140th Independent Radio Platoon (13A) - 131
DN • 23201-300, 乙 *Otsu*, 1st Army, Apr. 1945 distribution
DN • 23301-400, 仁 *Hito*, 12th Army, Apr. 1945 distribution
DN • 23401-500, 戊 *Bo*, Mongolia Garrison Army
DN • 23501-600, 波 *Nami*, 23rd Army, April 1945 distribution
DN • 23601-5000, Not Distributed
23971 進撃 133rd Division Artillery Unit (6A) - 205
DN • 25001-100, 東方 *Toho*, 1st General Army, April 1945 distribution
DN • 25101-200, 西方 *Seiho*, 2nd General Army, April 1945 distribution
DN • 25201-400, 徳 *Toku*, Kwantung (Kantō) Army, April 1945 distribution
DN • 25401-700, 栄 *Sakae*, China Expeditionary Army, April 1945 distribution
DN • 25701-900, 威 *i*, Southern Expeditionary Army, April 1945 distribution
DN • 25901-6000, 森 *Mori*, Burma Area Army, April 1945 distribution
DN • 26001-100, 達 *Tatsu*, 5th Area Army, April 1945 distribution
DN • 26101-200, 進 *Sunuma*, 11th Area Army, April 1945 distribution
DN • 26201-300, 幡 *Hata*, 12th Area Army, April 1945 distribution
DN • 26301-400, 秀 *Syo*, 13th Area Army, April 1945 distribution
DN • 26401-500, 楠 *Kusunoki*, 15th Area Army, April 1945 distribution
DN • 26501-600, 睦 *Mutu*, 16th Area Army, April 1945 distribution
DN • 26601-700, 築 *Kizuka*, 17th Area Army, April 1945 distribution
DN • 26701-800, 岩 *Iwa*, 3rd Army, April 1945 distribution
DN • 26801-900, 光 *Hikari*, 4th Army, April 1945 distribution
DN • 26901-7000, 守 *Mamoru*, 6th Army, April 1945 distribution
DN • 27001-200, 呂 *Ro*, 11th Army, April 1945 distribution
DN • 27201-500, 東北 *Tohoku* Army District units, April 1945 distribution

DN • 27501-800, 東部 *Tobu* Army District, Apr. 1945 distribution
27614 森 21st Independent Engineer Regiment (BAA) - 86
DN • 27801-100, 東海 *Tokai* Army District, April 1945 distribution
DN • 28101-400, 中部 *Chubu* Army Distinct, April 1945 distribution
28247 登 16th Trench Mortar Battalion (13A) - 131
28248 秀嶺 19th Trench Mortar Battalion (43A) - 158
28291 登 22nd Trench Mortar Battalion (13A) - 131
28371 秀嶺 18th Trench Mortar Battalion (43A) - 158
28372 登 20th Trench Mortar Battalion (13A) - 131
DN • 28401-700, 西部 *Seibu* Army District, April 1945 distribution
DN • 28701-9000, 北部 *Hokubu* Army District, April 1945 distribution
DN • 29001-100, Not Distributed
DN • 29101-300, 朝鮮 Korea Army, April 1945 distribution
DN • 29301-600, 湾 *Wan*, Formosa (Taiwan) Army District, April 1945 distribution
DN • 29601-900 臣 *Shin*, Minister of the Army
DN • 29901-30000 道 *Dō*, Inspector General of Military Training
DN • 30001-100, 燕 *Tsubame*, 1st Air Army, April 1945 distribution
DN • 30101-200, 松 *Mutu*, Asahikawa Divisional District
DN • 30201-400, 陸 *Riku*, Hirosaki Divisional District
DN • 30401-600, 仙 *Sen*, Sendai Divisional District
DN • 30601-800, 蔵 *Zō*, Tokyo Divisional District
DN • 30801-31000, 丸 *Maru*, Utsunomiya Divisional District
DN • 31001-200, 越 *Etsu*, Nagano Divisional District
DN • 31201-400, 澤 *Sawa*, Kanazawa Divisional District
DN • 31401-600, 張 *Hari*, Nagoya Divisional District
DN • 31601-800, 洛 *Raku*, Kyoto Divisional District
DN • 31801-32000, 攝 *Setu*, Osaka Divisional District
DN • 32001-200, 中国 *Chugoku* Divisional District
DN • 32201-400, 四國 *Shikoku* Divisional District
DN • 32401-600, 薩 *Satsu*, Kumamoto Divisional District
DN • 32601-800, 黒 *Kuro*, Kurume Divisional District
DN • 32801-33000, 津 *Shin*, Ranam Divisional District (Korea)
DN • 33001-200, 緑 *Midori*, Heijo (Pyongyang) Divisional District (Korea)
DN • 33201-400, 漢 *Kan*, Keijo (Seoul) Divisional District (Korea)
DN • 33401-600, 邱 *Kyū*, Taikyu (Taegu) Divisional District (Korea)
DN • 33601-800, 木 *Moku*, Koshu (Gongju) Divisional District (Korea)
DN • 33801-900, Not Distributed
DN • 33901-50, 隅 *Gū*, 1st Imperial Guard Division
DN • 33951-34100, 線 *Sen*, Homeland Rail Road Headquarters
DN • 34101-200, 路 *Michi*, Continental Railway Headquarters
34101 / 1231 路 3rd Railway Regiment, central China (CA) - 143
DN • 34201-400, 師 *Sui*, Air General Army, April 1945 distribution
DN • 34401-500, 羽 *Hane*, 2nd Air Army, April 1945 distribution
DN • 34501-600, 司 *Tsukasa*, 3rd Air Army, April 1945 distribution
DN • 34601-700, 鷲 *Washi*, 2nd Air Division
DN • 34701-800, 高 *Taka*, 5th Air Division

DN • 34801-900, 天鷲 *Amawashi*, 11th Air Division
DN • 34901-35000, 天翔 *Tensho*, 10th Air Division
DN • 35001-100, 天風 *Tenpu*, 12th Air Division
DN • 35101-200, 暁 *Akatsuki*, Army Shipping Corps Headquarters
DN • 35201-37200, 東部 *Tobu* Army District
36709 東部 8th Field Horse Remount Depot (8AA) - N/A
DN • 37201-38200, 徳 *Toku*, Kwantung (Kantō) Army
DN • 38201-400, Air Army Board
DN • 38401-500, 房 *Bou*, Tokyo Bay Army Corps
DN • 38501-40000, Not Distributed
79771 暁 3rd Sea Raiding Base Unit Headquarters (41A) - 115

Appendix

By November 1945 the Imperial Army had ceased to exist

Chart 1: **The Imperial Army ca. August 1945**

Organization	Code Name	Posting
Imperial General HQ	*Never had a code name*	Tokyo
General Armies:		
Kwantung Army	*Toku* 徳4570	Hsinking, Manchuria
China Expeditionary Army	*Sakae* 栄1490	Nanking, China
Southern Army	*i* 威1160	Saigon, Vietnam
1st General Army G.HQ.	*Toho* 東方8151	Tokyo, Japan
2nd General Army	*Seiho* 西方8152	Honshu, Japan
General Air Army	*Sui* 師500	Tokyo, Japan
Area Armies:		
1st Area Army	*Ei* 鋭1448	Mutanchiang, Manchuria
2nd Area Army	*Kagayaku* 輝16300	Manado, Celebese
3rd Area Army	*Kyou* 強9331	Mukden, Manchuria
5th Area Army	*Tatsu* 達8150	Sapporo, Japan
6th Area Army	*Tou* 統17700	Hankou, China
7th Area Army	*Oka* 岡1615	Singapore
8th Area Army	*Go* 剛7960	Rabaul, New Britain Is.
10th Area Army	*Wan* 湾 No #	Taipei Formosa
11th Area Army	*Sunuma* 進12300	Sendai, Japan
12th Area Army	*Hata* 幡12345	Tokyo, Japan

Organization	Code Name	Posting
13th Area Army	*Syo* 秀12480	Nagoya, Japan
14th Area Army	*Shobu* 尚武1600	Manila, Philippines
15th Area Army	*Kusunoki* 楠12490	Osaka, Japan
16th Area Army	*Mutu* 睦13500	Fukuoka, Japan
17th Area Army	*Kizuka* 築12701	Seoul, Korea
18th Area Army	*Gi* 義7970	Bangkok, Thailand
North China A. A.	*Ko* 甲1400	Beijing, China
Burma Area Army	*Mori* 森7900	Moulmein Burma
Armies:		
1st Army	*Otsu* 乙3500	Tiayuan, North China
2nd Army	*Ikioi* 勢16400	Macassar Is.
3rd Army	*Iwa* 岩3600	Yenchi, Manchuria
4th Army	*Hikari* 光4455	Tsitsihar, Manchuria
5th Army	*Shiro* 城5033	Yehho, Manchuria
6th Army	*Mamoru* 守1305	Nanking, China
11th Army	*Ro* 呂5500	Hankou, China
12th Army	*Hito* 仁4221	Chengchow, China
13th Army	*Nobori* 登7331	Shanghai, China
14th Army	*Shobu* 尚武1600	14th Area Army
15th Army	*Hayashi* 林1611	Rangoon, Burma
16th Army	*Osamu* 治1602	Batavia, Java
17th Army	*Oki* 沖9811	Buin, Solomon Is.
18th Army	*Mo* 猛7910	Madang, New Guinea
19th Army	*Ken* 堅9450	Batavia, Java
20th Army	*Sakura* 桜7907	Hankow, China
23rd Army	*Nami* 波8111	Canton, China
25th Army	*Tomi* 富8990	De Kock, Sumatra
27th Army	*Hokubu* 北部100	Kurile Islands, Japan
28th Army	*Saku* 策9410	Paung, Burma
29th Army	*Tei* 定9411	Taiping, Malaya
30th Army	*Bin* 敏25301	Meihokou, Manchuria
31st Army	*Sonae* 備7920	Truk Island
32nd Army	*Kyu* 球1616	Okinawa, Japan
33rd Army	*Kon* 昆7901	Bilin, Burma
34th Army	*Ten* 展 (*Robu* 呂武)	Hamhung, Korea
35th Army	*Shou* 尚18200	Cebu Island
36th Army	*Fuji* 富士18100	Urawa, Japan
37th Army	*Nada* 灘9801	Sangpong, Borneo
38th Army	*Sin* 信7950	Saigon, Vietnam
39th Army	*Gi* 義7970	Thailand
40th Army	*Yo* 陽21300	Kagoshima
41st Army	*Sugi* 杉 4732	South of Manila P.I.
43rd Army	*Shurei* 秀嶺12700	Shangtung, China
44h Army	*Sizume* 遠征14001	Liaoyuan, Manchuria
50th Army	*Shun* 俊21413	Aomori, Japan

Organization	Code Name	Posting
51st Army	*Ken* 建21410	Mito, Japan
52nd Army	*Sho* 捷13333	Susui, Japan
53rd Army	*Dan* 断21601	Tamagawa, Japan
54th Army	*Satsu* 颯21641	Shinshiromachi, Japan
55th Army	*Kai* 偕12475	Kochi, Japan
56th Army	*Shuu* 宗13580	Iizuka, Japan
57th Army	*Hou* 鋒13590	Takanabe, Japan
58th Army	*Toride* 砦21703	Cheju Island, Korea
59th Army	*Sanyo* 山陽32200	Hiroshima, Japan
Mongolia Garrison	*Bo* 戊5301	Wanchuan, Inner Mongolia
Tokyo Def. Army	*Hata* 幡 No number	Tokyo, Japan
Tokyo Bay Corps	*Bou* 房13300	Tateyama, Japan
Air Armies :		
1st Air Army	*Tsubame* 燕30001	Tokyo, Japan
2nd Air Army	*Hane* 羽8212	Hsinking, Manchuria
3rd Air Army	*Tsukasa* 司9813	Singapore
4th Air Army	*Shin* 眞15300	Manila, Philippines
5th Air Army	*Hayabusa* 隼2371	Seoul, Korea
6th Air Army	*Yasu* 靖19500	Fukuoka, Japan
13th Air Division	*Hayabusa Sakigake* 隼魁	Nanching, China
6th Air Division	*Yō* 洋	18th Army, New Guinea
Shipping and Rail organizations:		
Shipping Command	*Akatsuki* 暁2940	Ujina, Japan
1st RR Transport	*Sen* 線	Tokyo, Japan
Kwantung RR	*Michi* 路	Hsinking, Manchuria
Manchuria	*Manshu* 満州	Hsinking, Manchuria

Chain of command: A General Army controlled several Area Armies, which in turn controlled several Field or Garrison Armies. For a time the 13th Army was a defacto Area Army with the 6th Army its subordinate.

Japanese field armies were more or less the size of a U.S. army corps.

Chart 2: Army Activations and Movement from 1940 to 1945

In July 1937 the Marco Polo Bridge Incident precipitated the 2nd Sino-Japanese War (the China Incident). As fighting in China continued relations with the West deteriorated, diplomacy finally breaking down in 1941.
Vichy France agreed to allow Japan to occupy southern French Indochina, which threatened Allied interests in the region. The West retaliated in July. America, Britain and Holland placed an oil embargo on Japan, who could produce no more than 10% of its yearly consumption domestically and had less than one year's supply in reserve.
As Japan was already at war, and with an oil crisis looming, the speedy annexation of the British and Dutch East Indies, which together produced 50 million barrels a year, was the obvious next move.
In the months before Pearl Harbor Japan allied itself with Thailand and finalized plans for south Asia and the Pacific. Hope was that a swift victory would force the Allies to sue for peace and allow Japan to keep possession of her gains. Dec 8th was X-Day, the start date for the invasions of Hong Kong, Malaysia, Java and the Philippines.
Six months later, on June 7th, Japan's remarkable string of victories ended in the defeat at Midway.
Legend: **Bold is a** new army, *Italic* is an event and date.

1940:

1. Imperial General Headquarters:

1a. under direct control: Korean Army, Formosa Army, 1st Shipping Transport HQ became **Shipping Transport HQ** *June 7th*, **South China Area Army** *from July 25th*, **22nd Army** *from Jul 25th* and *deactivated Nov 19th*, **Indochina Army** *active Sept 5th*

2. Kwantung Army:

2a. under direct control: 3rd Army, 4th Army, 5th Army, 6th Army

3. China Expeditionary Army:

3a. under direct control: 11th Army, 13th Army, 21st Army *became South China Area Army on Feb 9th*

3b. North China Area Army: 1st Army, 12th Army, Mongolia Garrison Army

3c. **South China Area Army** *activated Feb 9th under I.G.HQ control from Jul 25th*: **22nd Army** *joined Feb 9th transferred with South China Area Army Jul 25th*

1941:

1. Imperial General Headquarters:

1a. under direct control: Korean Army, Formosa Army, Northern Area Army, **23rd Army** *joined Jul 5th, to China Exp. Army Aug 15th*, **25th Army** *joined Jul 5th, to Southern Army Nov 15th*, **South Seas Detachment** *joined Nov 16th*

1b. South China Area Army: Indochina Area Army

1c. Shipping Transport Command

2. Kwantung Army:

2a. under direct control: 3rd Army, 4th Army, 5th Army, 6th Army, **20th Army** *joined Sept 19th*, **Kwantung Defense Army** *joined July 12th*

3. China Expeditionary Army:

3a. under direct control: 23rd Army *from Aug 12th*, 3rd Air Corps *deactivated Nov 8th*, 1st Air Brigade *activated Nov 8th*

3b. North China Area Army: 1st Army, 12th Army, Mongolia Garrison Army

4. **Southern Expeditionary Army**: *activated on Nov 5th*

4a. under direct control: **14th Army** *joined Nov 6th*, **15th Army** *joined Nov 6th*,

1941: continued
16th Army *joined Nov 6th,* 25th Army *from Nov 15th,* 3rd Air Corps *joined Nov 15th,* 5th Air Corps *joined Nov 15th,* 1st Air Corps
5. **General Defense Army**: *activated Jul 12th*
5a. under direct control: Northern Army District, Eastern Army District, Central Army District, Western Army District
1942:
1. Imperial General Headquarters:
1a. under direct command: Korea Army, Formosa Army, 14th Army *IGHQ shared command w/Southern Army until June 29th,* **17th Army** *activated May 18th to 8th AA Nov 15th,* South Seas Detachment *to 17th Army May 20th,* **Gov. Gen. of Hong Kong Dept.** *joined Jan 28th,* **North Seas Detachment** *joined May 5th deactivated Oct 24th*, **Ichiki Detachment** *active May 5th to 17th Army Aug 10th,* 1st Flying Corps *deactivated June 6th,* 1st Air Army *joined Aug 10th*
1b. **8th Area Army** *activated Nov 15th:* 17th Army *joined Nov 15th,* **18th Army** *active Nov 16th*
1c. General Defense Army: Northern Army District, Eastern Army District, Central Army District, Western Army District
1d. Shipping Transport Headquarters: *deactivated Jul 14th*, **Shipping Command** *activated Jul 14th*
2. Kwantung Army:
2a. under direct control: Kwantung Defense Army, **Mechanized Army** *joined Jul 4th,* Kwantung Air Corps *dissolved June 10th*, **2nd Air Army** *joined June 10th*
2b. **1st Area Army**, 3rd Army, 5th Army and 20th Armies, **2nd Army** *all joined Jul 4th*
2c. **2nd Area Army** *joined Jul 4th*: 4th Army, 6th Army
3. China Expeditionary Army:
3a. under direct control: 11th Army, 13th Army, 23rd Army, 1st Air Group *dissolved Jul 10th*, **3rd Air Division** *activated Jul 10th*
3b. North China Area Army: 1st Army, 12th Army, Mongolia Garrison Army
4. Southern Expeditionary Army:
4a. under direct control: 14th Army *shared command w/I.G.HQ until June 29th,* 15th Army, 16th Army, 25th Army, **Borneo Defense Army HQ** *active from Apr 20th,* **Indochina Garrison Army** *active Nov 10th,* 3rd Air Corps *deactivated Jul 7th,* 5th Air Corps *deactivated Jul 7th,* **22nd Air Brigade** *active Mar 20th sent to 14th Army on Jul 15th,* **3rd Air Army** *activated Jul 10th*
1943:
1. Imperial General Headquarters:
1a. under direct command: Korea Army, Formosa Army, 14th Army, Governor General of Hong Kong Dept., North Seas Detachment *became the North Area Army on Feb. 5th*, 1st Air Army
1b. 8th Area Army: 17th Army, 18th Army, 4th Air Army *joined the 8th AA on Jul 28th*
1c. 2nd Area Army *from Oct. 30th,* 2nd Army *joined 2nd AA on Oct.30th*
1d. General Defense Army: **Northern Defense Army** *activated Feb 5th*, Northern District Army *deactivated Feb 5th*, Eastern District Army, Central District Army, Western District Army
1e. Shipping Command
2. Kwantung Army:

1942: continued

2a. under direct control: Kwantung Defense Army, Mechanized Army *deactivated on Oct 30th,* 2nd Air Army

2b. 1st Area Army: 2nd Army *to 2nd Area Army Oct 30th,* 3rd Army, 5th Army, 20th Army

2c. 2nd Area Army *to Imp HQ Oct 30th:* 4th Army *to 3rd Area Army Oct 30th,* 6th Army *to 3rd Area Army Oct 30th*

2d. **3rd Area Army** *joined Oct 30th:* 4th Army, 6th Army

3. China Expeditionary Army:

3a. under direct control: 11th Army, 13th Army, 23rd Army, 3rd Air Division

3b. North China Area Army: 1st Army, 12th Army, Mongolia Garrison Army

4. Southern Expeditionary Army:

4a. under direct control: 16th Army, 25th Army, Borneo Defense Army, **19th Army** *activated Jan 7th joined 2nd AA on Oct 30th,* **Thailand Garrison Army** *activated Jan 4th,* Indochina Garrison Army *joined the Southern Army Dec 10th,* 3rd Air Army

4b. **Burma Area Army** *joined Mar 27th:* 15th Army

4c. 2nd Area Army *from Oct 30th:* 19th Army *from Oct 30th*

1944:

1. Imperial General Headquarters:

1a. under direct command: Korea Army, Formosa Army *until Mar 20th,* 14th Army *shared command w/Southern Army, removed Apr 15th,* **32nd Army** *created Mar 22nd to the West District Army May 10th.* **31st Army** *created Feb 25th,* **Ogasawara Army Group** *from June 26th,* Governor of Hong Kong Dept. *to 6th Area Army on Dec 11th,* **36th Army** *activated Jul 15th, I.G.HQ to Gen Def Command Oct 27th,* 1st Air Army *until Mar 27th,* 10th Area Army *from Oct 25th*

1b. 2nd Area Army *to Southern Army Mar 27th:* 19th Army, 2nd Army

1c. 8th Area Army: 17th Army, 18th Army *to 2nd Area Army Mar 25th and to Southern Army June 20th,* 4th Air Army *to 2nd Area Army Mar 25th, to Southern Ex. Army Apr 15th*

1d. **5th Area Army** *created Mar 6th:* **27th Army** *activated Mar 6th*

1e. **10th Area Army** *created Sept 9th*

1f. General Defense Army: Northern Defense Army *became the* **5th Area Army** *under I.G.HQ from Mar 6th,* 36th Army *to 12th Area Army Feb '45,* Eastern District Army, Central District Army, Western District Army, **6th Air Army** *from Dec 25th*

1g. Shipping Command

2. Kwantung Army:

2a. under direct control: Kwantung Defense Army, 2nd Air Army

2b. 1st Area Army: 2nd Army, 3rd Army, 5th Army, 20th Army *until Sept 27th*

2c. 3rd Area Army: 4th Army, 6th Army

3. China Expeditionary Army:

3a. under direct control: 11th Army *until Aug 26th,* 13th Army, 23rd Army *until Aug 26th,* **34th Army** *until Jul 17th* 3rd Air Division *until Feb 15th,* **5th Air Army** *from Feb. 15th*

3b. North China Area Army: 1st Army, 12th Army, Mongolia Garrison Army

3c. **6th Area Army** *from Aug 26th*: 34th Army *from Aug 26th,* 20th Army *from Oct 19th,* 23rd Army *from Aug 26th*

4. Southern Expeditionary Army:

4a. under direct control: 14th Army *shared command w/I.G.HQ until Apr 15th,* Borneo Defense Army *became the* **37th Army** *on Oct 12th,* Thailand Garrison Army *became*

1944: continued

the **39th Army** *on Dec 10th*, French Indochina Garrison Army *became the* **38th Army** *on Dec 26th*, 3rd Air Army

4b. **14th Area Army** *created from 14th Army on Aug 4th*: **34th Army** *created Aug 4th*

4c. **7th Area Army** *created Mar 27th*, 16th Army *from Mar 27th*, 25th Army *from Mar 27th*, 29th Army *from Mar 27th*

4d. Burma Area Army: 15th Army, **28th Army** *from Jan 15th,* **33rd Army** *from Apr 11th*

4e. 2nd Area Army *from Mar 27th*, 19th Army, 2nd Army

1945:

1. Imperial General Headquarters:

1a. under direct control: Korea Army *became* **17th Area Army** *on Feb 6th to Kw. Army*, 31st Army, Ogasawara Army Group, 1st Air Army *until Apr 8th*

1b. General Defense Army *became* **1st General Army** *on Apr 8th:* Eastern District Army *became* **12th Area Army** *Feb 6th*, Central District Army *became the* **15th Area Army** *Feb 6th*, Western District Army *became the* **16th Area Army** *Feb 6th,* 6th Air Army *joined* **Air General Army** *Apr 8th*

1c. 5th Area Army: 27th Army *until Jan 22nd HQ became the* **15th Area Army HQ**

1d. 10th Area Army: 32nd Army, 40th Army *until Jan 16th and 16th Area Army on May 20th*

1e. 8th Area Army *abandoned in Rabaul on June 17th:* 17th Army, 18th Army *until June 17th transferred to the Southern Expeditionary Army.*

1f. Shipping Command:

2. Kwantung Army: *reorganized May 30th*

2a. under direct control: 4th Army *from May 30th*, 6th Army *to China Exp. Army Jan 25th*, Kwantung Defense Army *became the* **44th Army** *May 30th,* **34th Army** *created June 18th*, 2nd Air Army *to Air General Army on May 15th*

2b. **17th Area Army** *was Korea Army until Feb 6th, joined Kwantung Army Aug 10th:* **58th Army** *created Apr 8th*

2c. 1st Area Army *reorg. May 30th:* 3rd Army *from May 30th,* 5th Army *from May 30th*

2d. 3rd Area Army *reorg. May 30th:* 30th Army *from Jul 30th,* 44th Army *from May 30th*

3. China Expeditionary Army:

3a. under direct control: 13th Army, 6th Army *from Jan 25th,* 23rd Army *from Mar 10th,* 5th Air Army *to Kwantung Army on May 16th*

3b. North China Area Army: 1st Army, 12th Army, Mongolia Defense Army, 43rd Army *from Mar 22nd*

3c. 6th Area Army: 11th Army, 20th Army, 23rd Army *to China Expeditionary Army Mar 10th*, 34th Army *to Kwantung Army on June 18th,* Gov. Gen. of Hong Kong *to 23rd Army Mar 10th*

4. Southern Expeditionary Army:

4a. under direct control: 37th Army, 2nd Army *under the Southern Army from June 13th*, 39th Army *became the 18th Area Army on Jul 15th,* 38th Army, 18th Army *after June 17th*, 3rd Air Army, 4th Air Army *deactivated Feb 17th*

4b. Burma Area Army: 15th Army, 28th Army, 33rd Army

4c. 7th Area Army: 16th Army, 25th Army, 29th Army

4d. 14th Area Army: 35th Army, **41st Army** *from Apr 20th*

4e. 2nd Area Army *deactivated June 13th:* 2nd Army *to the Southern Army,* 19th Army *deactivated Feb 28th.*

1945: continued

4f. **18th Area Army** *was the 39th Army until Jul 15th:* 15th Army *from Jul 15th*

5. **1st General Army** *created Apr 8th:*

5a. **11th Area Army** *created Feb 6th:* **50th Army** *created Feb 6th*

5b. **12th Area Army** *created Feb 6th:* 36th Army *attached Feb 6th,* **51st Army** *created Apr 8th,* **52nd Army** *created Apr 8th,* **53rd Army** *created Apr 8th,* **Tokyo Bay Army Corps** *created June 19th,* **Tokyo Defense Army** *created June 23rd*

5c. **13th Area Army** *created Feb 6th:* **54th Army** *created June 19th*

6. **2nd General Army** *created Apr 8th:*

6a. **15th Area Army** *created Feb 6th:* **55th Army** *created Apr 8th,* **59th Army** *created June 15th*

6b. **16th Area Army** *created Feb 6th:* 40th Army *joined May 20th,* **56th Army** *created Apr 21st,* **57th Army** *created Apr 8th*

7. **Air General Army**: *created Apr. 8th*

7a. under direct control: , 1st Air Army *from Apr 8th,* 2nd Air Army *from May 15th,* 5th Air Army *from May 15th,* 6th Air Army *from Apr 8th*

Bibliography

Books

Anonymous. August 24, 2015. *A Dictionary of Military Terms and Expressions*: Sagwan Press

ATIS. 1947. (Allied Translator and Interpreter Section), Supreme Commander for the Allied Powers. *Report on surrendered Japanese personnel in U.S.S.R. territories*. CARL Digital Library EBook

ATIS. 1945. *Restoration of Captured Documents. ATIS Publication No. 10*: Allied Translator and Interpreter Section South West Pacific Area. CARL Digital Library EBook

ATIS. 1944 *The Exploitation of Japanese Documents*: Allied Translator and Interpreter Section, South West Pacific Area, Publication No. 6 CARL Digital Library EBook

Bullard, Steven (translator). 2007. *Japanese army operations in the South Pacific area, New Britain and Papua campaigns, 1942-43*: A.W.M. EBook

Bullard, Steven and Tamura Keiko (eds.). 2004. *From a hostile shore*: *Australia and Japan at war in New Guinea*. Canberra, ACT: Aust. War Memorial EBook

Frank, Richard B. 1990. *Guadalcanal*: *the definitive account of the landmark battle*. Penguin Random House

General Headquarters, Military Intelligence Section, General Staff. *Final progress of demobilization of the Japanese Armed Forces*, *December 31, 1946*: CARL Digital Library EBook. (PDF in four parts)

General Headquarters, South West Pacific Area, Military Intelligence Section, General Staff.1945. *Periodic Summary of Enemy Trends, No. 29*. CARL Digital Library EBook

Kai, Shunichiro. 1991. 日本陸海軍部隊要覧 *(Nihon Riku Kai Gun Butai Yoran)*: Shinpu Shobo

McNaughton, James C. 2006. *Nisei Linguists, Japanese Americans in the Intelligence Service during World War II*: Dept. of the Army, Washington D.C. (Chapter 3. EBook https://history.army.mil/books/Recent/Nisei/Ch3.pdf)

Military Intelligence Division. War Dept. 1945. *Guide to Maps of the Far East, Special Series N0. 31*. War Dept: CARL Digital Library EBook

Military Intelligence Division. 1945. *Japanese Recruiting and Replacement System.* War Department: CARL Digital Library EBook (PDF in two parts)

Military Intelligence Service. 1942. *Japanese Ground and Air Forces, Information Bulletin No. 14, MID 461*. War Department, Washington D.C.: CARL Digital Library EBook

Pacific Unit M.I.D. 1943. *Applied Tactics Japanese Army, Translation of Japanese Manual, Revised 1938*. War Department, Washington D.C.: CARL Digital Library EBook (PDF in six parts)

Pinyol, Joan. 2016. *The Rising Sun in Arms - Order of Battle of the Imperial Japanese Armed Forces, 1937- 1945*: Self-published 2nd Edition

Remmelink, Willem (translator). 2016. *Invasion of the Dutch East Indies*. Compiled by the War Office of the National Defense College of Japan 1967. Corts Foundation/Leiden University Press, 2015

Sledge, E.B. 1981. *With the Old Breed*: Presidio Press, a Division of Random House

U.S. War Dept. 1944. *Japanese military dictionary*: *Japanese-English*

United States. War Dept. 1944. *Handbook on Japanese military forces*. Washington: U.S. Govt. Print. Off.

The Japanese Monographs: Commissioned by the Historical Section, G-2, GHQ, FE. CA. Two-DVD disc set by LRA 2014, purchased from the late Jim Lansdale. The initial proposal for the Monograph series came from US Government *Instruction No. 126, Institution for War Records Investigation*. Begun in November 1945, Japan's Demobilization Bureau coordinated the project. Owing to essential missing operational records such as original orders, unit journals and plans the Japanese ranking and staff Army and Navy officers involved reconstructed missing details from personal papers and memory. Aside from a patriotic softening of adverse events, these accounts (which include many unedited translations) are believed to be substantially accurate.

Note: Monographs marked * are available as downloads from: http://ibiblio.org/hyperwar/Japan/Monos/

Monograph number – Title and details:

1 – Philippines Operations Record, Phase 1, Invasion of the Philippines, November 6, 1941 – June 30, 1942, unedited translation, 243 pages, unaccredited, undated

3 – Philippines Operations Record, Phase 2, Subjugation of islands, guerrillas and insurgents, the Philippines as a logistics base, December 1942 – June 1944, 56 pages by Col. Yasuji Okada, October 1946

4 – Philippines Operations Record, Phase III, 14th Area Army plans for defense, July 1944 – November 1944, 50 pages by Col. Shujiro Kobayashi and Col. Ryoichiro Aojima, October 1946

6 – Philippines Operations Record, 35th Army's defense of Leyte, June 1944 – August 1945, 171 pages by Maj. Masataka Iwano, Maj. Gen. Yoshihara Tomochika, editors Ryoichiro Aoshima and Rigai Watanabe, October 1946

7 – Philippines Operations Record, defensive preparations and U.S. invasion of Leyte, January – August 1945, 222 pages by Maj. Masataka Iwano and Col. Ryoichiro Aoshima, October 1946

8 – Philippines Operations Record, Shimbu Army Group in Southern Luzon, December 1944 – August 1945, 36 pages by Maj. Masataka Iwano and Col. Ryoichiro Aoshima, October 1946

9 – Philippines Operations Record, Shimbu Army Group defense of Clark Field, December 1944 – August 1945, 31 pages by Col. Yasuji Okada, November 1946

12*– Philippines Air Operations Record, 4th Air Army operations in Leyte, Luzon and Mindoro, August 1944–February 1945, 119 pages by Col. Matsumae, former 4th Air Army staff officer, Oct. 1946

13 – North of Australia Operations Record, 2nd Area Army, 1943 – 1945, 108 pages, unedited translation, unaccredited, July 1946

14 – Second Area Army Operations in the Western New Guinea Area (battle summary), May 1944 – January 1945, 18 pages, unedited translation, unaccredited, undated

15 – Outline of the Battle for Morotai (32nd Division), 15 September – 13 May 1945, 19 pages, unedited translation, unaccredited, undated

16*– Ambon (Amboina) and Timor Invasion Operations, January – February 1942, edited reproduced, 23 pages by Lt. Col. Tozuka Susumu based on diary notes, then expanded by Lt. Col. Kengoro Tanaka et al. January 31, 1953

17*– Homeland Operations Record, 1941 – 1945, 246 pages, rewritten and reproduced with the assistance of Susumu Nishimura: Monograph 17 by Maj. Gen. Yoshihide Kato et al., later compiled into one with Homeland Operations Monographs No. 18: Vol. II, 19: Vol. III, and No. 20; 16th Area Army, undated.

21 – Homeland Operations Record, Volume IV, Fifth Area Army, late 1943 – 1945, 50 pages, edited reproduced by Lt. Col. Risaburo Taguma from memory and documents in his possession, July 30, 1952

22 – Seventeenth Area Army Operations, 1941 – 1945, 46 pages by Lt. Col. Matsushige Ishibashi and Maj. Fusakichi Fueda, rewritten and reproduced by Col. Muraji Yano, July 23, 1956

23 – Air Defense of the Homeland, 1944 – 1945, 91 pages by Maj. Takejiro Shiba, rewritten by former Japanese officers Toshikazu Ohmae, Ryosuke Nomura and Tadao Shudo, June 5, 1956

24*– History of the Southern Army, 1941 – 1945, 159 pages, rewritten by the 1st Demobilization Bureau, July 1946

25 – French Indo-China Area Operations Record, 1940 – 1945, 40 pages by Lt. Col. Tateki Sakai with assistance from Lt. Col. Sakuji Ishimaru, Lt. Col. Kakuo Yamamoto, Lt. Col. Wasatatsu Shirai and Lt. Col. Isamu Hashizume, September 17, 1952

26 – Borneo Operations, 1941 – 1945, 98 pages by Col. Itsu Ogawa assisted by Lt. Col. Masashi Ino, rewritten and corrected incorporating extensive research by the Foreign Histories Division, Nov 20, 1957

27 – Jolo Island Invasion Operations Record, Dec. 1941, 3 pages by Col. Tsuneo Yano, edited, undated

28 – Tarakan Invasion Operations Record, Jan. 1942, 6 pages by Col. Tsuneo Yano, edited, Mar 4, 1952

29 – Balikpapan Invasion Operations Record, January 1942, 8 pages by Col. Tsuneo Yano, edited, March 31, 1953

30 – Bandjermasin Invasion Operations Record, February 1942, 7 pages by Col. Tsuneo Yano, edited April 21, 1953

31*– Southern Area Air Operations Record, 1941 – 1945, 37 pages, unedited translation, unaccredited, undated

32*– Southeast Area Air Operations Record, November 1942 - April 1944, 39 pages, unedited translation by Lt. Col. Koji Tanaka, undated

34 – Southeast Area Operations Record, Volume I, 17th Army on Guadalcanal, May 1942 – January 1943, 162 pages, unedited translation by Lt. Col. Norikuni Sadashima and Lt. Gen. Haruo Konuma, Sept. 1946

35 – Southeast Area Operations Record, Volume II, 17th Army's withdrawal from Guadalcanal, February 1943 – August 1945, 172 pages, unedited translation by Lt. Col. Norikuni Sadashima, Lt. Gen. Haruo Konuma, Lt. Col. Shiro Hara, Col. Toshihara Kamiya, Lt. Col. Matsuichi Iino and Maj. Isamu Tanaka, September 1946

37 – Southeast Area Ops Record 18th Army Ops, Vol. I, January 1942 – June 1943, 195 pages by Col. Shigeru Sugiyama, rewritten and reproduced by Lt. Col. Kengoro Tanaka, October 14, 1953

38 – Southeast Area Ops Record 18th Army Ops, Vol. II, June 1943 – February 1944,

212 pages, unedited translation, 1st Demobilization Bureau, unaccredited, September 1946

39 – Southeast Area Ops Record 18th Army Ops, Vol. III, Mar 1944 – August 1944, 191 pages, unedited translation, 1st Demobilization Bureau, unaccredited, September 1946

40 – Southeast Area Ops Record 18th Army Ops, Volume IV, Sept 1944 – June 1945, 321 pages, unedited translation, 1st Demobilization Bureau, unaccredited, October 1946

44 – History of the Eighth Area Army, November 1942 – August 1945, 114 pages, unedited translation by Maj. Gen. Kazuo Tanikawa, undated

45*– History of Imperial General Headquarters, Army Section, 1941 – 1945, 382 pages, unaccredited Nov 1946, corrected and rewritten by Col. Takushiro Hattori assisted by former general officers, May 11, 1959

54 – Malay Operations Record, November 1941 – March 1942, 104 pages, unedited translation by Col. Sugita, Lt. Col. Kunitake and Lt. Col. Hashizune, September 1946

58 – Burma Operations Record Phase II, early 1943 – summer 1944, 76 pages, unedited translation by Col. Fusa, Lt. Col. Minoru Kawachi and Col. Shigemoto Kobayashi, undated

66*– The Invasion of the Netherlands East Indies, November 1941 – March 1942, 59 pages by Col. Akimitsu Oda, read by Maj. Gen. Takashima and Lt. Col Yamashita. Owing to a number of inaccuracies and omissions it was rewritten later, April 10, 1958

67 – Palembang and Bangka Islands Operations Record, January – February 1942, 16 pages based on memories and personal papers by Lt. Col. Minoru Miyako, Col. Yoshimitsu Ake and Col. Seiichi Kume, April 28, 1953

76*– Air Operations in the China Area, July 1937 – August 1945, 220 pages by Maj. Takejiro Shiba based on documents from Co. Genichi Yamamoto, Col. Hiroshi Saso, Lt. Col. Hirokichi Mizuo and Maj. En Komatsu, rewritten and corrected by the Japanese Research division, December 10, 1956

78 – The Kwantung Army in the Manchurian Campaign, 1941 – 1945, 45 pages, unedited translation. Kwantung Army information is based on personal papers of Lt. Col. Ishiwatari and memories of Maj. Komuratani, Lt. Col. Mizumachi, Maj. Iwano and returnees from Korea and Manchuria. U.S.S.R. based on information contributed by Maj. Shishikura former I.G.HQ staff officer

130 – China Area Ops Record - 6th Area Army Operations, July 1944 – August 1945, 126 pages by Mr. Jiso Yamaguchi based on memories of Maj. Gen. Renya Mutaguchi, Lt. Col. Bun Hirai, Lt. Col. Iwaichi Fujiwara, et al., October 10, 1952. Edited, revised with assistance from Gen. Kawabe, Lt. Gen. Sato, Maj. Gen. HJayashi, et al., October 10, 1957

132*– Burma Ops Record 28th Army Ops Akyab Area, Nov 1943 – Sept 1945, 212 pages by Col. Aiichi Okamura (formerly 28th Army, written while interned in Burma), reviewed by Lt. Gen. Shozo Sakurai. Rewritten and corrected by Maj. Nizo Yamaguchi in employ of 1st Demob. Bureau, August 29, 1952

134*– Burma Operations Record, 15th Army Operations in Imphal Area and Withdrawal to Northern Burma, January 1943 – January 1945, 191 pages rewritten and revised, October 10, 1957

135 – Okinawa Operations Record, March – June 1945, 265 pages unedited translation by Lt. Col. Katsushiro Mizumachi, August 1946

138*– Japanese Preparations for Operations in Manchuria, January 1943 – August 1945, 190 pages based on war time notes and diaries of Lt. Col. Prince Tsunenori Takeda and prepared by Lt. Col. Katsushiro Mizumachi translated into English in 1951, final edit with assistance from Co. Muraji Yano, Lt. Col. Ko Takahashi and Lt. Col. Kengoro Tanaka, November 1953

143 – Southeast Area Operations Record Part I, January – May 1942, 19 pages, unedited translation, unaccredited, 2nd Demobilization Board (IJN), January 1950

148 – Burma Area Operations Record 33rd Army Operations, April 1944 – August 1945, 234 pages by Fumi Yamaguchi, reference materials from Maj. Hiroshi Kibini and Col. Tsuji's diary, August 1950, revised edition 1960

151 – Air Operations Record Against Soviet Russia, June 1941 – September 1945, 65 pages by Lt. Col. Katsuo Sato from memory, personal papers and available unit records, edited and corrected, March 3, 1952

154*– Record of Operations Against Soviet Russia, Eastern Front, August 1945, 364 pages by Lt. Col. Genichiro Arinuma, Maj. Kyoji Takasugi, 1st Area Army page 26 by Col. Hiroshi Matsumoto, 3rd Army page 60 by Lt. Col. Naotomo Hosokawa, 79th Division (and 112th Div.) page 110 by Col. Takaharu Shinabe, 127th Division page 139 by Maj. Masao Sakai, 5th Army page 148 by Col. Akiji Kashiwada, 124th Division page 225 by Col. Toyoharu Iwasaki, 126th Division page 246 by Col Masashi Tanaka, 135th Division page 274 by Col. Toshisuke Inouye, 132nd I.M.B. page 331 by Maj. Gen. Goichi Onitake. Edited, April 6, 1954

162 – 7th Area Army's Southwest Area Operations Record, April 1944 – August 1945, 186 pages by Col. Yutaka Imaoka based on fragmentary data and personal recollections, unedited translation, February 1951

164 – Railway Operations Record (overseas and homeland) 1941 – 1945, 209 pages by Lt. Col. Shigeru Kubota from memoranda and memory, unedited translation, March 1951

165 – Java Operations Record Part II, early 1944 - August 1945, 16th Army, 27 pages by Lt. Col. Shizuo Miyamoto from memory and fragmentary reports, unedited translation, April 1951

167 – Malay Operations Record, January 1944 – August 1945, 29th Army, 52 pages by Lt. Gen. Masuzo Fujimura and Lt. Gen. Naokazu Kawahara, unedited translation, May 1951

177 –Thailand Operations Record, 1941 – 1945, 39th Army and 18th Area Army, 37 pages by Col. Konishi Takeo with assistance from Lt. Col. Hachiro Tokunaga, rewritten November 30, 1953

180*–South China Area Operations Record, 1937 – 1941, 21st Army and South China Area Army, 139 pages by the Reports and Statistical Section of the Demobilization Bureau and from documents in the possession of Lt. Col. Heizo Ishiwari with fragments from other sources, maps supplied by the editor with assistance from Lt. Col. Tadao Shudo, rewritten, March 9, 1956

185 – 25th Army, Sumatra Operations Record, March 1942 - August 1945, 18 pages from the memories and personal papers of Lt. Col. Eiji Yamaguchi, Lt. Col.

Sakai Omura and Maj. Takuji Kuramasu, June 19,1953

JACAR: Japan Center for Asian Historical Records

The *Japan Center for Asian Historical Records* (*JACAR*) is the portal used for the majority of primary source material relating to Imperial Japanese Army code names and numbers (*Tsushogo*). Documents, for the most part, are in the Japanese language and require recognizable kanji phrasing (or a reference number) to search them out. Recently, the Center has incorporated an auxiliary English home page and search facility. A number of relevant documents in English have been preserved from MacArthur's time, JACAR reference numbers will provide quick access for any who care to explore further.

JACAR documents are held in either: A: *National Archives of Japan*. B: *Diplomatic Archives of the Ministry of Foreign Affairs*. C: *National Institute for Defense Studies of the Ministry of Defense*. All document reference numbers accessed through JACAR are preceded by one of the three letters denoting the institution that holds the document.

Wrong entry 17850 Correct entry 17650

Japanese army lists all have inaccuracies, in this example, the *11th Independent Machinegun Battalion* appears twice under different code numbers in the same list; 部隊通称番號一覽表 No. 1 Repatriation Bureau, Nov. 11, 1946, JACAR Ref. Code: C12121106600 (most accurate list I know of). Where possible the code numbers here have been checked and verified against at least two independently produced lists. Also note there are thousands of legitimate unidentified unit numbers.

Army Lists in English:

List 1:

JACAR Ref. C15011165100 End of October 1945. Field Marshal MacArthur's Headquarters submission *Japanese Imperial army units compilation table* (original record). *List 1*. National Institute for Defense Studies.

List 1, Download: 350 files (Total: 65.8 MB)

Cover: C15011165100
Inside Cover (English) C15011165200
Index C15011165300
Last file: Shipping Units: C15011200000

List 2:

JACAR Ref. C15011231900. End of October 1945. Field Marshal MacArthur's Headquarters submission, *Japanese Imperial army units survey compilation table* (original record) *List 2*. National Institute for Defense Studies.

List 2 Download: 103 files (Total: 45.7 MB)

Cover: C15011231800
Inside Cover (English): C15011232000
Index: C15011232100
Last file: Various Army Training Units: C15011242100

List 3:

JACAR Ref. C15011242300. End of October 1945. Field Marshal MacArthur's

Headquarters submission *Japanese Imperial army units survey compilation table* (original record) *List 3*. National Institute for Defense Studies.
List 3 Download: 88 files (Total: 22.5 MB)
Cover: C15011242300
Inside Cover (English): C15011242400
Index: C15011242500
Last file: Kwantung Army Misc. Units C15011251000

List 4:
JACAR Ref.C15011251200. End of October 1945. Field Marshal MacArthur's Headquarters submission *Japanese Imperial army units survey compilation table* (original record) *List 4*. National Institute for Defense Studies.
List 4 Download: 27 files (Total: 79.5 MB)
Cover: C15011251200
Inside Cover (English): C15011251300
Index (Army Districts): C15011251400
Last file: Shipping Units: C15011253800

List 5:
JACAR Ref.C15011254000. End of October 1945. Field Marshal MacArthur's Headquarters submission *Japanese Imperial army units survey compilation table* (original record) *List 5*. National Institute for Defense Studies.
List 5 Download: 19 files (Total: 16.2 MB)
Cover: C15011254000
Inside Cover (English): C15011254100
Index (Homeland Defense Units): C15011254200
Last file: Hokubu Units: C15011255800

Air Force:
JACAR Ref.C15011256100. End of October 1945. Field Marshal MacArthur's Headquarters submission *Japanese Imperial army units survey compilation Table* (original record). List in 4 parts. Japanese Army Ministry. National Institute for Defense Studies.
Download: 6 files (Total: 24.8 MB)
Cover: C15011256000
List 1: Air Unit HQs and Flying Units: C15011256100
List 2 (1 of 2): Air Service HQs and Units: C15011256200
List 2 (2 of 2): Air Service HQs and Units cont.: C15011256300
List 3: Air Army Ground Units: C15011256400
List 4: Air Army HQs Training Units, etc.: C15011256500

Other Primary Source Documents from JACAR in English:
JACAR Ref. C12121215800. November 11, 1945. (Document in Japanese and English, P. 10) *Rules on the war time code names of army units* and (P. 16) *Summarized history of code names*. National Institute for Defense Studies. 19 pages. Japanese Army Department. 19 files (Total: 88.0 MB)

JACAR Ref. C15011200300. *Japanese Army Ministry List 2 No.1 Table No.2 Part 1 (ground units, etc.)*. End of October 1945. Field Marshal MacArthur's Headquarters submission. *Survey table of the Japanese Imperial Army units, Compilation table (original record) List 2- (1) Japanese Army Ministry.* National Institute for Defense Studies. 315 files (Total: 50.7 MB)

JACAR Ref. C15011256800. *Abbreviations*. Field Marshal MacArthur's Headquarters submission *Japanese Imperial Army units survey table compilation table (original record) Japanese Army.* National Institute for Defense Studies. 2 of 5 files (Total: 8.3 MB)
JACAR Ref. C15011256900. *(1) General explanation about survey table as a whole.* National Institute for Defense Studies. 3 of 5 files
JACAR Ref. C15011257000. Field Marshal MacArthur's Headquarters submission. November 2, 1945. *(2) Japanese Imp. Army units unit types list.* National Institute for Def. Studies. 4 of 5 files
JACAR Ref. C15011257100. Field Marshal MacArthur's Headquarters submission *(3) Japanese Imperial Army Units alias and number list General explanation.* National Institute for Defense Studies. 5 of 5

Army Lists in Japanese:
部隊通称番号一覧表 *1001 to 38500* (Translation: *Unit Tsushogo Catalog 1001 to 38500)* 昭和21年11月11日 (Repatriation Bureau. November 11, 1946) 5 files (Total: 31.8 MB)
A list of sequential code numbers and units in abbreviated Japanese form (独 = 独立 Independent) some knowledge of Japanese will be needed to read them. Largest and most accurate of all the unit lists.
JACAR. Ref. C12121106500. National Institute for Defense Studies. Cover. 1 page
JACAR. Ref. C12121106600. National Institute for Defense Studies. Part 1. 50 pages
JACAR. Ref. C12121106700. National Institute for Defense Studies. Part 2. 50 pages
JACAR. Ref. C12121106800. National Institute for Defense Studies. Part 3. 50 pages
JACAR. Ref. C12121106900. National Institute for Defense Studies. Part 4. 18 pages

陸軍部隊調表 (Army Unit Survey List) Oct. 28, 1945, Prepared by the Army Ministry. These lists are by unit type.
Major Units List:
JACAR. Ref. C12121087200. National Institute for Defense Studies. Cover. 1 page
JACAR. Ref. C12121087300. National Institute for Defense Studies. Inside cover 1 page
JACAR. Ref. C12121087400. National Institute for Defense Studies. Contents. 1 page
JACAR. Ref. C12121087500. National Institute for Defense Studies. Segment 1 Index, list. 50 pages
JACAR. Ref. C12121087600. National Institute for Defense Studies. Segment 2. List. 50 pages
JACAR. Ref. C12121087700. National Institute for Defense Studies. Segment 3. List. 9 pages
Independent Units List:
JACAR. Ref. C12121087800. National Institute for Defense Studies. List 2,

segment 1. 51 pages
JACAR. Ref. C12121087900. National Institute for Defense Studies. List 2, segment 2. 52 pages
Manchuria Units List:
JACAR. Ref. C12121088000. National Institute for Defense Studies. List 3. 46 pages
Air Units List:
JACAR. Ref. C12121088100. National Institute for Defense Studies. List 4, segment 1. 37 pages
JACAR. Ref. C12121088200. National Institute for Defense Studies. List 4 segment 2. 4 pages
北方鮮満部隊編成補充担任部隊一覧表. April 1947. Supplementary units organized for North Korea and Manchuria
JACAR. Ref. C1501004480. Cover. 2 pages
JACAR. Ref. C13010270000. Notes. 1 page
JACAR Ref. C13010269900. Manchuria (Kanto) Army direct control. 8 pages
JACAR Ref. C13010270200. 1st Area Army direct control. 3 pages
JACAR Ref. C13010270300. 3rd Army. 4 pages
JACAR Ref. C13010270400. 5th Army. 3 pages
JACAR Ref. C13010270500. 3rd Area Army direct control. 5 pages
JACAR Ref. C13010270600. 30th Army. 3 pages
JACAR Ref. C13010270700. 44th Army. 3 pages
JACAR Ref. C13010270800. 4th Army. 5 pages
JACAR Ref. C13010270900. 17th Area Army and 34th Army. 3 pages
JACAR Ref. C13010271000. Korea Army District. 3 pages
JACAR Ref. C13010271100. 5th Area Army direct control. 5 pages

Records Used for Most Unit Personnel Totals: (In Japanese)
Cover Pages:
JACAR Ref. C12120965900. (National Institute for Defense Studies). 兵籍異動通報綴 (*Military Register; Personnel Assignment Reports Binder*). 2 files (Total: 235.1 Kbytes)
JACAR Ref. C12120966000. February 1947. (National Institute for Defense Studies). 兵籍異動通報 (*Military Register; Personnel Assignment Reports*)
General Armies:
JACAR Ref. C12120966200 to JACAR Ref. C12120967000. July 1940 to 1945. *Kwantung Army organization; number of persons*. (National Institute for Defense Studies). 9 files (Total: 26.4 MB)
JACAR Ref. C12120968000 to JACAR Ref. C12120968200. July 1940 to 1945. *Kwantung Army organization; number of persons*. 3 files (Total: 13.0 MB)
JACAR Ref. C12120968400 to JACAR Ref. C12120969500. June 1937 to 1945. *China Expeditionary Army organization; number of persons*. 12 files (Total: 40.3 MB)
JACAR Ref. C12120971400 to JACAR Ref. C12120972400. July 1941 to 1945. *Southern Expeditionary Army organization; number of persons*. 11 files (Total: 33.8 MB)
JACAR Ref. C12121034100 to JACAR Ref. C12121036200. *1st and 2nd General*

Army organization; number of persons. 22 files (Total: 11.7 MB)

Area Armies:

JACAR Ref. C12120972600 to JACAR Ref. C12120973700. June 1937 to 1945. *Burma Area Army organization; number of persons*. 12 files (Total: 39.5 MB)

JACAR Ref. C12120969700 to JACAR Ref. C12120970600. January 1937 to 1945. *North China Area Army organization; number of persons*. 10 files (Total: 22.8 MB)

JACAR Ref. C12120974200 to JACAR Ref. C12120974700. July 1940 to 1945. *1st Area Army organization; number of persons*. 6 files (Total: 17.2 MB)

Note: 2nd Area Army demobilized. File missing

JACAR Ref. C12120974900 to JACAR Ref. C12120975900. *3rd Area Army organization; number of persons*. 11 files (Total: 25.9 MB)

JACAR Ref. C12120976100 to JACAR Ref. C12120977400. August 1941 to 1945. *5th Area Army organization; number of persons*. 14 files (Total: 47.7 MB)

JACAR Ref. C12120977600 to JACAR Ref. C12120978900. June 1938 to 1945. *6th Area Army organization; number of persons*. 14 files (Total: 37.3 MB)

JACAR Ref. C12120979100 to JACAR Ref. C12120979500. 1941 to 1945. *7th Area Army organization; number of persons*. 5 files (Total: 10.9 MB)

JACAR Ref. C12120979700 to JACAR Ref. C12120980600. July 1938 to 1945. *8th Area Army organization; number of persons*. 10 files (Total: 26.4 MB)

JACAR Ref. C12120980800 to JACAR Ref. C12120982800. July 1941 to 1945. *10th Area Army organization; number of persons*. 21 files (Total: 55.0 MB)

JACAR Ref. C12120983000 to JACAR Ref. C12120983700. January 1944 to 1945. *11th Area Army organization; number of persons*. 8 files (Total: 17.5 MB)

JACAR Ref. C12120983900 to JACAR Ref. C12120985000. July 1941 to 1945. *12th Area Army organization; number of persons*. 12 files (Total: 40.2 MB)

JACAR Ref. C12120985200 to JACAR Ref. C12120985800. June 1938 to 1945. *13th Area Army organization; number of persons*. 7 files (Total: 22.7 MB)

JACAR Ref. C12120986000 to JACAR Ref. C12120987700. *14th Area Army organization; number of persons*. 18 files (Total: 61.3 MB)

JACAR Ref. C12120987900 to JACAR Ref. C12120988400. *15th Area Army organization; number of persons*. 6 files (Total: 15.9 MB)

JACAR Ref. C12120988600 to JACAR Ref. C12120990300. *16th Area Army organization; number of persons*. 18 files (Total: 43.9 MB)

JACAR Ref. C12120990500 to JACAR Ref. C12120991300. *17th Area Army organization; number of persons*. 9 files (Total: 24.4 MB)

JACAR Ref. C12120991500 to JACAR Ref. C12120991800. *18th Area Army organization; number of persons*. 4 files (Total: 9.2 MB)

Armies:

JACAR Ref. C12120970800 to JACAR Ref. C12120971200. February 10, 1938 to 1945. *Mongolia Garrison Army organization; number of persons*. 5 files (Total: 7.4 MB)

JACAR Ref. C12120992000 to JACAR Ref. C12120992600. *1st Army organization; number of persons*. 7 files (Total: 11.8 MB)

JACAR Ref. C12120992800 to JACAR Ref. C12120994000. *2nd Army organization; number of persons*. 13 files (Total: 42.0 MB)

JACAR Ref. C12120994200 to JACAR Ref. C12120995000. *3rd Army organization; number of persons*. 9 files (Total: 22.4 MB)

JACAR Ref. C12120995200 to JACAR Ref. C12120996200. *4th Army organization; number of persons*. 11 files (Total: 25.9 MB)

JACAR Ref. C12120996400 to JACAR Ref. C12120997000. *5th Army organization; number of persons*. 7 files (Total: 16.9 MB)

JACAR Ref. C12120997200 to JACAR Ref. C12120997900. *6th Army organization; number of persons*. 8 files (Total: 15.2 MB)

JACAR Ref. C12120998100 to JACAR Ref. C12120998700. *11th Army organization; number of persons*. 7 files (Total: 22.8 MB)

JACAR Ref. C12120998900 to JACAR Ref. C12121000000. *12th Army organization; number of persons*. 12 files (Total: 20.5 MB)

JACAR Ref. C12121000200 to JACAR Ref. C12121001500. *13th Army organization; number of persons*. 14 files (Total: 36.8 MB)

Note: 14th Army organization; number of persons. File missing

JACAR Ref. C12121001700 to JACAR Ref. C12121002100. *15th Army organization; number of persons*. 5 files (Total: 8.3 MB)

JACAR Ref. C12121002300 to JACAR Ref. C12121002700. *16th Army organization; number of persons*. 5 files (Total: 7.2 MB)

JACAR Ref. C12121002900 to JACAR Ref. C12121003300. *17th Army organization; number of persons*. 5 files (Total: 8.1 MB)

JACAR Ref. C12121003500 to JACAR Ref. C12121004200. *18th Army organization; number of persons*. 8 files (Total: 29.4 MB)

Note: 19th Army organization; number of persons. File missing

JACAR Ref. C12121004400 to JACAR Ref. C12121005400. *20th Army organization; number of persons*. 11 files (Total: 22.0 MB)

JACAR Ref. C12121005600 to JACAR Ref. C12121007000. *23rd Army organization; number of persons*. 15 files (Total: 31.9 MB)

JACAR Ref. C12121007200 to JACAR Ref. C12121007700. *25th Army organization; number of persons*. 6 files (Total: 14.6 MB)

JACAR Ref. C12121007900 to JACAR Ref. C12121008300. *28th Army organization; number of persons*. 5 files (Total: 12.6 MB)

JACAR Ref. C12121008500 to JACAR Ref. C12121009200. *29th Army organization; number of persons*. 8 files (Total: 18.1 MB)

JACAR Ref. C12121010100 to JACAR Ref. C12121011100. *31st Army organization; number of persons*. 11 files (Total: 25.2 MB)

JACAR Ref. C12121011300 to JACAR Ref. C12121012300. *32ndArmy organization; number of persons*. 11 files (Total: 34.8 MB)

JACAR Ref. C12121012500 to JACAR Ref. C12121012800. *33rd Army organization; number of persons*. 4 files (Total: 9.2 MB)

JACAR Ref. C12121013000 to JACAR Ref. C12121013400. *34th Army organization; number of persons*. 5 files (Total: 10.7 MB)

JACAR Ref. C12121013600 to JACAR Ref. C12121014300. *35th Army organization; number of persons*. 8 files (Total: 20.4 MB)

JACAR Ref. C12121014500 to JACAR Ref. C12121015500. *36th Army organization; number of persons*. 11 files (Total: 23.3 MB)

JACAR Ref. C12121015700 to JACAR Ref. C12121016100. *37th Army organization; number of persons*. 5 files (Total: 9.5 MB)

JACAR Ref. C12121016300 to JACAR Ref. C12121017000. *38th Army organization; number of persons*. 8 files (Total: 17.8 MB)

Note: 39th Army, Thailand. File missing

JACAR Ref. C12121017200 to JACAR Ref. C12121017600. *40th Army organization; number of persons*. 5 files (Total: 9.5 MB)

JACAR Ref. C12121017800 to JACAR Ref. C12121018200. *41st Army organization; number of persons*. 5 files (Total: 15.8 MB)

JACAR Ref. C12121018400 to JACAR Ref. C12121019200. *43rd Army organization; number of persons*. 9 files (Total: 15.2 MB)

JACAR Ref. C12120967200 to JACAR Ref. C12120967800. July 1939 to 1945. *44th Army organization; number of persons*. 7 files (Total: 19.0 MB)

JACAR Ref. C12121019400 to JACAR Ref. C12121019800. *50th Army organization; number of persons*. 5 files (Total: 6.8 MB)

Note: 51st Army Organization; Mito, Japan. File missing

JACAR Ref. C12121020900 to JACAR Ref. C12121021500. *52nd Army organization; number of persons*. 7 files (Total: 14.6 MB)

JACAR Ref. C12121021700 to JACAR Ref. C12121022300. *53rd Army organization; number of persons*. 7 files (Total: 13.7 MB)

JACAR Ref. C12121022500 to JACAR Ref. C12121023200. *54th Army organization; number of persons*. 8 files (Total: 13.1 MB)

JACAR Ref. C12121023400 to JACAR Ref. C12121024000. *55th Army organization; number of persons*. 7 files (Total: 16.0 MB)

JACAR Ref. C12121024200 to JACAR Ref. C12121024800. *56th Army organization; number of persons*. 7 files (Total: 16.4 MB)

JACAR Ref. C12121025000 to JACAR Ref. C12121025800. *57th Army organization; number of persons*. 9 files (Total: 21.2 MB)

JACAR Ref. C12121026000 to JACAR Ref. C12121026500. *58th Army organization; number of persons*. 6 files (Total: 13.6 MB)

JACAR Ref. C12121026700 to JACAR Ref. C12121027100. *59th Army organization; number of persons*. 5 files (Total: 5.8 MB)

JACAR Ref. C12121027300 to JACAR Ref. C12121028900. *Air Army attached units organization; Number of Persons*. 17 files (Total: 38.7 MB)

Air Armies:

JACAR Ref. C12121029100 to JACAR Ref. C12121029600. *1st Air Army organization; number of persons*. 6 files (Total: 20.3 MB)

JACAR Ref. C12121029800 to JACAR Ref. C12121030000. *2nd Air Army organization; number of persons*. 3 files (Total: 15.6 MB)

JACAR Ref. C12121030200 to JACAR Ref. C12121031400. *3rd Air Army organization; number of persons*. 13 files (Total: 40.1 MB)

JACAR Ref. C12121031600 to JACAR Ref. C12121032000. *4th Air Army organization; number of persons*. 5 files (Total: 17.8 MB)

JACAR Ref. C12121032200 to JACAR Ref. C12121032600. *5th Air Army organization; number of persons*. 5 files (Total: 27.3 MB)

JACAR Ref. C12121032800 to JACAR Ref. C12121033200. *6th Air Army organization; number of persons*. 5 files (Total: 19.2 MB)

JACAR Ref. C12121033400 to JACAR Ref. C12121033500. *5th Area Army, 1st Air Division organization; number of persons*. 2 files (Total: 6.2 MB)

JACAR Ref. C12121033700 to JACAR Ref. C12121033900. *10th Area Army, 8th Air Division organization; number of persons.* 3 files (Total: 13.4 MB)

JACAR Ref. C12121050000 to JACAR Ref. C12121050100. *Miscellaneous air units; number of persons.* 6 files (Total: 5.2 MB)

Homeland:

JACAR Ref. C12121036400 to JACAR Ref. C12121036700 *Hokubu and Asahikawa organization; number of persons.* 4 files (Total: 7.2 MB)

JACAR Ref. C12121036900 to JACAR Ref. C12121037300. *Tohoku organization; number of persons.* 5 files (Total: 10.9 MB)

JACAR Ref. C12121037500 to JACAR Ref. C12121038200. *Tobu organization; number of persons.* 8 files (Total: 27.2 MB)

JACAR Ref. C12121038400 to JACAR Ref. C12121038800. *Tokai organization; number of persons.* 5 files (Total: 13.7 MB)

JACAR Ref. C12121039000 to JACAR Ref. C12121039400. *Chubu organization; number of persons.* 5 files (Total: 18.5 MB)

JACAR Ref. C12121039600 to JACAR Ref. C12121039700. *Chugoku organization; number of persons.* 2 files (Total: 6.1 MB)

JACAR Ref. C12121039900 to JACAR Ref. C12121040000. *Shikoku organization; number of persons.* 2 files (Total: 4.7 MB)

JACAR Ref. C12121040200 to JACAR Ref. C12121040800. *Seibu organization; number of persons.* 7 files (Total: 21.7 MB)

Articles:

Bradsher, Dr. Greg (Senior Archivist). December 19, 2017. *The beginnings of the United States Army's Japanese language training: From the Presidio of San Francisco to Camp Savage, Minnesota 1941-1942*: National Archives at College Park. Blog entry

Bradsher, Dr. Greg (Senior Archivist, NARA). August 10, 2012. *From Rabaul to Stack 190: The Travels of a Famous Japanese Army Publication.* National Archives and Records Administration at College Park. Blog entry

Tanaka, Professor Hiromi (Keiko Tamura translator). Undated. *AWM 82 Captured Japanese documents*: Australian War Museum: Australian-Japanese Research Project, Online article

Takizawa, Akira. 2004-2019. *Taki's Home Page.* http://www3.plala.or.jp/takihome/

Illustrations and Photographs:

Cover:

Design and artwork: Roderick Grigor hereafter (author)

Chapter 1: Pages 1 to 10

Page 8 dog tag and note (author)

Page 9 Guntai techo page(service record notebook page) (author)

Page 10 Troop convoy on way to P.I. (author)

Chapter 1: Pages 11 to 16

Page 12 Peleliu: 2nd Inf. Regt. artillery unit, gun crew papers (author)

Page 13 (1) Muddy clump of documents (ATIS, public domain)

Page 13 (2) Cover *Register of Army Officers on Active Service* (photo: US National Archives and Records Administration, public domain)

About the author:

Toronto born Roderick Grigor graduated from the Ontario College of Art in 1981. He became an award winning professional illustrator, producing work for advertising, packaging, newspapers and magazines. In the mid 1990s high-end illustration became a casualty of inexpensive digital image manipulation and soon Grigor turned to super-realism fine art painting. He has several solo art shows to his credit.

A lifelong fascination with military and Japanese history has over years transformed the artist into a serious student and collector of WW2 Japanese military history books and artifacts. In 2014 he took on the idea of creating a comprehensive overview of the Imperial Army in WW2. Original English and Japanese source material forms the basis for an unprecedented look into the long-vanquished Imperial Japanese Army.

www.ingramcontent.com/pod-product-compliance
Lightning Source LLC
LaVergne TN
LVHW010600100826
845148LV00014B/2786